ARCHITECTURAL PRINCIPLES
IN THE AGE OF HISTORICISM

ARCHITECTURAL PRINCIPLES
IN THE AGE OF HISTORICISM

Robert Jan van Pelt
&
Carroll William Westfall

YALE UNIVERSITY PRESS
NEW HAVEN AND LONDON

To Relling
Carroll William Westfall

In memory of Alan Urbach
Robert Jan van Pelt

Copyright © 1991 by Yale University

First published in paperback 1993

Set in Bodoni by Excel Typesetters Co., Hong Kong
Printed and bound in Great Britain by Biddles Limited, Guildford and King's Lynn

Library of Congress Cataloging-in-Publication Data

Van Pelt, Robert Jan.
   Architectural principles in the age of historicism / Robert Jan
van Pelt and Carroll William Westfall.
      p.   cm.
   Includes bibliographical references and index.
      ISBN 0–300–04999–4 (hbk.)
      ISBN 0–300–05788–1 (pbk.)
      1. Architecture—Philosophy.   2. Architecture—Historiography.
I. Westfall, Carroll William.   II. Title.
NA2500.V34   1991
720'.1—dc20   90–22752
                                                        CIP

Contents

Acknowledgements

I unknowingly began this book during the decade beginning in 1972 when I lived in Chicago. That city's architectural and urban form had drawn me to it, but the city I had moved to was then being replaced with a less worthy successor. My involvement in the local citizen-based preservation effort revealed to me the destructive role orthodox architectural history plays in our cities. After moving to another appealing setting, Mr Jefferson's academical village in Charlottesville, Virginia, I had both the vision to see the world in a different way and the opportunity and encouragement to develop the implications of what I saw.

This book exists because the then-Dean of the University of Virginia's School of Architecture Jaquelin Taylor Robertson provided the support and protection that made possible the collaboration it represents. My sections contain material provoked in part by his thought and that of people in residence for brief periods or already on the faculty. In quick succession Leon Krier, Demetri Porphyrios, and Michael Dennis appeared as Thomas Jefferson Professors while the regular architecture faculty contained Robert Dripps, III, Bruce Abbey, and others who were supportive, sympathetic, or at least tolerant of my explorations and of the joint enterprise Robert Jan van Pelt and I undertook among them. No less important were the students who were willing to hear one or another of us out. In Charlottesville, as well as in the School's summer program in Vicenza, I found a setting where students were eager to test ideas in studios, seminars, and other settings. Meanwhile, I received additional insight into the topic through discussions with colleagues in other institutions and with architects and others involved in building in our cities and rural areas, through observing and participating in the twice-yearly sessions of the Mayors Institute on City Design held at the University of Virginia, through serving on architectural design juries at the Universities of Virginia, Waterloo, Princeton, and Yale, and through the discussions and presentations of a stimulating week as a guest of the Faculty of Architecture at the Universidad Francisco Marroquin in Guatemala City.

A number of other people have designed, said, or written things that have made a great difference in the way I think. Among those I have known personally are Norris Kelly Smith, Allan Greenberg, and my long-time friend Hadley Arkes. The role of others I have not known personally from Socrates onward I leave to the reader to discover.

Carroll William Westfall

My contribution to this book began as a response to a frustration common to many architectural historians who teach in architecture schools. When invited to serve on architectural design juries they discover that their efforts to confront students with the best buildings have no impact on their designs for tomorrow's architecture. Most often the students who understand the *Architectural Principles in the Age of Humanism* best turn out to be the worst designers. I first noticed the lack of relevance of architectural history for architectural design when teaching at the School of Architecture of the National University of Singapore. Living in a city-state that had separated itself from its own past to embrace the elsewhere already abandoned myth of progress I began to consider the historiographical question which was to become the foundation of *Architectural Principles in the Age of Historicism*. Pinna Indorf was the first who engaged with me in the conversation about the use and abuse of architectural history in architectural education. Alan Urbach's engagement with this conversation, initiated in the most trying of circumstances, showed me that this discourse mattered beyond the limited confines of architectural education. During my last two months in Singapore Kong Chee Chong provided the setting where I wrote a sketch of Chapter One and a first draft of Chapter Five.

The conversation intensified when I moved to the University of Virginia. There I met Westfall, who was thinking on similar lines. We enjoyed the time and space to discover our agreements and disagreements in a dialogue facilitated by Jaquelin Taylor Robertson, Robert Dripps, III and Bruce Abbey. The colloquium broadened when I moved to the University of Waterloo. Two directors, Larry Richards and Rick Haldenby, actively supported the kind of questioning which structures this book. Many friends, colleagues and students helped me in various ways to face the practicalities involved in writing a book or engaged in the conversation. Among those were Tim Shortreed, Sandra Black, Relling Westfall, Mieke Delfgaauw, Leo Katz, Joanne Young, Helmut and Margaret Schade, Ena Wrighton, Eleanore Kaufman, Ryszard Sliwka, Donald Mackay, Val Rynnemeri, Thomas Seebohm, Andrew Kiel, Andy Ortwein, Michael Thorpe, Robert Magee, Lionel Ohayon and Rick Hopkins.

The book would not have come to completion without the help offered by Ken Marek, Miriam Marek and Deborah Dwork. Ken's generous hospitality provided the structured space where I could concentrate on the task of writing the penultimate draft of the text. Miriam Marek gave structure to my time. A one-year-old girl quickly teaches a bachelor the preciousness of uninterrupted time. She taught me to use the few hours that she spent in her play-school productively. Deborah gave structure to my thoughts and ambitions. She forced me to face my own confusions squarely, and helped me to overcome my inability to come to conclusions. Her "enough!" was instrumental in bringing my arguments to some kind of closure. For four happy months we shared the same study as true writing partners, each writing our own book, each engaged with the other's struggles and discoveries. I hope that some of the joy of that collaboration is reflected in my contribution.

The manuscript would not have been publishable without the constructive and candid criticism it received from George Hersey, Robert Wiljer and the late O.B. Hardison. Hersey showed me that I was on the right track. Wiljer made it clear that the road was longer than I thought, and helped me to come to terms with my failure to advance beyond the halfway point of Periclean Athens. When Westfall and I submitted the text for consideration by Yale University Press, the publisher approached O.B. Hardison as the first referee. The judgement of the first referee is often crucial in an academic press's decision to accept or reject a manuscript for publication. O.B. responded with a lengthy, perceptive, passionate and tough-minded criticism of the book which revealed to its authors many of its problems and to the publisher some of its possibilities. Four months after receiving a copy of his critique I had the pleasure to discuss with O.B. and his wife Mari-Frances my response to his observations and suggestions. It was a happy and, as I thought then, a propitious occasion: our conversation gave me confidence that the issues we had raised were valid and important. Less than two months later, O.B. unexpectedly died. The American academic community lost a great scholar, this book its first reader, and I a new friend.

The manuscript would not have been published without the trust, patience and good humour of the people at Yale University Press. Robert Baldock, our editor, remained for five years receptive to my often chimeric proposals, and he did not loose his temper when, instead of a promised manuscript, he received a new prospectus for an altogether different book. *Architectural Principles in the Age of Historicism* was such a cuckoo's egg. Baldock did not banish it to the slush pile, the publisher's rampart designed to protect editors from quixotic authors. Instead he graciously adopted the unbidden manuscript, and gave it his best. I am also grateful to

Patricia Rennie, Peter James and Ann Geneva for their expertise. guidance and enthusiasm.

Finally I would like to acknowledge the importance of you, the reader. When Westfall and I set out to write this book we intended it to be an open-ended conversation, and hoped that others would join it. This book is not meant to be a gospel which demands conversion. Instead it is conceived as a catalyst which, so we hope, will lead to a discourse which far exceeds the undoubtedly personal boundaries of this effort.

Robert Jan van Pelt

The authors and publisher acknowledge with thanks permission to reproduce passages as follows:

From Thucydides, *History of the Peloponnesian War* (transl. R. Warner)[1], from Plutarch, *The Rise and Fall of Athens* (transl. Ian Scott-Kilvert)[2], from Aristophanes, *The Birds and Other Plays* (transl. David Barrett and Alan H. Sommerstein)[3]: Penguin Books; from Sophocles, *The Three Theban Plays* (transl. Robert Fagles)[4]: Penguin Books USA Inc.; from Friedrich Hölderlin, *Poems and Fragments* (transl. Michael Hamburger): Cambridge University Press; from Friedrich Hölderlin, *Hymns and Fragments* (transl. Richard Sieburth), from W. Robert Connor, *Thucydides*: Princeton University Press; "The Birth of Architecture" from W.H. Auden, *Collected Poems*: Random House; from Karl Jaspers, *The Origin and Goal of History* (transl. Michael Bullock): Yale University Press; from Jean Améry, *At the Mind's Limits* (transl. Sidney and Stella P. Rosenfeld): Schocken Books; from Aeschylus, *The Oresteia*, (transl. Robert Fagles)[5]: Viking Penguin, a division of Penguin Books USA Inc.

1. Translation copyright © Rex Warner, 1954.
2. Translation copyright © Ian-Scott Kilvert, 1960.
3. Translation copyright © David Barrett and Alan H. Sommerstein, 1977.
4. Copyright © 1977, 1979 for *Oedipus the King*, © 1977, 1980 for *Oedipus at Colonus* and © 1982 for *Antigone* and entire volume: Viking Penguin, a division of Penguin Books USA Inc.
5. Copyright © 1966, 1967, 1975 by Robert Fagles.

Prolegomenon

The title of our book reverts to and reverses Rudolf Wittkower's *Architectural Principles in the Age of Humanism*. In this classic history of architecture, written during the Second World War, Rudolf Wittkower (1901–71) discussed the precepts that guided Renaissance architectural practice. These principles embodied a normative understanding of an abiding and unchanging world that was reflected in a modular system of architecture structured according to laws of proportion. Wittkower described a lost world, and with that an obsolete canon. Yet he also believed that his discussions could help architects to develop "new and unexpected solutions to this ancient problem [of proportion]."[1] In other words, while Wittkower did not abandon the historicist and relativist belief that the subject of his study, the principles that had informed Renaissance architecture, had been valid once, but were no more, he did not rule out the possibility that his record of past interest in certain architectural issues could inspire a new debate about these problems. The specific solution of 1500, however, no longer applied in 1950. The architectural principles of the Age of Humanism could not inform architectural thought in the Age of Modernism. If architects were to find some inspiration from the pages of Wittkower's book, it was only for the sake of "new and unexpected solutions." In short, they should not apply the principles formulated by Leon Battista Alberti (1404–72), but invent new ones that would fit the social, economic, scientific and technological conditions of the twentieth century.

Wittkower did not explicitly claim contemporary relevance for his book; he circumvented the issue of whether a literal application of the Renaissance principles of architecture to contemporary architecture was legitimate. Nevertheless, the book made a great impression on architects and became required reading in architecture schools. In the preface to the third edition, published in 1962, Wittkower reflected that it had been "a satisfactory

experience to have seen [the book's] impact on a young generation of
architects." There was no recognition that the main cause of its popularity
was the uncritical attitude of designers who had come under its spell. In
1962 such questions of legitimacy still seemed irrelevant: of Wittkower's
book, and the articles, books or buildings inspired by it, none challenged
the then still dominant modernist and historicist paradigm. For all the noisy
assent that sanctioned Wittkower's examination of the past as a source of
inspiration, the book, in the final analysis, offered a wholly self-sufficient
present with another reason to look confidently to the future.

More than a quarter of a century later, we have lost the confidence of the
Kennedy era. Critical theory and postmodern critique have unmasked the
metahistorical pretense of the twentieth-century architectural tradition
commonly known as the "Modern Movement," and so even architects have
now consciously entered the already two-centuries-old Age of Historicism,
that is the epoch when people operate(d) on the assumption "that human
affairs can be adequately understood 'historically,' that is, by tracing them
to their origins and describing their relationship to a process of development through time."[2] In fact they unwittingly had enjoyed the historicist
blessings all along because the ideology of Modern Architecture and
historicism issue from the same stem. Both define history as change. But
the machine-like or brutalist aesthetics of Modern Architecture, infused
with its explicit claims of honesty, utility and innovation, carried the
explicit connotation that this change was for the better, that we could
interpret the developments of our own time in an optimistic, evolutionary if
not eschatological perspective. The city of the future was the criterion of
truth, the measurestick that declared the naked aesthetics of the avant-
garde as progressive, and therefore valid and the inherited and often
ornamental forms of the past as stale, futile and reactionary. The postulate
of infinite social, economic, scientific and technological advancement
allowed the Modern Architect to identify the stripped and transparent
architecture of Paxton's Crystal Palace (1851) or Mies's Seagram Building (1958) with progress and, therefore, with the moral and the good. We
have lost that certainty and, as a result, the spurious values of Modern
Architecture. We have come to realize the forward-looking creed of the
Modern Movement was a pious sham all along, that, for architectural
history, the Age of Modernism was, in fact, the Age of a value-neutral
Historicism. Yet until some fifteen years ago it still seemed otherwise.
Wittkower still could write in the context of a self-evident structure. He still
could believe with sincerity that the promise of tomorrow effectively
resolved the contradictions between the design tasks of the present and
the architectural principles of the past. We have lost his innocence: the
promise has become a fictive pretext, the responsibility for the present a

simulated affectation and the principles of the past a fiction determined by time and place. *Architectural Principles in the Age of Historicism* has been written amid the ruins of the Modern Architect's pretension and Postmodern Architect's perversion. The question of possible effect has ceased to be an issue of surprised satisfaction and is recognized as a reason for solicitude. Today there is more at stake than in 1949 (or 1962): the wager of *Architectural Principles in the Age of Humanism* concerned the value of a period of the past of architecture; in *Architectural Principles in the Age of Historicism* the future of architecture is at stake.

Because we are in a condition of flux we ought to think about the possibility of an abiding and lasting code of architecture. *Architectural Principles in the Age of Historicism* addresses this problem in the context of the city. It explores the question whether the architect might make buildings that allow for the reification of a *civitas* (the city as a community) into an *urbs* (the city as a place to live). *Architectural Principles in the Age of Historicism* explores the identity of what is usually considered as being radically distinctive: the purpose of citizenship versus the form and disposition of buildings. There are different equally valid points of departure for such an investigation. It can begin with an examination of the way city councils take decisions that shape the physical fabric of the city according to anticipated voter behaviour, or the manner in which the mortgage and loan industry, from informed guesses of the expected financial and economic developments, decides what kind of buildings are to be produced and how they are to be built. This book focusses, instead, on the way the problematic relationship between the normative or enduring and the changing arises in architectural (history) education.

The two authors teach in architectural schools; they are architectural historians who also teach architectural theory. *Architectural Principles in the Age of Historicism* is their reflection on what they have been teaching and ought to be doing in a broader humanist perspective. Thus they conceived of this text as an arsenal of ideas, observations and, especially in Westfall's contribution, practical propositions that might help others to fortify architectural schools as places where young people prepare themselves to build *as citizen–architects* a new and truly human world within the chaotic totality that was disclosed when the confident facade of Modern Architecture crumbled. Their motivation is the persuasion that architects may still aspire to build what the late W.H. Auden (1907–73) identified as the Good Place, a city that as a moral, political, existential and architectural concatenation bridges the chasm that separates one person from the other and all of us from the world.

Contradiction and confrontation structure the book. Contradiction is implied in the title. It professes that this book will offer "Architectural Principles," in other words a stable and normative ground that offers a universal basis for architectural production. Yet this designation announces an exposition of primary truths that can and ought to inform the making of buildings in the context of contemporary culture, the "Age of Historicism." As observed above, the word "Historicism" refers here to the now universally held persuasion that humanity is the ever evolving and ever changing offspring of history. From this follows the conviction that "man" lacks a fixed nature. Therefore there is no intrinsic justification for any attempt to prescribe universal and permanent norms or principles to guide any field of human endeavour, including the making of buildings.

Architectural Principles in the Age of Historicism is also a work of Heraclitean confrontation. It is the record of a conversation that began when the two authors met in the spring of 1984. Of radically different backgrounds and persuasions they recognized in the other a citizen and a colleague interested in the practical ramifications of the teaching of architectural history. Beginning in January 1986, van Pelt taught for three semesters in Westfall's Department of Architectural History at the University of Virginia. Their discussions in Charlottesville are the context from which this book emerged. That colloquy focussed on the unwanted implications of the historicist assertion that humanity is in a state of constant evolution and that, therefore, there are and may be no fixed norms that can inform our actions. Those eighteen months confirmed the Heraclitean *topos* of the flux of time and the relativity of all achievements. And it endorsed Heraclitus' remark that "opposition concurs and the fairest connection comes from things that differ and everything comes about in accordance with strife."[3] When van Pelt left Virginia for Ontario in August 1987 they decided to continue the dialogue on the use and abuse of architectural history education in the design-studio. This resulted in two extended sessions: one in Charlottesville and one in Waterloo. These meetings gave them the opportunity to challenge each other's ideas in public. The positive response of those present suggested a broadening of the discussion, and this text is a means towards that end.

The format of the text follows the paratactical structure of the dialogue as held in Charlottesville and Waterloo (the word paratactical derives from the Greek παρα "beside" and τάσσειν "to arrange" or τάχισ "arrangement"). In the following chapter entitled "Heraclitean Heritance" van Pelt offers some of the general considerations that set then and now the stage for the dialogue. He analyzes the dominant paradigm of contemporary historical activity and describes how all thinking about architectural history and theory has changed from an indisputable, normative and prescriptive paradigm into a self-conscious discourse that, as a record or vehicle of a polemic, is adrift in the ever changing currents of time. In the following seven chapters of *Architectural Principles in the Age of Historicism* the authors try to find along the stream some sheltered places of anchorage. Undergirded by the post-Kantian and thoroughly modernist paradigm that grants us the freedom to choose our own perspective on the world, they propound two existing if time-scarred moorings that fit their purpose. Westfall's landing offers security because it reflects those aspects of human life that are firmly embedded in an unchanging order of things. Van Pelt's offers a different kind of surety. It does not provide refuge in an anchorage along the river, but in the knowledge that what seems an unruly torrent is in fact a stream of destiny that flows purposefully towards what the Judeo-Christian tradition proclaimed as a safe and inviting harbour and what modern reality revealed as an all-devouring cataract, a disillusive Fall that in all its apocalyptic power offers a measure of enlightenment and a standard of action. Thomas Hardy's aphorism that "if a way to the Better there be, it exacts a full look at the Worst"[4] permeates his contribution.

The even-numbered chapters present Westfall's views; the odd chapters contain van Pelt's reflections. The four even chapters have a necessary or hypotactical order, as do the odd chapters. The two narratives stand, however, paratactically side by side, which means that they are autonomous statements not subordinated to any overarching theoretical syntax.[5] This paratactical structure is intentional: it undermines through repeated thematic displacement the self-sufficiency of the discourse as a whole as well as the balance of each of the two tractates. The paratactic concatenation reveals how the inherent logic of each of the two propositions is, after all, propositional. And, at a crucial point in the book, a paratactical rift allows one of the authors to express a wholly appropriate disbelief in his own assertions. These discursive breaks allow for an approbation of Lord Acton's insight that a historian who decides to encounter a colleague in a polemic must begin with "appreciating and, if even if it may be, fortifying and strengthening the adversary's position, supplying the gaps and correcting the flaws of his argument before he declares it untenable."[6] And they reaffirm the basic fissure that sets apart Westfall's position from van Pelt's: the chasm that separates Greek from Hebrew thought.

This ought not to be otherwise. The political philosopher Leo Strauss (1899–1973) said more than once that the crisis of modernity suggested the need of *t'shuvah*, the Hebrew word for return or repentance. The goal of such a return would be "Western civilization in its premodern integrity." Yet Strauss conceded that this premodern integrity was not univocal. There have always been two voices, in radical disagreement with each other. The one is that of the philosopher, and points at Athens; the other is that of the theologian, and directs us to Jerusalem. "The whole history of the West can be viewed as an ever repeated attempt to achieve a compromise or a synthesis between these two antagonistic principles. But all these attempts have failed. . . . The Western tradition does not allow of a synthesis of its two elements, but only of its tension: this is the secret of the vitality of the West." And Strauss decided that because the life of Western civilization is the life between two competing ideas of citizenship, we should learn to live such a life again, we should learn to live the conflict between Athens and Jerusalem. To recover architectural principles in an age of historicism implies a return to Athens and a return to Jerusalem. One person cannot do this. "No one can be both a philosopher and a theologian," so Strauss concluded, "but every one of us can be and ought to be either one or the other, the philosopher open to the challenge of theology or the theologian open to the challenge of philosophy."[7]

Westfall is no philosopher, and van Pelt no theologian. Both are historians, and wrote this book as historians. Yet Westfall's argument has an unqualified philosophical bias, and van Pelt's contribution is theological in tone. This opposition charges the question that is asked in Chapter One, and that is investigated in the following seven chapters with a significance that transcends the contingency of the answers. This also clarifies why the book does not culminate in a unified proposition that resolves the contradiction in some convenient concluding consensus. There is no jointly authored Epilegomenon that compares with this common Prolegomenon. Like in real life, this encounter ends in a simple act of disengagement. Thus the substance of this book must be recovered from the actual course of the conversation—an often faltering exchange of thought, hope and agony that, like all communion among friends, offers instances of veracity in the paratactical stills which separate and connect the expository affirmations.

PART ONE

INTRODUCTION

ONE

Heraclitean Heritance

Robert Jan van Pelt

From gallery-grave and the hunt of a wren-king
    to Low Mass and trailer camp
is hardly a tick by the carbon clock, but I
    don't count that way nor do you:
already it is millions of heartbeats ago
    back to the Bicycle Age,
before which is no *After* for me to measure,
    just a still prehistoric *Once*
where anything could happen. To you, to me,
    Stonehenge and Chartres Cathedral,
the Acropolis, Blenheim, the Albert Memorial
    are works by the same Old Man
under different names: we know what he did,
    what, even, He thought He thought,
but we don't see why. (To get that, one would have
    to be selfish in His way,
without concrete or grapefruit.) It's our turn now
    to puzzle the unborn. No world
wears as well as it should but, mortal or not,
    a world has still to be built
because of what we can see from our windows,
    that Immortal Commonwealth
which is there regardless: It's in perfect taste
    and it's never boring but
it won't quite do. Among its populations
    are masons and carpenters
who build the most exquisite shelters and safes,
    but no architects, any more

> than there are heretics and bounders: to take
>   umbrage at death, to construct
> a second nature of tomb and temple, lives
>   must know the meaning of *If*.

W.H. Auden, "The Beginning of Architecture,"
from *Thanksgiving for a Habitat*

For it is not possible to step twice unto the same river, according to Heraclitus, nor to touch mortal substance twice in any condition: by the swiftness and speed of its change, it scatters and collects itself again—or rather, it is not again and later but simultaneously that it comes together and departs, approaches and retires.

Plutarch, from *On the E at Delphi*

In the Prolegomenon we described how architectural theory has changed from a normative and prescriptive paradigm into a self-conscious discourse adrift in the ever changing currents of time. The metaphor alluded to the idea of history as a powerful torrent. First formulated by Heraclitus of Ephesus (c.540–c.475 BCE), this disturbing notion was quickly buried by Platonists, Stoics and Christians alike to remain delitescent until it was resurrected at the beginning of this century by such prominent philosophers of history as Ernst Troeltsch (1865–1923) and Friedrich Meinecke (1862–1954).[1] They popularized the image of history as a "stream of becoming, which makes all relative and dissolves everything in waves"[2] to address the collapse of the Ciceronian dictum that knowledge of the past can help us to face the future. Heraclitus' heritage is the plight of the architectural historian–designer: she turns to the past to find the Archimedean point on which to build a new world; yet she only runs into the Heraclitean river of constant change and endless becoming. The architectural–historical–theoretical literature does not show awareness of this predicament.[3] Therefore I will delineate in this chapter the main thrust of a by now almost century-old philosophical discussion on the existential implications of the modern understanding of the historicity of time. This debate centers on the debilitating implications of what some call historical relativism, others the problem of relativism and historicism, and again others label as the "Historical Point of View."

Let us begin with the context: the historicity of our own culture. It is difficult for us today to see our own situation in perspective, and, for example, the battle between modernists and postmodernists seems important. If we take a wider perspective, however, and compare this confrontation to the larger development of architectural history, then it seems as relevant now as the quarrel among the champions of the Neo-Gothic, Neo-Classical or Neo-Byzantine styles in the nineteenth century. In other words, it is pretty insignificant as the paradigm of our architectural civilization is not at stake. This paradigm is some two centuries old, and it is the abiding and invisible ground of our understanding of architecture. Its main characteristic is the sense of being a part of that dynamic process known as architectural history. Postmodernist, modernist, futurist, eclectist, classicist: whatever the designation we give an architect, they have in common that they are empowered by history, and not by God, nature, guild or science. Nineteenth- and twentieth-century architects know that the past is prostrate at their feet; they know that they stand on the summit of the present, they look back at the cumulative accomplishment of centuries, and feel able to decide what is fit to be kept (remembered) and what may be destroyed (through oblivion). Like gods bound by no law they judge without being bound by any standard of judgement of what is good or bad except that of their own position in time. History has empowered them with a past that is relative to their own existence. Yet these architects also realize that posterity will judge them in the same manner as they judge the past.

Many have only an inchoate feeling about the historicity of their own production. A few develop a more articulated sense of history. A critical discernment of one's place in time is the first and perhaps the most important criterion that has separated in the nineteenth and twentieth centuries the prominent architect from the production slave. This knowledge of history might take different forms. It might focus on the time of the place or expand towards the aeon of the world as told in myth; it might survey in a broad sweep a thousand-year history of changing styles, or study the pulse of the changing architectural fashion as reported by architectural critics like Paul Goldberger or Adèle Freedman; it might attend closely on keeping just ahead of the discovery of others, or address in apocalyptic terms a desired future. Aesthetic, functionalist, ontological: whatever the nature of such knowledge, it is historical, allowing no space for doctrines that claim a supernatural and therefore enduring validity, as it is in the nature of things that everything (even the manifestation of Being) changes. It is no accident that the greatest architects in the last two hundred years proposed, each in his own way, some kind of theory about the relationship between his design activity and the unfolding development of architecture. It is no accident that architectural theory, as it informs the educational process in architecture schools, is in fact applied history. Anyone who has attended architectural juries knows that the worthwhile critic not only has a keen eye, a sense of logic and a measure of common sense, but also a vision of history. Without the historical perspective there is no norm as to the "meaning" of the work displayed on the wall.

As the idea of history has been the foundation of thinking about values and norms in the last two centuries, so the idea of a history of architecture has been the basis of the criterion that informs our view of architecture. Paraphrasing Troeltsch (whose insights on the historicist character of the last two hundred years framed the foregoing reflections), we may state that architectural history has been the medium that allows architects and architectural critics to reflect upon the nature, origins and purpose of architecture.[4] Therefore it seems to offer such promise as a basis for teaching design. Yet it is a false promise. In his poem "The Beginning of Architecture" Auden pondered the debilitating implications of the historiographical paradigms which, as a convergence of a historicism and a relativism, have shaped the historical perspective in the past two centuries, and the resulting fallaciousness of the claim that architectural history can offer a criterion for architectural practice. The epistemological ground of the modern (and postmodern) era and its historiography declare that, as far as we are concerned, "Stonehenge and Chartres Cathedral, / the Acropolis, Blenheim, the Albert Memorial / are works by the same Old Man / under different names." Auden understood more of the writing of history than most architectural historians, who prefer to think that we can know what the Old Man did, that we are able to reconstruct "what, even, He thought He thought," and who believe that the result of that labor will have some normative significance.

Yet few of them read Auden—after all he has become unfashionable. And few today would dare to acknowledge that they read and appreciated C.S. Lewis's *Screwtape Letters*, one of the more populist sources of Auden's musings. After all, in a time of TV evangelism it seems unsophisticated to state in public, as C.S. Lewis (1898–1963) did, that one believes in Satan. Yet the exile of the *Screwtape Letters* to the jubilant shelves in the "Good News" bookstores is undeserved. Almost fifty years after their first publication in the *Guardian* they remain one of the more entertaining and penetrating critiques of the human condition in general, and the modern (and postmodern) situation in particular. Lewis believed that the present historiographical paradigm served a satanic purpose. If people learn from history, they will realize that crime does not pay. Therefore it is in the interest of Satan to prevent them from learning from history. In the candid confession of a high-ranking bureaucrat in the kingdom of Satan, the devil Screwtape, Lewis described the success of the satanic plot. Screwtape instructs a low-ranking "Tempter" (his cousin Wormwood) on how to guarantee a steady supply of human souls to hell. Referring to "the intellectual climate which we have at last succeeded in producing throughout Europe," Screwtape notices scoffingly that Wormwood could rest assured that hell would remain fully booked as people have lost their ability to learn valuable lessons from the past. First the link between past and present is broken by the functional illiteracy of the masses. "Only the learned read old books and we have now so dealt with the learned that they are of all men the least likely to acquire wisdom by doing so." This brings Screwtape to explain to Wormwood the sterility of historical knowledge.

We have done this by inculcating The Historical Point of View. The Historical Point of View, put briefly, means that when a learned man is presented with any statement in an ancient author, the one question he never asks is whether it is true. He asks who influenced the ancient writer, and how far the statement is consistent with what he said in other books, and what phase in the writer's development, or in the general history of thought, it illustrates, and how it affected later writers, and how often it has been misunderstood (especially by the learned man's own colleagues) and what the general course of criticism on it has been for the last ten years, and what is the "present state of the question". To regard the ancient writer as a possible source of knowledge—to anticipate that what he said could possibly modify your thoughts or your behavior—this would be rejected as unutterably simple-minded. And since we cannot deceive the whole human race all the time, it is most important thus to cut every generation off from all the others; for where learning makes a free commerce between the ages there is always the danger that the characteristic errors of one may be corrected by the characteristic truths of another. But thanks be to our Father and the Historical Point of View, great scholars are now as little nourished by the past as the most ignorant mechanic who holds that "history is bunk."[5]

Applied to architecture Screwtape's observations would read more or less as follows: the historian cannot ask whether a historic building is good or bad (as we cannot know), is true or false, right or wrong (on the plea that we cannot know), but only report that so-and-so designed it, that he derived the inspiration for the form from such-and-such sources, that it resembled certain other buildings (or pictures in books, or descriptions in texts), that different architects were influenced by the building, that they imitated it, or readapted the original to a new purpose, that it became a national symbol or not, that it gained recognition as a masterwork and became the focus of costly restoration campaigns, or that it fell into ruin and that it was finally pulled down as a safety hazard to the public. This is an outline of what architectural historians consider a solid prospectus of an architectural–historical investigation.

Screwtape's Historical Point of View, which popularized the more academic observations of Troeltsch, Meinecke, Acton and Heraclitus, summarized the dominant ideology that has shaped the historiography of the West for the past two centuries. It informs the methodology and ambitions of the standard architectural history courses offered in architecture schools. As Heraclitus recognized already twenty-five centuries ago, relativism is the other side of the historicist coin that declares life as historical. Thus everything is relative to history and unrelated to anything else because every age must be considered in its own terms. It seems so innocent to think of history as a sequence of critical actions that bring a new present into existence. And no one is alarmed when we read that this new present makes "that which was present irretrievably past."[6] Yet it is pure nihilism that denies enduring and universally valid norms that connect the past with the present, and, therefore, the now with the future. Confronted with this turmoil it is not surprising that a knowledge of architectural history is so useless when a person sets out to puzzle as an architect (and not as a mason or carpenter) the unborn.

The Cause of the Historian's Predicament

When I read Screwtape's ruminations for the first time I got the uncanny intimation that the postmodern attitude to the past fits the (modern) relativist understanding of history. I felt that this attitude to historical knowledge as the purveyor of instantly retrievable and applicable accessories predated Venturi's trip to Las Vegas by a century or two. Years later I have become convinced that my first apprehension was correct. The question *Architectural Principles in the Age of Historicism* tries to address did not emerge from the collapse of the modernist dream. In fact the unresolved relationship between architectural history and architectural practice was the pitfall into which the moderns sank the foundations of their Crystal Palace, the quicksand that swallowed in rapid succession the architectures based on romantic reminiscences and teleological creeds. Venturi's commercial strip only disclosed what has been there for almost two centuries. This implies that the scope of our discussion should not be limited to the developments of the last twenty years. We must take issue with a two-century-old perverse and pertinacious evolution. I would like to stress this point, as it is otherwise impossible to appreciate Westfall's and my own propositions. The two of us are convinced that we must go back to the eighteenth-century *philosophes* and their immediate successors to see if a relationship between history and practice different from the historicist and relativist paradigm (which would be canonized as the result of their combined effort) is possible.

The story of the Historical Point of View finds its origin in Heraclitus' musings. It only became historically significant two hundred and fifty years ago. At that time Europe was (still) a patchwork of customary societies where people invoked time-honored customs as a justification for their actions. Each of these societies was held together by wholly natural authority based on tradition. Custom was an inheritance and therefore beyond doubt. It was accepted that this inheritance should be transmitted to the next generation. Edmund Burke (1729–97) stated that inside a traditional society people could act without reference "to any more general or prior right."[7] Habit was a sufficient foundation for authority as the societal usages of people seemed perfectly integrated in the periodic cycles of nature. For most people life was still a question of living the five or seven ages of man in a natural fashion, which meant a life structured by age-old rites of passage and enduring sacraments. Thus the customary order of society converged with the world understood as the nexus of tellurian mysteries, human artifice and divine order.

> Our political system is placed in a just correspondence and symmetry with the order of the world, and with the mode of existence decreed to a permanent body composed of transitory parts; wherein, by the disposition of a stupendous wisdom, moudling together the great mysterious incorporation of the human race, the whole, at one time, is never old, or middle-aged, or young, but in a condition of unchangeable constancy, moves on through the varied tenour of perpetual decay, fall, renovation and progression. Thus, by preserving the method of nature in the conduct of the state, in what we improve we are never wholly new; in what we retain we are never wholly obsolete. By adhering in this manner and on those principles to our forefathers, we are guided not by the superstition of antiquarians, but by the spirit of philosophic analogy. In this choice of inheritance we have given to our frame of polity the image of a relation in blood; binding up the constitution of our country with our dearest domestic ties; adopting our fundamental laws into the bosom of our family affections; keeping inseparable, and cherishing with the warmth of all their combined and mutually reflected charities, our state, our hearths, our sepulchres, and our altars.[8]

For a more theoretical assessment and justification of these and similar sentiments I refer the reader to Chapter Two.[9] Here I would like to consider only the historiographical implication of custom. Because it recognized its final authority in the knowledge that "these are the ways of our fathers, and it has always been so, and it therefore will remain so," the customary society did not think about the past as separate from the present. This did not imply that there was no change. Change was hidden. Because custom is not fixed, it could create a successful appearance of fixity because change happened by insensible degree. In other words the awareness of change was surrendered to oblivion. Human actions that transcended the cycles of nature were also subsumed in the order of things. This is well illustrated in Burke's interpretation of Stonehenge. Burke argued that this megalithic monument had become the most sacred of the English monuments *because* its original intention had been forgotten: oblivion of the particular intention had created a universal horizon of meaning framed by the natural authority of custom.

> The great stones, it has been supposed, were originally monuments of illustrious men, or the memorials of considerable action; or they were landmarks for deciding the bounds of fixed property. In time, the memory of the persons or facts which these stones were erected to perpetuate wore away; but the reverence which custom, and probably certain periodical ceremonies, had preserved for those places was not so soon obliterated. The monuments themselves then came to be venerated; and not the less because the reason for venerating them was no longer known.[10]

Two pillars of memory stood within this landscape of oblivion: the classical tradition and the Judeo-Christian inheritance. These two bodies of knowledge, which explicitly celebrated the remembrance of great deeds and cataclysmic events that had changed the world, had been largely dissolved into the traditions of society at large. Yet where they seemed to break the closed circle of custom, they did so only to offer a new horizon of unquestioning authority. The classical and the Judeo-Christian tradition were maintained on the assumption that there was no chasm that separated the past from the present. In the classical tradition there was no separation because change was merely illusionary; in the Judeo-Christian tradition change followed the divine plan, and the present, past and future were connected in God.

In Western Europe the legitimacy of custom had become increasingly problematical since the late fifteenth century. The voyages of discovery, the increased dissemination of information, the reformation and counter-reformation, the destruction of the Aristotelian worldview and the rise of Cartesian doubt and discourse had sapped the foundations of custom. Yet until the mid-eighteenth century most Europeans lived their lives as their ancestors had done: their intellectual horizon coincided with that of their eyes, and the traditional authorities still had authority. Very few realized that things were not so self-evident anymore. These people began to seek contact with each other, which in the beginning of the eighteenth century led to the emergence of a much more cosmopolitan attitude in the leading political, social, intellectual and economic circles in Western Europe. Norman Hampson described "this cosmopolitan society, with its ties of kinship and patronage criss-crossing Europe like telephone wires" as a network that offered many opportunities for the exchange of ideas. "Travellers and their books abounded—and the eighteenth century traveller was no hasty tourist, insulated within his national capsule. Once arrived at his immediate destination, his letters of introduction procured him access to local society."[11] Narrow-mindedness did not bring a person far in a culture dominated by such institutions as the Grand Tour, the Freemason's Lodge and the Salon, and the authoritative descriptions of countries and peoples abroad that seemed so reliable back home proved prejudicial when checked against the facts.

It is not surprising that the cosmopolitan milieu of the early eighteenth century favored Locke's empiricist epistemology, which firmly based knowledge on sense experience. Locke's *An Essay Concerning Human Understanding* (1690) tried to attract the reader to his argument through a reference to a common experience: travel. Locke (1632–1704) stated that he had begun to think about the discerning faculties of man and the way people gain knowledge of things when he noticed on his journeys the difference and variety of people's persuasions, and how each nation nevertheless asserts its beliefs with such "assurance and confidence, that he shall take a view of the opinions of mankind, observe their opposition, and at the same time consider the fondness and devotion wherewith they are embraced, and the resolution and eagerness wherewith they are maintained, may perhaps have reason to suspect, that either there is no such a thing as truth at all, or that mankind has no sufficient means to attain a certain knowledge of it."[12] Locke's relativist point was well taken, and his idea that "the senses internal or external, appear to be all the passages of knowledge to the understanding, and the windows by which light is let into this dark room"[13] became the psychological creed of the Enlightenment.

Yet the great European party turned sour when the travelling gentlefolk realized that their worldly discernment and sophistication had left them without an ethical code. Having declared an adherence to custom as the sign of small-minded insularity, the belief in religious doctrine as the result of superstitious bigotry and the regard for classical precepts as biased conservatism in an era of scientific progress, they found that they had lost the ability to identify the difference between good and bad manners, or, what was worse, between good and evil. Locke had argued that knowledge derives from the experience of our environment, from which others inferred that our thoughts and our actions are natural and thus admissible. This moral empiricism led to a disturbing set of discussions that gave a sinister edge to the festive gathering in the eighteenth-century salon.[14] Some concluded that the bad was but the mask of the good. They found elegant support in Pope's *Essay on Man*, which declared that nature was a work of art in which all partial evil cumulated in universal good. Others believed that one should not dismiss the problem of evil so easily. Denis Diderot (1713–84), for example, stated that he would have liked to believe that the eternal will of nature should prefer good to evil. Yet he could not accept that the bad was the mask of the good, and so he refused to sing Pope's hymn. Some lost their course completely in an increasingly confusing ethical discourse. A few of them, like Julien Offray de la Mettrie (1709–51), decided to break through the metaphysical deadlock, and disengaged the age-old connection between virtue and felicity. They declared that the pleasures of the mind are the real source of happiness, and because the foundation of ethics was the pursuit of happiness, it followed that the distinction between good and evil was a semantic one. De Sade (1740–1814) turned these currents of thought into an all-devouring intellectual maelstrom.

Some believed that science offered a new basis of truth, and hoped that Newton's philosophy would be an ensured source of light in what had become an increasingly dark age. After all, if Newton's simple and elegant equation provided an easy key with which a gentleman of moderate learning could come to understand the structure of the universe, then one could reasonably hope that Newtonian science would also give some guidance in matters ethical. Yet Sir Isaac Newton (1642–1727) disappointed them. His *Optics* revealed how the vast mathematical system described in the *Principia*, a universe of regular motions described in elegant equations, was disconnected from the world of experience. That world of pleasure and pain was but a delusion of the senses, while the world of truth was an indifferent quantity. The great propagator of Newtonism, Joseph Addison (1672–1719), summarized the disconcerting reality of the Newtonian world in the 413th issue of the *Spectator*. Assuming an acquaintance with Newton's discovery that "Light and Colours, as apprehended by the Imagination, are only Ideas in the Mind, and not Qualities that have any Existence in Matter," and confusing them through a problematic allusion to Locke's *Essay Concerning Human Understanding*, he described the human condition in disturbing terms.

> We are everywhere entertained with pleasing shows and apparitions, we discover imaginary glories in the heavens, and in the earth, and see some of this visionary beauty poured upon the whole creation; but what a rough unsightly sketch of nature should we be entertained with, did all her coloring disappear, and the several distinctions of light and color vanish? . . . I have here supposed that my reader is here acquainted with that great modern discovery, which is at

present universally acknowledged by all the inquiries into natural philosophy, namely that light and colours, as apprehended by the imagination, are only ideas in the mind and not qualities that have any existence in matter. . . . Our souls are at present delightfully lost and bewildered in a pleasing delusion, and we walk about like the enchanted hero in a romance, who sees beautiful castles, woods, and meadows; and at the same time hears the warbling of birds, and the purling of streams; but upon the finishing of some secret spell, the fantastic scene breaks up, and the disconsolate knight finds himself on a barren heath, or in a solitary desert.[15]

Thus even the Newtonians had to acknowledge that the eighteenth-century salon stood on Lear's heath, and like the dispossessed king they could have recognized themselves in Poor Tom who, as Lear inferred, "wert better in a grave" than to answer the "extremity of the skies" with his naked body. And with Lear even the Newtonians could not but ask if man was, after all, "nothing more than this," nothing more than a "poor, bare and forked animal." For all its elegant pretence that man lived in Dr Pangloss's best of all possible worlds, the cosmopolitan *philosophes* knew that reality was different. The human race had become a rudderless ship drifting on an ocean of purposeless causation, or a sad piece of wreckage floating down a torrent of terror. At the end of the century, after the guillotine had completed the project begun by Locke, the German poet Friedrich Hölderlin (1770–1843) was to write the epitaph for that enduring and self-sufficient world of eternal truths that had been lost. His oeuvre, which gave a new language and a new silence to the modern age, mourned the catastrophe that had ruptured the relationship between the gods and mortals. Looking at the formless world he had inherited he desponded as all had been abandoned to an uncertain end. "We are fated," so the protagonist of Hölderlin's *Hyperion* (1799) lamented,

> To find no foothold, no rest,
> And suffering mortals
> Dwindle and fall
> Headlong from one
> Hour to the next,
> Hurled like water
> From ledge to ledge
> Downward for years to the vague abyss.[16]

Looking back two hundred and fifty years later at the eighteenth-century crisis, it is remarkable how little has changed. And just as some of us today try to find a rudder and find a course, so did the Enlightenment *philosophes*.

They decided to take the future as one's standard. Realizing that the present was hardly ideal, and that the past had been even worse, some decided to transform the Judeo-Christian eschatological vision of history into a secular doctrine of progress. Because the moderns were superior to the ancients, so the tomorrow would be better than today. To live a meaningful life implied to live in the light of progress. The past was only a foil to the future. The chronicles that recorded it were but catalogues of crimes, barbarism, scarcity, stupidity and prejudice, evils in short which could be overcome through the application of enlightened "progressive" policies. Thus the old distinction between good and evil, which had become untenable, was replaced by the objectively valid and empirically affirmed differentiation between progress and reaction.[17] (With the collapse of the modernist ideal the dominance of the doctrine of progress came to an end; therefore the renewed relevance of the eighteenth-century struggle with the questions of good and evil.)

Yet even the champions of the future believed that the study of history had some use. Liberation from the shackles of the past required an understanding of what was authentic to (wo)man; definition of progressive policies implied the identification of (wo)man's potential for improvement. Thus the would-be reformers had to define some idea of (wo)man, a concept of human nature that was, in the words of R.G. Collingwood (1889–1943), "something static and permanent, an unvarying substratum underlying the course of historical changes and all human activities."[18] This idea was the foundation on which to erect the edifice of the future. Carl Lotus Becker (1873–1945) has described how the *philosophes* began "to go up and down the wide world with the lamp of Enlightenment looking, as Montaigne did before them, for 'man in general.'" They hoped to do so through an empirical identification and enumeration of that which people had in common. With this they would be able to create a new standard of judgement as to "what ideas and customs and institutions in their own time were out of harmony with the universal natural order."[19]

Two sciences were specially suited for this quest for a new ethical basis: anthropology and history. If the first surveyed the world as space, the second saw the world as time. The traditional notion of history was not very helpful. It was provincial, and closely linked the Judeo-Christian and classical traditions, which had lost their authority. Therefore the *philosophes* called for a new kind of history, a history enabling people "to make that distinction, which abstract reason was unable to make, between the naturally good and the naturally bad, between customs that were suited and those that were unsuited to man's nature."[20] Thus they approached the past to reconstruct the image of (wo)man. The first task they faced was to collect and organize information on the ideas, customs and institutions of all peoples at all times and in all places. Comparison of these data would allow them to distinguish between those facts or modifications that appeared contingent and those that seemed universally valid. These common aspects of human experience would disclose the constant principles of human nature which, the *philosophes* believed, offered a new basis for action. The high expectations with which the Enlightenment turned to history implied the importance of the highest methodological standards. Historiography had to become "scientific."

The *philosophes* were not the first to turn to the past to find guidance for action. Classical historiography had been explicitly normative and pre-scriptive. It had operated within an inherited, self-evident, well-defined and enduring metaphysical universe. This meant that (the old) history showed how (an already known) general law operated in specific situations. The purpose of the new history was to reconstruct, through study of specific situations, a scientific knowledge of the laws of history, which are the same as the laws that rule human behavior. The *philosophes* assumed that (wo)man and society were the same kind of objectifiable phenomenons as the marvels of nature examined by the new scientists, and they believed that a scientific understanding of human reality would help to undergird the dilapidating edifice of civilization that had been erected on the by now shifting bed of local custom, Greco-Roman and Judeo-Christian thought.

It made sense to turn to the philosophers of nature, as they had been the first to repudiate the traditional notion that ancient authority or innate ideas give a true knowledge of the essence of the world and its wonders. Assuming that the world is open to human inspection, they already had begun to substitute knowledge derived from Aristotle and the Bible by data derived from sense experience long before the publication of Locke's *Essay*. And the scientists had begun to link these facts to each other according to the laws of causality. This deterministic epistemology has remained the foundation of classical science. From its inception this epistemology had a strong historical component. The philosophers of nature argued that a valid explanation of any aspect of the physical world demanded an understanding of the etiology and genealogy that connect, over time, a cause from the past with an effect in the present. Aristotelian philosophy of nature described the universe through final causes and essences, and was, therefore, futile. Thus scientists stopped speculations on why things are as they are, and turned to reconstructions that describe how things had become the way they were. Scientific knowledge became historical.

The new empiricist epistemology suggested the potential and the form of a scientific approach to history. If it was feasible to see nature in historicist terms, then it was also plausible to think about history (and therefore [wo]man as a historical being and human civilization as a product of human history) from a scientific perspective through the formulation of some laws that explain why things developed the way they did. This possibility was, however, not fully exploited until the end of the eighteenth century. Before this time history did not become the study of the continual transformations because, as Becker explained, philosophers were not interested in the question. "They did not ask how society had come to be what it was, but how it could be made better than it was. There is no more apt illustration of this slant of mind than the famous opening sentences of Rousseau's *Social Contract*. 'Man is born free, and is everywhere in chains. How was this change made? *I do not know*. What can make it legitimate? I believe I can answer that question.'" Becker urged us therefore not to ask the *philosophes* that question which was to become so important in the nineteenth century: "How did society come to be what it is?" With Rousseau the *philosophes* would reply: "We do not know." And, as Becker speculated, "we at once feel they have it on the tip of their tongues to dismiss us with an impatient, 'and we do not care.'"[21] They cared about history so far as it gave them insight into the unchanging aspects of human nature. They mined it for useful information and were not interested in the historicity of the past. A historian like Vico, who was interested in questions of becoming and the processes of change, remained at the periphery of the historiographical discourse.

This changed at the end of the eighteenth century in Germany. From 1750 Germany had been the center of a (proto-)Romantic protest against the *philosophes*' attitude to knowledge and its utilitarian perspective on the world in general. The different repressive regimes that made up the patchwork of ambitions known as the Holy Roman Empire had readily adopted the ideals of the *philosophes*. In Germany the new ideas on human society were not adopted to further the emancipation of the people from the inherited structures of the past. Instead the reigning kings, princes, dukes, bishops and counts used the ideology of Enlightenment to create more enlightened and more efficient instruments of suppression. German society was characterized by the lack of access to the government of the educated bourgeoisie and the intelligentsia. Most burghers had accepted the decline of their position, which had started three centuries earlier, and had settled for a life of pettiness, spite and submission.

About 1750, however, a new generation arose from the pool of resentment and discontent to initiate a new approach to history.[22] Setting themselves up against the rulers and their pragmatic councilors, these young men who would label themselves *Sturm und Drang* (Storm and Stress) called for a spiritual reawakening of the sunken bourgeoisie. Trying to recover a link with their past greatness, they set out to create a bridge between their own situation and the Middle Ages, the Golden Age in the history of the German bourgeoisie. Attempting to restore a sense of continuity, the young radicals were more concerned with the genealogy of identity than with the possibility of utility. They agreed that the *philosophes* had given (wo)man a very distorted self-understanding: rejecting authoritative customs, their pragmatic and instrumentalist posture only reinforced the separation between the bourgeoisie and the organic totality from which they had emerged and in which they had blossomed. It seemed that their future was without perspective, that, as Johann Gottfried Herder (1744–1803) wrote, "this building of one age upon another renders the whole of our species a deformed gigantic edifice, where one pulls down what the other built up, where what never should have been erected is left standing, and where in the course of time all becomes one heap of ruins, under which timid mortals dwell with a confidence proportionate to its fragility."[23]

Against this the champions of the *Sturm und Drang* proposed a vision of human life that stressed its relationship to its own creative powers, a vision that understood (wo)man and society as being in a constant state of transition that served, despite such occasional lapses as the decline of the German bourgeoisie, a higher purpose. This purpose unfolded from a central core of identity, and aimed at the fulfillment of the creative powers of the nation. Thus Herder reminded his powerless friends that "with the lapse of ages many of your edifices decay, and much of your gold is sunk in the slough of forgetfulness; the labors were not in vain, for such of your works, as Providence thought fit to save, have been saved in other forms."

> In any other way no human monument can endure wholly and eternally upon Earth; being formed in the succession of generations by the hand of time for temporal use, and evidently prejudicial to posterity, as soon as it renders unnecessary or retards their farther exertion. Thus the mutable form and imperfection of all human operations entered into the plan of the creator. Folly must appear, that wisdom might surmount it: decaying fragility even of the noblest works was an essential property of their materials, that men might have an opportunity of exerting fresh labors in improving or building upon their ruins: for we are all in a state of exercise.[24]

These comforting words are taken from Herder's *Ideen zur Philosophie der Geschichte der Menschheit* (Ideas on the Philosophy of Mankind) published between 1784 and 1791.[25] The book was a catalyst in the development of historical relativism by bringing together a few until then disparate ideas. First, Herder described the history of (wo)man and human society as the final stage of a natural evolution that had begun with the evolution of the cosmos, the earth, plants and animals. Therefore there was a continuity between the development of nature and the rise and fall of civilizations. Yet Herder did not believe that these external influences explained a national character or cultural achievement. He believed that history was a dialectic in which (wo)man's actions were shaped by the clash of natural forces that come from the outside and from his innate natural powers. The most important of these internal powers was language, the source of a people's identity. "Speech alone has rendered man human, by setting bounds to the vast flood of his passions, and giving him rational memorials by means of words. No cities have been erected by the lyre of Amphion, no magic wand has converted deserts into gardens; but language, the grand assistant of man, has done these."[26] The history of (wo)man is thus the history of language. There are different families of languages, each giving rise to its own linguistic community or *Volk*. Each language has it own characteristics, and the people who speak that language share the traits associated with it. Thus the German language engendered a hypotac- tical organic unity of the people who are assembled in the German *Volk*; the English language created an English folk and so on. Herder considered language as natural, and therefore the folk was natural and organic. Because there were many languages, there were many folks, and thus many histories which stood paratactically side by side. And as there was in the history of a people a continuity of language, the past linked to the present. This cultural continuity was not always expressed in the art or literature of a people in a given period. These conscious forms of cultural production could follow foreign fashion, adopting the forms of an alien *Zivilization*. This was, for example, the case in eighteenth-century Germany, where architects, painters and writers aped the French. Yet even in such times the folk had preserved German *Kultur*. The folk embodied a deeper community of thought, shared traditions, and a collective memory through its folk-lore.

Herder's naturalization of history negated the intentions of the *philo- sophes*, who had had turned to the past to reconstruct an understanding of human nature. Herder argued that there was no such thing as "Man" or "Humanity." There were the Germans, and the English, and the Jews, and the Chinese, and so on. Neither these peoples nor their histories compared to each other. Thus he introduced a relativist element in the study of history. For the time being this relativism remained under control: the powerful notion of language as a unifying element bridged the ages within the history of a specific people. If it was not possible to compare an eighteenth-century Englishman to an eighteenth-century Frenchman, it was possible to compare the former to his fourteenth-century ancestor (if, of course, English-speaking).

Herder's historiography had great resonance in a time of increasing nationalism. In Germany it led to the beginnings of the painful and as yet unresolved search for a national identity—a quest that, as I will argue in Chapter Three and demonstrate in Chapter Nine, was to change the face of architecture. Johann Wolfgang von Goethe (1749–1832) described in his autobiography how the new understanding of the existential relationship between language and national character emerged in a nation that, for two centuries, "went to school among the French in order to learn manners, and among the Romans in order to express himself worthily," leading to a situation that they ended up being nowhere at home, "least of all with themselves." And he continued to sketch the great effect of Herder's ideas. "But as already in this epoch [that is the 1780s] works of genius had appeared, the German sense of freedom and joy also began to stir itself. This, accompanied by a genuine earnestness, insisted that one should write purely and naturally without intermixture of foreign words and in accordance with common intelligible sense." The results were, however, not so laudable. "By these praiseworthy endeavors, however, the gates and doors were thrown open to a wide national insipidity, nay, the dike was broken through by which the grand deluge was soon to rush in."[27] Turning to the dark recesses of one's own repressed past disclosed at times the faded splendors of long-forgotten glories. Yet the wish to be one's own also contributed to the dissolution of the cosmopolitan perspective of the Enlightenment. The deluge of mediocrity that penetrated the broken wall of internationalism led to the stagnant provincialism that characterized so much of nineteenth-century intellectual life.

The English translation of the *Ideen* appeared in 1799. It showed the validity of Burke's view of a customary society and was therefore seen as a defence against the internationalist ideals of the French revolution. Its influence spread with the restoration of the old regimes after the collapse of Napoleon's version of a unified Europe. Having suffered the rationalist regime that claimed to serve "Humanity," people decided that it was better to muddle on within the undoubtedly corrupt context that history had bequeathed them. Becker deemed this conservative reaction to twenty-five years of revolution, war and upheaval as the cause of a new interest in a nation's roots. "Most people felt the need of stabilizing society; and the most satisfactory rationalization of this need was presented by those historians and jurists who occupied themselves with social origins, who asked the question, How did society, especially the particular society of this or that nation, come to be what it is? The unconscious preconception involved in this question was that if men understood just how customs of any nation had come to be what they were, they would sufficiently realize the folly of trying to refashion them all at once according to some rational plan."[28] The historians of the restoration adapted Herder's historiography to their own end. As a rule they threw out its most radical part: the organic theory of language. Of course it was untenable, as a more critical study of the sources revealed that the same word may have different meanings in different ages. People think differently as they develop. Yet, with the amputation of what seemed a useless limb, the nineteenth-century historians removed from Herder's historiographical vision the one element that had connected the history of each folk with the past and the present. Now the relativism that had already divided the different folks from each other began to affect the relationship between a people and its ancestors.

Few historians seemed to deplore the act of self-destruction they had committed in the name of scientific objectivity. Historicism was applauded, not condemned. The great English historian John Dalberg Acton (1833–1902) cried that history had governed when there was no knowledge of history, and that "when the knowledge of history came, the power of history departed," yet no one cared to listen.[29] Instead the professional historians congratulated themselves on the discovery that it is impossible to judge a specific culture or its achievements according to such impartial measuresticks as a transcendent notion of truth or meaning. They felt at ease with the notion that every historical culture had its own distinctive content, its own inherent and characteristic meaning, it own incommensurable worth and, especially, its own law. The new rigidity allowed them to defend their territory from invasions by the lesser educated who still believed that one could learn from history. In Fustel de Coulanges' *The Ancient City* (1864) we read, for example, that "the last eighty years have clearly shown that one of the great difficulties which impede the march of modern society is the habit which it has of always keeping Greek and Roman antiquity before its eyes." The reference is to the First Republic and the Napoleonic Empire. The scholarly Fustel de Coulanges (1830–89) wanted to distance himself from the notion that his reconstruction of the Greek and Roman customs and institutions could have normative significance or contemporary relevance. He continued with the observation that he would "endeavor to make clear once for all the radical and essential differences separating the ancient peoples from modern society." He recognized that the omnipresence of their legacy makes it difficult to think of them as an alien people. "This has given rise to many errors, and errors in this field are not without danger. If one wants to learn the truth about ancient peoples it is well to study them without thinking of ourselves. We must consider them as if they were wholly strange, and we should do so with a mind as free and with as much objectivity as we would employ, say, in studying the ancient Indians or Arabians. Thus considered, Greece and Rome come before us in a wholly inimitable way. Nothing in modern times is like them; nothing in the future can ever be like them again."[30]

Most historians today would agree with Fustel de Coulanges, and declare that thinking and valuing depend on their time and culture. Most historians think that rigorous objectivism is the paradigm of sound scholarship. They follow the greatest of the nineteenth-century historians, Leopold von Ranke (1795–1886), in a search for "how it actually happened." Few agree with the Lord Acton's perception that von Ranke's "modesty" led to "variable ethics" and a "perverted conscience."[31] Most historians consider Lord Acton a celebrated failure, famous for the non-book *The History of Freedom*, a book that was never written. Von Ranke, however, is remembered as the founding father of critical history. Thus they feel that they may underwrite his maxim that every age is equally close to God, or, in other words, that the value of a specific historical civilization does not depend on its resonance in later developments, but solely on its own existence. Each civilization exists for its own sake.

In comparison with the earlier classical and Judeo-Christian historiographic traditions, the relativist stance canonized by Ranke seems cosmopolitan in scope and humble in attitude. Leo Strauss assessed relativism differently. He discovered an extremely provincial and narrow-minded core behind the liberal facade. He argued that a relativist historian may only describe another time or civilization in its own terms if he has sympathetic understanding for it. From this he inferred that the historian is "gripped by the values to which the society in question is committed" and this demands of the historian to "expose one's self in earnest, with a view to one's own whole life, to the claim of those values to be the true values." Because almost all cultures and civilizations have been characterized by a nonrelativist, absolute commitment to its own values, it follows that the relativist cannot have genuine understanding. The paradoxical consequence is that "the field within which relativists can practice sympathetic understanding is restricted to the community of relativists who understand each other with great sympathy because they are united by identically the same fundamental commitment, or rather by identically the same rational insight into the truth of relativism." And wryly Strauss concluded that "what claims to be the final triumph over provincialism reveals itself as the most amazing manifestation of provincialism."[32]

Few see with Strauss's (or for that matter Fustel's) clarity that in this universe of historical relativism history does not connect, but separates the historian from his object of study and the present from the past. Applied to architectural history this means that, as far as the observer in the present is concerned, buildings from the past are the work of "the same Old Man." Each building from the past reflected the specific conditions of its own time, but it is the same to us, as we cannot really distinguish among them because we cannot really know them. Thus Auden felt free to scramble in his "The Beginning of Architecture" the list of buildings, putting Chartres before the Acropolis. In so doing he stressed the point that, from the viewpoint of the present, each point in the past is cotemporal with each other point, because not one of them is cotemporal with us.

Architectural Style and the Historicist Paradigm

The contemporary chasm that separates the present from the past was an unintended outcome of Herder's historiographical revolution. His intention had been to do exactly the opposite, to change the old, nationless patrimonial world into one that stimulated an awakening of the past in the present. This paradox was to affect the nascent discipline of architectural history. Goethe's "rediscovery" of Gothic architecture, initiated by his visit to the once German city of Strasbourg in 1770, is one of the important moments in the development of the discipline. In one moment of revelation, recorded in an essay entitled "German Architecture, D.M. [*Diis manibus*] Ervini a Steinbach," published in 1772 and republished in 1773 as part of Herder's book on German customs and art, the enduring canons of the classical were declared of no use for Goethe's German understanding of German architecture (Gothic) built in times of German glory (thirteenth century) by a German architect (Erwin von Steinbach) on German soil (the French annexation of Strasbourg in 1681 had not affected the land). Nationalistic attachment, not aesthetic judgement, was the basis of appreciation. "Since now I found that the building had been based on old German ground, and had grown thus far in genuine German times, and that the name of the master on his modest gravestone was likewise of native sound and origin, I ventured, being incited by the worth of this work of art, to change the hitherto desired appellation of Gothic architecture, and to claim it for our nation as German architecture."[33] This historicist thesis had relativist implication. German architecture "should not be compared with the architecture of the Greeks and Romans, because it arose from an entirely different principle."[34]

Such thoughts, formulated in the last decades of the eighteenth century, constituted the basis of the nineteenth-century interpretation of the history of architecture as the record of a nation's physical, intellectual and creative history in stone. This interpretation, which still inspires the majority of architectural histories written today, centers on questions of style. The German architectural historian and theorist Gottfried Semper (1803–79) explained that style has an explicit historicist connotation because it refers to "the accord of an art object with its genesis, and with all the preconditions and circumstances of its becoming."[35] The stylistic identification of a work of architecture as "German" implies that it was built by a German architect in German times on German soil, and so on. Semper explained that the word "style" derives from the Roman *stylus*, the instrument that the ancients used to write or draw. If the style of a building refers to its genesis this means that it points to the hand that created it (the architect and the society that built it), the material that received the imprint of the style (Semper identified it as man "in all his relations and connections to the world") and the message that was written down, which is the spirit of a specific age.

Stylistic analysis allowed the historian to interpret old buildings as "fossilized receptacles of extinct social organizations," records of a historical development that traces the growth of a specific people's "understanding, observation of nature, genius, will, knowledge and power."[36] The result was an understanding of architectural history as a history of style and a history of culture. The nineteenth-century defined the knowledge of the past of architecture as that of the changing appearances of architecture over time. It defined architectural–historical research as the attempt to chart the sequence of changing circumstances that, on the one hand, caused stylistic changes and of which, on the other, those stylistic changes are symptomatic. This approach still predominates. A recent (and in general excellent) textbook has proudly announced, for example, that its purpose is to explain the change of architectural styles as a "cultural process." "This book is not a chronicle, encyclopedia, or catalogue," we are told, "but a history, and history is a dynamo of movement, influence, and climactic events." Therefore the authors decided not to discuss vernacular architecture as "the essence of vernacular building is its unchanging quality," and, therefore, it is an "architecture without history."[37] The approach suggests innovation (the statement that it is no chronicle, encyclopedia or catalogue suggests that other architectural histories are defined in those terms). Yet it merely reiterates what was already commonplace in the first decades of the nineteenth century. And in the authors' unwillingness (or inability) to deal with "architecture without history" the book aptly reveals the pitfall of modern historiography. After all before 1750 any architect or builder would have declared that his creation fitted timeless principles of architecture. This then means that a historian of architecture who refuses to discuss "architecture without history" cannot discuss buildings created before the Age of Historicism.

The Poet and the Architect

The architectural historian's solicitude about an "architecture without history" revokes the central idea of Herder's historiographical revolution.

The soul of a people's history, so Herder had argued, was not discourse but language: what mattered was not what people had said, but how they had said it. The truth of any history was not to be found through a study of the self-conscious philosophical debates in the academies or the declaratory royal propaganda imposed on the unwilling populations, but in the unmindful utterances of the peasants. Erwin von Steinbach had been a great architect not because his adoption of a French architectural system allowed him to overcome the particulars of his birth and upbringing, but because he had been able to root a monument to God in the vernacular traditions of "old German ground." Herder's legacy is therefore paradoxical: it produced the kind of stylistic analysis which describes architectural history as a "dynamo of movement," yet sanctioned a kind of approach which dissolves an interest in stylistic change into an intellection of the unchanging significance of the "spirit of place."

Does this alternative to historicism offer a way out of the relativist predicament? Some architectural historians think so. They base their conclusions on the work of the Swabian philosopher Martin Heidegger (1889–1976). In a lecture given on August 5, 1951, Heidegger laid the foundations of a new kind of architectural history, which stressed not change but permanence. His point of departure was a discussion of language. "Language," so he said, "tells us about the nature of a thing, provided that we respect language's own nature." This means that study of the etymology of, for example, the word "building" gave access to the unchanging meaning of a building—that is, the meaning a building has for those who call that thing "building" and not "edifice." Thus a *Bau* built by Germans has a different meaning than an *edificio* erected by Spaniards. The noun *Bau* derives from the German verb *bauen*, "to build." This word derived from the Old English and High German *buan*, "to dwell." Heidegger commented that "the real meaning of the verb *bauen*, namely, to dwell, has been lost to us. But a covert trace of it has been preserved in the German word *Nachbar*, neighbour. The neighbour is in Old English the *neahgebur*; *neah*, near, and *gebur*, dweller. The *Nachbar* is *Nachgebur*, the *Nachgebauer*, the near-dweller, he who dwells nearby." On this narrow basis Heidegger began to erect a new surrounding for architectural discourse. He observed that the word *buan* also suggested the meaning of dwelling. Dwelling is not an activity which people perform alongside other activities in the sense of "we work here and dwell there." No: dwelling is encompassing.

Bauen originally means to dwell. Where the word *bauen* still speaks in its original sense it also says *how far* the nature of dwelling reaches. That is, *bauen, buan, bhu, beo* are our word *bin* in the versions: *ich bin*, I am, *du bist*, you are; the imperative form *bis*, be. What then does *ich bin* mean? The old word *bauen*, to which *bin* belongs, answers: *ich bin, du bist* mean: I dwell, you dwell. The way in which you are and I am, the manner in which we humans *are* on the earth, is *Buan*, dwelling. To be a human being means to be on the earth as a mortal. . . . But "on the earth" already means "under the sky." Both of these *also* mean "Remaining before the divinities" and include a "belonging to men's being with one another." By a *primal* oneness the four—earth and sky, divinities and mortals—belong together in one.[38]

The modern city did not offer any space for such a dwelling. As an existential wasteland it did not deserve further study. Yet the vernacular architecture of the countryside preserved the essential meaning of *buan*. The great farmhouses and small cottages were embodiments of true *Baukunst*, architecture. Heidegger's analysis suggested a new kind of architectural history which described these examples of "architecture without history." Such a history would be true to the meaning of the Greek ἰστορία, *historia*: "a detached and systematic investigation." Most of the buildings which crowd the pages of the usual architectural histories would be absent. Yet some of the great monuments would find a place. Heidegger believed that the great temples of ancient Greece embodied the fourfold in an exemplary manner, that, in short, these buildings had been (and in a certain sense still were) true dwellings.

In a lecture entitled "The Origin of the Work of Art," given on November 13, 1935, Heidegger described the temple of Poseidon in the ancient Greek city of Poseidonia (Paestum), located 30 miles south of Naples. This building allowed the citizens of Poseidonia to dwell because it measured, according to Heidegger, the historicity of being as it is established in the duality of unconcealment and concealment and as it emerges in the strife between world (the realm of manifestation, of self-consciousness, culture and the tribulations of history) and earth (the domain of concealment, of unself-consciousness, nature and the unchanging destiny of a people). "A building, a Greek temple, portrays nothing," so Heidegger began his relation. In this one sentence he challenged that whole universe of discourse which reads building as records. Heidegger continued with an evocation of the buildings as it stands, on the earth, in the middle of the valley. Then he turned to the god and he spelled out how the sanctuary enshrined the statue of Poseidon and how this envelopment concealed the god from the world. Yet this concealment allowed also for revelation: only through his shrine did Poseidon acquire a presence which extended into the temple's precinct and which simultaneously delimited it as a holy precinct. This bounding of the sacred domain was important because only as a specific place could the temple become a dwelling. Only "there" could it order and gather "the unity of those paths and relations in which birth and death, disaster and blessing, victory and disgrace, endurance and decline acquire the shape of destiny for human beings." As the earth had pointed to the god, the god made it possible for people to establish a world of their own, that is that actual network of relations which defined in the sixth and fifth centuries BCE the world of the men and women who founded, built and preserved the city of Poseidonia. "Only from and in this expanse does the nation first return to itself for the fulfilment of its vocation."

> Standing there, the building rests on rocky ground. This resting of the work draws out of the rock's clumsy yet spontaneous support. Standing there, the building holds its ground against the storm raging above itself manifest in its violence. The luster and the gleam of the stone, though itself apparently glowing only by the grace of the sun, yet first brings to light the light of the day, the breadth of the sky, the darkness of the night. The temple's firm towering makes visible the invisible space of the air. The steadfastness of the work contrasts with the surge of the surf, and its own repose brings out the raging of the sea. Tree and grass, eagle and bull, snake and cricket first enter into their distinctive shapes and thus come to appear what they are. The Greeks called this emerging and rising in itself and in all things *phusis*. It clears and illuminates, also, that on which and in which man bases his dwelling. We call this ground the *earth*. What this word says is not to be associated with the idea of a mass or matter deposited somewhere, or with the merely astronomical idea of a planet. Earth is that whence the arising brings back and shelters everything that arises without violation. In the things that arise, earth is present as the sheltering agent.
>
> The temple-work, standing there, opens up a world and at the same time sets this world back again on earth, which itself only thus emerges as native ground. But men and animals, plants and things, are never present and familiar as unchanging objects, only to represent incidentally also a fitting environment for the temple, which one day is added to what is already there. We shall get closer to what *is*, rather, if we think of all this in reverse order, assuming of course that we have, to begin with, an eye for how differently everything then faces us. Mere reversing, done for its own sake, reveals nothing.
>
> The temple, in its standing there, first gives to things their look and to men their outlook on themselves.[39]

Heidegger asserted the awesome character of this dwelling as it had come to pass in the cultivation of the strife between the Mediterranean sky, the Italian earth, the Olympian gods and the inhabitants of Poseidonia. Yet this numinous truth had been distorted, vulgarized and finally lost in the subsequent centuries. It had been banished from the Roman *civitas*. The city became a place of *Zivilization*. The cultivation of the fourfold was, however, preserved in the countryside, the place of *Kultur*.

Did this mean that the peasant only remembered the principles of building? No: Heidegger suggested that the poet also knew the truth of dwelling. This was important, because the poet gave a voice to the silent wisdom of the farmer. In a lecture given a few months after his analysis of the meaning of the verb *bauen*, Heidegger turned his attention to the relation between poetry and dwelling. His lecture concerned an untitled poem which Friedrich Hölderlin had written after his mental collapse in 1806. One section of the poem he found especially significant.

> May a man look up
> From the utter hardship of his life
> And say: Let me also be
> Like these? Yes. As long as kindness lasts,
> Pure, within his heart, he may gladly measure himself
> Against the divine. Is God unknown?
> Is he manifest as the sky? This I tend
> To believe. Such is man's measure.
> Well deserving, yet poetically
> Man dwells on this earth. But the shadow
> Of the starry night is no more pure, if I may say so,
> Than man, said to be the image of God.
> Is there measure on earth? There is
> None.[40]

Heidegger expanded the paratactic "yet poetically" into a broadening of his philosophy of dwelling which specified that not mere language, but only "poetry first causes dwelling to be dwelling." First reading suggests, so he asserted, that human dwelling on earth is "well-deserving," and that, therefore, the paratactical "yet poetically" introduced a restriction on that meritorious dwelling of man. Yet it is just the reverse: the "well-deserving" restricts. Therefore Heidegger invited us to add to it "to be sure." The truth of dwelling was to be found in poetry. This, so he argued, was already initiated by the question which began the fragment under consideration: "May a man look up / From the utter hardship of his life / And say: Let me also be / Like these?" Heidegger commented:

> Only in the realm of sheer toil does man toil for "merits." There he obtains them for himself in abundance. But at the same time, in this realm, man is allowed to look up, out of it, through it, toward the divinities. The upward glance passes aloft toward the sky, and yet it remains below on the earth. The upward glance

spans the between of sky and earth. This between is measured out for the dwelling of man. We now call the span thus meted out the dimension. . . . The nature of the dimension is the meting out—which is lightened and so can be spanned—of the between: the upward of the sky as well as the downward to earth. We leave the nature of the dimension without a name. According to Hölderlin's words, man spans the dimension by measuring himself against the heavenly. . . . The godhead is the "measure" with which man measures out his dwelling, his stay on earth beneath the sky.[41]

This act of gauging the dimension does not demand the instruments of surveyors. Instead it calls for the poetic word, which is the measure for all measuring. Because poetry is the authentic appraising of the dimension of dwelling, it is the primal form of building. "Poetry first of all admits man's dwelling into its very nature, its presencing being. Poetry is the original admission of building."

The statement, *Man dwells in that he builds*, has now been given its proper sense. Man does not dwell in that he merely establishes his stay on the earth beneath the sky, by raising growing things and simultaneously raising buildings. Man is capable of such building only if he already builds in the sense of the poetic taking of measure. Authentic building occurs so far as there are poets, such poets as take the measure for architecture, the structure of dwelling.[42]

Thus architecture resulted from the poetic word.

Does this mean that buildings are also the place where poetry dies? Heidegger did not address that question. Yet Hölderlin himself expressed such an apprehension in one of his most famous poems. In the first strophe of *Half of Life* the poetic word glorifies a world of dwelling. It celebrates the organic unity and plenitude of the landscape, a oneness in which the land hangs in the water.

With its yellow pears
And wild roses everywhere
The shore hangs in the lake,
O gracious swans,
And drunk with kisses
You dip your heads
In the sobering holy water

Yet the second and last strophe is of another mind. Nature, flowers, the sun and the earth are absent. What remains are meaningless artifacts, mute objects, works of architecture.

Ah, where will I find
Flowers, come winter,
And where the sunshine
And shade of the earth?
Walls stand cold
And speechless, in the wind
The weathervanes creak.[43]

Heidegger called Hölderlin the poet's poet. *Half of Life* can be read as
the poem's poem. Eric Santner described how, when a person reads the
German text of the first strophe, the plenteous "o" and "u" sounds "gently
open the mouth as if to make it ready for nature's offerings."[44] Thus the
language conveys "a physicality that enacts the strophe's imagery." In the
second strophe, however, there is "a war between harsh frictatives and
sibilants, ending in the bleak 'a' sounds and violent gutturals of the last
three lines."[45] The syntax of the poem supports violent change of mood
also. According to Santner the structure of the first strophe is "an almost
invisible, diaphanous hypotaxis" which contains basically paratactic structures in which the words and images melt into a dynamic totality. In the
second strophe all of this has changed.

> Not only is there no more melting of borderlines . . . but the existence of the
> borderlines now seems to condemn what is individuated to isolation and a
> silence unredeemed by any intimation of the sacred. "Die Mauern stehn /
> Sprachlos und kalt, im Winde / Klirren die Fahnen." The chiasmic arrangement
> of these final images, rather than redeeming the despair they invoke, contri-
> butes to a general sense that these artifacts are somehow all that remains: the
> walls, the weathervanes; the weathervanes, the walls. The existential integrity
> of things fills the poet, at least in this poem, with horror.[46]

Thus Hölderlin passed posthumously judgement on the project initiated
by Heidegger and followed through by architectural historians like the
Norwegian Christian Norberg-Schulz. Paratactically juxtaposed in space,
even buildings erected from the most poetic of intentions were fated to
point, in the end, only to themselves.

Anagkê

Architectural Principles in the Age of Historicism is not the first book to
address the negative implications of a study of architectural history as the
history of cultural expression in stone or the ἱστορία of a poetic intention
in marble. Victor Hugo (1802–85) understood our predicament more than

a hundred and fifty years ago when he presented the then new understanding of architectural development in his *Notre Dame de Paris* (1832). Like all of his mature work, this book was informed by Hugo's realization that the historicist interpretation of history was the ground of evil. Hugo believed that the eighteenth-century abandonment of an enduring order of things, which had culminated in historicist thought, had opened a flood-gate through which an all-devouring torrent of sequentiality had begun to pour. This river of endless change had shattered the ancient structures of meaning. Hugo did not limit himself to the observation that history did not offer meaning. The situation was worse: history was evil. Victor Brombert observed in his *Victor Hugo and the Visionary Novel* that "what is involved is not a banal inventory of history's horrors—the brutalities, contusions, fractures, mutilations, and amputations attributed to man throughout history by the narrator of *Notre-Dame de Paris*. . . . More fundamentally, evil is linked to the very notion of sequentiality. Hugo even inverts the proposition. Not only is history evil, but evil is to be defined by its historical status: 'Le mal . . . est essentiellement successif.' The corollary follows: ultimate values are outside historical time."[47]

This evil became manifest in Hugo's reading of the meaning of architecture. He agreed with Herder's idea that human beings were expressive creatures, and that architecture was one of their most important forms of self-expression. "Indeed, from the origin of things down to and including the fifteenth century of the Christian era, architecture is the great book of humanity, the principal expression of man in his various stages of development, both as regards force and intellect."[48] He used different examples to prove his point. "The generating idea, the word, was not alone at the foundation of all these structures, but also to be traced in their form. The temple of Solomon, for example, was not only the binding of the holy book, but was the holy book itself. Upon each one of its concentric walls, the priests could read the Word, interpreted and manifested to the eye; and thus they followed its transformations from sanctuary to sanctuary until they seized it in the inner tabernacle, in its most concrete form, which was still architectural, the Ark itself. Thus the Word was concealed within the edifice, but its image was upon its envelope, like the human form upon the sarcophagus of a mummy."[49]

Yet even such a monumental and famous form of expression as Solomon's temple stood along that linear path of infamy known as history. Therefore if the ancient Hebrews understood their temple as revelation, it was unavoidable that later generations would lose their ability to read the message suggested by its form, and should come to the conclusion that the temple obviously must conceal a (secret) doctrine of heaven and earth.[50] "This reveals That" intimated a future statement that "This conceals That," which, as Hugo concluded, must at one moment or another turn into the conclusion that "This effaces That." The causality of this development converged in Hugo's *Notre-Dame de Paris* to produce a sense of malaise and even doom that transformed the buildings that are the setting of the drama. In the preface to *Notre-Dame de Paris* Hugo set the tone for such a pessimistic understanding of architectural history in his description of a discovery in one of the dark recesses of the Notre-Dame of an inscription of the Greek word Ανάγκη, *Anagkê*. "Those Greek capitals, black with age and cut pretty deep into the stone—a certain Gothic peculiarity of form and attitude, showing them to have been the work of some hand of the Middle Ages—and, above all, their grim and fatal meaning (Doom)—impressed the author profoundly."[51] The term *Anagkê* was to become the word upon which *Notre-Dame* was built. It affected all the structures in which the novel is set. This realm of doom is difficult to find in space. It emerges time after time in hallucinatory encounters. In one of them Hugo explicitly referred to Goethe's experience in 1770. "It was indeed the steeple of Strasbourg, it was the steeple of Strasbourg two leagues high; something unheard of, gigantic, immeasurable; a structure such as no human eye ever neheld; a Tower of Babel." Sixty years later the joy of a rediscovered identity and a heaven-mounting self-confidence was dissolved into a historian's nightmare of a chaotic, shimmering and fundamentally evil world. "Claude, in a state of hallucination in which he then was, believed that he saw—saw with his bodily eyes—the pinnacles of hell. The innumerable lights gleaming from one end to the other of the fearful tower, seemed to him to be so many openings of the vast furnace within; the voices and the sounds which arose from it like so many shrieks and groans."[52] The same Dom Claude who realized that towers that reach to heaven must have foundations that sound the depths of hell coined the famous maxim "Ceci tuera cela" ("This Will Kill That"). At one point in the novel—which is set in the middle of the fifteenth century—Dom Claude encounters the first printed book. He realizes that the book (as an instrument of cultural expression) will kill the building (the book of earlier civilizations), as the new will always kill the old, as each new example of material progress will obliterate something that served a similar purpose earlier, and as each style will kill its predecessor. In a chapter entitled "This Will Kill That" Hugo described the formation, blossoming and decay of the different architectural styles. It is still interesting reading, yet it leaves one empty-handed as Hugo was not willing to offer the reader any other conclusion than that all is change, that "Ceci tuera cela."

After Hugo, many refined our understanding of the history of architecture as a cultural process that works not through an even development, but through a series of periods defined by a time and a place (Ottonian

Germany, Gothic France, Renaissance Italy etc.) After an initial effort to describe stylistic development in aesthetic terms, the interest of architectural historians turned to a study of the manner in which buildings document the character of each period. No historian, however, has dared to address the disturbing message of Hugo's *Notre-Dame de Paris*. No one has been ready to consider in public the possibility that the history they so carefully have described is a meaningless sequence of events, nay worse: a body of evil. Hugo would have been amused by Screwtape's confession. And he would have taken it seriously.

Hugo's pessimistic posture is hardly typical. Most architectural historians are people of kind, optimistic and moral disposition who seem incapable to see their historicist and relativist interpretation of history as the manufacture of evil. It is bad form to argue *ad hominem*. Nevertheless architectural histories are written by real people who cannot but imprint the stamp of their personality on their reconstructions of the past. Architectural historians are nice people, who conceive the good and the beautiful as the essential and universal aspect of human civilization. They have chosen the study of art and architecture not because they want to divert their attention from the darker and disturbing sides of our temporal existence, but because they simply believe that their best of all possible histories, with its pre-established harmony, has more truth than the evil and the ugly. Their species is perfectly exemplified by Kenneth Clark (1903–83) who, at the end of his television series *Civilization*, revealed his and his colleagues' healthy-minded disposition: "I believe that order is better than chaos, creation better than destruction. I prefer gentleness to violence, forgiveness to vendetta. On the whole I think that knowledge is preferable to ignorance, and I am sure that human sympathy is more valuable than ideology."[53] And thus the history he described was one of order, creation, gentleness, forgiveness, knowledge and sympathy; chaos, destruction, violence, vendetta, ignorance and ideology are merely foils that reveal the greatness of their enduring negations. In one paragraph he noted, without details, the modern urge to destruction, only to affirm in the next paragraph that he does not believe that we are entering a new period of barbarism. The disposition of Nikolaus Pevsner was not much different: having escaped Nazism, he ended up in London where wrote his *An Outline of European Architecture* in the middle of the Blitzkrieg. Undaunted by the destruction around him, he stated that "the recovery of a true style in the visual arts, one in which once again building rules, and painting and sculpture serve, and one in which form is obviously representative of character, indicates the return of unity in society."[54] One simply cannot expect such habitual optimists to interpret heaven-reaching towers as pinnacles of hell.

Unlike Clark and Pevsner, Hugo did see through the optimistic facade of the modern age. He believed that the cataclysmic and catastrophic event of his own time, the French Revolution, had brought the evil of Heraclitean history into focus and himself under obligation. Hugo realized that the revolution issued from a historicist understanding of society. An interpretation of medieval Paris as a theatre of change could not but look ahead to the year 1789 and, in the end, to the choices the writer had to make in his own time. Victor Brombert explained how Hugo used the aesthetics of stylistic fusion to suggest a medieval city pregnant with the cataclysmic event of the French Revolution. Hugo described the cityscape of *Notre-Dame de Paris* as the accumulated sediment of change. The novel "insistently proposes hybrid forms and figures, suggesting mixture, incompleteness, and processes of becoming." The most obvious example of this hybridity is the architecture in the novel. Architecture itself is affected by hybridity. It shapes the sinister Place de Grêve, the place of executions. This site offers a simultaneous display of architectural evolution and centers on a hybrid construction that unites justice and torture. "The cathedral, too, looms as an extraordinary composite in time and space. Unlike other constructions, which correspond to a moment in history or represent a perfect type, Notre Dame, in which several styles exist and commingle, is no longer a Romanesque and not yet a Gothic structure. It is an edifice in transition, the product of a grafting process."[55] Hugo interpreted the stylistic imprint of time as the mark of the immanent and irrecusable evil of temporality. Stone was unable to contain and arrest the flux of time. "This very special concern for historical mutation, this transitional perspective on both past and future," Brombert observed, "explains the cultural anachronisms that stud the novel . . . as well as the number of political allusions to the far-distant fall of the Bastille. The year 1789 looms both as a projected future in relation to the narrated time (1482) and as a relevant past for the author and his reader from the perspective of the time of writing (1830). The French Revolution, which is not the overt subject of *Notre-Dame de Paris*, is nonetheless its mythical time: it lies both behind and ahead."[56] Hugo realized that a world subject to irredeemable time was fated to become imprisoned under the ever growing accumulation of unresolved injustice. Having eliminated a supernatural and metahistorical system of justice, the revolutionaries were doomed to fall back into the retaliatory cycles of crime and vengeance. Cancelation of the recompensive Last Judgement in the heavens could not but bring about a vindicatory day of reckoning on earth that, in its turn, was to beget new days of doom, presided over by the earlier indicted. Hugo realized that a pack of unappeasable Furies runs along the Heraclitean flux of time.

In premodern days all roads led to Rome; in the age of historicism all rivers gush into a maelstrom of terror. Hugo found the heart of the historicist vortex in the Year of Terror, 1793. In *Notre-Dame de Paris* he alluded to that year. In his last novel, *Ninety-Three* (1874), Hugo removed the facade from the cathedral. In the wake of the destruction of the Franco-Prussian War and the carnage that followed the suppression of the Paris Commune, and about to reach the measure of his days, Hugo decided that the time for the mediation of allusion and camouflage had passed. "This Will Kill That" revealed itself now explicitly as the fundamental of the age of historicism. On it the revolutionaries erected a new kind of architecture that expressed the principled activity of effacement in a straightforward way. The tectonics of the architecture that was to wreck the whole fabric of civilization resembled those of the printing press that had symbolically razed cathedrals three centuries earlier: it was "a sort of trestle having four posts for feet."

> At one end of the trestle, two tall joists, upright and straight, and fastened together at the top by a cross-beam, raised and held suspended some triangular object which showed black against the blue sky of morning. At the other end of the staging was a ladder. Between the joists, at the bottom, and directly beneath the triangle, could be seen a sort of panel composed of two movable sections which, fitting close to each other, left a round hole about the size of a man's neck. The upper section of this panel slid in a groove, so that it could be hoisted and lowered at will. For the time, the two crescents, which formed the circle, were closed, were drawn apart. At the foot of the two posts supporting the triangle was a plank turning on hinges, looking like a see-saw. By the side of this plank was a long basket, and, between the two beams, in front and at the extremity of the trestle, a square basket. This was painted red. The whole was made of wood except the triangle which was iron. One would have known the thing had been constructed by man, it was so ugly and evil looking; at the same time it was so formidable that it might have been reared there by evil genii. This mis-shapen thing was the guillotine.[57]

Yet the guillotine was not erected by some evil demon; it was not an aberration in space, and in time. It was built in front of the tower of La Tourgue, a relic of the feudal and aristocratic past. It was "a monster of stone standing in companionship with the monster of wood. . . . La Tourgue was that terrible offspring of the Past, called the Bastille in Paris, the Tower of London in England, the Spielberg in Germany, the Escurial in Spain, the Kremlin in Moscow, the Castle of Saint Angelo in Rome." In the confrontation of the tower and the guillotine the architectural principles of the age of historicism emerged from the veiled realm of allusion which Hugo had explored more than forty years earlier. The aesthetical became the ethical. "In La Tourgue were condensed fifteen hundred years, the Middle Age, vassalage, servitude, feudality; in the guillotine, one year, '93, and these twelve months made a counterpoise to those fifteen centuries. La Tourgue was Monarchy; the guillotine was Revolution. Tragic confrontation." Follows a protracted and poetic evocation of this confrontation that ends in the recognition that the guillotine was the inevitable outcome of the history amassed in La Tourgue. "The sinister tree had germinated in the fatal ground. Out of the soil watered by so much of human sweat, so many tears, so much blood, out of the earth in which had been dug so many trenches, so many graves, so many caverns, so many ambuscades, out of this earth wherein had rotted the countless victims of countless tyrannies, out of this earth spread above so many abysses, wherein had been buried so many crimes, terrible germs, had sprung, on the appointed day, this unknown, this avenger, this ferocious sword-bearer, and '93 had said to the Old World: 'Behold me.' And the guillotine had the right to say to the tower: 'I am thy daughter.' "[58]

Strife

Architectural historians have chosen to circumvent the genealogy of historicist architecture. They happily discuss Hugo's *Notre-Dame de Paris*, but they ignore *Ninety-Three*. Guillotines have no place in their accounts of the past, and neither have the German deathcamps. But the primitive hut is the object of a whole discourse. The mythical beginning of architecture is undoubtedly less disturbing than its historical end. The simple hut does not challenge the moral innocence of the architectural historian. It shelters the academic outlook that transfigures relativist predicament into academic accomplishment and suggests that the aesthetic view of history is still relevant.

The philosopher Karl Jaspers (1883–1969) concluded in his *The Origin and Goal of History* that the aesthetic consideration of history is at best a way to stimulate and satisfy our curiosity. "One thing is beautiful, and so is another." This perspective leads to a relativist stance that declares that everything is of equal value. Therefore "nothing has any longer any value at all." Yet Jaspers believed that the past is not free of obligation. "Our true approach to history should be to wrestle with it."[59] Jaspers's understanding of historiography as the historian's struggle with the past fits an age framed by the Heraclitean epistemology of historicism and relativism. Jaspers's observation reflects the truth of Heraclitus' dictum that all things come about by strife.[60] Therefore it is time to prosecute this introductory discussion to its conclusion and begin the engagement.

PART TWO

THE DEBATE

TWO

Politics

Carroll William Westfall

"Crito, we owe a cock to Asclepius; please pay it—do not neglect it."

Socrates's last words, reported in Plato's *Phaedo*.

The Limited Scope of the Present Investigation

The body of ideas which I will present in the even chapters of this book is
the opposite of what Bernard Bosanquet called aesthetic theory. Aesthetic theory, he said, "is a branch of philosophy, and exists for the sake of
knowledge and not as a guide to practice."[1] Love of knowledge (or *philosophia*) has certainly been an important motivation for my contribution to
Architectural Principles in the Age of Historicism. Yet that love was but the
condition of my desire to develop some fundamental rules which can guide
the architect in the practice of design. These rules cannot come from practice alone, nor can they come from philosophy alone, although having said
that I have said all I can about the parity of practice and philosophy.
Practice needs philosophy because it can do what practice cannot do,
namely, overcome the limitations of working in the here and now. To apply
to practice, philosophy must confront and interact with practice. The practice I speak of is my own and that of others I can have accurate knowledge
about. Practices that are different because times, places or people are different require a different exploration of philosophy.

The aim of applying philosophy to experience gained through practice
is to formulate general propositions which are generally valid in my own
subsequent experience and practice and in the experience and practice of
others. The fact that what I formulate is extracted from my necessarily
limited experience necessarily limits their formulation and thereby their

applicability. This limitation need not invalidate them as guides to the practice of other historians or of critics, architects or builders wishing to know something useful about the past in order to act more knowledgeably in the present, and it cannot invalidate the use of the principles upon which they are based. To derive guides to practice in the very different circumstances of, say, present-day Italy, Canada, Guatemala or China requires using philosophy to confront and interact with the options, conventions and practices operating in those very different circumstances and formulating general propositions appropriate for application in them. It may or may not turn out that the general propositions valid there are the same as the ones valid within the circumstances of my experience. Judging whether or not that is the case requires more than an individual lacking intimate knowledge of those places can know on his own, which is not the same as saying it is unknowable.

This should be enough to suggest that this study is not constructed within current conventions. To follow it requires that the reader leave behind some of the conventional knowledge about the topic it treats. To assist in this task a brief presentation of the study's most important word, "city," might be useful.

A Brief History and Definition of the City

The city is not the product of the marvelous workings of nature, history, or culture. The first city was neither Ur nor Babylon, which were mere settlements, but the place where the Greeks imagined it possible to live the political life. The city, then, was invented by the Greeks when they invented politics, and they invented politics when they recognized that a city or *polis* is different from and superior to a settlement. The best city is, of necessity, a utopia. The actual city we live in is the best imitation we can make of that city.

The Romans linked a particular form of the political life to a particular place called an *urbs*. This produced the concept of the city as a legal, *civic* entity and identification of each particular entity with a particular *urban* locale. Now, for the first time, the physical character of a place was linked to its political life with the one seen in terms of the other. One could not be urbane in an ancient Greek city. The Romans brought the idea of the city down from the imaginings of the philosophers and rendered it in brick and marble.

The Roman knew he was a citizen and he knew what that meant. The post-Roman world diffused an individual's citizenship into a number of different civil realms, each of them using the art of politics as the means by which its citizens lived together. Now the individual could at the same time be a "citizen" of a variety of regimes—e.g., a family, a guild or estate, a city, and the larger civil entity (nominally the Empire; actually a princely state or a chartered municipality or *civitas*)—while also belonging to a range of religious ones (e.g., a pius confraternity, a parish and the larger ecclesia).

This legal structure was adapted in the United States to allow recognizing a "city" in any political entity given legal form within the national polity and contributing to the ends of that lesser polity. Such an entity would rightly have a higher claim on the citizen than whatever the market of the settlement offered.

From Renaissance theorists the new Americans learned this: as it is in politics so is it in city building and in architecture. The purpose a people have in living together defines the civil form they will find useful, and the civil form defines what is required of the architectural and urban form.

The new nation formed from the former British colonies was founded within this tradition on three principles we still acknowledge as true. One principle cut the political life loose from the religious one. Another established the self-evident truth that all men are created equal. The third acknowledged that the form of government best able to guarantee justice, property and liberty and to "secure the public good and private rights" is that of a large, representative democracy (*Federalist #10*).

The American city is an example of the classical city because only the classical tradition distinguishes between the city and the settlement and places the civic life above that of the market. The forms both city and market can take are diverse, ranging from what in other contexts might be called nations and in others nothing more than a cub-scout pack. To be clear here and avoid confusion with common usage, the word "polity" will be used here to refer to the place within which a political life can be, lived. The polity is unique among formalized societies because only polities embody the most important thing in the lives of people, namely, the authority of a government organizing the political lives of people who aspire to live justly and nobly and therefore happily. (Authority here means the lawful exercise of power, so in speaking of authority one is also speaking of power.) In both the traditions and the Constitution of the United States, the distribution and exercise of authority requires the consent of the governed. Because that consent can be given and used for a variety of purposes, there will be a variety of governments, some closer to the market and other similar arrangements in their purposes and others with the more important purposes only the most important institutions make possible, all of them satisfying at least the normative standards found in the Constitution and administered through the federal government which is itself restrained by those same normative standards.

In the United States, then, we can find the classical city in a broad range

of polities—from, say, a bicycle club and a condominium association to a
university, a municipality (or city, in strict usage), a county or a state, all
culminating in the federal government. What scale of entity is intended
when using the term "city," "polity" or even "state" cannot be determined
on the basis of merely seeing the word. What is intended depends upon the
context within which the term is used.

That having been said, it is possible to define the polity in general: The
primary purpose of any polity (no matter its scale) will be to serve the
purposes of its citizens while providing justice in their administration of
authority, order in the arrangement of their affairs and beauty in the form of
the parts and whole of the physical architectural and urban entity housing
it. This leads to a useful and flexible way of defining a polity:

> A polity is an entity in which three things are brought into coordination as
> people live together: a shared purpose, a government they construe in order to
> exercise power justly while reaching for that purpose, and a physical setting
> which serves their purposes and facilitates their governing themselves.

That definition contains a necessary hieratic order beginning with the
people and ending with the polity as a legal and, finally, a physical entity.
That is, the order necessary for good city building is not a circular order
made up of interchangeable parts found in the mantra of the modernist
historian which runs city, culture, civilization, society, style, city, culture,
civilization, society, style—and so on.

On Architecture and Government

Alexander Hamilton's words apply as well to the world of architecture as
they do to the political world he was addressing in *Federalist #1*: "the vigor
of government is essential to the security of liberty . . . in the contemplation
of a sound and well-informed judgment, their interests can never be
separated . . . ." In the world of Hamilton and the other Founders these
sentiments about government could be applied equally well to architecture,
and in the practice of many of them they were. They stood within a tradition
in which politics and architecture were different expressions of the same
principles. That tradition, the classical tradition, is unique. Like the city,
in which it was to be embodied, it was founded in ancient Athens,
developed in ancient Rome, recovered and extended during the Renaissance, and subjected to a new penetrating and invigorating scrutiny during
the lifetimes of those who brought forth the new United States.

Today it is difficult to take seriously or literally much of what Hamilton and the other Founders wrote. Is there a political issue today over which architects as architects would say that they "mutually pledge to each other our Lives, our Fortunes, and our sacred Honor?" No—but there never was. Those who did mutually pledge did so as citizens involved in politics, not as professionals involved in a profession. When we participate in politics today, whether in its easiest form, that of voting, or in its most extreme, that of going to war, we do so as citizens, not as lawyers, doctors, teachers or architects, because political activity, by which I mean participation in government, is the most important activity, even for those who consider themselves independent of government and free from its constraints. The vigor of government is essential even for the security of *their* liberty.

An ear attentive to the defense of current architectural habits will recognize that liberty is valued more highly than government, and eyes sensitive to the appearance of cities, towns, villages and rural areas will see ever less evidence of love for the fruits of government and an increasing desire for the product of free expression—unless it is merely tolerance of someone else's liberty—i.e., unless it is merely the fruit of pluralism. A mind that gives thought to what one hears and sees in the world of architecture must conclude that architecture is thought to be about liberty and not government and that architects respond secondarily to the world of government, and then usually only as a restraint in the form of building codes and ordinances, and primarily to whatever they call architecture. Architecture, in other words, is taken to be independent of government. It was not always so, and because it was not, it need not be so today. In what follows it is my intent to outline a way of thinking about architecture that was familiar to a string of architects who were able to do what we have become increasingly unable to do—namely, to build liveable, loveable, just and elegant cities, towns, villages and rural areas.

In all of what follows I plan to say nothing new but only to repeat a few basic propositions:

politics is more important than architecture;
content is more important than form;
the enduring and general is more important than the unique and particular.

The first of these can be put aside for the moment so that attention can be devoted first to the other two.

On Content and Form

Current orthodoxy in the practice, theory, history and criticism of architecture prizes form over content and uses formal qualities as the route to knowing about content. To know an object is to begin with its formal qualities and impute a content for them.

This legacy of the eighteenth-century *philosophes* and their intellectual partners and successors began in a proper suspicion of all inherited thought. A major project of the nineteenth century was to fill the void they left and give objects and events more than formal meaning. The result was the imputation of meaning on the basis of formal qualities. Foremost among these were those of style, culture, the symbolic form investigated through iconographic and iconological analysis, and various semiological approaches of more recent invention. These provide surrogates for what used to be understood as the intrinsic content of objects or events. They are alike in that each belongs to its own world and not to the object or event. Because this is so, whatever content is imputed to the object or event must remain extrinsic to it in a way that the intrinsic content of the earlier world did not.

This triumph of the so-called historical school, which began with Herder, remains in two aspects of modernism's orthodoxy. One is that the putative content is merely the symptom of the circumstances surrounding its generation. The object or event, therefore, is of interest not for itself but for what it points to—for example, the *Zeitgeist,* the will to form, the expression of the architect, the nature of the material, the *genius loci* etc. When that world changes (as the *Zeitgeist* marches on; as new forms are willed etc.), so too does the object or event in that its importance changes. As "time" "marches" away from the object or event ("time" "marching" in a straight line is history; history leaves the object or event behind), it becomes "out of date" and therefore either unimportant as something useful for the present or newly important for belonging to some time other than the present.

The other effect is that, as the world of the observer changes, so too must the putative intrinsic content of the object or event change. For example, a change in the way historians think about buildings will change the building's content. There were no "mannerist" buildings until historians invented that stylistic category. Before its invention, the buildings later identified as mannerist were considered deficient Renaissance designs that were unattractive and unworthy of attention. After the style was invented and there suddenly "were" mannerist buildings, the formal qualities they embodied were considered attractive and worthy of study and, eventually, of emulation. The happy result was that the sight of the eye was sharpened. The unfortunate thing was that locating certain formal qualities in a specific past time made them inappropriate for a present moment except as polemic.

The dominant position modernism has assumed cannot be justified on the basis of its honoring the promises made in its name. On the contrary, the more we see of the effects of its desire for the new, the more wary we become of it. The more wary we become, the more we recognize the value of the old. The sponsors of modernism, as Edmund Burke said of the supporters of modernism's first great political edifice,

> have no respect for the wisdom of others; but they pay it off by a very full measure of confidence in their own. With them it is sufficient motive to destroy an old scheme of things, because it is an old one. As to the new, they are in no sort of fear with regard to the duration of a building run up in haste; because duration is no object to those who think little or nothing has been done before their time, and who place all their hopes in discovery.[2]

For our purposes the traditional way of thinking about form and content, the way Socrates was the first to explain and which Kant sharpened, is valid. The formal qualities that make something, say, an object, status or event available to perception provide a knowledge of its extrinsic content, or form, and a means of knowing its intrinsic content. That means of knowing is available in one's experience with instances of it. This experience is determined by the laws of nature operating in the sensible world, while the actual knowledge of the intrinsic content comes only through reflection in the intellect and its participation in the intelligible world. That reflection occurs around certain principles we know prior to our experience and which determine the intelligible world's logic and reason or coherence. More will be said about these principles later.

Without encountering instances or reports of instances we can have no knowledge of the intrinsic content of what we encounter. An object such as a rock or a building and an event or a status whether brought about or established by nature or by people has an intrinsic nature (or character, or essence, or way, etc.) which exists because of the type or types (or kind or kinds, or sort or sorts, etc.) of thing it is. For example:

> We know a red object when we see it, but without red objects we would know nothing about redness. (That the object may also be spherical is irrelevant to its redness, but must be mentioned to identify the particular thing as a red ball.)
>
> We know a just act of government when we encounter one, but without just acts we would know nothing about justice. (That the act may also have been an act limiting someone's liberty, say, to build something that would be considered alien and indecorous within its setting, is irrelevant to its justice, but that aspect must be mentioned to identify that specific act.)
>
> We know activities revealing the presence of freedom when we see them, although we never encounter anyone who is completely free. (That the restraint on complete freedom is knowingly and willing self-imposed in order to assure

the enjoyment of freedom must be understood as an aspect of the way instances of freedom can appear.)

We know a well-designed building when we see one, but without well-designed buildings we would have no knowledge about the qualities that constitute good design. (That the building may be a student residence is not necessarily relevant to its being well designed, but its designation as a particular kind of domestic structure must be mentioned to identify that particular well-designed building.)

There is, in other words, something in an object or event that is generally shared by other objects or events (redness; justice; freedom; well-designedness) that unites it with other objects or events each of which is unique and particular. These general qualities or types have an intrinsic content that is universal and knowable in the intellect while the single instances are examples of them possessing the extrinsic characteristics that we apprehend with our senses. The object or event has the form that provides the perceptions, and the intellect provides the knowledge of that intrinsic content. That content is more important than the merely external knowledge one gains at first blush when encountering a particular example of the thing. Indeed, that content is not knowable by having only a brief experience with only one example of the type of thing it is or even with long contact with many of the most recent examples. Old people of sound mind and broad experience should (but will not necessarily) have a better knowledge of what is important about objects or events than young people of impulsive intellect and an ongoing freshness in their contact with the world.

On Knowing the Content

A building (or event or anything else) is important for both extrinsic and intrinsic reasons—extrinsically for what it offers to the senses (what we can see, hear, touch, taste or smell it to be) and can be immediately apprehended, and intrinsically for what it embodies and for what, through that embodiment, it refers to, connects with and incorporates. This intrinsic content that be known only through ratiocination or some other intellectual process that does not provide immediate results. The perceptions or thoughts of historians or anyone else are incapable of changing either the extrinsic or intrinsic content. A change, in other words, in the way historians think about buildings will not change the building's content. Thus, for example, when the value of a building is vested in the general and universal, when, that is, its value resides in its actual rather than in its putative intrinsic characteristics, its importance will not change merely because historians or others have changed their minds about something. For example, a change in the regard with which historians or critics hold a stylistic category such as mannerism will not change the importance of existing old buildings called mannerist. A devaluation of mannerism would make mannerist buildings less fashionable and allow them to recede into the background, while a person's "partiality for certain eras" may open our eyes to their intrinsic stylistic qualities, make those qualities fashionable and give them a prominence that leads architects to alter the way they design new buildings.[3] But that change does not affect the extrinsic characteristics of mannerist buildings, unless their fall from fashion leads to their neglect and deterioration.

That this issue is important not only for critics and historians but for architects, builders and anyone else with an interest in our cities, towns, villages and rural areas becomes clear when we substitute the words "modern," "postmodern" or "classical" in that sentence. A change in what we mean by one of these terms used to describe the "style" of current practice must perforce under current orthodoxy lead to a change in what buildings look like. The building must display the change more prominently than it reveals its continuity with what preceded it. The appearance of newness must be the most prominent aspect of the building's design—more important than its embodiment of what has always been important in the appearance of a building of its type, and regretfully more important than whatever allows it best to serve the ongoing, important activities that lead people to build buildings.

The intention here is to outline a way of reversing this emphasis—a way, that is, for knowing and dealing with an extrinsic content embodied in the particular and unique and an intrinsic content that is general and universal so that buildings will no longer be only as important as the ideas of current "critics" and "historians" make them, ideas that change according to impulse and are justified on no other grounds than partiality—ideas, that is, that are nurtured in liberty but which ultimately undermine the vigor that reason uses to govern a healthy, just and happy person and people.

The Question of Time and History

The intent here is to unhitch architecture from a history in which "time" "marches." When "time" "marches," it has a place to begin and a place to end, and the route from the one to the other is linear.

The most common form of history today is one that assumes it knows where that end is. This form began in Christian history when the end was salvation, the present was assessed relative to the place man occupies in God's plan for salvation, and the past was a linear progression beginning in Creation and ending in the future Apocalypse. This history of ends as it may be called was secularized during the nineteenth century by substituting the perfect state of man on earth for the perfect state of bliss for the soul in heaven. This is the form most common in the history of architecture and of cities. It tells how we are doing in reaching the end of the happy life by showing how far we have come in the past and what in the immediate past provides the basis for present action.

The history of beginnings is another legacy of the post-Enlightenment world. A linear history like that of ends, it says that the ends are contained in the beginnings. Know the beginnings and you will know the nature of things. The world-historical process works on beginnings to produce ends, as in the progression of myth to philosophy, of ritual to religion, of the rustic hut to the Sears Tower. Anthropologists are the major colleagues of historians in the history of beginnings.

Historians share a general agreement about what is important in the history of ends and of beginnings and devote most of their attention to the history in between which can be called the history of the middle. This is, after all, the only history with adequate material to support sound historical inferences.

The alternative form of history, the history of origins, works with the same material, but it is radically different from the histories of ends, beginnings or the middle. It is not linear (although because it is an imitation of events in nature it is of necessity sequential), and it does not take the beginning or the end of the thing to be inexorably linked to its later or earlier form. The historian's interest in a thing arises from a current concern for which he wishes to find an origin or a way it originally was. Like the other two kinds of history, the discoveries the historian makes provide a narrative with a beginning, a middle and an end. But unlike the history of ends, its end is unknown because it lies in the future and the future cannot be known.[4] Similarly, it has a beginning, but because its present status is not entailed in its earlier form—and hence not in the first form it had at its beginning—the beginning is in the original form of the thing in the sense of the primary form. Of interest to the historian is this form independent of circumstances, outside history. It is not the same as the form at the beginning of its career in history. It is knowable as a narrative about the present moment. It concerns what preceded that moment relative to what one hopes will become of that moment.

It would be wrong to think that a history of origins is merely a history rebuilt on old foundations and ignoring what the Enlightenment taught.

Nothing current can ignore its own past. To suggest this is to formulate the attempt in terms of the historicism that is being rejected here. Under historicism, as Leo Strauss has explained, a "return to an earlier position is believed to be impossible. But one must realize that this belief is a dogmatic assumption whose hidden basis is the belief in progress or in the rationality of the historical process."[5]

Strauss is not saying that a return to an earlier position is possible. To say that would be to frame a statement that can only be made within a context of historicism. It means merely that what was true at an earlier time remains true, that the form in which the thing will be known will be different, and that therefore the way of formulating the truth of the thing will be different.

To put this in another way: The intent here is to rebuild our understanding of the world in a way that recognizes the atemporality of types, or whatever we might call the part of the intrinsic content that interests us, and the temporality of the instances which bear the extrinsic content. In doing so we must account for the lesson of the Enlightenment that spirits and other "ideas" do not inhabit objects (the dogginess of a dog instanced in Fido; the idea of beauty in a building we find attractive) while at the same time accepting Kant's recognition that there are certain true things that can be known about objects (there is a class of thing that constitutes dogs and excludes cats; the attractiveness of a beautiful building resides in traits in that building which it shares with all other beautiful buildings and is in more than our reaction to it). In this world architecture is not hitched to the march of time. Instead, it is connected with what is true about architecture.

On Historical Knowledge: The Conventional

The history of origins provides access to knowledge of what is true about redness, justice, freedom and well-designedness. This form of history teaches the most important things for a person to know whether that person be acting in the role of citizen, historian or architect, for it teaches how to separate the extrinsic, circumstantial and transient from the intrinsic, enduring and true. It does so by providing instances within which the conventional can be separated from the natural and showing how the conventional and natural are connected in different, varying, circumstances.

The conventional exists in two main forms: it is generally agreed upon knowledge gained through hearsay rather than through seeing with our own eyes, and it is embodied in things (acts and artifacts) made by people rather than in something outside them.

Modernism accepts knowledge of the conventional as adequate knowledge. It raises conventional knowledge and things to positions of primacy and treats them as the best that can be. As a result, whatever can be done is done, or at least is allowed, because in the realm of the conventional there is no way to ask whether such things ought to be done. Facts become values; there are no values independent of the facts. Because it is possible to build very tall buildings, very tall buildings are built. Because it is possible to build and sell a great number of houses along wiggly streets, suburbs replace a rural landscape. Because this is the architectural style now in fashion, this is the style that is to be used.

On Historical Knowledge: The Natural

Modernism's conventionalism remains within the realm of what the circumstances of a time and place allows. It cannot have knowledge of things outside the present. Outside modernism the conventional is also the realm in which that which is is that which circumstances allow, but its simple being neither justifies its existence nor sanctions its use. Instead, the conventional is recognized as linked to and subordinate to the natural.

The conventional is the individual, circumstantial, contingent, dependent, particular, etc. Its complement, the natural, is the typical, universal, essential, principled, ideal, etc. Except in modernism, the conventional provides us a tentative, circumstantial knowledge of the natural when the natural is taken to be that which resides in the repository of that which is. Simply put, nature is the sum of coherence in the realm of the nature of objects and the categories of knowing while the conventional contains information arising from experience that makes knowledge of nature possible.

The *philosophes* dislodged this from being the common view of nature. Following them, nature has acquired such a multitude of meanings that only a broad range of conventions lacking the coherence of classical thought can organize our speech about it.[6] The most serious impediment to our knowing nature comes from the post-Enlightenment world's investment of the term with two antithetical meanings. One was given by the Romantics to refer to an arena free of the constraints of society or civilization where men could behave as willful, independent beings. The other was formulated by their predecessors who thought that the nature of man and society was like the nature of anything else whose secrets could be unlocked by the application of the new empirical science. As the individual's nature came to be thought of as something determined by a set of natural laws and his life in society to be knowable, predictable and ultimately determinable by the "laws" discovered by the social sciences, nature increasingly became the place outside man where people could find what was unique about themselves. This nature offered freedom. It did not, however, require the assumption of responsibility. Here nature stood opposed to society.

The meaning used here is quite different. Nature is the realm that conventions point to. In it is a diversity of things, all of them true, enduring and coherent with one another. One is the law of contradiction: two things that are contradictory cannot both be true. For example, one cannot claim that the statement "There is no truth" is true without contradicting the claim.[7] This is a necessary (or apodictic) truth and not an "analytical" statement such as the one that a triangle has three sides. Other necessary truths are the various axioms of geometry in which, for example, we recognize that no matter the shape of a triangle, the sum of the interior angles will always be 180 degrees. Necessary truths must be understood before we encounter instances illustrating them, for without that a priori understanding, we will have no knowledge of the logic, or reason, or coherence, of experience. We will, for example, not be able to understand that because of the law of contradiction truth cannot coherently be denied. And neither would we grasp the congruence between speech, geometry and numbers capable of rendering, each in its own way, the statement about the interior angles of a triangle no matter the language, the time or the place in which it is spoken, whether it is rendered in as many geometric diagrams and other instances as are needed to make the point, or whether it is formulated entirely in numerical form to make it commensurate with other numerological expressions. The realm holding those is the same one containing the laws and the God evoked in the statement that only by dissolving the political bonds that have tied the colonists to the mother country can they assume the station "to which the Laws of Nature and of Nature's God entitle them." From its pattern "we receive, we hold, we transmit our government and our privileges. . . . The institutions of policy, the goods of fortune, the gifts of providence, are handed down to us, and from us, in the same course and order. Our political system is placed in a just correspondence and symmetry with the order of the world, and with the mode of existence decreed to a permanent body composed of transitory parts. . . . Thus, by preserving the method of nature in the conduct of the state . . . we are never wholly new, and . . . we are never wholly obsolete."[8] It is the repository of the diversity and order which, as the Ionian philosophers of the sixth century BC first recognized, are "entirely accessible to human intelligence."[9] Indeed, "Nature was discovered when man embarked on the quest for the first things in the light of the fundamental distinctions between hearsay and seeing with one's own eyes, on the one hand, and between things made by man and things not made by man, on the other."[10] The coherence of nature extends to "the logic and language of morals" which, as Hadley Arkes reminds us, "are simply built into us. As Thomas Reid would say, they are part of 'the constitution of our natures,' and for that reason they are as much a part of our natural world as trees, rocks, air, and water."[11] To that list of things forming the coherence of nature we might add the physical laws concerning the movement of bodies, the properties of materials allowing them to be polished or not and to deteriorate or remain stable depending upon what one does or knows, and relationships people have to their governments, the changing forms of governments in relation to the changing characters of those who are governed, and other topics available through knowing what citizens, historians and architects need to know if they are to build well.

The history of origins provides access to this nature and to knowledge about how people live and build in it. In this history, if something is true once it is always true; the same thing in a different circumstance cannot be not true. In that statement the term true refers not to a mere descriptive or factual truth. These are empirical matters of fact providing the instances historians examine and belonging to the realm of synthetic statements referring to logically coherent but discrete events and things: e.g., these men signed that document in July, 1776, and it says this and that; this building was completed in 1826, it is built mainly of brick and wood, and it resembles the Pantheon. There is nothing necessary about the factual. Any of these things could have been otherwise: they might not have signed the document; the building might never have been built. But the veracity of the statements that they did sign and that it was build may be verified by the appropriate kind of experience with it, as, for example, seeing it oneself or accepting the report of those who are trustworthy. The character of factual information is that it is unique and refers to change. It is about time, place, circumstance, material, the contingent and so on. Factual accounts narrated within a structure based on sequence over time amount to a recounting of the *historical*, in the terms Robert Jan van Pelt uses (see section in the following chapter: "*Historie* and *Geschichte*").

The necessarily true exists in a different realm and is different in character. It concerns things that cannot have been otherwise and therefore cannot be other than they are. It is true prior to and independent of instances that might correspond to it. For example, it is true that all people are created equal, and it is equally true that there has been and continues to be slavery and other forms of inequality. The necessary truth of the equality of people is not controverted by factual evidence to the contrary. The realm holding these necessary truths is the *historic*. It stands in relation to the historical as value does to the factual and as the is does to the ought. The true, historic and valuable is immanent in nature, in aspects of individual examples and in what may be known about how we can know about the examples, as well as in whatever it is we know when we know that similar examples of something possess something—redness, justice, freedom, well-designedness—in common. It also exists even if there is no factual example of it, as in the following statement which is necessarily true although it has never been factual: The best world is one in which all individuals possess freedom and assume responsibility for their actions. Utopia is of necessity the image the actual city imitates. Unless we are blinded by skepticism and nihilism, we know this world to be possible even though there is no historical account that can verify it has been. It is more important to act on the basis of what one knows to be true than it is to be guided by the factual, although knowledge of the true is available only through factual information. The history of origins provides access to that knowledge.

Practical Knowledge

Tracking the history of origins provides a dialectical process for winnowing conventions and opinions important in the present and accessible in the past. Those who undertake the study are informed people of good will who know there is a right way, or a good way—a redness, a justice, a freedom, a well-designedness—and desire to know it. They also know that to the extent they acquire practical knowledge usable in the world, they will attain only the best knowledge possible at the moment. Their knowledge, like any conventional knowledge, is conventional. The conventional embodies that which a people agree to be the case while acknowledging that it can be otherwise, that in different circumstances it properly would be otherwise, and that the best possible conventional aspect of a thing is that which most closely approaches its natural character.

The implicit tentativeness of non-modernist convention must not be confused with the relativism found in the conventions of post-Enlightenment historiography. That approach subjects objects and events to scrutiny within certain conventional categories such as the stylistic characteristics of objects or the cultural content of events and considers the conclusions it draws to be "true" or "good" for the period that manifests them but "untrue" and "bad" if found in another. In other words, whatever is (or was), is (or was) "true." In this scheme contradictory things can be "true" and "good" so long as they do not appear at the same time. The Baroque was good when produced in the seventeenth century but bad when done in the nineteenth; cannibalism is acceptable for some but not for others. Both these claims are spurious, the former by confusing questions of taste with questions of ethics ("Baroque" refers to a certain conventional appearance which in itself

cannot be good or bad), the latter by contradicting the law of contradict
(cannibalism is bad no matter where it occurs or who commits it).

This historiography's relativism is achieved by analyzing only the c
ventional aspects of objects and events, that is, of nothing more than th
extrinsic, formal characteristics. One parallel in an analysis of polit
would be to assert that the eighteenth-century claim that all men are crea
equal and endowed by their creator with certain unalienable rights is
longer true in the twentieth, or that while it may be true in what beca
the United States it is not true in China or Poland and that a regime will
to promulgate laws that do not seek to embody those rights is neverthel
a legitimate regime because that's the way things are in China or Pola
or that until a government grants those rights, they cannot be said to ex

Another parallel in politics would be to conduct affairs on the basis
opinion polls, which yield up conventional knowledge, rather than on
basis of conventional knowledge tested against the principles of natu
law. It is one thing to say that because a majority of the colonists think
British king is a tyrant we therefore declare our independence from him
order to set up our own government; it is quite another to present the ar
ment that follows the analysis of circumstance recounted in the Declarat
of Independence: "When in the course of human events, it becomes n
essary [not merely desirable] for one people to dissolve the political ba
which have connected them with one another . . ." etc. In the Ameri
colonies, a particular government, not government in general, was tyr
nical, and the colonists believed that a different government would
able to provide security for liberty. It is in the nature of people to h
government—indeed, they must, if they are to secure those rights v
which nature endowed them—but the form of that government will alw
be conventional.

On Progress

People live with the hope that things will be better in the future.
Christianity, that future is one of salvation. In its secularized form in
histories of the middle it is assumed that history chronicles the progres
mankind. This assumption resides in the realm of dogma and conventi
not knowledge and nature, and must be rejected from the premises of
history of origins. To reject it is not to reject the idea that there is prog
or that history is irrelevant to the art of living happy lives. There is p
gress. More people than ever before live longer, with less misery and v
a greater abundance that makes life not only bearable but enjoyable.
social and political institutions are framed to assure that this form of p

gress, which is chronicled in the history of the middle, continues. In addition, more people than ever before know, or can know, certain things that are true within the logic of morals, although we pay increasingly little attention to this progress. Thus, while we can see that our life *is* improved, it is difficult to be certain that it is improving in ways that it *ought* to. The history of origins provides a way for placing an interest in moral progress above the interest in material progress.

Entailed in the history of origins is the assumption that the most important things an individual can attain are liberty and responsibility for his actions. Possessing liberty means a person is free to act, while assuming responsibility for his actions means that he will act in a way that is good by nature for him in so far as circumstances allow. To know what is good for him, the individual must seek knowledge of what is good by its nature, and once having learned something worth knowing, he must incorporate it into his way of life. In general terms, this means that knowledge derived from acts in the past becomes binding on those who come later.

An example of such knowledge is that slavery is categorically wrong. Once we know this there is no basis for condoning slavery whether the slaveholder be an ancient Greek or an American Founder. Their having practiced it in no way justifies our doing so no matter how much we admire other things they did. In like manner, knowing this does not warrant our condemning all that they did. We are not condoning or approving their position on slavery when we accept and value those parts of their thought that do not stand on their ignorance about slavery.

Similarly and conversely, some good thing that is known but neglected for reasons that cannot be explained by circumstance provides a just ground for condemning those who are neglectful. If living justly and nobly and therefore happily is the most important thing, it is obvious that whatever interferes with living in that way is to be avoided. A person in need cannot be a happy person. If a people have the means of feeding and succoring those who are unable to do so themselves but neglect doing so, simple justice may properly condemn them for failing to do so. Similarly, if an architect knows examples of beauty and utility that are superior to what he designs and he has the wherewithal to produce designs with that beauty and utility, he is open to contempt if some misguided understanding of architecture (e.g., a belief that good design is a matter of style) prevents him from doing so.

These ideas are staples in the classical tradition. The belief that there is progress and that history can provide knowledge that will assist in attaining it underlies the very foundation of the United States. The Founders did not consider progress to be an automatic accompaniment of the "march" of "time" (they spoke instead of the "course of human events") and they did not think that the knowledge necessary to secure it is easily acquired. Hamilton spoke optimistically in *Federalist #9*, "The science of politics . . . like most other sciences, has received great improvement. The efficacy of various principles is now well understood, which were either not known at all, or imperfectly known to the ancients." After cataloguing these, he concludes, "these are wholly new discoveries, or have made their principal progress towards perfection in modern times." In a similar manner Jefferson, in the maturity of his long and active life, observed that "forty years of experience in government is worth a century of book-reading. . . . laws and institutions must go hand in hand with the progress of the human mind. As that becomes more developed, more enlightened, as new discoveries are made, new truths disclosed, and manners and opinions change with the change of circumstances, institutions must advance also, and keep pace with the times."[12] Time moves, but men make the improvements.

The Founders, armed with a knowledge not available to the Greeks, Romans, Dutch, Swiss, British and others providing examples for their study, produced a superior form of government. They drew useful examples from wherever they were to be found. The most recent examples were not necessarily the best ones. They acquired knowledge piece by piece in what retrospectively could be (and now may be) seen as a necessary sequence recognizing at the same time that in different circumstances things would have been otherwise. As it was for the Founders, so was it for their predecessors: At each point in the sequence—in the thought of Socrates, Aristotle, Augustine, Machiavelli, Locke and the Founders—it was thought that the then current state of knowledge was superior to the earlier one and that, paradoxically, there could be no better state given the circumstances than the one they could imagine. Utopia is of necessity the image the actual city imitates. This is the classical idea of progress, an idea which stands in sharp contrast to the modernist one which sees each current moment as inferior to what is yet to come and sees the future as superior to any present or past.

The status of human knowledge is revealed in the conventions guiding the political life of a society. A city's constitution is its principal convention, and constitutions need constant amendment so that the knowledge of what is true and therefore binding can be adapted to changing circumstances and perhaps even be improved. Because politics is more important than architecture, it follows that as there is amendment and improvement in the forms organizing political life, so too there must be change in the buildings that serve it. Similarly, as there is progress in the human sciences affecting the way buildings are designed and progress in the natural sciences affecting the way they are built, the way we think about and practice architecture and building must be amended and thereby improved.

Because these improvements are available—because it is always possible to improve the fit between what we know and the pattern of nature that knowledge imitates—it is the responsibility of people to seek them. To avoid that responsibility either by avoiding politics or by using cities for purposes that do not hold that purpose as primary is to be less than human. The most effective instrument available for acting on that responsibility is intellect when it is applied to the art of living together in cities—in short, through living the political life.

Purpose and Buildings

The modernist idea of progress renders the question of purpose or destiny mute by entailing it in progress. Once we dismiss the dogmatic belief in progress we must confront the question of purpose.

The history of origins allows us to confront the question anew. Modernism's histories of the middle lock purpose into the positivist or historicist sequence they chronicle. This subjects the individual to the tyranny of the historical process or of the "laws" of the social sciences. A person freed from that tyranny is a person restored to full stewardship of that which makes him uniquely human, namely, his freedom and his assumption of responsibility for his actions. Now a person can assume the purpose that is unique to people, namely, to seek to perfect their individual natures and thereby find their unique pleasure. In confronting the world the person now puts this question in first place: How does this object or event contribute to this purpose? When the question is posed by the client or patron facing the need or desire for a new building, the architect charged with designing it or the critic or historian interested in guiding the outcome of their actions either directly or indirectly, it takes this form: How will this building assist the individuals responsible for it and those for whose use it is intended in finding their happiness? These are universal questions outside time and therefore questions whose answer in the present can be enlightened by knowledge of earlier answers.

These are primarily and fundamentally political questions when politics is understood in its classical sense, namely, the means by which the individual perfects his nature. Politics is the art of living together and is the first and most important task of people. Building requires working together which necessarily makes building a political activity. From this we can formulate the following axiom:

> Just as there is only one politics (the art of living together in order to perfect the nature of each individual) so too is there only one architecture (the art of building that serves that politics).

That axiom can be misunderstood, ignored and willfully misapplied, but we must acknowledge the necessity of its truth for the same reasons that we accept the self-evident truth "that all men are created equal, that they are endowed by their creator with certain unalienable rights, and that among these are life, liberty, and the pursuit of happiness—that to secure these rights, governments are instituted among men, deriving their just powers from the consent of the governed." Those reasons are in the logic of morals and are illustrated in the body of knowledge constituting the classical tradition running from the pre-Socratics to the present. In different times and places it has taken different forms, but its intrinsic content has always been the same. Its earliest formulation in architecture was perhaps in the first book and chapter of Vitruvius' treatise where he outlines the wide range of knowledge the architect must command. The reason that "human nature can master and hold in recollection so large a number of subjects" is because these studies "are related to one another and have points of contact" (I, i, 12) not in the particularities of craftsmanship and execution but in that of principles and reason. (I, i, 15; *opus* versus *ratio*). The formulation that is perhaps most important for us today in the United States is in the formulation it has received in the nation's founding documents and the body of knowledge extending from it.

Whether in Vitruvius or in the Founders, whether in architecture or in politics, there is a connection between the natural and the conventional. As we have seen, the connection or, better, interchange at the level of the true, that is, of the intrinsic and concerning the nature of things, is an interchange at the level of principle. That interchange is accessible to the intellect through dialectic, and its content is true no matter the circumstances of time or place although the instances in which we may know it depend absolutely on those circumstances.

The example of the connection between politics and architecture is more than merely a convenient illustration—architecture is, after all, connected to many other activities as well. This connection is the most important one because it is necessary for activity in both politics and building. A moment's reflection proves this to be so: Note that people do not go about searching for purposes for existing buildings; rather, buildings are built to serve existing purposes. This is true no matter the purpose, the time, the place, or the individuals involved (except in the realm of preservation which is a product of modernism).

A consequence of this observation is that the city is the supreme example of architecture. By city is meant any polity larger or smaller in size and reach, existing as the locus of politics, and existing because and when politics exists. In the classical tradition, the polity has one purpose to which all others are subordinate, namely, to allow the nature of the individual to reach and enjoy its perfection. Just as there is only one primary purpose for politics, so too there is only one purpose for architecture. Architecture is composed of buildings, and buildings differ from one another according to their primarily architectural character, that is, according to the purposes they serve. Each of these purposes is served by a particular type of building no matter the circumstances of time or place that surrounded their design and construction. These types are not conventional inventions of men but true forms in nature which exist whether men know about them or not. They will be discussed in the next chapter. Just where they are in nature is not a topic that must be pursued to agree that they exist. Suffice it to say that they exist in the same realm as the one that holds the law of contradiction, the congruence of the words, the geometric figurations and the mathematical formulation concerning right angles as well as the political types that see to it that political forms range from monarchy in which one person is at the head to democracy in which authority is vested in all the citizens.

These thoughts lead to a conclusion that begins with a useful, brief definition of a building:

> A building is an instrument a polity's members use for reaching their purposes which are sometimes public, sometimes private, and always coordinated through politics with other purposes.

That which we can call architecture is the generalized nature of the buildings built to serve an instrumental, political purpose and standing on the same basis of a rational connection to the same principles as the politics that aspires to build the good polity. The forms, or content, of buildings make this clear in that they embody and explain what purpose that building serves in the polity.[13]

To penetrate more deeply into the nature of architecture and buildings we must look again at the nature of politics.

Political Forms

Political activity is natural for people but the political forms that structure those activities are conventional forms. The best among them approach the natural as closely as circumstances allow. The purpose of political forms or governments is to serve the people. Those that serve people who seek to perfect their natures and thereby enjoy the uniquely human pleasures, that is, those who serve people who aspire to live justly and nobly, are legitimate; those that are served by the people are illegitimate. A legitimate government, regime or form of political activity satisfies two criteria: first, the individual citizen must enjoy and be guaranteed the freedom to be responsible for his actions, and second, the laws must conform to the imperatives found in the logic of morals and in natural right.

The life of the person seeking to live nobly and justly is the good life. Politics is the only way available for seeking this happiness. This good life is also the civil life, a term which itself shows that the good life can be lived only in cities, although the term city here means not so much a particular *urban* form but a general *political* one and hence is usually used in the form polity rather than in the form city. The basis for the good life lived in cities and other polities is in having actions correspond, in so far as circumstances permit, with what is good by nature for individuals. Such actions are based on the principles of morality or ethics.

Different circumstances — different times, different places, different material conditions — provide different ways for people to live together in civil society. The form a government takes in organizing the political life of its citizens in some particular time or place is its constitution.

Because a constitution, whether in the "unwritten" form of the British constitution or in a formal document such as the one in the United States (which itself is effective only because it swarms with unwritten customs), deals with the here and now and attempts to account for circumstances whose appearance and character cannot be predicted, it is conventional. But because it is supposed to ballast a regime with the equipment required for its members to attain happiness, it must draw on the natural or, as Burke observed, work "after the pattern of nature." Briefly put, it provides a predictable, organized, coherent relationship between the various activities required for reaching the purposes that people have when they live together.

Not all people have the same purposes for living together. So long as governments serve people and rest on the consent of the governed, each citizen must tolerate the legitimate ends of other citizens. And each citizen must define his own form of happiness. The Founders recognized the complementarity of these points. Blessed as we are with the gifts of Providence, Jefferson said in his First Inaugural, there is one more thing necessary to make us a "happy and prosperous people . . . — a wise and frugal government, which shall restrain men from injuring one another, which shall *leave them* otherwise *free to regulate their own pursuits of* industry and *improvement*, and shall not take from the mouth of labor the bread it has earned" (emphasis added).

In general, the differences in purpose fall into two broad categories, one of them inferior to the other. The inferior purpose is to allow the citizens to survive and perhaps even to prosper. To do so they form a settlement, but a settlement is not the same thing as a city or polity. A polity serves the other, superior purpose. Its superiority lies in its unique ability to allow its citizens to live the good life. To have a polity there must first be a settlement because only when people are secure and are fed and clothed and when those who need assistance receive it can they build a polity in which the good life is available to all.

Constitutions may (but do not necessarily) acknowledge this differentiation by distinguishing between what can be called arrangements and institutions. Arrangements build settlements while institutions build polities. An arrangement facilitates activities intended to accomplish a utilitarian task. Examples are markets, departments of public works and hotels where non-citizens take up temporary residence. An institution is the enduring form given through custom, practice, tradition or law to a principled activity that a group of people undertake in common; its most distinctive characteristic is that it accounts for the moral character of people.[14] A judicial system is the most obvious example. A system of education that includes attending to the moral character of citizens is another.

A polity contains a great number of different organized activities, some of which of necessity are institutions, some of which cannot be, and some of which may be institutions or may be arrangements. Constitutions organize these activities into an articulate whole. For our purpose, which is that of understanding how buildings serve polities, these activities can be divided into four classes.

One may be called *primary activities*. The name is chosen because these activities come first and are necessary for both settlement and polity. Their purpose is to perpetuate the race and sustain life, to use the language Aristotle used in the *Politics*. One group of such activities includes the things done in the family or household, that is, producing and rearing children, while another group of activities is found in units organized for some particular purpose related to sustaining life—a farmstead, a factory, a business venture.

Some of the primary activities assure that the citizens are fed, clothed and sheltered. Others provide care for the sick, infirm and inept. Others protect lives and property. The primary activities are necessary for any settlement be it that of a family, monastic community or university, or an American city, town, village or rural area, and even if it takes the form of a mining camp or gang of pirates whose members pursue what they consider to be the good life or a consortium of merchants who pursue the same end but with just practices rather than merely sweaty, wily or violent ones. The customs of families and the constitutions of monks, university students and Americans provide for ways to operate at the level of institutions and therefore may (but will not necessarily) form polities. But bands of miners, pirates and merchants, and mixtures of these groups, will never form a polity even if they number in the millions unless they have a more just and noble purpose than merely achieving prosperity. (Nevertheless, lest the language become impossibly contorted in this text, if it is not important for the sake of the argument to separate them from polities, they will be treated as if they are polities.) There is nothing inherently wrong with desiring a prosperous life. Indeed, prosperity may even provide a means of supporting the vigorous government necessary to secure liberty, although both Socrates and Jefferson thought that the polity was threatened when its members seek satiety in prosperity alone. Arrangements are as diligent in building build-ings for their use as institutions are.

To move beyond security and to use prosperity properly requires pol-itical wisdom. Political wisdom emerges from the play of reason among well-informed people of good will united in their desire to live happily and acting within the second class of activities, the political ones. The *political activities* through which the polity exercises its authority over its members form the core of a constitution. Current constitutional thought benefits from the sharp scrutiny given politics since the Renaissance, a scrutiny benefiting from a renewed and insightful study of the larger political legacy of Athens and therefore a direct extension of the Western tradition founded there. Although earlier periods were vague about this, the sharpened knowledge that became available through the eighteenth century's acuity makes it clear that there are three conventional forms providing for the three natural, fundamental political activities: a legislature with the authority to formulate just statutes, an executive authorized to administer them with prudence, and a judiciary with the authority to assess the con-gruence of questionable acts with statutory standards of justice. These are the activities that must be institutionalized if the regime they serve is to make a polity out of a mere settlement.

Political wisdom and not happy accident led the Founders of the United States to vest all authority in the polity they established with the written, federal Constitution in these three activities. Their wisdom arose from their knowledge of the nature of things, in principle, atemporally. Their artfulness, which grew out of their knowing how things are and how people act in practice in actual circumstances in particular times and particular places, is revealed in their decision to constitute the new regime within a balanced interweaving and segregating of the three separate spheres of ac-tivity and in the relationships they established between arrangements and institutions. For example, they did not provide instruments to police and defend citizens but mandated (in Art. I, Sect. 8 and II, 2) that these be among the tasks assumed by those vested with the authority to engage in the three political activities they did institutionalize. Similarly, by guaran-teeing "to every state in this union a Republican form of government" (IV,

4) they forfended against allowing authority to fall into the hands of "aristocratic or monarchical innovations," as James Madison explained in *Federalist #43*, and against letting the three political activities escape the control of the citizens in the states constituting the union. Similar defenses against abuse of rights by lesser governments such as those of states and cities and by any and all other arrangements and institutions were established by various constitutional procedures and articulated in the Bill of Rights. These procedures have been amended as changing circumstances have brought greater (or lesser) clarity to our knowledge of the relationship between the rights that are ours by nature and the conventions of the Constitution and statutes intended to secure them.

Religious activities are the third class. Most religious activities occur within institutionalized groups ranging from sectarian communities such as Baptists or Roman Catholics which are embedded within a polity, monastic communities seeking to insulate themselves from the earthly city, or other collections of people who come together to live the good life founded in belief. These are distinct from the purely political entity called the city. Membership in them is voluntary while that of the city comes about by nature. The members of a civil, political community accept the necessity of conducting their lives first and foremost according to what politics prescribes, whereas the members of religious communities accept the authority of pronouncements accessible only in revelation, divination, sacerdotal office or some other realm beyond the play of reason which provides the substance of the political life.

Religious communities are generally devoted to a life that its members believe exists better in some world other than the current one. Nevertheless, they must still exist in this world where they must perpetuate their kind, produce and exchange the necessities of life, and police and defend themselves. They must, therefore, organize the same primary activities as any other settlement. They also need to distribute authority among their members and, if they are to be more than a mere settlement, they must seek to do so with justice and nobility. They therefore must institutionalize the political activities into a constitution, although the constitution may simply vest all political authority in a religious leader.

Church and state do not easily cohabit in this world. Only the political theory, and occasionally the practice, of the Western tradition has had much success in separating the religious and political lives of citizens. The issue first came to a head when the Hellenic and Christian traditions collided in Rome. Since the time of Augustine, who saw Christian history as the fulfillment of the history of the Jews and who took Rome to be an instrument provided by God to give the church a civil form, we have known that it is possible for a religious community dedicated to something outside time to coexist with and within a purely political one that exists within a history. This knowledge provided an important precondition for the Enlightenment achievement of separating church and state. That separation grew from the knowledge that the greatest dangers to the good city are posed by the fanatical church, that the greatest dangers to the holy church are posed by the corrupt city, and that the good city can exist only when the pure church and the good city accept the separate claims each has on the individual who is himself responsible for his own moral character. A church is not a city, but neither is a city a church. Socrates knew this, and so did Machiavelli, but the separation was realized first in Virginia and soon thereafter throughout the new states in America. Asclepius' repayment for Socrates' sacrificed cock is embedded in two parts of the Constitution: "no religious test shall ever be required as a qualification to any office or public trust under the United States" (Article VI); and "Congress shall make no law respecting an establishment of religion, or prohibiting the free exercise thereof . . ." (First Amendment).

This separation recognizes that religion and politics offer different ends and pleasures. The political realm does not see these as necessarily incompatible with one another, although the religious realm does from time to time. The American polity does not accept a claim of superiority by Jerusalem, but neither does it suggest that Athens can disprove and thereby disallow the claim that Jerusalem may have on those who encounter and accept its revelation. The injunction "Render unto Caesar that which is Caesar's" comes from Jerusalem, not from Athens, and can be made only when Jerusalem recognizes that Athens is essential for the church's survival and protection. The result of this insight leads to the conclusion that in the best circumstances, an established religion is incompatible with a just state and to its corollary, that no state may ban any religious exercise that poses no threat to the state's offer of a means for its citizens to live happily in the justice and nobility the secular life offers.

This tolerance, which will take different forms within the conventions of different states, is necessary if each citizen is to enjoy political liberty and hence possess moral responsibility, even, if not especially, in the personal existential universe van Pelt presents in the odd chapters. Only when state and church are separated will people remain free of whatever presumed providential order they seem to encounter in revelation. Having encountered revelation, they nonetheless remain, as van Pelt will argue in the next chapter, free and responsible agents both in their openness to that revelation, in their actions in history and in their construction of history. Those who have received and accepted a revelation that brings them together as coreligionists will live within the institution their belief establishes while those who do not need not.

In their broadest sense, religious activities are responses to the recognition that there is something superior to oneself which one cannot explain and whose hold one cannot resist—not only God which institutionalized religions claim as their well-spring but also other things such as learning which fills us with respect, the law whose majesty we respect, or a thing, event or person that strikes us with awe. The activities that give rise to these feelings are organized within political activities and produce universities, court houses and museums, although the part of religious institutions that organize their members' political activities may also operate these institutions.

The final group of activities found in polities are *civic activities*. Unlike the political activities, a polity can exist without them, although it would be a rather dreary place, and unlike the primary and the religious activities they are not necessary for the individual, although they add to the pleasures that are uniquely human. They allow people in a society to reach special purposes called for by the special character of their political life. While a polity should have some of these, having too many may dangerously dilute the citizens' devotion to the necessary political activities.

An understanding of a polity's civic activities will always be more hazy than the one we can have of the other three classes of activities. The intention in inquiring into them is not to seal them into separate boxes which isolate them from the other classes of activities but to understand their relationship to those other activities. The position taken here is that civic activities have value to the extent that they reinforce and expand activities that are most clearly lodged among the other classes. What follows is framed within that context.

Like anything else in a polity, civic activities exist within a graded hierarchy of importance. The highest place is occupied by those most energetically and clearly devoted to the edification of the citizen's moral character. These are clearly institutions, and as such they participate in the atemporal and universal. At the opposite extreme are those which merely facilitate some desired, proximate, timely end and are therefore arrangements. Among examples of current civic institutions are school systems running up to college level (during this period of growth, the pupils are not yet responsible for their own moral character but are being trained to assume that responsibility), universities and liberal arts colleges (their liberal arts curricula have as their purpose that of educating the student's moral character; if this purpose is not central, it is a mere trade school), and organized churches (so long as these are not merely fanatical sects). Among examples of current civic arrangements are trade schools (they train people to flourish within arrangements such as the building trades, hospitals and hotel industry), most museums (the sensate aesthetic providing the criteria for collecting and displaying works of art is divorced from any concern with moral character), chambers of commerce (they merely promote commerce), professional organizations such as the American Institute of Architects (they control and supervise the credentialing of members and seek to regulate the terms for their members' conducting business), and banks (ever since the reforms from earlier in this century, demonstrable creditworthiness rather than assessments of moral character has provided the basis for making loans).

Many of these activities are now commonly called cultural activities, but there are three reasons for avoiding the term "culture" here. First, it carries the meaning given by nineteenth-century positivist social scientists to refer to the variety of conventions that they took to be the distinguishing characteristics or products of a civilization. There are numerous catalogues of these conventions; Ernst Gombrich's can serve as an illustration: religion, constitution, morality, law, customs, science, technology and art.[15] Know them, and you will know the civilization as a unique thing existing back there in the past. But that is not the interest being pursued here. Calling them civic rather than cultural activities prevents suggesting that there is a broad overlap and general compatibility between now orthodox cultural history rooted in these conventions and the interpretation being outlined here.

This leads to the second reason for rejecting that term. The interpretation that collects various organized activities under the umbrella term of "culture"—museums, schools, churches, governments, etc.—has no interest in relating the activities to the most important thing polities do, namely, allow citizens to pursue happiness. It fails to distinguish between arrangements and institutions, and it assumes that if something was, then it had to be, that if it is, then it ought to be, and that whatever comes next is already wrapped within the ongoing historical process.

These two points are illustrated in Lewis Mumford's influential discussion of the city. "Like the rulers of the Bronze Age," he tells us,

> we still regard power as the chief manifestation of divinity, or if not that, the main agent of human development. . . . Organisms, societies, human persons, not least, cities, are delicate devices for regulating energy and putting it to the service of life.
>
> The chief function of the city is to convert power into form, energy into culture, dead matter into the living symbols of art, biological reproduction into social creativity. . . .
>
> The final mission of the city is to further man's conscious participation in the cosmic and the historic process.[16]

The final and most substantial objection is that in interpretations using the concept of culture, the city is considered a cultural artifact. The city is nothing more than the sum of its conventions and is itself nothing more than an artful, conventional structure. When that is the case it is impossible to stand outside the city and assess it as a whole composed of parts and to see the parts that compose the whole. It cannot, for example, be seen as a polity. If the only view is from within, as Plato explained in his allegory of the cave, the only thing available for perception is conventional, extrinsic content—and then only as a shadow. In the cave there can be no knowledge of the most important thing which is its nature because confinement within the cave prevents a person from obtaining the many views needed to learn the nature of a thing. Even if the entire history of a moment may be presented for scrutiny, no other moment is. Whatever is seen must be taken as true, which means that there is no way to know what truth is. If the lawmakers say the law is just, on what basis might they be disputed? If the architect says the building is well designed, how might one disagree? Within the cave, that which is is what it is, no matter what that might be.

In light of these comments it seems most prudent to think of civic activities as ancillary and subordinate to one or another of the various activities in the other three classes. The political needs of a government ought to determine what form of schools it needs, although churches might also operate schools. A religious community may operate a hospital or day-care center, but so too might a unit of government or even a business arrangement seeking a profit. But even if civic activities are subordinate to other activities that dictate the purpose they are to serve, it is useful to have a category like this one so that activities of the institutions and arrangements located within the other three classes not be too narrowly circumscribed. Civic activities provide places in the public realm where units of government, religious communities and entrepreneurs can reinforce one another and strengthen and enliven the polity.

Recapitulation: Political Forms

Throughout this explanation the role and relative importance of an activity has been predicated on the extent to which it promotes or embodies aspects of the atemporal, universal, typical, enduring and true. The extent to which it does so is also the extent to which it serves the best purpose of politics and the highest end of the polity. The several activities can be understood in a number of ways. One places them within a hierarchical scheme in which lesser activities serve settlements while greater ones support polities. Another sees them as ranging from arrangements to institutions. Yet another sees them in action within the polity's constitution: Dominant in the polity are the political activities because they alone embody the several essential components that allow the individual to perfect his nature and take his pleasure as a person. Only they acknowledge the individual's freedom and his assumption of moral responsibility for his actions. The form they take is the one that allows men to render reasons and justify themselves as political individuals. They account for types of activity that are universal, enduring and atemporal while involving citizens confronting the circumstantial, contingent and temporal.

The other classes of activities are different in character. Primary activities are not necessarily embedded in the logic of morals, although they may be. Religious activities are by definition outside the reach of reason and therefore must occupy a special relationship to the polity. And civic activities are not in their nature universal, enduring and atemporal. Nevertheless, without primary and political activities, there is no political life, and without religious activities there is no possibility of acknowledging that political life is inadequate to provide the highest possible perfection of the individual. This means that these three (the primary, political and religious) are necessarily entailed in the good city, and it also means that what they are in or by nature (i.e., what they are as types) must exist not merely in convention but in the natural realm of the atemporal, universal, typical, enduring and true principles. Not so the civic activities. They do not serve the citizen directly but only through the service they render to one or another of the other three activities. It follows, therefore, that their character will derive from that of the institution they serve and that they remain conventional in character.

THREE

Prophetic Remembrance

Robert Jan van Pelt

Chapter One described the origin of what the German historian Friedrich Meinecke identified as "one of the greatest intellectual revolutions that has ever taken place in Western Thought."[1] The result was an antinomy. On the one side there emerged a tendency to ascribe a normative significance to history, and on the other side there was the Historical Point of View that denied the validity of the Ciceronian idiom that *historia magistra vitae* ("history is the teacher of life").[2] One way to encounter this contrariety is to make a choice. We may either surrender to the dynamism and complexity of the Historical Point of View, and abandon all hope to find in the recorded past (or the experienced present, or the anticipated future) a normative basis for architectural production. We may decide, in other words, to float with the restless stream of endlessly shifting and changing, intersecting and overlapping historical configurations through the uncharted territory of the future. Or we might try to transcend or subscend the horizontal flow of history through the formulation of some abiding and universal order or normative ground.

Westfall proposes a return to the historiographical paradigm of the premodern age. His four terse chapters construct a hierarchical and utterly reasonable universe, a system of secure rules that instruct architects how to build within a general and abiding order. To overcome the modern chasm between the acting subject and the objective world, Westfall advances the idea that it is possible to return to a pre-Kantian morality and epistemology that held that a timeless knowledge decides (wo)man's relation to a meta-historical world. People can discover a knowledge of the enduring, the general and the ideal by distilling the chronicles that describe the temporal, the particular and the partial. This is useful because it allows people to discriminate between what is good and what is harmful, salutary and injurious, useful and useless, incidental and exemplary.[3] It suggests what is the proper stance to take in relation "to the tasks for which

we are specially suited—for example, that of building and teaching."[4]
Westfall's contribution to this book offers a model of such useful knowledge. Since it is an organized self-contained totality it offers a utopian
prospect that, in very real terms, resurrects the ideal of the Hellenic polis.
The foundations of this reconstruction is the classical understanding of
history.

Westfall has begun his reconstruction of architectural history with a
reflection on the nature of politics (Chapter Two: "Politics"). This seems
odd, yet it is in accord with the principles that guided classical historiography. The classical view of history was rooted in a vision of politics.[5] It
assumed that the task of the historian was to provide leadership in the polis.
He was to study political deeds and their effects. The historian was to show
what kind of stance had been beneficial to the common wealth, and which
actions had proven to be detrimental to the whole. Since classical
historiography derived from the Hellenic understanding of politics, so it
shared in the Greek assumption that politics are the domain of reason.
Historical reflection can discern how reason orders the universe at large,
how it can order human society and how, when it does so, it allows people
to modify their behavior in such a way that it will fit the larger order of the
city, or the universe. As time was the stage on which the unchanging truth
of reason disclosed itself—at times more and at times less clearly—the
discovery of the past could become *Paideia*, an effort capable of guiding
human reason to truth.

This truth was first and foremost pragmatic. If people can discover in
history the contours of some unchanging human nature they can also learn
lessons from history. Therefore the historian may formulate rules that have
an enduring value. To reconstruct the past meant to construct a stable
foundation from which to face the future. Studying the chronicles that
recorded the actions of men, classical historiography tried to hit on the
bedrock of natural truth that underlies the conventions of human behavior
and action. Yet beyond the pragmatic use of history there was also a higher,
metaphysical dimension. Revealing the eternal within the actual, history
ranked with poetry and philosophy as a discipline that could give human
beings insight into the very purpose of human existence. Therefore the
writing of history was not to be motivated, as Thucydides wrote, by the
desire to "meet the taste of the immediate public," but by the desire to
create something that was "to last forever," an assumption based on the
concept that people can learn from history since "the events which
happened in the past" will, "human nature being what it is," "at some time
or other and in much the same ways be repeated in the future."[6]

This and related assumptions led to an understanding of history that
denied history's historicity because the events that occur in history do not

really change people, or the nature of the city, or the cosmos. In the classical view history did not ascend to some kind of goal. Like the world of space it was a cosmos, a closed universe in time ordered by a regular and predictable recurrence of events. As winter follows summer, and night follows day, so corruption follows achievement. From the classical perspective the occurrences of history are regularly returning opportunities in which each individual might find occasion and material for unfolding and shaping his or her own timeless nature. Thus people were essentially independent of time in realizing their own nature; they did not believe themselves to be qualified by their past; they did not convey their past into the present because this past — history — was to be left behind for the sake of the timeless and the immutable. They believed history to be a storehouse of examples that have no ontological significance as such. Barry Cooper concluded in his succinct review of the state of history within the tradition of the *philosophia perennis* that the discourse, "for which history provides rhetorical confirmation through illustrations," gave meaning. "History, to use a famous image, is a cave from which the philosopher seeks to escape."[7]

History as Choice, History as Destiny

If classical historiography described (wo)man as a political agent confronting the forces of fortune and fate, the Judeo-Christian understanding of history depicted a community in its struggle to reach a promised destiny.[8] The classical view of history projected human life within a context of necessity, and tried to show how people may aspire to a formal freedom, located in the man-made cosmos of the polis. The Bible set (wo)man in a world of possibility, a world that was conceived as creation. Creation is not identical to nature. It is first of all an unprecedented act, willed in freedom, a free act that happened at a moment that we know not merely as the beginning of time, but also as the beginning of history as the unfolding story of the relationship between a people and their God. This relationship was to be a mutual destiny. If the Greeks invited (wo)man to assimilate himself to the enduring order of things, the Jewish and Christian tradition confronted people with the responsibility to make a new world, a new creation. Greek historiography tried to reveal the enduring and universal within the temporal and the particular; Judeo-Christian historiography tried to show how individual choices and decisions conceived in freedom and made in the actuality of the historical moment could and would bring about a dialogue between time and eternity. It proclaimed the essence of human existence to be in its historicity, understood not in the relative terms of post-Enlightenment historiography, but in the absolute terms that are generated by the need to make choices.

The Judeo-Christian tradition in historiography did not consider either (wo)man or history in terms of an abiding *logos* that transcends the circumstances of the material and the sensual world. Instead it considered individuals in their relation to the absolute authority of one's responsibility for the world, a responsibility that can only be experienced in the present, and which was created and which will be fulfilled in history. Thus the Hebrew, Jewish and Christian historians thought about history as the concrete life of a community that is constituted by its own past. Reminding the people of a past that was their own making, the successors to the Yahwist writer implicitly issued the ever actual call to face one's responsibility for the future. This sense of responsibility for history connected the past with the future, and made history into a unified story of redemption, a redemption that would be fulfilled at the end of time.

The future-directedness of Hebrew historiography seems paradoxical, yet the idea of an eschatological history, which is a history that looks primarily to the future and not to the past, might be understood if we assume that its ground is God's fidelity to Israel as a historical community. Another way to make the idea more familiar is to remember that the prophetic vision of history as future actually shapes our sense of history. When we ask about the meaning of history, or even of a particular event, we infer a meaning in relationship to the future. We do not see history as something finished, a collection of facts. It is open-ended. Westfall's ideology does not allow for that, yet his practice shows that history is, indeed, essentially of the future. His effort to resurrect Alberti's theory of architecture shows that Alberti's *De re aedificatoria* is *not* a fact, but still a possibility.

In his comprehensive study of the biblical foundation of modern thought entitled *Religion of Reason* (1919) the German–Jewish philosopher Hermann Cohen (1842–1918) appraised the concept of history as the creation of the prophetic idea. "What the Greek intellect could not achieve, monotheism succeeded in carrying out. *History* is in the Greek consciousness identical with knowledge simply. Thus history for the Greek is and remains directed only toward the past. In opposition, the prophet is the seer, not the scholar. To see, however, is to gaze. . . . The prophets are the idealists of history. Their vision begot the concept of history, as being of the *future*."[9] The result was that in Hebrew thinking time becomes the future in which the past and the present submerge. "All existence sinks into insignificance in the presence of the point of view of this idea, and man's existence is preserved and elevated into this being of the future. Thus the thought of *history* comes into being for human life and for the life of the peoples." The Greek inability to make the future the core of history had prevented them to conceive of a universal history that embraced all people. Since there was no unity in the past and since there is no unity in the present any attempt to write a universal history must be future-directed. "This is the meaning of the future as the establishment of true being, that is, God's being on earth; the future, this idea of existence, represents exclusively the *ideal* of history, and not the Golden Age, or Paradise. Both have already been."[10]

Cohen's interpretation of the future-directedness of Hebrew historiography might be seen like an echo of some of the ideas formulated by the Danish philosopher Søren Kierkegaard (1813–55). Like Cohen, Kierkegaard thought about history as a prophetic challenge. Study of the past was an existential confrontation with the uncertainties that earlier generations (the so-called contemporaries) had faced. This encounter, if genuine, was to become the uncertainty of the present. Therefore the historian's mind "will be in a state of suspense exactly as was the mind of a contemporary."[11] Kierkegaard pronounced his prophetical view of history as the confluence of a biblically inspired, existentially apprehended and philosophically pondered understanding of the fallacy of the classical notion of education as postulated in Plato's *Meno*. In this work Plato described Socrates' attempt to prove that knowledge is recollection. Socrates contended that everyone knows the same, but the measure in which people are in touch with that innate knowledge differed from person to person. He understood learning as the discovery of that which people already know (but do not yet realize) and he compared the educator's task to that of a midwife who assists through questioning in the spontaneous recovery of knowledge defined as the recollection of origins. (The even numbered chapters of *Architectural Principles in the Age of Historicism* are a good example of knowledge as recollection.) Kierkegaard rejected this classical notion of the eternity and continuity of consciousness because it did not allow for change. Every event, all new insights and discoveries were doomed to be swallowed up in the timeless and boundless realm of recollection. The result was an inability of the individual to set himself free, to choose, convert or repent because there was no opportunity to interrupt the continuum of recollection. There was no call to confront the world as a responsibility and there was no need to make a choice because "every point of departure in time is *eo ipso* accidental, an occasion, a vanishing moment."[12]

Judeo-Christian epistemology offered an alternative to Socratic thought. If classical philosophy sought to deny history, the prophets concentrated all their energy on the effort to understand the nature of change and becoming, of fall, repentance and redemption. The prophetic tradition stressed the importance of the moment of existential decision. In his *Philosophical Fragments* (1843), Kierkegaard described that moment as one of "a peculiar character. It is brief and temporal indeed, like every moment; it is transient as all moments are; it is past, like every moment in the next moment. And yet it is decisive, and filled with the eternal. Such a moment ought to have a distinctive name; let us call it the *Fullness of Time*."[13] This designation reveals how Kierkegaard thought about each moment of decision in relationship to the event when time had come to its fullness: the passion and crucifixion of Christ.

In his famous and influential meditation on the anthropological dimensions of freedom, *The Concept of Anxiety* (1844), Kierkegaard expanded his analysis of the moment. "The moment is not properly an atom of time but an atom of eternity. It is the first reflection of eternity in time, its first attempt, as it were, at suspending time." Again he censured the classical tradition for its inability to grasp this. It mistakenly considered the atom of eternity as eternity, and thus "neither time nor eternity received what was properly its due." Kierkegaard reiterated that the classical obsession with the enduring as it might be found in nature like so many atoms of eternity had been challenged by the Judeo-Christian teaching on the importance of repentance and conversion. The return to God implies the need for a moment where people can choose between the immanent reality of the world and the transcendent promise of salvation.

Such an understanding of the significance of each moment of true decision allows for a reconstruction of history as a realm of meaning. "The moment is that ambiguity in which time and eternity touch each other, and with this the concept of *temporality* is posited, whereby time constantly intersects eternity and eternity constantly pervades time."[14] Therefore the history that is generated by the moment of decision carries a prophetic signature. Kierkegaard observed how the intersection of the eternal in time, which generates the usual distinction of present, past and future, is future-directed. The division of time reveals that "the future in a certain sense signifies more than the present and the past, because in a certain sense the future is the whole of which the past is a part, and the future can in a certain sense signify the whole." This comprehensive significance of the future derives from the circumstance that the moment as the locus of decision is future-directed. Thus "the eternal signifies first the future," an apprehension that is reflected in the linguistic usage to identify the future with the eternal. The moment generates the future, and the two posit the past. Kierkegaard criticized the classical tradition for not having understood the genesis of the past. It considered past time not in its proper relation to the future and the moment, but "as a qualification of time in general, as a passing by." Therefore "the eternal lies behind as the past that can only be entered backwards."[15] And he concluded that, "on the whole, in defining the concepts of the past, the future, and the eternal, it can be seen how the moment is defined. If there is no moment, the eternal appears behind as the past. It is as when I imagine a man walking along a road but do not posit the step, and so the road appears behind him as the distance covered. If the moment is posited but merely as a *discrimen* [division], then the future is the eternal. If the moment is posited, so is the eternal, but also the future, which reappears as the past."[16] Christian doctrine recognized the importance of this understanding of the moment. Its notion of the "Fullness of Time" glorified the moment as the origin of the future and the past. And he warned that without such an understanding of the pivotal significance of the moment the Christian ways to address the failures of the past (conversion, atonement and redemption) or the hopes of the future (resurrection and judgement) would become meaningless.

This uncertainty vis-à-vis the future translates into a new comprehension of the past as the domain where the future reappears. Already in his *Philosophical Fragments*, Kierkegaard had pondered the implications of this position. "What happened has happened, and cannot be undone" so he introduced a consideration on the immutability of the past. And he asked if this meant that the past carried the (Hegelian) signature of the necessary. His answer was negative: because the future was uncertain, and the realm of freedom, thus the past was uncertain too. The past "did not become necessary by coming into being, but on the contrary proved by coming into being that it was not necessary. If the past had become necessary it would not be possible to infer the opposite about the future, but it would rather follow that the future was also necessary. If necessity could gain a foothold at a single point, there would no longer be any distinguishing between the past and the future." The result of the identification of the immutable with the necessary was a contradiction, because a necessary past "would no longer belong to freedom, i.e., it would no longer belong to that by which it came into being." Consequently freedom would become an illusion, nay worse, it would turn into "witchcraft" and "a false alarm."[17] Kierkegaard maintained that the past is the result of free choices and not of historical necessity. Therefore "whoever apprehends the past, *historico-philosophus*, is therefore a prophet in retrospect. That he is a prophet expresses the fact that the certainty of the past is based on an uncertainty, an uncertainty that exists for the past in precisely the same sense that it exists for the future, being rooted in possibility . . . out of which it could not *emerge* with necessity, *nam necessarium se ipso prius sit, necesse est*. The historian thus again confronts the past, moved by the emotion which is the passionate sense for becoming: wonder."[18]

Kierkegaard's reflections on the prophetical character of historical study offer the contemporary student a profitable introduction to the structure and intensity of Judeo-Christian historiography. Yet the very tensions and anxiety that give his voice a measure of prophetical authenticity also pose a problem. A scholar (like myself) who uses the observations of other scholars (like Löwith or Cohen) to create an answer to a troubling question may dispense with the (wo)men who formulated these answers the moment that they have offered what they had to give. It is not so easy to turn one's back to Kierkegaard. The few lines which I borrowed from his oeuvre do not fit easily academic discourse. Forged in contradiction and despair they conclusively point beyond a tentative theoretical and ultimately secular understanding of the nature of the prophetical reflection on the past towards an unconditionally committed leap into the future. Having turned to Kierkegaard's *Philosophical Fragments* in order to find an answer to a question of scholarly interest I ended up with another and infinitely more troubling question in turn. The end of the *Philosophical Fragments* confronted me with a disturbing moral of the relationship between knowledge and time. At that point Kierkegaard asserted that his project had gone beyond the Socratic, but doubted whether this meant that it was therefore more true. This, so he believed, "cannot be decided in the same breath, inasmuch as a new organ has been assumed here: faith; and a new presupposition: the consciousness of sin; and a new decision: the moment; and a new teacher: the god in time." And he acknowledged that without these he would not have dared to compete with Socrates. Yet he also recognized that "to go beyond Socrates when one nevertheless says essentially the same as he, only not nearly so well—that, at least, is not Socratic."[19] Kierkegaard's question about the truth of his proposition survives unresolved; his challenge to at least my faith remains unanswered. Still.

But the clamor of a freely accepted intellectual joust overwhelms such an unheralded muttering of doubt. And thus I turn my back to the unwanted dare, and return to the pleasures of my earlier engagement.

The Hebrew prophets wrote history; Hebrew historians wrote prophecy. Since history was meant to be eschatological (*eschaton* referring to a doctrine of the "last things" or the ultimate destiny of a people), it offered a criterion that allowed people to choose their future. Prophecy pronounced a possible future as the result of choices made in the present, choices that were informed by a knowledge of how the present had come into being as the result of decisions taken in the past. For the prophet history was normative because it was motivated by personal choice, by the freedom to begin something and the freedom to abandon one's course. This possibility of choice gave people a genuine responsibility vis-à-vis the creation of their future by making them answerable for the past as the condition of the present. Prophets addressed the future destiny of the people in addressing the reality of the present. They showed what could be in order to confront the people with the urgency of actual decision. In meeting the ruins of the past in which the present generation lives, they hoped to avert the ruin of the future. A classical example of the historiographical dimension of prophecy is the sermon Haggai gave after the Jews had returned from the Babylonian exile. He discussed the prospects for the future in its relationship to the past. The connection of past, present and future was a responsibility for history that began, as Haggai explained, with the responsibility for the rebuilding of the Temple.[20]

Prophecy took the form of applied history, and historiography was applied prophecy: thus it is no accident that one of the greatest historians the Hebrews ever produced was the prophet Jeremiah. He was, as has been argued recently, responsible for the so-called Deuteronomist redaction of the history of the covenant between the Hebrew people and their God.[21] He turned historian after his prophecies, meant to prevent Judah's revolt against the Babylonians, had failed. The rebellion under Zedekiah had ended in Nebuchadnezzar's destruction of Jerusalem and its temple. Amid the ruins Jeremiah began to reconsider the history of his people. He realized that it had to be edited so as to explain how the recent disasters could have happened despite the unconditional fidelity of Yahweh to the covenant. How could a pagan king destroy a temple that tradition claimed was the seal on the everlasting covenant between God and David? Jeremiah added small passages to the existing history of the temple to cover the possibility of the temple's destruction despite the everlasting covenant. Jeremiah's additions explored the theme of mutuality. He included, for example, a paragraph in the description of the dedication of the temple which linked its future to the manner in which the people would uphold their covenant with God.

When Solomon had finished building the Temple of Yahweh and the royal palace and all he had a mind to build, Yahweh appeared to Solomon a second time, like he had appeared to him in Gibeon. Yahweh said to him, "I grant your prayer and the entreaty you have made before me. I consecrate this house you have built. . . . But if you turn away from me, you and your sons, and do not keep the commandments and the laws I have set before you, and go and serve other gods and worship them, then I will cut Israel off from the land I have given them, and I will cast out from my presence this Temple that I have consecrated for my name, and Israel shall become a proverb and a byword among all the nations. As for this exalted Temple, all who pass by will be astounded; they will whistle and say, 'why has Yahweh treated this country and this Temple like this?' And the answer will be, 'Because they deserted Yahweh their God. . . .' "[22]

Various episodes in the history of the Hebrew people needed major revisions also. The core of the Book of Kings, which Jeremiah inherited, was the idea that God had created an eternal and unconditional covenant with the people through David and his dynasty. The monarchy had fallen. Did this imply that God did not keep his word? Jeremiah decided to reinterpret the Davidic covenant in conditional terms. The shift from the originally unconditional Davidic covenant to a conditional one is illustrated in Jeremiah's redaction of Yahweh's second revelation to Solomon, discussed above. Though the first part of Yahweh's speech stressed that God will set his name for all eternity in the house that David built, the part added after the destruction of the dynasty made this promise conditional on the people's observance of the covenant. God would exile the Hebrews from the promised land if they failed to keep the covenant. To stress the unity of the history that connected the building of the temple in 970 BCE with its destruction in 587 BCE Jeremiah included, at appropriate places, references to the revised covenant and the implications of its conditional character. We read, for example, the effect of King Manasseh's decision to place the idol of Asherah in the temple's Holy of Holies.

> He placed the carved image of Asherah which he had made in the Temple, of which Yahweh had said to David and his son Solomon, "In this Temple and in Jerusalem, the city I chose out of all the tribes of Israel, I will give my name a home forever. *I will no longer make Israel's footsteps wander from the land I gave their fathers, provided they observe all I have ordered them in accordance with the whole Law that my servant Moses prescribed for them.*" But they did not listen, Manasseh led them astray, so that they did more evil than those nations Yahweh had destroyed before the sons of Israel. Then Yahweh spoke through his servants the prophets, "Since Manasseh king of Judah has done these shameful deeds, acting more wickedly than all the Amorites did before him, and has led Judah itself into sin with his idols, Yahweh, the God of Israel, says this, 'Look, I will bring such disaster as to make the ears of all who hear of it tingle. I will stretch over Jerusalem the same measuring line as over Samaria, the same plumb-rule as for the house of Ahab; I will scour Jerusalem as a man scours a dish and, having scoured it, turn it upside down.' "[23]

The Benighted Age

The prophetic interpretation of the past as the gate that leads from the ruins of the present into the *eschaton* of the future transcends the cultural realm narrowly defined with the epithet "Judeo-Christian." It gives structure and direction to, for example, Herder's vision of history. In Chapter One I discussed Herder's conversion to history as a renunciation of an awful present. Herder hoped for a national and universal regeneration through the formation of "humanity," the eighteenth-century version of the New Jerusalem of the prophets. Herder defined humanity as "reason and equity in all conditions, and in all occupations of men."[24] It was the very end of history "to which all the meaner wants of this Earth are subservient, and which they are all contrived to promote."[25] This supremely rational and equitable goal was the axis of history: there the various histories of the different *Volks*, which had emerged from many particular beginnings and which cumulatively had given expression to the infinite scope of human creativity, were to be united in a common matrix. Yet humanity was not only history's end, but (in so far as we understand history as the story we tell about the past) also its origin. Contemplating humanity, the historian would be able to give meaning to history "as a school, for instructing us in the course, by which we are to reach the lovely goal of humanity and worth."[26]

Herder's teleological vision of history was prophetic in structure, but it missed the eschatological passion that drove and inspired the Hebrew prophets. It did not resound with the moral vigor and political vitality of an Isaiah or Jeremiah. The ethical moment remained hidden behind the blithesome mask of destined progress. In the thought of Herder's compatriot Friedrich Hölderlin the grin turned grim. As far as Hölderlin was concerned, the late eighteenth century was scarcely enlightened, and the last twenty centuries of history had scantly been illuminating. The only lesson to be drawn from the study of two thousand years of European history was that society had been enveloped in the darkness of night. The catastrophe of the Peloponnesian War had brought the day of Hellas to an end and inaugurated a benighted, alienated, fragmented and barbaric epoch marked by a separation between the human and the divine.

These ideas were commonplace in late-eighteenth-century Germany. They structure, for example, Friedrich Schiller's seminal *On the Aesthetic Education of Mankind* (1795). Hölderlin's mentor, protector and critic Schiller (1759–1805) described the disintegration of Periclean Athens "in which every individual enjoyed an independent existence but could, when need arose, grow into the whole organism," and analyzed the rise of a new society designed like "an ingenious clock-work, in which, out of the piercing together of innumerable but lifeless parts, a mechanical kind of collective life ensues" in which each person is "everlastingly chained to a little fragment of the whole," a fate that reduces man "into nothing but a fragment."[27] Schiller analyzed how the progress of civilization, applauded by Herder, had led to a severance of the inner self from the objective purposes of society. The result was self-alienation and fragmentation which, however, could be overcome through an adoption of the program of

moral education through art proposed in Kant's third and, as far as the
Romantics were concerned, greatest Critique: *The Critique of Judgement*
(1790). The goal of this reformation was, of course, Herder's *Humanität*.

Schiller's examination of the crisis of European civilization assumed
prophetic intensity in Hölderlin's hymns and elegies. Hölderlin saw the
vocation of the poet in prophetic terms. In his hymn to poet "As on a
Holiday . . ." he exclaimed to his fellow poets:

> us it behooves to stand
> Bare-headed beneath God's thunderstorms
> To grasp the Father's ray, no less, with our own two hands
> And, wrapping in song the heavenly gift,
> To offer it to the people.[28]

The poet mediates between the moment (the grasping of the ray) and
eternity (God) when he wraps the heavenly gift of revelation in the song of
history, a *Lied* sung in the German language.

In his *The Archipelago* (1800) Hölderlin brought the poetic word to
Schiller's argumentation. He recited the contemporary dissipation of the
self in the confinement of its own creations.

> Ah, but our kind walks in darkness, it dwells as in Orcus,
> Severed from all that's divine. To his own industry only
> Each man is forged, and can hear only himself in the workshop's
> Deafening noise; and much the savages toil there, for ever
> Moving their powerful arms, they labour, yet always and always
> Vain, like the Furies, unfruitful the wretches' exertions remain there.[29]

Yet there was hope in desolation. Unlike Schiller, who merely argued for a
program of education, the poet's poet Hölderlin actually announced the
coming end of darkness and proclaimed the new day, the beginning of the
spirit's liberation from its twenty centuries of nightmarish exile.

> Not a moment longer! Already I hear on far foothills
> Choric song, the feast day's, and hear the green groves all re-echo,
> Where the young men more deeply breathe, where the soul of the people
> Quietly gathers in freer singing in praise of that god whose
> Realm is the mountain heights, but the valleys also are holy.

The poet knew that the day was to come again because it had been day
once. While the godless age of fragmentation and alienation had been
ordained by a higher power in order to give the world a brooding-time that

would open to an epoch of regeneration, its continuation was unnecessary: Hölderlin believed that Europe was ready to be reawakened, and the call was to come from Germany and in German tongue. The new appreciation of things Greek over things Roman or Christian and the crucial role of German thought in this world-historical conversion heralded the new era. Looking at the Periclean Age, the consummation of the Age of Daylight when the greatest individual freedom had been grounded in a most profound sense of communal belonging, the German nation would be able to summon the confidence to begin again, and reestablish the Parnassus amid the German mountains. Therefore he demanded that:

> When our autumn
> Comes, when you all, grown mature, you genii known in the ancient
> World return—and, look, the year's consummation approaches—
> Then may the feast-day preserve you also, great era long ended,
> May the people look towards Hellas and thanksgiving, weeping,
> Make the proud day of their triumph gentle with solemn remembrance![30]

Hölderlin's call to remember Greece was undoubtedly elegiac in character. He longed for it as Germany's lost home. At times the nostalgic pull towards the enchanting past proved almost seductive, and the ensuing grief for its utter destruction seemed unbounded in scope and fathomless in depth. At such moments he characterized the loss as overwhelming and the historical ideal as irretrievable.

> Tell me, where now is Athens? Over the urns of the masters
> Here, on your shores, on the holy, sorrowing god, has your city
> Dearest of all to you perished, utterly crumbled to ashes,
> Or does a token, a trace remain, just so much that a sailor
> Passing by will mention her name, will notice the site and recall her?

Yet Hölderlin never fully surrendered to nostalgia; he always returned to the crisis of the present and the tasks of the future. The threnodic mood always gives way to prophetic aspiration. Athens's splendor may be lost, but its substance proves enduring. That spirit, which the poet preserves, is one of commitment to one's patrimony and resistance to the forces that seek to usurp it. In short the Athens that remained in the poetic imagination (and that could be revived in the humiliated German lands) was the community that had chosen in 480 BCE to deliver its dwellings and temples to the Persians in order to save the polis. Hölderlin's Athens was a site of physical desolation, a ruined homeland to which the victors of Salamis returned, a city:

                                    like a time-ravaged mother
When the child long ago given up for lost after years comes
Back alive to her breast, no child but a fully grown youth now,
But with grieving her soul has withered, and joy comes too late for
Her, exhausted with hoping, and hardly she hears and can follow
What her loving son in gratitude hastens to tell her;
So to the people come back now seemed the old soil of their homeland.
For in vain after grove and garden the pious enquire now
And no friendly door is waiting to welcome the victors
As it used to do once when, happy, a man voyaged homeward
From the islands and, blessed, the fortress of Mother Athene,
Distantly gleaming, appeared to eyes uplifted in longing.
Yet familiar enough, though stripped and deserted, the streets are,
All the gardens that mourn within and beyond the Agora,
Where the portico's pillars and limbs of the gods lie in pieces,
There, stirred up in their souls and rejoicing in faith, now the people
Lovingly klink their hands in token of newly pledged union.
Soon the man, too, will seek and find the old site of his dwelling
Under the rubble; his wife, recalling the look of their bedroom,
Weeps and embraces him; the children excitedly ask him
For the table at which they'd sit in a circle at mealtimes
Watched by their ancestors, by benevolent gods of the household.
But the people raise tents, and neighbours renew their old friendships,
Choosing familiar sites, and true to the heart and its habits
Airy new habitations fall into place on the hillsides.

Hölderlin's poetic reconstruction of classical Athens did not focus on the Periclean Acropolis or Agora, but on the ruins that (quite literally) were to be their foundations. In the patriarchal existence amid the rubble he found the lesson to be followed, the sense of community that preceded the glory of achievement, the prophetic program of renewal to be enacted in the German lands. In an almost Isaian vision of natural, national and urban regeneration, Hölderlin evoked the reconstruction of the city as the cooperation of mortals, the earth, the sea and the sky.

But to please the maternal earth and honour the god of the waters
Now the city revives, a glorious artifice, firmly
Founded as galaxies, wrought by genius that readily thus will
Make himself fetters of love, and thus in majestic constructions,
Raised for his restless self, maintains a durable dwelling.
Look, and the forest serves that creator; Pentele, like other

Mountains near by, provides rich ores and offers him marble,
But alive as he is, and glad and splendid it seems to
Leap from his hands, and his work seems easily done, like the sun's work.
Fountains rise from the ground, and over the hills in pure conduits
Quickly the spring is conveyed and rushes to fill the bright basin;
Round about them, bright, as heroes dressed up for a banquet
Gleam round the communal cup, a circle of houses; above it
Looms the Prytanean hall, and now the gymnasia are open.
Temples are built for the gods and, near to immortals, a thought as
Holy as it is bold, the Olympion rises to Aether
From the sacred grove; still many a heavenly hall rose,
From its affliction, and long it flourished there, also for your sake,
God of the waters, yours too, and happily gathered your loved ones
Often yet would intone their paean to you on the foothills.[31]

These lines gather the enduring world of gods, sky and earth and the historical world of the Greeks into the moment of the poetic utterance. The image of the timeless citadel where the gods gazed down on the people and the memory of the life of the Agora retreat in a poetic reenactment of the city's reconstruction, an instauration brought about through the German word.

Historie and *Geschichte*

As the story of Jeremiah's or Hölderlin's historiographical activities show, the prophetical view of history was less concerned with scientific accuracy than with questions of meaning. Neither Jeremiah nor Hölderlin thought about history as the totality of events that constitute the past. For them history was the story about those events that they considered to be of normative significance. Or, to use the classic terminology, history is not a science of the *res gestae* (the science of *deeds*), but a *historia rerum gestarum* (the *story of deeds*).

English vocabulary does not offer a terminology that allows for a clear lexicographical distinction between these two different understandings of the noun "History." The German language offers, however, two different terms: history as the science of the *res gestae* is known as *Historie*. Its corresponding adjective is *historisch*, which translates as "historical." A *historia rerum gestarum* is labeled as *Geschichte*. The adjective of *Geschichte* is *geschichtlich*, which may be translated as "historic."[32]

Classical historiography and the historical school (which follows the precepts of the Historical Point of View) aim at the reconstruction of the past as *Historie*. While the former differs from the latter in its explicit search for a "useful" history, they confront the past like an object. The two perspectives explicitly aim at an "objective" method, though the classical historian has a different understanding of what objective means than his historicist and relativist counterpart. Each, however, searches for a truth that is independent from the interpreter. The story they write is a means to put the recovered truth of history on record. A result of such an application of the science of *res gestae* to the past is that it does not allow the historian to take responsibility for the past, because responsibility presupposes a genuine relationship among the participating entities. This relationship is *a priori* absent in a subject–object pattern. Historians who aim at the reconstruction of the past as *Historie* tend to stress the specialized nature of their work. They understand the evidence as ambiguous, relative and causal; therefore only those who have endured years of education may deal with it. They claim that the past is ambiguous because our knowledge and reconstruction of the past constantly changes; it is relative because the past may be understood only with the help of proper categories; and it is causal because it can understand events solely like the effects of some identifiable cause.

Those who understand history as *Geschichte* tend to be less concerned about academic degrees than about the question of whether the story has been well told. If *Historie* tries to tell "how it actually has been," *Geschichte* is an account that includes the facts (and the *factum*) and their resonance within the consciousness of subsequent generations (which includes the historian's encounter with them). In a *Historie* we expect to find clearly defined boundaries that separate the true from the likely, and the likely from the fabulous. We also expect explanations that declare what happened to be the expected outcome of some law of history or nature. In *Geschichte* we expect a horizon of meaning that addresses the future and the past as a possibility.[33] *Geschichte*, in other words, is not so much about the facts than about the way we care to remember them as the elements of a story that also affects our own lives and destinies. The narrative, which was only a means from the perspective of *Historie*, becomes an end when considered within the terms of the historic. That story which carries the past as *Geschichte* into the present bridges the chasm between the historical event and the present through its concentration on the question of meaning. It defines its content as historical and declares it also as historic, which means important to us. Because it is the locus of communal recollection, *Geschichte* differs radically from the science of *res gestae*, which assumes the autonomy of the historical events vis-à-vis subsequent interpretation.

One text might be both *Historie* and *Geschichte*. The Bible, for example, may be thought about as a collection of various sources that allow us to reconstruct the political and religious life of the ancient Hebrews. Such a reading interprets it as *Historie*. It might also be read as a history that has some prophetic or existential meaning for us. Then we approach it as *Geschichte*. Hölderlin's poems partake also in the two modes of history. They are *Historie* because they record a specific development in German Romantic literature, and they have also historical significance if used as source material for a study on the German infatuation with classical Greece. When considered as an interpretation of the character and meaning of Hellenic civilization as a guide for life in the benighted age, Hölderlin's evocation of Greece becomes *geschichtlich*. These two examples illustrate that *Geschichte* is not the exclusive territory of the PhD historian, but of anyone who approaches the past as an address that is directed at ourselves. In the story we tell about it, the past loses its ambiguous, relative character, and must become clear and absolute; what was explained as a causal connection must become a plot that pronounces fate to be that inescapable judgement through which our freedom manifests itself. *Geschichte* is a proclamation that speaks existentially to every individual. It preserves the complexity and relativity of the historical, yet simultaneously informs and delimits our interpretation so that we become able to see within the equivocal and relative the contours of the conclusive and the absolute. Within the existential encounter of *Geschichte*, the skeptical, the problematical and the causal will retreat, though only for a moment, behind a face that is decisive, simple and unique. The Judeo-Christian tradition identified that face as the mask of God. Hölderlin recognized it as the sculptured head of Zeus and Hegel saw it as the reflection of ourselves in a mirror. Whatever name we give to it, it is a presence that confronts us with the need to be decisive; it calls us to take responsibility for our destiny, and therefore for history.

One of the consequences of the absolute character of *Geschichte* is its legitimate claim to universality. This seems paradoxical, since its historical basis is often rather narrow. Why would the story of one or two small semitic nations (or one Greek city) be all-inclusive, and a multi-volume history of the world not? The answer is simple: the story of the Israelites and Judahites (or classical Athens) tells all that needs to be known. Hebrew history begins with a universal perspective when it describes the creation of the world and Adam. It follows world history until the Tower of Babel. *Historie* and *Geschichte* are still united. With Abram/Abraham the two separate. When God makes his covenant with Abram, the history of the world retreats in the background, since from that point there was only one meaningful history: the story of the covenant between God, Abraham and his descendants. Because it is the story of God's relationship with the world, it is a story that encompasses all that deserves the designation of "knowledge." What happens to the other nations is merely "information." This history of redemption, or *Heilsgeschichte*, will merge again with the history of the world, *Welthistorie*, only when the nations will gather around the reconstructed temple in the new Jerusalem. The ingathering of the nations terminates the end of darkness, the night of exile, the ordeal of *Geschichte*. Now history as *Geschichte* will come to an end. The river of *Historie* will still move, but nothing new will happen, since nothing new can happen.

> No more will the sun give you daylight,
> nor moonlight shine on you,
> but Yahweh will be your everlasting light,
> your God will be your splendour.
> Your sun will set no more
> nor your moon wane,
> but Yahweh will be your everlasting light
> and your days of mourning will be ended.[34]

Thus God will have made a new heaven and a new earth, bringing redemption to the old. The story of the covenant is completed, the promise fulfilled.

Geschichtliche Historiography and the Historical Point of View

At first sight it seems that relativist historiography cannot accommodate the demand for a *geschichtliche* understanding of the past. Yet, as the Italian philosopher Benedetto Croce (1866–1952) has argued in his *History as the Story of Liberty* (1941), the relativist historian might reveal the explicit historic aspect of any historical fact if she tries to reconstruct the choice or "freedom" inferred from that fact. Croce's understanding of history might be summarized in his assertion that "the two pronouncements, that history is the history of liberty, and that liberty is the moral ideal of humanity, do not allow of contradiction. They can indeed be contradicted verbally, but only by those who thus deny history or stifle the witness of the moral consciousness, by denying freedom."[35] Croce did not think about this history within the terms of a Hegelian development of the spirit, which described *Weltgeschichte* as liberty's birth in the Orient (one person is free), its growth in the classical world (some are free), its maturation in the Germanic world (all are free) to its final fixation and fulfillment in the self-consciousness of Hegel's own philosophy. Croce remained firmly committed to the relativist position that each age should be considered in its own terms and, therefore, that a historian cannot describe the relationship of epochs in terms of progress (of liberty) or regress (into bondage). In fact, Croce radicalized the relativist position when he asserted that "humanity in every epoch, in every human person, is always whole."[36] Throughout history, Croce professed, people have been the same in their relationship to the future as the field of action, the past as the domain of judgement and the present as the realm of decision. Croce did not deny the validity of the historicist assertion that historical situations are determined by the past. But he also recognized that every historical situation is open to the future, that it is a horizon of competing possibilities framed by the actuality of decision.

The German theologian Rudolf Bultmann (1884–1976) summarized Croce's "deeper understanding" of historicism as an almost prophetical apprehension of man as a being "who can never possess his genuine life in any present moment, but is always on the way and yet is not at the mercy of a course of history independent of himself." Croce had rightly understood that every moment is the *now* of responsibility and of decision. This universal *now* gives history its unity. "In this responsibility, as responsibility over against the past as well as over against the future, the unity of history is grounded."[37] Croce insisted that we run into the same dialectics of necessity and freedom within the determinate and historical tasks that our ancestors faced. Like them we have to decide which of all the possibilities open to us are relevant to our choice and action. Therefore we also have to decide which interpretation of history, of all possible readings of the past, is relevant to the task we are to fulfill. Thus if the classical historian identifies the sameness of people to be located in their nature, Croce saw it in the relationship between people and their world understood as a task to be performed. "Therefore in the accomplishment of that task, humanity expresses itself in its wholeness, and when other tasks supervene it will express itself in these from time to time, always in its entirety."[38] Within the actual moment of decision, faced by real people who are confronted with real tasks and real choices, the past and future gather each time anew, each time in the same way.

The result of this thorough and radical analysis of the relativist paradigm was a *geschichtliche* understanding of the past in terms of decision. Because choice presupposes freedom, history is nothing but the story of liberty. Each moment in history is marked by the sign of liberty. This liberty does not have significance because it shows an ideal, universal configuration of freedom. Croce alleged that such a blueprint for pure and perfect liberty is "the phantom projected into our imagination by our infinite desire, by our moral ardor, by our anxiety for purity and perfection, and it is not to be met with in the world of facts." Therefore the historian should adopt a relativist and historicist posture, and study liberty within "the circle in which it exists and not in that in which it does not exist or does not yet exist." Only thus will the historian be able to appreciate "the fact that there were slaves does not destroy the reality of the great works that the free men of Athens achieved in politics, in thought, in poetry, in the other arts, in the whole of culture and civilization."[39] Thus the historian will always face the task to distill the absolute, the normative or in short the historic from the relative, the contingent and the historical.

A Judeo-Christian History of Architecture

When we try to apply the Judeo-Christian understanding of the past to the history of architecture we run into problems. The construction of buildings does play an important role in the Bible, and the erection and destruction of the tabernacle in the desert, and of the first and second temples mark significant moments in the history of the covenant. Yet the results of those acts of construction, the actual buildings (or their ruins) were seen as obstacles that impeded the spiritual progress of the people. When the temple stood, its presence invited paganism (as with Manasseh) or suggested that the covenant could be maintained by ritual observances and donations instead of through repentance and conversion. In the years immediately before the destruction of the temple in 587 BCE Jeremiah identified the trust the people had in the almost apotropeic power of the building to be a potential cause of national and spiritual disaster. Standing before the temple he preached: "Put no trust in delusive words like these: *This is the sanctuary of Yahweh, the sanctuary of Yahweh, the sanctuary of Yahweh!*" The building did not matter, the people's actions did: "But if you do amend your behavior and your actions, if you treat each other fairly, if you do not exploit the stranger, the orphan and the widow (if you do not shed innocent blood in this place), and if you do not follow alien gods, to your own ruin, then there in this place I will stay with you, in the land that long ago I gave to your fathers forever."[40] Jeremiah's message was clear: the mere presence of the temple itself and of its cult did not give security. Only the people's attitude to the temple and the cult counted, or, with other words, their response to God. This did not mean that Jeremiah favored the abolition of the temple and its cult. Such an act of destruction would raise the question of whether the covenant was still valid. So one had to rebuild the temple, in an ever simpler form. Such an ideology supported an interpretation of the historic development of architecture that defined spiritual progress in terms of architectural reduction. At the beginning of architectural history there was a great emphasis on size and structural achievement (the Tower of Babel); as time progressed the architectonic qualities became less and less important, allowing the spiritual qualities to become predominant. The Christians were to draw the final conclusion when they stated that the new temple was to be the (mystical) body of Christ. With the crucifixion of the historical Jesus and the resurrection of the historic Christ the history of architecture, understood as a *Geschichte*, had come to an end. After that only the "fabric within" was to count.

In the twentieth century Sigmund Freud was to give a contemporary turn to this prophetic apprehension. In his *Civilization and Its Discontents* he suggested how the physical fabric of cities allows us to curb our instinctual aggression and egoism and sublimate our death instinct. This act of sublimation allows us to build civilizations, but at the price of a measure of self-alienation.[41] Thus it is possible to think about the city and its architecture like a museum of accumulated sublimation built on a landfill of accumulated guilt. Norman O. Brown judged the temple buildings that dominated the first cities to have been "monuments of accumulated guilt and expiation." These buildings reified the process of expiation into a mass of stone and gold. "Hence a city is itself, like money, crystallized guilt. . . . In monumental form, as money or as the city itself, each generation inherits the ascetic achievements of its ancestors; not, as Joan Robinson says of the gold fund, as a 'free gift from history,' but as a debt to be paid by further accumulation of monuments. Through the city the sins of the fathers are visited upon the children; every city has a history and a rate of interest."[42] The Judeo-Christian tradition tried to liberate people from this guilt by turning them away from the idea of a physical community gathered around temples made of stone to the idea of a spiritual community experienced in the temple of the heart. For a man like Jeremiah this architectural history of self-effacement had not yet ended. The posthistorical or "New Age," identified with the "New Jerusalem," had yet to come. Christian theologians thought differently. Christ's resurrection had superseded the history of man-made architecture. The resurrection had ended *Architekturgeschichte* since it had ended all *Geschichte*. His act of self-sacrifice had atoned for the guilt accumulated over time, fulfilled life's meaning and completed history.[43] It had initiated the fullness of the "New Age," the final time that connected the saving event to the actual end of *Historie*.

This "New Age" was the epoch located between the end of *Heilsgeschichte* and the end of the concurrent *Welthistorie*. It was characterized by the tension which the Swiss theologian Oscar Cullmann identified as the result from being already the time of the end, and not yet being *the* end. "The present period of the Church is the time between the decisive battle, which has already occurred, and the 'Victory Day.'" And Cullmann warned that,

to those who do not understand this tension, the meaning of the New
Testament must remain opaque, "for this tension is the silent presupposition that lies behind all it says."[44] The battle had been the passion, when
Jesus had gathered all time within one moment, and opened up through his
sacrifice the temporality of the world to the eternity of God. It allowed the
opposites of a historic past and a posthistorical future to coincide in an
everlasting present. Such a present is not without its own tribulations and
developments. Cullmann used the example of the Second World War to
illustrate this point. After Stalingrad the military leadership of the Axis and
the Allies knew that the war had been decided, yet the populations did not
know it, and, from the perspective of the individual, the last two years of
the war, with its bombings, the mass exterminations in Auschwitz and the
mass expulsions of peoples were undeniably the most dangerous. Yet in a
world-historical sense the war was over in January 1943. The crucifixion
and resurrection constitute the Stalingrad within the Christian *Geschichte*
(assuming that the Christians interpret the event from the Allied side). With
the saving event the world as a whole, and all that it constitutes, including
architecture, had entered the posthistorical age, linked to the everlasting
present of Christ's crucifixion and resurrection. After the resurrection
nothing really new could happen in the world: the redeeming deed had been
done, and all had been saved. All that remained to be done was to bring the
message of the already founded eternal Kingdom of God to the rest of the
world. Yet the successes or tribulations of the church militant would not
change the ahistorical character of the era after Christ, because his
redemption, as a universal redemption, contained within itself all valid
possibilities. The crucifixion and resurrection, culmination of a *Geschichte*,
would arrest further development because, as Niebuhr observed, they had
become "the pattern of all subsequent confrontations between God and
man" (that is the pattern of all that was worthwhile to record). "They must
contain the crucifixion of self-abandonment and the resurrection of self-
recovery. Men must die to sin with Christ and arise with him to newness of
Life."[45] Those born after Christ have no destiny to look forward to: their
destiny had already arrived and was preserved by the church.

   The Christian architect faced a dilemma: his faith told him that the
history of architecture had come to an end. How does one build after the
end has come? The tasks performed for good or evil by the builders of
Babel, Bezelael (the architect who built the tabernacle) and Hiram Abiff
(the architect of Solomon's temple) had been fulfilled in Christ. One
approach was to see the making of buildings in terms of the crucifixion and
resurrection.[46] This had become possible just at the moment that the
question of a posthistorical Christian architecture had acquired urgency:
i.e. during the reign of Constantine the Great. The recovery of Golgotha

and Christ's tomb, which had been buried under rubble for three centuries, was, as Eusebius recorded it in his *Vita Constantini*, an event which contemporaries interpreted within the context of Christ's passion and resurrection. "The cave, the holy of holies, was, in a manner so similar to that of our Savior, restored to life in that, after lying buried in darkness, it again emerged into the light."[47] Soon another discovery would be added: the discovery of the true cross. The basilica of the Holy Sepulchre, built over the site of Golgotha and the tomb, embodied the two themes in a new kind of posthistorical architecture explicitly conceived with the terms of crucifixion and resurrection. The Holy Sepulchre provided the (metaphorical) place where a posthistorical architecture could be securely grounded. Its "discovery" offered the elements of a building ritual; its plan and elevation a pattern to be followed.

Throughout the Early Middle Ages clerics and rulers desired to interpret their own important building projects in terms of the passion and the resurrection.[48] Since Christ's resurrection had been "translated" and "preserved" in Constantine's act, so Constantine's restoration could be "translated" and "preserved" in the architecture of the Occident. One of the most famous surviving examples is Charlemagne's Palatine chapel, which explicitly refers in its architecture to the Holy Sepulchre in Jerusalem. In the monastery church at Centula (or as it is known today Saint-Riquier), which was built by a nephew of Charlemagne at the end of the eighth century, the west tower consciously imitated the Holy Sepulchre in Jerusalem. This *Turris Sancti Salvatoris* consisted of a crypt or tomb, which contained twenty-five relics of Christ, with a chapel above it, surrounded on three sides by multi-storied galleries. The spaces of the passion and the resurrection were superimposed. Nichols found that this architectural ensemble did not suffice "to provide the sole commemoration of the Holy Sepulchre." On Easter Sunday the worshippers would apportion themselves in the west tower in such a manner that the building, the people and the relics merged into one liturgical symbol of the resurrection. "In the ritual, the human participants became figurations of the 'lignum vitae' of the cross, as well as of the human/historic aspects of Christ transposed, in a paradigm of grace that would have import for all humans in the belief of the time, by the miracle of the cross."[49] Centula's unity of historic ideation, eschatological aspiration and architectural disposition was unprecedented and proved to be a turning point in the history of architecture. The powerful typological symbolization, the dramatic massing of the various parts of the church's exterior and the complex spatial organization inside transfigured the architectural scene. Before the creation of Centula no building built in Western Europe after the collapse of the Roman empire could stand comparison with even the most humble relics of imperial provincial architecture; with Centula this had changed. Nine centuries after the passion and nine centuries before the French Revolution, European architecture came into its own.

Typology

The story of the Christ's passion and resurrection and the sign of the cross were comprehensive in meaning, yet poor in imagery. This aesthetic poverty limited their application to, for example, architecture: the complex magnificence of Centula's architectural and liturgical celebration of Christ's passion and resurrection exceeded the resources of most other communities. An alternative, the simple cruciform church, was too much part of tradition to evoke the drama of death and salvation. A specific Christian historiographic tradition developed to amplify the storehouse of imagery available to those who lived in the posthistorical age. If, indeed, all was to be seen in terms of the passion and resurrection—that is, in terms of salvation—then it was also legitimate to claim that the events that constituted the *Heilsgeschichte* before its final fulfillment could and should be seen in the same terms, and that therefore one's actions could embody the passion and resurrection through a reference to, for example, the transfiguration of Christ on the mountain.

Mark recorded the transfiguration as follows: "And he [Jesus] said to them, 'I tell you solemnly, there are some standing here who will not taste death before they see the kingdom of God come to power.' Six days later, Jesus took with him Peter and James and John and led them up a high mountain where they could be alone by themselves. There in their presence he was transfigured: his clothes became dazzlingly white, whiter than any earthly bleacher could make them. . . . As they came down from the mountain he warned them to tell no one what they had seen, until after the Son of Man had risen from the dead."[50] The reference to the passion and the resurrection is clear. Around the year 1000 theologians and architects discovered the potency of the story. To create a "dazzlingly white" mantle of churches would refer through the transfiguration to the end of history without remaining trapped in the imagery offered by the Holy Sepulchre. An eleventh-century Benedictine monk, Rodolphus Glaber, interpreted the white garments as "the language by which Christ clothes the world in the present age,"[51] which means the posthistorical Kingdom of God. "At the approach of the third year following the year 1000, it was possible to see almost everywhere in the world, but particularly in Italy and Gaul, the reconstruction of church buildings, even though the greater part of them, very well constructed, did not need rebuilding. . . . One might have said that the world itself stirred to shake off its old garment in order to cover itself everywhere with a white cloak of churches."[52] Thus not only were Jesus' passion and Christ's resurrection normative, but also those events within the *Heilsgeschichte* that prefigured the end of history. Some of these episodes could be found in the life of Jesus. The majority of motives, however, was derived from the Old Testament.

Christian theologians developed a comprehensive system of exegesis to decide which events had been normative. Their historiographical method is known as typology, and it seemed that their typology could offer a way to identify within the history of architecture those buildings were normative as architectural types.[53] The Christian typological understanding of history had, after all, successfully transformed the implicit unity of the past, the present and the future, posed by the Hebrew historians, into an explicit theory of the unity of the *Historie* of the world, the *Geschichte* of the covenant, the eternal moment of the passion and the resurrection and the posthistorical condition of the church. Its foundation was the metahistorical significance of Christ, who had gathered time and eternity in himself, becoming in the words of Revelation the "Alpha and the Omega, the Beginning and the End." On that basis Christian typology identified the normative events within time as it had stretched from the world's beginning to its end and made them valid beyond the chasm that separated a normative history from the posthistorical world. In a typological interpretation a historian tries to connect some event in history—for example the transfiguration—to the passion and resurrection of Christ, and through that with the situation in the present. The earlier event is interpreted as a figure, shadow or type of redemption wrought by Christ. The word "type" is derived from the Greek τνπον, *tupos*, which is the principal noun formed from the stem of τνπτειν, *tuptein*, "to strike." It refers to a mark that is left by a blow, and its specific use was that of an impression made on wax by a seal. The second event (that is the passion), the antitype, is seen as a fulfillment or actualization of the (concealed) content of the first one. The antitype recapitulates the type, and makes its hidden meaning manifest to all. Just as the passion and the resurrection are normative as to one's actions in the posthistorical age, they are also normative for one's interpretation of the *Geschichte* that preceded it. In the following pages I will use the designation "historic type" whenever I refer to the Judeo-Christian interpretation of the word.

Historic type and antitype do not relate to each other as cause and effect. They are the (material) imprints in history of some larger (spiritual) matrix that propels human destiny. This *mentalité* demands that the historian interpret historical change "from above." She is not required to reflect on the individual events within a historicist context, but thinks about them in their individual relationship to that larger spiritual order, simultaneously present and hidden. This matrix is not an unchanging order of things, but a sense of destiny steered by divine providence.

The typological perspective on history was developed to offer a rationale for the seeming absurdity of the belief that Christ's passion and resurrection marked the end of a particular history and the beginning of a universal redemption. On the one hand they accepted that Jesus' ministry on earth and his suffering on the cross was a fulfillment of biblical prophecy and, therefore, of the eschatological *Geschichte* of the covenant. On the other hand, they also believed that it was something more. Christ's passion may have ended the history of the covenant that had begun with Abraham, his resurrection, however, fulfilled the *Historie* of the world at large. These universalist aspirations made it imperative to break with what was for non-Jewish Christians the irritating particularism of Jewish *Geschichte*. Nevertheless one could not break with the Jewish legacy altogether, since Jewish prophecy formed the justification of the Christians' claim that Christ was the promised redeemer. Thus the theologians had to create an understanding of history that allowed them to interpret Christ simultaneously as being part of an existing *Geschichte*—the Jewish—and as having overcome that history. Typology offered the solution. A host of learned men began to interpret events described in the Tenach, which became now the Old Testament, as historic types of the passion and resurrection. The relationship between historic type and antitype provided the basis that linked and separated the *Geschichte* of the Jews and the posthistorical condition of the Kingdom of God. Christ was the link and the separation.

For an understanding of typology it may be helpful to think about a specific dilemma that the early Christians faced and that they tried to address through a search of a typological linkage between some event in the *Heilsgeschichte* described in the Old Testament and a question that was unique to the posthistorical age. My example comes from the Epistle to the Hebrews. This document had a crucial significance in the history of typology because it specifically addressed the question of how the metahistorical inner life of the posthistorical Christian was prefigured in the *geschichtliche* outer or observant life of the Old Testament Jews. The name of the document indicates that it was addressed to Jews. Its purpose was conversion. Its method was to prove to observant Jews that the passion and resurrection had brought their history to a fulfillment, which implied also the end of the legitimacy of the old temple cult in Jerusalem and the various old observances connected to it. The message of the epistle was that the whole world and every individual believer would be a temple of the posthistorical era. The writer of the Epistle to the Hebrews explained Christ as the highpriest of a New Covenant, a role that had been foreshadowed by the highpriesthood of the Old Covenant. He explained how "the first covenant also had its laws governing worship, and its sanctuary, a sanctuary on this earth. There was a tent which comprised two compartments: the first, in which the lampstand, the table and the presentation loaves were kept, was called the Holy Place; then beyond the second veil, an innermost part which was called the Holy of Holies to which belonged the gold altar of incense, and the ark of the covenant, plated all over with gold."[54] The writer of the epistle assumed that those who would read it were aware of the commonplace interpretation of the structure as an allegorical image of the universe.[55] The allegory designated the Holy Place as a symbol of the earth. The Holy of Holies represented heaven. The tabernacle as a whole was an earthly reflection of the true heavenly temple. Since the Holy of Holies represented the heavenly realm, it was forbidden to all humans except the highpriest who, after an appropriate sacrifice, was permitted to enter it for a few moments on the Day of Atonement. There he was to seek reconciliation between the people and God. The epistle describes this ritual in some detail.

> Under these provisions, priests are constantly going into the outer tent to carry out their acts of worship, but the second tent is entered only once a year, and then only by the highpriest who must go in by himself and take the blood to offer for his own faults and the people's. By this, the Holy Spirit is showing that no one has the right to go into the sanctuary as long as the outer tent [the Holy Place] remains standing; it is a symbol for the present time. None of the gifts and sacrifices offered under these regulations can possibly bring any worshipper to perfection to his inner self; they are rules about the outward life, connected with foods and drinks and washing at various times, intended to be in force only until it should be time to reform them.[56]

The writer assumes that the reader can believe that the existing cult and existing highpriesthood would be substituted for a new cult and a new highpriesthood, after some general reformation. In messianic circles such ideas were popular: the messiah, to come at the end of history, was to be a priest–king superior to the old Davidic kings and the Aaronite priesthood. He was to be the ideal priest, who would, in the end of days, fulfill the task of the office and overcome the imperfections and inadequacies of the existing priesthood. This resulted however in a polemical proposition that defined the task of the priest–king in contradiction to that of the existing highpriest in Jerusalem.[57]

This preunderstanding, and the assumption that the readers would be aware of the common allegorical interpretation of the Holy Place as earth and the Holy of Holies as heaven, allowed the writer to identify the first space as a symbol of the observances of the Jews; the Holy of Holies refers to the inner life and the liturgy of the messianic age. Jews had been unable to penetrate through the shells of ritual and enter the new, posthistorical age because they had been unable to enter that Holy of Holies. Christ's passion and resurrection had opened that space to all. This follows from an application of a seemingly insignificant detail of the passion to the allegory. Matthew records that, when Jesus died, the veil that separated the Holy Place from the Holy of Holies in the Temple of Jerusalem had parted in two. Thus it was legitimate to interpret the crucifixion as an opening of the Holy of Holies. The ritual on the Day of Atonement was linked with Jesus' passion and resurrection, and with the initiation of the posthistorical Kingdom of God.

> But now Christ has come, as the high priest of all the blessings which were to come. He has passed through the greater, the more perfect tent [the celestial archetype of the tabernacle represented by the Holy of Holies of the earthly tabernacle], which is better than the one made by men's hands because it was not of this created order; and he has entered the sanctuary once and for all, taking with him not the blood of goats and bull calves, but his own blood, having won eternal redemption for us.[58]

The conclusion was simple and straightforward: the Jewish highpriest was the historic type of the true highpriest, Christ; the actions of the former were fulfilled in those of the latter.

Each typology addressed only one aspect of salvation. The typological exegesis of the Jewish ritual of atonement solved the problem why Jesus of Nazareth was the promised messiah. In fact the evidence pointed against such an assertion since Jesus of Nazareth had not been born into the priestly tribe of Levi. This made it difficult to substantiate the claim that he could assume a priestly task: either his messianic action had no priestly character or he had been an imposter. It was clear that a priestly interpretation of Jesus' messianic deeds could not be avoided because the more traditional military—heroic interpretation of the messiah, which had been validated and popularized by Judas Maccabeus, was irrelevant for the sort of salvation Jesus had offered. Again typology provided the solution; the exegesis centered on another historic type of Christ, Melchizedek, an early Canaanite king of [Jeru]Salem. "When Abram came back after the defeat of Chedor-Laomer and the kings who had been on his side, the king of Sodom came to meet him in the Valley of Shaveh (that is, the valley of the King). Melchizedek king of Salem brought bread and wine; he was a priest of God Most High. He pronounced this blessing: 'Blessed be Abram by God Most High, creator of heaven and earth, and blessed be God Most High for handing over your enemies to you.' And Abram gave him a tithe of everything."[59] The writer of the Epistle to the Hebrews identified Melchizedek as a historic type of Christ the true highpriest.

You remember that Melchizedek, king of Salem, a priest of God Most High, went to meet Abraham who was on his way back after defeating the kings, and blessed him; and also that it was to him that Abraham gave a tenth of all that he had. By the interpretation of his name, he is first "king of righteousness" and also king of Salem, that is, "king of peace"; he has no father, mother or ancestry, and his life has no beginning or ending; he is like the Son of God. He remains a priest forever.

Now think how great this man must have been, if the patriarch Abraham paid him a tenth of the treasure he had captured. We know that any of the descendants of Levi who are admitted to the priesthood are obliged by the Law to take tithes from the people, and this is taking them from their own brothers although they too are descended from Abraham. But this man, who was not of the same descent, took his tenth from Abraham, and he gave his blessing to the holder of the promises. Now it is indisputable that a blessing is given by a superior to an inferior. Further, in the one case it is ordinary mortal men who receive the tithes, and in the other, someone who is declared to be still alive. It could be said that Levi himself, who receives tithes, actually paid them, in the person of Abraham, because he was still in the loins of his ancestor when Melchizedek came to meet him.[60]

The pattern and the justification of typological interpretation is obvious: it only works if the reader assumes that the Bible is a unified work of divine revelation. During the Middle Ages the unity of the Bible was not questioned, and typological exegesis offered a secure means to reflect on many different practical issues *sub specie crucis*. The interpretation of the saving event in terms of Christ's entry into the Holy of Holies formed the foundation of a theory of the church that identified the Holy Place of the tabernacle as a historic type of the terrestrial or militant church, while the Holy of Holies became a historic type of the heavenly or triumphant church. The veil, which had separated the two spaces in the tabernacle, became a historic type of the body of Christ, and thus of the eucharist. Because of this exegesis it was legitimate to interpret all the other elements mentioned in the description of the tabernacle, Solomonic temple and Ezekiel's temple in ecclesiastical terms. Because the church building embodied in form the teachings of the church, church architects could refer back to the tectology and morphology of the biblical architecture without losing the vital connection with the crucifixion of Jesus and the resurrection of Christ.[61]

Thucydides' Typological History

Typological historiography is not limited to the Hebrew tradition. The greatest of classical historians employed it also. Thucydides' narrative technique stresses the similarity of historical situations. The dramatic force of Thucydides' account of the Peloponnesian War is the direct result of his ability to tell the story of the war in such a way that it includes the reader through an intelligent use of repetition. Walter Robert Connor explained in his succinct and superb critique of Thucydides' *History of the Peloponnesian War* how the father of scientific historiography introduced in his narrative the dialectics of necessity and freedom that determined the field of decision of the Athenian and Spartan leaderships. "Throughout the *Histories* episode recalls episode and language echoes earlier phrases and ideas. Such recurrences shape not only the form of the work but also the responses and attitudes of its readers. We pause, interrupt the forward movement of our reading, break through the surface linearity of the text to recognize underlying patterns and structures." The effect of these typological recurrences is the reader's participation with the events. She is confronted "with questions of judgement and evaluation. But they pose these questions in an especially historical way. Judgements within the *Histories* are commonly concerned not with clear-cut contrasts but with minimal variations. We are presented with cases that are ostensibly very similar, but that on closer examination contain significant differences."[62] The text becomes drama and drama turns into the self-consciousness of criticism. Later events assimilate the memory of earlier ones, which generate, as Connor noted, "reassessments of old attitudes and the development of new responses as the complexity and implications of patterns become clear." Some, so he acknowledged, would identify Thucydides' technique in terms of a sophisticated form of indoctrination. Yet he argued that "a more supple view of the nature of historical writing recognizes the advantages, as well as the dangers, in Thucydides' technique, above all its ability to represent the complexity of historical developments and the cumulative effects of changes that are individually almost infinitesimal."[63] A good example of this might be found in Thucydides' relation of the destruction of Melos in 416/415 BCE. The Athenian expedition to Melos was only one of the war's minor operations, yet it became in Thucydides' typological universe one of the pivotal points in the war. It refers back to the Athenian destruction of Plataea and Mytilene, and forms the prologue to the narration of the disastrous Athenian expedition to Sicily. The core of the account is a dialogue between the representatives of the Athenian expeditionary force, who have come to offer the Melians terms of surrender, and the Melian Boule. For a full assessment of the Melian dialogue I bring Robert Connor's analysis of this episode to attention. Here I will only point at one of the most salient features of the dialogue: the typological relationship between the Athenian siege of Melos and the Persian attack on Greece in 480 BCE.

Athens's claim to moral leadership derived from its willingness to sacrifice the city and become a people of sailors to resist Xerxes' imperial ambition. The Athenians had refused to give in to Persian might. Sixty-four years later the Athenians demanded that the Melians would give in to them, not because of some moral right, but because of naval might. The Athenian representatives submitted their case bluntly before the Melian Boule.

> We on our side will use no fine phrases saying, for example, that we have a right to our empire because we defeated the Persians, or that we have come against you now because of the injuries you have done to us — a great mass of words that nobody would believe. And we ask you on your side not to imagine that you will influence us by saying that you, though a colony of Sparta, have not joined Sparta in the war, or that you have never done us any harm. Instead we recommend that you should try to get what is possible for you to get, taking into consideration what we both really do think; since you know as well as we do that, when these matters are discussed by practical people, the standard of justice depends on the equality of power to compel and that in fact the strong do what they have the power to do and the weak accept what they have to accept.[64]

This part of the Athenian speech elicited the following observation from Dionysius of Halicarnassus, an early commentator of Thucydides' histories who lived in the first century BCE. "Words like these were appropriate to oriental monarchs addressing Greeks, but unfit to be spoken by Athenians to Greeks whom they liberated from the Medes, to wit, that justice is the normal conduct of equals to another, but violence is the law of the strong against the weak."[65] For Dionysius it was another proof of the stylistic weakness of Thucydides' narrative. The reader with a sense of typological construction cannot but disagree: these words were fit, not for what the Athenians had been, but for what they had become. The former champions of Hellenic freedom had assumed the tone, the manner, the policies and the logic of Xerxes, and the stubborn Melians had become, de facto, the defenders of Greek liberty. And, as Connor noted, Thucydides confronts the reader with the question "What if the Athenians had acted against the Persians as they now urge the Melians to act?"[66] Thus the typological construction allows history to become in Croce's sense a history of liberty. The choice of the Melians in 416 BCE was ultimately not different from the choice of the Athenians in 480 BCE, or the choice of the English in 1940 CE.

At the end of the dialogue the Athenians had a last admonition to the

Melians. "This is the safe rule—to stand up to one's equals, to behave with deference towards one's superiors, and to treat one's inferiors with moderation. Think it over again, then, when we have withdrawn from the meeting, and let this be a point that constantly recurs to your minds—that you are discussing the fate of your country, that you have only one country, and that its future for good or ill depends on this one single decision which you are going to make." The Athenians withdraw, and the Melians and the reader are left to themselves. Historical time has stopped at its historic center. Then the decision: "We are not prepared to give up in a short moment the liberty which our city has enjoyed from its foundation for 700 years." The fate of Melos was sealed and, Thucydides' interest in the story wanes. He follows the lengthy exposition of the debate with a terse description of how the Athenians began the siege and how after a few months the Melians were forced to capitulate unconditionally to the Athenians, "who put to death all the men of military age whom they took, and sold the women and children as slaves. Melos itself they took over for themselves, sending out later a colony of 500 men."[67]

Authentic and Inauthentic Types

Thucydides' magisterial use of typological constructions in his narrative does not refute the general proposition that typology as a comprehensive historiographical construction is bound up with the Judeo-Christian tradition. Therefore any assertion that typological exegesis can provide a basis of a new kind of useful architectural history has to address the assumption that typology is obsolete as a hermeneutical device. When in the nineteenth century a school of historical and literary criticism emerged that showed that the Bible was an amalgamate of writings by different hands from different ages, the typological method of interpretation became a historical curiosity. It follows that the theologian who wishes to restore the typological approach to the Bible, or the architectural historian who believes that typology can excavate the layers of experience that sustain the normative ground of architecture, has to ask whether the typological method can still be legitimately employed in the "postcritical" age. G.W.H. Lampe (1912–80) argued in his essay entitled "The Reasonableness of Typology" that a typological interpretation of history, be it biblical or secular, can still be legitimate. He based his argument on the assumption that the foundation of the typological view of the scriptures—the unity of the Bible—still applies if that unity is considered as a consistency of perspective of the different writers who contributed to the writings of the Old and New Testament. The authors of the gospels and the different epistles addressed the same existential questions that guided the different narratives of the Old Testament and they also referred to the imagery of the older writings. This line of thought led to Lampe's distinction between an "authentic" typology, which is still valid and legitimate, and an "inauthentic" variety, which has become obsolete. The former operates within the prophetic view of history that the writers of the Old and New Testaments shared. The latter conceives of the Bible as a storehouse of oracles and riddles, "a huge book of secret puzzles to which the reader has to find clues."

Using the Epistle to the Hebrews discussed above for a comparison of genuine and far-fetched false typologies explained the difference between them. Lampe acknowledged that it is nevertheless not always easy to assess the legitimacy of a particular example of typology. The typological interpretation of Melchizedek is an example of a false typology. It lacks force "except as an apologetic argument directed to a particular class of readers in a particular situation." Because there is no clear correspondence between the [historic] type and the fulfillment, "the point that Melchizedek is a figure of Christ as the eternal priest rests upon a piece of sheer allegorizing about his lack of genealogy, and the idea that in Abraham the ancestor of the Aaronic priesthood, Levi, paid tithes to this [historic] type of the eternal priest depends on fantasy. The correspondence here is unreal, useful as the point may have been in the anti-Jewish controversy." Lampe also censored the patristic expansion of the Melchizedek type that interpreted Melchizedek's offering of bread and wine as a type of the Christian Eucharist. "Historically considered, his action in doing so has absolutely no part in the pattern of God's redemptive activity, and what Christ did at the Last Supper has no relation whatever to what Melchizedek did for Abraham."[68] The story lacks the tension that allows the event of sharing a meal to become a landmark in the history of salvation. The significance of the Last Supper derives from the fact that it is the "last" supper; the celebration of the exodus from Egypt becomes the opening act of the Passover of the world. The story of Abraham and Melchizedek stands on it own, without a link to Abraham's covenant, his circumcision or the binding of Isaac.

If unauthentic typology encourages the reader to ignore history, authentic typology traces those parallels that are "naturally suggested" by the text. Lampe thought the typology of the tabernacle to be genuine and appropriate because there is a genuine correspondence within the pattern of history between the historic type and the antitype. "The theme of redemption and an identical concept of expiation runs continuously through from the ritual provisions of the Old Law to the fulfillment of its intentions and aspirations by Christ's entry, through the shedding of his blood, into the heavenly sanctuary as man's representative. Because the correspondence is real and clear the ancient rite becomes an illuminating means of interpreting the meaning of Christ's high-priestly work, while the fulfillment in Christ enables the Christian reader to grasp more fully the meaning, the aims and the relative deficiency of the Temple and the sacrifices."[69] Lampe concluded that, therefore, authentic typology must derive from real history. For the Bible this means that it is applied within the specific biblical perspective on history as the history of salvation, that it cannot ignore the literal sense of the biblical narratives or the findings of critical scholarship. Applied with these constraints, typology might be something more than homilic embellishment. Lampe's insistence on the preservation of the historical character of the events subjected to typological interpretation is important because it preserves the specific intelligibility that belongs to history.

The Post-War Revival of Judeo-Christian Historiography

The historiographical assumptions and techniques described above were abandoned in the Enlightenment. The Christian creed, which postulated that the historic events of the passion and the resurrection provided a criterion of judgement and action, was replaced by von Ranke's relativist creed that history should not be "assigned the office of judging the past, of instructing the present for the benefit of future ages," but should limit itself "to show what actually happened."[70] Von Ranke's maxim had worked well in the age of progress when the achievement of tomorrow offered an answer to the question of today. Two world wars and the consequent disintegration of the old regimes changed all that. Every tomorrow brought only new dilemmas, and no answers. Once again, as in the Enlightenment, it was the historians who were called to give some kind of explanation.

A first response to the inability of historical relativism to provide guidance in the present was offered by Croce. We have seen how he tried to reassert the contemporary moral significance of the past through his reconstruction of history as a moral drama. His achievement was important, as Robert Caponegri noted. Caponegri acknowledged that Croce's "vision of human history as moral drama is certainly not new; it is rather the first, the immediate and spontaneous intuition of western man concerning history, and the most constant." Yet Croce's work was significant because of its "re-evocation of this vision of history at a juncture when it had all but vanished and when western man was most in need of it to revive in himself the sense of his own humanity and spirituality." Thus the quality and character of Croce's achievement was to be judged "not by reference to the vulgar norm of novelty, but to the clarity and power of expression of that constant vision of history and by the magnitude of the forces against which he reasserted it."[71] Yet Croce's effort to restore an ethico-political view of history as moral drama ultimately did not find the resonance it deserved. Part of it was his tendency to assimilate and domesticate the classical and especially prophetical content of his vision within the discourse of liberalism; part of it was his refusal to critically engage historical relativism. Croce's attempt to adopt the historiographical legacy of the nineteenth century as the foundation of his reconstructivist enterprise limited, in the end, its effectiveness.

The Russian Orthodox philosopher Nicolas Berdyaev (1874–1948) was straightforward in his rejection of historicism. In his classic *Meaning in History* (1936) he explicitly called for a revival of a (Christian) philosophy of history. "Catastrophic moments in world history have always proved an incitement to speculation," so began the first chapter of his book. "They have stimulated attempts to define the historical process and to build up this or that philosophy of history. It has been so always. St Augustine's was the first notable philosophy of history. . . . It coincided with one of the most catastrophic moments of world history—the collapse of the ancient world and the fall of Rome."[72] The image appealed: to see the present in terms of Rome's fall did not deny the validity of the thesis that the West faced a decline in, for example, power; the invocation of the memory of St Augustine offered, however, the paradigm and the prospect of a spiritual renewal. Many were willing to become the St Augustine of the twentieth century. St Augustine's major work, *The City of God*, had been a work of history. This suggested that the spiritual future of the West was to depend on a reassessment of the past in spiritual (read Christian) terms.[73]

Three years after the publication of Berdyaev's *Meaning in History* there was another war to illustrate the need for a historiographical revolution. Among the philosophies of history that issued from the ruins of Europe was one which proposed a reconstruction of the Judeo-Christian paradigm on a broad cross-cultural basis. *Vom Ursprung und Ziel der Geschichte* (1949), published in English translation in 1953 under the title *The Origin and Goal of History*, did not have an explicit Christian signature. Its author, Karl Jaspers (1883–1969), had been educated as a psychiatrist and was a philosopher with the reputation of being an "existentialist." This was enough to frighten theologians and historians. None seriously took issue with Jaspers's book. When Rudolf Bultmann referred to Jaspers in the ninth of his Gifford Lectures, held in early 1955 at the University of Edinburgh, he limited himself to the remarks that Jaspers's views were too singular to offer a contribution to the existing discourse. Yet he acknowledged implicitly the relevance of the book when he admitted that "Jaspers endeavors to understand history as the history of men who are responsible for the future, and he gives an analysis of our present time with its threatening problems in order to make the responsiblity urgently felt. This stress upon responsibility also shows, as it seems to me, that Jaspers strives to overcome the relativism of historicism."[74]

The singularity of Jaspers's proposition at first seems hidden. The opening paragraph of the Introduction invoked the well-known theme (by 1949) that the extent and depth of crisis "requires the whole history of mankind to furnish us with standards by which to measure the meaning of what is happening at the present time."[75] The first chapter of *The Origin and Goal of History* narrowed the theme to the historiographical discourse begun by, among others, Berdyaev. To write the whole history of mankind is to have a philosophy of history, and "in the Western World the philosophy of history was founded in the Christian faith. In a grandiose sequence of works ranging from St Augustine to Hegel this faith visualized the movement of God through history. God's acts of revelation represent the decisive dividing lines. Thus Hegel could still say: All history goes toward and comes from Christ. The appearance of the Son of God is the axis of world history."[76] With that the text arrived at the central notion that Jaspers explored and expounded in the rest of his book. It is the idea of an *Achsenzeit*, of a normative epoch within the development of (wo)mankind that may be identified as the "axis of world history."

We have seen how in his 1955 Gifford lectures Bultmann labeled the idea of an axis of world history as "strange." As a theologian he should have had more empathy with Jaspers's thesis, which explicitly acknowledged a Christian inspiration for the notion of a rupture within history. Yet theologians tend to judge heretics more harshly than unbelievers, and Jaspers belongs to the former group. He began the second paragraph of the first chapter with the relative assertion that "the Christian faith is only one faith, not the faith of mankind." Therefore Christian *Geschichte* could not be *Weltgeschichte*. Jaspers could have made it easy for himself by following the lead taken by Bultmann. He could have amalgamated the in German thinking by then usual distinction between *Geschichte* and *Historie* with the Historical Point of View into a philosophy of history that would allow Christians (read Europeans and Americans) to regain a grasp on the events that had passed. Jaspers did not seek this relatively facile solution. He declared in his Introduction that his view of history derived from the belief that "mankind has one single origin and one single goal." Therefore the question "what is the meaning of history?" could only be answered through an *empirical grasp* on the "unity of the whole of history."[77]

Jaspers's demand for an *empirical grasp* on the *unity of history* introduced a new challenge to the philosophers of history. Until the 1930s it was widely acknowledged that the foundation of any philosophy of history was the assumption that over time the spiritual took increasing possession of the material. Therefore the philosopher of history had to overcome the empirical in the past. Beginning with a plenitude of historical facts, she had to set up a process that would show the emergence from the manifold of that one fact that refused to remain *factum*, done. One concise *Geschichte*, with a beginning, a middle and an end, had to emanate from the infinitely large *Historie*.

Oscar Cullmann explained the transformation of the empirical of *Welthistorie* into the spiritual of *Heilsgeschichte* as a process of continual reduction, substitution and intensification.[78] In the beginning there was only Creation. Then God created mankind in order that it would "stand" for Creation. Mankind "fell" in Adam. Then God called from all the nations the Hebrews, so that they would stand for all the others. Just as world history had substituted for the timelessness of Creation, so now the history of Israel was now to substitute for world history. Because the people of Israel as a whole did not measure up to their world-historical task, God selected a remnant to represent the nation as a whole. The history of Israel became the history of the remnant. This remnant was further compressed until its history finally fixed on the Son of Man. Thus Christ recapitulated in his own history (that is the passion and resurrection) the history of the remnant, the history of Israel, the history of the world and Creation. Until the advent of Christ the history of salvation developed in terms of a progressive reduction of the breadth of its concern (the empirical) for the sake of its depth (the spiritual): after the saving event had passed it would develop in the opposite direction. Only thus could the Christians claim that the crucifixion and the resurrection marked the center of *Heilsgeschichte* and *Welthistorie*. From the moment the women witnessed the empty tomb history began to proceed from the One to the Many, but in such a way that *the Many represent the One*. This is possible because this reverse action takes place within the church, which is the body of the One. The church's unity would ensure that the movement from the One to the Many, which mirrored the earlier one of the Many to the One, would remain true to the posthistorical character of the time between the first and second coming, the time between history and eternity that Cullmann identified as that of the "even now—not yet."

Hegel's philosophy of history operated on a similar principle, though he replaced the Christian process of continual substitution and reduction with a notion of substitution and continuous movement. History, understood as the *Geschichte* of the development of consciousness, had "moved," so Georg Wilhelm Friedrich Hegel (1770–1831) explained, from ancient China to modern Prussia. When the spirit had "passed" a nation on the road from Peking to Berlin, it had galvanized the empirical of *Historie* into the spiritual of *Geschichte*. After it had moved on to the next stop on its westward course, a nation's history had fallen back into *Historie*, and often a pretty insignificant one at that.

Jaspers's demand for an empirical grasp on the unity of history was a reaction to one of the implications of the Christian and Hegelian scheme of interpretation: the increasing concentration of world-historical responsibility on one nation, group or even individual (Christ) or its transference from one nation to another (Hegel). Jaspers did not agree with the explicit paternalism of the Judeo-Christian or Hegelian scheme of world history. He believed that all people at every place in all epochs were responsible for history at all times. That universality of responsibility had been discovered by different individuals in the axial period, and it had become a practical reality in the modern age. Therefore Jaspers substituted the Christian scheme, which runs from the Many (Adam or [wo]mankind) to the One (Christ or the New Adam) to the Many as One ([wo]mankind as gathered in the universal church), for a scheme that runs from the One (the common origin of [wo]mankind) to the Many (the axial period) to the One (the common goal of [wo]mankind). Neither the common origin nor the common goal can be known empirically. "Origin and goal are unknown to us," Jaspers declared, they are "utterly unknown by any kind of knowledge. They can only be felt in the glimmer of ambiguous symbols."[79] Yet the history that connects the origin to the goal might be empirically known. Like the Christian philosophers of history, Jaspers realized that the story that connected the origin and the goal could not include everything. It had to concentrate on one theme if it were to be intelligible. That theme was to be the discovery of our responsibility for history. Jaspers believed that the proper way to tell the story of history was not to follow the development of the theme over time. This would imply the outdated and unacceptable ideology of successive "elections." The alternative was to replace a sequential mode with one of spatial amplification. The task of a philosophy of history was not to follow the trail, but to identify the one moment in history in which the unity of mankind realized itself universally.

This moment was to be the true axis of world history. Unlike the Christian philosophy of history, which identified that moment in the death and resurrection of a carpenter born at the periphery of a marginal country in a corner of the Roman empire, Jaspers believed that the axis would be felt universally by all people all over the world. Therefore it was not "the concealed interior, round which the foreground of phenomena at all time revolves, that element which is itself timeless, but which extends through all the ages and is enveloped by the dust-clouds of the solely present."[80] It did not need to be disclosed by revelation and preserved by dogma, but could be experienced by all who used their common sense. Therefore he could state that a historiographical axis only made sense if it could be discovered empirically, "as a fact capable of being accepted as such by all men, Christians included." Jaspers asserted that "this axis would be situated at the point in history which gave birth to everything which, since then, man has been able to be, the point most overwhelmingly fruitful in fashioning humanity; its character would have to be, though not absolutely empirically cogent and evident, yet so convincing to empirical insight as to give rise to a common frame of historical self-comprehension of all peoples."[81] The crucifixion of Jesus of Nazareth obviously did not meet the requirement of universal intelligibility. It was, at best, a very specific instance of the manifestation of the axis.

Jaspers found that the year 500 BCE met his call for empirical verification. That year was the mid-point of a period that lasted for a few centuries in which "man, as we know him today, came into being." It was the age of Confucius and Lao-tzu, the Upanishads and Buddha, of Zarathustra, of Isaiah, Jeremiah and Second Isaiah, the age of Homer, Heraclitus, Aeschylus, Thucydides and Plato. It was the age in which the mythical world came to an end, a world of self-evident truths and unquestioned customs. In this epoch people began to ask radical questions. "Face to face with the void he strives for liberation and redemption. By consciously recognizing his limits he sets himself the highest goals. He experiences absoluteness in the depths of selfhood and in the lucidity of transcendence. All this took place in reflection. Consciousness became once more conscious of itself, thinking became its own object. Spiritual conflicts arose, accompanied by attempts to convince others through the communication of thoughts, reasons and experiences. The most contradictory possibilities were essayed."[82] Thus, Jaspers concluded, the axial age gave rise to the basic categories within which we still think today. It has given us the foundation on which the whole edifice of civilization is built, an origin to which we return each time of crisis. It is in that sense the beginning of our history, which separates us from what we would call at first sight our prehistory. It offers us a criterion with which to judge our own achievements and it provides us with the questions with which we approach the age before it. The axial time itself marks a rupture, which divides (wo)man as we know her today, a (wo)man who is conscious of his history, from the being that preceded him. The year 500 BCE is, in the common sense of the word, the beginning of the story of modern (wo)man. In the Judeo-Christian sense it marks the beginning of the essentially posthistorical situation of the "even now—not yet." Jaspers argued that we haven't really moved beyond it because we can't move beyond it. We might only realize its potential. I believe that Jaspers was right. As we have seen, even that ultimate manifestation of modernism known as the Historical Point of

View can be traced back as a "Heraclitean Heritance" to the axial period.

In the period that Jaspers labeled as the axial period of world history a great spiritual revolution affected the major civilizations of the world. The revolution had different emphases in the various places where it occurred. In that sense it was, like every historical fact, bound by the relativist law that events may only be understood within their proper context. Yet during the axis period the boundaries that separate place from place and context from context merged, if only temporarily, into a common horizon. And while the universality of perspective discovered by Lao-tzu, the Buddha, Isaiah, Heraclitus or Plato was easily obscured by the particular concerns of later times, it remained the standard by which to judge subsequent achievements. Jaspers's axial period borrowed a great deal from the Christian understanding of the historic significance of Christ's crucifixion and resurrection. Expanding the Christian understanding of a normative center of history from one particular event to a whole epoch meant that it could now include other cultures also, and address other themes, such as architecture.

An Axis of Architectural History?

Jaspers's axial period within world history opens a new perspective for a normative architectural history. The spiritual breakthrough in Palestine took place within the context of a polemic against architecture.[83] In China, India and Persia it was unconcerned with architecture. In Greece this was different: the polis, and very specifically the polis of Athens, was the condition that made the decisive breakthrough possible. Unlike the Hebrews, the Greeks decided that there was an essential and existential relationship between the polis as a political community, its institutions and its architecture. (The Greeks did not formulate a theory about the relationship between *civitas* and *urbs*, and therefore were unable to summarize their discovery in a comprehensive theory. See my discussion below and the section "City and Urbs" in Chapter Eight.) The new consciousness would be pertinent only if it could become politically relevant, and for the Greeks this meant that it had to acquire some kind of spatial and architectural articulation (see Chapter Two: "Politics").

Thus we find ourselves at the threshold of an exciting and also paradoxical prospect: it is the potential of a reconstruction of a normative understanding of architectural history through the application of the Judeo-Christian historiographical paradigm to the architecture and urban form of the classical Greek city. A specific typological method of interpretation promises a justification of Westfall's understanding of building types on the basis of the history of architecture that preceded the creation of the Greek polis. In such an interpretation the polis (as *urbs* that is) becomes a universal archetype, a new beginning and an end, an axis of architectural history "for which everything that preceded it would appear to have been a preparation, and to which everything subsequent actually, and often in clear consciousness, relates back."[84] Jaspers's contemporary Martin Heidegger agreed. He, too, understood the polis as a caesura in history, a new beginning that ought to be taken seriously because "the beginning is the strangest and the mightiest. . . . If this beginning is inexplicable, it is not because of any deficiency in our knowledge of history. On the contrary, the authenticity and greatness of historical knowledge reside in an understanding of the mysterious character of this beginning."[85] Consequently I would like to propose that architectural history derives its structure from the new beginning that was the Greek polis, most perfectly embodied in classical Athens. This axis ought not be given a permanent, absolute and unique significance, since it is ultimately nothing but a historiographical tool to give history a plot. Yet it may fulfill our purposes in providing a center and organizing principle for architectural history. It discloses its power to reconcile opposites in showing the mutual ground between Westfall's application of classical historiography and my adaptation of the Judeo-Christian understanding of the past. Even Westfall's radical thesis that "the first city was neither Ur nor Babylon which were mere settlements but the place where the Greeks imagined it possible to live the political life" acquires resonance within the "axial" understanding of architectural history.

The Axial Period and the Crisis of the Present

Before we can proceed with an exploration of these domains of possibility we must reflect on the legitimacy of Jaspers's understanding of history. At times in our dialogue I challenged Westfall's approach to politics and history on the ground that its pre-Kantian epistemology, which declared knowledge to be our relationship to the world, did not address the twentieth-century experience of catastrophe and alienation. The classical assumptions of the reality of an abiding order of things and an unchanging human nature bore no relationship to the historicist and relativist world in which we live, and the chasm between Westfall's "truth" and the common apprehension of the world gave an ephemeral quality to his musings. Yet one could ask if an axial period located some twenty-five centuries ago addresses the questions and dilemmas of contemporary society in any more substantial way. I believe it does. Jaspers wrote *The Origin and Goal of*

History as a response to the catastrophe of the Second World War. The
central part of the book is, therefore, an analysis of the modern situation
that had made that war possible. Considering the triumph of a scientific
worldview, the increase of human power through technology, the emergence of a mass society and the concomitant rise of ideology, Jaspers
concluded that we were in the midst of what seemed to be a new axial
period. This age had been initiated by the combined efforts of the
philosophes, the French revolutionaries and the German idealists beginning
with Herder.[86]

As we have seen in Chapter One, the radical transformation of the world
had commenced when those people had begun to take an exclusively
historical view of human affairs — a matrix of understanding that was to
shake the naïve certainty held by people who lived in customary societies
that their own value systems were beyond doubt. The power of arms and the
international financial market ensured that the full effect of the eighteenth-
century discovery of the historicity of our own existence was indeed felt by
peoples all over the world. This physical unification of the world on a
historicist foundation was the beginning of a new epoch. Jaspers believed
that this had brought a new urgency to the study of history. Confronted with
an insecure and daunting future, we know that Revelation and Natural
Reason do not offer a perspective on our situation, and we return our gaze to
the past. "To the question: have such radical metamorphoses taken place
before? our answer was: we know nothing of the events of the Promethean
Age, when man first came into possession of his world through tools, fire
and speech. But within history the greatest turningpoint was the Axial
Period, which we have discussed."[87]

The new axial period, which we had entered in the mid-eighteenth
century, was different from the first one. If the earlier one had been
"relatively universal" in which developments in China, India, Palestine
and Greece were mutually related in meaning but separate in fact, now, in
the modern age, everything that happens anywhere is of concern to all. The
world has become a single whole in continuous intercourse. And if the
earlier period had been characterized by spiritual development, we face
spiritual regression. So why bother with the axial period of the fifth century
BCE? In an age of radical technological and political change the first
technological and social revolution of what Jaspers identified as the
Promethean Age seems to offer more guidance. And, indeed, there are
many today who believe that study of the Mesolithic and the early Neolithic
ages allows us to gain a firmer grasp on the ills of our society, especially the
phenomenon of the *homo hostilis*, the "enemy-making man" who continual-
ly tries to turn the world into a killing ground.[88] Jaspers did not deny that
study of the Promethean Age could offer useful insights into the dangers of

the present age. His point was that this was limited, that a useful history should not be a diagnostic tool alone, but should point to the path of reconstruction as well. It should reveal and also instruct. If we were to meet the future with confidence, then the axial period that centered on the fifth century BCE could teach us more. "The fact that we are tackling the high task of reconstructing humanity from its origin, that we sense the fateful question as to how we can, in faith, become specifically human beings is . . . evinced in the current tendency, which is becoming increasingly strong, to look back toward our origin [that is the axial period]." This origin, so Jaspers argued, was "the deep matrix from which we sprang, the specific reality which was concealed by the veil of secondary cultural constructions, turns of phrase, conventions and institutions." Yet historians and philosophers were to articulate its essence once more. Jaspers hoped that such study of the apprehensions that shaped the axial period would offer "essential assurances."[89] When Jaspers turned to that period he did not see harmony within harmony. Jaspers's Greece was quite unlike Hölderlin's enchanted Hellas where the gods, the sky, the earth and the people lived in a state of original and organic community. Jaspers's Athens was a city of crisis; human self-consciousness emerged amid the breaking up of old structures and certainties. We will see in Chapter Five how the world-historical reforms of Solon, which provided the constitutional basis for the Athenian polis, were a pragmatic response to an immediate crisis. Jeremiah and Second Isaiah built their new worlds of thought on the ruins of Solomon's temple. Jaspers ascertained that all these men met the events of their time as catastrophes that could be overcome through "insight, education and reform." "The endeavor is made to dominate the course of events by planning, right conditions are to be re-established or brought about for the first time."[90] Thus people like Confucius, the Buddha, Jeremiah, Solon and Sophocles revealed that (wo)man was better than the havoc he created. Their experience applies to our own time. Jaspers believed that we are in need, more than ever, of an assurance that the future will not become a "sombre malignancy destitute of humanity."

What man may come to has today, almost in a flash, become manifest through a monstrous reality that stands before our eyes like a symbol of everything unspeakably horrible: the national socialist concentration camps with their tortures, at the end of which stood the gas-chambers and incinerators for millions of people. . . . A chasm had opened up. We have seen what man can do—not according to a plan drawn up *in toto* at the outset, but in a circle along which he moves at ever increasing speed once he has set foot on it. It is a circle into which the participants are dragged without the majority of them knowing or desiring what they will suffer or do as they advance unceasingly around it. . . . Man is capable—under conditions of political terror—of becoming something of which no one had any inkling. . . . Seen from without the impression we gain from the phenomena is that men ceased to be human: almost without a doubt in the case of the active elements, more questionably as regards the tortured victims, who suffered different and greater agonies than those which every man undergoes in the torments of disease and which reduce us to wretched creatures. . . . This reality of the concentration camps, this interaction in the circular process between torturer and tortured, the manner of this dehumanization, is an intimation of future possibilities, before which everything threatens to vanish.[91]

These few paragraphs are the physical and ideological axis of Jaspers's *The Origin and Goal of History*. They constitute the core of the first philosophy of history created as a response to the reality of total catastrophe. They are to be taken seriously, if only because Jaspers was the only German-speaking philosopher of international repute who had the moral courage to face the question of German guilt directly.[92] Jaspers's vision of history is as much determined by the awareness of evil as was that of Victor Hugo. Unlike Hugo, however, Jaspers did find a normative ground: he located it in the axial period. He acknowledged that it was difficult to remain optimistic after reading the reports of the camps. He considered them a greater peril than the atom bomb because they menace the soul of man. "We may easily fall prey to the consciousness of utter despair." Yet there was some reason for hope. "Those individuals who, in all the frightfulness of suffering, although they could not save themselves from being miserable creatures in bodily anguish, yet refused to participate in their souls and who, although they could not avoid injury, yet remained intact as human souls, encourage us to hold fast to the ancient faith in man."[93] This led Jaspers to formulate his creed, a formula of faith that was essentially a reiteration of the principles adduced by various people in different places during the axial period. Jaspers believed that despite the menacing spectre of the camps, which "weigh down upon us like an incubus," we may still believe that our future will be different *because* the camps weigh upon us. "Man cannot get lost entirely," Jaspers argued, "because he is created in the 'image of the Deity'; he is not God, but he is bound to Him with oft-forgotten and always imperceptible, but fundamentally unsunderable ties." This means that he will never become an ape, ant or reflex machine, "save in the horrifying circumstances that brought him to this brink, from which he returns to himself, if he does not die as an individual."[94]

The philosopher Jaspers believed that the idea of individual freedom and its concomitant, the idea of individual responsibility, had not been destroyed in the camps. The self-consciousness arrived at by the great thinkers and teachers of the axial period was still intact and, therefore, the "idea of man" transcended the destruction of a people and a civilization. Elie Wiesel, who went through the world of the camps as an inmate, disagreed. He was to write, some decades later, that the catastrophe had made us unintelligible to ourselves, because "at Auschwitz, not only man died, but also the idea of man. . . . It was its own heart the world incinerated at Auschwitz."[95]

Jaspers and Wiesel represent opposite views: according to the former "we almost committed collective suicide, but the memory of Athens (or Jerusalem) saved us;" while the latter declared "we committed suicide, and we destroyed Athens (and Jerusalem) along with ourselves." Wiesel's statement challenges the purpose of this book, because if indeed the "idea of man" died in the camps, then the "idea of architecture" died too, and with it the notion that the past might have a normative significance in the post-Auschwitz world. A mediating position is taken by the Canadian philosopher Emil Fackenheim. When Jaspers wrote *The Origin and Goal of History*, he addressed the evidence of the holocaust that was within his reach. This included the material that surfaced in the Nuremberg Trials and some memoirs written by survivors. Jaspers's observations on the world-historical significance of the camps were more the result of his intuition than of a prolonged philosophical consideration. A generation younger than Jaspers, Fackenheim had more time to absorb the event, to reflect on it and to integrate it fully into his philosophical understanding of the world. The younger philosopher witnessed the Eichmann trial, and realized the shattering significance of Eichmann's claim that he had always obeyed Kant's categorical imperative. Fackenheim concluded a long discussion of the implications of Eichmann's statement with the observation that, if we are to take Kant's idea of humanity seriously, it "*must* have, and according to Kant *does* have, a matrix or *Boden* in *actual* humanity. Kant, in short, *believes* in humanity: *but is that belief warranted?* Perhaps it was so in Kant's time. Arguably it was once warranted at *any* time if only because, while undemonstrable, this belief was at least also irrefutable." Auschwitz had changed all that. It refuted Kant's belief in humanity through the systematic anihilation of the object of that belief, man. In Auschwitz "one kind of common man—the *Muselmann*—was made into a uniquely uncommon victim, while the other, the manufacturer of the victim, was made—*let himself* be made—into a uniquely uncommon criminal. And 'uniquely uncommon' in both cases was this, that personality was destroyed." This effacement of the personality repudiated the idea of humanity. "That this was possible is the awful legacy of Auschwitz to all humanity. The awful legacy for philosophy is that the annihilation of human personality robs the Idea of Humanity of its indispensable basis."[96]

Like Wiesel, Fackenheim came to the conclusion that Auschwitz paralyzed the whole metaphysical capability. Because one part of the world had become unintelligible we could no longer think "the world as such." Auschwitz was, in Fackenheim's words, "the precise point that marks the limit of penultimate rational intelligibility."[97] In that sense it acquired the character of a new axis, though it resembled more the axial structure of a black hole that engulfs all philosophical thought including the Historical Point of View. The relativist historian explains events by showing how they were possible. The four decades that have passed since the publication of Jaspers's *The Origin and Goal of History* have taught the champions of historical relativism a lesson in humility. Their rational musings slowly begin to lose their focus and direction. They come to grief when it becomes clear that the more plausible the explanation seems, the more absurd the event becomes. Fackenheim stated that the mind can accept the *possibility* of Auschwitz solely because it actually was. The result is that "the more the psychologist, historian or 'psychohistorian' succeeds in explaining the event or action, the more nakedly he comes to confront its ultimate inexplicability. In the paradoxical formulation of the philosopher Hans Jonas, 'much more is real than possible.'"[98]

There is no way to understand it because it is singular. This is difficult to accept, because it is difficult to accept that the axial period was unique. And even if, after some thought, we might acknowledge the unicity of the latter period of history, it is much harder to persuade ourselves that a unique event of catastrophic import would have happened in our own lifetime, all the more so when we are personally touched by it. It is more reasonable to apply a relativist perspective to one's own pain by supposing that the feeling of uniqueness is the mere result of the self-centered response to a soul-shattering experience. Yet such objections do not apply. Auschwitz is an abyss in which all thought is absorbed in continuous negation. That does not mean that it cannot give meaning. Although it is impervious to all efforts to make it "habitable" through discourse, it speaks to us nevertheless. The memory of Auschwitz challenges us not to surrender to its implications of despair, or apathy, or resignation. Auschwitz calls us to resistance.

This resistance can take many forms and include many professions. I believe that architects are called too because they had a unique responsibility in the creation and the perfection of the death camps: professional architects designed the camps, the barracks and the crematoria. For almost fifty years the great majority of architects and architectural historians have circumvented the questions raised by the circumstances that not only were the men who designed Auschwitz fully qualified architects, but one of them, Fritz Ertl, was even a Bauhaus graduate. Intellectual vacuity,

emotional passivity and moral indifference have characterized their response to the most serious remonstrance the discipline of architecture has
ever faced—even if this challenge came in the shape of the largely
unmodified horse stables (known as *Pferdestallbarakken OKH-Typ 260/9*
and designed to house fifty-two horses) which the architects of Auschwitz
adapted to house a thousand prisoners. It seems easy to commit these flimsy
and shoddy buildings to the garbage-heap of architectural history. Yet at
least one person would protest. Pelagia Lewinska, a Polish inmate of
Auschwitz, recalled, after the war, how the physical (architectonic)
environment of these barracks spoke to her with the commanding voice of
revelation. I will show in Chapter Five that the ancient city was designed in
such a way that it allowed a mature person to find his own bearings through
direct observation. The German architects designed the camps in such a
way that their tectonics and their rites would destroy purposefully the
inmates' sense of meaning and direction. If Athens was conceived as a
place to develop the personality in a healthy body, Auschwitz was created
to annihilate the spirit and exterminate the body. Lewinska described in
her *Twenty Months at Auschwitz* (first published in 1946) how "at the outset
the living places, the ditches, the mud, the piles of excrement behind the
blocks, had appalled me with their horrible filth. . . . And then I saw the
light! I saw that it was not a question of disorder or lack of organization but
that, on the contrary, a very thoroughly considered conscious idea was in
the back of the camp's existence. They had condemned us to die in our own
filth, to drown in mud, in our own excrement. They wished to abase us, to
destroy our human dignity, to efface every vestige of humanity . . . to fill us
with horror and contempt toward ourselves and our fellows." This sudden
insight had significant consequences: "From the instant when I grasped
the motivating principle . . . it was as if I had been awakened from a
dream. . . . *I felt under orders to live.* . . . And if I did die in Auschwitz, it
would be as a human being, I would hold on to my dignity. I was not going
to become the contemptible, disgusting brute my enemy wished me to
be. . . . And a terrible struggle began which went on day and night."[99]

I don't know if Jaspers read Pelagia Lewinska's account of her own
struggle to preserve the legacy of what Jaspers would identify as the axial
period. It supports, however, his observation that those kinds of experiences encourage us to hold fast to the ancient faith in, now, woman.
Fackenheim would have agreed. For him the commandment of resistance,
issued in Auschwitz, has the potential to make a new beginning, founded
on a new kind of categorical imperative. He declared that a person should
not try to comprehend or transcend Auschwitz, "but rather *to say no to it, or
resist it.*" This resistance must derive from the insight that Auschwitz "*is*
(for it *has been*); but it *ought not* to be (and *not* to have been). It ought *not* to

be (and have been), but it *is* (for it has been)." This clarity about the
relationship between the ontological and ethical reality of Auschwitz in the
present age is important because it prevents our thinking from lapsing into
either escapism or paralyzed impotence. Consideration of the death camp
only in terms of the "ought not" results in a spiritual withdrawal from the
issue, while a naked confrontation with the devastating reality of the camp
can only lead to a cessation of all spiritual ambition. *"Only by holding fast
at once to the 'is' and 'ought not' can thought achieve an authentic survival.
Thought, that is, must take the form of resistance."*[100] Yet when our
thinking takes the form of resistance against the totalitarian aspirations of
an explicitly posthistorical regime, we can only think such thoughts when
we know a basis in the authority of memory. The "ought not" is a negation
of what "is" and an affirmation of that what "ought to be." As an abstract,
formal possibility the "ought" belongs to the brilliant realm of speculation
or hope. As a determinate substantive reality that calls for unconditional
responsibility and concrete action the "ought" belongs to the realm of
memory, in the recollection of the past when the "is" and the "ought" were
unified in the "good." If it does not hold fast to that memory, the "ought
not" of resistance might become the "is" it opposes, and the destruction of
Auschwitz will lead to the construction of Gulag. Thus the implication of
our obligation to resist Auschwitz is our duty to unite the unequivocal "No"
with a "Yes." This is the "Yes" of Jerusalem, the "Yes" of Athens.

Strauss, Schmitt and Athens

At this point I would like to discuss one philosopher who turned to the axial
period as a response to the crisis of the present. The political philosopher
Leo Strauss has been credited as the agent of the revival of classical
political thought in North America. And if Westfall's contribution to this
volume were to have a resonance in the way we think about the purpose of
buildings, then Strauss's teaching would also find an architectural embodiment. Westfall always has acknowledged that the philosophical articulation
of his original historical proposition owes much to Strauss. Strauss showed
Westfall how Alberti's understanding of the city embodied abiding principles formulated in classical political philosophy. Yet Strauss's "discovery" of the enduring value of the classical Greek understanding of the
political—which gave Westfall the basis to expand his architectural
historical scholarship into an architectural theoretical position—originated
as an act of resistance. It emerged from a prophetic understanding of the
crisis of modernity.

Strauss began his scholarly career in Weimar Germany. He was the
author of a dissertation on Jacobi (1921) and a classic study on the

theological–political problem as investigated by Spinoza (1930). By 1932 Strauss had acquired a solid reputation as a responsible, relativist historian, as was proper for an aspiring university professor. And Strauss was a modernist, as behooved a student of the great neo-Kantian Hermann Cohen, the most important German–Jewish thinker and the most prominent professor of philosophy of his time. Earlier in this chapter I included some of Cohen's observations on the prophetical character of history. Cohen was able to develop a sympathetic understanding of the future directedness of Hebrew historiography because he was deeply committed to an eschatological worldview. This understanding had a sacred and a secular aspect. Cohen thought about the idea of progress as a postulate of practical reason. Progress was the keystone of a rational worldview which, at the turn of the century, seemed a sufficient tool to make sense of the human quest for dignity and happiness. Strauss was to assess later that this secular aspect Cohen's thought "belongs to the world preceding World War I. Therefore he had a greater faith in the power of modern Western culture to mold the fate of mankind than seems to be warranted now. The worst things he had experienced were the Dreyfus scandal and the pogroms instigated by Czarist Russia: he did not experience Communist Russia and Hitler Germany."[101]

In the early thirties Strauss went through a significant "conversion," which turned the Saul who believed that a return to premodern philosophy (and prophecy) was reactionary and therefore unacceptable into a Paul who preached that such a return or t'shuvah ("repentance") was required. This conversion occurred in a memorable confrontation with a text that was to give some respectability for the confused meanderings that passed as the political philosophy of Nazism. This text was an essay entitled Der Begriff des Politischen (The Concept of the Political), published in 1927 by a law professor at Bonn University, Carl Schmitt. Schmitt tried to come to a new understanding of the nature of what he labeled as "the political," which is the ground of politics. His effort was a response to the crisis of the liberal state, exemplified by the Weimar republic. By 1932 the five-year-old essay had become very topical and the journal Archiv für Sozialwissenschaft und Sozialpolitik invited Strauss to write a review.

In his essay Schmitt proposed to restructure the state in such a way that its foundation would become "the political." "The political" did not refer to the art of living together, but to the situation that precedes it: the encounter between friend and foe. War, Schmitt claimed, defined the natural condition of (wo)man and, therefore, the abiding foundation of society.

The specific political distinction to which political actions and motives can be reduced is that between friend and enemy. . . . The distinction of friend and enemy denotes the utmost degree of intensity of a union or separation, of an

association or dissociation. . . . The political enemy need not be morally evil or
aesthetically ugly; he need not appear as an economic competitor, and it may
even be advantageous to engage with him in business transactions. But he is,
nevertheless, the other, the stranger; and it is sufficient for his nature that he is,
in a specially intense way, existentially something different and alien, so that in
extreme cases conflicts with him are possible.

The political is the most intense and extreme antagonism, and every concrete
antagonism becomes that more political the closer it approaches the most
extreme point, that of friend–enemy grouping. In its entirety, the state as an
organized political entity decides for itself the friend–enemy distinction.[102]

The art of politics originated, therefore, not in the desire to live together,
but with the identification of an enemy. Its potential was decided by the
willingness of a group to prepare for the extermination of the foe.
Commenting on how Schmitt's conclusions reflected some of the present but
repressed undercurrents of modern thought, Strauss concluded that the
self-destruction of reason, which had been formulated by Schmitt and
which came to pass in Hitler Germany, had been "the inevitable outcome of
modern rationalism as distinguished from premodern rationalism."[103] A
return to the premodern situation was perhaps reactionary (whatever that
meant in an age that had destroyed the modern belief in progress) but,
given the choice between Schmitt's and Aristotle's definition of the political
(or Schmitt's and Jeremiah's understanding of the existential), not un-
reasonable. And thus Strauss began to study the ideas that had issued from
classical Athens and the calls for t'shuvah that had been heard in Judahite
Jerusalem. Referring to his teacher's progressive ideology (and its assimila-
tionary implications) Strauss acknowledged that, unlike Cohen, he was far
more disillusioned with the prospect of modern culture. Alluding to Athens
and Jerusalem he wondered "whether the two ingredients of modern
culture, of the modern synthesis, are not more solid than that synthesis.
Catastrophes and horrors of a magnitude hitherto unknown, which we have
seen and through which we have lived, were better provided for, or made
intelligible, by both Plato and the prophets than by the modern belief in
progress." The "progressive" solution, first formulated by philosophers of
nature in the seventeenth century and given general political significance in
the eighteenth century, must therefore give way to older ideas, the so-called
"ingredients" of Western civilization. Strauss warned, however, not to
interpret either Athens or Jerusalem as an answer to the crisis of modernity.
"Since the two ingredients are in fundamental opposition to each other, we
are ultimately confronted by a problem rather than with a solution."[104] And
since Schmitt (and the Nazis) had disclosed the essence of modernity to be
one of struggle against a real enemy, Strauss responded with his call to live

the only conflict that truly mattered: that between the philosophical and the
biblical point of view.

The Ideality and the Actuality of Athens

Reflecting on the hidden "beginnings" of Westfall's contribution—
Strauss's encounter with the philosophical substratum of the Nazi politics
of hostility—it is clear that there is a basic agreement between the odd and
even numbered chapters of *Architectural Principles in the Age of Historicism*. Despite the practical objections that I raised at the beginning of this
chapter, I cannot but acknowledge that, because of Strauss's conversion,
Westfall's effort is legitimate, as long as he acknowledges the relationship
to the event that brought it about, and as long as we read it as an act of
resistance. In other words, we may profit from Westfall's perspective if we
think about it in relationship to its origin (Athens) and its beginning
(Auschwitz). This means that we have to consider it simultaneously from a
metahistorical and a historical perspective. Fackenheim commented in his
To Mend the World that the kind of philosophical recovery of what "once
was" is only legitimate if that what is to be regained is "no mere fleeting
appearance but rather 'what *always* was.'" At first this would seem to
support Westfall's insistence that we reconstruct our history of architecture
within an enduring order of things. Fackenheim added, however, the
following afterthought to his reflection on the possibility to "mend" our
broken civilization. He declared that what "once was" cannot "*quite* be
what *always* was, for it could be—and was—ruptured. And because it was
ruptured the recovery of it is an *act* that is not inessential and will not leave
the 'what was' unchanged."[105] This, then, puts a particular pressure on the
Athens that Strauss rediscovered shortly before, and Westfall tries to
rebuild after, Auschwitz. We may be able to recover the idea of (wo)man, or
the idea of the city, or the idea of architecture from the past. Yet we know
that it has become historical because it might be destroyed. The idea of
(wo)man (or the city, or architecture) may still be the measure of (wo)men
(or politics, or buildings). But the circumstance that the historical deeds of
(wo)men (or the actual working of Schmitt's "political" in Nazi Germany, or
the actual operation of an extermination camp) have raised the question of
"recovery" or "reconstruction" implies that the historical has become the
measure of the ideal.

Having arrived in Athens by way of Auschwitz and Jerusalem, I see a
different city than the one which has been given a normative significance in
Westfall's theory of architecture. He interprets Athens as a sign of the
symbolically ideal city delineated in classical political philosophy; for me it

is the actual city as it existed around the year 500 BCE. Westfall's Athens is a first imitation of the metahistorical "best possible city" that, so he believes, reflects a timeless and abiding order of things. My Athens is a historic axis of history. It is the place where, in the actual life of the citizens, a standard was set which justifies the ideal, and which allows us to recover it. The standard was set in the actual life; the actual life was not the standard. Athens was not a perfect city, especially if we think about the workings of Athenian democracy in the Periclean Age. Yet there was a standard. It was suggested by Heraclitus and it was set by a historian, Thucydides.

Leo Strauss remarked in an essay on Thucydides' historiography that the kind of daring innovation, the *mania* that transcended in the historical Athens the limits of moderation to cause the city's ultimate downfall, "comes into its own, or is legitimate, or is in accordance with nature, only in the work of Thucydides — not in Periclean Athens as such. Not Periclean Athens, but the understanding that is possible on the basis of Periclean Athens, is the peak. Not Periclean Athens, but Thucydides' history is the peak."[106] The historic Athens (as interpreted by Thucydides) may legitimately occupy an axial position in our history; the historical Athens (governed by Pericles) may not. Thucydides' interpretation of the history of Athens parallels the Judeo-Christian interpretation of the history of Israel, in which the historical Jerusalem, with its political intrigues and factional tensions set the stage for the biblical (or historic) Jerusalem, the city of redemption. The biblical Jerusalem has prophetic (and therefore historic) significance; the historical Jerusalem does not. The same applies to Athens. Periclean Athens belongs to the relativists, Thucydides' Athens lasts forever.

Thucydides' Athens is radically different from Plato's (or Westfall's) "Athens." They use "Athens" as a symbolic image to describe the ideal polis that is structured according to the political rationalism invented by Socrates and developed by Plato and Aristotle. This "Athens" stands for a political philosophy that assumes that it is possible to define a common goal of all citizens (the good life), that it is also possible to acquire knowledge of the best regime that might realize that goal, and that it is possible to found that regime. In other words, Plato thought and Westfall agrees that reason is sufficiently equipped to realize the full potential of (wo)man. "Athens" is the name of the city structured by reason. It can be built anywhere. Thucydides came to another conclusion. He believed that it was possible to understand the nature of politics, but that this understanding could not guide the political life. According to Strauss, the difference between Plato's and Thucydides' views of Athens was one of perspective. The former judged the low (the actuality of the political life) from the perspective of the high (the ideality of political philosophy); the latter judged the high (the aspirations of the Athenian polity) in the light of the low (the arrogance of its leadership). The following excerpt from his lecture on Thucydides, given as part of a series on "The Western Tradition—Its Great Ideas and Issues," explains the difference between Thucydides' and Plato's (or mine and Westfall's) Athens.

> Plato had no illusions about the fact that if we limit our observations to human affairs in the narrow sense, Thucydides is right: political life proves again and again its imperviousness to philosophy. But Plato demanded that we take a comprehensive view, that we see human affairs in their connection with human nature, and human nature as a part of the whole; and he contended that if we do this, we shall arrive at the conclusion that the higher is stronger than the lower. The ultimate reason why Plato and Thucydides disagree has to be sought, not in a different estimate of human affairs as such, but in a different view of the whole.
>
> Thucydides held that the primary and fundamental act is movement or unrest, and that rest is derivative; that the primary and fundamental act is barbarism, and that Greekness is derivative; in a word, that war, and not peace, is the father of all things. Plato, on the other hand, believed in the primacy of rest, Greekness, harmony. Plato and Thucydides agree as to this—that for man, rest and Greekness and peace are the highest. But according to Plato, the highest for man and the highest in man is akin to the highest simply, to the principle or principles governing the whole; whereas according to Thucydides, the highest in man is not akin to the highest simply. According to Plato, the highest in man, man's humanity, has direct cosmic support. According to Thucydides, the highest in man lacks such support: man's humanity is too remote from the elements to be capable of receiving such support.
>
> This difference explains the difference of moods conveyed by the Platonic dialogues on one hand and Thucydides' history on the other. The serenity of Plato corresponds to his gay science, to his comforting message that the highest is the strongest. A light veil of sadness covers Thucydides' somber wisdom; the highest is of extreme fragility.[107]

Given the choice between Plato's and Thucydides' Athens, Strauss opted for the more optimistic perspective, claiming that "it is safer to understand the low in the light of the high than the high in the light of the low. In doing the latter one necessarily distorts the high, whereas in doing the former one does not deprive the low of the freedom to reveal itself fully for what it is."[108] Fackenheim rightly identified Strauss's maxim as "a superb expression of a grandiose philosophical failure,"[109] which led, for example, Hannah Arendt to her conclusion that only good has depth, and that evil is

banal. Fackenheim concluded that Auschwitz reveals the limitation of
Strauss's (and therefore Plato's) perspective. Auschwitz "does not, alas,
reveal itself fully for what it is to an understanding of the high but rather, to
the extent to which it reveals itself at all, only (as we have seen) to a
thinking confronting it, shattered by it, and saved from total destruction
only if it opposes its horror with a sense of horror of its own."[110]

I can agree with Strauss and Jaspers that Athens *can* offer an answer to
Auschwitz, but it is the Athens of Thucydides, the city that was the
protagonist in the catastrophe that revealed the fragility of civilization: the
Peloponnesian War. For Thucydides this war had ruptured history. Before
it, he reasoned, people always had believed that whatever war they were
involved in created a fissure in time that separated the past from a radically
new present. Yet when such wars were over, they were able to restore the
link to a fondly remembered past. The Peloponnesian War was different. It
had made clear what miserable creatures men were, and this insight
separated the generation who had witnessed the defeat of Athens from
people who had lived before. Therefore the war could be justifiably
identified as "the greatest war," the war that ended the illusion that life was
anything but war. And Thucydides was right. The Peloponnesian War *as
described in his history* is indeed the war of wars: it still allows us to judge
essential aspects of all subsequent wars, and civilizations.

Robert Connor clarified the manner in which Thucydides' *History of the
Peloponnesian War* challenges, subverts and expands our understanding of
the war in particular and the nature of the political in general. Connor noted
how Thucydides seems to propose at the beginning of his narrative "a
highly rational view of history, a confidence in the ability of reason to
uncover the past and determine the sources and patterns of power." The
historian's self-assurance parallels Pericles' certainty that rational policies
can secure a victory for Athens. "Reason seems very much in command and
to justify both Athenian strategy and the claim of the *Histories* to offer useful
knowledge. The reader naturally concludes that 'since Thucydides presents
his work as useful . . . he must have regarded human nature, political and
military affairs, and perhaps even the natural environment as liable to
rational prediction and control, at least to some degree.'"[111] In other words,
the beginning of the account set up a solid base for what Thucydides'
successors would canonize as the paradigm of classical historiography.
The reader easily succumbs to the idea that Thucydides left us "a document of the Greek Enlightenment, a reminder of the importance of reason,
and, despite all the irrationality and horror it reveals, as a work ultimately
optimistic about the future, if only man will learn fully to use his reason."
Yet Thucydides' text refuses to play into the hands of those who uphold
the validity of the principles of classical historiography. The man who in-

vented the genre also showed its inadequacy when applied to catastrophe. Thucydides progressively undermined the confident assertions made in the opening chapters, allowing our certainty of the potency of reason to erode as the narrative develops. Events do not match the earlier predictions made on the most rational of grounds, and we become increasingly aware of the power of the unexpected and unpredictable. "We focus increasingly upon the *pathos* of the war—not just its emotional power, but its way of undermining planning, outmaneuvering prediction, and making sufferers out of those who thought they would be in control." Does this experience refute the analysis of power in the first section? Connor believes not. "The anatomy of power in the first book remains valid within limits of which we become increasingly aware. It is not rejected but transformed. Naval power and financial strength continue to be important throughout the work but they result not in progress and security but in expansion and vulnerability. Walls come to symbolize not security but siege and defeat. Boldness and innovation are crucial constituents of Athens's growth but also of her overextension and defeat. Greatness characterizes the war throughout, but comes to describe suffering, not accomplishments."[112] Thus the experience of the war becomes the experience of the readers, forcing them to rethink what they thought they had learned. Connor stated that Thucydides' history "forces us to engage, attacks our assumptions, lays siege to our certainties, and grants no quarter or settlement. *Yet at every stage we resist.* Like the Melians, we feel there must be some possibility, however remote, of rescue or escape. The unexpected, we know, has a great role in war—immense for the belligerents as well as for the reader of the *Histories*. In hope of the unanticipated, we refuse accommodation. More than that, we envision something better."[113]

Thucydides' Athens has more in common, in short, with Jeremiah's Jerusalem than with Plato's Athens. His history is prophetical in the authentic sense of the word, and its relativism is charged with Croce's sense of freedom. It challenges us to rethink what we thought we knew. It confronts the limits of reason, sounds the depth of evil, issues a call to resistance and opens the horizon to the future. It is the Athens that might have meaning in an age which is lost in the ruined city created two centuries ago by rational, progressive and historicist ideologies.

Thucydides' Athens is fragile, and subject to the sovereignty of Heraclitus' *kinesis*, movement. It is a city built on a volcano. In Periclean Athens the movement seemed retained: almost fifty years of peace provided the appearance of stability. The city gathered treasures and built its walls and temples. Yet each year of peace and accumulation was paid for by increased suffering. Because the city had become so rich and powerful it could sustain defeat after disaster without being forced to surrender. Thus the measure of its accumulated glory, partially embodied in its architecture, became a measure of suffering. It is here that the Heraclitean character of Thucydides' Athens is most apparent. "The path up and down is one and the same," Heraclitus taught, a truth which not only included the destiny of men but also affected the enduring world of the gods and, therefore, cities. "Immortals are mortals, mortals immortals: living their death, dying their life."[114] Because the city is enduring, it is doomed to fall.

An example of this Heraclitean apprehension can be found in Thucydides' description of the events of the first years of the war. Because the city was so strong and powerful, the Athenian leadership decided on a scorched-earth policy. The rural population was to withdraw within the walled perimeter of Athens, which was connected through the so-called Long Walls to the harbors of the Piraeus and Phalerum. Their decision was based on the assumption that an impregnable, well-armed, well-populated and rich citadel, supplied and protected by the most powerful fleet in Hellas, would guarantee victory. It was a rational policy. It was a policy justified and even celebrated in Pericles' famous funeral speech, given at the official celebration of the city's dead a few months after the evacuation had been completed. Yet the concentration of people in one place lead to a decline in hygienic conditions, which in turn contributed to the outbreak of the plague. The walls behind which people had sought protection became the confines of a deadly prison. Rather than the elaborate burial rituals there were now abandoned corpses everywhere in the city. And if at the outbreak of the war the temples had been associated with the gold amassed therein, now they were full of the dead bodies of those who had taken up shelter in the sacred precincts. Thucydides would have understood Hugo's description of Dom Claude's hallucinary vision of the Tour de Nesle as a pinnacle of hell; he would also have agreed with Norman O. Brown's interpretation of the city as a monument of accumulated guilt and expiation. And he would have sanctioned Jeremiah's warnings to the people of Jerusalem not to trust in the strength of the city's walls and the amassed might of its temple. In short, Thucydides' Athens is a city in which modern (wo)man might feel (sadly) at home.

The concept of home brings me back to a still unresolved conflict with Westfall. In Chapter Eight he will argue that while the Greeks invented the polis, they did not realize the full implications of that invention in the urban form of their cities. There was no "necessary" link between politics and architecture. "Because their city could be any place, it did not have any special or particular meaning when it was some special or particular place. As a result, there was nothing special about the configuration its political, secular buildings took, and nothing particular about the space which the polis inhabited." According to Westfall the Romans overcame this disjunction through their theoretical understanding of the relationship between the city as *civitas* and the city as *urbs*. This holds true as far as architectural theory is concerned: the Greek invention of a political definition of the city as a community of citizens in a constitution had only been able to succeed because political reformers and philosophers from Solon to Aristotle consciously avoided the question of the relationship between polis and place. This inattention could sometimes be exploited. For example, in situations of emergency, when the Athenians found themselves separated from their city, the lack of consideration could become an ideological proposition useful as a means to bolster their morale: the city would survive in its citizens wherever they happen to be. It was perfectly reasonable for the Athenian general Nicias to exhort his discouraged soldiers shortly before the Athenian defeat in Sicily with the admonition that they should reflect that they themselves are a city already.[115] But such lofty notions, valid as they may have been, do not reflect how people thought. The ideality of the polis evoked in a general's speech does not (necessarily) express the emotions of the citizens. Thucydides noted that when the Athenian citizenry evacuated the countryside at the outbreak of the Peloponnesian War, people "sadly and reluctantly" abandoned their homes and temples, "they prepared to change their whole way of life, leaving behind them what each man regarded as his own city."[116] It is undoubtedly true that the architectural and urban splendor of Athens was, as John Dunne phrased it, "accessory and incidental to the human substance of the city."[117] Yet it is also true that buildings and places were important in the Greek political life.

I say Greek, and not Athenian. When Thucydides wrote his *History of the Peloponnesian War* he did not write a history of Athens at war. His history encompassed both sides, and he tried to do justice to both camps. In fact, he wrote the history of a civil war that split the country of Hellas into two parts, represented by Sparta and Athens. The history begins with a cultural history of Hellas, describing its barbaric beginnings and the slow emergence of a linguistic and cultural unity that found its first political expression in the common Greek effort to conquer Troy. The Trojan War made Hellas and, to a lesser extent, the Persian Wars did the same. They brought Greeks together and created the idea of a common homeland. The Peloponnesian War ended the idea of a common Greek home. And because it was a civil war, it was the greatest and the most catastrophal cataclysm.

Thucydides interpreted the war as a battle between ideology and custom. At the one side is Periclean Athens, the polis which believed in rational politics, in the possibility to control the political life through the application of reason. This is the city that claimed it could survive in its men alone, the city that forced its citizens to evacuate their homesteads and puts its trust in a fleet and its future on the high seas. It is a city of innovation, a city of progress, a city of daring. In Westfall's terms, it is a community that recognized "that a city is different from and far superior to a settlement," and that, consequently, politics were more important than architecture. It is the city that was to lose the war (and win the peace because it is preserved in Thucydides' history). It is a city that symbolizes what Westfall identifies as the origin of architecture, even though it was an origin that did not discover the manner in which the political and the architectural might be connected. In my understanding of history, Athens occupies the axis of architectural history. It is a new beginning. This beginning compares to Westfall's origin, yet it is different in that for Westfall the developments that preceded the origin are of no significance, while for me they are as relevant and significant as the Old Testament is to the New. Thus the older traditions of place and home, which appeared obsolete because of the radical concept of a city that could exist anywhere Athenians found themselves, balanced the new ideology. Thucydides' history gives these older customs, the "other" Athens, a name: "Sparta." If *The History of Peloponnesian War* anticipates Dickens's *A Tale of Two Cities*, it is because Sparta balances Athens in the same manner as the customary society of England was to balance the revolutionary society of France. Sparta was old-fashioned and conservative. It was a city ruled by custom and moderation. In a metaphorical sense it was the Athens that was obscured behind the glittering facade of the Periclean buildings. The Corinthian delegation, addressing the Spartan assembly shortly before the outbreak of the war, compared Athenian activity to Spartan indolence, Athenian initiative to Spartan hesitation, Athenian public spiritedness to Spartan private mindedness.

> As for their bodies, [the Athenians] regard them as expendable for the city's sake, as though they were not their own; but each man cultivates his own intelligence, again with a view to doing something notable for the city. . . . In a word, they are by nature incapable of living a quiet life themselves or of allowing anyone else to do so. That is the character of the city which is opposed to you. Yet you still hang back. . . . Your idea of proper behavior is, firstly, to avoid harming others, and then to avoid being harmed yourselves, even if it is a matter of defending your own interests. . . . Your whole way of life is out of date when compared with theirs. And it is just as true in politics as it is in any art or craft: new methods must drive out old ones. When a city can live in peace and quiet, no doubt the old-established ways are best: but when one is constantly being faced by new problems, one has also to be capable of approaching them in

an original way. Thus Athens, because of the very variety of her experience, is a far more modern state than you are.[118]

In the *History of the Peloponnesian War* the conflict between Sparta and Athens is a war between custom and ideology, between a society that values private morality higher than the public gain and the society that defines itself in terms of the public realm. As a historian Thucydides sides with the Athenian polis, because its daring makes the kind of history that is worthy of remembrance. He knows that as a historian of Athens he has been endowed with a tremendous responsibility: in his account the city will remain, even after it has become the past. "It will be remembered that of all the Hellenic powers we held the widest sway over the Hellenes, that we stood firm in the greatest wars against their combined forces and against individual states, that we lived in a city which had been perfectly equipped in every direction and which was the greatest in Hellas."[119] Because of Thucydides' history the Athenians "do not need the praises for the moment, but whose estimation of facts will fall short of what is really true."[120] Therefore, too, did he conceive of his history as a work that did not seek applause, but that was intended to create a lasting contribution.[121] As a citizen, Thucydides has more sympathy for Sparta: the very audacity and fragility of the Athenian polis, which gave meaning to his calling as a historian, led him back to the customary society in Sparta.[122] Thucydides was well aware of the dangers a society faced when it left the old customs. An extreme example of this was found in his analysis of the Corcyrean revolution of 427 BCE, a revolution in which a society radically rejected all the customs and conventions that had guided them until then.

> What used to be described as a thoughtless act of aggression was now regarded as the courage one would expect to find in a party member; to think of the future and wait was merely another way of saying one was a coward; any idea of moderation was just an attempt to disguise one's unmanly character; ability to understand a question from all sides meant that one was totally unfitted for action. . . . The simple way of looking at things, which is so much the mark of a noble nature, was regarded as a ridiculous quality and soon ceased to exist.[123]

The simple way of looking at things teaches us that a city is not only in its (wo)men, but the nexus of people and place. Thus Thucydides followed Nicias' assertion that wherever Athenians settle there would be an Athens with a description of the stone quarries where the Athenian soldiers were imprisoned after their surrender to the Syracusans.

> There were many of them, and they were crowded together in a narrow pit, where, since there was no roof over their heads, they suffered first from the heat

of the sun and the closeness of the air, and then, in contrast, came on the cold autumnal nights, and the change in temperature brought disease among them. Lack of space made it necessary for them to do everything on the same spot; and besides there were the bodies all heaped together on top of one another of those who had died from their wounds or from the change of temperature or other such causes, so that the smell was insupportable. At the same time they suffered from hunger and from thirst. During eight months the daily allowance for each man was half a pint of water and a pint of corn. In fact they suffered everything which one could imagine might be suffered by men imprisoned in such a place.[124]

Obviously the gathering of the dead and the still living in the quarry is not a polis, and the suffering of the Athenian men gives the lie to Pericles' proud assertion, eighteen years earlier, that "this, then, is the city for which these men, who could not bear the thought of losing her, nobly fought and died. It is only natural that every one of us who survives them should be willing to undergo hardships in her service."[125] Just as eighteen years of war had revealed the pretense of seemingly rational ideology, the unburied corpses in the quarry exposed the sanctimony of a "noble death."

In conclusion, the radical side of the Athenian understanding of architecture, which led Westfall to the conclusion that "the city was so thoroughly a being of political character that the locale of that politics could be a matter of indifference," had, at the same time, a self-destructive, anarchic side. For Westfall this is no problem, as the subsequent development of the idea that politics is superior to architecture (first in ancient Rome, later in Renaissance Rome and finally in eighteenth-century America) resolved the initial opposition between the political space of appearance and the urban space of existence. What was a revolutionary and disproportionate idea in 450 BCE has become through the succeeding twenty-five centuries the basis of a moderate and prudent theory of architecture. I believe, however, that the axial significance of Athens is located in the dialogue between the historical reality of Periclean Athens and the historic significance given to it in Thucydides' account of it. Therefore the relationship between ideality and ideology, between the customary and actuality is of crucial significance.

Martin Heidegger pondered the complex and paradoxical relationship between the Greek understanding of human community as a placeless venture and a historical place in one of the lectures that he delivered in 1935 at the University of Freiburg. Commenting on the first ode from Sophocles' *Antigone*, Heidegger interpreted its first line—"There is much that is strange, but nothing that surpasses man in strangeness"—as the "authentic Greek definition of man." Man is the strangest of all "not only because he passes his life amid the strange understood in this sense [of the unhomely] but because he departs from his customary, familiar limits, because he is the violent one, who, tending toward the strange in the sense of the overpowering, surpasses the limit of the familiar." (Wo)man is strange because she is the most vulnerable to the power of fate and, simultaneously, challenges its power for the sake of destiny. In a second passage from the ode the chorus describes (wo)man ·as *pantoporos aporos ep'ouden erchatai*, "everywhere journeying, inexperienced and without issue, he comes to nothingness." Heidegger explained that "the essential words are *pantoporos aporos*. The word *poros* means: passage through transition to . . . path. Everywhere man makes himself a path; he ventures into all realms of the essent, of the overpowering power, and in doing so he is flung out of all paths . . . and befallen by *ate*, ruin, catastrophe."[126]

> The interpretation is completed by the third salient phrase, line 370: *hypsipolis apolis*. In construction it is similar to *pantoporos aporos*, and its situation in the middle of the antistrophe presents another parallel. But it moves in a different direction. It speaks not of *poros* but of *polis*; not of the paths to all the realms of the essent but of the foundation and scene of man's being-there, the point at which all the paths meet, the *polis*. *Polis* is usually translated as city or city-state. This does not capture the full meaning. *Polis* means, rather, the place, the there, wherein and as which historical being-there is. The *polis* is the historical place, the there *in* which, *out of* which, and *for* which history happens. To this place and scene of history belong the gods, the temples, the priests, the festivals, the games, the poets, the thinkers, the ruler, the council of elders, the assembly of the people, the army and the fleet.[127]

The polis is, therefore, a place because it is at the site of history. Yet history is created by human beings who, "pre-eminent in the historical place," are fated to become as historical actors "at the same time *apolis*, without city and place, lonely, strange, and alien . . . at the same time without statue and limit, without structure and order, because they themselves *as* creators must first create all this."[128] Thus it follows that the polis is ultimately fated to be without place, adrift in the course of time.

I will return to the implications of Heidegger's observations on the unhomely / homely character of the polis in Chapter Five. The purpose of that chapter is to investigate how the problem that the Athenians defined as irrelevant at the theoretical level (because it did not fit the ideology of the "portable" and therefore daring polis) did find a day-to-day resolution at the level of custom and tradition. I will argue how at the level of the practical the true greatness of the Athenian achievement must and can be measured: classical Athens is not the axis of architectural history because it offers us a superb demonstration of some doctrine. And I will show that, as a real-life answer to the question of life, death and, indeed, immortality, a daring answer wrought in strife, Athens deserves to be remembered as the city where the history of architecture found a new beginning.

But yet . . . It is in the nature of hindsight that my reconstruction of the historic Athens will be biased towards what was at the time daring and disproportionate. Even Thucydides recognized this. Discussing the veracity of Homer's account of the Trojan War—the only serious competitor to the Peloponnesian War for the dignity of "the greatest war"—he examined the reliability of archeological evidence. His conclusion was that the unprepossessing appearance of Mycenae in his own time neither supported nor denied the historical validity of the *Iliad*. To illustrate his observation he invited the reader to think about the future of Sparta and Athens.

> Suppose, for example, that the city of Sparta were to become deserted and that only the temples and foundations of buildings remained, I think that future generations would, as time passed, find it very difficult to believe that the place had really been as powerful as it was represented to be. Yet the Spartans occupy two-fifths of the Peloponnese and stand at the head not only of the whole Peloponnese itself but also of numerous allies beyond its frontiers. Since, however, the city is not regularly planned and contains no temples or monuments of great magnificence, but is simply a collection of villages, in the ancient Hellenic way, its appearance would not come up to expectation. If, on the other hand, the same thing were to happen to Athens, one would conjecture from what met the eye that the city had been twice as powerful as in fact it is. We have no right, therefore, to judge cities by their appearances rather than by their actual power.[129]

Time proved Thucydides to be right. The historian who saw the world in terms of a Heraclitean *kinesis*, movement, rightly saw that *Architekturgeschichte* can never reflect *Welthistorie*, if only because the potency of great architectural monuments and urban ensembles to resist decay and destruction is, in the final analysis, disproportionate to their contemporary political and existential significance. This problem cannot be resolved except in the effort to discern in the buildings that became part of Athenian *Geschichte* tendencies towards an understanding which comprehends the nature of the Greek transformation of architecture and which includes the "homely" values of, for example, Sparta. The task which I have set myself is, therefore, to show how the architecture and urban form of Athens, which reached its perfection in the great monuments (the Acropolis, the Agora) which resulted from daring political innovations achieved in a very particular situation, remained also true to the values that were at stake in the Peloponnesian War. Only in this way might a study of Athens provide us, twenty-five centuries later, with an approximation of what is true, ultimate and universally valid in architecture (in Sparta, in Rome, in Charlottesville, Waterloo, Berlin and Auschwitz). Therefore, I will draw together the most significant areas that articulated the political and civic space of classical Athens, and I will measure their significance according to the measure provided directly or in disguise in Thucydides' dissection of the city. I will base this procedure on the supposition that sound judgement and not blind chance was responsible for their being recorded or implied.

We may now begin to investigate the significance of classical Athens as the normative Axis of a Judeo-Christian interpretation of architectural history. The city we will investigate is a historic yet actual city. This examination of the universal center of the history of urban form will offer a criterion that will allow us to judge consequent developments *and* the different possibilities open to the architectural designer today.

FOUR

Building Types

Carroll William Westfall

On Nature, Types, and the City

It is in the nature of things that the superior governs the inferior. In human affairs, the same axiom says that those things which better serve the purposes of people who seek to perfect their natures ought to govern those things that do so less directly. We have seen that, in attempting to perfect the nature of people, politics is superior to architecture. It follows, then, that the political service buildings can render must be the dominant thing in building.

The historian wishing to know about old buildings and the architect (or patron, client, government official or whomever) responsible for building a new one have the same interest: They want to know what building will best serve the purposes that will bring them together on the building site. The best is in the typical, or that which it is in the nature of the thing to be, while the purposes that are most important are the political ones. Knowledge of politics provides a parallel for thinking about buildings. Following how Aristotle taught us, while we study cities and their political forms in order to learn things of general validity, each city provides us with a unique experience and hence different knowledge of those forms. But the wise citizen who thinks about such things knows that it is in the nature of political bodies to fall into types (or categories or classes, etc.) ranging from the vesting of all authority in one person, or monarchy, to vesting it in all citizens, or democracy. No matter what names, ranges of authority or bases of legitimacy may be claimed or found for such types, things cannot be arranged otherwise (although they may be given different names and arranged in a different conventional context); it is in their nature to be that way; it always has been and always will be. These types may be taken to be true forms existing even before there were people to be the participants in states that would follow the forms and thereby become knowable.

As a parallel in buildings we ought to be interested first of all in things that are of general validity, that is, that which must be included in the design of any building no matter the time, place or materials in which it takes actual form. That validity is in the political purpose the building is to serve. The purpose a building is to serve defines the type of building it is.[1] The building's type embodies what is true about it. This true content or aspect is independent of the effects of time, place and material. A useful way to define *building type* is as a generalized, unbuildable idea of a building knowable only in the intellect and containing within it all the possible examples of actual buildings of that type that have been and can be built.

In actual experience we encounter not types but examples of buildings. Each building is unique, embodying within it the circumstances of the time, the place and the materials in which it was built. This makes it conventional, circumstantial, contingent, dependent, individual, specific and transient. A building, then, combines the general and the particular, and it also combines the purposive and the material. It satisfies certain particular functions by imitating the essential nature of the type of building it is. It also becomes an example of architecture and not an instance of mere building by embodying the typical aspects of the tectonic realm within its actual construction. In this chapter attention will be paid to the first point, or buildings functioning as instruments the citizens of a city or other polity use for reaching their purposes which are sometimes public, sometimes private, and always coordinated through politics with other purposes. In the next chapter van Pelt will reinterpret these types in a historicist sense. In Chapter Six I will return to the enduring universe established in Chapter Two and in the second part of this chapter, and examine the other, architectonic aspects of buildings.

Central to both arguments are the ideas each author conveys with the term "type." Both authors of this book value the term's ability to remind the reader that the fundamental issue in discussing architecture is not style. But there is more to it than that, as an important strain of current architectural discourse makes clear. In current discussion different applications of the term have simultaneously contributed to the liveliness of discussion and produced considerable confusion. Because the concept of type plays a central role in both a literal and intellectual sense in *Architectural Principles in the Age of Historicism*, it is essential that the reader be able to distinguish our uses of the concept of type from the uses others give it. The excursus which follows will offer a short review of the various meanings the term has been given over time.

Excursus: A Short History of Typological Thought in Architecture[2]

The Use of the Term "Type" before 1800

The decades around 1800 mark a rupture in the history of the understanding of the term "type" as it applies to architecture. In the earlier epoch architectural theorists used the word "type" often interchangeably with a number of other terms such as "class," "mode" or "kind." It was a collective noun which organized a designated class of buildings within the larger category of architecture. Vitruvius, for example, used the term *genus* with a considerable latitude in his *De Architectura*. Using it to refer to any kind of grouping, he employed the term to designate differences between buildings—in for example his discussion on the different *kinds* of temple plans and elevations (III, iii, 3), the differences between elements of buildings—there are five *kinds* of courtyards and various *kinds* of rooms (VI, iii, 1; VI, iv, 1), and the various systems which order architecture as a whole—there are three *kinds* or *orders* of columns: Doric, Ionic and Corinthian.

Alberti adopted the term *genus*, which Vitruvius had employed with such a lack of clarity and precision, to indicate the different classes which one could use to define and describe architecture as a coherent, comprehensive and articulated body of knowledge. Unlike Vitruvius' grouping, Alberti's categories of buildings were based on clear differences in the purposes of buildings within the context of the city as a political community. The first of these distinctions was that between the sacred and the secular, the second that between the public and the private. Then he differentiated between more and less ornate buildings, and between those which are bigger and smaller, those which occupy a central position in the city and those which are at the periphery. It seems odd that Alberti failed to develop a consistent terminology to set these different classes apart in his discussion. Yet the inherited term *genus* seemed sufficient as the explication of the topic was complete in itself. The text of his *De re aedificatoria* provided everything a person needed to interpret what the term meant each time it was employed, and it was not necessary to create a more precise terminology.

Typological terminology remained imprecise during the sixteenth and seventeenth centuries. Alberti's successors tended to simplify his discussion, yet they also showed a propensity to use more terms. This linguistic erosion did not alarm contemporary observers, as they shared with the authors of the treatises a general understanding which held that the value and the beauty of the thought was conveyed in the form of the whole rather than in the logical interconnection of all the individual parts. Sebastiano

Serlio, for example, referred in one discussion in Book V of his widely distributed treatise to the "various forms of ancient and modern temples,"[3] while in Book IV he promised to speak of the "many modes of temples designed in various forms."[4] When in the same Book he referred to the differences that arise from using the different orders and their ornaments, he wrote of the "five manners of building and of their ornaments."[5]

Cartesianism was to destroy the classical paradigm which allowed for a flexibility in terminology. Proceeding from a situation of radical doubt, Descartes sought to clear his mind of received opinions and establish certainty by means of "long chains of very simple and easy reasonings, which geometers customarily use to arrive at their most difficult demonstrations."[6] The new edifice of thought he built became paradigmatic for relationships between wholes and their parts that would eventually transform architectural theory. Descartes promulgated four rules of discourse which allow us to reach that kind of certainty which provides basis for action (1. never accept anything as true if you do not have evident knowledge of its truth; 2. divide each of the difficulties into as many parts as possible; 3. direct your thoughts in an orderly manner, moving from the simple to the complex; 4. make your enumerations as complete as possible). In so doing he turned the epistemology of the classical theories upside down. In Alberti's theory the unity of his theoretical universe was a basic assumption.[7] Descartes' demanded that a person should include nothing more in his judgement than that which presented itself to his mind so clearly and distinctly that he had no occasion to call it into doubt.[8] Thus a movement began which would favor reductionism. Instead of the classical dictum that architecture imitates the whole of nature, it now became fashionable to specify within nature one thing which in the architectural discourse could take the place of the Cartesian ego. This thing, which presented itself to the mind so clearly and distinctly that one had no occasion to call it into doubt, and which provided a basic definition of good architecture, would turn out to be the rustic hut.

One of the first to found architecture on such Cartesian foundations was Francesco Milizia. In his *Principii di architettura*, first published in 1781, Milizia proclaimed that architecture "lacks a model formed by nature," yet that men, "following the natural industry in constructing their first habitation," had provided architects with a basis for certainty when they made the rustic hut, "the origin of all beauty in *civil architecture*."[9] The hut recapitulates the "beautiful nature" in a wholly "imaginary" form, yet "its basis is entirely natural."[10] Having defined the basic element, or as Milizia labelled it the best archetype, "produced by nature and ingenious man,"[11] it is possible to develop a conditionally infallible typology which proceeds from the fundamental division of civil architecture in public and private buildings. After a few more divisions, which separate for example private architecture in two groupings on the basis of location—either in the city or in the country—Milizia reaches a point where he can distinguish forty-two kinds of buildings, all brought together in a table that reveals the logic and completeness of his discourse "at a glance."[12]

In Milizia's theory of architecture we can already observe that tendency to construct a theory of architecture on the basis of a clear understanding of its fundamental archetype. Such a methodology implies the necessity to define the nature of the basic element precisely. In a Cartesian epistemology it is unacceptable to leave confusion as to the exact nature of the basic element of certainty. Thus, so one would expect, forty-two types would develop from the one archetype. Yet Milizia does not make that jump yet. And he does not need to do so, as his Cartesian reformation of classical architectural theory still operated within that classical tradition. The understanding his predecessors had established could be carried on in his discussion. The same applies to Laugier's theory of the primitive hut. In his *Essai sur l'architecture* (1753) Laugier completed Milizia's project when he stripped the discussion of architecture to those components which seemed absolutely certain and, as such, as a firm basis for architecture. Laugier believed those principles to be those which primitive man had wrested from nature when he set out to construct his rustic hut. The column, the entablature and the pediment were the essential parts of that hut. "I can only see columns, a ceiling or entablature and a pointed roof forming at both ends what is called a pediment. So far there is no vault, still less an arch, no pedestals, no attic, not even a door or a window."[13] Yet his Cartesian reconstruction of architecture was less radical than his initial reductionist move suggested. Laugier did not reject the classical tradition, as is illustrated, for example, by his unquestioning acceptance of the Vitruvian trilogy, as a topic for substantive discussion. "One must build with solidity, for convenience and according to *bienséance*."[14] The last term refers in Laugier's discussion to the appropriateness of a building to its purpose. "*Bienséance*," he explained, "demands that a building is neither more nor less magnificent than is appropriate to its purpose, that is to say that the decoration of buildings should not be arbitrary, but must always be in relation to the rank and quality of those who live in them and conform to the objective envisaged."[15] In order to facilitate the discussion of the topic of *bienséance* Laugier comes close to what could have become a typological distinction based on use when he introduces the fundamental distinction between public and private buildings. Yet this distinction does not become the first move which allows him to erect a fundamental typology based on the firm foundation provided by the archetype of the rustic hut. Instead he picks up into his discussion whatever understanding his predecessors had established. The groupings of buildings which Laugier distinguishes is based on the architectural order used in building them. This Vitruvian notion is also reflected in the "Dictionnaire" which he provided in the second edition of his *Essai*. It did not include entries for terms such as "kind" (*sorte*)—which was supposed to be clear from his usage within the text—or terms like "type" or "style," that would preoccupy the next generation. The only term of substance he included was "order." This referred to "a system of columns and entablature with their distinctive proportions, ornaments, and character. There are only three Orders, the Doric, Ionic and Corinthian."[16] Thus Laugier believed that orders were one thing, and the buildings in which they were used something else. He could discuss the differences between the orders while being indifferent to the different "kinds" of buildings.[17]

Laugier did not challenge the received classifications within the classical tradition. He did however establish a different basis for discussing questions within that tradition. The Cartesian foundation of the rustic hut was not exploited to erect a radically new discourse; yet it provided a new kind of standard, to which other buildings could be compared. ". . . [T]ake note of this: never has a principle been more fertile in its effect. From now on it is easy to distinguish between the parts which are essential to the composition of an architectural Order and those which have been introduced by necessity or have been added by caprice. . . . Let us never lose sight of our little rustic hut."[18] The hut became normative. It allowed any person endowed with common sense to judge that the "parts that are essential are the cause of beauty, the parts introduced by necessity cause every license, the parts added by caprice cause every fault."[19] Armed with this knowledge anyone could see that, for example, Greek buildings were better than Roman ones, or that Soufflot's Sainte Geneviève was far superior to Michelangelo's Saint Peter's. Thus his theory could be prescriptive for practice and his prescriptions could be independent of whatever was the most recently available precedent.

Laugier's reductionism allowed eighteenth-century architects to maintain some sense of intellectual control over a field which was being assaulted with a rapid expansion of information about architecture through, for example, archaeology, travellers' reports and views, precise measured drawings of formerly unknown or poorly known buildings, and new ways of thinking about the structural behavior of building materials. The field devoted to architecture began to overflow the traditional boundaries which had circumscribed it as a distinct body of knowledge. The primitive hut made it possible that, during the last half of the eighteenth century, a person could be reasonably well informed about architecture with less actual knowledge than at any other time between 1450 and the present. Through the hut, architecture, which had been mysterious to the outsider, could become common. Looking at the rustic hut he could declare that only the column, the entablature and the pediment form an essential part of the composition of each architectural order. Place each of these parts in a suitable relationship to each other, and the work will be perfect. In the hut its principles revealed itself to the eyes of all, common men and learned alike. Laugier's archetype suggested that everybody could participate in the discovery of the laws of architecture. Thus Laugier realized for architecture what the *philosophes* had done for knowledge in general. As everyone with common sense could call himself a philosopher, so everyone who understood the primitive hut could call himself an architectural theorist. Architectural theory, therefore, became more or less sound and practiced common sense, which on the basis of a few simple principles ventured to enter upon the universal. The only requirement was that the amateur of architecture would not "lose sight of our little rustic hut." As an object-lesson of how to make it possible to master an increasingly complex field in a few easy steps, Laugier's archetype of the rustic hut was to inform the typological discourse of the nineteenth and twentieth centuries.

Style and Type in the Modern Age

The expansion of our information about architecture led to a substantive change in what people thought architecture to be. A building ceased to be a demonstration of something which was true and which could not be known except through the evidence it itself provided. Instead a building (or a painting, or a text, or a deed, or a rite) became an illustration of something outside itself and for which it was not essential. In the new relativist and historicist epistemology, buildings reflected (and consequently contributed to) culture just as art, literature, politics or religion did. Buildings became cultural artifacts, and to know a building meant that one had to know the culture, and vice-versa.

This new awareness radically broke with the earlier assumption that buildings imitated the enduring order of nature. The kind of architectural theory Alberti promulgated, a theory which had tried to describe the nature of architecture within its own terms, could not provide a framework for understanding buildings in the new relativist and historicist universe. Histories of architecture would fill the lacuna. Historians classified and designated buildings not on the basis of their *genus*, but according to the categories of style and character.

Two notions of type survived the wholesale surrender of the once autonomous body of knowledge of architecture to the limitless field of cultural inquiry. Formulated around 1800, J.N.L. Durand and Quatre-mère de Quincy developed their different notions of type as alternatives to the dominant relativist and historicist attempt to reduce the knowledge of architecture to that of a history of architectural styles. Durand's definition of type has become an important part of the current thought about the theory, history and practice of architecture. It permeates most talk about architecture by both lay people and professionals. During the last two decades Italian architectural theory has rediscovered the potential of Quatremère's understanding of type. As popularized by Aldo Rossi, it has recently become the staple of the more elevated, or pretentious, current discourse in North America.

The earlier notions of type did not survive their absorption into modernism unscathed. Used before 1800 to refer to classifications of (architectural) material within a body of knowledge that was complete in itself, the term came to be used to create a bridge between the system of thought that described the cultural activity of building and the larger matrix of culture which informed that activity. In the classical theory of architecture everything which required understanding was provided within the body of knowledge defined as architecture. Words which referred to a certain class, kind or group of buildings or elements, i.e., words that could be translated as type, were merely devices used for organizing that thought. Those words did not refer to material outside the body of knowledge of architecture as it was described in one or another theory. This changed around 1800. As architecture lost its autonomy as a body of knowledge and became dependent on a potentially infinite amount of information, so the words used to distinguish certain distinct aspects of architecture acquired a new function. A word like "type" ceased to designate certain classes of things within the ordered universe of architecture, and became now a tool to refer to something outside the traditional body of architectural knowledge. This "something outside" was complete without reference to architecture. With the disintegration of the traditional boundaries of architectural discourse, it became important that the words which were used to create a bridge between the sub-field of architecture and the larger field of culture (or science, or technology etc.) would have a precisely defined meaning which could not be conveyed by other words. The imprecise terminology, which had worked so well within the limited discourse of classical architectural theory, now became unacceptable. Both Durand and Quatremère felt it necessary to define the notion of type precisely.

Durand's Notion of Type

Durand's definition of architectural typology occupies the core of current theory and practice. Durand defined a type in relativist utilitarian terms when he stated that the utilitarian significance of a building as determined by the current interests of society defined its type.[20] To understand Durand's utilitarian typology it is necessary to make a brief excursion into his theory of architectural representation.

The two most important sources of Durand's architectural theory were located outside the traditional body of architectural knowledge. The first of these sources was the newly developed technique and attendant science of descriptive geometry. Descriptive geometry had been developed by Gaspard Monge who, as professor at the Institute Polytechnique in Paris, had been responsible for the appointment of Durand as a teacher of architecture within its department of applied geometry.[21] Monge's descriptive geometry displaced the by then traditional way of producing a facsimile of a building, which had originated in Alberti's explanations of perspective and theory of architecture. Alberti had shown how a person could render or design something as it was accessible as an object of sight—as a building if it was built or as a rendering of one if it was only intended or designed and not yet built. This implied that the building was seen (if built) or read (as a representation) in terms of the surfaces that bound material and that reflected the light that allowed a person to see it with his own vision. This understanding of the building had already been challenged by eighteenth-century aesthetic theory. The Newtonian separation of the world of mathematical truth (described in the *Principia*) and the world of (visual) sensation (described in the *Optics*) found its final philosophical expression in the first book of Kant's third critique when he declared that design and not appearance is the essential part of architecture. "Here it is not what gratifies in sensation but merely what pleases by its form, that is the fundamental prerequisite of taste."[22] Color and texture were to be considered to be part of a building's charm, but not of its design. Monge's descriptive geometry broke the relationship between vision and knowledge. With the help of the new manner of depicting buildings one produced a facsimile composed of sharp, precisely measured depictions of the edges or outlines of the plans, elevations and sections of buildings. This produced a sharp divorce between what one could encounter with vision (the surfaces which reflect the light) and what one could know only through a precise, scientific investigation of things. This separation between vision and description appealed to the architectural community as it gave a building an objective reality or truth which was independent of the variations that come from the subjective understanding of different individuals. The new description of buildings suggested that architecture acquired the same kind of scientific reality as, for example, the Newtonian universe. The lines which measured the edges of the planes described a truth about the building in the same manner as the lines which Newton had drawn to describe the movement of the heavenly bodies. It did not matter whether or not these lines could be seen with the eye.

Durand expanded his attempt to create a scientifically valid architectural theory on the basis of scientific methodologies when he adopted Baron Georges Cuvier's new method of classification within the natural science. This method provided Durand with a model of how to organize the things described with the help of descriptive geometry. The result was an easily teachable and applicable method of design. Using a combination of Cuvier's method of classifying things and Monge's method of describing things, one began with teaching (or designing) the parts (say, stairs, doors, windows) and moved into ever larger wholes (say, entire cities) with the assemblage of the parts into the whole controlled by the regularities of descriptive geometry (plan, elevation, section etc.). This methodology was steered by the ambition to achieve the greatest economy in the thing constructed and the ambition to establish an absolute control over the parts by means of the design controls Durand found in descriptive geometry, viz., the grid and the axis.[23]

Durand's method of architectural design was not dictated by the purpose the building was to serve. It could be applied to any kind of structure. The task of designing a specific kind of building was to be dictated by knowledge largely outside the control of the architect. This knowledge was presented to the architect in the form of the building's brief or program which defined the end or utilitarian role the building was to play in the society. The brief was given architectural substance by defining the appropriate type through selecting from a catalogue of buildings which had served, or still served, a similar function and which provided the data from which characteristic compositional patterns could be extracted. Thus a list of functions provided a list of types. In Durand's theory, then, a building type was a characteristic composition of a design capable of the most economical satisfaction of some particular function or end.

The union of a design methodology circumscribed by the sciences of descriptive geometry and classification and a typology based on function created a separation between on the one side the technological and functional rationale of the building and, on the other side, its ornament and other details of appearance. As things developed, the design's general form and construction (including its material) would become a question of engineering, while the question of its appearance would become a matter of style. As a result type and style became understood as unrelated. Type referred to the compositional pattern relative to function while style referred, as Anthony Vidler put it, to "clothing for an otherwise 'naked' object" and capable of being changed at will.[24] Thus the production of a building came to depend on two specialized realms of knowledge which lacked any necessary connection and which themselves were composed of a number of separate fields of expertise which are unconnected to each other.[25]

All this should be familiar to those who are conversant with current orthodoxy in architectural theory, history and practice as it provided the foundations for modernism in architecture. One might quibble about the relative importance of the various components, but there is a general consensus that Durand's understanding of the production of buildings describes the way things are and ought to be. This understanding, which is less than two centuries old, favors a one-sided discourse which concentrates on the stylistic aspect of buildings. This is the result of the fact that style is the object of judgement, while the constructive and utilitarian side of the building are objects of proof. There is not much to say about the structural efficiency or the economic viability of a building after one has concluded that the one is sound and the other cost-effective. As judgements on style change rapidly, it has produced a mass of literature which forms the core of the current "knowledge" of architecture (as it relates, of course, to the history of culture in general). Stylistic discussions have not only the advantage of remaining up to date. They also facilitate the writing of history as style places buildings most clearly within a historical sequence. And they also provide ample space for the industry of architectural history which establishes for each building or group of buildings "necessary" precedents and "influences," and its relationship to works of art in other media.

More recently some architectural historians have begun organizing some of their materials according to type with the discussion of the type then organized according to the concept of style.[26] One of the most popular books resulting from this approach was *A History of Building Types*, a monograph purporting to be the first of its kind, and written by Nikolaus Pevsner, a person who had devoted a major portion of his life to expounding on architecture as style.[27] These studies do not challenge the basic assumptions of orthodox modernism as formulated almost two centuries ago by Durand.

Quatremère's Understanding of Type

Quatremère de Quincy, "perpetual secretary" at the École des Beaux Arts, articulated an alternative understanding of architectural typology. Unlike his contemporary Durand, Quatremère affirmed the validity of the classical tradition as a basis for the production of buildings, albeit that the classical already had become in his time the self-conscious neo-classicism arising from a recognition of a chasm between its own time and the classical past. Quatremère's enterprise was therefore the hopeless one of attempting to recover something lost, although he thought that he renewed something enduring. The enduring he sought was that which was essential to architecture. This essence was in its origins which he took to be in or near the primitive hut. Much of this sounds as if it derived directly from Laugier. Yet there was also an important difference: if Laugier had postulated one primitive hut which as the essential type informed the one and only tradition of good architecture, Quatremère bowed to relativism and pluralism when he postulated at least three types: the cave, the tent and the hut. These corresponded to the three fundamentally different forms of acquiring food: the hunters shelter in caves, shepherds camp in tents, and farmers build huts. Quatremère believed that the Egyptians had developed the cave, the Chinese the tent, and the Greeks the hut. As the West had inherited the Greek tradition it knew the hut to be more important than the cave or the tent. Nevertheless the existence of alternatives was important, and their presence and justification reflected the relativist and historicist direction of Quatremère's theory.

Quatremère believed that in architecture (and in "every other field of inventions and human institutions")[28] the notion of type defined the original reason of a building. He used a type metaphorically, and not technically, because a type is an idea rather than an actual thing. Many people, so Quatremère observed, mistake a model for a type. A model is "the complete thing," "an object that should be repeated as it is." In a model everything is "precise and given." A type is different. It is "the original reason of the thing," "the object after which each [artist] can conceive works of art that may have no resemblance to each other." Unlike the model, the type is not specific but "more or less vague." As an origin the imaginative type and not the positive, material model offers a valid basis for imitation. Laugier's primitive hut was, in Quatremère's definition, not a type but a model. The hut which Quatremère postulated as the origin of Greek architecture did not have a precise form, and was not even an aesthetic canon, but "an elementary principle, which is like a kind of nucleus about which are collected, and to which have been coordinated over time, the developments and variations of forms to which it is susceptible." This elementary principle which Quatremère located at the origin of society is not yet a type; it is only the essence of a type. In each country the idea or essence of the type will develop differently according to the specific circumstances generated by a country's climate, its mores and its institutions. Therefore, there will be differences in the current examples embodying the idea contained in the type.

Quatremère's theory anticipated the relativist historicism that defined culture as the cause of artifice, be it a building, a work of art or an institution. Or so one could interpret him. The fuzziness of his explanations and the fact that he never produced an architectural design that might exemplify what he meant left his ideas open to any sort of interpretation. The functionalists of the later nineteenth century and the modern purists of Le Corbusier's generation found one subsidiary part of Quatremère's theory "extraordinarily attractive."[29] "One further applies the word 'type' in architecture," he explained, "to certain general and characteristic forms of the building which receives them." That is, "a great number of pieces of furniture, utensils, seats, and clothes have their necessary type in the uses one makes of them, and the natural habits for which one intends them. Each of these things has truly not its model, but its type in needs and nature. . . . Who does not believe that the form of a man's back ought to be the type of the back of a chair?" This last example of type illustrates also Quatremère's justification for his use of the term "type." He explained that his source for the word was in the "general acceptance" of the meanings given to the Greek word *typos*, which means "model, matrix, imprint, mold, figure in relief or in bas-relief."

The Current Revival of Quatremère's Notion of Type

Quatremère's approach lay forgotten until Giulio Carlo Argan rediscovered it thirty years ago. Since then typology has changed from an instrument for classifying buildings to a central topic in architectural discourse. Argan's article, which appeared in 1961 and was repeatedly republished within the context of the highly charged political atmosphere of Italian post-war architectural polemic, brought Quatremère's distinction between type and model back into view. Argan stressed that the type and not the model should be the point of departure for design. He suggested that types are the generative means by which buildings receive their configurations. These involve its complete configuration (what we might call its general formal properties especially as defined by its plan—e.g., centrally or longitudinally planned buildings), its major structural elements and its decorative elements.

Argan's ideas were most extensively developed in the rationalist, Hegelian, Marxist theories of Aldo Rossi. In that form they are virtually explicitly antithetical to the ideas underlying the polity of the United States, but this has not prevented them from being influential on American architects who indulge in theory. Rossi repeats Quatremère's definition of type, endorses it, and explains that the ideas the types contain are the irreducible elements in cities. These elements are cultural elements that have the character of necessity and which react dialectically with "technique, function, and style, as well as with both the collective character and the individual moment of the architectural artifact."[30]

American architects and theorists are apparently either blind or indifferent to the political implications of these theories. Their acceptance of architecture and cities as primarily cultural rather than primarily political could account for their attraction to these theories while their willingness to endorse them apparently arises from their allegiance to the present form of American pluralism as liberty without the restraint required for society to be civil. The result is a general incoherence in the use of the term—it means whatever the author wants it to mean and carries with it whatever material external to architecture the author wants to include. This vastly diluted meaning embracing the broadest tolerance of pluralism is embodied in Rafael Moneo's recent response to his question, "What then is type?" His answer:

> It can most simply be defined as a concept which describes a group of objects characterized by the same formal structure. . . . It is fundamentally based on the possibility of grouping objects by certain inherent structural similarities. It might even be said that type means the act of thinking in groups.[31]

Here architecture has become a purely formal exercise lacking any necessary connection to an epistemology or metaphysics. Now it is merely what the architect says it is, or, as Moneo says, "typology today has come to be understood simply as a mechanism of composition. The so-called 'typological' research today merely results in the production of images, or in the reconstruction of traditional typologies. In the end it can be said that it is the nostalgia for types that gives formal consistency to these works."[32] Moneo could simply have said that, today, without historicism (in the way Karl Popper uses the term) there is no typology.

In this way of thinking types are linked to culture and are based in whatever the author finds valuable within culture. An adherence to a lawless pluralism sees to it that disputation based on honest disagreement about what is valuable within culture is unacceptable—everyone, after all, has a right to his own opinion, and architects have the right to build it. Once the concept of types has reached this pass, it is essential to undertake the exercise found in Chapter One in which architecture and the city were distanced from the concept of culture and to find a different basis for discussing types. With this in mind it is now time to return to the argument of *Architectural Principles in the Age of Historicism*.

On Building Types

Knowledge of types as used here provides us access to knowledge of things that are of general validity, that is, things which must be included in the design of any building no matter the time, place or materials in which it takes actual form. In Chapter Two I argued that the validity is in the political purpose the building is to serve. Here the discussion will turn to the types serving politics and to the definition of a *building type* as a generalized, unbuildable idea of a building knowable only in the intellect and containing within it all the possible examples of actual buildings of that type that have been and can be built.

When one knows types as that which is true, normative and most important about buildings, one knows what it is that actual buildings ought to imitate. The true, as we saw in the chapter on politics, is not the same as the factual, just as the historic is different from the historical. The true and the historic are beyond the factual and the historical which they entail. In the same sense, a thing imitated is true and historic while a copy is in the realm of the factual and historical. The architecture being discussed here is one in which the design uses the facts to point primarily to the true. That is, it embodies knowledge about the adaptation of the true to the contingent, the general to the specific, the enduring to the transient, the principled to the circumstantial, the thing imitated to the copy. Similarly, it is one in which the true is embodied in the contingent, the general in the specific, the enduring in the transient, the principled in the circumstantial.

Those familiar with modernist ways of thinking will see that among other things, this proposition reverses the familiar order of things. Under modernism, the specific in the general leads to knowledge of style, the transient is found in what are taken to be enduring Platonizing abstractions of proportion and geometric purity, the contingent is governed by the true properties of materials to produce structural stability and perhaps even expression or the binding laws of economics to produce economically viable if not profitable buildings, while the principled is simply outside modernism's relativist concerns, which are in the conventional, the merely factual and, to the extent there is interest in history, the historical.

From the point of view of our interest in architecture and buildings, the thing we ought to wish to know about a building is the same thing we wish to know about anything else (an act, a law, a constitution, a poem, a snowman) people make: How does it serve the most important purpose, that of fulfilling the task that is unique to people, namely, perfecting their nature and pursuing the pleasures that are uniquely available to people as people. These things result from acts of volition and have the same kind of relationship between the typical and the particular as buildings do. They differ from one another because the constituent parts of both their typical and circumstantial contents are different, not because their purposes are different. To accomplish its purpose each example and each class of these things must satisfy the same three criteria as any other act of volition. It has to be adapted to its purpose. It has to aspire to timelessness, that is, to seek to last over time by lasting beyond the immediate circumstances that brought it into existence. And it has to do so with an appropriate grace.

These three criteria form the familiar Vitruvian trilogy of commodity, firmness and delight. To say that commodity, firmness and delight are something like current ideas about function, structure and beauty is to give only the most feeble suggestion of the vast gulf separating pre-Enlightenment understandings of architecture and the current ones. Commodity, for example, may now refer to the immediate utilitarian function to be served and need make no distinction between functions serving facilitating arrangements and those embodying ennobling institutions. In like manner, firmness refers to structural stability relative to the same criteria guiding judgements about commodity. Generally, that a building can stand currently provides adequate proof that it is firm, and the more cheaply it can be made to do so, the better. Firmness is not thought of as a necessary concomitant of beauty and complete and adequate bearer of beauty—if it were, there would be no separation between the task and method of the structural engineer and the architect. Similarly, beauty is purely arbitrary. It is taken to be a word that refers to what any person might find attractive and need not have any relationship to commodity or firmness, although it might if one likes.

In the approach outlined here, our interest goes beyond that of modernism, which is content with knowing what is. We want to know how things ought to be. To know that we must know the types which are the normative *exempla* imitated by particular buildings.

This knowledge is intellectual knowledge gained through experience. In our individual, personal experience our perception of things is prior to our knowledge of types, but in nature it is the reverse: types are prior to things. Our experience of things provides us with the material we need so that we may use our intellect to gain a knowledge of types. Once we have that knowledge, we have a knowledge of that which preceded nature's production of things. We also have a knowledge of that which is binding on us—that which we must acknowledge and conform to if we are to achieve the end we have in mind. If we do not, we either will not achieve our end, or we will satisfy a different, lesser end, or both.

As in our individual experience, so too in the accumulation of experience of a people living together in a political regime: The *is* (the factual, the historical) is in the individual, particular example of a building, an actual, physical, material entity which embodies opinions and conventions as well as the type. The *ought* (the true, the historic) is in what one comes to understand about the building. A particular example may be a persuasive model or even paradigmatic in its capacity to embody a particularly insightful opinion or high level of convention, but the most valuable, useful knowledge it contains is in its type. The types can be known only through reasoning about the data of the senses. They are atemporal and in nature where they have an existence that is like that of political wisdom and justice, the logic of morals undergirding just political activity, and the concinnity making it possible for buildings to be commodious, firm and beautiful.

The means of knowing the types precedes the means of making examples of the types; we must know before we can design and build. In other words, the means of engaging in the dialectic opening up knowledge of the types must precede the making of examples of the types (recall that knowledge of the types is impossible without examples). Because the complete knowledge of the types to which particular buildings aspire includes the opinions and conventions embodied in all buildings, it is knowledge of the origins of buildings and of buildings yet to be built. The types are coeval with nature, and so is the polity which is a construction in political form before it is an actuality in architectural form. The polity of former times as well as current ones is the most important source of the experience needed for engaging in this dialectic because only it includes the combination in political and architectural forms or the opinions and conventions needed for knowing the types.

This order of things is the reverse of the one to which the post-Enlightenment world has habituated us. Modernism's interest in the history of beginnings rather than of origins and in the is rather than the ought has led us to think of the city as a physical setting stocked with buildings where people come together to do what the buildings suggest they do or allow them to do. But modernism aside, the words people speak provide the basis for the knowledge about how people should live and hence what they should build. To build, therefore, requires the polity. Architecture serves politics.

This is in the nature of things. It is, after all, in the nature of people to form societies, to want to know and to exercise reason. But not all societies are the same, not all people know the same thing, and all conclusions of reason are neither the same nor necessarily true. There are, however, certain characteristics common to all societies and to all sources of information available through the senses to him who wants to know and to reason about what he perceives. Nature is the totality of those characteristics, and it is in the nature of people to want to know nature.

The polity is the instrument people use to inquire into nature in order to discover what is best for them. Among the things they find while searching into nature are buildings.[33] They discover that any particular building is an example of a type, a discovery that entails the distinction between types and examples and the recognition that the type exemplifies the true and the example embodies the circumstantial. This leads to the recognition that a building serves a political purpose and is therefore like an arrangement or an institution—an instrumental good and not an end in itself. To say it again: architecture serves politics when politics is the art of living well together. From this it follows that the political service buildings can render must be the dominant things in building.

Type

A building type is a generalized, unbuildable idea of a building containing within it all the possible examples of actual buildings of that type that have been and can be built. The types are discovered in nature which contains any number of other kinds of types including those embodied in the acts of men and the political forms of states.

The building types are not isomorphic with other types. The substance of the acts of men and of the political forms of states embody different kinds of material. Thus there is no one-to-one linkage between the various kinds of types discussed so far—the differentiation in political activities between institutions and arrangements, the organization of the various human activities into primary, religious, political and civic categories, or the schema of political forms running from monarchy through democracy. Nonetheless, the principles that organize the building types, activities and forms of states, as well as the combinations of material and types to be discussed later, will be compatible with one another because they all derive from the same nature which is the source of the very ideas of isomorphism and coherence.

A brief excursus at this point might prevent a possible misunderstanding of my meaning here.

In the currently orthodox historiography a particular political form entails a particular architectural form, and, conversely, a particular architectural form "symbolizes," "means" or in some other way embodies, points to, necessitates or requires a particular political form. This leads to the relativist claim that at times classical architecture is the architecture of centralized states and undemocratic regimes (e.g., Alexander, Augustus, Constantine, Julius II, Louis XIV and Hitler), at other times it is the architecture of the opposite pole of political organization (viz., Periclean Athens, Medicean Florence and the early Federalist period of the United States), and that either way, once the classical tradition atrophied and the modern period began, any use of classical architecture was anachronistic and therefore false. Classical architecture, in other words, is a style forming an indissoluble unity with the other cultural traits of a period including its political forms.

The evidence supporting these positions is the use of a similar formal vocabulary of classicism in the various states in which it appears. Such a use of that evidence proves nothing: architecture, whether called classical or anything else, is more than, and quite different from, a mere formal vocabulary through which the spirit of an age or even of a regime manifests itself. In addition, the selection of examples is arbitrary in that the same formal vocabulary of classicism was used by a variety of people operating very different regimes. And a direct linkage between an architectural form and political form is absurd. It suggests that a regime's buildings must be replaced or turned to different purposes when that regime is replaced and that the purpose and form of an institution must remain unchanged once it is provided with a proper building. These absurdities do permeate modernist thinking. It brought havoc to buildings during the French Revolution, and it occupies a key role in current preservation activities.

The problem with the modernist position is the directness of the linkage to both political forms and to historical moments. A building is the only and necessary embodiment of anything else produced at that moment and also carries forward a line of development that began in a historical past and is aimed at some historical future. What is must be. Here it is argued that a building imitates a type which is timeless. The type provides a symbol of the purpose which the building embodies, but the specific character of that symbol is provided by the conventions current at the time the building is designed. The particular building is a conventional sign within which is embedded the natural symbolism of the type. Signs point to particular meanings such as functions and the relative importance of similar things, while symbols embody the larger purposes that enliven the aspiration to live the good life of justice and nobility.[34]

The building types are classified according to the way they serve the political purposes of people in polities. A polity's institutions and arrangements are often the most important builders in it, so to know how a polity is constituted is to know who is likely to build. That inquiry will provide important historical information, but it will not be important historic knowledge useful to a person who wants to know what to build. To know that, he must know what the activities in a polity are and what purposes they serve. He then needs to know what building type serves which purpose and accommodates which activities. And he needs to know some important things about the types and conventions that actually operate when building. The first two points will be discussed here while the final one will be left for Chapter Six.

Experience with historical building and reflection about the historic within that experience as well as the knowledge available to us through our life in the present suggests that there are only six purposes for buildings, each with its own building type, and that all activities in all polities are accommodated by one or more of these types.

The enumeration comes directly from the analysis. A different understanding of the way political life is given conventional form in constitutions and a different interpretation of the activities that constitute political life would likely produce a different number and different understandings of each of them. The group identified here fits the analysis that has led to this point.

The types' identities are based on the four classes of activities found in the polity, but they do not simply equate a type to a class. Instead, they derive from the way in which people undertake the activities of the various classes and the way in which actual buildings can accommodate actual activities. None is necessarily superior to another; their relative status is determined by the constitution they serve. But each is based on a particular activity, so that each may be defined by a gerund describing the activity and a noun naming the type.

At one extreme are the types serving what are commonly called religious activities, although institutionalized religions are not the only fora for religious activities. Again, the place religious activities occupy in a city is established by the constitution. Essential for something to be called a religious activity is its capacity to allow the participant to acknowledge that there is something superior to himself which he cannot explain and whose hold he cannot resist. There may be any number of different activities calling for buildings, and it may be that they defined the earliest building types, but because we are interested here in the mature fruits of experience (origins) and not with the chain of inchoate changes that led to them (beginnings), we can move directly to the two religious purposes that define building types.

One purpose promotes veneration by allowing a person to be hushed and reverent in the presence of that which is superior to himself; venerating calls for a *tholus*.[35] The other is to celebrate that superiority with others; celebrating requires formal worship and calls for a *templum*.[36]

The religious uses of these types are clear enough—as for example in the *tholus* form for the tomb, baptistery and shrine and the *templum* form for fanes, houses of gods and basilical churches. Similarly, in a purely secular realm, when something is to be venerated, for example a political hero or the idea of union, a *tholus* is still the appropriate building type, as for example in the rotunda of the United States Capitol Building or at the Jefferson Memorial in Washington. Similarly, a *templum* can be found in a central greensward as occurs when graduates, faculty and honored guests process through it as at the Lawn at Thomas Jefferson's University of Virginia or when dedicated souls congregate for a special occasion at the

Lincoln Memorial or for the quadrennial inauguration occurring at the Capitol end of the great Mall in the capital.

At the opposite extreme from the religious types are those buildings that are most closely allied with primary activities. To dwell, to perpetuate the race in the household and to accommodate the extension of the household into the family—in short, activities whose purpose is to pursue domesticity—requires a *domus*.[37] To provide a place for making and trading things needed to sustain life, a purpose which, like that of practicing domesticity is necessary but is not the same thing as maintaining a domestic hearth, calls for a *taberna*.[38] (Growing things is a subordinate activity to trading them. Agriculture generally requires a place outside the polity and does not call for its own building type. Thus the *taberna* incorporates agricultural activities within its scope.)

Somewhere between the religious and the primary activities is the realm of political activities. Here there is an even looser fit between activities and architectural accommodation than in those of venerating, celebrating, dwelling or trading. This is as it must be: compared to those activities which remain relatively fixed in their form and thus provide a rather direct translation into building types, political activities require constant adaptation to the best, or the best possible, knowledge of circumstance. Political activity is the area in which men search for an accommodation between the *is* found in circumstances and the *ought* within the types. The three great divisions of political activity we are familiar with—legislating, administering and judging—have in common their dependence on confronting the disorder of unpredictable, time-bound, unique circumstances with the logic of morals found in the principles of justice. This commonality is not an activity but an aspiration on the one hand and a claim for authority on the other. The aspiration gives birth to a broad range of activities, as broad, indeed, as the variety of circumstances people confront and as varied as the knowledge of people who organize political activities into the conventional form of a constitution. The forms they are given in a constitution are too far removed from their sources in aspiration and authority to give themselves over to building types, and so the building types serving political activities do not represent the activities directly. Instead, they arise from the deepest and most fundamental purposes of those activities, one of which is that of providing a means of acting on the aspiration to live well by living politically, the other by providing a seat for the authority that binds the members of a polity.

One of the two building types serving political activity is the *theatrum*.[39] It acknowledges that one of the most important political purposes, indeed, the essence of politics, is aspiring to live the good life, a purpose that takes the form of joining with others in actively imagining things as being other than they are and predicating actions on the attempt to make them that way. Related to the *theatrum* is the *regia*,[40] the place where a governing, political authority resides, a place which in general is a residence of the person or body that governs. The *regia* need not be accompanied by a *theatrum*—note, for example, that in a monastery, the monks' residential complex complements a *templum*, not a *theatrum*. Similarly, any body claiming authority in the governing of affairs—no matter the affairs—will (may) use a *regia*. The *regia* is not necessarily domestic, that is, no one need live there, although someone will be known to reside there, even if only occasionally. Indeed, it stands at the opposite extreme from the *domus* in which those who are governed live. They live in *domus* because they lack the authoritative role of those who live in *regiae*. They may be slaves, serfs, aliens, or members of other classifications which are purely conventional designations that assume a category of citizenship where responsibility for them is lodged. The conventional category may have a base in a natural status, as is the case with children, the insane or the physically infirm. The only thing the resident of a *domus* may not be is a vagabond or other transient with no stake anywhere. A true, complete, unalloyed democracy would have no *domus* while at any one moment in a true, complete, unalloyed monarchy there would be only one *regia* in which one would find the monarch.

Two further comments are in order before moving on to the form these types take. One is that the names for the types have been introduced in Latin because the political theory in which they are embedded was first articulated in that language. Those terms sound rather clumsy in speech today, so for some their English equivalents or translations will perhaps serve better: *tholus* = tholos; *templum* = temple; *theatrum* = theater; *regia* = regia / regias; *domus* = dwelling (a word whose root has nothing to do with that of *domus*); and *taberna* = shop.

The other concerns the fourth class of activity, civic activities. These do not have activities requiring types. Civic activities serve the other activities in ways spelled out in the polity's formal constitution and traditions. Because they are subordinate to those activities, the religious, primary or political activity a civic activity serves will provide the type for the particular building to imitate. For example Jefferson established the University of Virginia as a place for training those who would govern and therefore included four of the six (or so) building types in its design. It uses the dwelling as the basis for residences for students who are to be governed by knowledge, accommodating them in the cells of the colonnades and ranges and incorporating part of the space in front for public access and including access, albeit not direct, to the private gardens between the colonnades and the ranges. His design locates the authority of professors in the regias of the ten dominating pavilions. Theaters are within the lower-floor rooms of the pavilions and Rotunda. And the tholus-library in the Rotunda where students could venerate the knowledge they sought caps the entire scheme. No temple was needed for the informal, independent life the students were to lead, although later the Lawn would be made into one on special occasions. Similarly, a University isolated from the marketing and manufacturing disrupting life in polities needed no shops.

The types exist in the realm of thought, not of matter or even of image. Nevertheless, a type and its example are connected, as is a thought and its material embodiment, and thus the thought and the image. The image is not the type but merely an aspect of it. The type's image is pregnant, however. It suggests what can come from the yet-to-be-born thing it can be taken to be. That embryo is found in the reflection flowing from experience with the examples, and thus contains within it something about the activities it serves and accommodates as well as the materials appropriate according to varying circumstances. In this sense it is a natural symbol of the political purpose it accommodates. In both the most simple and most complex way, then, the type's character is embodied in its plan diagram, and that plan diagram is about a purpose which is virtually a diagram of how actions achieve the purpose the building serves.

For each type there is a single plan diagram, two of them with three variations on the same form. They look like this:

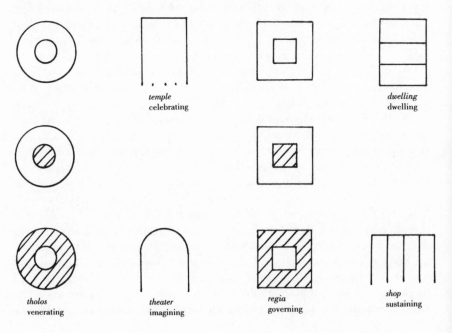

temple
celebrating

dwelling
dwelling

tholos
venerating

theater
imagining

regia
governing

shop
sustaining

The Normative Character of the Building Types

These plan diagrams are quite far from furnishing the plans for buildings but they provide the basic character of what the plan of the finished building must be if it is to serve its purpose. Similarly, the gerunds designating the various purposes—venerating, celebrating, aspiring, exercising authority, dwelling, trading—are too broad and general to provide direct assistance in understanding the functions a building must satisfy. To design and build requires a much more particular knowledge not only of uses or functions for the building but also of the particular means available for building. If it is to be valuable knowledge, this particular knowledge will address mere changing circumstances and fall into the trap of historicism if it is not disciplined by that which stands outside history, namely, the normative qualities of the types.

The types are normative relative to purpose, but, as anyone with the least experience with actual undertakings in the world in which we live knows, we must in practice accept a somewhat loose fit between the type and particular activities or uses. A parallel in politics is this: The purpose served by a particular activity is not always clear, and it is not always easy to find the proper activity to reach a particular purpose. If the purpose is to live in peace, is it better that the activity be that of practicing ongoing diplomacy or engaging in preemptive war? Because fitting the means to the end is the most difficult task of people engaged in political activity, prudence is the chief political virtue.

In the realm of architecture, while the building types suggest how certain purposes *ought* to be accommodated by a building, circumstances do not always allow it to *be* so. Consider this analogy: Children ought to be reared in families, but in some situations orphanages may serve that purpose. Similarly, the cella of a temple can be used as a theater, a governor's house can be used as a bazaar, and so on. Indeed, it is perhaps the case that such aberrant uses are more common than the proper ones, and investigating why they exist may provide one of the most telling interpretive tools for our understanding of architecture and the polity. Similarly, we receive a powerful suggestion about how or how not to design an actual orphanage, temple or governor's house when we consider what the normative fit is between purpose and type or purpose and activity.

It might be the case that in the normative world of nature each type ought to be used alone, but in practice, in the world we know and live within, there is often the justification for combining two or more into a composite. Indeed, some combinations are quite common, and quite revealing. It might be said that they reach the status of being conventional combinations. The most common kind of Italian Renaissance church combines the tholos and the temple. Some versions of Renaissance palaces in Rome commonly insert shops into the regia type. The United States Capitol building (and thereby the conventional state capitol building) is clearly a composite of a tholos flanked by two theaters with facades based on the fronts of temples, but to have mentioned facades is to have gone beyond the realm of building types.

The importance of knowing circumstances and conventions as well as types becomes apparent the moment we notice the departure from the norm to accommodate an actual situation and observe that many important buildings combine different types into a single design. These departures are responses to the various circumstances any particular building incorporates and are of two kinds. One is in the program or the uses and functions the building is to satisfy. These are usually known better by the patron than by the architect. The other is in the particular means of building (i.e., the art of *building* as opposed to the art of *designing*), a knowledge of specifically architectonic things that I will discuss in Chapter Six.

The final arbiter for patron, builder and architect is the political purpose the building is to serve. The standards that must be satisfied in so far as circumstance allows are embedded in the normative world of nature containing the typical forms for buildings, the acts of people and the political forms of states. Bringing activities and designs into congruence in the service of the political life must be the most important task of the designer. When designing, the first and most necessary question one asks must be, Which one or more of the six (or so) purposes is to be accommodated? From that question flows the entire process of designing and building.

On Particular Buildings

The most distinctive characteristic of any building's design is the plan diagram identifying the type of building it is. But an actual plan, much less a plan diagram, does not necessarily tell what a building's elevations and coverings or roofs will look like. The variety of possible relationships between a building's actual plan and its elevations and coverings are much more extensive than the variety existing in the connection between the plan diagram and the actual plan. These relationships and the extension of the plan diagram into an actual plan are governed by conventions which arise from experience with the art of building. These conventions themselves yield knowledge of types, this time architectonic ones, entailing certain normative standards. I will discuss those standards for *architectonic means* in Chapter Six. Here, where attention will be focussed on the relationship between plan diagrams and actual plans, material will be introduced which also applies to the plans' three-dimensional embodiment in buildings.

To move from plan diagram to actual plan requires knowledge that derives from the experience with the uses and functions of buildings and of the ways they are built in different circumstances. This is quite specific knowledge predicated on particular conditions that change with time, place and knowledge. They range from the way the various activities a constitution organizes are structured in various institutions and arrangements to the relative importance of architect, patron and public in designing, and from the relative wealth or poverty of a people to the extent to which the available technical skill is able to make the best use of available materials. Everywhere and every time, these conditions differ, but they are easily, or at least readily, available in the *regional tradition* builders follow as they produce buildings ranging from the most august monument to the most humble vernacular.[41] These buildings can be divided into various categories within a schema based on the six (or so) building types and the relative positions they occupy within the constitution they serve. The buildings within any particular category can be called versions where the term *version* refers to a conventional subdivision of a type that allows the type to be made useful by specifying the two important things about it—the first being the various functions entailed in the purpose and the best way of satisfying those functions in the circumstances of that region, and the second being the building practices used to give material embodiment to building types. Put briefly, versions embody the general characteristics of regional *uses* for buildings and the *means* of building them. Another word for regional traditions is style (the Tuscan style of Florence's Baptistery, San Miniato al Monte, and Leon Battista Alberti's facade of Santa Maria Novella; "commercial style" used to refer to Chicago's first tall commercial buildings when new) so long as the term is understood as a synonym for manner (*mos; maniera*) and not as an attribute of culture (e.g., early Renaissance style for Alberti's facade; the Chicago School style for the commercial buildings).

Converting a plan diagram into an actual plan requires knowing the uses intended for the building and the addition to the diagram of specific things which may be called *utilitarian components*. These components usually derive from traditional practice, although inventions occasionally provide something useful. A plan diagram expanded into an actual plan becomes identifiable as a particular functional type of the sort J.N.L. Durand presented. Some examples will be useful:

The several versions of temples may be differentiated by the way their plans arrange any or all of what tradition has supplied: stylobate (in Greek usage) or podium (in Latin), pronaos or portico, naos or cella, colonnade, apse, transept, crossing, chapel, sacristy, nave, aisles, narthex, vestibule and atrium. Among regia, the utilitarian components include, for the Italian palace version, the *androne* (entrance passage), *cortile* (open, interior court), loggia, chapel, greater and lesser halls, service rooms and stable, while the type's and version's adaptation to the uses of American commerce, as in Chicago's commercial-style buildings, draws from the same list while adding a cortile skylight and elevators.

Except when governed by modernism's impulse for originality, designers draw on particularly forceful examples which provide an especially clear knowledge of a version's conventional forms. These can be divided into two classes according to the proximity in time to the use by a designer and the degree of literalness with which they are used.

One of these is the *model*, or an example produced in relatively close proximity to the designer who draws on it and which, because it illustrates intelligent and useful solutions to concrete problems that are still prominent in the art of building, he can follow relatively literally. Models are rare and appear only under especially propitious circumstances, the most important of which are the following:

1) By the time construction is undertaken, previous practice must have made available a clear knowledge of the type. This requires a high level of articulation in theory or practice or both about the relationship between a people's purposes and their constitution's conventions on the one hand and the principles of architecture and the embodiment of political purposes in various versions of the building types on the other.

2) By the time the building is undertaken, current architectural practice must have made available a strong and clear conventional knowledge of the means of investing the type with a properly articulated design composed of properly designed components. A discussion of these architectonic means will be presented in Chapter Six.

3) The builder (i.e., the patron, not the architect) must have adequate wealth and time to build a large, well-finished structure on a prominent site, and the builder's status must warrant such a building.

4) The builder must have available an architect with the requisite knowledge, talent and skill.

Conditions seldom conspire to allow an example to reach the status of a model, although luckily all four conditions have occasionally been present.

The other class of model is comprised of *paradigmatic buildings* which are models that are more remote from the designer. That distance means that the conventions they use to convert the type into an actual building are so far from current practice it is difficult to use the building as a model. Yet for various reasons it is important that the building represent the nature of the type of building it is or even of the version it embodies, and thus very different architectonic means are used to build it.

Buildings become paradigmatic because they show how to solve recurring, unavoidable problems encountered whenever one moves from a purpose dictating a building type to the particular circumstances that call for a building to serve certain particular uses to be built at some particular moment. For example, as we will see in my next chapter, it is necessary that in a building, the plan and elevations must be congruent with one another. There is often but not always a great flexibility available in the way the elevations of a plan can be arranged and still be congruent with it, just as there is a flexibility available in the way a plan can be arranged and still be congruent. The least flexibility, or the greatest restraint, in these matters generally occurs with buildings at the very highest level of the hierarchy of buildings, that is, in the design of those buildings serving a constitution's most important institutions. When properly designed, they display a plan, elevations and coverings, and a relationship between plan and elevations and coverings, that are both right and which practice has made canonic within that version. It is, for example, possible to imagine widely different plans for the Parthenon and still have it identifiable as the Parthenon but it is more difficult to imagine a wider range of elevations. It is also possible to imagine a wide range of different uses for a building following the paradigm of the Roman Pantheon, but no matter what else it may carry with it, it is so clearly a tholos it will always evoke veneration.

Both model buildings and paradigmatic buildings embody a rightness in the relationship they illustrate. The difference between them is in the temporal and geographic reach each class has. Models affect a narrower range of versions than do paradigms. As a result, a paradigmatic building is a model of a very special status. For reasons that may have as much to do with non-architectonic aspects as architectonic ones, these rare buildings present an example of the integration of form and material that people accept as binding on subsequent practice. Again, the example of the Pantheon is instructive. It was a model for Bramante's tomb tholos at St Peter's, where the similarity of its meaning is clear, as well as for Andrea Palladio's Villa Rotonda, which, because it is generally considered to be a signorial dwelling, one would expect to be a regia but because it is clearly based on an example of a tholos a special explanation is required.[42] Greater differences between earlier and later examples are evident when the model is paradigmatic. A paradigmatic use is always less literal but the source is no less ambiguous. Examples of the Pantheon as paradigm are the rotunda under Thomas U. Walter's great dome in the United States Capitol Building, Jefferson's Rotunda at the University of Virginia, R.M. Hunt's Administration Building for the World's Columbian Exposition in Chicago

in 1893, and John Russell Pope's Jefferson Memorial in Washington or his
central space in the National Gallery.

Buildings based on paradigms are generally built for more august
purposes and are therefore more rare than buildings based on models.
Models generally initiate a string of examples that gradually accumulate
into a version which can be narrowly defined when its relationship to the
model is more literal (fifteenth century Florentine palaces; a Palladian villa)
or broadly defined (Renaissance palaces) when less so. The material most
commonly presented in the history of architecture is a sequence of models:
Alberti's 1456–72 facade for the Florentine church of Santa Maria Novella
as the first in a string lasting for centuries, Michelozzo's Palazzo Medici
from 1446 as *the* Florentine palace and San Gallo and Michelangelo's
Palazzo Farnese as its successor in Rome, the Palladian winged villa house
as seen at Palladio's villa Barbaro at Maser (c.1555–9), and Fr Mansart's
Maison (1635) as the epitypical French château. The string need not be
continuous. Note how at a greater distance of time and place the Palazzo
Farnese reappears in buildings as diverse as Sir Charles Barry's Reform
Club in London from 1837 and in the commercial and apartment buildings
filling the blocks in the Burnham and Bennett *Plan of Chicago* from 1909.
These buildings call to mind a canonic assemblage of motifs and elements
forming the facade and in perfect or at least studied concinnity (or
congruity) with the plan, although none is a copy of another. In the same
way that any particular building imitates a type, so too does it follow the
lineaments of a model, unless it succumbs to the modernist impulse to be
original.

This suggests an additional way to define versions, one that is compatible with the earlier one but with a different emphasis: a *version* is a
traditional and canonic but nonetheless conventional pattern or composition of actual plan, elevation and covering in which the three parts are
inseparable in some cases and separable in others.

Recapitulation

To recapitulate the points presented in this chapter: The activities a polity's
constitution organizes vary from being arrangements to institutions and
range across four classes. These activities can in turn be divided into the
six (or so) purposes that buildings serve. Each purpose has a corresponding building type with a characteristic plan diagram. The type embodies
the continuity between the present and the past. It is that which endures
because it is true. Because it is true, it exists outside the time marked by
history, and it has symbolic value—it symbolizes some particular political

purpose. Every building is an example of some one or more types which it imitates.

An actual building is an example of a type embodying the unique and never-before-known circumstances that come from the here and now. The plans of actual buildings are based on the types' plan diagrams, used singly or in combination and with the addition of various utilitarian components. The variations fall into general groupings called versions which embody conventions derived from the differing response to specific, unique circumstances. These conventions concern the way the type's general purposes are converted to specific functions (a building's uses) and the extension of a plan into a three-dimensional, material building (the architectonic means). Versions understood as styles or manners of building provide the most immediately available or most important source of knowledge concerning the conventions required under particular circumstances for imitating the type to produce particular examples of buildings. Buildings persuasive in ongoing practice are models, while those that find themselves embodied in more august buildings and in more diverse times are paradigms.

As an imitation of the type any particular building is a sign of some universal political purpose. As an example of a conventional version it tells a person specific things about a particular time and place. And as a material object—as a fact—it is an interpretation of the general and the specific made by some particular person or political body in a specific time and place.

FIVE

Athenian Assurance

Robert Jan van Pelt

There are a growing number of "histories" of individual towns, Greek and Roman, from the archaic age to the end of antiquity. With scarcely an exception, however, they lack a conceptual focus or scheme: everything known about the place under examination appears to have equal claim—architecture, religion and philosophy, trade and coinage, administration and international relations. The city *qua* city is flooded out. . . . But what questions do we wish to ask about the ancient city, whether they can be satisfactorily answered or not? That is the first thing to be clear about, before the evidence is collected, let alone be interrogated. If my evaluation of the current situation is a bleak one, that is not because I dislike the questions being asked but because I usually fail to discover any questions at all, other than the antiquarian ones—how big? how many? what monuments? how much trade? which products?

M.I. Finley, "The Ancient City," in *Economy and Society in Ancient Greece.*

Introduction

The Cambridge classicist Sir Moses Finley (1912–86) was undoubtedly one of this century's most important and perceptive students of ancient Greek society. Therefore his censure of the traditional descriptive and positivistic histories of ancient cities carries weight. It provoked the following essay about the urban form of democratic Athens. And it gives it a measure of justification: after all, whatever its flaws, my reconstruction of classical Athens derives from an unequivocal question. "Might classical Athens

bequeath to us a normative understanding of the purpose of architecture?"
This problem gives structure to the following examination. It has, so I hope,
guided me around the historicist and relativist labyrinth created by an
attitude to scholarship that has continued to transform the city that
twenty-five centuries ago opened our intellectual horizon into what the late
Sir Moses aptly labeled as an intellectual cul-de-sac.[1] My answer derives
from the proposition (discussed in Chapter Three) that the development of
Athens's architectural and urban form in the three centuries after Solon's
constitutional reform marked an axial period in the history of architecture.
In this chapter I will show why classical Athens may be judged as a
complete city, a nexus of stone and people that fulfilled the idea of the city
as a bulwark of stability within a torrent of change. And I will begin with an
examination of how the Athenian answer to the great question of life and
death, time and eternity, change and meaning still has normative
significance for an understanding of the task of the architect in the
twentieth century. Focus will be the manifestation of six architectural types
in the historical cityscape of ancient Athens.

The Fivesquare City

Athens' architectural and urban form fulfilled the idea of the city. This
idea had been developed over the twenty-five or so centuries that separate
the building of cities such as Gilgamesh's Uruk (or Lagash, Ur, Nippur or
Akkad) from Pericles' completion of the Athenian Acropolis. The ideology
of these early cities was expressed in the symbolic image of a geometric
square divided by two streets (the *cardo* and the *decamanus* as the Romans
labeled them) into four smaller squares. The square was symbolic of city's
ramparts, which separated the city from the countryside and which
proclaimed to those who desired entrance to the city the importance and
might of its inhabitants, of its king and, most importantly, of its gods.
Elaborate gateways gave access to the city where mortals and immortals
cohabited in a not always easy union of interests. The neighborhoods of the
people surrounded the temple of the gods, the ultimate crossroads of all the
winding alleys that made up the early city's streetscape.[2] Some cities had
one gate, and other cities a multitude of entrances. In some cities the
sacred precinct occupied the center of the built-up area, in other cities the
temple was part of the rampart. Some cities were round, some were oval,
some were irregular and others were quadrilateral. Be that as it may, all of
these archaic cities could be symbolically represented by the twice-divided
square. It indicated, as James Dougherty explained, that "the devotee who
enters its gates approaches 'the center of the world,' sometimes a miniature

of the cosmos laid out in a quadratic geometry emphasizing the points of the compass and usually having a fifth point, the center, a shrine or tower where the union of earth and heaven, man and god, is ritually consummated."[3] This image of heaven and earth, god and man, traditionally has been interpreted as a quincunx (four points forming a square, with a fifth point in the middle) or fivesquare (four squares that center on a point, the "pivot of the four quarters," as Paul Wheatley styled it).[4] What is important here is that in the archaic period the center was simultaneously occupied (by the immortals) and forbidden (to mortals). It was the *templum*, the precinct of the gods. There the vertical of the transcendent cut the horizontal of the immanent, leaving a mark or fissure contained by the temple.

In the axial period there was a shift in the interpretation of the diagram of the quincunx or fivesquare. With the transformation of the myth into discourse people began to look more critically at the idea of the center with its cosmological claims and associations. In Chapter Three we saw Jeremiah's criticism of the temple, and the spiritualization of the topos until it had lost all presence within the physical space of the city. The Book of Revelation expressed the new attitude quite well with its vision of a messianic Jerusalem, perfectly square and without a sanctuary.[5] The city's center as a sacred cosmic axis, barred to ordinary mortals, became irrelevant. Therefore the symbolical image of the city was given a new depth and meaning. The quincunx became now literally a fivesquare, consisting of four smaller, identical squares arranged in such a pattern that a fifth one appeared, which surrounded the four smaller ones. In this new configuration the periphery took the place of the center, the horizon overcame the notion of place, a sense of destiny triumphed over a foreboding of fate, the idea of empire surmounted the palace and a knowledge of history wrested itself from the embrace of nature. And as the centripetal emphasis had been transformed into centrifugal concern, so the old cosmological axis where heaven, earth and underworld met within a precinct controlled by king and priests became a metaphor available to all. I will show in the following pages that the urban and political form of classical Athens was a large square, which physically embraced four districts, which in turn were dramatically recapitulated in another realm that transformed the common boundary into a common horizon.[6]

The Emporium

The first square, which enclosed all the others, is the most problematical. As a figure of separation, it seems to allude to the walls that set the city apart from the countryside. In the cities that were erected before the axial period the walls were indeed understood as boundaries, which divided an abiding realm of order, owned, ruled and protected by the immortal gods who occupied their temples in the city's center, from the chaotic and changeable world of nature. Those who dwelt within the city walls could hope to share the immortality of the gods; those outside were delivered up to the cycles of birth and death.[7] Within the city walls there was the promise of destiny, and therefore the experience of history. Outside the walls was only fate, and the cycles of time. Within the city people obeyed laws; outside they responded to fortune. This did not mean that all the territory outside the walls was irrelevant. As we will see below, parts of it belonged *de iure* to the city. Nevertheless, the popular notion of what constituted a city was centripetal: it converged on the visual might of the walls to concentrate on the sumptuousness of the city's shrine. A good example is to be found on the first tablet of the Gilgamesh epic. The description moves from Uruk's outer wall "whose brightness is like copper" via praise of the inner wall "which none can equal" to a glorification of the shrine of Ishtar "which no later king, no man, can equal."[8]

In the axial period the understanding of the city's boundaries changed from a separation from the countryside to the notion of a bridge to the territory outside the city. The *civitas* ceased to be identical with the *urbs*, and began to encompass all the land under its effective control. As François de Polignac has shown in his seminal *La naissance de la cité grecque* (1984), the creation of sanctuaries at the edge of a particular city's sphere of influence created the conditions within the thus bounded land that allowed for the civic and political integration of city and countryside, of city-dwellers and farmers, of urban civilization and peasant culture.[9] Thus the *demos*, the "people," emerged from the conciliation between the until then opposite realms. The centripetal movement towards the city-center was replaced by a dialectic between center and periphery, which acknowledged the reality of relationship between city and countryside.

This bond was, in the first instance, simply physical: a city needs a steady supply of food and cannot produce it. The city is a parasite. Not everyone will agree with Jacques Ellul's judgement that the city is "like a vampire" that preys "on the true living creation" and that gives nothing in exchange for all the food and people it consumes because "what the city can produce for the country is absurd and ridiculous compared with what she receives." But there is undoubtedly some validity to his observation that the city's spiritual worth, "her ferment of ideas will be of use nowhere but in the city. . . . The very character of the city, in the economic field or the intellectual, artistic, or humanitarian, is to receive from the outside, to consume, and to produce things without value or meaning, usable only inside the city and to her gain."[10] It is true that the city cannot live without the countryside, and the political recognition of that fact in Solon's unification of the inhabitants of Athens and Attica into one *demos* or people (around 590 BCE) and the subsequent strengthening of the relationship between the rural *trittyes* (literally "thirds" of the ten "tribes" or constituencies set up in 508 BCE) and the political life of the city under Peisistratos and Kleisthenes, created the condition for the polis as a viable existential proposition. The splendor of the Acropolis helps us forget that the Athenian polis was, in the days of its greatness, a basically rural community. As Chester G. Starr concluded, "by 500 the solid backbone of the citizenry of most Greek *poleis* [cities] consisted of small and medium farmers who cultivated their *kleroi* [the land sufficient to support a family] in ancestral fashion, but were intimately connected to the urban centers, where they existed, and to the religious and political machinery of the state."[11] Farmers filled the Athenian assembly; farmers filled the ranks of the Athenian army.

This had been different from the situation before Solon's reform. Solon's biographer W.J. Woodhouse ascertained that in the closing years of the seventh century Attica's agricultural population was "groaning in hopeless poverty, ground down by heartless oppression and exploitation, and goaded to the verge of overt revolution."[12] Solon's economic and social legislation transformed a destitute rural population into the solid core of a citizenry that would, in time, save Athens during the Persian invasions and provide the economic basis for its rebuilding under Pericles. The subsequent political development of Athenian democracy was "in no sense a willed or foreseen development, but was in reality a by-product of Solon's reforms and regulations."[13] Whatever one's understanding may be of the nature of politics, all will agree with Solon that an empty stomach or a diseased or ill-housed body do not encourage people to take responsibility for a political community that is so obviously incapable of protecting its citizens from hunger and deprivation. Such a breakdown commonly occurs when the relationship between city and countryside is disturbed. This is illustrated by events that occurred during the first two years of the Peloponnesian War (431–404 BCE).

In response to the Spartans' and their allies' preparations to invade Attica (431 BCE), Pericles advised the rural population to evacuate the land and retreat into the city. His strategy depended on the strength of the navy, the core of the Athenian empire and the umbilical cord that connected the city to its sources of supply. Pericles' policy was based on the experience of 480 BCE, when the army's defeat at Thermopylae had been overcome by the navy's victory at Salamis. The legendary proportions of the latter battle had initiated the fateful transformation of Athens from a city rooted in its countryside to one that relied on an infrastructure of international trade and financing. The architect of this ultimately ill-starred policy was Themistocles. A shrewd military commander without much empathy for the countryside and its ancestral customs, Themistocles had turned the city to the sea. Plutarch recalled that he developed "the Piraeus as a port, for he had already taken note of the natural advantages of its harbors and it was his ambition to unite the whole city to the sea."

> In this he was to some extent reversing the policy of the ancient kings of Attica, for they are said to have aimed at drawing the citizens away from the sea and accustoming them to live not by seafaring but by tilling and planting the soil. It was they who had spread the legend about Athena, how when she and Poseidon were contesting the possession of the country, she produced the sacred olive tree of the Acropolis before the judges and so won the verdict. Themistocles, however, did not, as Aristophanes the comic poet puts it, "knead the Piraeus to the city": on the contrary, he attached the city to the Piraeus and made the land dependent on the sea.[14]

The Piraeus, laid out on the basis of a gridiron scheme and connected to Athens by the famous long walls, became the central business district of Athens. It centered on the Emporion, an economic zone that ran along the harbour, and that was separated from the rest of the Piraeus by a set of boundary stones. Within this perimeter all the goods imported by ship were stored, taxed, displayed and sold. Within the emporium citizen and foreigner, Greek and non-Greek were equal. The law of the emporium was the rule of money.[15]

The arrangement was highly innovative on an economic and symbolic level (for example, the walls that in the pre-axial period used to separate the city from the countryside now quite literally connected the city to its source of supply: the Piraeus). The new departure in urban form suggested a novel strategy in time of war: as the city theoretically could survive as long as the Athenian fleet controlled the seas, it seemed logical to withdraw the population within the Athenian–Piraean citadel, which as Themistocles had argued, "could be perfectly well defended by a few troops of inferior quality, so that the rest would be able to serve in the navy."[16] The Athenian fleet was meant to force the enemy for a decisive engagement à la Salamis.

At the outbreak of the Peloponnesian War this strategy, conceived shortly after the Persian War, led to Pericles' decision to evacuate the rural population to the Athenian–Piraean stronghold. Thucydides recorded that "the Athenians took the advice he gave them and brought in from the country their wives and children and all their household goods, taking down even the wood-work on the houses themselves. Their sheep and cattle they sent across to Euboea and the islands off the coast. But the move was a difficult experience for them, since most of them had been always used to living in the ·country. . . . It was sadly and reluctantly that they now abandoned their homes and the temples time-honored from their patriotic past, that they prepared to change their whole way of life, leaving behind them what every man regarded as his own city."[17] When they arrived in the Athenian-Piraean citadel they found a city with full stores and a full treasury, but also a city that had insufficient accommodation. Whatever open areas were left within the walled area were quickly occupied, and people even settled in temples, and in the towers along the walls and "wherever they could find space to live in."

The overcrowded city became a biological time-bomb. Within a year the plague broke out. Thucydides noted that the displaced persons were especially hit as "there were no houses for them, and, living as they did during the hot season in badly ventilated huts, they died like flies. The bodies of the dying were heaped one on top of the other, and half-dead creatures could be seen staggering about in the streets or flocking around the fountains in their desire for water. The temples in which they took up their quarters were full of the dead bodies of people who had died inside them. For the catastrophe was so overwhelming that men, not knowing what would happen next to them, became indifferent to every rule of religion or law." Within the overcrowded city, civic resolve began to weaken. The first signs of anarchy occurred at funerals. Thucydides surmised that the multiplication of deaths in individual families exhausted the financial resources of many. People could not afford to bury their dead anymore, and "they would arrive first at a funeral pyre that had been made by others, put their own dead upon it and set it alight; or, finding another pyre burning, they would throw the corpse that they were carrying on top of the other and go away." This was only the beginning: the anarchy that manifested itself in the disposal of the dead also began to affect the posture of the living. Those who could afford to do so began to indulge in whatever pleasure was still available. "As for what is called honor, no one showed himself willing to abide by its laws, so doubtful was it whether one would survive to enjoy the name for it. It was generally agreed that what was both honorable and valuable was the pleasure of the moment and everything that might conceivably contribute to that pleasure."[18]

Thucydides' description of the civic disintegration of the besieged city depicted what will happen if the delicate relationship between the productive and purgative expanse of the countryside and the consuming and pestiferous body of the city is ruptured. It showed that the cunning of men like Themistocles or Pericles, who believed that a strongly fortified harbor, a powerful fleet and large warehouses could compensate for the loss of direct contact with the countryside, did not measure up to the wisdom of Solon. Nor did it match the insight of the Sumerian kings who built the first cities, twenty-five centuries earlier. These early cities consisted of three interrelated parts: the first was the city proper (*uru*), the walled area with its temple, palace and houses. Then there was the port of trade (*kar*), the place of commercial activity and a center of river and / or overland trade. In this section of the city foreign traders worked and lived under a special dispensation. Finally there was the outer city (*urubarra*), a large stretch of irrigated land that surrounded the walled city and the commercial district. The outer city, with its farms, fields, cattle folds and gardens supplied the two other parts of the city with food and raw materials.[19] All of these three constituent parts were essential to the city. Nevertheless this unity was never adequately embodied in the city's architecture or urban form. The economic aspect of the emporium has always overshadowed its existential significance, and its prosaic if not commonplace character has tended to obscure its symbolic importance. The very irregularity of the economic process has allowed the spontaneously created marketplace—the vagabond forum of goods—to elude the organizing grasp of tax-collectors, statesmen and architectural historians alike. Therefore the marketstalls tend to be lost in the information that describes the gross national product, the policy decisions of empire builders and the surveys of the history of urban form. Only the large emporia, set up as part of well-defined imperialistic policies, have been absorbed into strategical thinking, be it that of Pericles or of Stalin.

In a very pragmatic sense the emporium constitutes the first architectural type. Without it there can be no city, there can be no politics, there can be no civilization and there can be no history. The shop, the booth, the stall, the newsstand, the bazaar, the professional office, the railway terminal, the airport or any other manifestation of Westfall's *taberna* converge on the idea of a place of exchange or emporium as the urban type that replaced the city wall in the axial period. The emporium makes that which is produced elsewhere (food, tools, information, knowledge, people) available to the inhabitants to the city. It connects and separates the city from its sources of supply, be it the fields of the farmer, the factories or the world at large. Neither the farm nor the factory, nor the roads, water-, rail- or airways belong to the city. The place of exchange does, and it offers the farm, the factory and the transportation network an urban "facade." Yet it is no more than a facade. The ideological, political and architectural unauthoritativeness of the shop is evident to all. No city can be without its shops and warehouses, but emporia are not enough to make a city. Auden realized this when he wrote that a city which centers on a mall or business district will never be boring, but, also, that it won't quite do. For an agglomeration of houses will only be a city when it knows the meaning of *if*.

When in 431 BCE Pericles surveyed the city of Athens he saw well-defended walls, full warehouses and the most powerful fleet in Greece. From the logistical point of view there was no *if*, or so it seemed at the time. A year later he, too, learned that it didn't quite do. It was a lesson that brought the historical Athens down, and allowed Thucydides to erect another, historic Athens. As a place where people assign values to things the emporium is unable to acquire value itself. Thus it is unable to validate a settlement as a city.

The City as Second Nature

The polis was not built on the separation between nature and artifice, or the countryside and the walled town. Its basis was the distinction between the private and the public, the household and the *civitas*.[20] This differentiation of the polis into two radically separate domains, marked not by a city gate, but by the threshold of any dwelling, articulated and clarified the relationship of an individual's personal affairs to his civic responsibility and the manifold concerns of the community. The reduction of the city into two distinct realms reflected the general development of Greek thinking, which sought to grasp the world through the identification of the basic oppositions that give it its form. Setting off chaos from cosmos, the transient from the eternal, the artificial from the natural, convention from nature, myth from philosophy, opinion from knowledge, matter from form, space from place, the Barbarians from the Greeks, the tyrannical from the political and human impulse from ethics, the Greeks were able to reduce complex issues to simple choices that could be understood by all who belonged to the *demos*, the people. This made it possible to entrust ordinary people with political responsibility. Westfall's approach follows the Greek precept: proceeding from the simple distinctions offered in his contribution to this book he hopes to make it possible, again, to entrust ordinary people with the task of making buildings.

The fivesquare city embodied and expressed the twofold structure of the polis. These five squares manifested themselves symbolically in five architectural types. Only one of these types, the place of exchange, did not articulate the distinction between the public world of the polis and the private world of the household. It served the private needs of the public at large, bringing questions concerned with housekeeping into the physical and, to a certain extent, political realm of the public domain. In Hannah Arendt's terms, it belonged to the social domain.[21] (On the basis of the difference between the civic ambiguity of the place of exchange and the politically intelligible character of the other types I originally assumed that the emporium was not an architectural type, but that it was a sub-category of another type, the house. Subsequent reflections on the relationship between the countryside and the city, summarized above, affected my initial assessment of the place of exchange.) Four of the five types contributed to the creation of an urban environment that allowed people to live what Westfall labels "the political life," or, as John Dunne called it, to "satisfy one's desire to live."[22] These types are related but not necessarily identical to Westfall's dwelling, tholos, temple and regia (see Chapter Four). In the following sections I will explore each of them, not as they embody some aspect of a theoretical understanding of the political life, but as they structured the actuality of classical Athens.

The House

Only one of these types, the dwelling or house, embodied exclusively the idea of the private realm. The house was the location of the household and, as such, the domain where the people labored in order to manage the necessities of life. The equality of the polis (that is: of all the male citizens) stopped at the threshold of the house. Inside, the *paterfamilias* ruled with absolute authority. The house was his property. As Hannah Arendt explained, "property meant no more or less than to have one's location in a particular part of the world and therefore to belong to the body politic, that is, to be the head of one of the families which together constituted the public realm. . . . To own property meant here to be master over one's own necessities of life and therefore potentially to be a free person, free to transcend his own life and enter the world all have in common."[23] The size of the house was irrelevant: it could be one room, or it could be relatively large (but it should not appear too large, as it would otherwise assume a "public" character). What did matter was that it offered the owner a physical foundation for a sense of dignity and self-respect. In providing a foundation of the public realm the house related to the place of exchange: if the latter supported the body, the former nourished the mind.

We have seen how the Athenian polis was a largely agricultural community until the Peloponnesian War. Most of the citizens were farmers and, therefore, the majority of the dwellings were farms. When Solon was elected archon in 594 BCE, he was faced with a catastrophal social situation in Attica. In the seventh century farmers had become increasingly indebted to wealthier families. In order to feed their families they had been forced to mortgage their farms and their person, and everywhere markers or *horoi* indicated the mortgaged status of the land. Most farmers had become *de facto* tenants on their own farms. If the farmer failed to pay the annual installment, he became a serf or, in the worst case, a slave. The land fell to the lender. A sequence of bad harvests at the end of the century had brought serfdom and slavery to many, and many farms had fallen to the lenders. Solon realized that, if Athens were to have any future, he had to rescue the rural population and restore its freedom and self-respect.

Solon's legislation, which unified the city and the countryside and which was to bring the rule of law all over the polis, began with the passing of the *seisachtheia,* the "shaking off of burdens" or the redemption of the land and the people. All debts were cancelled, and it became illegal to obtain loans with oneself and one's family as security. W.J. Woodhouse judged this legal protection of one's personal freedom, which denied an individual the liberty to offer his own body as security of a loan, to be the decisive element of Solon's reform. "In this decree was enshrined the true palladion of Attic liberties, and very rightly does Aristotle with forcible simplicity set it in the forefront of what he says by way of summary of Solon's great work."[24] The *seisachtheia* also worked retroactively: those who had been reduced to serfdom in the past or sold into slavery were set free. Even those who had been sold abroad were traced and redeemed. Solon proudly claimed that "many brought I back to their God-built birthplace, many that had been sold, some justly, some unjustly, and others that had been exiled through urgent penury, men that no longer spoke the Attic speech because they had wandered so far and wide; and those that suffered shameful servitude at home, trembling before the whims of their owners, these made I free men. By fitting close together right and might I made these things prevail, and accomplished them even as I said I would."[25] All could return home, and begin a new life of freedom and dignity. The signs of servitude, the *horoi* that had marked the mortgaged fields and the ruined households, were removed. As Solon superbly stated, "right good witness shall I have in the court of Time, to wit the Great Mother of the Olympian Gods, dark earth, whose so many fixed landmarks I once removed, and have made her free that was once a slave."[26] The boundary line that enclosed one's property, the *nomos,* was from now on to be sacred. Without this protection of a citizen's place in the world there could be no guarantee of justice. The only markers that the city imposed as a collective on the land were to be the sanctuaries at the edge of the political realm of the polis and, in the center of the polis, the *horoi* that separated the political meeting places from the neighborhoods.

The most important element of the house was, as can be inferred from Solon's legislation, the threshold that separated the private realm within from the political domain without. It was also important that the house did not display the wealth of the owner, which means that it did not distinguish itself architecturally from the other houses in the city. One visitor to Athens rated the majority of the houses as undistinguished, if not poor. "If strangers were to come upon it suddenly, they would scarcely believe that this is the talked-of city of the Athenians."[27] These strangers would not have understood that the poor aspect of the houses was the very foundation of the city's greatness. Only thus could the citizens act like *isoi*, equals, and only thus could the political life be structured by the law of *isonomia*, the equal participation of all citizens, rich and poor, in the act of decision.

The idea of the home, embodied in the type of the house, established a person's autonomy and, therefore, his responsibility. It defined a person's place in the world. The depth of the resentment of those who Pericles forced to evacuate their lands in 431 BCE now becomes clear. The abandonment of their properties affected the legitimacy of their citizenship. The Christians were to solve the dilemma differently from Solon. In their faith the Domus Dei (the Church) offered a home to all citizens of the Civitas Dei (the people of God), and thus gave the destitute and the homeless a basis for dignity. No one was a slave in the house of God since it offered a place for all. The church's spiritual answer to the dilemma Solon had addressed became the foundation of the modern ideology of property. If for the church a person's property had its source in a baptized soul, in the modern age it became one's possession of one's own body, or one's "labor-power."[28]

The modern substitution of the body (or the mind) for the house is, in an odd way, appropriate. I already mentioned in passing that the city emerged as an answer to overcome the "problem of death." As John Dunne and Robert Lifton have argued, a consciousness of one's own mortality is the foundation of the city and urban civilization. The former explained how we create cities not because we hope to escape death, but because we wish, notwithstanding death, to satisfy our desire for life. He showed how each urban civilization offered a different answer, yet that all provided some kind of "symbolic immortality," some sense that our lives have meaning despite the certainty of death. Lifton explained that we affirm life in the face of death through the construction of cities: "the human problems of mastering death anxiety and achieving a sense of immortality are tasks that individuals cannot accomplish alone. These are issues at the common boundary of the individual life project and the collective historical project."[29]

I will return to the issue of symbolic immortality in the next section. What is important here is the idea that the problem of death is located "at the common boundary" of the house and the polis. Though the polis gives the answer, the house is the place where the question germinates. When the Greeks separated the public from the private realms, they did so partly to preserve the house as the place where death could be sovereign, a place where each human being could die her death and, therefore, live his own life. Without such a place where one might face the ultimate questions, there could be no freedom, no autonomy, no responsibility and, therefore, no citizenship. The Greeks realized that a consciousness of one's own mortality created a secure boundary around the house. The house thus became a private holy place that offered the space in which the dialectics of living and dying, and birth and death, were resolved. It was only with the resolution of these issues that the civic conciliation of individual mortality and collective immortality was possible.

The Typology of the Public Realm or the Second Nature of Tomb, Temple and Stoa

The threshold that leads to the hearth within the house also offers an entrance to the gathering places of the polis. It is in these places that the citizens might begin to overcome their own finitude as mortals. It is there that they enter history. Neither the place of exchange nor the house really belong to the history of architecture, or its foundation, the history of the city. That history, understood as *Stadtgeschichte* (and not *Stadthistorie*) may be summarized as the history of the various ways in which the city has structured and architecturally embodied its public realm as a forum where individuals assemble and act in order to gain, retain or regain what Lifton identified as a collective sense of immortality.[30] That forum is public, and therefore deserves to be remembered and recorded. In the archaic cities this forum was the temple precinct that allowed mortal people to consort with the immortal gods. In the medieval cities it was the cathedral and the market, the places where people participated in the Kingdom of God and where, through an application of their God-given skills and knowledge, manifested the plenitude of God's creative powers. And in our age the forum exists in the gatherings of those who decide to resist the totalitarian claims of the metropolis.

In classical Greece the forum that allowed the citizens to overcome their mortality comprised three places: the cemetery, the acropolis and the agora. Each of these political places was characterized by its distinctive type: the cemetery by the stela, the acropolis by the shrine and the agora by the portico or stoa. As I will discuss below, the stela or a grave marker equals Westfall's tholos, my shrine his temple and the stoa relates to his regia. Amid the haphazardly scattered shops and houses these types helped to define the places where people met their ancestors who made the city into what it had become (stela), their gods who guaranteed its future (shrine), and other citizens of their city (stoa). All these fora embodied areas of concern that are (or ought to be) free from the troubles of daily life. Taken together, the gravestone in the cemetery, the temples on the acropolis and the stoas around the agora demarcated the political domain where citizens could pursue meaning or "symbolic immortality." In the private realm each person confronted his own mortality and the problem of survival every day, in the public realm he could reach beyond his individual mortality through immortal deeds. Hannah Arendt interpreted these spaces as the "space of appearance," the place where people emerge from the discretion of the house into the public. There they might find greatness and immortality. "The task and potential greatness of mortals lie in their ability to produce things—works and deeds and words—which would deserve to be and, at least to a degree, are at home in everlasting-ness, so that through them mortals could find their place in a cosmos where everything is immortal except themselves."[31] Those who had a house could acquire a place in the city through action in the midst of the assembled company of fellow citizens. The public nature of these deeds ensured that non-perishable traces of those acts would be preserved in the memory of those who were witnesses to these acts. The presence of the others sug-gested that those acts would also be remembered by the following genera-tions as being part of the enduring order of the city. The public realm was the place where people could act and where the memory of those who had deceased was preserved. Thus the inhabitants of the city knew that as citizens they could gain public immortality, their individual mortality notwithstanding. The public realm was a two-way street: the citizens could attain immortality within the context of the city and the city as a community acquired a place within the enduring order of things.

This was the official ideology of the Athenian polis. As we have seen in the Chapter Three, the reward of an enduring place within an eternal order was not always so self-evident as Hannah Arendt would like us to believe. First of all the axiom of a stable order; Thucydides' archeology of the city, recorded in the First Book of his *History of the Peloponnesian War*, revealed that if such a cosmic order existed it was difficult to perceive it within a world of constant movement. This was obviously a problem, because the foundation of the Greek polis was not divination on the basis of oracles, dreams and omens, but direct observation. As in Homer's *Iliad*, "blind-ness" predominates as the root of disaster, only in Thucydides' history the blindness is not caused by the gods, but by an unwarranted trust in the power of vision. Pericles himself fell victim to the luster and aura of the rhetorical image of Athens that he presented in his own orations. As Thucydides showed, civic affirmation led to governmental assertion, and governmental assertion to imperial presumption. At that point Pericles ceased to distinguish between authority and power, and began to justify the disastrous policy to evacuate the countryside as a prudent move because Athenian sea-power was far more important than the continued occupation of the land. "This [naval] power of yours is something in an altogether different category from all the advantages of houses or of cultivated land," he argued to the Athenians in a speech in which he tried to defend his policy of evacuation. "You may think that when you lose [your houses and land] you have suffered a great loss, but in fact you should not take things so hardly; you should weigh them in the balance with the real source of your power [the navy] and see that, in comparison, they are no more to be valued than gardens and other elegances that go with wealth."[32] Thucydides explicitly juxtaposed the idea that the polis would be anywhere where its citizens (or its ships) happen to be to the attachment to a house: only blindness could lead a politician to assign a practical significance to what ought to have remained a pious abstraction. This inversion of values was made within the context of a speech contrasting the virtues of action against the vice of apathy. But, as we have seen in Chapter Three, Thucydides' history of Athens revealed that a philosophy of action tended to interpret prudence as languor, leading to brazenness and impudence. From the perspective of twentieth-century political science, which demands a system of checks and balances, the Athenian constitution as it was reflected in Athenian policy was indeed relatively unsophisticated: the institution charged with the protection of the constitution, the Areopagus, proved itself surmountable by the radical mob, and its effective demise as supreme moderator of the political life in 458 BCE opened the way to an ultimately self-destructive policy of unrestrained imperialism. For all its inherent fragility and its consequent failing, the Athenian constitution did have one great virtue: it was set within a general understanding of the condition of the political life that made (and still makes) sense and that was (and still is) superbly open to architectural articulation. It is within this qualified context that the urban arrangement of Athens's public space discloses the universal within the contingent.

There are many ways one might interpret the threefold division of Athens's public space. Here I would like to reflect on their significance as a matrix of the unfolding of civic time, which is the temporal structure of the political life. Time is to the city what space is to the settlement. We build settlements in space and constitute cities in time. We build settlements in order to render a smaller or larger bit of space into a place where we can find shelter, and we make cities in order to overcome our own temporality. All settlements that deserve to be called cities share this essential purpose, yet until the axial period the temporal problem was given spatial articulation and spatial definition. To live in communion with the immortal gods meant to overcome death in at least a symbolic fashion. Thus the nature of citizenship was located in the actuality of one's residence within the temenos that centered on the temple and which was bounded by the city walls. As I discussed in Chapter Three, a prophet like Jeremiah had criticized such an interpretation of the city's nature, and he had begun to reinterpret Jerusalem in temporal terms: it was still a city (and not a mere settlement) because of the covenant that formulated the Hebrew destiny in metahistorical terms. Thanks to their understanding of the polis as being located primarily in its people, the Greeks reached such an intellectual distance to the actual place of the city that they became able to reinterpret the three most important districts of the public domain in temporal terms.

The citizens' present, future and past acts made up the city's public realm. This translated into a threefold public time, which comprised the time of the living, the time of the city and the time of the dead.[33] The time of the dead was the immutable past. It was a paradigm for the time of the living, the present. The dynamism of the present together with the immutability of the exemplary past were the foundations of the time of the city, which was its enduring greatness, the future of eternity. The immutable past, the dynamic present and the enduring future were embodied in three special places: the cemetery was the place where the dead were venerated, and through them the immutable past; the agora was the place where the citizens acted and governed and the acropolis was where the enduring greatness of the city was celebrated.

The Stela

We have seen how the place of exchange is an important but essentially "private" point of transfer between the city and the countryside. The stela or marker on the grave is (or, better, ought to be) its public counterpart. In classical Athens it was the place where the citizen returned into the order of nature, and where his actions, undertaken for the city, were subsumed into an immutable past.[34] The Athenian necropolis was the physical boundary between the city and the countryside: it was located in front of the western and most important entrance to the city, the place where three roads (the way to Eleusis, to Colonus and Phyle and the Demosian Sema that went to the Akademia) converged on three juxtaposed gates (the Sacred Gate, the Eriai Gate and the Dipylon Gate). The older graves were covered by low mounds. Those from the sixth or fifth century BCE usually were marked by stone or marble stelai, gravestones or statues. From the middle of the fifth century, the central part, which bordered the Demosian Sema, was a reserved strip for the graves of heroes and statesmen. Pausanias' description, which dates from the second century CE, lists memorials to those who died for their city, including the men who surrendered in Syracuse. All their commanders were inscribed, except Nikias, as he was "despised as a willing prisoner and a man unfit for war."[35] Furthermore there were the tombs of Kleisthenes, Pericles and many other lawgivers and leaders. All of these men had been buried with great pomp and circumstance at the city's expense.

The annual public funeral of the citizens who had fallen in war for the city's sake was one of the most important civic events in ancient Athens. Thucydides described it as a context for his account of Pericles' funeral oration. The ceremony started with the *prothesis*, the laying out of the remains of the deceased.[36] This occurred in a large tent that had been erected in the Agora, the civic center of the city. The *prothesis* lasted for two days, giving the mourners ample opportunity to bring offerings to their own dead. The *prothesis* was followed by the *ekphora*, the conveyance of the bones from the city of the living to the city of the dead. In this procession "coffins of cypress wood are carried on wagons. There is one coffin for each tribe, which contains the bones of members of that tribe. One empty bier is decorated and carried in the procession: this is for the missing, whose bodies could not be recovered. Everyone who wishes to, both citizens and foreigners, can join in the procession, and the women who are related to the dead are there to make their laments at the tomb." That citizens and foreigners were permitted to join the cortege might be interpreted as a demonstration of Pericles' assertion of the laudable "openness" of the city, or of its imperial strength. The train moved through the Dipilon gate to the Demosian Sema. There the bones "are laid in the public burialplace, which is the most beautiful quarter outside the city walls. Here the Athenians always bury those who have fallen in war."[37]

The formal presence of the ten tribes in the procession, symbolized by the ten coffins, emphasized the civic character of the funeral. The ten tribes had been set up in the Kleisthenic reforms of 508/7 BCE, which had completed and perfected the constitutional project begun by Solon eighty years earlier. Key to this reform was the abolition of the four old Ionian tribes which embodied traditional regional loyalties that preceded the establishment of the Athenian polis. In Solon's constitution each of the Ionian tribes sent one hundred members to the council that prepared the meetings of the popular assembly, and as the tribes had not emancipated themselves from aristocratic influence, the rich had been able to maintain an extraordinary measure of informal control over the Athenian polis (I will come back to this issue in a later section of this chapter). Kleisthenes successfully broke the aristocratic hold on power when he made ten new and completely artificial (or conventional) tribes that had no relationship to any specific region or clan. These tribes, or constituencies, completed the unification of city and countryside initiated by Solon. Citizenship implied membership in one of the tribes, yet which that would be was arbitrary. As before, a citizen served in the council, or Boule, as a representative of his tribe, and the army was organized on the basis of tribal contingents. The funeral procession, therefore, symbolized the civic and military structure of the polis: it represented the constitutional context in which a man had lived, acted and died as a citizen.

The most important part of the ceremony was the funeral oration that followed the deposition of the bones in the earth. It was a great honor to be chosen to give the funeral oration. In 431 BCE the Athenians chose Pericles to deliver the eulogy. The purpose of the funeral oration was to recapitulate, justify and glorify the essential aspects of the city's political life, for the sake of which those who had been interred had sacrificed their lives. When Pericles mounted the rostrum to deliver his speech, the Peloponnesian War had raged for one year, and many Athenians already had lost their lives. The question of why it was appropriate to risk one's life for the sake of the city had become very topical. The answer was to be found in the ideology of the polis: to live in a city (as opposed to a settlement) meant to live within the city's collective body after the death of one's physical body. Therefore Pericles invited the gathered people to fix their eyes "every day on the greatness of Athens as she really is." Much of his speech was a celebration of the Athenian constitution and the life that it had made possible. And he concluded that anyone who reflected on the city's greatness would recognize that it was "men with a spirit of adventure, men who knew their duty, men who were ashamed to fall below a certain standard" who were responsible for its present glory. "If they ever failed in an enterprise, they made up their minds that at any rate the city should not find their courage lacking to her, and they gave to her the best contribution that they could. They gave their lives, to her and to all of us, and for their own selves they won praises that never grow old, the most splendid of sepulchres—not the sepulchre in which their bodies are laid, but where their glory remains eternal in men's minds, always there on the right occasion to stir others to speech or to action."[38] The dead lived on, as an example of excellence that provided a normative foundation for the political life of the city, enacted in the speeches delivered and the deeds undertaken in the Agora, the center of the city of the living.

It is in this context significant that the Akademia, the most significant educational institution of Athens, was located at the north-western end of the necropolis. It was connected to the city by the Demosian Sema, the stately avenue alongside of which were the graves of the famous, the worthy and the noble. Every time they went to school the young would walk the course of Athenian history. This journey along the past was the best lesson in citizenship they could receive. In fact, the funeral orations and eulogies, which explained the meaning and significance of the city and adduced examples of lives lived in a truly civic manner, provided the young men with the core of their educational program. The educational system also pointed to the universal of the past that was represented in the graves along the Demosian Sema and embodied in the polis. As Athens was "an education to Greece," and Hellas a school for the world, so it was appropriate that a person's contribution to the life of the polis aided the universal transformation of chaos into cosmos. In the words of Pericles, "famous men have the whole earth as their memorial: it is not only the inscriptions on their graves in their own country that mark them out; no, in foreign lands also, not in any visible form but in people's hearts, their memory abides and grows."[39] That these men had died while carrying out undisguised imperialistic policies did not matter: the Athenian understanding of what their city was all about suggested that a war waged by the polis was, per definition, a civilizing war. This belief was sanctioned by the city's patroness, Athena. She was the deity of (political) reason, a goddess celebrated in the Agora and the Akademia, and the champion of the civilizing war, the war fought to extend the order wrought in the polis over the whole of Hellas. Her patronage warranted a prudently managed imperialistic war as an important civic task. (The other kind of war, the reckless and impudent adventurism fought for the sake of war, was the ward of Ares.)[40]

Pericles skillfully linked in his funeral oration generally accepted notions of the nature of civic life with the war effort when he recalled how "mighty indeed are the marks and monuments of our empire which we have left." The extent of the Athenian empire attested to Athens's greatness. "We do not need the praises of a Homer, or of anyone else whose words may delight us for the moment, but whose estimation of facts will fall short of what is really true," Pericles stated proudly. A factual history (such as that written by Thucydides) that described how "our adventurous spirit has forced an entry into every sea" and how Athenians have left everywhere "everlasting memorials of good done to our friends or suffering inflicted on our enemies"[41] would preserve the city's memory and, with that, of the men who nobly fought and died on her behalf. Thus, in the final analysis, the cemetery was not only symbolic of the city, or the world at large (as interpreted in the Akademia), but also of the empire.

Thucydides' account of Pericles' funeral speech is one of the most important sections of his *History of the Peloponnesian War*. In his merciless study of the pathos of the polis, it is one of the few episodes of affirmation and celebration. The speech and the necropolis explicitly celebrate the ideology of the polis as a society that sustains prosperity, liberty and personal fulfillment and, in turn, is sustained by the citizens' willingness to live and die a civic death. This ideology was, of course, ubiquitous: it informed the ideology of the house, it was embodied in the shrines of the Acropolis and shaped the matrix of the political life of the Agora. But in the house it could not be part of the political discourse, and on the Acropolis it was shrouded in a veil of ancient myth. In the Agora citizens could perceive the relationship of polis and citizen at work, which meant that they were confronted with the fragility of the whole proposition. In the necropolis the inherent instability of the polis was overcome. Only there did the political ideology of the city reign supreme, uncontested by the pressures of the private life and unchallenged by the realities of the political process. The space that celebrated the immutable and irrefutable past was therefore the most important of the city's civic spaces.

The necropolis was the moral and the pragmatic foundation of the public realm. The Athenians realized that feuds among families and clans easily became timeless vendettas that destroy the fabric of the city's social and political life (I will return to this issue in my discussion on the symbolic significance of the Areopagus). In order to break the endless cycle in which evil is returned for evil, Solon instituted a law that forbade "anybody to speak ill of the dead, for piety requires us to regard the dead as sacred, justice to refrain from attacking the absent, and political wisdom to prevent the perpetuation of hatreds."[42] Thus a very simple rule of conduct subsumed the dead under the order of the public domain, effectively removing them as sources of justification for private maneuvering.

Finally, the public cemetery was also a gage of the moral character of the citizen as a private person. One of the consequences of the radical separation between the private and the public realms was the disjunction of a citizen's public stance from his behavior at home. Did it matter if the brilliant statesman was a petty husband and harsh father? These questions have remained important, as the story of Senator Hart's candidacy for the Unites States Presidency has shown. The necropolis offered a kind of transition zone between the public and the private realms where these kind of issues could be resolved. In classical Athens the validity of one's kinship to another person was attested by the care one paid to his grave. Robert Garland observed in *The Greek Way of Death* that a person who did not fulfill the proper rites of interment, or failed to visit the grave regularly, could be denied his inheritance as the omission proved that he had no genuine kinship with the deceased. "Conversely it was of vital concern to an Athenian that he should leave someone behind who would not only attend to his burial but also perform the customary rites at his grave. The anxiety with which he contemplated the omission of these rites could be so acute that it might induce a childless man to adopt an heir with the express object of ensuring that his mortal remains did not want attention from the living."[43] The household took care that the dead were properly remembered through private devotions. Yet these took place in the public realm: in the graveyard. As the whole idea of the household converged on the way in which the surviving took care of the dead, it was proper to assume that the manner in which a person fulfilled his duties at the grave was an indicator of his moral character. Hence "before a citizen could pass the examination which he had to undergo before appointment to public office, he had to prove to the satisfaction of his assessors that he had regularly discharged this obligation."[44]

The civic, urban and architectural significance of the necropolis has eluded architectural historians who studied the elements of the Hellenic city as architectural expressions of the Greek "way of life." A good example is R.E. Wycherley's otherwise useful *How the Greeks Built Cities*. The book describes the city structure and its constituent elements in detail, but in the main body of the text there are only two short references to it: once it mentions that approaching the city a visitor would pass "interesting monuments by the wayside, including shrines and tombs;" and the text notes that the abodes of the dead, "clustered thickly together or strung out along the roads," appealed to Pausanias, a writer of a famous travelogue from the second century CE.[45] Neither the city plans that illustrate Wycherley's book, nor all other accounts of Hellenic cities, include the cemeteries, as they are located outside the city's walls. These plans thus obscure the real nature of Greek urban form.

The architectural type affiliated with the necropolis was the stela, the solid marker of a grave.[46] Architectural historical studies do not assign the stela architectural significance. Art historical classifications corroborate this blindness when they classify the stela under sculpture. The stela does not offer the kind of inhabitable space that we associate with a work of architecture. Yet as we had to expand our notion of the polis until it includes the necropolis, so we have to broaden our definition of architecture. The dead rest below the surface, in the earth. The mass of the earth is their habitation, yet the earth is not architecture. The stela is. Why so? A comparision of the spatiality of the world of the living with the spatiality of the world of the dead will give a clue.

The world of the dead is the world of nature; the spatiality of the cemetery is identical to the primordial spatiality of nature. The space of nature is vertical: it derives from the contrast of the solid mass of the earth to the space of air above. Mass and space meet at the surface of the earth. All things material fall to the mass of the earth on account of their weight, and vegetation emerges vertically from the mass of the earth into the world of air. Human beings are the only living beings who truly resist this vertical spatiality of nature. Their intellect and upright position create a condition that allows them to emancipate themselves from that order and stand out against the spatiality of the world of nature. Human beings *ex-sist*, "stand out." They are conscious of a space that is oriented upon themselves as center, a space that is stretched over the surface of the earth from the center to the horizon. This space connects a person with another person, or a thing, or a destiny. This connection is a path, a horizon(t)al axis. Therefore the experiential space of human beings is horizon(t)al. And therefore the political space of people is horizon(t)al.

Works of architecture define the political space of the city, connecting countryside to settlement and dividing the public from the private, the realm of the dead from the domain of decision from the time of the city. Buildings define the polis by vertical walls that are erected on the horizontal surface of the earth. Through the disposition of the solid of vertical walls within the void of horizon(t)al space architects explore the relationship between the here and there, the common and the sacred, their own and the inimical. Architects build on the earth because people cannot live in the earth: human beings need air to live, and a void to move their bodies. They need the horizontal of the earth's surface to create a destiny. The horizontal spatiality of architecture opposes the vertical spatiality of nature. If we reintegrate the dead within our understanding of the city, then we must also account for the spatiality of nature within our appre- hension of architecture. When people die, their bodies become part of nature. The living *ex-sist*, stand out; the dead fall back to the surface of the earth We surrender our dead to the spatiality of nature when we bury them horizontally in the mass of the earth. For the dead there is no horizon.

Architects who build exclusively for the living, and who define stelai as pieces of sculpture, think about the horizontal of the earth as a neutral datum. They only consider what happens below the surface in so far as it might affect the stability of what is erected above. They ignore the past that is gathered below the surface. Their universe fits that of their clients, who do not like to think of what is below their feet. They do not like to think that the seemingly solid and neutral earth is in fact one great cemetery, a layering of pasts that were once presents just like ours. City fathers who plan for the living ban cemeteries to the countryside, as these spaces remind the city's inhabitants that there is a world below, a world repressed but nevertheless there. The cemetery addresses that world below: the stones that mark the graves are the boundary stones that separate the horizon(t)al space of the living from the vertical space of the dead. Unlike the boundary stones that separate one property from another, the stelai do not define one part from the other in a game of relative difference. They separate the domain of the living from the realm of the dead in an absolute fashion. The stelai are immutable. When Solon removed all the *horoi* from the land he did not touch the stelai but protected them through his legislation to safeguard the sanctity of the dead.

A viable city articulates the radical difference between the space of the living, which is the space of the *now* and the *here*, and the space of nature, which is the space of the immutable past. Only when it consciously creates space for the vertical world of nature can it come to terms with it. The stela cautions and admonishes. It portends of the "Also you, but not yet." And the "but not yet" is the location of our freedom towards the future and our responsibility for the past. It might take many forms, but it always points to the earth and the heavens, disclosing the presence of the absolutes of death and immortality, of fall and salvation in an otherwise relative world. In the Middle Ages church towers were like gigantic stelai, celebrating the passion of Jesus as in the monastery of Centula. And the skyline of the business district of any large North American city has an uncanny resemblance to the graveyards of old. Also the tholos, which in Westfall's typology serves the purpose of veneration, can be interpreted as a modified stela. Its dominant axis is not horizontal, but vertical, and as such the tholos affirms the spatiality of nature, be it as a man-made womb for fertility cults, as a sanctuary of chthonic mysteries or as a cosmic tomb of a city's heroes. [47] The tholos shares in the meaning of the stela, but also in that of the shrine. Its ambiguity and particularity attenuate its typological significance, which is fully preserved in the clear "other worldliness" of the stela.

The Acropolis

The next type is the shrine. It relates to Westfall's temple. In his city it refers to the verb "to celebrate." In classical Athens the Acropolis was the shrine of the city as it celebrated within the imperfect setting of the actual city the enduring idea of *the* city, of the city Athens ought to be. The Acropolis, the "city on the hill," was, in a certain sense, the city's constitution.

The Socratic questions, asked after the fall of Athens, mark the beginnings of political philosophy. Neither Solon, Kleisthenes nor Pericles operated on the basis of an abstract political philosophy that summarized the ideal of the polis and that served as a horizon of the actual political decisions to be taken. After one and a half centuries of classical scholarship, Hegel's conclusion that "the consideration of the State in the abstract . . . was alien to them [the Greeks]" still stands. Like Hegel we recognize that the grand object of the Greeks "was their country in its living and real aspect;—*this actual* Athens, this Sparta, these Temples, these Altars, this form of social life, this union of fellow-citizens, these manners and customs."[48]

However the Greeks were not without guidance. A different kind of imaginary construct of what the city was, or should be, preceded the rise of classical political rationalism. This was a kind of imaginary city that transcended the everyday realities of civic life. It was *he polis*, "*the* city" that refused to be reduced to the immediacy of "this actual city," the city subject to the tribulations of time and the ravages of history. "The city," characterized by Nicole Loraux as the "immobile prime mover," and the "irreducible kernel of meaning," is the polis celebrated in Pericles' funeral oration, as reconstructed and reworked by Thucydides.[49] It is a city that honors the ancestors who, "by their courage and virtue," created and preserved the city. It is a city that enjoys a system of government that is a model for the whole of Greece, a city in which all are equal before the law, where ability and not one's birth decided who will be elected in which office, a city in which no person, "so long as he has it in him to be of service to the state, is kept in political obscurity because of poverty."

And, just as our political life is free and open, so is our day-to-day life in our relations with each other. We do not get into a state with our next-door neighbor if he enjoys him in his own way, nor do we give him the kind of black looks which, though they do no real harm, still do hurt people's feelings. We are free and tolerant in our private lives; but in public affairs we keep to the law. This is because it commands our deep respect. We give our obedience to those whom we put in positions of authority, and we obey the laws themselves, especially those which are for the protection of the oppressed, and those unwritten laws which it is an acknowledged shame to break. And there is another point. When our work is over, we are in a position to enjoy all kinds of recreation for our spirits. There are various kinds of contests and sacrifices regularly throughout the year; in our own homes we find a beauty and a good taste which delight us every day and which drives away our cares. Then the greatness of our city brings it about that all the good things from all over the world flow in to us, so that to us it seems just as natural to enjoy foreign goods as our own local products.[50]

Pericles' summary of what kind of city Athens ought to be maps the different areas of civic concerns—some of which have been discussed above and some of which will be reviewed below: it was a city with well-supplied places of exchange, secure houses, a city where anyone could be chosen for an office in the stoa, a city where those who deserve praise were honored after their death at the stelai that marked their graves. Yet all these places were subject to the pressures of life as it actually was

lived. Even in Athens people gave their neighbors black looks. Nevertheless the imaginary ideal city that was evoked in transient speeches had
one permanent foothold in the actual city. The purpose of the Acropolis, or
"high city," was to tower over the bustling city below as an autonomous
presence and, as such, to offer a stable point of reference. Before the
invention of political philosophy it constituted "the city," the enduring
paradigm that framed the polis as though it were a constitution. In short,
the Acropolis testified to the enduring nature of the city.

To assert the enduring nature of the polis was to affirm something that
was impossible. The laws of nature, as the Greeks know, decided that
everything that had been generated would degenerate, that everything
that had been put together would fall apart, that a building that had been
constructed could be destroyed. Therefore they did not speak of the
beginnings of the polis, but of its origin, the act that had transformed
settlement into city. An origin has a miraculous character: it cannot be
explained as that which was generated out of its presuppositions. There is a
magical aspect to an origin, a suspension of the laws that rule the world of
beginnings and ends. The Acropolis embodied and expressed this magical
and miraculous quality of the polis. The necropolis showed the natural
history of the city, a history of beginnings and ends, of birth and death. The
Acropolis revealed the supernatural origin of the city. It was the place
where the city had been founded.

Plutarch recounted one of the myths of the city's origin. When the
legendary hero Theseus arrived in the city of Athens, he found a community
"plunged into disorder and strife, and the affairs of [King] Aegeus and his
household in great distress." Theseus liberated the city from its subjection
to Crete, and on his return to Athens found himself king (the old Aegeus
had committed suicide because he thought that Theseus, who was inci-
dently his long-lost but since recovered son, had been killed in Crete). This
then set the stage for Theseus' decision to establish Athens anew, as a city
that brought order where had been chaos, and peace where had been war.

> After Aegeus' death Theseus conceived a wonderful and far-reaching plan,
> which was nothing less than to concentrate the inhabitants of Attica into a
> capital. In this way he transformed them into one people belonging to one city,
> whereas until then they had lived in widely scattered communities, so that it
> was difficult to bring them together for the common interest, and indeed at times
> they had even quarreled and fought one another. So he now travelled around
> Attica and strove to convince them town by town and clan by clan. The common
> people and the poor responded at once to his appeal, while to the more
> influential classes he proposed a constitution without a king: there was to be a
> democracy. . . . Some were convinced by his arguments without any difficulty,

and others . . . preferred to be persuaded rather than forced into agreement. He then proceeded to abolish the town halls, council chambers, and magistracies in the various districts. To replace them he built a single town hall and senate house for the whole community on the site of the present acropolis, and he named the city Athens.[51]

This wonderful founding myth, which summarized in symbolic language the Solonic and Kleisthenic reforms, describes the Acropolis as the site of an unprecedented act, a radical political innovation that proved to be extremely vital and enduring. The political magic of Theseus was to be embodied in the buildings that Pericles erected on the Acropolis. As Plutarch recorded, centuries later people still took pride in the miraculous origin of those buildings.

> So the buildings arose, as imposing in their sheer size as they were inimitable in the grace of their outlines, since the artists strove to excel themselves in the beauty of their workmanship. And yet the most wonderful thing about them was the speed with which they were completed. Each of them, men supposed, would take many generations to build, but in fact the entire project was carried through in the high summer of one man's administration. . . . It is this, above all, which makes Pericles' works an object of wonder to us—the fact that they were created in so short a span, and yet for all time. Each one possessed a beauty which seemed venerable the moment it was born, and at the same time a youthful vigour which makes them appear to this day as if they were newly built. A bloom of eternal freshness hovers over these works of his and preserves them from the touch of time, as if some unfading spirit of youth, some ageless vitality had been breathed into them.[52]

Unlike the actual city of Athens, which was located between the necropolis and the Acropolis, the temples on the Acropolis were designed to ensure the memory of Athens even after the actual city would have disappeared. Thucydides conceded that the Acropolis could preserve the memory of Athens. His pessimistic vision as to the city's future must have been shared by many. Few had any doubts that the city would disappear one day, that its unity and power was to dissolve into its constituent parts. The necropolis— a collage of urban fragments set in a landscape of ruins—prophetically represented the unavoidable physical fate of the actual city. Unlike the houses of the city, which were made of brick, rubble, wood and plaster, the sepulchral fragments would last, as they were solid pieces of poros and marble. The Acropolis, ruined or not, would offer later generations the model that showed how with these fragments the historical city could be reassembled in the memory of the historic Athens, the city in which the vision of "the city" that is would have merged with the memory of "the actual city" that was.

The Acropolis framed the polis of the present and preserved the polis in the future. It was, it would be and, as is implied by its metahistorical character, it also always had been. It reached far into the future and back into the past, to the origins of the city. On the Agora were the statues of the Eponymous Heroes, who were remembered as the heroic founders of the ten constituencies that formed the actual city of Athens.[53] On the Acropolis was the statue and the temple of Athena Polias, the patron goddess of the city. The Athenians did not believe, like the inhabitants of the cities before the axial period, that the immortal goddess actually dwelt in her temple, and that her presence on the Acropolis made it possible for the citizens physically to consort with her and thus share in her immortality. The polis was the location of one's (symbolic) immortality. The only thing that mattered was that the polis would endure. Athena Polias was, of all the gods and goddesses, most closely associated with the idea of the political life. She was the instigator of action. Vincent Scully characterized her in his brilliant analysis of the Athenian Acropolis as "the embodiment of what the city state might be—the polis which helped to liberate men from their terror of the natural world with its dark powers and limiting laws. As such, Athena held the fortified places. . . . Above all, she held the Acropolis of Athens."[54]

The Acropolis was the place where Athena Polias had sanctioned the founding of the actual city in the past. The myth of the founding of Athens related how the goddess competed with Poseidon for the protectorship of the city to be. Her victory over the god who controlled the violence of the waters imprinted on the city the destiny to become the place where people could develop all their faculties within the context of the polis. There, on the limestone rock that arose from the Attic plain, the Athenians erected an ensemble of buildings that "still stand at the frontiers of human consciousness and can still touch the imagination of modern man more intensely perhaps than any other works of art done before this time."[55] If classical Athens as a city occupies an axial significance in the history of urban form, then its Acropolis concentrates this significance in one creative moment in which the political, urban and architectural imaginations of Pericles, Phidias, Iktinos and Mnesicles transcended the political and ideological oppositions of this actual Athens to converge in a vision of *he polis* in which city and nature, earth and heaven, land and sea and mortals and immortals were reconciled in an image of enduring perfection. The Acropolis was, so Vincent Scully judged, the place where "human striving and natural law," where "old and new ways" were reconciled. This appeasement could be observed in its two main sanctuaries. "In the asymmetrical, gently scaled

Erechtheion the old traditional earth cults are humanized and made extra-ordinarily articulate, lucid, and civil, while in the Parthenon what might be called the human view of Athena becomes unexpectedly splendid, dominant, and divine."[56]

The Acropolis gave the political life in Athens a broad basis of justification and legitimized its equanimous and self-confident stance within Hellas. The difference between assurance and arrogance is one of degree, however, and many believed that the enormous wealth and energy absorbed in the reconstruction of the Acropolis testified more to Pericles' hubris than to political wisdom. I would argue that Pericles and the Athenians had become prisoners of the empire they had created. Norman O. Brown wrote that a city is crystallized guilt, and that each generation inherits "the ascetic achievements of its ancestors . . . as a debt to be paid by further accumulation of monuments."[57] He could have had Periclean Athens in mind. When Pericles defended his strategy of concentrating all the resources in the fleet, he asserted the importance of the Athenian empire over the polis. The general argued that it was proper for the Athenian citizens to support the imperial dignity of Athens—which meant that they had to maintain and reinforce the fleet—because their fathers had won it to hand down to the present generation. And he reminded his fellow citizens that "the reason why Athens has the greatest name in all the world is because she has never given in to adversity, but has spent more life and labor in warfare than any other state, thus winning the greatest power that has ever existed in history, such a power that will be remembered forever by posterity."[58] With power came income in the form of tributes, and military responsibility. The Athenian Acropolis is a supreme example of the type of the shrine because it was atypical: no other Hellenic city could afford to erect buildings of such quality and on so grand a scale because no other city had an empire to pay for its public works.

The Athenian Acropolis was atypical: its very splendor engendered discontent, which ultimately led to the destruction of the very polis that it was meant to perpetuate. Plutarch recorded how the conservative citizens, who looked more to the land than to the sea, objected to the lavishness of the new Acropolis on moral grounds.

They cried out in the Assembly that Athens had lost her good name and disgraced herself by transferring from Delos into her own keeping the funds that had been contributed by the rest of Greece, and that now the most plausible excuse for this action, namely, that the money had been removed for fear of the barbarians and was being guarded in a safe place, had been demolished by Pericles himself. "The Greeks must be outraged," they cried. "They must consider this an act of barefaced tyranny, when they see that with their own contributions, extorted from them by force for the war against the Persians, we are gilding and beautifying our city, as if it were some vain woman decking herself out with costly stones and statues and temples worth of money." Pericles' answer to the people was that the Athenians were not obliged to give the allies any account of how their money was spent, provided that they carried on the war for them and kept the Persians away. "They do not give us a single horse, nor a soldier, nor a ship. All they supply is money," he told the Athenians, "and this belongs not to the people who give it, but to those who receive it, so long as they provide the services they are paid for. It is no more than fair that after Athens has been equipped with all she needs to carry on the war, she should apply the surplus to public works, which, once completed, will bring her glory for all time, and while they are being built will convert surplus to immediate use."[59]

Was it lack of judgement, arrogance or neurotic ambition, or was it that there was no other option for Pericles than to use the money under his custodianship to create an acropolis that would give the city, as Scully phrased it, "a sense of action with nature's consent, of conquest without folly or guilt, pride without loss of reverence"?[60] Whatever the lofty reasoning, the building of the Acropolis created employment opportunities, filled the Emporium and gave Pericles' populist party the votes it needed to remain in power. Yet the Acropolis represented the peak of Athenian wealth and power and the cause of her political disintegration. Meant to recapitulate the actual city in an ideal image, its very expense also prepared the battlefields that would end its history. Thucydides alluded to this when, at the beginning of the *History of the Peloponnesian War*, he described the Acropolis as the future ruin it indeed became. For the historian, the future remains of Pericles' dream of an enduring city suggested the transitoriness of political power and cultural achievement.

The modern, historicist perspective is not much different. As heirs to Herder, who described human history as the torrent of change that only revealed "wreck upon wreck, eternal beginnings without end, changes of circumstance without any fixed purpose," and that postulated that "no human monument can endure wholly and eternally upon earth; being formed in the succession of generations by the hand of time for temporal use, and evidently prejudicial to posterity,"[61] we know that the enchanted cityscape of ideality and eternity generated in the heat of imperial ambition was indeed but an illusive and elusive spell. The Roman architects had luck: even the smallest fragment of their mediocre temples acquired in premodern architectural theory a normative and enduring significance. Neither Alberti, Serlio, Palladio nor Scamozzi ever travelled to Greece (or for that matter to Paestum or Sicily, with their Greek temples). And even if they had had the opportunity to do so, they would not have bothered as they believed that Roman understanding of the principles of architecture had been superior to that of the Greeks.

When in 1762 the initial volume of the first reliable description of the architectural remains of the Acropolis appeared (Stuart and Revett's *The Antiquities of Athens*), ancient Greece already had been assigned its proper historicist designation within a general context of relativist resignation. My own copy of the second edition of the popular pocket version, issued in 1841, appropriately begins with a long lamentation of how the "two great devastators, time and the conqueror," have done their work on the Acropolis. And it sighs how "those unrivalled constructions which, in their finished beauty and grandeur, were the pride and marvel of antiquity, might have remained nearly entire, but for the persevering encroachment of domestic and dilettante depredation." After a catalogue of disasters that covers three pages it concludes that "instead of marvelling that so few [monuments] have been preserved to the present time, it may well excite our special wonder that so many survived the casualties to which they have been exposed."[62] The Acropolis, which had been conceived as the apex of civilization, became the silent and suffering witness to the fragility of the polis.

The romantic interpretation still predominates, and with Vincent Scully we prefer to forget that the historical Acropolis was more likely the result of neurotic ambition and self-idealization than of Socratic wisdom. With him we prefer to read the historic Acropolis as a mystery in which a cosmic stillness transcends the world of change. "There is only being and light," so Scully enunciated. "Time lies dead in the white and silver light of the outdoor room between the Parthenon and the Erechtheion. It dies upon the Parthenon's white and golden columns, so that Athena takes her own step forward and outward forever." In this light the particular and the contingent acquire a measure of universality. "What remains is beyond action, too instantaneous for reverie, too deep for calm. It is silence, the sweet deep breath taken. Time stops. Fear lies dead upon the rock. The column is. It stands."[63] Scully's ontological reading conjures the image of the lonely poet in search of meaning. Perhaps he has had the privilege to experience the Acropolis in Byronic fashion. I have never been able to avoid the crowds up there. And so I learned to understand the Acropolis as a place designed for crowds, today and twenty-five centuries ago. It was, after all, nothing but a tasteful version of Disneyland's Main Street USA.

The Acropolis is the most problematic district of the fivesquare city because its glorification and idealization of urban civilization also reveals its shadow side. Created to ensure the city's everlastingness, it could not but summon our death anxiety to the surface of our consciousness. Victor

Hugo never saw the Acropolis, but I believe that he would have recognized in the notion of *Anagkê* ("Doom") the mutual foundation of his Notre Dame and the Parthenon. In his *Civilization and Its Discontents* Freud used the image of the "eternal city" of Rome to explore the contradiction between immortality and death that is at the core of any civilization, any institution and, ultimately, any work of architecture. Yet I believe that his observations on the unresolved and irresolvable relationship between our desire to become immortal and our assimilation of death into our lives also apply to the Acropolis. Thucydides realized this well: when he described the future state of the Acropolis he conjured the vision of a ruined Parthenon set in the midst of a vast necropolis.

The Agora

Halfway between the necropolis and the Acropolis, along the road that connected the immutable city of the past and the enduring city of all times, was the Agora.[64] The Agora was the political center of "this actual Athens." There the citizens decided on the future of the city and acted upon their decisions.[65] In the Agora the citizens converged as equals (*isoi*) to realize in speeches and deeds the city's destiny as portrayed in the Acropolis. The Agora was a place structured by the law of equality (*isonomia*). This meant that all the citizens could participate equally in the process of decision. At the Agora they could choose from all the alternatives open to them those which would ensure the future of the polis. These rival possibilities were presented in the form of a competition: different speakers would propose and defend in often heated debates the various competing resolutions, and all who were enfranchised could vote as to who was to be the winner. Thus the basis of the Athenian democracy was the freedom of speech as it was at work in the Agora.

The political center of Athens originally was located at the foot of the north slope of the Acropolis.[66] This so-called Agora of Theseus was a small open space surrounded by a few small buildings that housed the three most important offices defined in the Athenian constitution adopted in 683 BCE, the year that the monarchy was officially replaced by the archonship. An elected Archon Basileus ("king–archon") was responsible for the cult of Dionysius and was the judge of all matters religious. He had his headquarters in the Boukoleium. The Archon Eponymos ("archon who gives his name [to the civic and religious calendar]") was the chief executive officer in charge of the city of Athens and supreme judge of all civil affairs. His office was the Prytaneion. This building housed the public hearth of Athens. The Prytaneion was the official reception center of the city: there the Archon Eponymos entertained at public expense ambassadors of other cities and those who rendered service to the polis. It was also the place where important civic relics were kept, and where murder cases were tried. Finally, there was the Archon Polemarch ("army-commanding archon") the commander of the army and the judge entrusted with all cases involving non-Athenians. His office was the Epilykeium. Dracon's constitutional reform of 624 BCE created six more archons who joined the initial three in a College of Archons (Thesmothetae). The Prytaneion, the Boukoleium and the Epilykeium remained the offices of the Archon Eponymos, Basileus and Polemarch. A new and large building, the Thesmotheteion, was to offer space to the six new archons. Built at some distance from the other three buildings, it was also to serve as the chief banqueting hall of the city.

Solon's reform of 587 BCE opened the political structure of the city to all free men within Attica: they could vote in the popular Assembly and those who had a yearly income that exceeded 200 measures of corn, oil or wine were eligible for office.[67] Responding to the demand for a large meeting place, the city authorities moved the political center 350 meters to the north-west, to a spacious and level area that recently had been enclosed within the new city walls but which was still unused because it had been a cemetery. This site had been from prehistoric times the place where the Athenians came together to celebrate festivals and hold contests in honor of their heroes and ancestors. The decision to move the political center to this place unified the celebrations in honor of the dead and the gods—which included athletic, dramatic, musical and equestrian contests in which the living could testify to the civic significance of the immutable past created by their ancestors—with the idea of government. Democracy was to be a celebration and a contest. Therefore the road used for the annual festival of the Panathenaia, which celebrated Athena Polias in a procession starting at the western entrance of the city and ending at the Acropolis—unifying the immutable past, the dynamic present and the enduring future of the city in a linear fashion—crossed the open space diagonally and, by the same token, the middle of the Agora was the orchestra. This was the round place used for dramatic and musical contests, which when used was surrounded by wooden grandstands.

The Agora was the place where the popular assembly (Ecclesia) met *es to meson*, in the middle of the community. The sole legislative body of the Solonic democratic constitution met once a month, and decided on war and peace, elected the army commander and the college of nine archons. Later in the sixth century the meetings of the assembly were moved 400 meters to the south-west; at the even more spacious hill-site known as the Pnyx there was ample space for all the 25,000 members of the Ecclesia. Because of its natural cavea, the Pnyx allowed everyone to see and hear what was proposed. As Thompson and Wycherley observed in their monumental study of the Agora, the Pnyx should still be regarded as an "offshoot or appendage" of the Agora.[68] The Agora remained assuredly the ideological location of the Ecclesia: the office of its chairman was there, and it was there that the various councils and committees that did most of the assembly's work convened. At the periphery of the Agora the city offered meeting and office space to the various democratic institutions. The Bouleuterion, which housed the elected council of first 400 and later 500 members (Boule), was there. The Boule prepared the business for the Ecclesia, dealt with urgent matters and acted as a kind of general ministry to the polis. The Bouleuterion gave the council a spacious covered theatre-like meeting hall. Members of the Boule, on a rotating basis, served on its inner council or executive committee (Prytany), which represented the Boule publicly. The city erected a new Prytaneum next to the Bouleuterion for their use. The Prytaneion served as the office of the chairman of the Prytany, who was also the chairman of the assembly. In him the assembly remained present at the Agora even after it had moved to the Pnyx. South of the Prytaneion were the military headquarters (Strategeium) where the military council met. The Athenian supreme command consisted of ten generals (Strategoi), who after the Kleisthenic reform were elected by each of the tribal regiments. The Solonic constitution provided for several people's courts, which met in the different stoas around the Agora. These buildings also housed the offices of other officials, and the archives of the city.

South of the Agora was the Areopagus or "Hill of Ares," a bare rock that was believed to be the original meeting place of the Areopagus, a prestigious Council of Elders. Its members were men who had served the polis as archon, and they were appointed for life. As "Guardians of the Law" they embodied the continuity of tradition. The Areopagus exercised wide and not very well-defined responsibilities that included, among other things, the protection of the constitution. As an essentially conservative body at odds with the radical innovations of the Periclean Age, the Areopagus was stripped of almost all of its powers between 463 and 459 BCE. The council was left only with jurisdiction in homicide cases. Yet it preserved its symbolic significance as a force of moderation, of reconciliation and of the supremacy of the polis over the blood feuds of the past. This is illustrated by the fact that the prosecutor and the defendant who pleaded before this council were under a solemn oath "in which, as the penalty of perjury, they invoked destruction on themselves, their houses and their families; and this oath was taken in the name of the Semnai, a trinity of female divinities worshipped in a cave on the slopes of the Areopagus as the presiding deities of the Court."[69]

The Semnai were Erinyes or Furies, the daughters of the earth and the night. Before the founding of the polis these winged maidens meted out revenge as a primitive kind of justice. Aeschylus' third and last play of his *Oresteia*, *The Eumenides*, describes how these Furies were persuaded by Athena to civilize themselves, limiting their revenge to those who committed acts of perjury and leaving a duly established court, the Areopagus, to dispense justice. They became the Eumenides, the "Kindly Ones." *The Eumenides* describes the trial of Orestes, the man who, under strict orders of Apollo (who in turn had given voice to the wish of Zeus), had killed his mother Clytaemnestra in order to avenge the death of his father Agamemnon at her hands. Pursued by the Furies, Orestes fled to Delphi. There he found a temporary refuge in the sanctuary of Apollo.

At the beginning of the play, Orestes kneels in prayer at the Omphalos, the Navelstone. Around him are the Furies. On entrance into the shrine Apollo had beaten them temporarily down with sleep. Representative of the Olympian patriarchy, Apollo shares with Orestes his feelings for the female spirits of below.

> They disgust me.
> these grey, ancient children never touched
> by god, man or beast—the eternal virgins.
> Born for destruction only, the dark pit,
> they range the bowels of the Earth, the world of death,
> loathed by men and the gods who hold Olympus.

Apollo predicts that Orestes will be pursued by the Furies until he reaches the city of Athens.

> And once you reach the citadel of Pallas, kneel
> and embrace her ancient idol in your arms and there,
> with judges of your case, with a magic spell—
> with words—we will devise the masterstroke
> that sets you free from torment once for all.[70]

This masterstroke is, as we will discover, the creation of the polis.

Orestes flees to Athens. The Furies, roused by the ghost of Clytaemnestra, follow him. They all meet again on the Acropolis, where Orestes has found sanctuary at Athena's statue. Athena enters, and observing the impasse suggests a trial. After the exchange of verbal hostilities the prosecuting party, the Furies, the council for the defence, Apollo (who has followed the party to Athens) and the defendant, Orestes, agree, and Athena summons the court whose judgement will end the spiral of unatoned guilt, revenge and civil war. This court is to meet on the Areopagus, a hill where once the Amazons pitched their tents "when they came marching down on Theseus, full tilt in their fury, erecting a new city to overarch his city." Where destruction once loomed for Athens now a new foundation for justice was to be created. The terror of the Areopagus, "The Crag of Ares," was to protect the constitution and serve the peace of the city.

> Here from the heights, terror and reverence,
> my people's kindred powers
> will hold them from injustice through the day
> and through the mild night. Never pollute
> our law with innovations. No, my citizens,
> foul a clear well and you will suffer thirst.
>
> Neither anarchy nor tyranny, my people
> Worship the Mean, I urge you,
> shore it up with reverence and never
> banish terror from the gates, not outright.
> Where is the righteous man who knows no fear?
> The stronger your fear, your reverence for the just,
> the stronger your country's wall and city's safety,
> stronger by far than all men else possess
> in Scythia's rugged steppes or Pelops' level plain.
> Untouched by lust for spoil, this court of law
> majestic, swift to fury, rising above you
> as you sleep, our night watch always wakeful,
> guardian of our land—I found it here and now.[71]

The myth of the founding of the Areopagus recorded a third version of the founding of Athens as a true polis. The first was the myth of Athena's victory over Poseidon. It described the founding of the polis against the horizon of the enduring. The second narrated the deeds of Theseus, and described the creation of the settlement as the unification of all the towns in Attica as a historical act. The third myth stressed the decisions that each citizen confronted in the present. For the classicist E.T. Owen the specific significance of this myth was that it offered the institution of Athenian trial by jury as a solution to the problem of pain and sin. "The committal of [Orestes'] case to a legally constituted tribunal of men is the apotheosis of law, of civilization, of the polis and ordered life." Aeschylus showed how the polis is a "gracious and humane, but infinitely precarious" compromise. In it some kind of equilibrium has been achieved between human instinct and the pressures of the outside world. The result is a work of art structured by the harmony "which holds, and just holds, all the discordant elements of the universe together."[72]

Thus the Areopagus symbolised the axis of (Athenian) history. The rule of law replaced the rule of the blood feud. In a very literal sense the low hill, which was left in its original state, symbolized the Acropolis and the necropolis, and made them subservient to the civic life of the Agora. Physically it rose above the civic center like a lower version of the Acropolis, but instead of columned temples there was a bare scored, marked and pitted summit that carried unmistakably chthonic associations. At this no-man's land between the sky and the earth, the gods of the Olympus and the divinities of passion, the Furies, had been reconciled by the goddess of political reason, Athena. From now on the goddesses of wrath were to be known as the *eumenides*, the "well-disposed" or the "goddesses of good will." There the enduring future and the immutable past had surrendered their power to the judgement of men; there the sky and the earth had agreed to grant a measure of space to the authority of the city; there the desire for immortality and the death instinct appeared to have found some kind of balance. Halfway between the Acropolis and the necropolis, the barren height of the Areopagus, with its cave-sanctuary of the Semnai, was the democratic successor to the mythic cosmic axis. If the latter had suggested man's power to achieve a measure of physical control over his fate, the vantage point of the Areopagus allowed people to acquire a comprehensive view of their destiny. The Areopagus was (and still is) the best place to appreciate the way the necropolis, the Agora and the Acropolis relate to each other. From the viewpoint of the Areopagus, the city was one of peace and prosperity. When she founded the Areopagus, Athena described the city that was to grow in its protective shadow.

> Nothing that strikes a note of brutal conquest. Only peace—
> blessings, rising up from the earth and the heaving sea,
> and down the vaulting sky let the wind-gods breathe
> a wash of sunlight streaming through the land,
> and the yield of soil and grazing cattle flood
> our city's life with power and never flag
> with time. Make the seed of men live on,
> the more they worship you the more they thrive.[73]

The precinct of this mountain—the seat of a monarchy of Awe—was the Agora, the place where debate and suffrage was to reach a reconciliation between foes.

If the architecture of the Acropolis represented the enduring aspects of the polis, and if the deserted and gutted crown of the Areopagus embodied its integration within the world of nature, the Agora embodied its political dynamism checked by the moderation of the Areopagus. There the repercussions of the political vitality of the Athenian polis was not a summation of societal, financial and artistic forces to create temples that would last forever, but a never ending program of alteration, adaptation and renovation. Some of these changes in the built environment were the result of political and social developments. Buildings were put up and pulled down, or meeting places expanded or even turned around to satisfy the specific needs or ideologies of the moment. For example, Plutarch recorded a tradition that linked the radical transformation of the Pnyx at the end of the fifth century BCE to collapse of democratic government. In the original Pnyx the speaker faced the Piraeus, the stronghold of the democratic faction. The arrangement suggested that the assembly gathered at the Pnyx could feel itself backed by the sailors, boatswains and pilots from the Piraeus. "This was also the reason," Plutarch wrote, "why the platform of the people's Assembly in the Pnyx, which had been built so as to look out over the sea, was later turned round by the Thirty Tyrants, so that it faced inland, for they believed that Athens's naval empire had proved to be the mother of democracy and that an oligarchy was more easily accepted by men who tilled the soil."[74] True or not, the story illustrates how no building or spatial arrangement associated with the Agora was sacrosanct. This was different in the Acropolis. Rhys Carpenter has brilliantly reconstructed in his *The Architects of the Parthenon* (1971) the way party politics influenced the design and building history of the Parthenon in specific and the Acropolis in general.[75] The result, however, transcended the infighting of its beginning, and the Thirty Tyrants who turned around Pericles' arrangement of the Pnyx did not try to do the same with the Parthenon: the aesthetical and material quality of the buildings on the Acropolis attested to the enduring greatness of the city irrespective of the nature of the government in power or the amount people with political franchise. The situation in the Agora did not compre to that on the Acropolis. The workmanship with which the buildings were erected was of no importance whatsoever. Many of the structures, such as wooden grandstands that could be erected and removed at short notice, were temporary. What did matter was that each structure fitted the specific function that it had to serve. If it lost its function, the structure was either adapted to a new one, or unceremoniously removed.

Functional demands were important in the architecture of the buildings around the Agora. Yet even there function did transcend into purpose. We have seen how in the necropolis a unified foundation of the polis emerged from the rupture of death, and how on the Acropolis the instantaneous and miraculous transformed into the enduring and the divine. On the Agora the chain of contingencies and circumstances transcended into the symmetrical order of civic time. There was nothing haphazard or random as to who was to serve on which council for what period of time. The calendar that divided the year into ten periods of either thirty-six or thirty-seven days imprinted an invisible rhythm on the comings and goings within the Agora. These ten civic "months" related to the ten civic constituencies or tribes. Aristotle's description of the Athenian constitution records that "there is a council of five hundred appointed by lot, fifty members of each tribe. Each tribe's members in turn, as decided by lot, form the prytany, the first four for thirty-six days each and the remaining for thirty-five days each. First the members of the prytany eat together in the Round House [Prytaneum], at the state's expense. Then they convene meetings both of the council and of the people: the council every day, except when there is a day of exemption, the people four times in each prytany."[76] Thus the polis ensured that a stable temporal order of equality or *isonomia* reigned supreme over the vicissitudes of political change.

Jean-Pierre Vernant summarized the significance of this regular rotation of offices on the Agora as the basis of a coherent social system, "governed by numerical relations and correspondences that permitted the citizens to declare themselves 'the same,' to enter into relations of mutual equality, symmetry, and reciprocity, and together to form a unified cosmos." Standing in the middle of the open space, and surveying the different offices at its perimeter, the citizen could see that power and government were no longer concentrated "in a single figure at the apex of the social structure, but [were] distributed equally throughout the entire realm of public life, in that common space where the city had its center, its *meson*." In that configuration power and authority passed according to a fixed schedule from constituency to constituency and from individual to individual. The result was a situation in which "command and obedience, rather than being opposed to each other as two absolutes, became the two inseparable aspects of one reversible relationship." The principle of equality structured this centered and circular domain "in which each citizen, because he was like all the others, would have to cover the entire circuit as time went round, successively occupying and surrendering each of the symmetrical positions that made up civic space."[77] Seen from Vernant's perspective, the rearing up and pulling down of buildings at the Agora's edges might be interpreted as a symbolic reflection of the dynamic order of the Agora. Within the context of my reading of Athens's public space it is no less appropriate. The Agora was located halfway between the necropolis and the Acropolis, between the city of eternal ends and the city of eternal beginnings. The Agora brought the two together, in the actuality of time as experienced by the living generation.

The Agora was the location of the government and the seat of sovereignty. This suggests that its affiliated architectural type compares to Westfall's

regia. Indeed, a quick comparison of the plan-type which Westfall gave for
the regia (the so-called "square donut") to the Agora shows a remarkable
similarity. Westfall's diagram shows two concentric squares. The central
open space of the Agora, the place of gathering and decision, might be
compared to the inner square of the regia, while the strip with the buildings that house the various offices and councils that defined the perimeter
of the Agora corresponds to the space between the inner and outer square
of Westfall's regia.

The political archeology of the Agora as recorded in myth and reconstructed by historians supports an interpretation of the precinct as regia.
Homeric myth described the beginning of Greek civilization as a palace
culture. It depicts the megaron or central hall of the king's palace (regia)
as the locus of deliberation and judgement, decision and action. There
the king and his council gathered around the hearth. There the council's
deliberations converged in a collective judgement that either assented to or
dissented from the monarch's policy. This meeting around the fire, which
symbolized the common spirit, resembled the congregation of the gods on
the Olympus. In fact, the conclave of king and council was more than mere
reflection of the divine assembly. As John Dunne has argued in his *The City
of the Gods*, it actually replaced it. Dunne explained how every councilor's
"wisdom in matters of fate placed him on a level with the gods and put him
in touch with the powers to which it belonged to determine destiny."[78] The
council of the living did not only sit in joint session with the gods. It also
sat with the dead. The council's collective wisdom was based on foresight
and hindsight, of a knowledge of history. Therefore the meetings of the
assembly were framed by chanting the myths in which the paradigmatical
lives, decisions and destinies of the ancestors were recalled as the immortal
deeds that had created a moral universe within the fated world of nature.
The stories suggested that struggle was more important than achievement
and glory more important than wealth. They suggested that what really
mattered was the kind of history individuals made for themselves and their
people. The mythic past, as described in Homer's *Iliad* and *Odyssey*,
supports the identification of the Agora, the successor of the megaron as
the place of deliberation and decision, as a manifestation of Westfall's
regia. Like the megaron it was located between the council of the dead
and the gods, now symbolically represented by the public cemetery to the
north-west and the Acropolis to the south-east. The mythic origin of the
Areopagus, the guardian of the Agora, underlined the latter's royal ante-
cedents. Aeschylus' *Oresteia* began with the destruction of the Royal House
of Atreus, and ended with the construction of the House of Athens.

The historical archeology of the Agora also justifies its designation as a
regia. Athens was the only Greek city where the so-called Dark Ages did

not result in a total severance between its Mycenean beginning and its classical origin. Aristotle's *The Athenian Constitution* records how the office of Archon Basileus was the remnant of actual kingship, and how the office of Archon Polemarch had begun as that of a military aid to the king. Speaking of the time before Dracon, the text mentions that the oldest offices were that of Archon Basileus, Archon Polemarch and the Archon (Eponymos).

> The oldest office was that of the *basileus*, the traditional ruler. Secondly the office of polemarch was added, because some of the *basileis* were not strong warriors. . . . The last to be created was the office of archon. . . . That the office of archon was the last of these was confirmed by the fact that the archon is not responsible for any of the traditional festivals, as the *basileus* and the polemarch are, but only for the newer creations. This is how it has more recently become the principal office of state, being augmented by newly created functions.[79]

Jean-Pierre Vernant has argued convincingly that the Agora, as a concatenation of assembly and office holders, succeeded the Mycenean palace as democracy had replaced kingship. With the creation of the Archon Eponymos the notion of *arche*, command, was severed from the king—archon; "it became independent and determined the province of a strictly political reality. Elected for a period of ten years, the archons were later replaced every year. The election system, even though it kept or borrowed some features of a religious proceeding, implied a new conception of power: *arche* was delegated every year by human decision, through a choice that presupposed confrontation and discussion. This stricter delimitation of political power, which took the form of civic office, was complemented by *basileia* [kingship], which was now relegated to a specifically religious sphere."[80]

The Agora metaphorically transformed and expanded the megaron. The kingship that had been exercised in the megaron was now divided into different offices, and its origin ceased to be the decision of the gods (or the dead), but the deliberations of the assembly. These fragments of kingship were held together by something that transcended them all, a kingship that was no longer embodied in a person, but in a principle that united all the different aspects of the city—its laws, its religion, its morality and its customs. This normative principle was the Nomos. Its symbolic seat was the Areopagus, the hill at the south side of the Agora. The Nomos ruled over the Agora, and prevented it from becoming a pell-mell of anarchy. Victor Ehrenberg described the Nomos, which translates as custom, as the flexible synthesis of the various sacred and profane, written and unwritten norms that ruled the city. "Venerable in age, yet new every day, the Nomos could be experienced by every citizen as a tangible reality; it preserved the sacred traditions of his ancestors, originating from the aristocratic tradition as it did, and kept the past alive; as the will of the gods it ensured its future; it expressed, in fact, a sense of eternity that united the citizen with his ancestors and his descendants." And as the Nomos comprised the legislation by the assembly, ancestral customs, religious traditions and the perceived order of the Olympian world, so it was embodied by the institutions that preserved these laws and usages. Therefore the Nomos could overcome the antagonism between monarchy and democracy. "The citizen assembly as the political ruler and the god of the state as the divine king, were brought together in what expressed the will of both—in the Nomos, which really became 'Nomos the King.'"[81] The polis was Nomos' kingdom of Awe, the Agora its court and the council of the Areopagus its habitation. Yet just as the Nomos' kingship was of a spiritual kind, so was its palace. Westfall's regia fits the Mycenean royal citadel, an architectural mass around which the houses of the commoners lived and within which the king and council gathered. The square-donut of Palazzo Farnese—an object in the city—is, therefore, a paradigmatic model of a regia. Such a reading of Westfall's diagram implies that the larger square defines the exteriority of the regia, and the inner square its interiority. At the Agora this hierarchy was reversed: what in the Mycenean palace or in the Italian Palazzo was the interior courtyard has become *to meson*, the public space, and what used to be the public face has become the location of the more private parts of the various offices. The Agora's inversion of its Mycenean prototype may be explained as the result of the transposition of a building type into an urban form. Such an exposition implies that the Athenian Agora was a less paradigmatic example of the regia than, for example, Palazzo Farnese. A purely formalistic or architectural–theoretical comparison of the Agora and the palazzo in question certainly legitimizes such a judgement. In my historiographical universe the Athenian situation as a whole is normative and the Agora shares in that value judgement. While I do not deny that Palazzo Farnese is a paradigmatic example of Westfall's regia, I maintain that the example of the Athenian Agora has a normative significance because of its location at that nexus of contingencies known as classical Athens. As we have seen, the Athenian Agora fits the square–donut diagram of Westfall's regia, and it also carried its royal associations. The kind of building that defined it as an urban space was not a solid set in space, but a form that defined, bounded and protected the open space of the middle. Originally the Athenian Agora was surrounded by all kinds of different buildings, but one architectural form came to predominate as a special type that connected and separated the center of deliberation from the periphery of administration: the stoa or portico.

The stoa was a long, free-standing portico, generally open on one side and closed on the other. The open side fronted a public space; its length gave that area a regularized boundary and the rhythm of its colonnade imprinted a sense of order on the precinct. The closed side was often penetrated with doors that gave access to different rooms that were part of the stoa, or to various buildings located behind the stoa. The stoa itself was used as a courthouse and as a place for informal discussion. Whatever its function, the stoa provided, in Scully's words, "a finely unaggressive shell to contain the positive action of human beings."[82] In J.J. Coulton's monumental *The Architectural Development of the Greek Stoa* the stoa is described more as a reservoir of power than as a place of action. Stoas were "the natural resort for people wanting shelter from the rain or sun, people waiting for a friend or talking to acquaintances met in the agora, or people just wanting to see what was going on in the city. Of these the most notable, of course, are the philosophers, who found that they could most convenient-ly survey life and talk to their followers in a stoa." Stoas also served as shelter for the homeless. "In view of all of this," Coulton continued, "a stoa was a natural place to display something to the public notice, such as the text of a law or decree." And he concluded that "the general usefulness of stoas was in fact such that they are frequently listed among the necessary amenities of any proper city."[83] The stoa was a vital reservoir of thought and discussion, from which the assembly in the agora and the elected leaders in the various councils and offices derived new inspiration and energy. The stoas were storehouses of human vitality that could be activated in the meetings in the Agora or in the exercise of responsibility in the different councils and offices that it screened. The Stoa, in short, provided the broad and solid foundation of the two political spaces it separated and connected. These early corridors of power occupied the true center of the civic space of Westfall's regia; they allowed the center to remain in control of the periphery, and suggested in the measured beat of the doors leading into chambers and cabinets the circuit of responsibility described by Vernant. In its twofold relationship to the precinct of the Agora and the buildings at its periphery, the stoa became an architectural embodiment of the Nomos—the law that defined the political life in the Agora—the Nomos of which Heraclitus wrote that "people should fight for the law [Nomos] as for the city wall."[84]

The Gilgamesh epos attests how the building of massive brick ramparts marked the beginning of the history of the city: Gilgamesh built the walls to protect men and a sacred enclosure to protect the goddess Eanna. The erection of stoas—inhabitable envelopments of discourse—completed the architectural definition of Athens's public realm, and brought the urban form of the city and the history of architecture to completion. It did so in a very unprepossessing way. After all, the stoa recapitulated at a political level the form and function of emporium, the first type that I discussed earlier. If the emporium consisted of a market place for goods, surrounded by stoas that functioned as storehouses, the stoa defined as foundry of foresight and the storehouse of hindsight the Agora as a place where council leads to wisdom and reason informs decision. The two were connectors: the one of the people to the rest of the world, the other of the people to the remembered past and the anticipated future.

Therefore I believe that the word "regia" is a misnomer for the urban type of Westfall's square donut, embodied in Athens by the Agora. While it correctly identifies its palatial origin, it does not express its essential architectural concept: the stoa or portico. Therefore I will adopt the designation of "stoa" for Westfall's regia. This designation does not preclude a typological analysis of the Italian palazzo. It suggests, however, that the French chateau, with its long galleries (which served as symbols of the owner's sovereignty), is a more paradigmatic example of the regia than the Italian palazzo. This is not an altogether absurd proposition: for all its aesthetic flaws and hygienic deficiencies, Versailles occupies a much more important place in the cultural imagination of the West than Palazzo Farnese. And what is the palace of Versailles but an elaborate stoa that opens on one side to the precinct of France (the garden), and on the other side to the chambers of power, the royal apartments?

The Fivesquare City Reconsidered and Recapitulated

Athens was a fivesquare city. At the beginning of this chapter I described the larger square that originated and bounded the four smaller ones as the settlement that centered on the emporium. I proposed that the four remaining squares were four realms of concern, each with its own political and existential significance, each with its own affiliated architectural type. There was the neighborhood with the house, the cemetery with the stela, the acropolis with the shrine and the agora with the stoa. Closer study of the nature of these five realms revealed, however, that the question of which four were circumscribed by which fifth is not as straightforward as I originally suggested. Brecht's proposition that the grub precedes ethics, and that a crowd of disembodied spirits do not make a polis has remained as valid as it was before. Yet we ate in order to become capable of exploring new horizons. Thus we should feel free to reinterpret the diagram.

In fact, I would like to argue that the figure's receptivity to reevaluation is the touchstone that offers an important criterion of judgement as to the normative significance of each of the designated types. Each of the four types which I related to the smaller squares—the house, the stela, the shrine and the stoa—can fulfill the purpose of the fifth (or first) and larger square. Each of these types recapitulates some important aspect of the city as a whole. Without the private realm of the house, there can be no citizenry and there can be no city. Thus the house encompasses the four others, interpreted now as that which is not private. Without the remembrance embodied in the landscape of stelai, there can be no loyalty and attachment to the city as a historical community. As the foundation of civic commitment, the stela contains the four other districts of the city. Without the aspiration and hope embodied in the shrine, the idea of the city as a collective affirmation of life in the face of death becomes if not hollow than certainly inaccessible. Therefore the shrine contains the city as an ideal to be ministered. And without the vagabond forum of the stoa, which separates legislation from administration and which connects the discourse of politics and the practice of government to the ordinary citizen, there will be no freedom. Thus the stoa, accessible to all, encompasses the foursquare city in order to open it up to the boundless horizon of possibility.

Twenty-five centuries after it came to completion, classical Athens still offers the urban designer and the architect a criterion of what a city and its architecture can and ought to be. This does not mean that the Athens that we reconstructed was in its own time so self-evident a proposition as it is for us today. In my discussion of the emporium I already referred to Themistocles' founding of the Piraeus as the commercial district of Athens. There, too, was the naval basis. The founding and the urban development of the Piraeus challenged the viability of the old city of Athens, or the Asty as the Greeks called it. When in 479 BCE the decision was taken to build the Piraeus, the memory of the battle at Salamis was still fresh. At that occasion Themistocles' command had been challenged on the basis of the Athenian abandonment of the city of Athens that made him a man without a city and a leader without authority. Themistocles had answered that "It is quite true . . . that we have given up our houses and our city walls, because we did not choose to become enslaved for the sake of things that have no life or soul. But what we still possess is the greatest city in all of Greece, our 200 ships of war."[85] The creation of the Piraeus applied this principle in a situation of peace. This is absurd.

Robert Garland observed in his history of the Piraeus that the creation of the coastal suburb (which was incidentally larger in population and surface area than the Asty) *logically* called for the abandonment of the (in 480 BCE largely destroyed) Asty in favor of wholesale migration to the easily defensible and providable harbor. And this would have happened, so he believed, if the Asty had been at a greater distance from the Piraeus.

"Fatally for Athens . . . the Asty was close enough to the coast to enable fairly rapid communication with the port town. Had the distance been greater, the case for abandoning the old city would have been unanswerable and the future course of Athenian history would have been very different. That such a move does not seem to have been contemplated was due to emotional attachment, vested interest, religious scruples, and the sheer force of public inertia."[86] In other words, the fivesquare city of Athens had *de facto* become, even before its architectural completion, a military liability and if one would follow Themistocles' understanding of politics, a political absurdity. The Athenians who believed that shrines can have a life and houses a soul got tired of their leader who had saved their city but who, afterwards, did not have the wisdom to see that a city at war is different from a city at peace, and thus they banished him. Themistocles died in exile. His remains were later brought back to Athens, and, as Plutarch recorded, buried on a promontory near the harbor of the Piraeus. It was an appropriate resting place for the man who had effectively urged the Athenians to leave the place where their ancestors had lived and were buried for the convenience and safety of the harbor. Appropriate, too, because at the city's most important port of entry it announced to all who arrived from abroad that Athens was a city that faced the grotesque, extravagant and contradictory consequences of democracy.

This brings me back to the fivesquare city. The triad of the necropolis outside the Asty, the Agora—Areopagus and the Acropolis celebrated the threefold time of the polis as manifested in the immutable past of history, the dynamic present in which citizens transcend a concern for private gain for the sake of the city, and an enduring future that frames the collective aspiration of the citizenry. The discourse of reason dictates that these three urban spaces made the public space of the Hellenic polis, conceived as a bulwark in time, complete. But the Athenians knew that life as actually lived and experienced by each individual citizen did not follow the dictates of an architectonic reason. Their decision to send Themistocles into exile could not have been taken if not on the basis of a clear sense of the dramatic. These people realized how the unanticipated, the improbable and the paradoxical quickened the pace of everyday existence in directions that often ran counter to the one proposed by that of the civic realm. The all-encompassing sense of belonging and of destiny, generated during the great public festivals, did not match the irrational reality of urban existence. Any inhabitant of the democratic city could see the abyss between the dignified remembrance of the necropolis and the lofty ideology of the Acropolis and, on the other hand, the workings of "this actual city" as embodied in commercial practices within the emporia, inappropriate behavior within the homes and dirty deeds within the Agora. And they knew, too, that notwithstanding the authority of the Areopagus, the Furies with their relentless and inflexible memory of evil done loomed behind the civic facade of public funerals. And they knew that on the acroteria of the Parthenon sat the Moiras, who weave the thread of time and decide the fate of cities and men. The polis was not utopia realized, and did not embody the ideal of the perfect life as formulated by Aristotle and resuscitated within architectural discourse by Westfall. Despite its elegant completeness, ancient Athens was no more able to meet the needs of the individual people than, for example, the contemporary North American city. This is the price of freedom. Between the heroic immutable past and the illusion of the enduring future, citizens did not find only the rational dynamism of the political constitution, but also false rhetoric, irrational political compulsions, criminal injudiciousness and ambiguous abjection. They witnessed the success of the unworthy and the random destruction of the heroic. And behind the revolutionary facade of the various reforms they found an impregnable and shady world of ancient custom, an imperishable world in which the officially rendered ties of blood and soil, once embodied in kinship and tribal affiliation, had persisted as impenetrable but powerful motivations. They knew that the emporia and houses, the stelai, shrines and stoas were often not the landmarks of a comprehensible destiny, but the sinister *scaenae frontes* that masked a fated doom, Ανάγκη, *Anagkê*, necessity, Doom.

The Hellenic city had to address the reality of frustration, the inevitability of failure and the certainty of suffering. It was not sufficient to state at funeral orations that the sacrifice the dead had made for the sake of the city ensured in itself their everlastingness. Death in battle always means defeat, even if the individual's downfall ensured the city's victory. Only in exploring and presenting the tragic potential of human existence in general and that of the lives of the heroes in particular would the polis be able to bridge the tragic abyss that existed between the rational understanding of what the city was about and the absurdity of the actual working of the city, between the city's claim that the private realm was of no importance and the citizen's experience that his private anguish determined to a large extent the way he acted in public. Therefore the Greeks, and especially the Athenians, who more than others faced the dichotomy between lofty ideal and dirty reality, developed a specific civic institution in which the threefold nature of the public realm was related to the being of every citizen, in which personal suffering was brought on the public stage, and civic responsibility was revealed in its relationship to private tragedy. This institution was drama. As Vernant explained, Greek drama was fully integrated in the civic life of the Greek city. "By establishing, under the authority of the *archon eponymos* in the same civic arena and following the same institutional norms as the assemblies or the popular ribunals, a performance open to all citizens, directed, played and judged by qualified representatives of the various tribes, the city makes itself into a theater; in a way it becomes an object of representation and plays itself before the public."[87] The architectural type of this most important of the city's political institutions was the open-air theatre. The theater is the sixth and last architectural type. Unlike the others it *explicitly* and *purposefully* recapitulated the emporium, the house and, most importantly, the three types that gave architectural form to the public realm: the stela, the shrine and the agora. As will be clear, the theater relates to Westfall's theatre.

Attic Tragedy

Athenian drama began with tragedy, the drama that explored the world of contradiction and inevitable defeat for the sake of self-knowledge. Karl Jaspers described the emergence of tragic knowledge as the quintessential achievement of the axial period. In his major philosophical work, *Von der Wahrheit* (*Concerning Truth*), published in 1947, Jaspers included an important discussion on the historic and existential significance of tragedy. In this section, published separately in English translation under the title *Tragedy Is Not Enough*, Jaspers took up the central theme of his *The Origin and Goal of History*. He described how "history was rent asunder by the birth of Tragic Man."

> The greatest chasm separates those civilizations that never achieve tragic knowledge—and consequently its vehicles, tragedy, epic and the novel—from those whose way of life is determined by poignant awareness of the intrinsic part tragedy plays in man's existence. . . . Man seems only truly awake when he has such knowledge. For now he will face each realization of his ultimate limits with a new restlessness that drives him beyond them. Nothing that is stable will endure, for nothing that is stable will satisfy him. Tragic knowledge is the first phase of that historical movement which takes place not only in external events but in the depths of man himself.[88]

As we have seen in Chapter Three, Jaspers identified the axial period as an age of anxiety. Between 800 and 300 BCE the stability of the mythic world, with its fundamental security, disappeared in a great maelstrom of change. Yet this general breakdown and the pervasive sense of failure had led men like Solon, Aeschylus, Sophocles and Thucydides to search for the true nature of things. All of them agreed that life's reality is not lost in failure. Instead they discovered that especially in failure the layers of illusion are stripped away until it discloses the core of being where life makes itself wholly and decisively felt. Jaspers summarized their findings in the statement that there is no tragedy without transcendence. "Even defiance unto death in a hopeless battle against gods and fate is an act of transcending: it is a movement towards man's proper essence, which he comes to know as his own in the presence of doom."[89] As Aeschylus explored in his *Oresteia*, Sophocles in his *Oedipus Tyrannus* and Thucydides showed in his *History of the Peloponnesian War*, a people's confrontation with the ruin of the world around might become an encounter with the reality and truth of the infinite. To the open-minded observer the experience of a particular disaster suggested that every configuration, fivesquare or not, was ultimately doomed. Yet it also revealed that this ultimate destiny of ruin brought them in touch with the very core of Being, the ground of all existence. "The spectator discovers that doom itself is the triumph of reality, a reality so fundamental that it forever outlives all destruction: in prodigality and in destruction, in danger and doom, this reality becomes aware of its own supreme power."[90] Thucydides wrote a history of the "greatest war" in order to discover the truth that was concealed beneath the reality of his native city. He realized that even the minds of bright men like Themistocles and Pericles were destined to break down in the very wealth of its potentialities. As we have seen, the measure of Athens's greatness became the measure of her suffering because, as Jaspers observed, every one of these potentialities, as it became fulfilled, provoked and reaped disaster. Few of his fellow citizens read Thucydides' work. But all of them witnessed the tragedies staged in the Theater of Dionysius, located in the sacred precinct of Dionysius Eleuthereus on the southern slope of the Acropolis. Tragedies (and later also comedies) allowed them to experience the reality of the city, and led them back into that reality. It allowed them to overcome the tragic through the creation of an awareness of the larger context of reality. For Aeschylus' *Oresteia* this larger context was, as we have seen, the Nomos as embodied in the polis. Tragic knowledge is ultimately political.[91] It always contains, as Jaspers argued, "the final release from tragedy, not through doctrine and revelation but through the vision of order, justice, love of one's fellow man; through trust."[92] Yet this vision does not deny the inexorable limitations of our understanding and our power to act upon that understanding. Ultimately the actions taken in response to our discovery of reality leave the question as such unanswered. Even the order of law embodied in the Areopagus is, in the end, a limit.

The tragedy originated in the two annual festivals of Dionysius: the Lenaea and the more popular City Dionysia, which was the most important urban festival after the Panathenaia. The City Dionysia had been founded by Peisistratos in 534 BCE. It was intended to consolidate as a folk festival the political unification of Attica, wrought fifty years earlier, by a social integration of the citizenry. If the Panathenaia celebrated the political constitution with processions that connected the necropolis, the Agora and the Acropolis, the City Dionysia stressed the idea of the social unity of all the people. When Peisistratos instituted the City Dionysia, the old affiliations of kinship and region were still very powerful, which meant that Athens's political constitution was at odds with the social reality in Attica. As we have seen, Solon had given constitutional significance to the traditional four Ionian tribes, but within these tribes there was a core of opposition to the new democracy. These were the clans. Each of these aristocratic old-boy networks comprised the lineal descendants of a common heroic ancestor. Alan Little described these clans, which were closed to commoners, as bulwarks of stout conservatism. "They maintained their solidarity in the old ceremonial way through common religious rites in honor of their common ancestors, by owning a common burial place and by reciprocal obligations of help, defense and redress of injuries." The tribal groups had lost their economic significance, a divestment that affected their significance as channels of social reciprocity. Nevertheless the democratic institutions had not been able to encroach the tribal taboos. "Here was a psychological stronghold which had to be stormed before the democratic process was complete, and this is precisely the function to which we see tragedy bending its energies in the beginning of its history, using the tribal forms, the tribal thought patterns which alone were intelligible to the group, but carrying to the conscience of the people as a whole what had previously been the ethical problems of the tribal clan."[93]

The City Dionysia were instituted as a means to create a stable social basis for the political superstructure of the polis. This social integration had very practical aspects. The Dionysia were first and foremost a big party, a national holiday held at the beginning of the spring. It began with a great procession, in which dancing girls accompanied huge phalluses that were carried to symbolize the idea that all Athenians had come from the same seed. The festival lasted for a week and transformed the city into one great emporium. Founded to bring the people of Athens together, the City Dionysia soon became a great Panhellenic fair. As it coincided with the beginning of the sailing season, ships with visitors from all over Greece converged on Athens. Many came voluntarily. Others did not. During the days of Athenian imperial glory, the festival was also the time when embassies from the allied cities had to pay their obligatory call on Athens to surrender the annual tribute. They had to bring the money to the middle of the theater where it was counted by the city treasurers. In return, the city invited the delegates to attend the remaining days of the festival, for free.

Their luck was that the last three days of this festival offered some most appropriate reflections on their misfortune. Every day a different playwright, selected by the Archon Eponymous, had to present a tetralogy (such as Aeschylus' *Oresteia*) consisting of three tragedies (in the case of the *Oresteia* these were the *Agamemnon*, *The Libation Bearers* and *The Eumenides*) to which was added one satyr play (*Proteus*). These plays were presented as part of a competition, judged by ten judges selected by lot from the ten tribes. The winner received an award.

Apocalypse

The earlier dramas, like those of the *Oresteia*, remained committed to the conflict between passion and reason, tradition and innovation, aristocracy and democracy, the ties of blood and the ties of the polis. Their metaphorical location was the Areopagus, the hill where the Nomos resided and where the Furies (now also known as the Eumenides) lived. Their apocalyptic zenith was the work of Sophocles. Two of the seven surviving tragedies (of a total of 123) are particularly significant: *Antigone* (442 BCE) and *Oedipus Tyrannus* (429 BCE). In these two plays Sophocles explored the limits of the polis and the breakdown of politics. Significantly, Sophocles did not choose Athens as the primary location of his tragedies, but the city of Thebes. The classical scholar Froma Zeitlin explained the meaning of Thebes as that of being a kind of Mr. Hyde to the Athenian Dr. Jekyll: it was the place where the impossible could become real. "Thebes functioned in the theater as an anti-Athens, an other place. If we say that theater in general functions as an 'other scene' where the city puts itself and its values into question by projecting itself upon the stage to confront the present with the past through its ancient myths, then Thebes, I suggest, is the 'other scene' of the 'other scene' that is the theater itself. Thebes, we might say, is the quintessential 'other scene,' as Oedipus is the paradigm of the tragic man and Dionysus is the god of the theatre. There Athens acts out questions crucial to the *polis*, to the self, the family, and society, but these are displaced upon a city that is imagined as the mirror opposite of Athens." The adoption of Thebes as the locus of tragedy preserved the Aeschylean ideology, manifested in *The Eumenides*, of Athens as the place where the opposites could find reconciliation. And the fiction that the stories of Antigone and Oedipus applied in first instance to the history of another city also allowed for a relentlessness which would have been unacceptable if applied to, for example, the history of Themistocles. Zeitlin described Thebes as the shadow self of Athens where the tragic action could be pushed "to its furthest limits of contradiction and impasse. As such it also furnishes the territory for exploring the most radical implications of the tragic. In other words, Thebes, the other, provides Athens, the self, with a place where it can play with and discharge both terror and attraction to the irreconcilable, the inexpiable, and the unredeemable, where it can experiment with the dangerous heights of self-assertion that transgression of fixed boundaries inevitably entails."[94] This shadow Athens was the setting of both the *Antigone* and *Oedipus Tyrannus*. The *Antigone* touched on the increasing separation between the individual and the institutions of the state that had accompanied Athens's imperial achievement. It centred on two protagonists: Creon, the King of Thebes, representative of the interests of the state, and Antigone, who defies Creon's legal authority because the political structure that he embodies is indifferent to the claims of humanity. The story describes the aftermath of King Oedipus' abdication and death. His two sons, Eteoclus, and Polynices, had assumed the rule over the city together with their uncle Creon when Oedipus—having discovered that he had involuntarily killed his father Laius and married his mother Jocasta—had left Thebes in order to wander the highways of Greece as a beggar. The two brothers quarreled over their rights of succession. Creon supported Eteoclus, and Polynices left Thebes. He returned with an army, and in the resulting battle the two brothers killed each other. The responsibility for the state fell now to Creon, who ordered a state-burial for Eteoclus, and decreed that the corpse of the "traitor" Polynices was to be thrown out unburied, a prey for the dogs and vultures. Defiance of this order was punishable by death. Antigone, the sister of the two brothers, disregarded Creon's edict and buried Polynices. Arrested and brought to Creon, Antigone defended her actions in a ferocious manner, and thus sealed her fate. She was condemned to be imprisoned in an underground tomb, where she was to starve to death.

Having committed a living being to the world below and ordered a dead body to remain in the world above, Creon has disturbed the cosmic order. Having assumed the role of a god, Creon has deified the city and subverted the hierarchical order of the universe.[95] This becomes clear to him (and the audience) when the blind seer Tiresias appears, who recognizes that Creon has blocked the communication between the immortals and the mortals. He urges Creon to change his mind as the birds and dogs have begun to foul the public altars and sacred hearths of Thebes with the carrion flesh of Polynices' corpse.

And so the gods are deaf to our prayers, they spurn
the offerings in our hands, the flame of holy flesh.
No birds cry out an omen clear and true—
they're gorged with the murdered victim's blood and fat.

Take these things to heart, my son, I Warn you
All men make mistakes, it is only human.
But one wrong is done, a man
can turn his back on folly, misfortune too,
if he tries to make amends, however low he's fallen,
and stops his bullnecked ways. Stubbornness
brands you for stupidity—pride is a crime.
No, yield to the dead!
Never stab the fighter when he's down.
Where's the glory, killing the dead twice over?[96]

Creon rejects Tiresias' advice, who then turns from a counselor into a seer, who, possessed with sacred powers, threatens Creon with doom.

Then know this too, learn this by heart!
The chariot of the sun will not race through
so many circuits more, before you have surrendered
one born of your own loins, your own flesh and blood,
a corpse for corpses given in return, since you have thrust
to the world below a child sprung from the world above,
ruthlessly lodged a living soul within the grave—
then you've robbed the gods below the earth,
keeping a dead body here in the bright air,
unburied, unsung, unhallowed by the rites.

You have no business with the dead,
nor do the gods above—this is violence
you have forced upon the heavens.
And so the avengers, the dark destroyers late
but true to the mark, now lie in wait for you,
the Furies sent by the gods and the god of death
to strike you down with the pains that you perfected![97]

Tiresias' proclamation of the divine verdict turns the minds of Creon's advisors. They realize that the future of the city is now at stake. They persuade Creon to countermand his own decree, but it is already too late. When the men of Thebes open Antigone's prison-tomb, they find that she hanged herself.

In the confrontation of Creon and Antigone Sophocles revealed how political authority might usurp human right and challenge divine justice. Yet the ethical crisis can still be resolved within the existent polis. As Cedric Whitman observed, "the *Antigone* unquestionably reflects one of the earliest phases of the rift between city and citizen; Creon, drawn in tyrannical and oligarchic colors, embodies the moral atrophy of civic institutions, while the heroine herself presents the ideal of individual moral perception. Her tragedy is a tragedy which Sophocles, writing at the peak of Athenian greatness, could envision as a possibility." Yet Sophocles did not condemn the polis. It remains a flexible and vital structure that might ultimately resolve the contradictions, if only in the theatre. "The *Antigone* is 'political' through and through, in the broad Greek sense of 'pertaining to the polis.' For the religious adherences of Sophocles are profoundly interwoven with the whole concept of the city-state, and neither could exist without the other. Somewhat as the Sophoclean hero stands alone by his own moral force, the city-state looked to its inner, organic structure for its justification; it could live only through the individual political conscience of its statesmen and citizens, and it would last only so long as there was someone strong enough to understand it."[98]

Sophoclean tragedy posited the question of understanding, of truth and illusion (or vision and blindness, knowledge and ignorance, unconcealment and distortion, being and appearance or *noumenon* and *phenomenon*) as the foundation of the polis. Creon did not understand that the laws of the living were only valid in so far as they did not confound the laws of the immortals and the dead. His blindness brought him doom. In *Oedipus Tyrannus*, written thirteen years after *Antigone*, the sense of crisis deepened to such a degree that it seems as though it locates the very chasm that separates Jaspers's "Tragic Man" from the being that preceded him. When Oedipus blinded himself when he had seen what he was, he rent (architectural) history asunder.

In *Oedipus Tyrannus* Sophocles turned to the events that preceded those described in *Antigone* in order to uncover the tectology of illusion that separates truth from reality. The drama begins in the fifteenth or twentieth year of Oedipus' reign. Sophocles characterizes Oedipus as a king of greater stature, intelligence and insight than Creon. His wit had earned him his kingship when he had solved the riddle of the Sphinx and so delivered Thebes from its despoilment. The Thebans had offered him the city and the hand of its queen Jocasta, whose husband King Laius had been killed on his way to the oracle at Delphi shortly before Oedipus' arrival in the city.

After a happy marriage that produced four children and years of enlightened government things begin to go wrong. The plague hits Thebes. Oedipus sends his brother-in-law (and, as he will later learn, his uncle) Creon to Delphi to consult Apollo's oracle. Creon returns with the message that the Delphic oracle commands that Laius' death must be avenged if the suffering is to cease. Oedipus accepts the task to find and kill Laius' murderer. He summons Tiresias. The seer, who knows the secret of Oedipus' parentage and his past, initially refuses to tell the King the repugnant truth. But when he is mocked by Oedipus Tiresias utters the horrible accusation that Oedipus himself killed the King. Oedipus does not believe him. His first reaction is to assume that this uncanny accusation is politically motivated, conceived as part of a sinister plot to overthrow him as King of Thebes. Yet he does not cede his quest for the truth and, as the play progresses, Oedipus discovers that he indeed killed Laius when they met in a skirmish shortly before his own arrival in Thebes—the reason for his earlier ignorance of this fact was the assertion by the only and extremely confused witness that Laius had been killed by a band of thieves; Oedipus had engaged the man who now turned out to have been Laius in a one-to-one combat, and hence he had never sought to relate the two events to each other.

Yet this is not all: the truth is even more hideous. Oedipus is a regicide and a patricide. He did not only kill his predecessor as king and husband, but also his father. He learns that at his birth it had been prophesied that Laius would be killed by his own son, and therefore his parents had sent the baby from Thebes to be raised in Corinth. Oedipus realizes that he was that baby, that he had killed his father and that he lived in incest with his own mother for the duration of his reign. As the Sophoclean scholar Bernard Knox wrote, "that discovery is the most thoroughgoing and dreadful catastrophe the stage has ever presented. The hero who in his vigor, courage and intelligence stands as a representative of all that is creative in man discovers a truth so dreadful that the chorus which sums up the results of the great calculation [of all human achievement] sees in his fall the reduction of man to nothing."[99]

O the generations of men
the dying generations—adding the total
of all your lives I find they come to nothing . . . [100]

Oedipus Tyrannus reveals abjection to be the murky limit of the polis and its institutions. The perverse truth that Oedipus discovered about himself defies the structure and scope of the city's institutions. As we have seen, the foundation of the polis was the idea that a system of human justice, symbolized by the Areopagus, could in the end overcome the accumulation of guilt. The triumphant end of the *Oresteia* was the establishment of due process. Yet the enormity of Oedipus' life is, in a sense, beyond the reach of human and divine justice. His abomination has broken human and cosmic order, and thus also the only foundation for judgement. True: an Athenian court of the fifth century would most likely have acquitted

Oedipus. When faced with an unprovoked assault by a stranger, Oedipus had acted in self-defence, ignorant that the stranger was his own father. The crime had been involuntary, as had been the sin of marrying his own mother. A ceremonial purification would probably have sufficed to resolve the whole incestuous affair.

Yet the jury's verdict would not have touched the black hole of the play: the question of culpable innocence, the question that has fueled so much of the Sophoclean debate. The German scholar Karl Reinhardt (1886–1958) commented in his *Sophokles*—completed in the fateful month of January 1933—on the remarkable silence with which Sophocles surrounds that most important issue of Oedipus' responsibility. Reinhardt acknowledged that Oedipus speaks of himself in words that are used of a criminal who is guilty of another's death. "But," so Reinhardt argued, "that does not mean that any question was raised about the guilt." And he invited us to reflect on the possibility that *Oedipus Tyrannus* would have ended like *The Eumenides*, with a court that exculpates Oedipus. Such a verdict would have been meaningless to Oedipus himself, "for what meaning would such an acquittal have in the face of the contradiction between what he has imagined he is, and what he is?" Reinhardt believed that the issue at stake was not who was responsible, but what is the truth about Oedipus. And no judgement can release Oedipus from what he has learned about himself. "So there is no decision here about justice and atonement—nothing would be more misguided than to regard Oedipus' blinding as an atonement—or about freedom or necessity. What we have to consider is illusion and truth as the opposing forces between which man is bound, in which he is entangled, and in whose shackles, as he strives towards the highest he can hope for, he is worn down and destroyed."[101] If Aeschylus' *Oresteia* revealed how the question of justice undergirds the political life, then Sophocles' *Oedipus Tyrannus* disclosed how justice itself is shaped by the mystery of fate.

The play was for the first time performed in the year 430 BCE, when Athens was still in the grips of the plague. That year the Athenians had learned that the rational policies created by Themistocles and applied by Pericles had turned against them, that the city that had seemed a refuge had become a lethal trap. The whole play is pervaded by this sense of powerlessness: Oedipus, the man who had saved the city from the sphinx through his cunning, was, in the end, wholly ignorant as to the cause of its destruction. He was powerless when the plague arrived. Few in the audience would not have recognized in Oedipus, a man of action, courage and intelligence, the kind of qualities and temperament that they prized in the democratic leadership, and especially in Pericles. As Knox observed, "Oedipus the King is a dramatic embodiment of the creative vigor and intellectual daring of the fifth-century Athenian spirit."[102] Yet these qualities did not give Oedipus the means to save Thebes, as it did save Athens. This realization that reason is ultimately powerless to shape the world as we want—a realization that shaped Thucydides' *The History of the Peloponnesian War*—became an integral part of the Athenian experience in the last decades of the fifth century. This apprehension is wholly contemporary. Knox commented that "Sophocles' play has served modern man and his haunted sense of being caught in a trap" because it confronts us with "our own terror of the unknown future which we fear we cannot control—our deep fear that every step we take forward on what we think is the road of progress may really be a step toward a foreordained rendezvous with disaster."[103]

Ultimately the play is about truth and illusion, about knowledge and ignorance. The man who knows so much, who solves the riddle of the Sphinx, is in fact ignorant. He even doesn't know who his parents are. But ignorance can be overcome, even though Oedipus realizes that the price he has to pay for this is tremendous. And so in the end he is a victim of fate, to necessity, *anagkê*. Yet within it he reasserts the one, two-sided freedom that is left: the freedom to search for the truth, the truth about the prophecies, about the gods, about himself and the truth about freedom itself. It is a freedom that will compel him to endure the knowledge he gains in his search, because without that endurance he will not be able to continue that search. The German scholar Reinhardt believed that we experience this freedom in shackles, that is one which wears us down, one which will destroy us. It fitted the apocalyptic mood of the early thirties. Writing fifty years later, the American Bernard Knox judged this freedom in more optimistic terms. The freedom to search for the truth, so Knox asserted, "is the key to the play's tragic theme and the protagonist's heroic stature." And he saluted the lonesome hero who, against all reasonable advice, did his utmost to find the truth. "And in this search he shows all the great qualities that we admire in him—courage, intelligence, persever-ance, the qualities that make human beings great. This freedom to search, and the heroic way in which Oedipus uses it, makes the play not a picture of man's utter feebleness caught in the toils of fate, but on the contrary, a heroic example of man's dedication to the search for truth, the truth about himself. This is perhaps the only human freedom, the play seems to say, but there can be none more noble."[104]

Caesura

Having begun his descent into thirty-five years of silence, Friedrich Hölderlin completed in 1804 his dark, dissonant and disturbing transla-tions of *Antigone* and *Oedipus Tyrannus*. These emotionally naked and powerfully irrational "translations" are the core of his last creative period:

the first six years of the nineteenth century which gave birth to that remarkable oeuvre that many critics today recognize as a primary source of modernism.[105] Yet his translations did not only cast their shadow on the twentieth century; in an epoch marked by such catastrophes as the French Revolution and the Napoleonic empire they brought to light a new and appropriate reading of Greek civilization marked by crisis and catastrophic dislocation. In short, Hölderlin broke with the neo-classical celebration of ancient Greece as that untroubled realm of Apollonian perfection and authoritatively restored to the European memory that seemingly irrational and ultimately Heraclitean apprehension that had guided Thucydides' unsettling assessment that the true measure of achievement is the profundity of the cataclysm that it brings forth—that, as Tiresias tells Oedipus, great good fortune results in total ruin—that the scope of freedom is its horizon of fate. Indeed: Hölderlin's (unusual) interpretation of the cause of Oedipus' abjection corresponds in many ways to Thucydides' understanding of the fall of Athens. If the School of Hellas fell victim to its own intellect, so also Oedipus. According to Hölderlin Oedipus' fault was that he interpreted the instruction from Delphi "too infinitely." The enormity that brought Oedipus down was not the murder or the incestuous marriage, but his compulsive need to know the truth, that "sick-minded hankering after consciousness" which was to lead to destruction because "knowledge, once it has broken through its bounds . . . excites itself to know more than it can bear or comprehend."[106]

In a short commentary on *Oedipus Tyrannus*, Hölderlin pondered how the adjacency of greatest exaltation and deepest abomination, represented in the fate of Oedipus himself, emerged from the structure of Greek drama. Tragedy had an order, so he argued, and the principle of this order was the alternating and rhythmic succession of *Vorstellungen* or representations. Representation referred to the ethical or moral issue that a tragic hero embodies in the play. The alternation of representations is, then, the strife that occurs when a hero like for example Antigone suffers the collision of two conflicting and unappeasable ethical demands, of the divine and the mortal, the boundless and lawless infinite and the rule-bound finite. This conflict between freedom and necessity can only deepen into an irremediable and monstrous situation as the play progresses, a dialectic of discourse against discourse that cannot but lead away from a possible synthesis and a satisfactory resolution in a Hegelian sense. Hölderlin believed that tragedy ought to create an equilibrium between these two demands. In *Oedipus Tyrannus* this balance is to be found at the moment when Oedipus realizes that his quest for truth has resulted in the discovery of the enormity of his life, a moment at which he takes responsibility for all his acts, even the most horrible, even though they were committed in innocence.

This quest for an equilibrium necessitates a moment in the drama when the conflict is in a state of suspense, an event when, as Hölderlin phrased it, the truth of the conflict of representations appears. That instant when tragedy turns upon itself Hölderlin identified as the *caesura*, "the pure word, the counter-rhythmic rupture" that counteracts and meets "the onrushing change of representations at its highest point in such a manner that very soon there does not appear the change of representation but the representation itself."[107] This foreboding moment of counter-rhythmic suspense, the silent center of the tragedy when rhythm and *logos* meet in an interruption which, paradoxically, makes it possible for the tragedy to continue, occurs in both *Antigone* and *Oedipus Tyrannus* at the moment that the seer Tiresias appears as he "enters the course of fate as the custodian of the natural power which, in a tragic manner, removes man from his own life-sphere, the center of his inner life into another world and into the excentric sphere of the dead."[108] Indeed: Oedipus, who mocks the seer's knowledge as blindness, ceases to be a whole person at the moment that he refuses to see himself for what Tiresias and the whole audience know him to be. The blind seer speaks "the pure word" that ends the beginning and begins the end.

                                                       So,
you mock my blindness? Let me tell you this.
You with your precious eyes,
you're blind to the corruption of your life,
to the house you live in, those you live with—
who *are* your parents? Do you know? All unknowing
you are the scourge of your own flesh and blood,
the dead below the earth and the living here above,
and the double lash of your mother and your father's curse
will whip you from this land one day, their footfall
treading you down in terror, darkness shrouding
your eyes that now can see the light!

                                            Soon, soon
you'll scream aloud—what heaven won't reverberate?
What rock of Cithaeron won't scream back in echo?
That day you learn the truth about your marriage,
the wedding-march that sang you into your halls,
the lusty voyage home to the fatal harbor!
And a crowd of other horrors you'd never dream
will level you with yourself and all your children.[109]

Thus the development of the plot, conceived as a strife between the opposing principles is, if only for a moment, arrested in an opening up of the world to the infinite. The caesura thus marks an element that is common to all religions and all cities. It signifies the cleft caused by the vertical insertion of the divine into the horizontal of the world. It denotes the fissure in time where the historical was shattered by the eternal. The caesura in the drama is like a restoration in time of the sanctuary in space that archaic civilizations located at the fifth point of the quincunx of the city. The caesura in the play succeeded to the legacy of the heaven-embracing shrine, which had became obsolete in the axial period.

Yet the caesura did not appropriate only the temple's divine aspects. A building that touches the heavens must have foundations which reach into infernal depths. This has remained the root of architectural symbolism from the Mesopotamian zigguraths to Dom Claude's vision of the Tour de Nesle (see Chapter One). It was also essential in Hölderlin's assessment of the significance of the caesura in Sophoclean tragedy: the opening up is simultaneously a being thrown back to the realm of the finite. "The presentation of the tragic rests primarily on the tremendous—how the god and man mate and how natural force and man's innermost [essence] boundlessly unite in wrath—conceiving of itself, [rests] on the boundless union purifying itself through boundless separation."[110] Dark language and dark thoughts: tragedy purifies the moment of contact in that it reveals how the moment of union is also the moment of total abandonment, how consummation is in fact betrayal, how revelation is in the final analysis concealment. Yet there is a logic to this paradox, a logic that emerges from the boundlessness of the divine and the finitude of mortals. When a finite being runs into the infinite, the infinite can only be experienced as abyss or nothingness. Thus the moment of unification is felt as a withdrawal of the divine from that very union. Was this the truth which Jeremiah saw when he warned the people of Judah not to assign a transcendent significance to Jerusalem's temple? Did the polemic against the man-made temple emerge from a realization that the very power of architecture and liturgy to summon a feeling of mystical union was doomed to turn into its opposite?

I don't know, but such caution makes sense as the immediacy with the divine of the caesura (be it in space or time) is ultimately the realization that God turns away from the world, that God betrays the world. This, so Hölderlin discovered, was as much the ground of Sophocles' *Oedipus Tyrannus* as it had been the yield of his own life. In *Hyperion's Song of Fate* Hölderlin expressed a first apprehension that the serene city of the Olympians was unconnected to the fragile encampments of the mortals, and that the gods were unresponsive to the latter's desire to partake in their moral order. While people were "fated / To find no foothold, no rest," the immortals existed in an enchanted and "fateless" realm all of their own, a luminous and self-sufficient world that cannot be but disinterested in the benighted and troubled domain below.

You walk above in the light,
Weightless tread a soft floor, blessed genii!
Radiant the gods' mild breezes
Gently play on you
As the girl artist's fingers
On holy strings.[111]

This initial foreboding of a fissure that separates human tragedy from divine comedy was to deepen into a profound sense of crisis. By the turn of the century Hölderlin had begun to explore the explicitly prophetic vocation of the poet. I quoted in Chapter Three the lines from his "As on a Holiday . . ." in which he placed the poet bare-headed beneath a numinous thunder-filled sky. He was to grasp the god's ray, wrap it in song and hand it over to the people. Yet he was unable to retain this daring vision of the poet's awesome mission: the poem breaks down halfway in the following strophe as its maker suddenly realized that contact with the gods can only be bought at the price of self-destruction. The poem records the poet's cry "But, oh, my shame! when of . . ." Then silence. Again: "My shame!" And the poem breaks down for a second time.

And then a few last, fragmentary lines.

And let me say at once

That I approached to see the Heavenly,
And they themselves cast me down, deep down
Below the living, into the dark cast down
The false priest that I am, to sing,
For those who have ears to hear, the warning song.
There[112]

A year later, in 1801, Hölderlin seemed to have accepted that the immortals do not communicate with mortals in the benighted age as an expression of wisdom. Only through their silence were they able to save humanity from the cataclysm evoked in "As on a Holiday . . .". In the seventh strophe of his elegy *Bread and Wine*, Hölderlin assented to an uneasy standoff wrought in mutual resignation.

But, my friend, we have come too late. Though the gods are living,
Over our heads they live, up in a different world.
Endlessly there they act and, such is their kind wish to spare us,
Little they seem to care whether we live or do not.

For not always a frail, a delicate vessel can hold them,
Only at times can our kind bear the full impact of the gods.[113]

These issues crowded Hölderlin's mind when he worked on his translation of *Oedipus Tyrannus*. Oedipus' fate found resonance in his own life. Like Oedipus he had found that resignation is the only possible response to what human beings can only characterize as a turning away of the divine, the revelation of nothingness, the catastrophe. Yet he also discovered that this renunciation amounts in fact to apostasy. The person who has discovered in the vision of God the emptiness of the heavens has no choice but to turn back to the earth and betray God in turn.

George Steiner speculated that this betrayal was, in the end, the only appropriate way to force God to announce her presence: "to fill the gap, certain human beings—Oedipus—must be made, must make of themselves, *Verräter*, 'traitors to God'. They must, as it were, commit treason against the natural, against the ontological boundaries which separate mortal being from the divine." This treason may only be committed at that boundary, in a situation of union. Only the poet who stands bare-headed beneath God's thunderstorm can become the false priest; only the most ardent disciple can commit the treason of Gethsemane. And Steiner continued with the speculation that "these sanctified and self-sacrificial betrayers *compel* the divine to manifest its offended, overwhelming power and thus restore it to man's awareness."[114] Oedipus blinded himself and left Thebes to wander Greece as a beggar. Hölderlin became mad in 1806 and, after a year's treatment in a clinic run by a man whose claim to fame is the invention of a mask to prevent screaming, lived for another thirty-seven years in semi-confinement in a tower of Tübingen's old city wall. Judas hanged himself. The child born from his fateful kiss, the church, was however not content with this historical token of divine wrath. Assuming the divine power of vengeance they committed a whole people for two thousand years to the fate suffered by men like Oedipus and Hölderlin.

The caesura is an enormity that cuts through all the categories and concepts, ideologies and propositions with which we give meaning to the world and our lives. And Hölderlin, the prophet who turned into the false priest, reflected that "at such a moment, the man forgets himself and the god and turns around like a traitor, naturally in a saintly manner.—In the utmost form of suffering, namely, there exists nothing but the conditions of time and space." In a situation in which knowledge is reduced to its bare essentials the mortal forgets himself as he is wholly immersed in the moment, and the god forgets himself "because he is nothing but time; and either one is unfaithful, time, because it is reversed categorically at such a moment, no longer fitting beginning and end; man, because at this moment of categorical reversal he has to follow and thus can no longer resemble the beginning in what follows."[115] Philippe Lacoue-Labarthe, professor of philosophy at the University of Strasbourg, commented on these disturbing thoughts that "the scansion of the tragedy thus opens a temporality that is both irreversible and discordant (or out of tune): what follows the caesura will never be the same as what went before; the end will never again resemble the beginning."[116] This insight of the necessity of the withdrawal of the divine at the moment of the greatest immediacy with the divine was the insight that Sophocles gave the Greeks, an insight that was to become also central in the prophetical theology and which might help us to understand the cataclysmic events of our own age.

To add only a suffix.

The caesura is an axis in time, and as such it introduces an understanding of history that we explored in Chapter Three. Yet within it is a Heraclitean moment that gives rise to a different, historicist history. In Hölderlin's reading of the Sophoclean caesura, Zeus betrays humankind: he becomes nothing but time and voluntarily surrenders to meaninglessness because, as George Steiner observed, "pure temporality is tantamount to incomprehensible crisis. Man, in turn, is forced to follow, to move with the incomprehensible, seemingly 'senseless' whirl of time. Thus he becomes fragmented into a succession of broken-edged moments and impulses, and is severed from the responsible roots and limitations of his being."[117] This, then, is the paradox that underlies the tragic understanding of time, the Judeo-Christian construction of history and the modern notion of change. In classical historiography the caesura was suppressed; the historicist tendency was arrested before it could gain momentum. The Judeo-Christian tradition that centered on the caesura of the Exodus and the crucifixion, unleashed it onto the world. The words spoken during the crucifixion— "'*Eloi, Eloi lama sabachthani?*' which means, '*My God, my god, why have you deserted me?*' "[118]—attest simultaneously to the authenticity of the caesura on Golgotha (in so far as Jesus of Nazareth was a man) and typologically foreshadows the historiographical revolution of the eighteenth and nineteenth centuries. This suggests, then, why any attempt to restore a Judeo-Christian understanding of time, or for that matter one that fits that of a Hellas which knows itself to be centered on the theater, must remain in an unresolvable and double-minded relationship to historicism. It is imprisoned in a situation of collision that cannot be overcome, a situation that characterizes my own absolutist / relativist interpretation of the Judeo-Christian tradition, Thucydides' evocation of Athens and, as we will see in Chapter Nine, the Nazi philosophy of history. Hence the ambivalent and, at times, even tortured character of the odd chapters of this book.

To Continue on a Lighter and More Constructive Note

The greatness of Sophocles' *Oedipus Tyrannus* masks in fact the decline of Attic tragedy in the latter part of the fifth century. As in the history of architecture, also the historical development of drama followed the rule that its greatest manifestation only came into being when the institution that had nurtured it had passed its zenith. Sophoclean tragedy compares in this respect to those other great monuments that testify to the greatness of an age just lost: the Parthenon, the Pantheon and the cathedral of Amiens. Already by the middle of the fifth century it had become clear that the old oppositions that had given rise to tragic knowledge had started to become outdated, and the metaphorical location of Athenian drama moved from the Areopagus to the Agora. Comedy emerged as an alternative to tragedy as the social safety valve of the polis. Alan Little observed that the problems of the city were by now utterly different. The contradictions between taboo and law or being and appearance had been brought to terms. "More insistent were the problems of the hour, the outcome of a war-torn democracy. It thus became more necessary than ever to preserve the precarious balance of society, and as aids to such stabilization both tragedy and comedy had related functions to fulfill."[119] One of the many forces that contributed to the pressures within Athenian society was the demand of the democratic system on the time and energy of the Athenian citizens. There were many people who must have felt that the political life, and especially the time-consuming jury duties, was not worth their trouble, and that it should be possible to reform the state in such a way that it would become a "really comfortable city: warm and welcoming, like a soft, fleecy blanket."[120]

These last words are taken from Aristophanes' comedy *The Birds*, which was performed during the City Dionysia of 414 BCE. The subject of the play is the flight from political responsibility of two old Athenians, Euelpides and Peisthetaerus. While looking for a city where they might live in peace and comfort, Peisthetaerus got the idea to suggest to the birds that they build a city in the sky. This city, Nephelococcygia ("Cloudcuckooland"), was to be free from the troubles of politics. In fact, Nephelococcygia was to be one immense emporium: as it would occupy the realm between gods and men, the birds would be able to impose transit duties on the sacrifices that the people offer to their gods. Peisthetaerus took charge of the design and building of this literally utopian city of leisure and pleasure (the inhabitants will enjoy for free the fragrant odors of the sacrifices). One of the characters who offered his services to the founder of Nephelococcygia is the mathematician Meton, who pretended to be an urban designer.

METON: I propose to survey the air for you: it will have to be marked out in acres.

PEISTHETAERUS: Good lord, who do you think you are?

METON: Who am I? Why, Meton. *The* Meton. Famous throughout the Hellenic world—you must have heard of my hydraulic clock at Colonus?

PEISTHETAERUS [eyeing Meton's instruments]: And what are those for?

METON: Ah, these are my special rods for measuring the air. You see, the air is shaped, how shall I put it?—like a sort of extinguisher; so all I have to do is to attach this flexible rod at the upper extremity, take the compasses, insert the point here—you see what I mean?

PEISTHETAERUS: No.

METON: Well, I now apply the straight rod—so—thus squaring the circle; and there you are. In the center you have your market place: straight streets leading into it, from here, from here, from here. Very much the same principle, really, as the rays of the star: the star itself is circular, but it sends out straight rays in every direction.

PEISTHETAERUS: Brilliant—the man's a genius. . . . [121]

For Aristophanes the architect was one of those many pretentious specialists who were called on to advise on the future of the city. The average member of the Assembly faced (then as much as now) the task to decide on the basis of information that he hardly could understand. Aristophanes presented the dilemma very well: it was obvious that Meton's proposal was absurd, yet, in the play itself, there seemed to be some ground for it. Standing in the middle of the theater's orchestra, at the bottom of a large cone (Meton's metaphorical fire extinguisher), the actor who played Meton only had to point at the figure of the theater to explain the diagram of Nephelococcygia. Meton's dramatic identification of the theater with a city had authority because the architectural form of the theater explicitly recapitulated the essential elements of Athens.

The theater where *The Birds* was performed was the Theater of Dionysius, located in the sacred precinct of Dionysius Eleuthereus. [122] Originally there was only a shrine at this site; until the middle of the fifth century the Agora hosted the dramatic and musical contests of the City Dionysia. One year, however, the wooden grandstands surrounding the orchestra on the Agora collapsed, and it was decided to create a permanent home for the contests. The musical contests were to be held in a specific building, the Odeion. The tragedies were to be performed in a permanent theater on the slopes adjacent to the sanctuary of Dionysius. An existing dancing floor, which occupied the level ground between the hill and the temple of Dionysius, was transformed into a perfectly round orchestra. The slope surrounding the orchestra was turned into a hollow, shell-like auditorium (*theatron*) that could seat 12,000 people.

The architecture of the theater recapitulated the threefold nature of the public realm for each private individual, seated in the *theatron*, the auditorium. First, there was the immutable past, the world of kinship, of chthonic impulse, the domain of the unconscious represented in the *Oresteia* by the Furies who seek revenge for the slain mother, Clytaemnestra. This was the world of the hidden caves below, of the earth and the necropolis, of the womb from which all came and the place to which all will return. The *theatron*, the auditorium carved out of the rock, actualized this world in the theater. Then there was the enduring future, the domain of the conscious represented in the *Oresteia* by Apollo Patroos, the radiant "fatherly" Apollo who champions Orestes' case and, in so doing, the idea of patriarchal government. This was the world of light, the sky and the acropolis, the realm that Jaspers identified as the inexhaustible Encompassing which, as the background of all backgrounds, defines our field of action and knowledge. This was the vertical plane of the landscape and the sky that, as a cosmic *scaenae frons*, terminated and transformed the cone-like enclosure of the *theatron*. Between the worlds of below and above was the plane where the social and the political met. This was the world of political discourse and tragic knowledge, the domain founded on the distinction between the private and the public, the realm that mediated between the subconscious and conscious represented in the *Oresteia* by Athena. Athena was the delicate and heavy-armed goddess of the polis who resolved the competing claims of the Furies and Apollo Patroos through the creation of the civic structures that house the authority that prevailed over the thrust of the angry mob and the power of the autocratic monarch. This was represented by the orchestra, the stage that had been built first on the Agora. Thus the building of the theater brought the fivesquare city to completion.

When, in *The Birds*, Aristophanes interpreted the Hellenic theater as the figure of the city that, suspended between earth and heaven, was to offer a perspective on the troubles of Athens, he capitalized on a deeply rooted symbolism. And while Nephelococcygia did not turn into the warm and welcoming place for which Euelpides had hoped, it did, however, give some insight as to what was important and what superfluous. I will forego the inclination to add some philosophical speculations to this chapter and limit myself to the lesson that can be found in *The Birds*. At the end of the play Peisthetaerus won the hand of a girl named Sovereignty, Zeus' aide who "holds the key to the Gifts to Mankind department, where Zeus keeps all the blessings of civilization: good government, wise politics, law and order, dockyards, endless slinging matches, public assistance officers and the half-drachma they pay out for a day's jury service."[123] Neither Meton's star-shaped city nor Hippodamos' gridiron city plan were included under the blessings of civilization. I assume that Aristophanes thought that the combination of an informal fivesquare division of the urban space with a well-designed theater would suffice as a means to create a comprehensible and therefore habitable city between earth and heaven, tomb and temple. Classical Athens supports the assertion that a city founded with a knowledge of the tragic, structured by a measure of compassion, administered with a dose of common sense and celebrated with a sense of humor does not need the geometric chimeras proposed by men like Meton, Hippodamos, Filarete, Ledoux or Le Corbusier. When Burke observed that "the legislators who framed the antient republic knew that their business was too arduous to be accomplished with no better apparatus than the metaphysics of an undergraduate, and the mathematics and arithmetic of an exciseman,"[124] he did not think about architects. Yet I believe that, on the basis of the foregoing discussion of Athens's civic and urban form, we may safely apply his censure of modernist legislation to the making of cities as well. And thus we have rediscovered that wisdom that, more than twenty-four hundred years ago, Peisthetaerus shared with his fellow Athenians.

PEISTHETAERUS: Brilliant—the man's a genius. But—Meton!
METON: Yes?
PEISTHETAERUS: The people here are like the Lacedaemonians, they don't like strangers. And feeling's running rather high just at the moment.
METON: Party differences?
PEISTHETAERUS: Oh no, far from it: they're quite unanimous.
METON: What's happening, then?
PEISTHETAERUS: There's to be a purge of pretentious humbugs: they're all going to get beaten up. You know what I mean: like this. [He begins to demonstrate.]
METON: Perhaps I'd better be going.
PEISTHETAERUS: I'm not sure you're going to get away in time. [His blows get progressively harder: meanwhile the Chorus advances menacingly.] Something tells me that someone's going to get beaten up quite soon!
[Meton hastily gathers up his instruments and makes for the exit, pursued by the Chorus.]
I warned you! Go and measure how far it is to somewhere else.[125]

The Forlorn Stranger

Meton was thrown out of the city. The citizens passed judgement on his ambition, but they also brought judgement on themselves. This brings us to the most difficult and perhaps also the most important part of the fivesquare configuration of classical Athens: the perimeter of the fivesquare figure. This edge might be interpreted in two ways. First of all it bounds as a border the different types in one civic and political figure. If we take the outline as a frontier, we have completed our reconstruction of Athens. As a pale that delimits the civic domain it also opens the fivesquare city to a realm which does not (yet) partake in the city's freedom. The circumvalla- tion offers protection for the political society and suggests an irreducible and ultimate confrontation with its limitations, its shadows and its victims. The line ought to be interpreted as a moral proposition. If we do not think about the line in that way, it becomes possible to reflect on the fivesquare arrangement without reference to the fact that, for example, the preserva- tion of Athens's liberty demanded that it unjustly enslaved other popula- tions. However, if we choose to take the moral significance of the boundary seriously, then we discover that the actions of the city as a whole become an important gage of the truth of the political process as it is founded on the private realm and given shape in the threefold of the necropolis, the Acropolis and the Agora. Thucydides realized this and explored the topos in the Melian Dialogue.

The extermination of the Melians is the turning point in Thucydides' account of the Peloponnesian War. Before it the Athenian actions seemed justified by the city's leadership in the Persian war; after it Athens was perceived to have cut itself from the moral source of its legitimacy as a big power. Only imperial aspiration remained. The Athenian delegation acknowledged this. "This is no fair fight," so they admitted, "with honor on one side and shame on the other." Honor had ceased to be important, as was fair play and just dealing. Sixteen years of war and almost war had taught the Athenians that international relations were not ruled by the Nomos, but by the "general and necessary law of nature to rule whatever one can." Unlike the laws of the polis, "this is not a law that we [Athenians] made ourselves, nor were we the first to act upon it when it was made. We found it already in existence, and we shall leave it to exist for ever among those who come after us. We are merely acting in accordance with it, and we know that you or anybody else with the same power as ours would be acting in precisely the same way."[126] Thus the common good of Athens had ceased to apply to Hellas as a whole. Though within Athens all had been made equal in order to create freedom, within Greece the unavoid- able inequality in power between the different cities resulted in the scan- dalous assertion that Melian surrender would serve the common good of the Hellenes.

> MELIANS: And how could it be just as good for us to be the slaves as for you to be the masters?

ATHENIANS: You, by giving in, would save yourselves from disaster; we, by not destroying you, would be able to profit from you.

MELIANS: So you would not agree to our being neutral, friends instead of enemies, but allies of neither side?

ATHENIANS: No, because it is not so much your hostility that injures us; it is rather the case that, if we were on friendly terms with you, our subjects would regard that as a sign of weakness in us, whereas your hatred is evidence of our power.[127]

The Athenians had built a far-flung empire in order to preserve their own liberty and the other cities' freedom in the face of Persian might. Now they realized that the preservation of this empire meant the destruction of others. The very existence of the neutral yet friendly Melian community offered within this distorted perspective a radical challenge to Athenian freedom. Therefore they had to come to terms with it. In 416 BCE coming to terms meant extermination.

The paranoid Athenian position was deplorable, yet it touched upon a basic truth. When the Athenian configuration of liberty entered into communication with another, deeply rooted and autonomous form of freedom, the Athenians perceived a sinister threat to their own freedom. They were unable to constructively address the moral dilemmas that the Other, the stranger imposed on their political notion of liberty. The prophetical perspective on the outsider (in this case Melos) was alien to a civilization that defined itself in terms of particular beginnings instead of in terms of universal ends. The laws of ethics operated within the polis, but did not rule the relationship between the city-states. This was the hideous default that brought an end to the glory that was Greece. Thucydides suggested so much in the ending of his account of the destruction of Melos. As Connor observed, "although the Melians are destroyed, the episode is never rounded off with a neat sentence of the sort that concludes the Plataean or Mytilenean affairs. We never hear 'Such was the end of the Melian affair.' Instead, with the destruction of Melos fresh in mind, we move directly to the great Athenian expedition against the island of Sicily."[128] Indeed: the disastrous Sicilian expedition was the ultimate outcome of a policy that defined the national interest not as the common good of the population as delineated in the fivesquare configuration of the Asty, but as an imperial ambition as defined by the city's maritime capability. If the Asty stood for an unselfish civic idealism derived in political discourse, the Piraeus manifested an egoistic imperial realism that sought containment of disorder.

The Melian Affair brings some of the issues raised earlier in this chapter into focus. It reveals that the seemingly perfect fivesquare configuration is flawed because of a thoughtlessness in its interpretation. First of all the Agora: while the stoa seemed hospitable to the stranger, allowing each person, citizen or not, to contact those in office, the inability of the constitution to accommodate within the confines of the political center the voice of the other Greek cities implied the paradoxical situation that the individual altruism of the citizens could not but result in a collective selfishness. In other words, the Agora was incomplete as it did not accommodate the embassies of the other cities. The opposite was true for the Acropolis. There the architectural ambition expressed in the grandeur of the monuments exceeded the measure proper to the city. The Parthenon, financed by the tributes of the cities under the protection of the Athenian fleet, wrongly suggested that Athens's future depended on fear or respect of lesser powers. Within the context of Athens's foreign policy, the Acropolis was a tool that manifested the forcefulness and munificence of the city. The cemetery escapes this censure, as do the neighborhoods and the theater. These domains of the city's life accommodated the stranger in a much greater degree. It is significant, however, that these realms preserved in the Periclean age their archaic meaning to a much larger degree than the Agora and the Acropolis.

These thoughts lead to the French philosopher Emmanuel Levinas. Levinas has made the issues which Thucydides raised in the Melian Dialogue into the focus of his philosophical enterprise. He scrutinized the prophetical character of the meeting of such totalitarian configurations of freedom as the one that structured the Athenian polis with the other, the stranger. Levinas has argued that the access to the stranger is inescapably ethical. The stranger does not belong; he is forsaken, exposed and menaced. His wretched presence defies the order of the polity. Therefore it arouses the citizenry's aggression and its desire to assert its power. Yet, simultaneously, the stranger's destitution forbids the polity to kill.[129] The dejected and abject other, who does not partake in the liberty that the citizens enjoy, commands and begs. It commands, "Thou shall not kill," and it begs for mercy. As a master and a slave, the stranger delimits the polity's freedom.

The stranger delimits the city's freedom and pronounces judgement. Levinas described the meeting with the other as the origin of the awareness that freedom is based on injustice. "At no time can one say: I have done all my duty. Except the hypocrite. . . . It is in this sense that there is an opening beyond what is delimited; and such is the manifestation of the infinite."[130] The confrontation with the other implies a judgement that manifests itself not as a "theoretical consideration . . . in which freedom would spontaneously take up its rights again," but as "a *shame* freedom has of itself, discovering itself to be murderous and usurpatory in its very exercise. . . . The life of freedom discovering itself to be unjust, the life of freedom in heteronomy, consists in an infinite movement of freedom putting itself ever more into question."[131]

Levinas' observations parallel the account of the Melian Affair. They suggest that an analysis that pronounces that freedom as configured in the typology of the city to be the ultimate and normative essence of architecture ought to include an awareness of the responsibility without which liberty becomes injustice. I will discuss the more practical architectural– theoretical implications of this discovery below. Here it is important to look at one of the basic assumptions of Levinas's argument. Levinas contends that this responsibility for the other, be it neighbor or stranger, precedes the covenant on which society is based and in which freedom is to be found. Responsibility for the other "comes to me from what is prior to my freedom, from a non-present, an immemorial. . . . ' If I interpret responsibility as a duty that proceeds from freely negotiated contract or covenant, then I am like Cain. Asked by God about the whereabouts of Abel, Cain answered that he was not his brother's keeper, i.e., that he had not accepted responsibility for Abel and that therefore he was not responsible for him. "But responsibility for another comes from what is prior to my freedom . . . . The proximity of a neighbor is my responsibility for him; to approach is to be one's brother's keeper; to be one's brother's keeper is to be his hostage. Immediacy is this. Responsibility does not come from fraternity, but fraternity denotes responsibility for another, antecedent to my freedom."[132] Thus Levinas urges us to see the measure of a person's freedom as the sense of responsibility from which it generated.

Levinas discussed this acceptance of responsibility in terms that recall Kierkegaard's analysis of the moment (see Chapter Three). The discovery of the *a priori* of our responsibility suspends the progress of time and confronts us with the eternal as the horizon of destiny. We appropriate the eternal in the moment "by giving a sign of the giving of signs, of the 'for-the-other' in which I am dis-interested: here I am [*me* voici]! The accusative [*me* voici!] here is remarkable: here I am, under your eyes, at your service, your obedient servant. In the name of God. But this is without thematization; the sentence in which God gets mixed in with words is not 'I believe in God.'" Levinas does not affirm that the absolute necessarily reveals itself in the other, and neither does it inevitably disclose itself in the "Here I am!" Yet this announcement *testifies* to the Infinite perforce. It is a testimony. Levinas insists that testimony, and not the dialogue, precedes all dis- course. "It is the 'here I am' said to a neighbor to whom I am given over, by which I announce peace, that is, my responsibility for the other."[133] In the unconditional commitment of the "Here I am" a person acknowledges the limitations of freedom to be the presence of the other. And thus the person becomes a witness. The Athenians did not realize this when they disembarked on Melos. When they announced their presence they did not pretend to be a testimony to the infinite as it manifested itself in the transcendent helplessness of the Melians. It was but the necessary and logical outcome of an immanent worldview that thought about strife in natural and not conventional terms.

Yet the heinous extermination of the Melians—the first of genocides committed for ideological reasons—was not without response. Fifteen years after the Melian affair the issue of the destitute stranger became the focus of the city's attention. In 401 BCE the defeated city of Athens hosted as usual the City Dionysia. Three years earlier, when the city surrendered to the Spartans, the citizens of Athens had faced the fate that they had meted out to the Melians: the Thebans and the Corinthians demanded that the city should be razed and the population enslaved. The Spartans preferred to treat the beaten foe with moderation instead. They compelled the Athenians to give up what remained of their fleet, destroyed the Long Walls that connected the Asty to the Piraeus and imposed a puppet regime. Three years later the Thirty Tyrants had fallen, and democracy had been restored. That year the audience in the Theater of Dionysius saw Sophocles' *Oedipus at Colonus*. In this play Sophocles showed how Oedipus found a place to die after years of wandering that followed his self-blinding, his abdication from the throne and his departure from Thebes. In political sense this place was Athens; in topographical sense the deme of Colonus, located within sight of Athens's walls. In Sophocles' day the site was part of the city's necropolis. The play begins with the arrival of disgraced Oedipus and Antigone in the grove of the Eumenides, the Furies who had once pursued Orestes to Athena. Oedipus rests on a rocky ledge beside the grove, not knowing that he commits an act of sacrilege. An inhabitant of Colonus passes by, and is shocked to see the trespasser in the sacred domain. He orders Oedipus to leave the place. Yet Oedipus refuses when he learns that the grove is dedicated to the Daughters of Darkness, as he knows that he has reached his final destination. In his prayers to the Furies he recalls how:

> When the god cried out those lifelong prophecies of doom
> he spoke of *this* as well, my promised rest
> after hard years weathered—
> I will reach my goal, he said, my haven
> where I find the grounds of the Awesome Goddesses
> and make their home my home. There I will round
> the last turn in the torment of my life:
> a blessing to the hosts I live among,
> disaster to those who sent me, drove me out. [133]

When the inhabitants of Colonus learn the ignominious identity of the man who refuses to leave, they threaten to expel him. "Out with you! Out of our country—far away!" so they cry. Yet Oedipus begs for compassion, reminding them that the measure of their city's greatness is its treatment of the wretched beggar, the miserable stranger, the humble suppliant.

> Then what's the good of glory, magnificent renown,
> if in its flow it streams away to nothing?
> If Athens, Athens
> is that rock of reverence all men say it is,
> the only city on earth to save the ruined stranger,
> the only one to protect him, give him shelter—
> where are such kindnesses for me?[134]

The inhabitants of Colonus recognize the truth of Oedipus' words, and decide to refer the final decision to Theseus, the King of Athens. When Theseus arrives, he recognizes in Oedipus a fellow traveller who deserves compassion.

> Tell me all. Your story, your fortunes
> would have to be grim indeed to make me turn
> my back on you. I too, I remember well,
> was reared in exile just like you,
> and in strange lands, like no man else on earth,
> I grappled dangers pressing for my life.
> Never, I tell you, I will never shrink
> from a stranger, lost as you are now,
> or fail to lend a hand and save a life.
> I am only a man, well I know,
> and I have no more power over tomorrow,
> Oedipus, than you.[135]

He grants Oedipus his request for a place where he may die in peace and a place where his shattered body may rest. And so a destitute stranger was the first person to be interred in what became the national cemetery, the place where the men were buried who had contributed to the city's greatness. His grave was to be unmarked, known only to Theseus and his successors. The knowledge that the city's immutable past centered on an untended grave was to be the secret of its future greatness, providing "a bulwark stronger than many shields, stronger than the spear of massed allies."[136] Yet it was a wisdom that the Athenian leadership had forgotten, twelve years earlier. Their inability to see with Theseus' eye the stranger as one's other had led to the city's destruction. In the year 401 BCE a new

beginning had been made with the reestablishment of democratic government. *Oedipus at Colonus* reminded the citizens that this new beginning
ought to be seen within the context of the charitable decision taken by the
city's founder.

With Levinas and *Oedipus at Colonus* the elements of the program
initiated in Chapter Three begin to fall in place. The ideology of the
stranger offers, for example, an answer to the issue of "authentic" and
"inauthentic" types raised by Lampe. If we take classical Athens as a
source of useful knowledge of architectural types, then we must come to
terms with the problem of authenticity raised in Chapter Three. If we look
at the fivesquare configuration without any reference to the area without,
then it is difficult to define an uncontested line that separates pertinent from
forced typologies. Lampe's analysis suggests an approach to the problem
that stresses that the political significance of the stela, the shrine, the stoa
and the house depend on traditional and historical associations of the
grave, the temple, the center of government and the home. In classical
Athens each of these types—or better antitypes—embodied an ideology
specific to the time and place. Yet each of these articles of the Athenian
constitution belong to a larger realm of concern that is not specific to
Athens. These frames of reference can be characterized as four of the five
great orientations discussed in this chapter. The stela can be seen to refer
to the idea of one's habitat as an authoritative environment founded on a
valued past, the shrine to the idea of one's community as a dedicated group
of people bound by common destiny and mutual responsibility, the stoa or
agora to the idea of one's city as the locus of humanly significant alternatives—that is, alternatives that empower an individual to make a
decision, act on it, and accept the consequences—the house to the idea
of one's domicile as the abode of a personal liberty that is free from
the environing situation. In other settlements, towns and cities before
Athens, people had used tombstones and monuments, temples and sacred
precincts, political power houses such as palaces and, finally, private
dwellings to explore the scope and the depth of these important value
orientations from which had emerged the specific but comprehensive civic
configuration embodied in the Athenian antitype. The Athenian example
stands in each of these instances at the end of a development because each
of the Athenian types implicitly recapitulates all the others. Thus it seems
legitimate to interpret the circles in Avebury, the sanctuaries of Uruk, the
palace of Argos or the house of Odysseus as historic types of respectively
the Athenian necropolis, the Acropolis, the Agora and the neighborhoods,
and each one *per se* can be seen as a historic type of Athens as a whole.

There remains the problem of the fifth type. We have seen how the
theater occupies a special place in the fivesquare diagram, interpreted now

as the Athenian antitype. It was the only one of the building types that explicitly recapitulated the other four. A first exploration in typological analysis reveals another aspect of its quintessential significance: of all the architectural types, the theater was the only one without history and therefore without its historic type. It was invented in Athens in the fifth century. This clarifies why it could assume its inclusive and encompassing character. The unquestioned and unqualified relationship between the other types and the reality they embodied was absent in the theater. Instead it offered qualities of mediation and reflection. Therefore the invention of the theater marked the moment when architecture could become the realm of theory. (I was not surprised to find that the most interesting and theoretically satisfactory parts of Vitruvius' discussion of the various architectural types concerned the geometric and acoustical design of theaters.)

The theater not only offered the possibility of a *historia*, but also of a *theoria*, a comprehensive view of the city and its architecture as an authoritative environment structured by authority and liberty. In the architectural posthistorical age, initiated by the invention of the theater, thinking about buildings was to be in constant dialogue with either philosophy, which assimilates life in nature, or theology, which anchors life in God. Philosophy and theology were to disclose the hidden reason that connects the life of humans, the city's political realm and the world of nature or the world of the divine. Philosophy was to unite the authority of the past, and the threefold liberty of the present and the future with the *Logos* or reason that rules all. Theology was to show how the stela (the relics of martyrs and saints), the shrine (the *Ecclesia Triumphans*), the stoa (the *Ecclesia Militans*) and the house (the *Domus Dei*) were but parts of that theater of salvation called the world and medieval master masons were to show how these principles were a sufficient basis to create a powerful image of the *Civitas Dei* in the form of a cathedral. (NB typological analysis shows that the medieval cathedral was indeed a city, but not a settlement; it did not include an emporium.) In both instances the quintessential architectural type of the theater is the paradigm for the theoretical unification of the world, of civic consciousness and thinking about architecture. The theater shows that architecture was to be more than an embodiment of Norberg Schulz's "spirit of the place" (stela), Pevsner's object of aesthetic intention (shrine), Heidegger's domain of dwelling (house) and Westfall's manifestation of politics (stoa).

As an architectonic form the theater reconciled the different aspects of the city in one image. This synthesis of the different histories that comprise the city's life within one ordered space has been the foundation of all architectural theory, and therefore of all architecture in the architectural posthistorical age. With the invention of the theater architecture has become philosophy or theology because it shares with these realms of discourse the task and the power to create a unified representation of the whole world that can be taken in at once. It *represents* the world, but it has ceased to *be* the world. Divorced from Aeschylus' drama, Sophoclean tragedy or Heraclitus' antinomy-play, the theater has all to easily surrendered its contesting character to become the serene emblem of a thinking about architecture and the city that revels in the creation of such Parmenidean oppositions as *civitas* and *urbs*, content and form, government and architecture, the natural and the conventional and so on. The flux is arrested in a definition, the becoming has become the prelude of a bounded, finished, immobile, balanced and perfected truth.

These considerations on the vital distinction between genuine and false typology are more than a flimsy gossamer. When Lampe raised the issue he relied for an answer on the tabernacle. The shrine of the Jews is an authentic type because both the type (the Hebrew liturgy of atonement) and the antitype (the cosmic implications of the crucifixion) powerfully connect to the traditional image of life as a task and a pilgrimage. Entrance in the Holy of Holies implies a return to God; conversion follows a decision for good against evil. Therefore the allegory of the tabernacle contains a moral significance that gives depth to its authenticity as a type. Our reflections on the relationship between the fivesquare figure and the world outside of it provides, so I believe, a valid way to infuse the types that are derived from Periclean Athens with a measure of authenticity in so far as it proclaims that false typology deals with the other as an obstacle, a challenge to be overcome while genuine typology reveals the other as suffering and helpless *and* as a manifestation of the infinite who sizes up the finite totality of our architectural constructions and places it under judgement. In short authentic typology defines the configuration of the polis as a form of judgement and, consequently, of responsibility.

Repetition and Recollection

A question remains: does the newly forged relationship between liberty and an ethical imperative connect to the typological method as such? In other words: may we consider a concern for the relationship between the dispensation of freedom and the consecration of justice as the necessary implication of the Judeo-Christian understanding of history as a series of typological repetitions of an axial figure? I believe so. My confidence derives from Kierkegaard's analysis of the ethical significance of repetition. In his *Repetition* (1843), Kierkegaard reflected on the difference between the Judeo-Christian theology of repetition, the classical philosophy of recollection and the Hegelian ideology of mediation. The purpose of the book was an investigation into the existential possibilities of life in the Heraclitean flux. "One solution," he said, was frankly to acknowledge "that the individual has no business in the flux and, after making one's excuses, to make a quick exit." This approach neatly summarized classical historiography and the Socratic notion of knowledge as recollection. "Christianity, on the other hand, summons up the nerve metaphysics has lost. Taking time and flux as its element, it puts its hand to the plow of existence and pushes ahead—for eternity lies ahead, not behind—to create for itself such identity as life allows."[139] Christianity overcame the Heraclitean curse that forces events to rush headlong on each other's heels by repetition. Kierkegaard claimed that the question of repetition ought to be as important to modern (i.e., Christian–existentialist) philosophy as the notion of recollection had been for the Greeks. "Just as they taught that all knowing is a recollecting, modern philosophy will teach that all life is a repetition. . . . Repetition and recollection are the same movement, except in opposite directions, for what is recollected has been, is repeated backwards, whereas genuine repetition is recollected forwards."[140]

Kierkegaard's notion of repetition developed from his understanding of the decisive character of the moment (discussed in Chapter Three). At any moment in time, people have the opportunity to make a new beginning. This idea went right back to the core and the mythical beginning of the Judeo-Christian tradition. For example, the Jewish tradition teaches that the secret that God gave man was that of how to start anew. "It is not given to man to begin," Elie Wiesel wrote in a commentary on the new beginning Adam and Eve made after they had been thrown out of Paradise. Beginning is God's privilege. "But it is given to man to begin again—and he does so every time he chooses to defy death and side with the living."[141] Such moments of choice and decision comprised the eternal foundation of the Judeo-Christian tradition. They were real moments in which the beginning is repeated, moments when people decided to take up their existence. These moments of resolution, which could and ought to be repeated in the future, were occasions of possibility. As such they were, in the words of the Kierkegaard critic Pat Bigelow, moments when the eternal was summoned into time, moments when time was released into eternity. "In the act of repetition, time always and ever begins anew, and this ceaseless beginning anew is the eternal taking the temporal up into itself upon itself."[142]

Every decisive moment was repetition, yet the moments that were recognized as repetition (through for example a typological understanding of its significance) stood out in time. As Kierkegaard observed, the nature of world-time is to change. Novelty, development or innovation were therefore normal and expected in the world of nature in which everything rushes on and presses on as if steered by a dazed fatalism. Repetition was unexpected, beyond the laws of causality. It broke the ruthless mold of scientific logic and historicist causality. "The dialectic of repetition is easy, for that which is repeated has been—otherwise it could not be repeated— but the very fact that it has been makes the repetition into something new. When the Greeks said that all knowing is recollecting, they said that all existence, which is, has been; when one says that life is a repetition, one says: actuality, which has been, now comes into existence."[143]

Life as it comes into existence in repetition is marked by the sign of freedom. To see life, and therefore history, as a rhythm of new beginnings entails a recognition of the reality of freedom. "Freedom's supreme interest is precisely to bring about repetition, and its only fear is that variation would have the power to disturb its eternal nature. Here emerges the issue: *is repetition possible?* Freedom itself is now repetition. If it were the case that freedom in the individuality related to the surrounding world could become so immersed, so to speak, in the result that it cannot take itself back again (repeat itself), then everything is lost."[144] If the purpose of history (understood as *Geschichte*) is to make it possible for us to stand out against the world of necessity, i.e., to *ex-sist* as human beings, then it is through repetition that people make a history for themselves. This history interrupts the time of nature, and makes a home for humankind in a re- currence of beginnings, repetitions and new beginnings. And it is because of this bold periodicity that history can become a teacher. It does not teach as a midwife, initiating a retreat into transcendental recollection. To the contrary: it discloses the concrete situation as a moral responsibility, an existential ability and an ethical possibility. Caputo summarized the im- portance of Kierkegaard's understanding of repetition as an affirmation of the reality of the situation in which a person could find herself. It is em- phatically not "an ethical gymnastics which thinks anything is possible," and neither is it freedom as an abstraction. To the contrary: it is the free- dom to realize the particular moment into the fullness of time. "It does not depend on the favor of world-history to give it an opportunity, but it knows how to find the possible in any situation in which it is put. . . . The ethical does not require one to be in the right place at the right time, for the es- sentials of ethical repetition are at hand at any time or place. . . . In sum, repetition on the ethical level is the constancy and continuity of choice by which the self constitutes itself as a self, by which it returns again and again to its own innermost resolution and establishes its moral identity."[145]

Kierkegaard insistently stressed the ethical character of the act of repetition. He did not assign either ontological or aesthetic significance to this recurrence. Kierkegaard insisted that repetition's renewal marked a real development, "for consciousness raised to its second power is indeed no meaningless repetition, but a repetition of such a nature that the new has absolute significance in relation to that which has gone before, is qualitatively different from it."[146] The forward-directed thrust of repetition (in contrast to the backward-directed sentiment of recollection) implies that repetition recovered a partially realized historical past into the fullness of historic time. This means that the Jew who cites the figure of Exodus during Passover and the Christian who cites the figure of the passion in the Eucharist think these two "saving events" to be incomplete. Only in their affirmation of the contemporary significance of these events can the participants in the seder meal or the liturgy of the mass bring to completion the liberation of the Jews from slavery and the redemption of all from hereditary sin. In other words, something is "added" to these events, a kind of existential *donum superadditum* or gift of grace that augments the historical so that it transfigures into the historic. This *donum superadditum* is grounded in the ritual act of repetition and given substance in the ethical resolve to fulfill the responsibilities of the thus accepted heritance. Because repetition is an act of grace there is a rupture in the ontological identity of the figure and its repetition: the ritual of passover cites the Exodus from Egypt, but it *is not* and *ought not* be that Exodus, but another one. Jesus of Nazareth realized this in that passover celebration some 2000 years ago which Christians remember as the Last Supper: a repetition that according to the church ended one history and began another.

Of Day and Night

All of this effectively combines into a coherent proposal to universalize Athenian *Architekturgeschichte*. Typology allows the historian to broaden its scope until the fivesquare city has become the matrix of the whole of architectural history; the question of justice allows the architect to make effective distinctions between authentic and inauthentic types, and an understanding of repetition allows the reader to describe the normative significance of the appropriation of historical types into the present. Only one issue remains: the claim of relativism. "If one wants to learn the truth about ancient peoples it is well to study without thinking of ourselves. We must consider them as if they were wholly strange."[147] These disturbing words of Fustel de Coulanges have remained with the debate all along, and their annoying truth begins to call more and more attention to itself as the successful completion of the project Westfall and I have begun seems closer. Yet it is only a partial truth. To study the ancient peoples "without thinking of ourselves" is obviously an impossibility: why study them at all if not because we think we might learn something from their *Geschichte*? And what holds true is badly formulated: the Greeks were undoubtedly different from us, but does this imply that they are "wholly strange," or perhaps the Other?

This new perspective on the two-centuries-old problem of relativism points to the man who was one of the first to grasp its devastating implications: Friedrich Hölderlin. In Chapter One I described how he mourned the fate of modern (wo)man to fall "Headlong from one / Hour to the next, / Hurled like water / From ledge to ledge / Downward for years to the vague abyss." He was a historicist, and a relativist. In his poem dedicated to the Greek goddess of memory, Mnemosyne, Hölderlin put the following disillusive lamentation in the mouths of the Greek statues that filled the museums of his own times.

> A sign we are, without meaning
> Without pain we are and have nearly
> Lost our language in foreign lands.

All the heroes had died:

> By the figtree
> My Achilles dies,
> And Ajax lies
> By the grottoes of the sea,
> By streams, with Skamandros as neighbour.[148]

And a description follows of the necropolis of Hellas' past, a history lost to the present generation.

Yet, paradoxically, the man who fully realized the chasm that separated his present from the ancient peoples also believed that it was possible to repeat Greek beginnings in the German lands. He did not intend this repetition to be of an aesthetic nature: it simply was not feasible in the impoverished Germany of the early nineteenth century.

> I want to build

> and raise new
> the temples of Theseus and the stadiums
> and where Perikles lived

But there's no money, too much spent
today. I had a guest
over   and we sat together. [149]

And neither was this repetition to be ontological in nature: Hölderlin did
not assume that a repetition was possible because Greeks and Germans (or
better Hesperians, from the Greek name Εσπέρα, "the Land of the West")
shared a common nature, that, in fact, the rule of relativism only applied
in certain poetic moods. To the contrary: a follower of Herder, Hölderlin
remained fully convinced that Greeks were as different from Germans as
the Greek language from the German tongue. So what was the relationship
between a Greek and Hesperian if not one of identity as the champions of
the Enlightenment had wanted to believe? Hölderlin pondered this issue in
a letter dated December 4, 1801 which he sent to his friend the (failed) poet
and playwright Casimir Ulrich Böhlendorff (1775–1825). [150] (Böhlendorff
has been described as a "wrecked idealist" or Hölderlin's "weird shadow-
self or double" [151] — like Hölderlin, Böhlendorff was to become mad; unlike
Hölderlin, Böhlendorff was to take his own life.) Hölderlin complimented
his friend for his final draft of *Fernando or the Baptizing of Art: A Dramatic
Idyll* (1802). Hölderlin noted that Böhlendorff had achieved precision,
clarity of presentation and "effective flexibility" that made the play "like
a good blade." This he judged an achievement, as Hölderlin had learned
that "we learn nothing with more difficulty than to freely use the national."
With this cryptic remark he initiated a profound reflection on the relationship between Greek and German or Hesperian culture. Hölderlin posited
that it is "precisely the clarity of the presentation that is so natural to us
as for the Greeks the fire from heaven. For exactly that reason they will
have to be surpassed in beautiful passion—which you also have preserved
for yourself—rather than in that Homeric presence of mind and talent for
presentation." Hölderlin acknowledged that this sounded paradoxical.

Yet I argue it once again and leave it for your examination and use: in the
progress of education the truly national will become the ever less attractive.
Hence the Greeks are less master of the sacred pathos, because to them it was
inborn, whereas they excel in their talent for presentation, beginning with
Homer, because this exceptional man was sufficiently sensitive to conquer the
Western *Junonian sobriety* for his Apollonian empire and thus to veritably
appropriate what is foreign.

   With us it is the reverse. Hence it is also so dangerous to deduce the rules of
art for oneself exclusively from Greek excellence. I have labored long over this
and know by now that, with the exception of what must be highest for the

Greeks and for us—namely, the living relationship and destiny—we must not share anything identical with them.

Yet what is familiar must be learned as well as what is alien. This is why the Greeks are so indispensable for us. It is only that we will not follow them in our own, national [spirit] since, as I said, the *free* use of *what is one's own* is the most difficult. [152]

It is a difficult letter that has invited much learned comment. What seems important is Hölderlin's explicit rejection of the neo-classical tendency to imitate the products of Greek cultural and artistic achievement as a means to bring Hellenic Enlightenment in Hesperian darkness. Hölderlin did not urge the Germans to *imitate* Greece. They were under obligation to *repeat* the Greek experience, and this repetition was to be found in an unconditional absorption of an existence alien to one's own culture and heritage. Hölderlin believed that the Greek art did not reflect Greek nature, but its opposite. The character of the Greek was not serene and rational. To the contrary: it was wild and mad, a bright and boundless whole that had been touched by "the fire from heaven" and that expressed itself in "sacred pathos." Yet this inner fire had been repressed in an almost Freudian sense by a civilized superstructure that the Greeks had borrowed from Egypt: there they had found the "clarity of presentation" and the "Junonian sobriety" which they lacked. [153] The result of this assimilation of Egyptian form to Hellenic content was Greek civilization. Yet the Greeks had not remained stuck at that experiential plane defined by rational politics, rational philosophies and rational architecture. They knew how to break out from there and rise even higher: the superstructure of civilization allowed them to reappropriate, in turn, their own passionate and irrational nature, but now in an authoritative, superbly crafted fashion: Heraclitus' antinomies, Thucydides' histories and Sophocles' tragedies were the most important examples of this reification of their own nature— concretizations of an inner truth that allowed the Greeks to overcome the alienation of civilization. In other words: the paradoxes of Heraclitean thought, the Thucydidean identity of greatness and disaster and the Sophoclean caesura were the bridges which spanned the abyss of civilization in order to connect the Greeks to themselves. Yet these bridges had been erected at a price: as Hölderlin realized, "the free use of what is one's own is the most difficult." That price had been the very destruction of the civilization that separated and connected the pinnacle to its foundations. And this could not have been different.

The Greeks had only been able to become themselves through assimilation of that which was alien to their own nature (i.e., Junonian sobriety). The same applied to the Hesperians or, more specifically, the Germans.

Like Herder and all the other Romantics and Idealists, Hölderlin believed that the unique task of the German people was to become themselves. The Greeks had shown the way how this could be done: the Germans had to assimilate a civilization that was radically different in order to rediscover their own nature. But whose nature were they to absorb? Hölderlin had a straightforward answer: that of the Greeks. He believed that the Germans and the Greeks were complementary: what came naturally to the Germans ("clarity of presentation" and "Junonian sobriety") had not come easily to the Greeks, and what had been natural to the Greeks ("sacred pathos") was alien to the Hesperians. As the Greeks had assimilated "Junonian sobriety" in order to come to terms with their "sacred pathos," so the Germans had to assimilate "sacred pathos" in order to come to terms with their "Junonian sobriety." Greece was to be Germany's teacher, but not Greek civilization. The Greece that could initiate the German process of self-discovery, self-affirmation and ultimately self-assertion was the irrational world that had been repressed, a Greece which surfaced in, for example, the caesura of *Oedipus Tyrannus*.

In short the Greeks and the Germans stood in a complementary relationship in so far as the Apollonian sublimation of Greek art could teach the German what came naturally to him, and the violent compulsions that it tried to suppress could show the German the road to completeness. But this lesson could only be fully understood after the Germans had learned the meaning of Heraclitean philosophy, Thucydidean history and Sophoclean tragedy. Therefore Hölderlin could state in the same sentence that Germans and Greeks shared a similar destiny, and simultaneously did not share anything identical with them. Applied to architecture Hölderlin's proposition could be summarized as follows: the German architect should overcome classicism (i.e., the imitation of Greek forms) in order to appropriate the classical (i.e., the "holy fire" that gave the architecture existential meaning as a caesura) so that he would be able to create a truly national (i.e., German) architecture, a classical architecture, which is in fact German architecture.

Hölderlin's insights offer a final justification for a theory of typological repetition of the Athenian center. His thoughts accommodated the relativist understanding of the incommensurability of various cultural epochs and national characters; yet his vision also offered a perspective on the use we ought to make of that contrast. He had a keen understanding of the importance of the Other as the basis for self-recovery, and proposed a national freedom that began, appropriately, with an almost Kierkegaardian act of repetition. His thoughts are also useful in acquiring a different perspective on a typological understanding of Greek architecture. Aren't after all the issues explored typological? Thus it seems that our own assimilation of the typology of Periclean Athens might liberate us from the deadlock in which we find ourselves, providing us with a radically different perspective that, ultimately, may lead us back to our own origin, an origin that was reflected in the rational tectology of classical architecture. In other words a reading of the pathos of the architecture and urban form of classical Athens might be the gate to a proper enjoyment of the Hesperian sobriety of Westfall.

And finally Hölderlin explains why the move from Jerusalem to Athens has been legitimate and necessary. He made clear why the Judeo-Christian tradition may only recover its own integrity and vitality if it recognizes itself in the classical world, if it is prepared to come up (in the words of Peter Szondi) against its own origin *as if it were a foreign one*. This proposition is, of course, not alien to the Judeo-Christian tradition. In fact it reflects the prophetical apperception of the Other as the center of concern, the axis of our own *Geschichte*. And what makes the Other special is her complete otherness. To give but one example: Christ is not the center of Christian history because he is the same, but because he is wholly different.

Some Concluding Remarks

"I could jubilate about a new truth, an improved outlook of what is above us and around us." With these words Hölderlin finished his discussion of the relationship between Greece and Germany in the letter to Böhlendorff. And he added a note in which he expressed his anxiety that he "might end up like the old Tantalus who received more from the Gods than he could take."[154] His foreboding came true in his own life. It also casts an ominous shadow over the odd chapters of *Architectural Principles in the Age of Historicism*. Yet for now I will give no heed to the Thucydidean insight that the measure of any achievement is the suffering it engenders. I review my findings with a measured sense of jubilation. Thucydides' crafty narrative, Kierkegaard's existential discernment and Hölderlin's dialogal intention all reaffirm Lampe's assessment that typological historiography is legitimate and useful. Typology deals with history, but this history is a *Geschichte* that refuses to be imprisoned in the past. It reaches into the future through the perceived repetition of an event or situation that we recognize as the rupture or *caesura* that sundered the historical past from the post-historical present. Thus typology originates in the paradoxical apprehension that the only way we can make a connection to the past as *Geschichte* is through the very event that has disconnected us from the past as *Historie*. This paradox does not fit the universe of causality revealed by the Historical Point of

View. It seems to offer, however, new opportunities to overcome the very limitations of a causal interpretation of history.

This is significant, as causality structures the great majority of contemporary historical writing. This makes sense if a historian wants to know why certain things happened as they did. She must invoke a historiographical method that is based on an investigation of causality when she investigates why Abbé Suger "invented" the Gothic in the twelfth century, or why Goethe "rediscovered" it in 1770. Yet such a perspective on history does not tell her what to do with such information. Typology promises a useful perspective because it is future-directed. The writer of the Epistle to the Hebrews interpreted the crucifixion and resurrection in terms of the Jewish liturgy of atonement because he was still uncertain as to what the later event meant, but assumed a correct knowledge of the significance of the earlier one.

The study of a historic type gives a handle on the totality of the antitype. The typological interpretation of the ritual and allegorical significance of the various spaces of the tabernacle offers a complete story with a beginning, middle and end, as it explores the *geschichtliche* significance of the crucifixion and resurrection. There are, of course, other historic types that refer to the (universal) antitype of the passion, like the binding of Isaac, or the Exodus from Egypt. All of these historic types, however, are narratives complete in themselves and therefore permit interpretation of the saving event as a story with a beginning, middle and end. And as a story it is hospitable. A causal explanation is not so fertile. An enumeration of the various known causes of the Gothic (Suger's infatuation with the writings of Dionysius Areopagita, or his ambitions as regent of France, or certain technological developments etc.) might help a historian to understand why the abbey church of St Denis was built as it was, but does not contribute to her understanding of the building's "meaning" because each of the causes was so radically different from the result in which they converged.

In short: a typological interpretation of the present in light of the past offers a real prospect of a useful history. Such an *Architekturgeschichte* is to center on classical Athens. As an axis of architectural history it transformed, in its own unique way, a historical epoch into an era that *as far as architecture is concerned* bears the mark of the posthistorical. The fivesquare city is the unifying factor in the history of architecture that has preceded that central event. And typological interpretation of the fivesquare configuration may help us to recover from the historicist and relativist torrent of *Architekturhistorie* a normative and profitable *Architekturgeschichte*.

Six

Architectonics

Carroll William Westfall

Introduction

In Chapter Four I presented buildings as ideas or objects of thought taking
the form of plan diagrams. But a building is more than an idea or a type's
plan diagram. It is an actual, physical, substantial object resulting from
the application of thought, craft and labor to actual, physical material in a
process of building or construction. This process participates in principles
of nature that are appropriate to building just as the process of governing
does. As a result, a building represents an understanding of those principles as they are embodied in the particular time and place they document
just as a political act does. Earlier we saw that the liaison between the
principles of nature, the process of governing and any particular political
act is a polity's constitution. Here we will see that the liaison between the
principles of nature, the process of building and any particular building
is a building's architectonic substance which might be thought of as a
building's constitution.

A building is both a natural and a conventional object. As the useful object discussed in Chapter Four it embodies the natural types derived from
the political purposes it serves in the conventional forms that allow it to
serve the specific functions that lie within the circumstances of a particular
time and place. Designing the example of the type requires knowing the
particular functions serving those purposes in the particular circumstances
that include the here-and-now of living and building. As an example of
artifice requiring various architectonic means for its production, it embodies two aspects of architectonic content. One aspect is the natural types
inherent in the laws governing the behavior of physical material and the
conventions deriving from regional practices. The other is in the formal
properties that make the building congruent with the order of the polity it
serves and the pattern of natural beauty it imitates.

Proceeding in the sequence used here puts more emphasis on the building type and its connection with political purposes than on the production
of the particular example, which is the topic of this chapter, and its relationship to other buildings to be discussed in Chapter Eight. This is as it
should be if architecture is first of all a civic art and only secondarily an art
devoted to architecture. But that secondary aspect of architecture is not
unimportant—to build any particular building one must know not only the
nature of the type but also the rules one must follow in the art of building.

There are two sets of rules, one dealing with structure, the other with
beauty. The two sets have much in common because they both arise from
the nature of actual buildings. As we saw in Chapter Four, actual buildings
accommodate particular functions in the service of the enduring purposes
symbolized in the plan diagram for the type of building it is. Analogous to
the relationship between purpose and function in the art of building is the
relationship of form and material. In the art of building as in the art of
politics, there are certain true, enduring, atemporal types or forms that can
be known incompletely at best and only in the intellect, in words, symbols
and images independent of material. Actual buildings include matter, but
matter alone is as unbuildable as form alone is. Matter, in other words, is
formless—it is something like mud, smoke, a combination of mud and
smoke, or something else which can only be known through analogy. While
sensible (that is, the senses make its presence known), it is unknowable
because, lacking form, there is nothing within our perceptions of it for the
mind to grasp. Bridging the gap between form and matter is the architectonic substance of building. As was the case in the differentiation between
the settlement and the polity, architectonic substance consists of two levels
of importance, one in structure, the other in beauty.

The present chapter will deal with the rules related to artifice, first the
rules of structure and then the rules of beauty. For two reasons these topics
will be given only the most cursory treatment. One is that in this study
polities are more important than the individual buildings serving them,
and the greater importance of the topic means that it deserves a larger
treatment. The other is that the way the rules become embodied in actual
material derives in great part from regional traditions of building. To discuss one of these extensively in order to illustrate how the rules are translated into practice would seem to enshrine that tradition above others,
while to discuss a number of them would put a labor on the reader disproportionate to the place the topic occupies in the argument. Instead, I will
provide examples, and only brief ones at that, from two strong and important traditions and leave an exposition of other traditions and a more elaborate formulation to any of them to my fellow architects and architectural
historians.

Structure

Structural types

Structural types provide the contact between the building and the laws that operate in the material universe. A *structural type* is a generalized, un-buildable idea of a complete structural unit or any of its components containing within it all possible actual examples that have been and can be built and possessing an analogue in those parts of nature that are law-abiding and which it imitates. A type is atemporal and true, while an example of it is time-bound and only as valid as current knowledge can make it. An *example* of a structural type or component is the product of artifice fulfilling the job it must fulfill in order for the building's form to take on actual material presence.

Practice produces a plenum of conventional solutions to particular structural problems that contain the general rules, canons and propositions embodying the types. Investigating them provides access to the rules of structure. The analogy here is to the versions that mediate between the building types and particular examples. In discussing the art of building, the various versions can be called the various architectonic or structural versions (or styles, a term that is, unfortunately, dangerous to use because of its possible confusion with the term used in positivist architectural history, or manners, or kinds) of architecture. The architectonic versions stand in a different relationship to the structural types than the political versions do to the building types. This is because building types belong in a class with political forms, not with material forms. To put it in terms of Kant's distinctions, the political versions belong to the intelligible world of moral law rather than to the sensible world of natural law where the architectonic versions reside. As a result, knowledge of the building types alone cannot teach a person how to contrive the architectonic structure of an example. Knowing the type does not lead directly to the design. Knowing this is to be a temple does not produce the Parthenon every time. Because the connection between building types and structural types is one of contingency rather than necessity, each building must be designed anew.

The art of building requires knowledge of the sensible world which contains the natural laws that the examples of the structural types and their components imitate and thereby make intelligible. Acquiring this knowledge begins with the examination of actual buildings and of the properties of materials supplied by nature for building them. It ends (in so far as it ever ends—because circumstances change, revision must be constant) in providing a coherent manner of organizing the material within which the enduring content of the building is embodied.

As we have seen, the enduring content of a building imitates the pattern of nature which is a coherent pattern. What is the analog in understanding the relationship between the structural types and their various examples? In answering that I will work with two ideas that are embedded within the classical tradition.[1] One concerns imitation. All buildings and other results of artifice are imitations of a model of some kind. The model is knowable only in the intellect; that is, it is a type. When an actual thing provides the model, the act is one of copying, not imitating, and the result is a revival, a neo or new classicism, not a classicism, in which the adjective indicates the primacy of time and thus of the circumstantial in the copy. The copy contains nothing new because it can contain no more than the examples it depends on. The imitation looks through the examples into the pattern of nature they reveal and extracts something new. In imitating, the substance and the material of model and example are different, and each retains its own identity. In copying, the model and example are confused with one another. In the most extreme form of copying, that is, in making a replica, the intent is to make the two indistinguishable. This is never the intent of imitating. All this may be summarized by saying that an imitation is to nature as a copy is to an example and as the historic is to the historical and the valuable is to the factual.[2]

The other idea is a premise of the classical tradition—that the enduring forms, the pattern of nature imitated in specific acts and examples, is a coherent pattern, and that the coherence in the imitation derives from its extraction from that pattern. From this it follows that a coherent organization of the material embodying the structural types must be, and must appear to be, congruent with the natural forms embodying the order and coherence of nature's pattern. If material is to be, and appear to be, orderly and coherent, it must be stable; if it is to be stable, it must be able to, and appear to be able to, resist motion acting against it. The motion that is important to architecture is visible motion. Not visible are abstractions of the natural sciences applied to building but invisible within the strictly architectonic realm of architecture—bending moments, shear, moments of inertia, atomic motions within crystalline forms, etc. The important motions acting in nature, and appearing to act in nature, were never more clearly defined than they were by Aristotle, who divided them into seven directions: back and forth; right and left; up and down; and circular. The structural types, then, must imitate those parts of nature that are able to resist these forces in nature.

One additional point must be made before proceeding. In order to make contact with its source in actual nature, the material from which the actual example is made must be evident either actually or virtually (that is, fictively). Clay will be seen as the origin of brick and tile, quarries of building stone and forests of timber unless plaster, paint and other devices of artifice playing no actual structural role are used to establish the necessary connection between the appearance and its origin in some particular time and place. Without either an actual or fictive representation the design lacks conventional content and therefore cannot provide a way of knowing how it is congruent with the world it serves. The practices of modernism demonstrate the importance of this point: the glass and crystal buildings and cities used to provide apocalyptic visions of things like the Heavenly Jerusalem or the diverting, healthy, happy city of modernist bliss are independent of time and place and therefore unable to tell the time of this place.[3]

The Three Structural Types

There are only three structural types capable of this mimesis. One is the *wall*, which is capable of resisting any of the paired linear motions. The second type is the wall fragmented to produce a sequence of piers and gaps spanned by left-over fragments of wall taking the form of the *arch*. Like its parent, it is capable of resisting any of the paired linear motions, while the arch makes it possible to account for circular motion as well. Because the arch is the only structural type able to do so, it must be seen as the origin of the *vault* and *dome*. *Trabeation* is the final structural type; it is an orderly assemblage of smaller pieces of material organized to form vertical uprights (perfected as columns) spanned by beams (perfected as entablatures). This type when elaborated can produce a hypostyle grid.

The Five Classes of Material Components

Producing an actual example of a structural type—building a wall, turning an arch, raising a colonnade—requires artifice. Artifice is the means by which formless material is given form to make it useful to the important purposes of people. It is the architectonic means or middle term between the structural type which lacks material and the formless material in which it will be rendered as the actual plans, elevations (or facades) and coverings (or roofs) of buildings.

The discussion of artifice and the structural types has been anticipated in the discussion of how plan diagrams of the building types are fleshed out with the various utilitarian components required by the various versions of specific examples. In doing the same with the structural types the designer's artifice draws on a knowledge of the canonic, conventional form of material, a form, that is, that belongs to the architectonic versions (or styles). This artifice has the capacity of embodying a building's type in a structural type (at one extreme) and in material (at the other extreme) to make a building that is useful to people.

The best knowledge of the conventions governing the art of building with the structural types is knowledge of the canonic conventions. The *canonic* is something more than the merely conventional. Like the conventional, its use is sanctioned by experience, but in addition it is also explicable or justifiable in a theory that is grounded in the same principles as the politics that provides the purposes governing the choice of the building types. It is, in other words, both traditional (as opposed to innovative) and rational (as opposed to arbitrary).

Knowledge of the various canonic conventions is for the architect what knowledge of the best actual states is for the citizen active in politics. In architectural theory as in political theory, this knowledge is systematic knowledge in which things of the same class are treated alike and the classes of things are articulated within a larger scheme of things. There are five classes of things in the conventional forms in which artifice renders the structural types: piece, element, motif, covering and structural component. Each of these will be defined in turn.

A *piece* is a smaller, constituent part of an element. Examples from the world of classical masonry forms are bases and capitals which stand as the feet and heads of shafts; a shaft is another piece; these support the three pieces of the entablature: architrave, frieze and cornice. Such forms are not limited to the marbles, granites and other stones used in Mediterranean examples. There is a long American tradition of rendering them in wood with the best examples illustrating how the masonry forms can be translated into forms appropriate for their imitation in wood.

Another realm of examples in the world of wooden construction in America derives from the experience gained in using machine-made lumber and nails and exemplified in what is loosely encompassed within the term Western or platform framing, an outgrowth of the balloon frame and now a vernacular construction form in domestic and small-scale construction. Its pieces include sills, studs, plates and sheathing.[4]

An *element* is one complete, canonic structural unit composed of smaller *pieces*. An element is the fundamental, smallest complete class of thing.

Two examples from masonry construction are the wall and the Order. The complete masonry wall includes a base and mudsill, a shaft and a topping cornice to keep the rain out or the stringcourse which receives the flooring (i.e., covering; see below) in a multistory structure. The wall's pieces are the blocks of brick or stone and may include many other pieces (beams, stucco or stone revetment, etc.) depending upon the regional tradition. The Order of classical architecture is most commonly thought of in its trabeated form composed of the canonic pieces of pedestal, base, shaft, capital, architrave, frieze and cornice or, in the humblest construction, a wooden lintel. Another type used to span openings included within the Orders is the arcuated one which may be thought of as a beam bent or as a wall opened up in a way that allows it to remain stable and with the span over the opening itself composed of smaller pieces, either bricks or voussoirs. Its pieces are therefore like the ones of the trabeated and wall systems.

The American wood vernacular also provides examples of elements. As is also the case with masonry, the most common element is the wall, this time assembled from lumber and sheathing with its outer layer normally made from clapboards, shingles or stucco and its openings for windows and doors made as lintel-headed frames puncturing the wall's membrane. An arched opening cannot represent structure directly because there are no smaller pieces giving themselves over to being laid up in a circular configuration, as there is with bricks or stone voussoirs. Thus arched openings are commonly used only if the construction is meant to represent masonry forms, a practice which accounts for the tendency of wood-framed construction with arched forms to be coated with stucco rather than clad with boards and for the design to make stylistic references to something often called Spanish or Mediterranean. The "Shingle Style" produced a tradition of thinking of the entire wall as pliable with shingles forming an outermost skin. A representation of stone construction with stucco produces a copy rather than an imitation and therefore is of a lesser dignity than the linteled forms of Western framing or the arched forms of masonry. The shingle tradition does not suffer from this deficiency and has been used effectively for important buildings, for example, town halls and churches.

A *motif* is a traditional or canonic combination of elements. Examples in the masonry construction of classicism are a temple front, a triumphal arch, the combination of the trabeated and arcuated systems to produce the Colosseum motif, a colonnade, an arcade and a frame for a hole in a wall (for example a tabernacle or aedicular window or a portal).

America's classical wooden construction easily renders these same motifs. They can be used in a wide range of applications running from highly finished forms complementing masonry construction—think of the entrances to brick colonial (Georgian) houses such as Westover in Charles City County, Virginia, from 1730ff.—to the very diluted ones as, for example, in the simple frames around openings and as components added onto the "Shingle Style" buildings the balloon frame made possible. These imported motifs are not necessary to complete Western frame buildings. As the simple and effective combination of walls and roofs with the simplest framed openings common in much of American wood construction demonstrates, simple buildings can be completed handsomely with only the simplest forms of canonic motifs used to enframe openings. Ultimately, a tabernacle window stands behind the sill–jamb–header motif of Western framing's and "Shingle Style's" window surrounds just as it does behind the sill–jamb–lintel (or arch) combination used to make a window in the simplest brick wall.

A *covering* is the structure spanning across supports enclosing the upper part of an interior from the sky or the upper space of a floor level from the next floor level. Generally, the uppermost covering, or the roof, forms an important part of the building's visible design. Elements and motifs stand vertically and bear the loads of the coverings. The design of the covering must be integrated with its supports, but the covering and the supports are separable. Some coverings are simple, others are quite complex. In masonry construction they can run from the vault to the very complicated combination of crossing arches, pendentives, drum and dome. In wooden construction the range runs from shed and pitched roofs to complicated intersecting pitched roofs interlaced with towers and turrets. In both masonry and wood construction, experience gained in building teaches how best to arrange the pieces (brick, stone, etc.; joists, rafters purlins, etc.) in accordance with the nearest approximation to the structural types to make the most efficient use of material.

In the most important, perfectly designed building, all material would be disposed within structural types. But just as utopia is impossible to realize, so is such a design. There is always something required for structural stability that cannot be incorporated within a structural type. The components answering to these needs may be classed as *structural components* composed of things that do various tasks in a coherent manner without being absorbed within a structural type. They are to the structural types what the utilitarian components are to the building types.

Practice teaches what these are. In masonry construction, one example is the string course. Relative to the height of a multistory wall, it is neither a mudsill nor a fragment of entablature, but relative to an individual floor it serves the same role as they do by providing a base or a capital for an element (a wall). Another example is a pediment or, more precisely, the raking cornices of a pediment, since the horizontal cornice would be part of an entablature, and the fastigium it caps. The pediment in a temple front motif or on the top story of a church is primarily representational of structure in that it suggests the form of the covering (a timber truss roof or a vault) obscured by the wall whether there is such a thing or not. The pediment atop a tabernacle window motif or aedicular portal is different; one might think of it as decoration, a term to be discussed more fully below. The examples in masonry construction are also found in wood construction which has perhaps only the bracket and railing to add to the list, although both of these are also found in masonry forms.

Rules of Structure

The structural types, like the building types, are natural symbols and contain all possible examples including past, present and future ones. The actual architectonic or structural *versions* (or styles), however, are conventional. They imitate both structural types and the nature of the materials in which they are constructed. Their conventional character, which is organized within the five classes of component parts (pieces, elements, etc.), immerses them in the world of the here-and-now, the contingent and circumstantial world of change and transience which they must represent if they are to provide conventional knowledge for discovering the nature of the structural forms they embody and the political forms they serve. The best design most completely imitates the form. The best imitation represents the coherent pattern of nature, the same nature the political constitution imitates. That pattern is based on rules which are congruent with the rules in other activities based on nature. Because they are activities, they take the form of verbs. The rules of structure, then, are based on the linkage between type and example that occurs in active verbs. This allows the architect to imitate nature not by imitating its products but by imitating its processes.[5]

Processes operate over time. They not only build up but also tear down. Nature provides the material that artifice makes useful in building, and it provides the forces that lead to a building's deterioration. Effort is required to provide stability. The natural principle of economy which states that means must be proportionate to ends requires a proportionality between the expenditure for stability and the relative importance of the building. A building must be as (or only as) enduring as its purpose—flimsy buildings should not be raised up for enduring purposes, and buildings that might, or appear as if they might, last forever are hardly appropriate for transient uses. Achieving that proportionality connects the designing of buildings to the political realm that calls them into being, and it also connects the rules of structure with the rules of beauty which will be discussed in the second half of this chapter.

Working with the conventional forms of structural types and contriving the proper level of stability requires a level of knowledge that raises the art of building above mere craftsmanship and puts it in the realm of artifice. Following the Renaissance formulation of the classical tradition, we can say that craftsmanship uses the hand to apply tools to material and make it conform to the forms required for the design while artifice requires the head to extract the principles and their rules and to apply them to formulating the designs that direct the hand. Craftsmanship was found only in the reformed material. Artifice, however, encompasses not only the reformed material but the appearance produced by that material. This set artifice apart from craftsmanship by making artifice a form of knowledge. Thus the appearance of the forms of things which gives access to its intrinsic content or nature is as important as the extrinsic forms things actually have.

These observations can be formulated as the principle of stability which says that the design of a building must provide the appearance of an appropriate actual stability and actually possess an appropriate actual stability. That is, a building needs to look as strong as it is and be as strong as it needs to be.

Central to this principle is the maxim that classical architecture makes a vivid representation of structure. This representation includes two classes of formal presentation, one actual, the other virtual (or fictive, or apparent). Actual structure is the name given to the part of the design in which one sees the actual form of the material that does the actual job of providing for a building's stability. If removed, the building would lack something essential to stability and the building would eventually collapse. In virtual structure, the forms of the material have only a visual purpose.[6] A pilaster, for example, only appears to lend support to a wall. Remove it, and the wall is actually as stable as ever, although it will appear to have been weakened. In architecture, both actual and virtual structure are necessary and each reinforces the other. Neither necessarily has a higher value than the other, although in some conventions a hierarchic distinction is made between the two.

Both actual and virtual structure provide access to the conventions in which the structural types are embodied. But the types are also embodied in words and images independent of buildings, for example, in drawings made before or after the actual building has been built. A building's translation into an image produces a substitute for the actual building, but its translation into words transposes it into other terms that make it comportable with other things known through words. If the thing translated into words is an imitation of a type in nature, it will join with other types in the principles that are common to the various types, but only if the words can be rendered as coherent speech. Because in this way a building is a form of speech, the rules of speech can provide a model for the criteria the rules of structure must satisfy if they are to be rules extending from principles and not mere prescriptions.

This understanding of the rules of structure suggests that if a design is to have a coherent structure it must be possible to name each of the things in the design and to attach active verbs to the role they play and in the process produce complete sentences. This allows for speech to produce a facsimile of the building in the form of a coherent description revealing how it is linked to other aspects of nature—for example, the purpose its users serve in a state and the representation it makes of the world of nature including the processes controlled by its laws.

The material used for describing buildings is simple enough. The material constituting the descriptions of what one sees in the actual or virtual structure has already been given. These include the names of pieces such as bases, capitals, shafts and entablatures, and sills, studs and plates; of elements such as the Order and the arch; of motifs such as the temple front, the triumphal arch, the colonnade or the arcade; and of coverings such as the roof and the dome. It also includes the role each plays. As we have seen, elements support; motifs support, enclose and enframe; and coverings span and enclose. When dealing with actual structure, the description deals with the thing actually playing the role whereas descriptions of virtual structure must add something about the means of achieving the facsimile of actual structure—for example, by indicating that the trabeation uses pilasters, the stone is actually stucco, and the apse is actually rendered in perspective.

This speech about buildings (whether in verbal or architectonic form) will be very diverse—as diverse as the buildings it is about. All but a handful of elevations lack a precise terminology that evokes their appearance with the same clarity that a plan's name (basilica; palace) evokes a type or a version of a type. Thus the best way to describe an elevation is to define which elements and motifs appear where and specify what structural job they are doing. Thus one example of a precise precis of a description taken from church design (Brunelleschi's San Lorenzo or Santo Spirito) is to say that a basilica's nave elevation is composed of a columnar arcade supporting a wall punctured by aedicular windows and itself supporting an open timber roof. Another example (Brunelleschi's Santa Maria degli Angeli): An octagonal plan is enclosed by solid walls opened with arches seemingly carried by pilasters and extended into handkerchief-domed chapels while the arches support a tall entablature and carry a segmental dome. Similarly, a description of John Russell Pope's Jefferson Memorial would refer to the eight-column temple front standing before the rotunda composed of fifty-four Ionic columns supporting a Pantheon-like dome covering the central space. My wooden house in Charlottesville has a front facade of frame construction rising two stories with horizontal cladding on the lower floor and a flared shingle wall above with a single pedimented, shingled wall dormer rising into the low-pitched roof on each side of the center where a pair of doors (only one of them still operable) is sheltered by a shed-roofed porch supported by posts, evidently an addition from the 1920s to the original 1870 (1889?) building.

On the Architectonic Versions

Having traversed the rules of structure we may return to their application
in the various versions (or styles, or manners) of buildings. As explained
earlier, among actual buildings, the architectonic versions are to the
structural types as the political versions are to the building types. Furthermore, because the connection between building types and structural types
is one of contingency rather than necessity, each building must be designed
anew. The designs will fall into classes according to conventions guiding
the way the architectonic versions are combined with the actual plans.

The most important conventions are the ones contained within the buildings serving as models or paradigms. As explained in Chapter Four, a
model is an actual building produced in relatively close proximity to the
designer who draws on it and which, because it illustrates intelligent and
useful solutions to concrete problems that are still prominent in the art of
building, he can follow relatively literally. Paradigmatic buildings are
models that are more remote from the designer and require a less literal
adaptation of the architectonic means it illustrates.

Models and paradigms are useful in showing how to solve recurring,
unavoidable problems encountered whenever one moves from a purpose
dictating a building type to the architectonic means found within particular
circumstances. Because plans support elevations it is in the nature of
building for the plan and elevations to be congruent with one another, but
the means of achieving that congruence reside in conventions, not types.
The limitations governing the design of plans are generally more rigid than
the ones concerning elevations. Buildings serving the most important
purposes tend to follow models in which there is relatively little flexibility
in contriving plans or elevations, and they generally call for a relatively
close fit between the elevation and the plan supporting it. Similarly, their
elevations tend to follow the conventional, architectonic versions more
closely and to present a more literal or traditional rendering of elements and
motifs in which canonic usage is most prominent.

With these general observations we have again come to the point where
the political purpose of the building becomes the most important determinant of its design. That being the case, we can move to the heart of that
issue and discuss the rules of beauty.

Beauty

Nature provides the pattern which a building must imitate if it is to be
beautiful. An analogous statement has been made earlier for the use and
the structure of the building, so with this treatment of beauty we will cover

the third of the three Vitruvian "conditions of well building," commodity, firmness and delight. In congruence with the premodern understanding and as discussed in Chapter Two, the position held here is that whatever we take to be the beauty of a building we come to know from its appearance and that whatever it is we see derives from qualities in the building. The beauty, in other words, is in the building, not (merely) in the eyes of the beholder. That which gives rise to what we see resides in two aspects of a building's appearance, one pertaining to its use, the other to its structure. Each of these will be dealt with in turn.

In the beautiful building each of these two aspects of appearance is guided by the appropriate rules of beauty. The rules of beauty are conventions congruent with general, broad propositions that define how things are in our experience. Unlike the character of the building types, they cannot claim to be based on true principles of the way things simply are because they deal with things like relative placement of things and relative finish of material, which means they already depend upon circumstantial conditions for their appearance. What is true in them is the orderly pattern they imitate or, more precisely, what is true in them is that they can be understood to derive from an orderly pattern. Beauty exists when a building represents the orderly pattern that is right for it and when a person can see that that is the case. Beauty is in the object. If the observer does not see it, the observer, not the building, is deficient.

Decorum and the Rules of Dilution

Not all buildings are equal. Inequality produces hierarchy. Since the political purpose a building is to serve is the most important determinant in its architectural design, it follows that the hierarchical distinctions between buildings must first and foremost represent the hierarchical distinctions between their political purposes. The task of the architect is to design so as to lodge his building in the proper position within the hierarchy.

The inherent inequality of purposes had been firmly established in politics from the very moment there was politics—and even before that, when God gave His commandment to Adam. In commanding Adam, he was telling Adam that he was less than God. The principle of hierarchic distinction in politics had its parallel in architectural practice, but it was first articulated into architectural theory during the quattrocento and was first explained in Alberti's *de re aedificatoria*. It is both the earliest and also the clearest explication of the implications of architecture's ability to represent the hierarchical distinctions between buildings serving political purposes, and therefore I will make extensive use of it.

The first proposition concerning this articulation is this: the building's purpose defines its status, which is not absolute but relative to that of other buildings. For its status to be legible, it appearance must relate it to other buildings serving the same general purpose if the comparisons that establish status are to be read. Buildings, in other words, are to be seen in relationship to one another in their political setting, that is, in the polity.

A corollary of this is that the assemblage of buildings serving a polity represent the constitution, and if one is to know the specific purposes and functions and the hierarchical gradations of a polity's buildings, one must know the constitution. The way the constitution will be represented in buildings will depend on what kinds of connections there are between the constitution's conventions and the conventions deriving from its parallel among the political and architectonic versions of buildings serving it. Together, these embody such things as the character of traditional building practices (there may be more sophistication in dealing with building than with politics), economic means available for building (building is a discretionary expense for governors, and people may be unwilling to pay the price of building well), and the formal conventions of various political and architectonic versions (buildings may represent the most lofty aspirations by imitating the Heavenly Jerusalem, or they may represent the most humdrum quotidian ambitions of merchants). These conventions differ from region to region and from time to time, but they establish the actual conditions within which buildings are built. When properly handled, they can establish the relative importance of buildings serving a political regime with the same clarity that allows a person interested in shopping to distinguish a Niemann-Marcus from a K-Mart (or Harrods from Woolworth).

The rules of dilution provided a systematic method for representing the varying status of buildings. They exist in a formulation which has general validity and the specific forms that make them useful guides to practice. The general statement, which Alberti first formulated but which would apply anywhere (and already had existed, since he based his formulation on his observations of existing buildings), is this:

Lesser buildings borrow their forms from more important buildings.

To design any building in the polity requires that one know the design of the most important buildings, even those that have not yet been built within the current knowledge and conventions of a place.

In answering the question about what forms are to be borrowed and how that borrowing can occur, the general formulation can be expanded in the following way:

1. something bigger is more important than something smaller
2. a more central site is more important than a peripheral one

3. something free-standing is more important than something embedded
4. something well designed and highly finished is more important than something that is less so
5. conventions provide a means of knowing the relative status of similar things that allow comparison with other things

Only the last two of these have much to do with what the architect controls in the design. The others are largely established by forces that operate to site buildings and provide the resources for construction. The architect's task is most evident in the last two propositions.

These last two propositions make a great deal of the relatively greater status of artifice compared to craftsmanship and of the essential importance of conventions operating within ongoing traditions. These are both central to the concerns of the classical that was made conventional in ancient Greece and subsequently expanded within various canons ever since, in the same realm that has been preoccupied with the political ideas that have the same origins. One of the great benefits of classical architecture is its ability to be articulate within these rules. That also accounts for its appeal whenever it is recognized that politics is more important than architecture.

Only a pair of specific formulations of the use of these rule are needed to illustrate them. One concerns the structural types and members and is found in Alberti's formulation: trabeation is superior to arcuation, columns are superior to their projection on the wall as pilasters, and marble is superior to stone. Another concerns the relative status of the Orders. In what sequence should any or all of what we think of as the five canonic Orders—Tuscan, Doric, Ionic, Corinthian and Composite—be used to reveal the status of buildings relative to one another? And what is the proper level of finish for the various orders in various circumstances?[7]

These formulations and others like them hold whether the structural types and the conventional Orders are rendered in the traditional masonry forms that ancient legend tells us were developed on the basis of imitating wooden building in stone or in the later step of translating those masonry forms into American wooden construction. A very different series of rules guides the representation of status in Western framing.

This means of construction offers a much less extensive variety of ways for representing status. There are a number of reasons for this. In contrast to classical architecture, Western framing is a very recent invention and therefore lacks the accumulation of experience that more articulate systems contain. It is difficult to imagine how its potential can be expanded given its current dependence on a very limited range of actual building materials—basically lumber and boards or stucco—although one should never preclude the possibility that succeeding generations of designers might find additional richness in it. After all, a system that can produce the undulations of the "Shingle Style" might also come up with an arcuated system that imitates the nature of arches rather than merely copies the arches of masonry. And it is impossible to find in Western framing a paradigmatic building of the highest status that can be diluted to produce lesser buildings, although there might be a Parthenon somewhere in Western framing's future. According to the legends that gloss its theory, classical architecture derives from the problem of building houses for the gods, while the founding myths explaining the beginnings of Western framing in balloon framing refer to the mechanics and boys who combined machine-made nails and machine-cut lumber to produce a church that did not even have a permanent site or longevity. St Mary's Church in Chicago, according to the Homer of modernism, was "Razed and reërected three times during its short life."[8] The outstanding designs of its subsequent career have usually been limited to regias in the form of the American free-standing residence, one range of which is noted for the economy and rapidity of production as at Levittown, another for the ingeniousness of unique designs as in any number of houses from the time of Andrew Jackson Downing forward. The limitations of Western framing as an architectonic means becomes evident when it is used to produce a higher status building. To raise its status the designer is forced to reach outside architecture and to pull other content into the design. An example is Charles Moore's Kresge College at the University of California at Santa Cruz which the architect said draws on the shopping center and the village treated as a formal model shorn of political content and replaced "by aspects of make-believe, or an urgently important four-year-long operetta."[9] There is nothing in the architectonics of the design suggesting either shopping center, village or operetta stage because there cannot be—those are terms referring to functions and not purposes or architectonic content. Thus, when people no longer recall that that is what the place is supposed to be, the only content left from the original architectural design will be the limited content of the Western framing system.

That content is limited not only because of the currently limited potential of Western framing but also because of the particular use it was given in this example. The design exploits the potential of blank, planer, unarticulated stucco walls to emulate the minimalist abstractions of the then current styles in painting. It therefore illustrates what happens when the unique character of the medium of architecture is put into the service of other media of expression and representation. Buildings cannot imitate anything other than nature and the nature of building. When their design is based on what is being done in another medium, the result is copying, and when buildings copy the style of another medium, in this case painting, the result must be a curtailment of what building and architecture can contain. When the style of that other medium is antithetical to the aims of art, as has recently been the case, the result is doubly damaging to architecture: Not only is the attempt to extract additional content from the architectonic potential of architecture neglected, but architecture is pressed into the service of positivism and historicism that are antithetical to the political life defined as the art of living together in order to live nobly and justly.[10]

It remains to be seen whether Western framing has the potential to become a rich architectonic means for building. There is no question that the tradition embodied in classicism does, but it is difficult to use the standards and achievements of classicism as a basis for assessing the potential of Western framing. For example, in classicism, one of the ideas consistent with its rules is that something more difficult to do is more valuable than something that is easier. Thus, because there are more design problems in combining arcuation and trabeation than there are in using either one independently, a well-designed trabeated pier arcade would elevate a building above those with only trabeation or only arcuation that are equally well designed. But in Western framing this problem does not arise, and perhaps never can. Meanwhile, it has been the tendency ever since its invention to look to other systems for solving difficult structural problems—for example, by combining Western framing with skeletal steel construction with the result that something other than a skillful solution to a difficult architectonic problem—such as depending on analogy or hoping for metaphor, as is the case in Kresge College—has been used to elevate the status of a building. Because this is, but need not necessarily be, the case with other aspects of Western framing as well, it is fruitless to pursue this parallel inquiry into it and classicism.

In classicism, complementary to the idea that something more difficult is more valuable than something that is easier is another idea: the better of two things is the one with the higher degree of finish produced with better craftsmanship and better and more expensive materials. Wide variations are possible within this formulation, however. Renaissance architects and theorists were punctilious in maintaining that rich materials do not compensate for poor craftsmanship and that an ignorant design cannot be rescued from ignominy by using expensive craftsmen and materials. A successor of this idea can be seen in American colonial practice where wood self-consciously simulates stone in important buildings or parts of buildings. Everyone is familiar with the pseudo drafted ashlar at George Washington's Mount Vernon. Less familiar is its use at Thomas Jefferson's Monticello, where the area within the porch flanking the entrance in the east front is not only treated as pseudo drafted ashlar but is painted and then coated with sand to reinforce the simulation. One of the deficiencies of current practice in Western framing is its failure to be hospitable to the addition of highly skilled craftsmanship to the elements and motifs which it prefers to leave at a minimalist level of abstraction. Contrast this with the virtuosity of "Shingle Style" architects who revelled in making roofs move about, walls undulate, windows bulge and surfaces come alive with textures made from a variety of cleverly handled shingles, slats, boards and other wooden pieces intrinsic to the construction system. In this case the artful use of craft fitted within general rules appertaining to the style (in the sense of regional practice). It was therefore teachable, and it provided an index of individual talent in the way the performance of an aria in an opera does. More recently, craftsmanship has been absorbed by an attitude toward architecture that sees it as the basis of design and in the service of an individual genius. Thus, as the brilliant works of architects as diverse as Mies van der Rohe (I have in mind his Farnsworth House in Plano, Illinois, from 1949) and Carlo Scarpa show, the art of their craft is not used to elucidate a design that is already rich and intelligible at a more general level, and it is not composed of aspects that can be used in other circumstances; and neither can it produce acceptable results when used by others who are less talented than themselves. A mediocre "Shingle Style" house is not deficient in the way a mediocre Miesian box or Scarpa storefront is. Without having the art of craftsmanship serve a larger purpose within design, it cannot do its job, which is to lodge a building at a particular level of status among other buildings, something now achieved primarily through richness of materials and sheer size, not only of the building but also of the elements and motifs composing it.

In implementing these rules of dilution, elevations demand more attention than plans do because a greater amount of a plan's design is established by the building's purpose and function and by considerations such as location and size that usually lie outside the control of the architect. From this we can conclude that elevations always, and coverings less often, provide a very precise representation of the status of the building within the relevant rules of dilution and a very learned presentation of current knowledge concerning artifice. As a corollary we can say that because the structural types are necessarily more limited in number than the ways available for rendering them, the structural type will address the general while its specific design will present the particular. Taken together, these propositions show that, to take the example of an exterior elevation, the choice of a structural type, selected in coordination with the regional practices found in various versions of the architectonic and building types, will locate the building in the hierarchy of buildings while its precise detailing will produce a detailed gloss on that status.

The Rules of Congruity

What has been said so far serves as prelude to the final, most important consideration of a building's beauty. As we have seen, in serving purposes buildings provide commodity and in being stable they satisfy firmness. The third term in the canonic, Vitruvian trilogy is that delight which results from the appearance of things. We have been dealing with appearance all along, but not yet with appearance the purpose of which is to provide delight. So far, the appearance has been serving the purpose of clarifying and explaining how a building serves a larger political purpose with other buildings and how it embodies an intelligent understanding of the natural world of which it is a part and fits the particular region in which it is built. These necessarily precede the final aspect of beauty and must be well handled if beauty is to be present. But they do not in themselves provide a presence for beauty.

Beauty is a special delight deriving from the fundamental law of congruity in classical thought: the means is proportionate to the end and is congruent with the means for reaching other, related purposes. Congruity refers to more than proportion or mere numerical commensurability just as purpose embodies more than mere function. Beauty is the culmination of design, and it is found in a mean. In classical theory, beauty is explored under several headings, the most important of which are decoration, ornament and the four aspects of congruity, namely, number, finishing, collocation and congruity itself, each of which will be discussed more fully below.

This way of thinking about beauty is clearly stamped with traditional classical thought, and is clearly inimical to modernist thought. In modernist thought, beauty, to the extent it is said to be present, is thought to be in an extreme—an extreme of, say, structural daring-do (think of the exhibitionism of Richard Rogers' Lloyd's of London building in London) or of razzle-dazzle spectacle (for example, of theories pushed to logical but absurd ends as at Bernard Tschumi's Parc La Vilette in Paris) or, at the one end, of a vast reduction to some sort of putative essence (as in the Miesian canon and its reductionist derivatives in the work of, say, Caesar Pelli, or of buildings said to complement older ones, as in I.M. Pei's banal East Wing of the National Gallery in Washington, which simply turns a blind eye to most of what John Russell Pope's original building presented to vision).

The modernists' preoccupation with extremes has prevented the exploration of the mean where classical thought located beauty. In modernism as in classicism, the prevailing ideas of what constitutes the beautiful has been most thoroughly explored in the most important buildings. As a result we now look to the bank towers and museums to find comparisons to an earlier era's temples and palaces.

An important and unwelcome consequence of the preoccupation with the extremes has been the development of ways of providing designs with the decoration, ornament and aspects of congruity any building necessarily has in ways that cannot be used in less important buildings forming parts of the same city. The towers and museums of America's central cities become ever more enriched with whatever is thought to constitute beauty in architecture while the surrounding suburbs produce vast numbers of buildings forming a jarring disjunction with their superiors. Many of these buildings simply trivialize what the most valued buildings present. Others, for example those built in Western framing, are left without any means of incorporating ornament, decoration or aspects of congruity that locate them within the same universe of architecture. The choice currently most easily accessible to the inventive designer is to make these buildings either decorated sheds or ducks, although neither choice is inherent in the order of things governing design using Western framing as their architectonic means. At least, that is the lesson taught by a great number of buildings in America's later nineteenth-century towns, villages and even suburbs. They were something richer and more civic-minded than decorated sheds and ducks because their design was diluted from current examples of their civic-minded superiors. More recently, however, with the superiors' designs eschewing any intention of representing their purpose within the larger civic complex of the city and instead exploiting extremes that simply cannot be incorporated into its architectonics of other methods of construction, Western framing has been left as an impoverished panhandler picking up whatever its richer neighbors have thrown its way. Because this is the case, it is fruitless to continue the exploration in this essay of the ways it embodies beauty.

As classical architecture so clearly shows, beauty derives from establishing the mean between excess and deficiency—although another way of writing that sentence is equally valid: An architecture that, among other things, seeks beauty through establishing a mean between excess and deficiency may be called a classical architecture, the most familiar examples of which derive from that practice connected with the theories elucidating it running from Vitruvius through Alberti and onward, although other examples also embody the same principles with different rules suiting their circumstantial particularities. Whether classical or otherwise, satisfying the rules of stability and dilution are necessary conditions for a building's being beautiful but they are not sufficient conditions. This is perhaps most clear in Alberti's famous definition of beauty, the first, more familiar and more simple of the two he gave in his architectural treatise:

Beauty is the reasoned harmony of all the parts within whatsoever subject it appears such that nothing could be added, diminished or altered, but for the worse.[11]

Stability and decorum both individually and in relation to one another do not constitute the whole of the reasoned harmony. They allow a building to represent and to speak but being stable and decorous does not produce eloquence. To provide eloquence requires attention to the rules of congruity which will bring modifications to a design already satisfying stability and decorum. Beauty dictates to structure and function in the same way that political wisdom governs a people's navigation through circumstances.

The rules of congruity are enmeshed within the rules governing the previous parts of the design. The rules of dilution properly lodge it within the hierarchy of buildings, and the rules of stability provide a proper relationship to the structural types. The same rules indicate what kind of beauty is appropriate to each building, and the principle of proportion provides the means for providing that beauty. Beauty itself is in the realm of the enduring and therefore is of only one kind, but because beauty is only available to us in phenomena and these require particular circumstances, there will be various kinds of beauty. The rules of structure and of dilution provide ways of assuring that the building possesses the appropriate kind of beauty. Its means of doing so are with decoration and ornament.

Decoration and ornament are not the same thing, and neither is either one an option that can be left off according to the whim, "taste" or ideology of the architect or builder. Decoration and ornament are necessary parts of the design (all buildings have them, even if they were not put there as the result of an architect's design) and provide its completion in the way the nose completes the nostrils and therefore the face. The utilitarian components serving function and the material components composing the structural types provide ample opportunities for the embellishment (embellishment = literally, making beautiful) of decoration and ornament.

Authors on architecture do not always distinguish between them, and even when a distinction is made, it may be other than the one made here, which follows what I take to be a conventional distinction. The difference between them is easily seen in the differences between the functional and structural parts of the building. Ornament belongs to function. As John Onians has recently said, its principal function, and the function of the orders in particular, "is to articulate the characters and values of individuals and institutions and to express and affect states of mind."[12] In its origin it "has little to do with beauty," as George Hersey has explained. "It means something or someone that has been equipped or prepared, like a hunter, soldier, or priest. . . . The word has implications of honor, achievement, religious duty. The ornamented temple is one prepared to honor the god."[13] It therefore is related to the rules of dilution. Decoration is to structure as ornament is to decorum. In a variety of written pieces and in lectures, Demetri Porphyrios has explained how the architectonic character of buildings derives from their imitation of the art of building. In the terms used here, decoration clarifies stability by glossing the rules of structure.

A building can function well without ornament and can be stable without decoration and it therefore can possess a beauty in its function and structure, but that beauty will be clarified and made evident only after the proper luster of decoration and ornament has been added to the design's beauty. Ornament is an enrichment that explains and clarifies function and purpose, while decoration does the same for aspects of actual and virtual structure. The extent to which either is used depends upon the relative importance of the building and resides in the conventions that may be learned by consulting the versions of the building types and structural types. In some instances, for example for a less important building, a design might properly have a simplicity that is inadequate for more important buildings which require a more far-reaching grace. No matter the level of the beauty, decoration always plays a crucial role in making the material qualities of the building evident. The most important aspects of its doing so are in two different roles. One of them is clarifying the character of the material's use, and thereby marking the relationship between craftsmanship and artifice—how extensively a material is worked, how different materials are connected, etc. The other is calling attention to those places where the loads of a structure change direction—at the base and capital in trabeated and arcuated systems, at the springing of a vault from a wall, around an opening in a wall for a window or door. These qualities allow the conventions of architectonic versions to provide insight into what is known about nature.

Just as a decorous and stable building is a source of knowledge, so too is a beautiful one. Beauty itself is a form of knowledge, and a beautiful building teaches. While people take delight, that is, pleasure, in beauty, beauty is more than pleasure and is based on more than mere attractiveness. This understanding must be stressed today because classical ideas of beauty are nearly the direct opposite of many current and popular today. Currently and commonly, beauty, or whatever the term is for that which provides pleasure, is thought to be found in the senses, period. This has three important results: because the senses quickly become sated, the architect must reach into extremes of the kind mentioned above if he is to produce something thought to be beautiful; it puts beauty in a category of experience that is incompatible with reason (as is evident in a comparison between current rock music and, for example, Mozart); and it removes beauty from being in the thing perceived and makes it instead a property possessed by the person doing the perceiving (to "increase" the beauty, the mind might be altered—say, with drugs—and the beauty increases without further reference to the object).

In classical aesthetics, beauty arises from judgement based on the evidence of the senses and not from sensation alone, and it is within the object or the source of sensations even if there is no one doing any perceiving or sensing. At different times in different theories, the faculty for making those judgements, which are called judgements of taste, is located differently. Common despite the differences is agreement that the faculty is not one of sensation but of mind, that is, of intellect, and that the form the judgements take is that of reason or understanding. Judgements of taste are different from other kinds of judgements. There is no *a priori* argument or condition that can prove a thing is beautiful. As a result, as Alberti puts it, judgements about the beauty of a thing proceed not "from mere opinion, but from the workings of a reasoning faculty that is inborn in the mind,"[14] a comment with which Kant would not take exception.[15]

Knowing the beauty of a thing tells a person about its purpose and design, and, conversely, knowing the purpose of a thing tells a person what beauty is appropriate to it. To see this beauty in architecture requires that one know the building through one's personal perception of it and that one exercises reason, that is, thinks, about it. To be an object of reason it must be a form of speech; to be a beautiful object, it must be eloquent speech. To put it another way: For a building to be beautiful, it must be visible and open to the inquiry of reason. Its purpose must be just and noble, and its form must be, and must appear to be, appropriate to its purpose.

The beauty of an object resides in its congruity with the pattern of beauty in nature. In imitating that pattern, the architect follows the rules of congruity. Each architect, critic, historian and theorist develops his own understanding of the rules of congruity. A useful digest is the one provided by Alberti, whose discussion of this topic, as with many others, set the stage for all subsequent discussions and will be followed, sometimes generally, sometimes quite closely, in what follows. He gave four aspects of congruity, or proportion as he called it, three of them leading to the application of reason to design and based on rules, the fourth the result of a special talent (*virtù*) possessed by good architects and beyond the reach of rules.

Alberti called the first aspect number. Seemingly simple-minded, number prescribes that there be the proper quantity of components and that those quantities be based on what one finds in nature. In buildings as in animals, supports such as columns should be in even numbers and openings in odd numbers. The importance of this aspect is not in the analogy to nature but in the necessity that things in a design be of such a discrete nature that they can all be known as discrete parts and as classes of things—supports that are columns or walls, openings that are doors or windows, etc.

Alberti's second aspect, finishing, establishes a more complex correspondence between buildings and other productions of nature and of men. Finishing refers to proportionate correspondences between length, breadth and height. The parts of a building and the building as a whole must have a discreteness that allows them to be measured. The capacity for mensuration is essential. The proportions within which the measurements are to be cast is an additional matter that need not be taken up here except to say that the proportions used for regulating the dimensions of buildings must be derived from the same rules of proportion used for making harmony in music and in geometric figures. Alberti explains the standard three systems of proportion: arithmetic $(b - a = c - b)$, geometric $(a:b = b:c)$ and harmonic $((b - a) / a = (c - b) / c)$.[16]

Number guides the disposition of utilitarian components and of various material components in structural types. Finishing pertains to their combination in the fabric which gives material embodiment to the versions of the type. The third aspect, collocation (or arrangement, or even composition), attends to details of design within the larger framework established by the first two sets of rules and takes the design back into the realm of function and structure.

Collocation refers to the proper situation or placement of the several parts called for by the general conventions found in the versions of building types or of structural types and in the particular functional and structural problems the design is addressing. It runs from controlling the disposition of the utilitarian components to make an actual building out of a plan diagram to supervising the placement of the smallest moldings on capitals. Alberti makes it clear that there are no rules for guiding one to proper collocation beyond the ones provided for number and finishing and by the rules of dilution and of artifice. Proper collocation derives not from rules but from judgement. All men are naturally equipped to see and be repelled by poor collocation: "if a puppy had an ass's ear on its forehead, or if someone had one huge foot, or one hand vast and the other tiny, he would look deformed."[17] A good architect is a person nature has equipped with the innate talent or capacity to design with proper collocation.

Collocation can be assisted by numbering and finishing. However, the final aspect of the rules of congruity,[18] which is congruity itself, is beyond the reach and guidance of rules. Following the rules establishes the basis for including this final aspect in a design, but something more is needed than can be provided by merely following the rules. The source for that something more is once again the innate talent of the learned, practiced architect who can exercise the judgement required to design.

"Congruity," Alberti says,

> is nourished with every grace and splendor. It is the task and aim of congruity to compose parts that are quite separate from each other by their nature, according to some precise rule, so that they correspond to one another in appearance. . . . when the mind is reached by way of sight or sound, or any other means, congruity is instantly recognized. . . . I might call it the spouse and the soul of reason . . . it runs through man's entire life and government, it molds the whole of Nature.

These observations led Alberti to his second, more comprehensive and final definition of beauty:

> Beauty is a form of sympathy and consonance of the parts within a body, according to definite number, finishing and collocation, as dictated by congruity, the absolute and fundamental rule in Nature. This is the main object of the art of building, and the source of her dignity, grace, authority and value.[19]

Part of the beauty of that definition is that for the word "architecture" it is possible to substitute any number of others that reside in the realm of the conventional in their role as liaison between the true and the actual without any change of meaning or force—for example,

> This is the main object of the political life guided by the constitution of the polity, and by this it obtains its dignity, grace, authority and value.
> This is the main object of the acts of the citizen, and by this the citizen obtains his dignity, grace, authority and value.
> This is the main object of a polity's urban form, and by this the city obtains its dignity, grace, authority and value.

This last sentence may provide an apposite prelude to Chapter Eight, the final part of my contribution to this volume.

SEVEN

Paratactical Dejection

Robert Jan van Pelt

Hälfte des Lebens	*Half of Life*
Mit gelben Birnen hänget	With its yellow pears
Und voll mit wilden Rosen	And wild roses everywhere
Das Land in den See,	The shore hangs in the lake,
Ihr holden Schwäne,	O gracious swans,
Und trunken von Küssen	And drunk with kisses
Tunkt ihr das Haupt	You dip your heads
Ins heilignüchterne Wasser	In the sobering holy water
Weh mir, wo nehm'ich, wenn	Ah, where will I find
Es Winter ist, die Blumen, und wo	Flowers, come winter,
Den Sonnenschein,	And where the sunshine
Und Schatten der Erde?	And shade of the earth?
Die Mauern stehn	Walls stand cold
Sprachlos und kalt, im Winde	And speechless, in the wind
Klirren die Fahnen.	The weathervanes creak.

Friedrich Hölderlin, "Hälfte des Lebens / Half of Life" from *Hymns and Fragments*, transl. Richard Sieburth.

Deject revocation.[1]

---

1. Hölderlin's "Half of Life" takes the place of Chapter Seven. In the original outline Chapter Seven was not meant to be a suspension of discourse: its purpose was to follow the discussion of the five-square city of Athens with the kind of practical speculations which constitute so much of the second

part of Westfall's contribution. Yet things turned out differently. The discussion of the quintessential type at the end of Chapter Five, intended to be the pivot of the odd chapters of the book, did not provide the hoped-for solid ground. That final and steady base on which theoretical reflection could erect a tower that would reach to heaven proved to be cracked, and subsequent investigation disclosed an infernal rift. Also the theater succumbed to the tectonic law which postulates that any tower which touches the heavens also sounds the sinister depths of hell. Sophocles' *Oedipus Tyrannus* opened that unfathomable chasm, and Hölderlin's interpretation revealed its inevitable and irresistible character. The discussion of the caesura implied a helpless surrender of worn ambition: it revealed that a pious fiction—such as the one which proclaims Jaspers's vision as a valid and useful perspective on an otherwise refractory past—was after all nothing more than a polished fabrication. Continuation of the discourse as if nothing had happened was to move from blind error to manifest falsity. And so began a weary process of renunciation. At first it was camouflaged by the hubris of Aristophanes' Meton. Yet even gaudy wit could not do more than gloss over the uncanny crack. The fissure remained, and remains. It is the proper place to recall Hölderlin's observation that a man who stares into the horror of a caesura will turn around as a traitor—"naturally in a saintly manner." And it is the proper time to remember how Hölderlin asserted how time is reversed in that confrontation, "no longer fitting beginning and end." And it is the time and the place to ponder Hölderlin's intellection of the ensuing conversion, "because at this moment of categorical reversal he has to follow and thus can no longer resemble the beginning in what follows." And Hölderlin concluded, "thus Haemon stands in 'Antigone.' Thus Oedipus himself in the tragedy of 'Oedipus.'" And so the argument rests at an unexpected junction in our debate.

My dispute with Westfall has come effectively to an end.

And so my contribution to the debate ends with a few pieces which were meant to have been brought into a unified design—fragments of a historiographical ambition which shattered on the sudden discovery that the completed edifice would have been a sinister and dissolute abomination. In Chapter Eight Westfall will build his city, uncontested now. And thus the debate will end in a clear victory for him who resolutely perserved to follow the chosen path. In the third part of this book, appropriately entitled "The Remainder," I will offer those who are still interested to discover my motivation for this paratactical chapter of renunciation the shattering intuition which brought the debate so crudely to an end. This disclosure will only reproach and repudiate the main assumption of this book: the idea that it is possible to (re)discover architectural principles which allow architects to build in an age of historicism. Therefore it is proper that this bitter allegation will be offered in Chapter Nine, a reckless excursus located in a third part of this book outside the perimeter of the tilting-ground proper. Isolated from the main text I will offer a rendering of the ignoble and spectral puppet show which, standing at the rift, I saw suspended from the Sophoclean stage into the yawning void.

Robert Jan van Pelt

EIGHT

Cities

Carroll William Westfall

The polity is the name we give to the arena of political activity in which we seek to live the good life. In it the actual, unique, unpredictable activities of citizens meet the tests of justice and legitimacy put to them through the means provided by their constitution, a conventional instrument embodying the best available knowledge of the true and enduring on the one hand and of the actual and circumstantial on the other. To form the city of the classical tradition we have added a great deal to the knowledge taught by the Greeks. This knowledge tells us what we need to know about what the city ought to be. Only it can take us outside and beyond the provincialism our immediate experience and past provide for us. A brief review of the development of the classical understanding of the city supplementing the one van Pelt has provided will bring us to an understanding of what it can and ought to be today.

City and Urbs

Our city is the name we give to the place we call our home, our *patria*, our *Heimat*, our *città felice*. In it are those things that are most dear to us. The Greeks of the classic period, the ones who fought the Persians but not the ones who destroyed Melos, thought this was the political life which meant the city was transportable. When a city such as Athens, when overwhelmed by an enemy such as the Persians, was destroyed as a physical entity, the citizens could seriously consider whether to return and rebuild or to build elsewhere, doing so when all the citizens were refugees but without any doubt that the city was still intact. And more commonly, when a polity thought it necessary, it would send a body of citizens off to a new place to found a city. This was not a colony but a new city that was at best allied with the place from whence its citizens had come but not a part of that polity.

The Greeks had no way in their language or in their politics to distinguish between the city as political form and the city as physical locus and entity. The city was so thoroughly a being of a political character that the locale of that politics could be a matter of indifference. There were favored places but not unique and necessary places—Athena preferred the Athenian Acropolis, but she had other homes. The Athenians were especially favored by Athena's gifts, but politics was an affair of a different temporal and locational nature from the one she and the other gods dealt with. Her home was a temple, always a fine and well-finished building, while the home of an Athenian was a rugged dwelling, his place of business was in a shop called a stoa, and the seat of the most important of the city's political institutions was a regia. For reasons van Pelt has explained, the Athenian Agora of the classic period can itself be seen as a regia, although not with the same clarity as the Palazzo Farnese can be. In like manner, examples of individual civic buildings also lack the clear relationship to the types that later examples would have, just as they also lacked the monumental and finished architectural treatment of the Acropolis' buildings until the institutions they housed had become mere rigid and inflexible hulls around formerly fresh fruits, although the relationship to the regia of the *prytaneion* and, along with its interior theater, of the *bouleuterion* in Athens and elsewhere are clear from an early period.

Whatever connection there was between these civic buildings was found in the conventional, not in the necessary. The polis was not the same thing as an acropolis or any other sacred place with its sacred, religious buildings. These existed, and they were precious to the Greeks, but they belonged to all Greeks in one way or another while the city did not. The polis was particular. It was made by people who had become responsible for their own fate and who tended to their affairs through the constitution directing their political life.

The Greeks' invention of the regime or constitution provided a hint that a First Amendment was possible. The regime their constitution defined was a conventional affair of their making and subject to their changing it within the framework of the nature of states, not an establishment given by the gods, by old men, or men of olden times and immune from change. This invention freed people from the domination of a place and left them free to forge their own destiny. But it also left them bereft of a place which they could identify with their destiny. Because their city could be any place, it did not have any special or particular meaning when it was some special or particular place. As a result, there was nothing special about the configuration its political, secular buildings took, and nothing particular about the space which the polis inhabited. Indeed, there was most likely no concept of space as we know the term, and no notion a city's buildings were connected to one another in a place.

In the classical tradition, this disjunction between polis and place did not extend beyond the period of Greece's golden age. The relationship between polis and place that we know is based on the one prevailing in the Roman world.

The Roman thought that became canonic was formulated at the turn of the millennium during a period of political troubles when the republic collapsed and was "restored" by the principate we know as the empire. At this time the past was hauled into the present and installed as an empty but effective shell to give legitimacy to circumstances that everyone knew ought to have been otherwise. One of the restoration's most important components was the distinction between, and unity of, polis and place or, in Latinate terms, of civil form (*civitas*) and its urban setting (*urbs*). From now on, a city inhabits an urban area and, complementarily, the normative condition for an urban area is that it be civilized.

Unlike the Greek city which had been mobile (or moveable), the Romans considered a people and a place to be connected to one another. Thus Romans have a word *urbs* for which there is no Greek equivalent: An *urbs* (an urban area) is the physical setting wherein a particular, legal political order exists. The concept should strike us as being entirely reasonable in that we know that it is important to demarcate where certain legal forms prevail and where they do not. But reasonable as it is, it did not come about as an extension of a reasonable understanding but of a mythic, mysterious one. Its origins reveal that peculiar genius of the Romans, that of adapting the practices of various peoples to an orderly and workable assemblage which at times had at least the appearance of something just and legitimate and at times was actually just, or at least legitimate.

The linkage between the civic and urban realms was derived from the Etruscan practice of divination which existed in the realm of mysteries and hence is difficult for us to understand today.[1] In Etruscan, and eventually in Roman rite, the site for a city was established through divination: an augur used signs provided by the gods (flight of birds, entrails of animals, etc.) to discover a site that people could inhabit and that they then made into a miniature version of the world. To do this the site was enclosed with a circle (even if the actual physical form was different, for example a square) and quadrated (divided into four: the result will eventually be the familiar set of cross streets, the *cardo* [N / S] and *decumanus* [E / W]). The product of the rite was what in Latin is called a *templum*,[2] that is, an enclosed and ordered locus, a consecrated place, an *urbs*.

To prepare this place for habitation, those who would reside there dug a hole (*mundus*) in its center and cast into it those things necessary for its life and for their own lives: relics, good things, wheat and wine, earth from previous places of their habitation, and so on. A flame was kindled on an altar,[3] and the land within the bounds was divided and distributed (usually by the gods, i.e., by lot), and the bounds were set by a ritual plowing of a bounding furrow. This plowing became the base of the walls immediately inside of which was the sacred strip boundary (the *pomoerium*) while the gates were placed where the plow was carried (to carry = *portare*; gate = *porta*). This left the gates under civil jurisdiction while the walls were under sacred protection.

When a city is founded in this way the civil and urban forms must be coordinated, a task the Greeks had not been constrained to do. As was the case with so much of the Roman world, the manner in which they could coordinate the physical components within the walls was available in Hellenistic Greece. In places such as Pergamon, Priene and Miletus enclosed precincts were marked off and devoted to a particular purpose marked by a dominant structure whose placement was predicated upon its appearance from a particular point, usually the entrance to the precinct. The result in Greek practice was a series of precincts which were inward looking and bounded, with one precinct connected to another not by interconnected design devices but by a topography over which people could not exercise dominion. The Romans perfected the design of precincts by using a wider variety of architectural devices. In this sense it may be said they invented the possibility of urbanism, or the design and construction of a setting meant to support a particular political or civic realm.

Like the civil forms it contained, this urbanism was limited and not universal. We misunderstand the Roman world if we think of it as a single government, politics or civil form extending across the entire world or the entire extent of the known or controllable world. Quite the contrary: The Roman state was a legal entity composed of treaties meant to establish concord between the various parts of which it was composed, each with its own rights and prerogatives. The most important of these forms was the *civitas*, and the most important *civitas* was Rome. As St Augustine said with full awareness of Cicero's teaching: "What is a *civitas* except a multitude of men brought together in a sort of bond of *concordia*," a *concordia* that was assured through justice and the rule of law.[4] Here was the object of the Roman's love.

An *urbs* extended only as far as the boundaries of the *civitas* it housed. Within it was a concord established between its components both within the same class of things, be they civic or urban, and between components from each of the two classes. The most important of the civil components was the family, and the most important urban one was the precinct. The precinct might contain a family in a regia or a dwelling. It might hold a forum with its temple, which was a miniature of the *templum*, which was itself the city, and the basilica which was simply an adaptation of a pair of shop rows fronting on an open space and roofed over, i.e., an elaboration of a Greek stoa and like it following the type of the shop. Or it might contain any of -the various elaborations of the building types that make Roman urbanism so filled with paradigms of urban pieces—shrines (tholoses, temples); forum or temple precincts with temples and shrines (tholoses and temples), basilicas and assembly halls (regias and theaters), shops, and triumphal arches and other commemorative structures; baths (regias, often with shops); houses of the wealthy (*domus* in Latin but a regia in this typology, often with a garden and a front of shops); *insulae* (piles of dwellings sometimes configured as regias with shops along their fronts); gardens (walled precincts and platforms, to be discussed below); etc. The relationship between these versions and the types need not detain us. What is important is their use within the urban setting. These buildings were always arranged in precincts or formed whole precincts, and they were always collected into *ad hoc* assemblages. Between them and filling out the urban area were the gaps that were simply "empty." What was outside the precinct was left-over space that was not a part of any precinct and had only a very vague relationship to the *urbs* containing the *civitas*. In a sense we can understand but the Romans could not have, it is possible to say that the precincts were never coordinated into designs that ranged across a continuous space conterminous with that of the *civitas*.

Other connections were made, and these ultimately proved to be more important. The Romans joined the Greek idea that a people and its politics are synonymous with the Etruscan idea that a people are identified with a place. In doing so, they produced the ideas that have subsequently become canonic and may be said to constitute the classical city. These ideas may be summarized in this way: Place, people and politics form a unity; the purpose of that unity is both to govern and perfect the individual according to his nature; and the political form of that connection is the constitution while its architectural form is the urban structure. The perfection of the individual is found in his actions, actions he undertakes in an area where he can achieve present renown and future fame.[5] We know the success of the Romans. It is easily available in buildings and in reports that were never lost because they were always of value to someone, among them Cicero's "Dream of Scipio" and St Augustine's *City of God*: "There are those two things, namely, liberty and the desire of human praise, which compelled the Romans to admirable deeds" (V, 18).

The Romans had not separated the sacred and secular worlds. They interpenetrated one another in many ways. Only after the empire was Christianized was a separation sought. St Augustine (354−430) and St Benedict (480?−543?), both trained in the philosophy and law of antiquity, carved out of the Roman world the basis of separating the demands of religion, which one accedes to through a willful act, from those of politics, which one joins perforce through birth. They recognized that there were four components that needed attention: the true, the contingent, the political and secular, and the religious or sacred. For the time being the political and religious would remain indissolubly bound while attention was focussed on sorting out the various claims of the true, typical and natural from the conventional, contingent and circumstantial. This task continued for a millennium with relatively little change in the way the terms and their relationships were formulated. Attention that was fruitful for building in the world did not return to the relationship between the *civitas* and *urbs* and the location of the political and the architectural until Italians took up the issue, first in Florence and then in Rome in the fifteenth century. A part of that inquiry, which was assisted by an avid interest in antiquity and a wealth of easily available information about it, had to do with the relationship between the political and the religious. When it seemed that modern Italians knew as much about the ancient way of thinking about these topics as the ancient Romans had, the inquiry was suddenly given an entirely new frame of reference in the works of the Florentine, Niccolò Machiavelli (1469–1527). Machiavelli made it clear that the political life was the life of the city and that the city was the place wherein that life was lived. But, beyond that, he taught that in the affairs of the citizen the will, or the faculty a person used to make choices for which he would be held accountable and therefore had to justify, was at least as important a faculty as the intellect, and that in a polity things could be other than they were or had been. The immediate sequel to these ideas of major interest to us in the United States would be written in England, particularly by Thomas Hobbes (1588–1679) and John Locke (1632–1704).

Were this a positivist history I would present the sequence of people and events that contributed to the major reformation in the understanding of the relationship between polis and place, the understanding that is the basis of current knowledge and practice. But because I am instead providing only a sketch of a paradigmatic history, I need only to present the content of that reformation.

Space for the City

We think of space and what it holds not as the Greeks and Romans did but in ways that were discovered in the fifteenth and sixteenth centuries. These discoveries constituted an historic change that was as important as the

Greeks' invention of the polis and the Romans' invention of the coordination of the civil and urban structures. What the Italians did in the Renaissance was to discover that the political, architectural and urban forms of a place were based on the same principles and could and should be coordinated with one another, as a copy is to its models and, more importantly, as a conventional example is to the type it imitates. The pair of lost panels Filippo Brunelleschi (1377–1446) used for showing his fellow Florentines the perspective representation he had invented may stand for the beginning of these important discoveries. Its culmination might be taken to be in the work of another Florentine, Michelangelo (1475–1564). In the 1540s he had shown in his design for the Capitol in Rome how space and solid can be subjected to the same discipline of architectural design.[6] Later, in about 1562, he showed that a street, in this case the via Pia, now via XX settembre, in Rome, could be subjected to the same rigor as any architectural problem. Cities would, or could, now be built as buildings, squares and streets and not simply buildings and empty voids as had been the case before Brunelleschi. From now on, no one could ignore what the Renaissance masters of political, architectural and urban thought had taught: To have a noble, just and beautiful city requires that the political, architectural and urban be organized according to the same natural principles.

The principles are in the nature discussed earlier—the place within which one finds true things (as opposed to merely factual ones), things such as the logic of morals, natural right, the 180 degrees which, no matter the form (verbal, oral, visual, tall examples and short ones) constitute the total of the interior degrees of a triangle, the six (or so) building types, and so on. The Renaissance architects and theorists discovered that among those true things, or in nature, is the *homogeneity of space*; this would be the space within which the urban setting will be placed. The urban setting, however, was a conventional thing. It was immersed within the world of the contingent, factual and circumstantial. Their achievement was to find a way to coordinate the two. Once coordinated, they could place buildings within that space. The buildings were the ones serving political purposes, and their designs were contrived to promote those political purposes. Now, not only was architectural design congruent with political purposes, but so too, and within the same principles, the architectural design was congruent with the setting within which buildings serve cities. Cities occupied space which was now understood to be homogeneous. Renaissance theory and practice allowed buildings to be *homomorphic* with that space.

That theory also included the knowledge that among the conventional things are the versions of the building types appropriate to a particular time and place, that is, appropriate both to the particular urban setting in which it is to be built and to the particular conventional form given to the politics of that place in its constitution. It also acknowledged that in addition to buildings other physical components already found in cities or capable of being added to them were necessary to serve the constitution's regime.

Renaissance theory and practice provided all that one ought to know to design cities, although the form that theory and practice takes today is different because current circumstances surrounding building in cities is different. To clarify the content of Renaissance theory, a few more things need to be said about homogeneous space and homomorphic buildings.

The first evidence of the discovery of spatial homogeneity is in Brunelleschi's invention in about 1415 of systematic perspective which allowed a rational, three-dimensional grid to be laid on or imposed on the perception of the world. Leon Battista Alberti explained that this grid was like a "reticulated net of the finest threads" spread across a window through which we look at the world as if in a picture.[7] Space thought of in this way can be called perspective space. It allows us to know what can be seen (what is) within a realm that we know to be more regular and full of things than we can know (the ought), but in allowing that, it lets us know the limits of our knowledge, that is, that we know it as a facsimile of what is actually there.

This homogeneous space is marked by several characteristics. First, it is unlimited in extent. It is, therefore, unlike the two kinds of space thought to exist previously. One of these is precinct space, which is limited by the boundary around a precinct. Examples are the Roman complexes discussed above and the Roman system of centuriation where each city or town was surrounded by an extension of measured space that ended at the point reached by the measured space extending out from a center in the next city or town. This form of space is probably based on Hellenistic space, and, if it is to be named after a period rather than a characteristic, it should perhaps be called Hellenistic space. The second kind of space supplemented rather than supplanted Hellenistic or precinct space and might be called relational space. In it, an area is thought of as a bounded entity with boundary dimensions forming a proportional rectangle and with a proportioned relationship to its neighboring area. In its most sophisticated form, which it reached in the Florence Brunelleschi explored in his youth, the areas can be thought of as bounded in the third dimension so that the ground area is seen in relationship to a backdrop.[8] The result, however, is not a spatial volume but merely an area with a backdrop, the counterpart in spatial design to the trecento paintings Masaccio's spatial illusion made obsolete.

Second, homogeneous space is knowable, definable or measurable with a regular three-dimensional grid or matrix of some sort, one that embodies the same characteristics as a geometric definition that is translatable into mathematics, and vice-versa. This makes it possible for the character of space to be treated as a subject of ratiocination with the same logic as the one operating in any other form of reasoning from first principles, as, for example, in the logic of morals and the law. This characteristic was discovered through the invention of perspective—or, if one wants to turn it around, the invention of perspective was made possible through this discovery about space. This characteristic makes it possible to understand the profound difference between Roman centuriation, which is based on augury and divination, and the political, surveying and settlement system embodied in the universal grid system of the Northwest Ordinance of 1787. It is no mistake that perspective and global projections were both invented in mathematically and geometrically acute quattrocento Florence, a city with a self-conscious understanding of its history and constitution and the city that gave birth to Machiavelli, and that Thomas Jefferson, an architect fascinated by the *camera obscura* and a political man committed to thinking of the land as a place where the farms of patriots would spring up, provided the essential material for the two parts of the Northwest Ordinance, one defining how the land would be measured to produce an *urbs*, the other specifying how the now measured land would form states (polities) and join on an equal footing with the other states comprising the union.

The third characteristic of homogeneous space is that it is capable of being represented as orderly with mathematical (or artificial) perspective. As Norris Kelly Smith has taught, perspective is predicated upon having a particular, unique viewpoint on the world, one which puts the person at the viewpoint in direct confrontation with objects and actions in space. It links him with things and with others. It makes him morally responsible for the position he takes. The absoluteness of this situation, one in which the person is responsible for taking a position, contains the obverse—that a person cannot be held accountable for that which can be shown to have been outside his view. The point is that a person can now change his position, and in doing so he can change what he sees. But his changing position does not change what is there and where it is, although this is exactly what happened in the previous, conventional understanding of space. Nor does changing his position nullify the content of what he saw when in the previous position. The individual is responsible not only for seeing but for remembering certain things.

In the previous understanding of space, a space which was defined by what might be called *relational design*, the relationship between things changed when the position of the observer changed. The only order of things in that scheme was a conventional one extending from the opinions of the observer. It had no connection with the plenum of space within which they were actually arrayed. If a person did not arrange them, it could be said they did not exist. But in homogeneous space a *perspectival design*, whether as a picture or as an architectural design, records how things actually are or actually could be, and it puts them in a relationship to one another that depends upon their placement within a plenum and not within a phenomenological understanding made by and therefore valid only for the observer.

Relational design is the method used for disposing objects within precinct space. Its use stretches from the Athenian acropolis through Pergamon, Priene and Miletus to Rome, medieval cities and the quattrocento examples of Pienza, the Ptolemy views of Rome, Florence and other cities and the magnificent view of Nuremberg in that city's *World Chronicle* of 1493. In this kind of space it is difficult if not impossible to support the idea that the space fronting on a building belongs to that building. A building is instead an object that has an outer boundary that may be seen and an interior within that boundary, or an object in space comprehensible in a single glance, such as the Parthenon.[9]

Perspectival design is very different. It requires and works within homogeneous space. The object is fixed in space. The individual can turn away from it and disregard it (although that does not make it go away) or he can examine it from a different point of view, one that does not alter its placement or its relationship to other objects as they were known from the other point of view, although what he now learns will be different because he sees something different. When the information he receives from several points of view is coherent according to the standards of coherence contained within reason, the design can be said to be not only coherent but also homomorphic with space.

Homogeneous space assumes the possibility of objects that are homomorphic with it.[10] *Homomorphic buildings* are those whose forms are congruent with other buildings that can be seen to be congruent with them and in which the congruence defines a homogeneous spatial realm. These buildings are designed with an architectonic character that invests them with the best current knowledge available about the material world so that they may embody, indeed imitate, that which is true in the world of nature, as this was discussed in Chapter Six.

On Perspective

This interpretation of space puts a tremendous burden on perspective. It assumes that there is something "out there" which perspective reports about. There are a number of different ways to make that report. Why should the technique of producing virtual space named perspective be given a higher priority than other methods used for imitating the pattern of nature?

It may be that perspective is the most familiar convention and that we prize it more highly for that reason alone. Perspective space is familiar to us through the constant presentation to us of perspective images produced chemically and electronically in photography and television. Earlier, this magic of facsimile making was found in the mechanics of the *camera obscura* (cp. the one Jefferson played with, on display at Monticello) and, before that, in the learned technique Brunelleschi invented and Alberti and others taught painters and others who sought to produce facsimiles or actual imitations of the world. Ever since its introduction, and especially in its current excessive use, we have taken that view of the world to be true in a way that other views are not, even when we recognize its limitations (for example, in its substitution of a cyclop's view for that of creatures with two eyes).

But there is more to it than that. Perspective in the form Alberti explained in his treatise on painting, which was apparently the form Brunelleschi had invented, is not a convention but a geometric axiom with the same claim to truth as other axioms in Euclidian geometry. This does not mean that claims for what perspective can do should be extended beyond what it legitimately can grasp. As Ernst Gombrich explained, "perspective aims at a correct equation: it wants the image to appear like the object and the object like the image. Having achieved this aim, it makes its bow and retires."[11] From there on, the conventions of art and architecture take over and fill out what perspective has made possible.

Perspective's broad acceptance since the fifteenth century as the appropriate technique for producing virtual space in paintings and rational design in architecture and urbanism, as well as its continued force even after other techniques have emerged under modernism, indicates not only that it was thought of, and continued to be thought of, as an improvement over previous ways of seeing. Note that there is no evidence (indeed, the evidence argues for the other side) that people saw the world this way before Brunelleschi discovered within nature the view of the world perspective makes possible. Such an observation proves nothing: it is possible (indeed, likely) that people who saw the world in ways previous to the way Brunelleschi taught were simply not simultaneously clear-sighted and clear-headed.[12] Its acceptance and continued currency resides in its correctness, that is, in its ability to establish a true equation between the image and the object, and this correctness invests it with a superiority and authority over any other technique whenever coherence is sought.

Furthermore, the place perspective occupies among the conventions used for producing works of art, architecture and urbanism are no longer the ones within which it was ensconced during the Renaissance. As Norris Kelly Smith, Albert Pérez-Gómez, van Pelt and others have argued in various ways, the use we make of perspective is the one given us by the eighteenth century. The role it now plays is fundamentally different from the one it had played before that time. Earlier, it had provided a form of knowledge discovered in the world and available in no other way. It had, that is, provided people with some of the information they needed to know when deciding what moral stance to take relative to the phenomena they confronted, phenomena that were about a nature that included them. Later, however, it became merely a means of recording the visual relationships between things. This record did not necessarily touch any important part of the individual. It recorded relationships that could just as well be otherwise. And it was a record of relationships between things that were in themselves of interest in this record only for extrinsic and not for any intrinsic aspects or qualities. They simply *were* that way.

But the eighteenth-century attitude about perspective as about so many other things provided a welcome housecleaning that chased the ghosts out of the objects. In its new purity, as for example in Jefferson's version of it in the two parts of the Northwest Ordinance and in L'Enfant's design for Washington, it was a powerful tool for connecting politics with urban form and urban form with architectural form. That form of perspective design is still the normative form.

That normative role is difficult to accept now because the nineteenth century managed to stuff new ghosts into the apparatus of perspective (the *Zeitgeist* explanations for its emergence when and where it did, pure visibility, etc.), ghosts which modernist artists then set about exorcizing. The method of exorcism, however, called for the rejection of the perspective view of the world and its replacement with the spatial conventions of cubism and surrealism (and other conventions based on something non-perspectival). Their currency does not necessarily make the content of the previous view untrue and replace it with a view that is true (or "more true"). Indeed, by the standards that allow something, including the perspective view of the world, to be called true, the ones reared in its place following its rejection can be shown to be incapable of being true. They do not originate in the realm of knowledge that is congruent with truth,[13] and they seek their validity not in their congruence with the thing about which they report but in whatever context is contrived for them. "Ceci n'est pas une pipe." Nor, when rendered in some convention rather than in perspective, is it even a report about a pipe but about a convention. Such a view cannot be connected with the political life opening access to the virtuous and noble life. Only perspective, so far as we know, does that.

On the City's Form

In the circle of those who discovered the large realm of perspective design with its homogeneous space and contrived an architectural theory that could place homomorphic buildings in it were people equally adroit in political theory. They contrived an articulate explanation of political activity or theory of politics in which what occurred and what ought to occur were considered topics related to one another in principle and in narrative and presentable in media as diverse as prose, acts, paint and construction. It is no accident that among those alive during the same generation, and aware of and responsive to the works of one another, were Thomas More, Erasmus, Luther, Machiavelli, Julius II, Raphael, Bramante, Michelangelo, Leonardo and Cesare Borgia, all of them notable for the form they gave their encounter with the worlds of action and of knowledge. In one way or another, these people explored the ways there could be formed in the actual world a facsimile of what they knew about the best world men may live in, a city, that is, that was a *patria* in which men were at home, a polis in which they could seek to perfect their individual natures through politics, and a place which was both particular and therefore could not be otherwise and an embodiment of the best that could be.

More than a century ago Jacob Burckhardt, surrounded by evidence pointing to an approaching calamity in what he called culture, sought the beginnings of modernity and found it in the Italian Renaissance, and in particular in its statecraft:

As the majority of the Italian states were in their internal constitution works of art—that is, the fruit of reflection and careful adaptation—so was their relation to one another and to foreign countries also a work of art. . . . The purely objective treatment of international affairs, as free from prejudice as from moral scruples, attained a perfection which sometimes is not without a certain beauty and grandeur of its own. But as a whole it gives us the impression of a bottomless abyss.[14]

Burckhardt's Hegelianism led him to conclude that things could not have been other than they were and became. Our viewpoint is different. We are the heirs of the Renaissance recognition that the state is a work of art, "that is, the fruit of reflection and careful adaptation," but we add to that the recognition that in such a state people are forced to confront their "prejudices" or conventions and their "moral scruples" or what they think is right. Here we have the origins of our present form of classical political theory which sees states as conventional structures each one of which is given a unique form as existing circumstances determining that which is are juxtaposed against the pattern of nature that tells how they ought to be.

Burckhardt left out of his definition of the state as a work of art the other Renaissance discovery, that its urban form is a complementary, subordinate form of the same art. Like the constitution, the urban form must satisfy certain true, just, human purposes by applying thought to practice. This linkage had its origins in the Renaissance, most likely in the practice beginning with Brunelleschi. It reached a particular moment of intensity during the sixteenth century. And it ran on into the eighteenth century when it began to lose the reinforcing unity that had been giving it a special vigor. That unity was eventually nearly completely submerged within the tide of modernism in urban planning that swamped both Europe and America and then most of the rest of the world after the Second World War.

In its full maturity urban design was predicated upon a series of interlocking propositions that made it a theoretical and practical undertaking subordinate to a political life that sought to provide a way for people to seek happiness by living justly and nobly. These propositions, which might be called the conventions of urban design, can be presented as a series of six separate components, as will be done here, but in so doing one must remember that the separation is done only for analytical convenience. No one element can be discussed without acknowledging that what one knows of it is predicated upon its place within a scheme incorporating all six components. The parts form a whole that is like the whole formed by the beautiful building or any other beautiful thing of which Alberti spoke, one in which the parts are arranged such that nothing can be added, altered or removed without detriment to the whole. The legacy of Renaissance urbanism, for that is what we are talking about here, is that when we think about or comprehend an urban scheme with the intent of writing about it or modifying it by building in it, we carry all six components along with us as a unity, something we cannot do when we lay out a scheme in the form of a verbal explanation.

In what follows it will be useful to recall that the term "polity" refers to the political entity defined by a constitution of some sort and can range in scale from a bicycle club or condominium association to a sovereign nation-state.

1. All physical elements are accounted for and coordinated with one another within the design. Whatever is done for the polity is done for every element within it. The vast variety of physical things in polities, including open spaces and streets, reaching down to small houses and the outbuildings beyond an

urban area's central area and including people doing things within the polity, now claim attention and are brought into coordination within the design.

2. All of those elements within the polity are now thought to be worthy of the attention of design, a design that accounts at the same time for both the political and the architectural, the civic and the urban. Within the same scheme of design will be things that are public and private as well as sacred and profane.

Unlike pre-Renaissance urbanism, attention is no longer limited to the most important or most worthy or to the parts of the polity that signify its highest importance. Instead, if something, whether civic or urban, is within the polity or even in some way pertinent to the polity, it is worthy of the attention of design. The design it receives is specified by the contemporary, conventional functional and structural versions in play in the place.

3. The design imposed on the elements in the polity is contrived within the framework of homogeneous space and homomorphic objects. That is, it is used as a means of revealing the relationships that the various actual, material things in the polity have to one another and within the universally extensible realm of which this polity is a part. Nothing in the polity is designed as an isolated entity. Instead, each physical component is designed as a part of a larger whole that includes all the things within a polity. The main point of any design is not to produce a thing that in itself betrays attention to design but to reveal the relationship that the thing has to other things within the polity. Similarly, the polity itself is linked with the larger world beyond its civil and urban boundaries.

4. The main content revealed by the relationships is the relative importance of all of the polity's physical elements in their role of serving the purposes of the citizens. While this has always been the case when there has been what can be called design in polities, now, for the first time, the hierarchy embraces all the elements within the polity. Thus there is now a visible relationship from top to bottom and not merely, as had occurred in relational design within precinct space, a separation of the important from the unimportant, of the significant from the insignificant, of the institutional from the merely utilitarian. The rules of beauty guide the designer in revealing these hierarchic distinctions.

5. The primary content of the design is the constitution's distribution of authority. It makes transparent the relative importance of the physical elements rendering service to the polity's hierarchy of institutional purposes and utilitarian arrangements and of the role of each in the life of each citizen.

The urban form embodies the constitution. No two polities have the same constitution, but all polities have a constitution. The content, whether rendered in the coordinated urban design or in the fragment of such a design as represented in but a single new building, when these are conceived and designed according to the principles found within this systematic approach to urban design, is that unique constitution. This constitution is a contrivance of current knowledge and is therefore only conventional, but the knowledge it embodies is knowledge of nature, of the nature of things, of natural knowledge, just as the buildings that serve its parts are conventional embodiments of the natural building types they exemplify.

6. Within each institution and arrangement served by buildings there is a person whose character is most important for its character.

Everyone who knew the classical tradition knew this in the era before the social sciences invented ways to replace judgement with procedures in governing. In the broadest sense, this is the founder, the Theseus, Athena, Solon and Kleisthenes of Athens, the Founding Fathers of the United States, William Penn in Philadelphia, Jane Addams at Hull House. We still acknowledge the overarching importance of some one particular person's character as exemplary of official character when we inquire into the character of the office holder—is this president a worthy successor of Washington, Jefferson, etc., is this a Bramante in architecture? The classical, or Western, tradition teaches that the person will define his actions according to the character he brings to the office he occupies. This sense of office is a legacy of ancient Rome, and it made the representational republican form of modern government possible. An office allows an individual to become a facsimile of something needed in the polity's constitution—say, a good legislator—without his ceasing to be himself—say, a person not quite certain he knows all he needs to know in order to act, without ever denying that he is responsible for the actions done within and in the name of the institution or utilitarian arrangement of which he is an officer. On becoming President Jefferson revealed this in his First Inaugural Address by acknowledging "that the task is above my talents, and that I approach it with those anxious and awful presentiments which the greatness of the charge and the weakness of my powers so justly inspire." An institution is a corporate body, as, for example, the ancient College of Augers, the Benedictine Order or, in the modern world, the United States Congress, the Board of Visitors of the University of Virginia or the Pattington Condominium Association, but its members and officers are people, and, except in purely private undertakings such as David Henry Thoreau building a cabin at Walden Pond, individuals acting in an official capacity rather than corporate bodies build polities and build in polities. They do so as officers of institutions within constitutions, and they do the better job of it in proportion to the extent they do so with a knowledge of the power of urban and architectural form to make visible their character as officers, and to the extent they seek to represent the service their institution renders its members.

The Components of Urban Form

Urban design arranges the architectural and other pieces serving a people into a pattern serving their constitution. The arrangement exists in the time-bound and place-bound world of circumstance. There is no necessary correspondence between the longevity of buildings and other physical components and the institutions, arrangements and individuals which bring them into being and which they serve. At any particular moment the physical parts constituting the urban setting are out of temporal co-ordination with one another and with the polity they serve. For example, there may be important buildings housing institutions that are no longer as important as the building suggests, there may be very important insti-tutions not yet fitted out with buildings proper to their importance, there may be institutions that are still housed in a building type that was appro-priate for it at its foundation but is no longer the one suitable for it, and so on. In this way the urban form of a place presents a two-level historical narrative. For those interested in how things are, it presents a factual and historical account of the place, both past and present, which may be read in any number of ways—as, for example, in the variety of forms given useful histories of the middle. For those who wish to know how things ought to be and who know how to see through the conventions into the pattern of nature they imitate, it also presents historic ideas about the aspirations of people.

Within the narrative, including its most recent episodes, is embedded a diagram of the political constitution. The diagram is composed of physical things and of the means designers and builders use to dispose them homo-morphically within a homogeneous space in order that the rational connec-tion between the civic and the urban can be put to the service of citizens. Prominent among these urban components are the six (or so) building types. Their design according to the rules of beauty will assure that they are in a relationship to one another that is fitting and right for the time and place they occupy and will occupy into the future. In addition, there are two more classes of things in polities. They provide ways of coordi-nating the polity's buildings and other physical components with one another and they extend the range of physical things in polities beyond the limited extent controlled by the six (or so) building types.

Architectonic Means

One class can be called *architectonic means*. Encompassed within the class is whatever it is that design manipulates to produce coherence in the assemblage of physical components forming the polity. Some of them are aspects of architectural design that are equally serviceable in urban design. Some of these are found in the nature of things and are therefore natural means, but others are in the realm of convention. Nature cannot be known completely, and the extent to which there will be invention among conventions, being the product of man, cannot be predicted. Therefore, no complete catalogue is possible. They are means designers use, and designers are always more inventive in coming up with them than theorists, critics or historians.

The character of things in this class can be grasped by considering some examples. Some of the most conspicuous are the following:

1. *A regulating and controlling axis for actual or virtual movement or for the alignment of physical elements.*

As is the case with a ray of vision or a line as a shortest distance between two points, this is a natural means. It was made useful for conscious urban and architectural design when it was yoked for the service of artifice through the theories of perspective design broached by Brunelleschi and Alberti, although it had been used continuously in conventional ways in the earliest examples of architecture and urbanism whether classical or not.

2. *An enclosed and defined open area such as a piazza.*

Again, this is a natural means (or at least the openness that is not built on is provided by nature), but it could be incorporated into urban design only after homogeneous space had been discovered. Before that, this space was simply the place where there was nothing which meant it could not be designed or coordinated with the design of something material. That place in which there is nothing cannot be other than it is, although how it is depends upon the form it is given by the conventions of design. Named things such as piazzas and the forms these named things take are conventional. They could be otherwise.

3. *A reserved strip, or a place where some public purpose is served by forbidding or disallowing buildings.*

Examples of this are the *pomoerium* of ancient Roman polities, roads, streets and the free-fire area outside the walls of a polity. These are natural in the same way that axes and open areas are. But they are, finally, conventional when appearing in designs established by functions serving purposes.

Because this is so, and because the discovery of homogeneous space provides important new insights into handling them, there is no reason to assume that streets in polities were always capable of being designed or that the means of designing them in one circumstance were the same as those used in another. That the *via triumphalis* in the *forum romanorum*, the via XX settembre (via Pia), Pennsylvania Avenue, rue de la Opéra, and Fifth Avenue are not interchangeable with one another has as much to do with the different understanding of reserved strips as it does with the conventions guiding the design of the material structures belonging to and defining them.

4. *Controlled relationships in the placement of things.*

This too is a natural means in that things must have relationships of location relative to one another, but it is a device of artifice because these natural means are controlled through the conventions of design. The conventions found their way into design from a number of sources. Some of these are concerned with the representation of hierarchical relationships: if public dominates private and sacred dominates profane, the most important churches will be free-standing and in a more central location and the private dwellings of the irreligious will be imbedded within other buildings or among themselves and consigned to the periphery.

5. *Hierarchic differentiation in artifice.*

The more important things will be, and will appear to be, produced with what current conventions establish as higher and more important levels of artifice. To be legible requires the ability to compare things to one another. This in turn requires a continuity in artifice and in design conventions (i.e., a "stylistic" continuity) operating over time and among the several classes of things composed in polities. The main aspects of artifice providing for differentiation are in the value of materials, level of finish, and level of technology, all of which are determined by conventions.

Building Components

The other class of components composing the polity are things rather than means and may be called *building components*. They have much in common with actual buildings and may even be worked into the design of buildings, but they are built to serve special functions rather than particular purposes arising from the polity's arrangements and institutions. This removes them from the control of the six (or so) normative building types and puts their design entirely in the realm of convention (excepting the condition that their architectonic means will adhere to the structural types).

This conventional status gives their use a great flexibility in both architectural and urban design. They can join with utilitarian components to flesh out the building types. They might stand free of actual buildings. They might be material accessories to various of the architectonic means. They will always serve the political purposes embodied in the polity's constitution, playing the role in urban form that ornament and decoration play in architectural form.

As with the architectonic means, the building components are so thoroughly immersed in the conventional no complete catalogue can be made, but a brief listing and description of some of the most familiar of them can indicate their range.

1. *Tower.*

Towers hold bells, display clocks, provide targets for the eye, furnish lookouts over prospects, proclaim power, mark authority. They may be freestanding, but more commonly they will be incorporated into a building that otherwise follows the normative standards of a type.

2. *Platform.*

Among platforms are paved planes in an open area and bibs marking off the area immediately adjacent to a building from the space they front.

3. *Wall, colonnade or arcade.*

These architectural motifs can be used to define a reserved strip, frame an open area or perform some other useful task that is unconnected to their role in giving material embodiment to building types.

4. *Gateway.*

Whether filling a breach in a wall or standing free, gateways perform particular tasks, perhaps functional ones defined by arrangements, as for example fortified gates, perhaps commemorative ones connected with institutions, as for example triumphal arches.

5. *Parterre, greensward and bosket.*

From nature come various kinds of collections of living things that can be used as if they belonged to the same class of material used in actual buildings and in building components. To be part of an urban setting artifice must clearly be seen as the cause of the form they take, unless they are confused with that which lies outside the polity, in the empty, uncivilized wilderness. More about this group, which is probably the most recent addition to the catalogue of building components, will be presented below.

Different practices produce different conventions for using different items from these two abbreviated catalogues of components. Roman imperial architects were unexcelled masters in using these components, an accomplishment which comes as no surprise when one recalls that the ancient Romans thought of the polity as an arena in which one could act and thereby win renown and fame. Their example shows how many of these kinds of components there are and how richly and well they can be used. "Each city and town," William L. MacDonald has recently written, "is seen as formed around a clearly delineated, path-like core of thoroughfares and plazas, which . . . can be called an armature, that provided uninterrupted passage throughout the town and gave ready access to its principal public buildings."[15] The armature was articulated with an accumulation of things that did not result from a single campaign of design and execution—

gateways, pavements, curbs, colonnades, foursquare structures at armature junctions, public fountains, exedra, steps, platforms, porticos, terraces, column displays, elaborated walls, etc. It was more important to have these components play their role in the armature than it was to maintain the design integrity of the various buildings they touched; thus, when push came to shove, an armature's colonnade remained straight even if that meant that the rectangularity of the precinct it passed was distorted.[16]

Occasionally it appears that an armature was an elongated precinct, but since an armature's most highly wrought parts are usually at the point it and a precinct merge or intersect, it would seem that an armature is usually in the empty space outside the urban precincts. When perspective design with its homogeneous space and homomorphic buildings became dominant in urban design, precinct design was replaced by design using streets and piazzas to play the role armatures had in Roman imperial urbanism. Many of the same components served this new kind of urban design, as the Piazza San Marco in Venice, Bernini's great piazza in front of St Peter's and the Washington and Chicago pictured by Daniel H. Burnham and his colleagues in the first years of the present century show, but now a richer understanding of homogeneous space and perspectival design allow them to be more completely merged into and integrated with the design of the buildings defining the open spaces.

The spatial components of American urbanism belong within the same family as the best examples of postmedieval Europe. Here as in Europe, they can be read as rooms and streets formed by the solids of buildings and other components required for a city that works as a polity and not as a mere settlement.[17] But because the political situation and the tradition of building are very different in America, major translations are required to make the examples of imperial, papal, monarchical and other princely builders and cities appropriate for American practice which is dispersed and diffuse. The special character of American urban design is a topic to which, until recently, we have paid very little attention but which provides rich rewards for the diligent.[18]

Patterns

The physical components of polities—the matter of urban form—is buildings (examples of types), architectonic means (ways of organizing things, and some material elements), and building components (material elements that are not examples of types). Their organization does not necessarily stem from nature, although it used to be thought it did when the Romans consulted auspices and medieval Tuscans imitated the Heavenly Jerusalem.[19]

But once people discovered that they make states and that states build polities, they realized they had to look to the needs of the state to find the polity's urban form—unless building was put on the automatic pilot of positivism or determinism aimed at taking it to its end in the future.

Contrary to the tenets of modernism that produced designs for Bolshevik Moscow, German socialist *Siedlungen* and a contemporary city for three million residents as with the Berlin of Speer and Hitler, and unlike the positions taken by modernist historicism with its greater trust in the social than in the human sciences as exemplified in the works of Paul Zucker, Lewis Mumford or Spiro Kostof, the pattern guiding the placement of the components forming a polity's urban setting will follow no necessary, predetermined form but will be conventional. There is no necessary link between a political form and an urban form. Tyrants do not necessarily and inevitably use axes to connect buildings and star-shaped plans for arranging streets, and democrats do not always avoid axes and build grids. Seeing stars or grids is not enough to know whether one is dealing with a tyranny or a democracy. Similarly, an assemblage of the buildings, and the sequence in which they appear in a polity or appeared in the original polities, is a matter of convention flowing from the constitution and not a matter of historical sequence. Thus, in opposition to what van Pelt suggests in Chapter Five, a theater is just another building, albeit usually a very important one, and not a quintessential type that contains, arranges and gives destiny to some fateful historic development of a particular collection of building types (i.e., emporium, stela, shrine, stoa/palace, house and theater).

This conventionality should not be taken to mean that an urban form's pattern can be arbitrary and take any form one wishes it to have. A polity's urban form must be to the material world what the constitution is to the political and the actual building is to the natural—a representation of knowledge of the actual and of the true and an imitation of the pattern of nature. It reveals what a people aspire to achieve, what they love and what they know about how things are and how they ought to be. It embodies the history of the place by showing the historic and the historical. It is therefore the most powerful means of knowing both the history and the present condition of the place.

The Classical American City

My primary interest in this study concerns the history and current state of the world from the point of view of the United States today.[20] American citizens are the political heirs of the classical tradition which they use in the improved form it takes in the Constitution and the regime that Constitution governs. They are also the heirs of the urban history accompanying that tradition. To live the most happy life possible under that Constitution, they must make the best use they can of the best of that tradition, both in their political regime and in their city-building practices.

Jefferson was especially aware of this and of the intimate connection between political and urban forms. His grandest legacy in this field of activity is the universal, democratic grid of the Northwest Ordinance which the federal government laid on the land that would receive citizens who would raise up political entities within the protective compass of the Constitution. At one stroke, with the Northwest Ordinance there was a form on the land that had to be honored if a town or city was to be a part of the American polity. From that moment on, there was a means of divining through reason what the general character of the form of a town or city ought to be. To develop this point will require one more, final exploration.

The possibility of the good life, the political life in which people seek to perfect their natures, precedes any particular polity, whether it be at the scale of the smallest institution or that of the national government, as the place within which any particular individual participates in politics. What is true in principle is also true in fact: There has always been a preexisting condition within which the polity both as a civic regime and as an urban form is built. During most of man's past these conditions were thought to be outside the reach of people. One realm beyond their grasp was the immutable history which they honored and which established the base for their political actions as individuals and as citizens. Thus it was during the Renaissance, for example. History was a part of Revelation which simply was as God had made it to be. History and Revelation contained a past that predicated a certain future, or at least the larger lineaments of that future. Renaissance discussions of free will always hover on the edge of constraints imposed by belief in a final, superior judgement about how people used that most precious gift. Had it not been so, Machiavelli would not have been able to say that people can act as if it is not so and that they will be more successful in reaching purely secular ends to the extent that they act as if the past does not dictate the future.

In then current opinion, equally determined—that is, not absolutely, but largely determined—were the natural endowments within which that history had been enacted. Certain things were facts of nature that were often determinative of such things as the number of people a polity could sustain, the level of wealth they might enjoy and the rhythm of a day's or a year's activities and the sensitivity of people to it. It was also determinative in important aspects of the form and character of the buildings and other structures they might build to make an urban setting for their politics, as was the previous history laid on the place in the form of existing buildings and other urban components and the political constitution that existed in time-laden layers within the place.

The Enlightenment challenged both the inherited wisdom about what the nature of history was and the limitations that physical nature seemed to contain. When these presuppositions about man's place in history and in the physical world dissolved, post-Enlightenment thought had its task cut out for it. The reconstructed world of history and of physical nature took two antithetical forms. One is embodied in the thought connecting Rousseau, the French Revolution, positivism, historicism, the social sciences, modernism and urban renewal. The other is in the body that includes Burke, the American Revolution, Jefferson, Lincoln and the ongoing classical tradition. This is the tradition that interests me because it is the one that offers the best approach for reconstructing and building in the American polity.

This tradition does not disavow its revolution. The American Revolution had as its origin the desire to establish a *novus ordo seclorum*. This new order came to encompass the entire range of important things in a form whose contrast with the old order would be a prophetic and revelatory sign, in the sense van Pelt discussed these concepts in Chapter Three, that there would now be a new way of combining the civic and the urban, a new basis for the architectural and urban, and a new relationship between an urban form and the land and the larger nature of which the land was a part. The nature holding that land was the same that held the laws and the God that undergirded the Declaration that a new order could be established and that in the circumstances current in the summer of 1776 had to be established.

The nature holding that land and laws was the same nature that would supply the rest of the things needed for living a life in congruence with it. In Jefferson's understanding, this included the universal, democratic grid that political authority could lay on the land and which from there on would define the circumstances of the location within which people would settle. Within it would be political units ranging from farms through states and the lesser ones nestled within those larger political forms—the bicycle clubs, condominium associations and universities that would add pleasure and nobility to a just life. That grid became the one within which any subsequent architectural or urban construction must take place if that construction is to serve the polity. Whether the United States Capitol Building or a smoke house behind a cottage, the architectural design must acknowledge the presence of the Northwest Ordinance grid as the locus within which the American polity is given embodiment.

This way of thinking about buildings puts politics first and formal qualities last. As a consequence, occupying last place in this analysis is any *a priori* formal image used for assembling the urban components no matter what it might be called—prototype, schema, pattern or whatever. (It is important to include this corollary: Putting any of these formal devices first in an analytical procedure suggests that they occupy a primary place in the process that brought into being the thing that is being analyzed. When that is the case, it is to say that those who built were not free to do other than to follow the pattern that they followed. If that is the case, because what was true for them is true for us as well, it is pointless to have an analytical technique that suggests that things could be other than they are.) Every regime (or political organization) has had such a formal pattern (e.g., Roman centuriation and the *quadrata* of the Roman city as *templum*; the grid of the Northwest Ordinance and its miniaturization into the railroad town). The procedure sketched here, however, assumes that any particular formal pattern is conventional and is a product of useful knowledge and not something extracted from nature, although it does imitate the pattern of nature. Nature has no grids to copy. Instead, it contains regularity, congruity and mensurability, but to the extent that grids are regular, provide for congruence and are subject to mensuration, they imitate the pattern of nature. So do other patterns—say, the spirals and radials decorating the architectural treatises of Francesco di Giorgio Martini, Pietro Cataneo and Vicenzo Scamozzi. But these were not the patterns the American polity laid on the land. The grid was. Choosing the grid was not accidental: It alone offered the strongest link between the basis in principle of the political regime the land was to host and the construction of physical components beginning with boundary stakes and running to entire urban areas that had to be laid on the land to serve that polity.

The grid and the law of settlement it includes are products of the political life. They stem from the same nature, are aimed at the same purpose and are congruent with the natural rights the polity aspires to embody. They are therefore legitimate and binding, although subject to revision and amendment if circumstances and political wisdom call for changes—as it did in its long sequence of amendments ranging from providing bounty for railroad building to parcelling out the land in various homestead acts, and so on.[21] A point stated above can now be repeated: The American grid became the one within which any subsequent architectural or urban construction must take place if that construction, be it the Capitol or a smoke house, is to serve the polity.

In working backwards, that is, when looking to the past for examples, whether as models or paradigms, one can discover patterns that contain the physical components serving a regime. This discovery leads to useful knowledge. But such patterns do not enjoy the same kind of *a priori* existence in nature that the building types do. There is in urban form no equivalent to the building types. Whatever pattern exists emerges from the general experience a people have in governing and building in a particular place over a span of time. In doing so, they embody what they learn in conventions—versions of building types, versions of structural types, a repertoire of architectural means and building components that serve their purposes. This is true as well for the grid of the Northwest Ordinance. That grid need not have had the pattern it had. It could, for example, have been based on rectangles or hexagons instead of squares (although using squares made the mathematics much simpler, and a simpler mathematics was seen as a way of providing a more secure land title to the citizen-settler). But once the actual world was known to be composed of homogeneous space that could hold homomorphic buildings, the pattern's nature had to be as it is—geometrically and mathematically commensurable with the way buildings are built and integrated politically within the constitution of the polity.

It is necessary to make one qualification to this point: there is a true form for the ways people live on the land. To have towns and cities there must necessarily be a certain kind of place on the earth. That place cannot be in a setting that is un*civil*ized and that is therefore *wild*erness.[22] No person who seeks to perfect his nature as man lives there. Such a person lives instead in the *city*, a natural form that stands at the farthest extreme from the wilderness. Between the two is, simply, land, or landscape, which is nature put to the use of man in the city, void of the *wild*ness of wilderness but not endowed with the full *civil*ity of the city. It has the same character—or it lacks character in the same way—as the void between the precincts in pre-Renaissance understandings of nature. This sequence—wilderness, landscape, city—must not be overrated. It only provides a place for a polity but does not provide a formal type, schema or other pattern for the polity built in the part of nature reserved for the most important work of people, which is that of perfecting their nature through the art of living together. That form, like the forms given the political life, is in conventions.

On Building in American Cities Today

As we saw in Chapter Two, just as there is only one politics (the art of living together in order to perfect the nature of each individual) so too is there only one architecture (the art of building serving that politics). In that sense politics and architecture are both conducted according to normative principles. But, as we also saw, without examples there can be no knowledge of the principles, and examples emerge only within a circumstantial world immersed in the transitory events occurring over time and in particular places. Thus the political life and the art of building are pursued according to conventions embodying principles and forged by knowledgeable people from their experiences with the actual facts of existence. Having said that it was then possible to see that a building is an instrument a polity's citizens use for reaching their purposes which are sometimes public, sometimes private and always coordinated through politics with other purposes. Their purpose is to facilitate the good life, the life of happiness, the one in which the individual may aspire to reach the normative. In politics and in building, this means doing the possible while aspiring to do the best.

That résumé refers to ideas that are universally valid and therefore valid in all particular circumstances, although the form they take will be different in different times and places. The construction drawn from experience in the United States, or in some part of the United States, cannot be transported to and imposed upon some other place, say, Canada, Guatemala or Italy. Neither I nor anyone else with a limited knowledge of those places can formulate the manner in which these ideas are to be embodied in them. People who live in the city need to build it, just as those who built the city ought to live in it. My interest is in my city, in the United States and its lesser polities. In them it is abundantly clear that the current prevailing, canonic theory of architecture, practice of architectural history and understanding of building, of cities and of the political relationship between the art of living and the art of building is not based on those ideas. Thus, just as it is my hope that the foregoing pages have provided a basis for finding an alternative to current ways of thinking about buildings and cities, so too is it my hope that this final section will suggest ways to change current practice.

Basic to that change is this simple maxim: In political activity as in designing, one must know the best and the possible to produce the closest imitation of the best in the actual. Because knowledge is cumulative, current circumstances always have the potential for improved practice. We therefore always have available a more advanced knowledge within the classical tradition than was available to Iktinos and Callicrates, to Vitruvius and Hadrian, to Alberti and Bramante, to Philibert d'l'Orme or François Mansart, or to Jefferson, Stanford White and Daniel Burnham. The degradation under classicism is no more necessary than the improvement within classicism is inevitable. Both require effort. To benefit from the advance of knowledge those involved in building need to emulate the method the Founders used for drawing on new knowledge when they sought an improved polity. The new constitution they sought was present in their personal experience and in their knowledge of the past that bore on it in ways that as van Pelt has explained it are historic. They had only to extract the new polity through study, polish it through debate among people of good will, and use art to frame their discoveries with an ordered eloquence. A similar method can be used in designing to extract or excavate a polity's buildings, architectonic means and building components from their sites.

It is possible to excavate a building because all the conditions required to design a building are present within the site. The procedure is simple: first, political activity provides the program, and then architectural activity furnishes the building. The political activity comes first because politics is more important than architecture. It determines the political purpose that would be played by construction on that site. The architectural activity follows because it provides a means to an end and is not an end in itself.

There should not be any ambiguity about this. There is no longer any part of the United States lying outside the jurisdiction of government, nor has there been one for a century in actuality and in potentiality for more than two centuries, or ever since the Northwest Ordinance's regimen for settling and organizing the United States was put in place. Gently arrayed within it is a hierarchy of authorities. The federal government stands above all others as the Civil War taught it must and as practice continues to affirm it ought to. But in line with the Founders' experience leading to the Revolutionary War, that authority is strictly confined by the restrictions imposed through the Constitution. States stand next, but more immediately relevant to most building activities are the lesser polities of counties and municipalities established by state statute and possessing the potential for a more intimate political life. Within these three levels of government—federal, state and local—new polities are constantly chartered—state universities that might enjoy near autonomy, public bodies formed to display art, private corporations with no more lofty intention than producing a profit. And there are also the citizens themselves who build, sometimes merely a house in the form of a regia but perhaps something more grand and conspicuous such as a massive commercial structure based on the type of the shops.

No matter what body or person builds and no matter what is built, the thing built is touched with a public interest, and the builder is primarily a citizen and secondarily something else—a householder, an entrepreneur, a banking corporation, a church, a school district, a museum, a university. None of these is first of all a private entity. Each of them is first of all a public body even if the purpose it is serving is that of promoting a largely private end.

Put another way, building is an act of citizenship. Whether the building be by bodies or individuals, what is built can be built well only when the builder has a clear idea of how the thing being built will first serve the larger polity so that it may also and only secondarily serve particular, proximate, functional ends. Unless the intention of serving a good public purpose stands first, the building's service of the secondary goals of economy, profit, functional efficiency, self-aggrandizement or artistic expression will remain ungoverned. These latter goals cannot be dismissed, and neither can building take place without them, but cities, villages and rural landscapes are improved only when the authority of government is evident as the protector of the liberty of individuals to pursue those ends. If developers seek their justified profit and architects seek the expressive ends appropriate for art without first of all serving the public interest their activities touch, the result is the degradation of cities, towns and rural landscapes. The public interest cannot be served by seeking a change of the developer's heart or reform in the artistic impulses of architects, for those things either will not happen or would lead to atrophy if they were forced into being. Instead, the good of the polity is served by treating public ends reached through politics as superior to private ones reached through the special skills of individuals.

The most prominent current method of directing the art of the developer and the architect to accomplish a public good is through controls embedded in land-use and building codes. Their basis is in the legitimate interest in public health and safety, but their current form is purely modernist. They therefore cannot put first the larger purposes a healthy and secure people have for living together. Along with various protective and conservation conventions and other ordinances and statutes construed on the same basis, they are now largely accepted as necessary compromises to the widely held belief that in America with land ownership comes the "freedom" to do with it as one wishes.

Architects and developers generally accept the words and diagrams composing the codes as reasonable intrusions into their rights to be artists and to make a profit because they are thought of as neutral relative to the purely architectural results of the decisions they affect, and the general public accepts the premise that they protect them from the selfish ends of special interest-groups or avaricious individuals. But both groups are mistaken, for the codes directly affect the most important aspects of building. For example, they directly affect the image a person is allowed to embody in a design as he satisfies their restraints on use, size, siting, bulk, materials, access, egress, etc. They also impose on the use of land and the relationships between buildings and other urban components the various modernist standards that deal with secondary functions rather than with political purposes which are primary. And as their long use sanctions their continued use, they become either increasingly unresponsive to changing circumstances or increasingly divorced from embodying the political judgement of the public officials who stand behind them. Thus, in places where modernist codes define how political and architectural activities are meshed, cities, towns and rural landscapes become increasingly healthy in ways codes can manage and increasingly unhealthy as places to pursue the perfection of one's nature.

Modernist codes are antithetical to the imagery that supports building in the classical city, town and rural landscape. When the classical tradition is fresh and vivid, the most visible and conspicuous cement holding together the political and architectural and rendering it articulate in architectural and urban form is the image people have of the place they would build to serve their life in politics. The image can take many forms. One is the common, unarticulated consent held by villagers about what villages like theirs look like. Others are more particular, as for example the widely circulated engraved plans presenting Pierre L'Enfant's ideas for Washington, DC, the extensive collections of pictures and models produced by the McMillan Commission when it restored L'Enfant's plans a century later, and Leon Krier's suggestions for the addition of flesh to those bones and meant to guide the capital's third century of life. Washington is more richly blessed than other cities but, even there, that form of imagery has largely fallen into desuetude. The imagery replacing it is not imagery at all but the words and diagrams in codes, the discipline of the developers' bottom line, and the impulses that are mistaken for imperatives of artistic style in the practice of architecture.

The alternative is to have building activity embody the purpose a site ought to serve to the extent that is possible given the current circumstances. This requires political judgement to decide which of the six (or so) building types the proposed building should imitate and how that type is to be converted into a buildable program. Doing so calls for a complementarity between political and architectural activity: in both, the relationship between the lesser which is entailed (specific buildings for particular functions within unique circumstances) and the greater which entails (the principles and normative standards existing within nature) must be consulted when establishing the character of the design. A long experience with this procedure stretching back to its formulation in classical Athens suggests that the resulting building will serve the polity well in proportion to the breadth of participation by the informed, active citizens involved in good will within the political institutions entrusted with formulating the decision.

The political art of citizens establishes the program or the brief for the building while the special art of the architect translates that formulation into a material embodiment of the type of building it is. So far the architect has participated primarily as a citizen where he has a special expertise concerning the art of building but where that special expertise gave his voice no greater authority than that enjoyed by others. Now that actual building is to occur, his participation shifts in emphasis but not in intent because the art of the architect is an art of citizenship, not an escape from it.

In practicing the art that is uniquely his, the architect will be guided first of all by the polity's conventional architectonic or structural versions. As it was with the political art so too is it in his art: What he needs to know is already in the site, or nearby, or in the urban area of the polity. The broader the reach of the purpose the building will serve, the broader the range of versions of existing buildings are to be consulted: a regia in the form of a modest residence fits a neighborhood, but in the form of a court house, it fits not merely a county but also the state of which that county is an integral part, and it alludes to the national polity it helps form. The design of any building will thereby reveal the extent of the reach of that which it houses. As it is with place, so too with time: Buildings serving purposes with longer histories — say, a religion or an institution of justice — must reach longer into the past if they are to show the commitment to an appropriately attenuated future. The broader lineaments of design must establish a liaison of the purpose with what one learns about pursuing that purpose in other circumstances. Meanwhile, decoration and ornament will inevitably refer to the circumstances surrounding the moment of construction. When well done, the result will be a building that is homomorphic with the homogeneous space it occupies. Homomorphism refers to a political and architectonic fit between what is needed and what the homogeneous space calls for and allows. In their normative (and therefore never actual but always potential) condition, polities occupy homogeneous space filled with homomorphic buildings, architectonic means and building components all obeying the rules of beauty. At any one, particular moment the urban embodiment of a political regime will reveal the current knowledge of the nature of which it is a part and the current extent to which it reaches that which it aspires to be.

Crucial to this argument is the notion of fit. What are the allowable limits setting off the fitting from the ill-fitting? A brief exploration of this question will bring this essay to a close.

One side of fit is determined by the political activity bringing the building into existence. Museums provide instructive illustrations of how fittingly political entities have been able to do their part of the excavation, although the illustration they provide could be replicated *mutatis mutandi* in any number of other examples — railroad and airline terminals, schools, university buildings, libraries and even department stores, apartment buildings and any number of other kinds of buildings that emerged in the architect's practice as the public realm enlarged along with the range and reach of the architect.

The first museums in the current sense of the term appeared during the earliest years of modernism when works of art were shorn from their connection with churches and governors and were established as a form of public instruction and, later, of enjoyment. Government now took on the role of art's protector and perhaps even supporter, but art was no longer a gloss on religion or government and a form of instruction for the governor. It therefore had to move out of the church and palace and find a new home. From the beginning, the experience of finding a home for art illustrates the point that the greater the clarity of understanding of the place the museum fits within the polity, the better the fit has been with the polity's other buildings and that when that understanding is lacking, architects have filled the vacuum with their own uncivil ideas about what role architecture plays as an art.

When the polity had a clear purpose for the museum and exercised that purpose by extending a strong hand into the affairs of art, the building took a form that allied it with the polity's most important public buildings. These new buildings often embodied the same temple and regia types from which the art was being removed. Karl Friedrich Schinkel's Altes Museum (1822–30) is an example. It assumed the shape of the square donut that Germans, following Mediterranean practice, had used as the regia form, for example in the 1698 palace by Andreas Schlüter which the new museum faced. But he replaced the temple with a great Pantheonic tholos calling for veneration in the presence of the best works of art. This change reinforced the idea that what was important in the art came from the artist and not from God, and it erased the idea that the art received its sanction from an institutional organization that competed with the polity that was sponsoring the museum. He made this latter idea even more effective by housing the tholos' dome within a projecting cubic mass so that it could complement rather than compete with the palace across the way. In addition, Schinkel, working closely with the monarch, had designed a subtle spatial setting for the museum to link it with the palace and other institutional buildings. For the first time the heart of Berlin now had a homogeneous spatial setting,[23] a *sine qua non* for all of Schinkel's designs.

More than a century later John Russell Pope's National Gallery (1937–41) translated the same program into forms excavated from the nation's capital. Like the Berlin museum, the Washington building was based on the nearby regia that gave it its authority. The version of the type Pope followed was the five-part chateau (or villa) form found on Capitol Hill and in numerous earlier examples. Among these were the canonic Palladian villa, the vast building in Versailles which in 1682 Louis XIV had established "as the main royal residence and governmental seat of France,"[24] and at the homes of American planters and Founders such as George Washington at Mount Vernon and Thomas Jefferson at Monticello. The exterior of the Capitol building regia also included the temple fronts that Thomas Jefferson's Virginia Capitol (1785–99) in Richmond had established as appropriate for representing the status and purpose of regias like this, and it featured a conspicuous domed tholos. Thornton's proposal that that tholos serve as the tomb for the first Chief Executive and his wife raised fears about what the identity was of the new nation's foundation, but those fears were assuaged after 1806 when Benjamin Henry Latrobe, who was Jefferson's confidant in matters architectural, labeled its revised design the "Hall of the People" and after 1817 when Charles Bulfinch referred to it as "Grand Vestibule, Hall of Inauguration, Impeachment, and of all Public Occasions." It could now became accepted as the place where Americans might venerate the union.[25]

When Pope designed his museum the Capitol's form was the one Thomas U. Walters had been working on since 1850. His design was recognized as being less a personal taste than a response to the obvious public requirements already embodied in the extant building even as it brought the latest iron technology to the architectonic means. Although many thought that the iron the dome's construction required might better be devoted to the Union's war effort, Abraham Lincoln said, "When the people see the dome rising it will be a sign that we intend the union to go on."[26]

Pope's building was also made spatially, which it to say urbanistically, homomorphic by nestling it into the spatial structure originally laid on the land by L'Enfant and periodically rediscovered and restored. That quality completed the fit with the setting that had started in its homomorphism with the other institutional buildings with which it works to serve the larger purposes of government. Both buildings therefore illustrate how designs can be excavated from their sites through the requisite and patient political and architectural activity, even though a great deal of site preparation may have been called for before the excavation could be undertaken.

The contrast of these buildings to three recent museums is instructive. In none of them is the museum thought of first of all as a public institution as were Schinkel's or Pope's buildings. In each, the architect explored ideas that belong first to some aspect of current thought about architecture rather than to the building's role in its supporting polity. And in each case the result is a building whose program is as incommensurate with the larger purposes of good polities as its architecture is ill fitting with its site when its site is thought of as the urban setting of a political regime.

The Sainsbury Centre at the University of East Anglia (1974–8) by Norman Foster is ancillary to a university. It contains a gallery, accommodations for those teaching about art, and the eating facilities now required to supplement whatever else a public museum offers. The institution's public purpose is found in its service to the university which the architect's design indicates is distinctly different from whatever else the university offers the public. Art is first of all about seeing something, and this building pulls the then current technology into the service of making art objects visible while converting that technology from mere machinery into architecture. The result is a minor masterpiece of modernist architecture as technology presented as a fragment of a larger piece and disconnected from the institution that nourishes it.

The Staatsgalerie Building (1980–3) in Stuttgart by James Stirling was built to allow Swabia to compete with other polities seeking legitimacy through their support of art. Designed in a moment when historical allusion was popular, it evoked Schinkel's Altes Museum but did so without referring either to its typological origins in the regia or tholos or to the Mediterranean and especially Greek classicism the Germans used to invoke their mythological origins. Instead, the museum was evoked as a purely visual device and transformed into a subtly played-out series of abstract forms. To make architecture out of the abstraction, the architect drew on the ramps and pipe-rails of Le Corbusier, on the color from German Expressionism in the form of stone slabs which, by being thin and being used in ways that were clearly not structural, could also allude to the dissolution of mass, and on other elements of modernist style. Then-current thought required that it be "contextual," which meant, among other things, allowing an existing pathway to find a way to weave through the building. The result is a unique design, one with the power of the best modernist, abstract art, and one belonging so completely to its site and its moment it makes not even the slightest gesture to the larger plenum of political and spatial order surrounding it.

The Whitney Museum of American Art in New York began as a private collection but became a public institution with a public presence when in 1966 Marcel Breuer designed a conspicuous modernist structure for it. Moated, blank-walled, upside-down and massively scaled, the abstract block is clearly a regia, but one where art is given all the authority and therefore one that is aggressively and self-consciously destructive of all that is near it. Breuer's building quickly receded into the past where the landmark-preservation procedures based on historicism could categorize it along with other old things in the vicinity as valuable in or characteristic of things valuable in the past. That made it a protected historical landmark.

When the museum decided to build a vast expansion, it found itself in a paradoxical situation. The addition had to be compatible with the original building which it was to leave untouched, but to be compatible it had to be

destructive of the other components of the landmark district. To fit in, the
new building had to be ill-fitting. This paradox neatly illustrates the contradiction between two different, current ideas about the city, both of which
accept the city as a mere settlement rather than requiring it to be a proper
polity. Both ideas are encompassed within Lewis Mumford's understanding
that a city is a generator and protector of culture. The city Breuer contributed to is one that collects works of art when art is thought of as what
artists make, while the expansion is to be built in a collection which is
itself a work of art because it contains objects characteristic of the time
or style in which they were made.

The political process involving the museum and the authorized representatives of the people in New York has been unable to find a satisfactory
design for the addition. Nor will the participants in the process be able to
if they behave as reasonable people acting in good will with one another.
This is because there is no external viewpoint for assessing the relative
merits of the claims put forth by the museum on the one hand and others
with an interest in the outcome on the other. The failure is in the political
framework defining what purpose the building is to serve and how that
purpose is to be embodied in its architectural design, not in the skill of
Michael Graves, the designated architect who so far has had three proposals
rejected.

The architect who fails so spectacularly in New York succeeds when
he is given a workable brief. At the University of Virginia Graves has
proposed a design for a Liberal Arts and Sciences Building in response
to a program contrived by university officials newly awakened to their
responsibilities for making political judgements and not merely functional
ones when acting as commissioners of buildings. Jefferson first organized
the homogeneous spatial setting which he, Stanford White, Fiske Kimball
and other, lesser architects subsequently enriched with homomorphic
buildings. A program defined in these terms in a site with that kind of
continuity promises rich rewards to the talented excavator, which Graves
has turned out to be. His design promises to be both as personal and as
fitting for the polity it will serve as the best of those of his predecessors
are, an accomplishment that is impossible in the circumstances in which
he finds himself in New York City, where those responsible for building
have failed to understand that a city is not the same as a settlement.

Graves's minor structure at Mr Jefferson's University contradicts the
conclusions one might draw from the example of the museums, his included, and any number of other buildings suggesting that there is no
possibility of doing things in ways other than those which the strongest
forces of modernism dictate. Like its neighbors and its predecessors, the
civic buildings running back to the ones crowning Pericles' Acropolis, it

shows that a building is an imitation of the pattern of nature resident on the site in the form of the political purposes that are to be served and the normative standards guiding the use of materials put into the service of architecture to accommodate those purposes. The building was there on that site and in nature all along. Once the requisite political and architectural skills have extracted it from the site, the building turns out to be the right one for the time and the place in which it emerges. The buildings, architectonic means and building components serving the polity that are extracted or excavated from sites in this way represent both the true nature of the place and time and the particular circumstances of the place and time. Given current knowledge, one can say, this design cannot be otherwise. The good city is a collection of such things. Given current knowledge, the good city, the *patria*, is buildable.

PART THREE

THE REMAINDER

The remainder appears to be coextensive with the entire architecture of non-totalizing thought. In its view there is nothing that is everything; nothing that is exhaustive, there is a residue in every system—in cosmogony, food ritual, even sacrifice—which deposits, through ashes for instance, ambivalent remains. A challenge to our mono-theistic and mono-logical universes such a mode of thinking apparently needs the ambivalence of remainder if it is not to become enclosed within *One* single-level symbolics, and thus always posit a non-object as polluting as it is reviving—defilement and genesis. That is why the poet of the *Atharva Veda* extols the defiling and regenerating remainder (*uchista*) as precondition for all form. "Upon remainder the name and the form are founded, upon remainder the world is founded."

Julia Kristeva, *The Powers of Horror*

NINE

Apocalyptic Abjection

Robert Jan van Pelt

For if only we are pure in heart,
Like children, and our hands are guiltless,

   The Father's ray, the pure, will not sear our hearts
And, deeply convulsed, and sharing his sufferings
Who is stronger than we are, yet in the far-flung down-rushing storms of
The God, when he draws near, will the heart stand fast.
But, oh, my shame! when of

My shame!

   And let me say at once

That I approached to see the Heavenly,
And they themselves cast me down, deep down
Below the living, into the dark cast down
The false priest that I am, to sing,
For those who have ears to hear, the warning song.
There

Friedrich Hölderlin, "As on a Holiday . . . ," from *Poems and Fragments*, transl.
Michael Hamburger.

Prologue in the Academy

In the early 1930s the German philosopher Martin Heidegger initiated a
project that aimed to recover the truth of pre-Socratic Greece in his own

time and for his own people.[1] Heidegger had become convinced that such a "homecoming" was the only response to the rootlessness and mental exhaustion of the modern age. He believed that the Hellenic spirit had stood in a unique proximity to the simultaneously concealed and radiant principle of existence that he defined as *Sein*, "being." The domain of this manifestation of being had been the polis, the foremost creation of the Greeks. It had been the *Lichtung* ("clearing") that had gathered the fourfold of the gods, the sky, the earth and the people in one place. In the light of this clearing people had recognized the chasm that separates human mortality from divine immortality. Heidegger interpreted this discovery as the first disclosure of being or, in more common words, as the dawn of meaning. This awesome discovery of the fact *that we are* had transformed mere space into place, houses into dwellings and settlements into cities. The terrible content of this revelation of being meant that Greeks had been "perpetually compelled to wrest being from appearance and preserve it against appearance. (The essence of being is unconcealment.) Solely in the enduring struggle between being and appearance did they wrest being from the essent, did they carry essent to permanence and unconcealment: the gods and the state, the temples and the tragedy, the games and philosophy; but all this in the midst of appearance, beset by appearance, but also taking it seriously, knowing of its power." The story of Oedipus explored the terrible price the Greeks paid for their knowledge of being. Heidegger interpreted the story as it goes from a radiant beginning (when Oedipus has the appearance of glory) to its gruesome conclusion (when he is revealed as the murderer of his father and the desecrator of his mother) as "the struggle between appearance (concealment and distortion) and unconcealment (being)." This unconcealment Oedipus can only bear by blinding himself, by removing himself from the world of appearance, "by letting the cloak of night fall round him, and, blind, crying out to the people to open all doors in order that a man may be made manifest to them as what he *is*."[2]

Heidegger's understanding of Sophoclean tragedy and Greek civilization as a whole derived from Hölderlin's provocative vision. Like Hölderlin before him, Heidegger asserted that the awesome truth of being, which had come to pass in the strife among the Mediterranean sky, the Hellenic earth, the Olympian gods and the Greeks, had been distorted, vulgarized and finally lost in the later centuries. The Socratic–Platonic turn to metaphysics had mocked the almost miraculous equilibrium of disclosure and concealment in which the earth towered up through the world and the world grounded itself on the earth—a *phusis* that had given meaning and vitality to Periclean Athens. The spirit had fallen from the numinous grace and immediacy of the ineffable word when it abandoned the experience of being in its concrete historicity for the sake of theoretical discourse and speculation. Philosophers turned their back to the intuited gathering of the things that belong together in the clearing of life as lived, and began to make logical distinctions between object and subject or fact and value. They abstracted being into opposing concepts, and proclaimed the dialectic of abstract ideas and ideals as the source of meaning. Their exclusive concern for the timeless and the eternal destroyed the awareness of human historicity. And so they began the history of philosophical thought, a history that was nothing more than a long descent of misrepresentations that claimed to reveal the truth about beings, but estranged the people from being as such. The advent of Christianity had reinforced this renunciation of being for the sake of some recondite theological truths. The Judeo-Christian tradition was to seal the last few passages that had preserved the contact with the pre-Socratic apprehension of being.

In this benighted epoch only some small lights could be seen, clearings that suggested the possibility of a general homecoming in which people would learn again to set up a world and set forth the earth. Artists (and especially poets) had preserved the experience of setting up and setting forth. Hölderlin's late poetry had been one of these points of illumination as "all the poems of the poet who has entered into his poethood are poems of homecoming."[3] It was a homecoming to pre-Socratic Greece because of the strife it contained and the fate it engendered. Hölderlin's vision had been more than a dialectic of ideal and idea. He had lived the strife of being. Yet the strife between aspiration and limitation had overwhelmed the poet's resources, and this most promising attempt to repeat the Greek beginning had been aborted. The wretched poet stared into the horror of defeat, and flung himself down from despondency to dementia.

Heidegger appropriated Hölderlin's fragmented legacy and transformed it into a comprehensive metaphysical, historical and political proposition. He expanded for example Hölderlin's notion of the complementary relationship of Greeks and Germans and the resulting special responsibility of the German people as the guardians of the Hellenic discovery of being. Assimilating Hölderlin's shattered language to the better-known Nietzschean polarity of Dionysius and Apollo, Heidegger taught that the Greeks had been endowed with the Dionysian gift that had brought them into direct contact with the fire of heaven, a contact that allowed them to be touched by the might of being. Their anointed task had been to restrain the unsubdued, to bring Apollonian form and structure to the unbounded. This had resulted in the Apollonian and metaphysical world-structure that, in turn, had become the endowment of the Germans. The philosopher's ability for grasping, preparing and planning, his capability for order and organization came to them naturally. Therefore the Germans' anointed task was to emancipate the Dionysian from the Apollonian. "This is the 'paradox.' Since we fight the cause of the Greeks, but on the opposite front, we become not Greek but German."[4]

Like Hölderlin before him Heidegger began to call for a national renewal through a German repetition of the Greek beginning. Unlike the poet, who had lived at the margins of society, the philosopher spoke from the rostrum in the centre. In the lecture course that he delivered at the University of Freiburg in the summer semester of 1935 he recounted the Hölderlinian prophetical understanding of history. "The spiritual decline of the earth is so far advanced that the nations are in danger of losing the last bit of spiritual energy that makes it possible to see the decline (taken in relation to the history of 'being'), and appraise it as such." Heidegger declared that he was not a pessimist like, for example, Oswald Spengler (the author of the highly popular *The Decline of the West*). According to Heidegger "the darkening of the world, the flight of the gods, the destruction of the earth, the transformation of men into a mass, the hatred and suspicion of everything free and creative, have assumed such proportions throughout the earth that such childish categories as pessimism and optimism have long since become absurd."

> We [Europeans] are caught in a pincers [between Russia and America]. Situated in the centre, our nation [Germany] incurs the severest pressure. It is the nation with the most neighbours and hence the most endangered. With all this, it is the most metaphysical of nations. We are certain of this vocation, but our people will only be able to wrest a destiny from it if *within itself* it creates a resonance, a possibility of resonance for this vocation, and takes a creative view of this tradition. All this implies that this nation, as a historical nation, must move itself and thereby the history of the West beyond the centre of their future "happening" and into the primordial realm of the powers of being. If the great decision regarding Europe is not to bring annihilation, that decision must be made in terms of new spiritual energies unfolding historically from out of the centre.
>
> To ask "How does it stand with being?" means nothing less than to recapture, to repeat (wieder-holen), the beginning of our historical–spiritual existence, in order to transform it into a new beginning. This is possible. It is indeed the crucial form of history, because it begins in the fundamental event. But we do not repeat a beginning by reducing it to something past and now known, which need merely be imitated; no, the beginning must be begun again, more radically, with all that strangeness, darkness, insecurity that attend a true beginning.[5]

Thus Heidegger spoke in the seminar room. And he proclaimed this understanding of German vocation in the main auditorium. Repetition was the theme of the notorious address that he delivered on the solemn assumption of the rectorate of the University of Freiburg. In this speech Heidegger affirmed the spiritual significance of the National Socialist state. It offered an opportunity to recapture "the power of the *beginning* of our spiritual–historical being." This beginning had been the moment when Western man had risen "from a popular base" to stand up "to the *totality of what is*, which he questions and conceives as the being that is." This beginning had not been surpassed. "For if indeed this primordial Greek science is something great, than the *beginning* of this great thing remains what is *greatest* about it." Therefore he asserted that this Greek beginning still *is*. "It does not lie *behind us*, as something that was long ago, but stands *before* us. As what is greatest, the beginning has passed in advance beyond all that is to come and thus also beyond us. The beginning has invaded our future. There it awaits us, a distant command bidding us [to] catch up with its greatness."[6] When Heidegger spoke these words on May 27, 1933, the issue of repetition had ceased to be a matter of academic debate. He believed that National Socialism embodied a new beginning in which the not yet realized grandeur of Greek origins would be realized. Hitler's ascent to power was an unparalleled historical possibility to regain for Europe the Dionysian Greece that had been lost for almost twenty-five centuries, a Greece that had been rediscovered on a poetic level by Hölderlin and on a philosophical level by Heidegger himself. "I saw in the movement that had gained power the possibility of an inner recollection and renewal of the people and a path that would allow it to discover its historical vocation in the Western world."[7] Thus Heidegger reflected on his rectorial proclamation after the collapse in 1945. And he explained his rectorate as "an attempt to see in the 'movement' that had come to power, beyond all its failings and crudities, something that reached much farther and that might some day bring about a gathering of what is German unto the historical essence of the West. In no way shall it be denied that at that time I believed in such possibilities and for this reason renounced the thinker's proper vocation in order to help realize them in an official capacity."[8] In other words, Heidegger identified Nazism as the instrument to realize Hölderlin's prophetical vision. It, and it alone, was to bring about the German repetition of the deeper Heraclitean, Sophoclean or Thucydidean reality of pre-Socratic Athens.

The Necropolis of Nazi Germany

Heidegger's vision of National Socialism certainly applies to architecture. A comparison of the different domains of ancient Athens and the foci of architectural activity in the Third Reich offers a premonition of this awful truth; an effort to match the Attic theatre with its Nazi counterpart transforms presentiment into unambiguous certitude. This conclusion wreaked havoc with my own project and led to repudiation and capitulation. In short the attempt to rediscover architectural principles in an age of historicism led to the ineluctable conclusion that Adolf Hitler (1889–1945) had realized the program of renewal proposed in the odd chapters of this book. In the following pages I shall sketch the outlines of a fatally flawed effort to repeat the perceived inner truth of Periclean Athens.

We begin with the cemetery. When Hitler assumed dictatorial power on March 23, 1933 by the Gesetz zur Erhebung der Not von Volk und Reich (Law to Remove the Distress of People and State), he effectively abolished the constitution and the institutions of the Weimar Republic. The void was to be filled by a new kind of organic community, a *nationaler Rechtstaat*. Not a written constitution and its institutions, but the actual life of the *Volk* as it is engaged in its struggle for existence was to be the structure of the new state.[9] This new kind of state was a radical departure from the modern understanding of the polis, yet approximated the description that Heidegger was to give two years later of the Hellenic polis as "the historical place, the there *in* which, *out* of which, and *for* which history happens."

> To this place and scene of history belong the gods, the temples, the priests, the festivals, the games, the poets, the thinkers, the ruler, the council of elders, the assembly of the people, the army and the fleet. All this does not first belong to the *polis*, does not become political by entering into a relation with a statesman and a general and the business of the state. No, it is political, i.e. at the site of history, provided there be (for example) poets *alone*, but then really poets, priests *alone*, but then really priests, rulers *alone*, but then really rulers. *Be*, but this means: as violent men to use power, to become pre-eminent in historical being as creators, as men of action. Pre-eminent in the historical place, they become at the same time *apolis*, without city and place, lonely, strange, and alien, without issue amid the essent as a whole, at the same time without statue and limit, without structure and order, because they themselves *as* creators must first create this.[10]

Did Heidegger refer to Hitler? It seems likely. After all a little more than a year earlier he had publicly pronounced Hitler as the solitary being who defied the usual relationship between citizen and state because he embodied "the German reality of today, and of the future, and of its law."[11] He was, in other words, that lonely, strange and alien being who, fulfilled in being, defied the limits of normality. He was the man who, touched by "the fire from heaven" and fulfilled of "sacred pathos," would liberate the

Germans from their imprisonment within the matrix of "Junonian sobriety."

The Nazis shared a less sophisticated version of Heidegger's interpretation of Hitler. They proclaimed that the Führer was the enduring constitution of the *Volk* as it was gathered within and without the boundaries of the Reich was to be the state. Through the Führer the *Volk* could become conscious of itself and its destiny. He was the unifying link that joined the traditional manifestations of the state, the party and the *Volk* into a new and dynamic synthesis. This synthesis was to be the basis of his boundless power: the different offices that he held, such as the Chancellorship and the Presidency only served as illustrations of his power as the leader of the people. And thus that forsaken, anomalous and alien being became a German Christ, a parallel that the self-maddened German Protestant establishment sanctioned.[12] So Hitler's ignoble and murky autobiography became the surrogate of a written constitution. The state was completely embedded in the story of his own life, coloured by the spell of his own struggle. The title of the "Bible" of Nazism, *Mein Kampf* ("My Struggle"), already suggests this; the subtitle of the first part, "Settling Accounts," only reinforces the autobiographical character of the work. The first sentence recalls the beginning of the gospel. "Today it seems to me providential that Fate should have chosen Braunau on the Inn as my birthplace."[13] On the border of Austria and Germany, Braunau was the proper place of birth for a man who saw himself as the destitute outcast, a man who for the sake of a dream of national regeneration had defied the order of two empires to live forsaken, exposed and menaced.

The idea that many people thought about *Mein Kampf* as a German Bible seems fantastic. Yet a dispassionate analysis of its text discloses what the American theologian Michael D. Ryan labeled as a fundamentally theological logic. The book might be reduced to a few simple propositions. The first one asserts that Hitler learned the basic laws of life which determine the success and failure of nations in his own struggle or *Kampf*. His struggle for survival and recognition in Vienna had taught him that these basic laws of life have specific political implications. Life in the gutter had also revealed to him the cause and nature of the disease which affected European society. And it explained why the German Reich had collapsed in 1918: the German armies had not been beaten in the field, but the will of the people to continue the war had been weakened as the result of internal rot. This knowledge made Hitler into the physician who was qualified to treat the diseased body of the German *Volk*. He would be able to heal the community through politics. "Thus, properly understood, Hitler's personal struggle was really Germany's struggle for recovery, and so he was worthy to be the leader because he fought not for himself but for the whole people."[14] Ryan observed that the structure of *Mein Kampf* showed a logical relationship between the worldview that it presented and Hitler's claim to charismatic leadership. Hitler's *Weltanschauung* derived from his own experience of the reality of the Darwinian struggle for existence, and therefore validated his leadership because it had been obtained through struggle. On the other hand his accession to a position of charismatic leadership justified his worldview because it could now acquire an objective existence in the real world. In other words: the creation of a party or later state dedicated to the struggle for existence created a situation that was effectively ruled by these "basic laws of life" described in *Mein Kampf*. Once the Germans had accepted total war as the foundation of civilization the other nations were forced to respond in kind.

The unavoidable result of this self-authenticating *Weltanschauung* was that "strange, mystical relationship between the leader and the people, the true national community (*Volksgemeinschaft*), first in Hitler's mind, and then in the minds of the masses when Hitler's propaganda efforts took hold."[15] And as the masses which rallied around the Nazi banners became larger and larger, the perceived power of the Führer became greater and greater, until the stranger Hitler became that modern incarnation of a thaumaturgic king, a latter-day version of a messianic saviour who was believed to be endowed with magical powers unavailable to ordinary mortals. The source of his demonic energy was not God but the assembled masses of the German *Volk*; his instrument of conjuration was not faith, but the party, the mystical body of the leader through which the *Volk* struggles for its existence. Within this context Hitler's pronouncements on political matters swiftly ceased to be guidelines for political action and became prophecies that demanded fulfillment. Because Hitler had promised that the Jews were to be destroyed, the Nazis had to carry out this policy. Hitler's public conjurements about the progress of the Final Solution flaunted an autobiographical fixation. On November 8, 1940, he declared: "I have . . . again and again stated my view that the hour would come when we shall remove this people [the Jews] from the ranks of our nation." And on January 30, 1942, he told his audience in the Berlin Sport Palace that "on September 1, 1939, I have already gone on record in the German Reichstag—and I am careful not to make any hasty prophecies—that this war will not end as the Jews imagine it, namely with the extermination of the European peoples, but that the result of this war will be the destruction of Jewry." A month later he repeated that "my prophecy shall be fulfilled that this war will not destroy Aryan humanity but it will exterminate the Jew." And on September 30, 1942, he invoked the memory that "some time ago the Jews laughed about my prophecies in Germany, too. I do not know whether they are still laughing today or whether they have stopped laughing already. I can only assure you even now: they will stop laughing

everywhere. And I shall be proved right with these prophecies as well."
And so on.[16]

These incantations suggest that the pivotal events of Hitler's life (and not National Socialist ideology) disclose the meaning of Nazi architecture as a celebration of Hitler's rise to power within the (still) unburied past of Germany. One of the most important of these was the *Putsch* of 1923. Its memory was to be the necromantic foundation of all Nazi architecture. Hitler claimed, and Nazi propaganda asserted, that the failed coup d'etat gave legitimacy to Hitler's rule. This extraordinary claim can only be understood if we think about Hitler's relationship to the state and the party. Hitler did not take the state seriously except as a means to an end. "Its end is the preservation and the promotion of a community of physically and psychically equal living beings." Therefore "not the cultural achievements or relative power of a state but the part assigned to its people is the decisive factor in its evaluation. . . . A state is bad, no matter what its degree of culture, if it leads the racial bearers of this culture to their doom." Hitler considered the Weimar Republic as the ruination of the German people. Therefore the *Volk's* struggle for existence had begun with Hitler's struggle against the Weimar Republic. The *Putsch* was thus a legal act against an illegal regime. "Not the preservation of a state or a government is the highest aim of existence, but the preservation of the people." The Weimar Republic had not been able to protect the people from the ravages caused by the Treaty of Versailles, the French occupation of the Ruhr and the inflation. Therefore the question of legality had ceased to be important. "The ruling power may use a thousand so-called 'legal' means, yet the instinct of self-preservation of the oppressed is always the most sublime justification for their fighting with all weapons." In short: "human right breaks state rights."[17] The party was the body in which the *Volk* had struggled in the person of Adolf Hitler against the Weimar Republic, a struggle that was simultaneously interpreted as the struggle for existence of the German nation. The difference between the state and the party was that the former was static, the latter dynamic in character. It was an instrument of transformation. It was a movement, a marching column in which the masses of individuals were unified in the fighting body of the nation. This *Volk* was a *Volk ohne Raum* ("people without space"), a notion that referred to the idea that the German state as it had emerged from the First World War lacked sufficient land to support its increasing population and the generally felt feeling that the Treaty of Versailles had left the German nation without a place in the community of nations. The *Volk* had become homeless in the Weimar Republic, the illegitimate child of defeat, a forsaken, exposed and menaced alien among the nations. From this catastrophe Hitler had emerged as the unknown outsider to take charge of the destiny of the *Volk* and lead it from exile towards its proper home. He was to be the political leader in the anticipated struggle *and* the master-builder of German destiny.

The actual debacle that formed the basis of Nazi Germany was the armistice of 1918 and the Treaty of Versailles of 1919. Hitler believed that this treaty had been a dictation designed to destroy the German *Volk*. The Versailles *Diktat* had served the Nazis well as an object of attack during the years before 1933. After it had been overturned it had, however, limited symbolic significance as the cataclysm from which the Nazi movement had emerged. Another important date in the history of Nazism, February 24, 1920, had also limited appeal. That day the official history of the Deutsche Arbeiterpartei had begun in a mass meeting in the Hofbrauhaus in Munich when Hitler presented the twenty-five points of the party program. Yet the historical importance of February 24 did not translate into historic significance. Most important of all Hitler had not yet been party leader (this responsibility he only assumed on August 1, 1921) and the Deutsche Arbeiterpartei had not yet been renamed as Nationalsozialistische Deutsche Arbeiterpartei (the name of the party was changed in April, 1920). Therefore the Nazi mythographers identified another day as the symbolic beginning of the new Reich: this day was November 9, 1923, the day of the Beer Hall *Putsch*, a day in which the commemoration of defeat, the actuality of collapse and the promise of resurrection conveniently converged in the death of sixteen party members and the survival of the stranger who was destined to lead the German people towards the Thousand Year Reich. That day became, in the official history of the Nazi movement, the moment of the beginning of the National Socialists' armed struggle for the *Volk*.

The events that were to acquire great symbolic and magical significance began to unfold on the evening of November 8. The state commissioner of Bavaria, Gustav Ritter von Kahr, delivered a speech in the Bürgerbraukeller in Munich in the presence of a gathering of high officials. Hitler took advantage of this opportunity. Intent on toppling the (in his eyes) illegitimate government of Bavaria, he surrounded the Beer Hall with 600 stormtroopers and forced his way in to declare a national revolution. A chaotic night followed; von Kahr was able to escape with the other officials and by the morning it became clear that the *Putsch* was about to fail. Since Hitler had nothing to lose, he decided to imitate Mussolini's successful March on Rome, and set forth with his followers toward the Residenz, the seat of the Bavarian government. He hoped that the mere fact of this demonstration would exorcize the government from the city of Munich. At 11.00 AM the Nazis left the Bürgerbraukeller, crossed the River Isar and marched into the old city.

An official report prepared for a committee of inquiry described the events as follows:

> The column of National Socialists about 2000 strong, nearly all armed, moved on through the Zweibrückenstrasse across the Marienplatz towards the Theatinerstrasse. Here it split up, the majority going down the Perusastrasse to the Residenz, the rest going on along the Theatinerstrasse.
>
> The police stationed in the Residenz tried to cordon it off as well as the Theatinerstrasse by the Preysingstrasse. Numerous civilians hurried on ahead of the actual column in the Residenzstrasse and pushed the police barricade. . The ceaseless shouts of "Stop! Don't go on!" by the state police were not obeyed. Since there was the danger of a breakthrough here, a police section, originally in the Theatinerstrasse, hurried around the Feldherrnhalle to give support. They were received with fixed bayonets, guns with safety catches off, and raised pistols. Several police officers were spat upon, and pistols with safety catches off were stuck in their chests. The police used rubber truncheons and rifle butts and tried to push back the crowd with rifles held horizontally. Their barricade had already been broken several times. Suddenly a National Socialist fired a pistol at a police officer from close quarters. The shot went past his head and killed Sergeant Hollweg standing behind him. Even before it was possible to give an order, the comrades of the sergeant who had been shot opened fire as the Hitler lot did, and a short gun battle ensued during which the police were also shot at from the Preysingpalais and from the house which contains Café Rottenhöfer. After no more than thirty seconds the Hitler lot fled, some back to the Maximilienstrasse, some to the Odeonsplatz.[18]

The report did not mention the death of sixteen Nazis. And neither did it record that one of the flags the Nazis had carried had fallen in the blood of one of the victims. Grave omissions: twelve years later the sixteen would be sanctified as the martyrs from whose blood the Thousand Year Reich had arisen, and the flag, christened as "The Blood Flag," was to become the party's most important relic and instrument of divination.

The immediate sequel to the incident was, however, less triumphant. Those who survived the incident, including Hitler, were arrested and brought to trial. Hitler was condemned to five years' imprisonment in the fortress prison at Landsberg. He was paroled after nine months in December, 1924.

The whole episode seemed a badly written comedy, and even many Nazis felt uncomfortable with it, especially after the party had committed itself after the event to acquire power in a legal manner. Furthermore the whole march had been an example of gross miscalculation, and no one liked to be reminded of failure, especially if that failure was the direct result of the lack of judgement of the man who was believed to have the magical power to lead the German people into a bright, new future. For several years the event was buried in the National Socialist unconscious. Only Hitler held fast to that day as the alpha and omega of his autobiographical worldview. It was the day that Fate had spared him the lot of his sixteen comrades. Therefore he began the first part of *Mein Kampf*, written during his imprisonment in Landsberg, with a dedication to the sixteen dead. "As its blood witnesses, may they shine forever, a glowing example to the followers of our movement." He concluded the end of the second and last part of the same work, written between 1925 and 1926, with the theme of regeneration. "On November 9, 1923, in the fourth year of its existence, the National Socialist German Workers' Party was dissolved and prohibited in the whole Reich territory. Today in November, 1926, it stands again free before us, stronger and inwardly firmer than ever before."

Hitler's interpretation of the meaning of the day was to prevail. When the Nazis came to power legally in 1933, November 9 became the most important holiday of the new Germany. It was the day of defeat and death (1918: Germany; 1923: the sixteen men) and resurrection (1923: Hitler; 1933: Germany). Taking some clues from the New Testament, in which the death of Jesus of Nazareth had been depicted as the resurrection of mankind, the march against the Bavarian government was officially designated as the origin of the Third Reich. The *Putsch* marked the beginning of the party's armed struggle on behalf of the German *Volk*. The sixteen (dead) martyrs and the (living) Hitler became the founding fathers of the new Germany. From their blood and in his survival the Third Reich had emerged.

Like few before him Hitler intuited the political purpose of architecture, and therefore he commissioned the architect Ludwig Troost to transform the city into a worthy setting of the new national cult. The route that the Nazis had walked in 1923 became the spine of the urban redevelopment of Munich. It consisted of two parts with three nodes. At the beginning was the first sacred place, the Beer Hall, where the annual procession was to start at exactly 11.00 AM. From there the route to the Feldherrnhalle was marked with 240 pylons, each honouring one of the 240 men who had died in the struggle against the German state and the enemies of the *Volk* between November 9, 1923 and January 30, 1933. The Feldherrnhalle was the second sacred place. There a monument was erected in honour of the sixteen principal martyrs of the movement. Until that point the elements referred literally to the historic events of 1923. However, the march had gone further in a metaphorical sense, leading to the new Germany that had been instituted the January 30, 1933. Thus the processional road was extended from the Feldherrnhalle until it reached the splendid neo-

classical Königsplatz at the other side of the old city. This square, the
termination of the cultic route and the third sacred place, was to represent
the Third Reich. At the point where the processional road (the Briener-
strasse) met the Königsplatz, two "Doric" Temples of Honour were erected,
open to the sky. Each was to contain eight coffins. At its sides large and
monumental party buildings were erected along the Arcisstrasse, revealing
the essential unity between the sacrifice of the sixteen in 1923, which
formed the basis of the political constitution of the Nazi movement, and
the instruments through which the Führer absorbed the nation in the
constitution of the movement and his own person.

The buildings were an instant success. The party ideologist Alfred
Rosenberg applauded them as "the first attempt to realize the ancient
Greek ideal."[19] The architectural critic Wilhelm Lotz praised the transformation of the Königsplatz because it showed for the first time in the
modern age that "a deeper meaning can dwell in a city-square" as long as
its origin is a spiritual principle and not a desire for aesthetic variety in the
built-up area of a merely decorative intention. The Königsplatz had shown
that it was still possible to create an architecture that emerges from inner
principles of dedication and value instead of being derived from external
contingencies of use.[20] Troost's widow judged "the clear symmetry" and
the "austere ordering of every detail, the noble stone of the mighty walls,
columns and pillars" to be symbolic of the "fundamental strength which is
renewing the German *Volk*." The buildings embodied such Apollonian
principles as "natural clarity," "calm serenity" and "the strong, austere
determination produced by a heroic mood" which Hölderlin and Heidegger
had defined as the endowment of the German people.[21] Yet Hermann
Giessler, who in 1938 became chief planner for the reconstruction of
Munich as "Capital of the Movement," also recognized in Troost's architecture shadows of the anointed task of Germany, which was to be undertaken within the body of the National Socialist Party. For him the buildings
stood for the ideological struggle, "the uncompromising battle for power in
the country, and showed with 'Doric' austerity and severity the face of the
militant party. These representative buildings, therefore, were symbols
of both the party itself and what the party was fighting for: the highest
development of power and freedom of the German character with its innate
virtues."[22]

By 1935 these interventions in the fabric of Munich were completed,
and on November 9 of that year—four days before Heidegger delivered his
famous lecture on "The Origin of the Work of Art"—the great incantatory
festival of the Resurrection of the Dead started.[23] That morning Hitler and
his entourage left the Beer Hall to retrace the route taken by the putschists
in 1923. The head of the procession was formed by the leaders of the

surviving putschists. They carried their sacréd relic, the Blood Flag. The flag was the symbol of the new Germany, symbol of its constitution and its struggle for existence. And the masses sang how they were sworn to that flag, how it was their creed, "of God and *Volk* and Land."[24] It was like the host from the mass, which proclaimed that those who die will continue to live in the earth, that those who have recognized themselves through struggle will continue to live in blood.[25] Those who followed the flag in 1923 had marched straight into the realm of eternal life, embodied by the Führer. And those who marched in 1935 could share that destiny. "Whoever follows the flag, lives, / And in him live those who died for the flag."[26] The flag was a portable stela. The marching column a walking cemetery. The procession passed along the 240 pylons. Each time the flag passed one of them the name inscribed on that pylon was read out in a solemn fashion. The participants believed that with each name the spirit of the deceased was summoned to join the march. When the procession reached the Feldherrnhalle, the men met units of the newly created Wehrmacht, which had risen from the soil of the Fatherland and the blood of the *Volk*. The army guarded the coffins of the recently exhumed bodies of the sixteen martyrs, which had been placed there the night before. The coffins were loaded on gun-carriages and the procession of the living and the raised spirits of the dead moved on to the Königsplatz. There the bodies were removed from the gun-carriages, and consigned to the sixteen sarcophagi of the two shrines. Hitler placed wreaths on each of the tombs. He then began his funeral oration, or, better, his incantation. He stressed how their death had transcended into the regeneration of the *Volk*, symbolized by its instrument of struggle, the resurrected armed forces. "These sixteen men, who twelve years ago gave their lives as sacrifice for their people and their Führer, are today raised from the grave. Who does not feel the truth of this resurrection? Who does not see the glint of their eyes in the newly raised-up Wehrmacht? And the Reich, which is itself built around this consecrated ground, is it not their kingdom? The kingdom of their 'will' and victory?"[27] From there the procession entered the Königsplatz itself, where the mass of the *Volk* was gathered. A voice called one by one names of each of the sixteen martyrs one by one; each time the representatives of the new Germany responded with a loud "Here!" "Again and again the thousands roar 'Here!' . . . the testament of these first Blood-witnesses is thus raised up to our entire Movement, while their spirit lives and works for Germany as its Eternal Watch. . . . Each of the dead thus greets the assembled thousands, who are themselves the reflection and the carriers of their will to victory."[28]

The numinous ceremony came to an end, and reflection on the significance of what had happened began. The next day the *Völkischer Beo-*

bachter, the Nazi Party newspaper, wrote that "the dead of the Ninth of November [do not lie] in dark graves and tombs but in a beautiful building, in a well-lit hall, under God's free heaven. In these brass sarcophagi beats the heart of our revolution." The editorial went on to affirm that these dead had found new and everlasting life in the German nation gathered around the holy flag. It declared that the liturgy had dedicated the sacred mission of all Germans, a task for which God had given them the strength for work and victory. The fate of the sixteen, the struggle of their comrades and the celebrations in their memory were the inner experience of the Nazi movement from which Germany had gained eternal life. And the editors asked "How few marched off in the beginning? Today there are millions represented in the flags and standards who are witness to this celebration. How few had from the first a clear understanding of this German belief? Yet the way to victory was ever clear to our soldiers in those lonely, quiet hours." Concluding with an expression of gratitude, the editors said, "We old and young national socialists thank Adolf Hitler for this unforgettable day. We praise him and his holy symbol of the resurrection of Germany, for we have him and the flag of our struggle to thank. We go forward with open eyes and believing hearts under his direction."[29]

Four days later Heidegger delivered his lecture on the origin of the work of art. The philosopher told his audience that "whenever art happens— that is, whenever there is a beginning—a thrust enters history, history either begins or starts over again. History means here not a sequence in time of events of whatever sort, however important. History is the transporting of a people into its appointed task as entrance into that people's endowment."[30] The events in Munich a few days earlier must have given this reiteration of Hölderlin's insight a special edge.

For the next four years the November celebration was to be the most significant event of the National Socialist year. The annual march of the Führer and his comrades, dead and alive, was a thaumaturgic liturgy of actual regeneration. The symbol was reality. The exorcism was real. It is significant to note in this context that the worst pogrom in modern German history, the so-called Reichskristallnacht, began on November 9, 1938. Within this sorcerous realm architecture ceased to be merely representational. In the world of magic and sorcery, breaking the windows of Jewish shops and houses equaled the destruction of the houses itself, and of their inhabitants. The buildings that Hitler had willed and Troost had built were accredited with magical properties too. The shrines in which the sixteen had been buried were open to the sky and the world: thus the summoned spirits of the sixteen remained a part of the *Volk*'s continuing struggle for existence. The halls were opened, and empowered the continuation of that struggle, elsewhere, in Russia, Poland, France, the Low Countries. It seems a bad joke, but we know better: it was all for real. It was so real that when the death of the sixteen martyrs ceased to be persuasive, other corpses had to be found. By 1938 the story of the sixteen had lost most of its attraction. First of all, the sixteen had died in a *Putsch* against the state. By 1938 the amalgamation of party and state had become complete. Germany prepared itself for war. It was clear that the armed forces of the state, and not the party, were to struggle for German existence in far-distant lands. In July 1939 Hitler, who until then had been officially Leader and Federal Chancellor, adopted the one title of Leader, *Führer*. The party, the state and the *Volk* were now finally unified in one, single person. A subtle shift in the liturgy of the Ninth of November celebrations reflected this development. While in the original celebrations the theme had been the resurrection of the sixteen in the New Germany, now Hitler's "miraculous" survival became an issue of central importance.[31] Fate had chosen Hitler to fulfil his mission. The increasing centralization of the cult on the person of Hitler reached a climax on the eve of the November celebrations in 1939. As was the customary, Hitler joined his old comrades in the Beer Hall to remember the time when the party had struggled for power. Unknown to everybody present except the Führer and his immediate entourage, the Gestapo had planted a bomb in the room. Hitler left the gathering earlier than usual. The bomb exploded. Many died, but, again, Hitler "miraculously" survived. His survival became the principal theme of the liturgy of the next day. The bodies of the victims of the explosion were carried in the procession as silent witnesses to Hitler's survival which confirmed his election sixteen years earlier. There was only one difference: in 1923 Fate had operated through a historical accident; in 1939 Fate operated through Hitler's intention. The stela had become the execution ground.

The Nazi transformation of Munich into the necropolis of Germany assimilated the ideology of the Athenian cemetery and the Holy Sepulcher into the Nazi movement. Unlike these earlier examples, however, the German necropolis was only a sham. When Pericles reminded his fellow citizens of the city they had inherited from their fathers, and when the monks of Centula preached the resurrection of Christ, they had a reasonable or moral certainty that their pronouncements agreed with what their audience recognized as common sense. Their speeches did not contradict the way people in classical Athens or Carolingian Europe lived their daily lives. Considering the available evidence as fully and impartially as possible would lead a person from classical Athens to the ideals of the polis and a monk from Centula to the idea that Christ's death constituted a cosmic victory. Yet any German who watched the shamanic Munich rituals had to suspend reason. Only when submerged within the carefully manipulated atmosphere of collective hysteria did the proclamations make sense. However, this sense had no relationship with the proper common sense approach to the stela which might restore a relationship to the past in our cities.

Hitler's Acropolis and Agora

The same analysis applies to the other aspects of Hitler's misguided reconstruction of the fivesquare city. He made Berlin and Nuremberg into a mondial acropolis (Berlin) and a national agora (Nuremberg). We can be short about Speer's design for Berlin, or Germania as the city was to be called, and the grounds for the Nuremberg party rallies: the project for the north—south axis is well known, and a few observations will suffice to show the relationship between Speer's dreams and Iktinos' achievement.

Munich was a corruption of the Athenian necropolis; the city of Germania was to have become a perversion of the Acropolis. Hitler conceived of Germania as the city that was to anchor the National Socialist movement into the eternity of victory. The official date of the decree that initiated the construction of Germania was June 25, 1940 (in fact the document was written a few days later). In the first two paragraphs of the decree Hitler explicitly defined the replanning of Berlin as the final consolidation of the nation's military victory.

> As the capital of a strong, new Reich, Berlin is to be given in the shortest possible time-span by means of its architectural reconstruction an expression which is commensurate with the grandeur of our victory.
>
> I regard the accomplishment of these supremely vital constructive tasks for the Reich as the most important contribution to the final consolidation of our victory.[32]

Yet the victory as embodied in the new city plan was not that of the German people over its non-German foes, but the triumph of the stranger Hitler over all. Elias Canetti brilliantly grasped the meaning of the first of the two main elements of the central avenue which had been designed by Hitler himself: the propyleum. It had, appropriately, the form of a triumphal arch.

> Previously, Hitler and Speer had often discussed this Triumphbogen. It was to reach a height of 120 meters, i.e. twice that of Napoleon's Arc de Triomphe in Paris. "That will at least be a worthy monument to our dead in the World War. The name of every one of our 1,800,000 casualties will be carved in granite!" Those are Hitler's words as recorded by Speer. The defeat of World War I is not acknowledged, it is transformed into a victory and celebrated by a triumphal

arch that is twice as big as the one granted to Napoleon for all his victories together. The goal of outdoing Napoleon's victories is thus clearly announced. Since the arch is meant to last for all eternity, it has to be made of hard stone. But actually, it consists of something far more precious: 1,800,000 Germans. The name of each single one of these casualties will be carved in granite. They are thereby honoured, but are also close together, closer than they ever could be in a crowd. In this enormous number, they constitute Hitler's arch of triumph. They are not yet the corpses of his new war, planned and desired by him, they are the casualties of the first war, in which he himself served like anyone else. *He* survived it but he has remained true to it and has never denied that war. In the awareness of those dead, he has gathered the strength of refusing ever to recognize the outcome of the war. They were his crowd before he had any other; he feels they are the crowd that helped him to achieve power. Without the dead of World War I, he would never have existed. His aim of bringing them together in his Triumphbogen is an acknowledgment of this truth and of his debt to them. Yet it is *his* arch of triumph and it will bear *his* name. Hardly anyone will read many of the other names. Even if 1,800,000 names can actually be carved in, the overwhelming majority will be ignored. Their number is what will lodge in memories, and that enormous number belongs to *his* name.[33]

The emergence of the cipher from the 1,800,000 had brought the victory of National Socialism that, in turn, had transformed the catastrophe of 1918 into an everlasting victory. This victory was to be celebrated in the shrine that was to end the avenue that began with the Triumphbogen. The shrine was the Kuppelberg or "Dome-Mountain." This gigantic domed hall was the largest single space ever created, and it was to endure for the thousand years to come. It was to hold gatherings of a hundred thousand people at a time. The space was to be dedicated to Hitler's name, and for a thousand years German crowds were to gather there to celebrate him as the man who gave them an existence and a world. The hall was to be Hitler's temple. And as each temple unites human artifice with god-created nature, so also the domed hall: as a Kuppel-Berg it was to transform a (man-made) Dome into a (God-made) Mountain. Like the Athenian Acropolis, the Kuppelberg was to be part of the temporal city and the timeless geography of the world.

The vanity of Hitler's project reminds us of the Periclean reconstruction of the Acropolis. However, in Athens the fundamental distinction between mortals and immortals had remained intact. Pericles never tried to build a shrine to himself: he knew that the gathering of the people was different from the assembly of the gods. In Hitler's Germany the five-millennia-old distinction between mortals and immortals was circumvented. The unity of humanity, forged in face of the divine pantheon, was dissolved into a graduated continuum that ranged from animal to the *Untermensch* (the Jew), the *Mensch*, the *Übermensch* (the German) to the One who was beyond definition: Hitler himself. The theologian Michael Ryan has explained this deification of Hitler as the inevitable outcome of the Nazi vision of redemption. Salvation was to be the recovery of German heritage through a national program of biological regeneration. "This," Hitler had promised, "would result in the new age of the master race, the race of men and women who would create a new culture for the future—one that would last a thousand years." Germania was to embody that eschatology in stone. "What is striking here is that this *Heilsgeschichte* from beginning to end operates within the limits of time. . . . It amounted to a resignation to the conditions of finitude, while at the same time asserting total power for itself within those conditions. This is what makes the logic of *Mein Kampf* theological. By asserting total control within the limits of finitude, Hitler deified himself and made himself into the saviour of the German people." The result of this was "the deliberate decision on the part of mass man to live within the limits of finitude without either the moral restraints or the hopes of traditional religion."[34] The granite mass of the buildings, which were to stand for a thousand years, literally now became the symbolic content of Nazi architecture. Their meaning was the their permanence. And this, Thucydides had prophesied, would also be the final purpose of the Athenian Acropolis *after the gods had abandoned the site and withdrawn from the city*.

The rally grounds of the Nazi Party in Nuremberg reinterpreted the Athenian Agora in Volkish terms. In Chapter Three I observed how Carl Schmitt's analysis of the nature of the political influenced the Nazi understanding of the nature of the political life. The political, Schmitt had argued, was the identification and, potentially, the extermination of an enemy. This definition of the nature of the political had implications for the internal political situation. The state had to be strong because other states were possible foes. That meant that the state could not tolerate the political pluriformity that weakened its power to wage war. Schmitt thus proposed the kind of *Burgfrieden* or "Fortress-peace" which had been prevalent in Germany during the First World War. During this time all the political parties had been unified behind the Kaiser and the army. Schmitt maintained that those who refused to support the state in its confrontation with the enemy effectively aided the opposing forces. Therefore they became part of the enemy.

The state as the decisive political entity possesses an enormous power: the possibility of waging war and thereby publicly disposing of the lives of men. The *jus belli* contains such disposition. It implies a double possibility: the right to demand from its own members the readiness to die and unhesitatingly to kill enemies. The endeavour of a normal state consists above all in assuring total peace within the state and its territory. . . . As long as the state is a political entity this requirement for internal peace compels it in critical situations to decide also upon the domestic enemy. Every state provides, therefore, some kind of formula for the declaration of the internal enemy.[35]

The agora of the state structured according to the principles of Schmitt's political theory had a double purpose. It had to serve as an arena where the nation's combative strength could be mustered, and it was the place where the nation should declare its internal enemy. The Nuremberg party rallies fulfilled these purposes. Leni Riefenstahl's *Triumph of the Will* (1934) powerfully attests to the way Nuremberg embodied the first aspect of Schmitt's agora. The Reich Citizenship Law and the Law for the Protection of German Blood and German Honour, conceived, written and promulgated at the Reich Party Congress of Freedom in Nuremberg, fulfilled the second of Schmitt's demands. They were to protect the nation from a nation that, as the Jew-basher Julius Streicher put it, had traversed for millennia a path of murder and mass murder, a nation that had arisen from criminal roots or, even worse, "a pseudo-people welded together by hereditary crimi-nality."[36] The first of these so-called Nuremberg laws introduced a dis-tinction between the enfranchised citizen and the disenfranchised subject. Only those of German or kindred blood could be citizens. The law did not mention the Jews. The second law dealt explicitly with the perceived bio-logical threat which stood in the way of the national program of biological regeneration which was to recover the German heritage. Its preamble read:

> Imbued with the insight that the purity of German blood is a prerequisite for the continued existence of the German people and inspired by the inflexible will to ensure the existence of the German nation for all times, the Reichstag has un-animously adopted the following law, which is hereby promulgated.[37]

The first article forbade marriages between Jews and those of German or kindred blood; the second article forbade extramarital intercourse between Jews and Germans and the third stipulated that Jews were not allowed to employ "household female subjects of German or kindred blood who are under 45 years old." In the hurry that surrounded the creation of the Nuremberg laws—the first was written the night before its promulgation on old menu cards, the second law was hammered out "in the midst of commotion, to the accompaniment of music and marching feet and in the setting of flags,"[38] the authors had not been able to define who was actually a Jew. Through the First Ordinance of the Reich Citizenship Law, issued on November 14, 1935, the two Nuremberg laws were brought to bear upon each other. Article 4 explicitly stated that a Jew could not be a citizen, and that he therefore "is not entitled to the right to vote on political matters; he cannot hold public office." Article 5 defined a Jew as someone who had at least three grandparents "who are fully Jewish as regards race," or someone who had two Jewish grandparents and who belonged to the Jewish community, and/or was married to a Jew, or who was born from a Jewish parent, or who was conceived in an extramarital relationship involving a Jew after the entry into force of the Law for the Protection of German Blood and German Honour.[39]

Delusion and Reality

Nazi architecture and urban design were a consistent effort to reconstruct the classical fivesquare city within the age of historicism. The typological analysis of Nazi urban design initiated in this chapter can only be a beginning, and we may only draw a preliminary conclusion. My appraisal of the urban transformations of Munich, Nuremberg and Berlin / Germania converges on the notion of the theatrical. What had been real and legitimate in Athens, and what should be in our age credible to us, the Nazis used as a conscious trick. In Periclean Athens the necropolis, the Agora and the Acropolis anchored the reality of urban life in the consciousness of the people. In Germany architecture and urban design became tools of deception, a carefully designed stage for the rituals handed down by the Ministry of Propaganda. In Athens the architecture disclosed a world where people could be free from the rage of the Furies; in Germany the architecture aided a cynical leadership to shackle a people to the calculatedly aroused outbursts of collective hysteria. And as all had become a theater, and as everyone had been assigned roles as actors, no one felt guilty in 1945 when the proscenium crumbled, the backdrop burned and the performance came to it untimely end. Invoking the Heraclitean topos that all the world is a stage, and men merely players, the good citizens took off their masks. At worst the German considered everything that had happened as a tasteless comedy, at best they tried to understand it as some Sophoclean tragedy. A student of the plays and novels from post-war Germany commented that "the question asked was often not so much 'Why did no one manage to stop Hitler?' as 'Why were we the one to fall prey to this evil situation?' Turning the question this way put the experiences of the recent past into a particular pattern of thought. The German people were seen as the collective victim of a terrible fate, rather than as a group of morally responsible individuals. An entire historical epoch was reduced to merely one manifestation among many of the eternal struggle between good and evil; history came to be seen in terms of primal myth."[40] The resulting idea of the recurrence of history, in which everything changes while remaining the same, led from a pseudo-Sophoclean awareness of fate to a sloppy invocation of historical relativism. Reading the influential *Die deutsche Katastrophe* (*The German Catastrophe*), written in 1945 by the by then doddering octogenarian Friedrich Meinecke, the Germans learnt to see the Nazi years as a mistake of history, a discontinuity of tradition which had already been absolved in the Heraclitean flux of time. Meinecke's historicist and relativist analysis of the Third Reich made it all somehow palatable. The Historical Point of View confirmed that the thousands who in 1948 cheered Mayor Ernst Reuter and General Clay in the three besieged sectors of Berlin were somehow different from the thousands who had called some six years earlier for Total War: unlike the crowd which cheered Goebbels, the masses outside the Lichtenberg Townhall were the champions of the tradition of the true Germany, the Germany of Schiller, Schinkel and Schelling. And as a token of their gratitude the representatives of the true (that is Free) Germany appointed Meinecke as the first Rector of the first institute of higher learning which was to rise (untainted so people believed) from the ruins of the Nazi (that is the not so German) past: Berlin's Free University.

The dramatic histrionics of the city that Hitler built made the traditional theater obsolete. The abortive history of the *Thingplätze* illustrates this well.[41] The *Thingplatz* was to have been for the German city what the theater had been for the Greek polis: a place where the fundamental concerns of past, present and future, of soil, city and sky could be gathered in an experience of wholeness. Modeled on the ancient Greek theater, and deriving its name from the tribal gatherings of the ancient Germans, the *Thingplatz* was meant to become the center for the whole ceremonial, national–political and artistic life of each German community. These all-inclusive centers for "community experience and experienced community"[42] were meant to unite the chthonic and historical elements of the Munich festival with the universal cosmic character of the future city of Germania and the political dynamism of the Nuremberg party rallies. The writer Richard Euringer defined in the *Thingspiel* in 1934 as a festival in which the elements of fire, water, air and earth, and stones, stars and the sun's orbit were also actors, a drama in which the daily became mythical and the nameless mass a people. In the liturgy the fallen were to rise, the spirit was to march forth from stones and the community was to renew itself in a cultic celebration of the Day of Judgement.[43] A few people were impressed. A French visitor described the experience of a *Thing* drama as a *gemütliche* version of the Munich festival or the Nuremberg party rallies.

In the audience, one is drowned in the anonymous mass, rubbing elbows with one's neighbour; one sings with the others familiar songs, one reacts together and violently to the simple but marvellous episodes in the action [on the stage]: the appearance of the dead soldier, etc. . . . Then one becomes aware of an inchoate but omnipresent mass of Germans, in the audience, on the stage, and beyond the *Thing* place, one is reassured, happy in the certainty that all Germany is marching, that Germany is both its present and its ancient self: the old and romantic, tough Teutonic joy in [the] tribe runs through each of the spectators in the crowd; the miracle occurs; for several seconds, the *Volk* community is a living reality.[44]

But as the visitor noted, the illusion of unity only lasted for several seconds. Most participants in the *Thing* liturgies were bored most of the time, and by 1936 the Nazi leadership had abandoned the proposition of the *Thingplatz* as a serious successor of the Greek theater. The director of the Düsseldorf State Theater, Felix Emmel, analyzed the causes of the failure of the *Thingplatz* in 1937. He argued that the *Thingplatz* had been conceived by architects who had understood little of the demands of dramatic performances and that its form had not emerged from the essence of drama, but from an architectonic imitation of the Greek theater. Emmel admitted that some of the *Thingplätze* were of great beauty. Yet they were useless as there were no plays that could be performed within them. Only when large groups of actors marched on and off the stage did the theater function as intended. The individual actor, however, was lost. Emmel suggested that it would be better to forget the purpose of the *Thingplatz* as a repetition of the Greek theater, and use it as a political meeting place.[45] It was a proper suggestion: in a world in which politics had become theatrical, the theater had become the right location of the political.

Yet not all had been theater. Speer's sets had concealed a real world where the delusive themes acted out in Munich, Nuremberg, Berlin and the *Thingplätze* were earnestly and methodically applied to the lives of millions of people. This real world might be summed up in one word: Auschwitz.

Auschwitz was to the topsy-turvy city Hitler built what the theater was to the classical city, or the Thebes of Sophoclean tragedy was to the Athens of Periclean democracy. The difference was that if the theater (and Sophocles' Thebes) recapitulated the real into representation, Auschwitz gave reality to what seemed in Munich, Nuremberg and Berlin an innocent performance reprieved within the historicist court of academic historiography. Despite this inverted relationship between the real and the theatrical, Auschwitz does take the place of the theater in the political edifice of National Socialism if only because it offers an unmitigated instance of the Sophoclean caesura, the event in which a man is removed "from his own life-sphere, the centre of his inner life into another world and into the excentric sphere of the dead."[46] In Hölderlin's interpretation, Sophocles had depicted "man's understanding as wandering below the unthinkable."[47] This, in a nutshell, defines human existence in the shadow of an event that, as I discussed in Chapter Three, is fundamentally incomprehensible. Yet it is typologically apprehensible. To propose the hypothesis that the extermination camp relates to the rest of German society as the Attic theater to the polis does not imply an explanation. It offers merely another perspective on what Emil Fackenheim aptly defined as the whole-of-horror of the camps. Yet that vista does not mean that we give Auschwitz its proper place within the panorama of architectural history. As Fackenheim observed, such a placing-in-perspective "would *already* constitute a dissipation, not only blasphemous but also untruthful and hence unphilosophical, of either the *whole* of horror—the fact that it was not random, piecemeal, accidental, but rather integrated into *a world*—or else *of the horror* of the whole—the fact that the whole possessed no rational, let alone redeeming purpose subserved by the horror, but that the horror was starkly ultimate."[48] The typological equation of the extermination camp with the theater does not give an explanation because the truth of the very core of the theater, Sophoclean tragedy, is the brutal truth that it cannot be understood. In other words the extermination camp and the Attic theater are ruptured by a caesura; in the camps the caesura is real, in the theater it is symbolic.

Caesura

The American–Jewish theologian (and poet, and novelist) Arthur A. Cohen (1928–86) was the first to interpret Auschwitz as caesura. In his earlier theological work Cohen "avoided" (as he was to admit later) the challenge of Auschwitz. By the late sixties he discovered that it was impossible to confront the question of God without encountering the evil of the extermination camps. He knew it was an almost hopeless task. As he explained in 1981, "there is something in the nature of thought—its patient deliberateness and care for logical order—that is alien to the enormity of the death camps. There is something no less in the reality of the death camps that denies the attentions of thought. Thinking and death camps are incommensurable. The procedures of thought and the ways of knowing are confounded. It is to think the unthinkable . . ."[49] Yet he knew that he had to approach *the event* (of the Nazi destruction of the Jews) not because it had meaning, but rather because he was persuaded that "it has no meaning, because it denies meaning and makes mockery of meaning."[50] Cohen began to search for a language that would help him to address the issue.

Two terms became central in his thought. The first was the *tremendum*, the second the caesura.

Cohen derived the term *tremendum* from Rudolf Otto's classic *The Holy* (1923). Otto described God as the utter mystery, the enormous mystery, the terror mystery, the *mysterium tremendum*. This original and awesome holiness, from which all the other attributes of God emanate, is countered by the human *tremendum*. This *tremendum* Cohen defined as "the enormity of an infinitized man" who fears death so completely and denies death so mightily that he builds a mountain of corpses to the gods of the dead as if "to placate death by the magic of endless murder." Cohen identified the Nazi destruction of the Jews as the *tremendum* of our own times, "for it is the monument of a meaningless inversion of life to an orgiastic celebration of death, to a psychosexual and pathological degeneracy unparalleled and unfathomable to any person bonded to life."[51] Cohen believed that it had not been accidental that the victims of the *tremendum* had been the Jews: their four-thousand-year-long history was, after all, "a celebration of the tenacity of life."

This interpretation brought him to the second concept, the caesura. He borrowed it from the Jewish philosopher Martin Buber (1878–1965). According to Buber the four millennia of Jewish history had been without a midpoint, without a rupture or, as he also called it, a caesura. The motivation for this contention was rooted in Buber's polemical interpretation of the Christian tradition. As Cohen observed, "Buber regarded salvation out of incarnation and the empty tomb as an arbitrary insertion of the plumb-line of eternity into the vortex of time, with the result that History was broken open to the pre-Christ and the post-Christ and the marking off within Judaism of prophetic figurations and posterior stubbornness. Buber's insistence therefore that Judaism has no midpoints, that Jewish history is cantilevered from its moorings in creation toward an unfixed endtime, was part of his intellectual momentum *contra Christiana*."[52] Against the Christian understanding of an axis of history Buber asserted the traditional Jewish belief that there are no messianic moments because redemption is not an event but a never-ending process that can only come to a conclusion at the final end of the historical era. Cohen commented that "Buber's assertion that there is no caesura is accurate insofar as it concerns the eschatological vision of the perfecting and redemption of history, but wrong insofar as it misses the underside of history, the corrupting caesura, the abyss rather than the heavens of the historical."

For the Holy there may be no caesura, but for the unholy its name *is* caesura. The discontinuity of the abyss is precisely what insures that it is both caesura and *tremendum*. The abyss of history is in this view, also a gap in normal time, no less a gap, no less a decisive gap than would be the messianic redemption. In the time of human *tremendum*, conventional time and intelligible causality is interrupted. In that time, if not redemption, then the demonic tears the skein of events apart and man (and perhaps God no less) is compelled to look into the abyss.[53]

That abyss confronted them with the most terrible of their fears: the possibility of total annihilation. This carries the signature of absolute evil because it suggests that the Jewish doctrine of redemption as a process in time is invalid. The devout Christian knows the source of his mortality to be in the present reality of a living God, and can ultimately come to terms with catastrophes such as the mass destruction of peoples because the ultimate reality of salvation is not on earth but in heaven. For the pious Jew this is different. She trusts in the election of her nation, in the experience that the chosen people is eternal. In short she trusts in the God of the covenant. As Cohen remarked, "if there is one incontestable article of the Jewish unconscious, it has been the mythos of indestructibility and the moral obligation of tenacity." Yet the Nazi destruction of the Jews cracked this foundation of three millennia of Jewish existence. Auschwitz almost annulled thirty centuries of Jewish endurance. "Is it a wonder," Cohen asked, "that Jews should regard the *tremendum* as a caesural fissure that acquires with each decade a more and more profound meta-historical station as the counter-event in Jewish history, the source of its revisionist reconsideration and self-appraisal?"[54]

These thoughts initiated a project to construct a new theology that addressed the now questionable if not preposterous assertion of the unconditional fidelity of a biblical God to a centuries-old covenant. If the covenant still held, why had God remained silent when the Nazis built the fires of the crematoria? This project "to cross the abyss" culminated in a new theology that proposed that "God's speech is really always man's hearing, that God is not the strategist of our particularities or of our historical condition, but rather the mystery of our futurity, always our *posse*, never our acts."

> If we can begin to see God less as the interferer whose insertion is welcome (when it accords with our needs) and more as the immensity whose reality is our prefiguration, whose speech and silence are metaphors for our language and distortion, whose plenitude and unfolding are the hope of our futurity, we shall have won a sense of God whom we may love and honour, but whom we no longer fear and from whom we no longer demand.[55]

Many critics praised Cohen's essay. The American theologian David Tracy identified it as an example of "the rarest of human achievements:

genuinely theological thinking." Reading Cohen's work was to meet "thinking on its ownmost ground."[56] Yet not everyone agreed. Richard L. Rubenstein and John K. Roth came to the conclusion that Cohen's reconstruction ultimately affirmed the irrelevance of God. Therefore Cohen had failed to offer a credible post-Holocaust theology. Yet they admitted that Cohen's failure was more tragic and not personal. "Let us recall that the tragic is not so much the story of human error or folly as it is the inexorable unfolding of a destiny wholly resistant to human intention. When Oedipus learned that he was destined to kill his father and marry his mother, he did everything he could to evade that destiny. Nevertheless, every evasive measure only brought him closer to the fated denouement."[57]

This brings us to the second interpretation of Auschwitz as a caesura. It takes up the Hölderlinian interpretation of Greek tragedy. Its purpose is radically different from Cohen's adoption of the idea of caesura. Cohen's caesura addressed the significance of Auschwitz for the Jews. It suggested that it introduced within Jewish *Geschichte* a fissure that compared to the *geschichtliche* rupture of crucifixion and resurrection within Christian history. Yet the caesura of the cross had been one of salvation, while that of Auschwitz had been one of perdition. Nevertheless the two were primarily concerned with the victims of history: the primary group to be touched by these events were the Jews, and not the Germans or the Romans. In Philippe Lacoue-Labarthe's application of Hölderlin's analysis of *Oedipus Tyrannus* to Auschwitz the direction of concern turned towards the significance of the death camps as a caesura in German and European history.

Lacoue-Labarthe addressed the question of Auschwitz within the context of the so-called "Heidegger Case," the debate about Heidegger's relationship to Nazism. Like so many other French Heideggerians, Lacoue-Labarthe has tried to counter the challenge that Heidegger's unconditional commitment to the National Socialist movement had deep roots in his own philosophy. In his *Heidegger, Art and Politics* (1990) Lacoue-Labarthe acknowledged that Heidegger's response to the camps was "scandalously inadequate." Heidegger mentioned the death camps only once. In a lecture given in 1949, he observed that "agriculture is now a motorized food industry, the same thing in its essence as the production of corpses in the gas chambers and the extermination camps, the same thing as blockades and the reduction of countries to famine, the same thing as the manufacture of hydrogen bombs."[58] Heidegger's refusal to state the difference between the motorization of the agricultural industry and industrialized death is, as Lacoue-Labarthe rightly judged, "strictly—and eternally—intolerable."

This is so for an extremely *simple* reason: the extermination of the Jews (and its programming in the framework of a "final solution") is a phenomenon which follows *essentially* no logic (political, economic, social, military etc.) other than a spiritual one, degraded as it may be, and therefore a historial one. In the Auschwitz apocalypse, it was nothing less than the West, in its essence, that revealed itself—and that continues, ever since, to reveal itself. And it is thinking that event that Heidegger failed to do.[59]

Heidegger's unwillingness and inability to face the Nazi destruction of the Jews was significant because the annihilation of the Jewish people was the unintended yet inevitable consequence of the philosopher's assertion that a German repetition of the Hellenic beginning could bring an end to the benighted age. After all, the Judeo-Christian tradition separated Berlin from Athens, and while it was possible to convert German Christians back into the *Volk*, it was not so easy to do the same with the Jews. The successful effacement of Christianity as a metaphysical barrier depended on the annihilation of Judaism as a physical reality. If, as Heidegger asserted, the history of the West was the history of the first revelation of Being in the Greek polis and its later withdrawal, and if that history called for a new beginning, then it followed that the Judeocide was the doomed consequence of this history. Hence Auschwitz is the fissure where the West reveals its terrible essence.

Auschwitz, in other words, had been built in the shadow of Heidegger's teacher: Hölderlin. If Heidegger's project had been a response to Hölderlin's call to recover for the German present the holy pathos and heavenly fire of ancient Greece, then the key to Auschwitz was to be found in that moment in Hölderlin's thought that had made the holy pathos of the Greek world accessible to the kind of Junonian sobriety that we associate today with the name of Adolf Eichmann. That moment is to be found in his discussion of the Sophoclean caesura. The truth of Oedipus was, in the final analysis, the ontological origin of Auschwitz. Thus Lacoue-Labarthe felt free to discuss the two events in direct relationship to each other. Commenting on Hölderlin's "Remarks on 'Oedipus'" he observed that "a caesura would be that which, within history, interrupts history and opens up another possibility of history, or else closes off all possibility of history."

But two points absolutely must be made here:

1. We may only speak of a caesura in the case of a pure event, i.e. an empty or null event, in which it is revealed—without revealing itself—a withdrawal or the nothingness.

2. There is a caesura only where an attempt at immediacy (an excess) is interrupted or cut off, i.e. a crime against the—historical—Law of Finitude.

In the case of Auschwitz—which Blanchot calls that "event without response"—these two conditions are, as the sinister-sounding phrase has it, "satisfied." And this is so for the only time, so I believe, in modern history (this is why Auschwitz opens up, or closes, a quite other history than the one we have known up until now). With one small proviso—though this changes everything—that Auschwitz is the site of dissociation: those who suffer the "categorical turning away" in the unprecedented figure not even of death, but of a mere purging (an unutterable degradation of *catharsis*)—are not those who desired immediacy or committed a crime, but those upon whom those who did do these things literally discharged themselves (once again, an unutterable degradation of *catharsis*)—making of Auschwitz, no less literally, the *discharge* of Germany (and of Europe).[60]

Therefore we ought to think about Auschwitz as at once more and less than tragedy: "more because the infinite separation is absolutely hyperbolic: less, because no (re)presentation of it is possible."[61] I can agree with him as long as the word tragedy is qualified as Greek tragedy. As far as the modern city is concerned, the Judeocide is neither less nor more: it is exactly what it is: the tragedy of the West understood as the tension between Athens and Jerusalem.

The Camps and the Weltanschauung *of National Aestheticism*

The foregoing analysis suggests the quintessential significance of the death camp in the Athens that Hitler tried to restore in the German lands. Study of the *nationalsozialistische Weltanschauung*, the immediate ideological source of the camps, corroborates this first and hesitant understanding of the place of the camps within the Nazi polis. A *Weltanschauung* or worldview was not merely a belief or an ideology. It was, as Emil Fackenheim explained, something special.

> It deserved respect, even awe, if only it had the three characteristics a *Weltanschauung* requires: cosmic scope, internal coherence or *Geschlossenheit*, and a sincere commitment on the part of its devotees. . . . Hence when the *nationalsozialistische Weltanschauung* appeared, it was respected simply *because* it was a *Weltanschauung*: not despite the fact that it was cosmic but because of it; not despite the fact that it slandered "good" as well as "bad" Jews but—indiscriminate attacks on *das Judentum* being necessary for *Geschlossenheit*—because of it. And the pimp Horst Wessel became a saint, not despite the fact that he died needlessly but, having died because he had refused a Jewish doctor's aid, because of it.[62]

Unlike an ideology, which was created in the study of a philosopher, a worldview was forged in the actual struggle for existence. It owed its existence "not to the ideas of a few crazy ideologists, but to the knowledge and ruthless application of Nature's stern and ruthless laws." A worldview proclaimed that "to preserve a certain culture the man who creates it must be preserved. This preservation is bound up with the rigid law of necessity and the right to victory of the best and stronger in this world."[63] Therefore the victory of Hitler's life and the triumph of Horst Wessel's death could become the canonical stories that anchored the National Socialist *Weltanschauung* in the reality of life—a relationship which, as the Nazis maintained, the political ideology created by the Jewish bourgeois philosopher Karl Marx lacked. Yet this very link between worldview and real life as lived was problematic because events did not always fit the prognostications. In order for a worldview to work, it had to account for failure in the same manner as the Greek polis had done. Only thus could it be comprehensive or *geschlossen*. In Hitler's *Weltanschauung*, the nations of the world were all subject to the natural law that structures the Darwinian struggle for existence. In that struggle the English and the Italians were natural allies of Germany, while Russia was the natural enemy: the English were to rule the seas, Italy the south and Germany the east. Each had its own role within the larger destiny proclaimed and preserved in the worldview. Yet England did not affiliate its maritime power to German combative might. The British refused to surrender when they had been expected to do so. Churchill defied important elements of Hitler's *Weltanschauung*. Therefore an explanation had to be sought within that very same worldview to preserve its integrity. Not surprisingly this vindication of the Führer's vision was found in the perceived cause of all of Germany's mishaps: the Jewish conspiracy. Hitler's doctrine of a single enemy set out to destroy the natural order of the world with the help of the unnatural ideal of humanitarianism explained all misfortune which had befallen or was to touch the German nation. It was important that the Jew was the *single* cause of all disaster. Only thus could he become that symbolic keystone of the Nazi worldview. This led to the seemingly absurd proposition that the Jew could be held responsible for the Bolshevik revolution *and* American monopoly capitalism. The Germans believed this proposition because it fitted their image of Jewish cunning: once they had accepted the fundamental distinction between (existentially rooted) worldview and (abstract and artificial) ideology, it made perfect sense to suppose that the one people without a homeland (and therefore worldview) would try to set out to control their "hosts" with the help of an arsenal of seemingly opposing ideologies, be it communist, socialist, liberal. Thus, as Fackenheim observed, "if *der Nationalsozialismus* was the acting out of a *Weltanschauung*," then it had to include that conspiracy. The result was an edifice that recognized antisemitism as its "granite-like" core. Therefore "neither the Führer nor his 'decent' followers could be satisfied with a *Halbheit* that would have *Geschlossenheit* but stop short of confirming its truth. The 'solution' of the 'problem' posed by the Jewish 'poisoners' of the world, in that case, had to have *Ganzheit*, i.e. be 'final,' and remain so to the end."[64]

A *Weltanschauung* was, in short, a noetic work of art. A state based on a worldview was a *Gesamtkunstwerk*. As we have seen in Chapter Five, Periclean Athens had not emerged from a poetic intention: its origin, Solon's reform, had been the pragmatic response to a crisis. Yet it had been remembered as a political and existential work of art. Taken as a model to be repeated, it could only result in a hell. Auden reflected on this in an essay entitled "The Poet & the City." He warned that "society has always to beware of the utopias being planned by artists *manqués* over cafeteria tables late at night."

> All political theories which, like Plato's, are based on analogies drawn from artistic fabrication are bound, if put into practice, to turn into tyrannies. The whole aim of a poet, or any other kind of artist, is to produce something which is complete and will endure without change. A poetic city would always contain exactly the same number of inhabitants doing exactly the same jobs forever. . . . A society which was really like a good poem, embodying the aesthetic virtues of beauty, order, economy and subordination of detail to the whole, would be a nightmare of horror for, given the historical reality of actual men, such a society could only come into being through selective breeding, extermination of the physically and mentally unfit, absolute obedience to its Director, and a large slave class kept out of sight in the cellars.[65]

Written in the late fifties, Auden only alluded to the idea that Hitler's Germany had been an essentially artistic construction, and that the world of the camps were the keystone in the edifice, or the parataxis in the poem. Twenty years later artists and thinkers became more audacious: the German filmmaker Hans-Jürgen Syberberg explored in his seven-hour *Hitler, A Film from Germany* the unsettling thesis that Hitler was the greatest film maker of all times, the director who "made the Second World War, like Nuremberg for Leni Riefenstahl, in order to view the rushes privately for himself, like King Ludwig attending a Wagner opera alone."[66] At the end of the film, the narrator of *Hitler* summarized the Führer's vision of the state as a work of art which embodies an enduring truth and therefore proclaims the end of history.

> I believe and avow, I had a dream. The artwork of the state and politics and nation and each individual a part of it, each in his place. The attempt to lead the masses to victory with their inherent strength. In a beautiful race. A model for all others, according to the old pattern, two thousand years old and known

to every schoolboy from an early age. Like Darwin the Englishman's law of the struggle for survival, and Wagner's myth from *Rienzi* to *Parsifal*. The *Gesamtkunstwerk* of Germany, the model, I proclaim the death of light, the death of all life and of nature, the end.[67]

The implied idea of the Judeocide as the ultimate outcome of an essentially aesthetic *Weltanschauung* did not issue only from the fertile imagination of a man who Susan Sontag compared to Richard Wagner. Also a sober and meticulous historian like Raul Hilberg, who reconstructed the scope and the minutiae of the legal, administrative, organizational and technological mechanics of the "Final Solution" in a most scrupulous and unaffected manner, could not escape the apprehension that the Nazi destruction of the Jews had been conceived as part of a great edifice. Speaking in October 1987 at a symposium on understanding evil, Hilberg described how, shortly after Germany's surrender in 1945, he discovered parts of Hitler's personal library. He found books on two topics: Frederick the Great and architecture. "That was it, plus his old rent receipts from the 1920s. He didn't throw out the receipts. How were these books inscribed to Hitler? To Adolf Hitler, *den Erbauer des deutschen Reiches*, to the Architect of the Third Reich. For Hitler everything was architecture. The war itself was an aesthetic phenomenon, the destruction of the Jews an edifice, the whole *Götterdämmerung* a controlled Wagnerian process."[68] Lacoue-Labarthe, finally, concluded from his analysis of the relationship between the Heideggerian discourse with the National Socialist *Weltanschauung* that Heidegger's understanding of art (and architecture) "casts a precise light on the essence of National Socialism, which has remained more or less veiled in the dominant discourses on the subject. This is the reason why, I believe, one may venture the term national-aestheticism."[69]

The death camp was an integral part of the most grandiose edifice ever conceived. It was its essential, its type and its theater. If the Greek theater punctuates architectural history as the symbolic fissure that separated the architectural historic from the architectural posthistoric epoch, the camp marks the actual caesura that has ended architectural history as such. Like the classic theater Auschwitz recapitulated the city which it completed: it revealed the truth of what Germany had become.

Auschwitz had its emporium, its necropolis and its Acropolis, its Agora and its houses.

Kanada

It seems odd to discuss Auschwitz as an emporium, as it seems to be first and foremost the symbol of the city without emporia. This, in any case, was how Richard Rubenstein discussed Auschwitz in his *The Cunning of History*. In a reflection on the implications of the metropolitan destruction of the countryside, Rubenstein identified Auschwitz as the prophetic image of the ultimate destiny of urban history. "Auschwitz was perhaps the terminal expression of an urban culture that first arose when an ancient protobourgeoisie liberated its work life from the haphazard, unpredictable, and seasonable character of agriculture and sustained itself by work which was, in the words of Max Weber, 'continuous and rational.'" The German extermination camps, and their satellites such as the ghettos of Warsaw, Lodz and Vilna, offered for those who could see an apocalyptic image of the end of urban civilization. It is the time "when the city, deprived of the countryside's surplus food and bloated by the countryside's surplus people, feeds upon its own ever-diminishing self and finally collapses. The starving inmates of Auschwitz, consuming their own substance until they wasted away into nothingness, may offer a prophetic image of urban civilization at the end of its journey from the countryside to Necropolis." The Jews were the first exiles from the countryside, the pioneer inhabitants of the metropolis and the first inhabitants of Necropolis. Their fate prophetically suggested that "unlike current economic, social, and demographic trends are somehow reversed, there will be other citizens of the city of the dead, many others."[70]

Rubenstein was only partly right. In fact there was a lot of wealth in Auschwitz. It was to be found in a section of the camp known as "Kanada." There thirty large barracks overflowed with food, clothes, gold, diamonds and other goods taken from those who had arrived on the ramp. Kanada represented, as two historians of Canada's miserable record vis-à-vis Jewish refugees phrased it, "life, luxury and salvation; it was a Garden of Eden in Hell; it was also unreachable." The prisoners who had named the storehouses of unattainable wealth "Kanada" had done so rightly as "in effect, the barracks at Auschwitz symbolized what Canada was to all the Jews of Europe throughout the 1930s and 1940s — a paradise, enormous, wealthy, overflowing and full of life; but out of bounds, a haven totally inaccessible."[71]

A few "privileged" prisoners were allowed to work and live in Kanada. One of the inmates assigned to the task of collecting, sorting and despatching the effects of the deportees was the sixteen-year-old Kitty Hart. She remembered the conditions in Kanada as relatively comfortable. "Our huts were luxurious in comparison with those in the main camps. There were only three hundred girls to a hut. Inside were three-tier single bunks, with well-filled straw mattresses and two blankets each. There were even proper windows with a view — of the gas chambers and crematoria." The price for the privileged comfort of Kanada was a life right next to the gaschambers and the ovens. Kanada was situated between the four crematoria at the western edge of Auschwitz–Birkenau. These buildings also contained the gaschambers. Kitty Hart discovered the gruesome implications of this location within minutes of her arrival in Auschwitz's promised land. One of the other girls chosen to work in Kanada pulled her to the window of her barrack. "I did not want to look for I was too afraid of what I might see."

"You must see this, do you hear, you must," said Isa with whom I palled-up on the way, and who was now one of our little family of four.

I raised my head and there not fifty yards away was a sight that staggered me. I had seen much, but never, never anything like this. I stood as hypnotized. I could not move. I was actually witnessing with my very own eyes a murder, not of one person, but of hundreds of people, innocent people who had been led, mostly unsuspecting into a large hall. This was a sight that could *never* be forgotten. On the outside of the low building a ladder had been placed which reached up to a small opening. A figure in SS uniform climbed up briskly. At the top he pulled on a gas mask and gloves. Holding the opening with one hand, he pulled a bag out of his pocket, and swiftly threw the contents, a white powder, inside, shutting the opening immediately. In a flash he was down and, throwing the ladder on the lawn, ran away as if chased by a ghost.

At the same time the most terrifying screams echoed through the air, the desperate cries of suffocating people. I stood holding my breath, my hands pressed against my ears, but the cries were so loud, one would have thought the whole world must be able to hear them.

Someone shook me. "It's over. Do you hear me, it's quiet. They are all dead now."

It had taken about five to eight minutes. . . .

I was still unable to take my eyes off one point. Everyone stared at one thing and now it happened. Smoke was beginning to billow out of the tall chimneys and soon sharp flames shot up six feet high into the sky. The black smoke became thicker and darker and choking, bringing with it a most peculiar smell, that of burning bodies, a smell of a singeing chicken would be comparable, but this stench of burn fat and hair was unbearable. So what we had heard in the other camp really was true—the rumours were not exaggerated. Here were the death factories. As evening came, the whole sky was red, as if lit up. Smoke and flames poured out of all the chimneys which surrounded our little camp. It seemed as if blood was coming out, as indeed it was. No one slept that night, we just stood by the windows listening and watching. [72]

Yet even a life adjoining the daily ritualism of genocide became normal. After a few months in Kanada, Kitty's amazement and horror had waned and she began to adapt to a jumbled world in which the small comforts of

Kanada incongruously mingled with the extermination next door. In this insane, Kafkaesque realm, the horrifying had become a matter of course, and the grotesque an everyday normality that the privileged, well-fed and well-dressed inmates of Kanada tried to ignore. Kitty remembered that summer as beautiful. "It was very hot and we on night shift found it difficult to sleep during the day. We were usually up early in the afternoon and on fine days we lay outside on the lovely lawn that surrounded our hut, sunbathing and splashing ourselves with water to cool off. We would dance and sing and even form a little band. We began to laugh and joke again. In the evenings and Sunday afternoons the orchestra from the men's camp came over to play for us. Once we even staged a three-act play. I spent many hours reading the books that I had found while making up bundles." Yet this idyll was the minuscule eye of a hurricane of destruction. "All around us were screams, death, smoking chimneys making the air black and heavy with soot and the smell of burning bodies. I think our main fight was for sanity and so we laughed and sang with the burning hell around us."

> It was incredible, we lay sunbathing and not two yards away, divided only by a thin wire fence, columns of people of all nationalities were passing by on their way to the sauna and the gas chambers. . . . Most of them walked in unsuspecting. Only some looked uneasy. How could they imagine what was to come? Everything had been so cunningly disguised. They looked at us—we appeared well fed and well dressed, even sunbathing. It is true the queer building puzzled them and often they would ask us when passing, "Do you girls work in this factories over there?" pointing to the crematoria.
>
> Or they would ask, "What is being made in those factories?"[73]

The second question seems naïve, yet touches on a deep and disturbing truth. The combination of the crematoria and Kanada was a production line. The ashes of the deportees were only the waste generated in the production of philanthropies, charities and benefits. As far as the Germans were concerned, the western edge of Auschwitz–Birkenau was the core of one of the largest altruistic enterprises the world had ever seen. To understand this scandalous claim, we must think about the function of Kanada in more detail. Kanada—"our Canada, which smells not of maple forests but of French perfume'[74]—was an emporium that consisted of thirty large storehouses. It was the center of an enormous network for the redistribution of the last belongings of the deportees.[75] Throughout the killing operations the most valuable things (money, gold, gems and diamonds) found their way to the Reichsbank and anything that was still useful to selected charities such as the Volksdeutsche Mittelstelle—the Ethnic German Welfare Organization, VoMi. To give an idea of the gains: the value of the money, gold and precious stones "recovered" in 1942 and 1943 in the Operation Reinhard camps, the competition so to speak, was RM 178,745,960.59 (or about $70,000,000); in the year 1942 the VoMi took delivery of 211 freight cars of clothing. When the Germans evacuated Auschwitz in early 1945 they burned most of the barracks; the six warehouses that remained still contained an astonishing collection of goods which included 348,820 complete men's outfits, 836,255 complete women's outfits, 5525 pairs of women's shoes, 38,000 pairs of men's shoes, 13,964 carpets, innumerable sets of false teeth, spectacles, shaving brushes and so on.

The duly audited lists of valuables, goods and commodities and the barracks full of useful items served an important function in the process of extermination. The arrest, deportation and extermination of the Jews was a matter of administrative routine that the Nazis preferred to handle with a minimum of discussion. Thus these actions did not allow the perpetrators to receive a sense of confirmation through public acknowledgement. This was different with the booty. Peter J. Haas observed in his *Morality after Auschwitz: The Radical Challenge of Nazi Ethic* (1988) that in contrast to the extermination of the Jews the disposition of their possessions was given a lot of thought and, at times, even became a matter of heated debate.

> The considerable care taken to identify, legally collect, and then distribute the economic plunder is striking when seen in contrast to the almost nonchalant way in which the owners were dispatched. From the point of view of energy expended, the Holocaust in Germany was not a matter of killing Jews but a matter of appropriating and distributing their property, the murder of the owners being just a step in the process.[76]

The inventories of Kanada were, in fact, the last stage in a professionally managed process of expropriation that had began in the late thirties in Germany with the forced registration of enterprises, bank accounts, securities, insurance policies, trusts, real estate, art collections and that ended in the early forties with the removal of the gold caps and fillings from the mouths of the gassed victims. Not only institutionalized greed motivated this process of dispossession. The large-scale disendowment of Jewish property was understood as the justified repossession of the pilfered inheritance of the German people—the Jew was after all per definition a filcher, a swindler and a fence. While few were prepared to state unequivocally that the all Jews deserved to be killed—many "decent" Nazis preferred not to be told about the "unknown destination" of their Jewish neighbors—it was clear that the alienation of Jewish property and possessions and the proper restitution of these effects to the people through the state and selected charities restored a balance of justice. Therefore Kanada could become for the SS leadership a symbol of what was unconditionally right in the war against the Jews and, simultaneously, it also testified through its efficiency to the unselfishness and disinterestedness of the men who had managed the genocide.

Himmler's secret speech given at the Gruppenführer meeting at Poznań on October 4, 1943 makes this clear. The lengthy review of the achievements of the SS began with a recapitulation of the ethics of the SS. "One basic principle must be absolute for the SS man: we must be honest, decent, loyal, and comradely to members of our own blood and to nobody else. . . . Our concern, our duty is to our people and our blood; it is for them that we are to provide and plan, to work and to fight, and for nothing else. Towards anything else we can be indifferent."[77] In the course of the speech Himmler briefly touched on the extermination of the Jews. He acknowledged that even the slightest reference to this "really grave matter" was unusual, and that he raised it at all was exceptional. The Reichsführer-SS compared the silence that enveloped the war against the Jews with the silence that surrounded the role of the SS in the infamous "Night of the Long Knives," the purge against the SA in 1934. "We never talked about this and never will. It was the tact which I am glad to say is a matter of course to us that made us never discuss it among ourselves, never talk about it. Each of us shuddered." After this introduction he congratulated the SS men on having faced the horrors of the extermination. "Most of you must know what it means to see a hundred corpses lie side by side, or five hundred, or a thousand. To have stuck this out and—excepting cases of human weakness—to have kept our integrity, that is what has made us hard. In our history, this is an unwritten and never-to-be-written page of glory." The elimination of the Jews had prevented the military disintegration of Germany, so Himmler argued, "If the Jews were still ensconced in the body of the German nation, we probably would have reached the 1916–17 stage by now." Yet even Himmler felt uncomfortable with a justification of the "resettlement" which declared all Jews as "secret saboteurs, agitators and demagogues." And so he quickly turned to the question of the spoils. Kanada became a source of moral justification. Its existence and success proved that individual opportunism had (in general) not interfered with duty.

> The wealth [the Jews] had we have taken from them. I have issued a strict order, carried out by SS-Obergruppenführer Pohl, that this wealth in its entirety is to be turned over to the Reich as a matter of course. We have taken none of it for ourselves. Individuals who transgress will be punished in accordance with an order I issued at the beginning, threatening that whoever

takes so much as one mark is a dead man. A number of SS men—not very many—have transgressed, and they will die without mercy. We had the moral right, we had the duty toward our people, to kill this people which wanted to kill us. But we do not have the right to enrich ourselves with so much as a fur, a watch, a mark, or a cigarette or anything else. Having exterminated a germ, we do not want in the end, to be infected by the germ and die of it. I will not stand by and let even a small rotten spot develop or take hold. Wherever it may form, we together will cauterize it. All in all, however, we can say that we have carried out this heaviest of our tasks in a spirit of love for our people. And our inward being, our soul, our character has not suffered injury from it.[78]

The gaschambers were beyond speech and therefore beyond justification. Kanada fitted in the world of discourse, yet one which did not follow the usual patterns of cause and effect. As the origin of the goods and valuables was unmentionable, despoliation metamorphosed into reparation, robbery into charity. Kanada's role as the center of a network of charity and benevolence showed that the organizers of the genocide had acted "in spirit of love for our people," and that was the only thing that counted. The fate of the Jews was a matter of indifference and, if some did feel some guilt, then the giant potlach that issued from Kanada served as a powerful means of expiation. As Norman O. Brown wrote, "the man who has stolen someone's elses property usually seeks to get rid of his guilt by sharing it with others.[79] Kanada allowed the SS to transform the whole of Germany into a community of shared guilt.

Himmler's attitude also revealed another way that the bureaucrats of the Judeocide dealt with the question of guilt. Himmler did not reject the call of conscience. To the contrary: he actually suggested that the SS was the conscience of the nation and expected every SS man to be a decent person. He suggested that it was proper to limit the pertinence of conscience to one specific class of actions: those deeds that directly affected the life of the Volk. In his speech Himmler illustrated the range of his conscience as follows. "Whether 10,000 Russian females drop from exhaustion while building an anti-tank ditch interests me only insofar as the anti-tank ditch gets finished for Germany's sake. . . . If someone were to come to me and say, 'I cannot build the anti-tank ditch with women and children; it is inhuman, they will die in the process,' then I would have to say, 'You are a murderer of your own blood, for if the anti-tank ditch is not built, German soldiers will die, and they are sons of German mothers. They are our own blood!' "[80] Thus the question of guilt was discussed only in relationship to the German Volk, the community to which the acting individual was bound. The fate of the outsider was of no consequence as it was outside one's moral and ethical universe. And all Jews were per definition outsiders. Stripped of all their belongings they had become as superfluous as garbage. First placed out of view in the refuse heaps of the ghettos, the human waste that had issued from the assembly line of Kanada was finally dumped on the conveyer belt which led into the great incinerators.

The Barracks

Even garbage had still its use, especially after 1942. As the demands on the German war economy increased, its stock of natural and human resources decreased. And as more and more "Ersatz" products began to fill the shelves of German shops, so more and more "Ersatz" people began to fill the labour gap. An important German industry such as I.G. Farben invested 700 million RM in a large synthetic-rubber plant at Auschwitz (Buna IV). The money was spent on the factory, not on the inmates who built it or the slaves who laboured there. The average life expectancy of a prisoner "rented" out by the SS for a daily rate of between 1.50 and 5.00 RM was between three and four months.[81] The situation for those who slaved in the Krupp, the Siemens-Schuckert or the Herrmann Göring Works was not much better. One of the inmates who was selected for work in the Krupp factories at Auschwitz remembered how "beating and torture administered by the Krupp supervisory personnel was not uncommon. At work we were Krupp's charges. . . . Hungry, cold, stiff from hard labour, lack of sleep and beating, and in constant fear of our masters we were forced to exert all our remaining energies to make guns for our oppressors. We worked until we dropped." This witness, Theodor Lehmann (born Tadeusz Goldsztajn), summarized the situation as one in which the inmates were less than slaves. In ancient days masters had taken a minimal care to ensure the survival of their "property." In factories around Auschwitz such care was bestowed only on the mechanical equipment. "The machinery had to be operated with care, oiled, greased and allowed to rest; its life span was protected. We, on the other hand, were like a bit of sandpaper, which, rubbed a few times, becomes useless and is thrown away to be burned with the garbage."[82] Yet during their few months of productive existence the captives needed to be sheltered from the elements. And thus the theoretical interest in the minimum dwelling and the *Existenzminimum*, which had fuelled so much of the most enlightened architectural discourse in the late 1920s, found at last a most practical implication in the design of the barracks that were to house the slave population.

In Chapter Three I discussed how the architects of Auschwitz designated the standard design of army horse stables as a proper solution to the housing problem in the camp. Within these flimsy and shoddy constructions people were forced to live in a situation of abject degradation. They were heaped up as if they were goods in dirty and cold spaces too small to hold even the volume of their bodies. The Polish novelist Tadeusz Borowski (1922–51), who spent one year in Auschwitz, described in his essay "Auschwitz, Our Home" the living conditions in the barracks:

> If the barrack walls were suddenly to fall away, many thousands of people, packed together, squeezed tightly in their bunks, would remain suspended in mid-air. Such a sight would be more gruesome than the medieval paintings of the Last Judgement. For one of the ugliest sights to a man is that of another man sleeping on his tiny portion of the bunk, of the space which he must occupy, because he has a body—a body that has been exploited to the utmost: with a number tattooed on it to save on dog tags, with just enough sleep at night to work during the day, and just enough time to eat. And just enough food so it will not die wastefully. As for actual living there is only one place for it—a piece of bunk. The rest belongs to the camp, the Fatherland. But not even this small space, not the shirt you wear, nor the spade you work with are your own. If you get sick, everything is taken away from you: your clothes, your camp, your "organized" scarf, your handkerchief. If you die—your gold teeth, already recorded in the camp inventory, are extracted. Your body is burned and your ashes are used to fertilize fields or fill in the ponds. Although in fact so much fat and bone is wasted in the burning, so much flesh, so much heat.[83]

The situation in the barracks seemed extraordinary and totally discontinuous with the pretty *Siedlungen* that Hitler had built for the Aryan workers. It reflected, however, in a deeper sense the essence of what life in the Heimat itself had become. While Nazi propaganda made much of the "clarity, beauty and harmony" of the several hundred settlements created by the Labour Front,[84] it failed to mention that the price for the little red-roofed houses was the loss of all privacy. Referring to a persistent theme in the dreams of her patients, the psychiatrist Charlotte Beradt, who worked in Germany until 1939, defined the situation of the average German as that of "a life without walls." The metaphor referred to a dream one of her patients, a forty-five-year-old doctor had in the second year of the Thousand Year Reich.

> It was about nine o'clock in the evening. My consultations were over, and I was just stretching out on the couch to relax with a book on Matthias Grünewald, when suddenly the walls of my room and then my apartment disappeared. I looked around and discovered to my horror that as far as the eye could see no apartment had walls any more. Then I heard a loudspeaker boom, "According to the decree of the 17th of this month on the Abolition of Walls . . ."[85]

This Kafkaesque dream described, as Charlotte Beradt maintained, "the structure of a reality that was just on the verge of becoming a nightmare."[86] With the symbolic disappearance of the walls the sacred Nomos vanished also and with that the boundary that had given householders the rights of citizenship and the assurance of justice since the days of Solon. Beradt's investigations suggest that the Germans realized that the doomed world of the camps existed in a continuum with their own grotesque reality, a plenum of betrayal in which colleagues testified against colleagues, friends beared witness against friends and children informed on parents.

The Cemetery

The chimneys of the crematoria are the powerful symbols of Auschwitz. They stand for massive destruction, for effacement without trace. They proclaim the worldview that based its uncompromising stance and infallible truth on its ability to identify and purge the human waste from society. In a formal sense Auschwitz had no necropolis: the incinerators of Germany's garbage heap made a landfill unnecessary. The sacred soil was not to be poisoned with Jewish remains. Yet in an architectonic sense the death camp had its own graveyard. Just as the Athenian burial ground was outside the city's walls, so also was Auschwitz's necropolis. It stretched from its electrified barbed-wire boundary to the outermost borders of the German *Lebensraum*, only now the cemetery consisted not of tombs, graves and crypts, but of all the shtetls and villages, towns and cities of Europe.

The metaphor might be explored at different levels, but its most obvious meaning will suffice. In classical Athens the necropolis had stood for the notion that an accommodation with the immutable past was the foundation of the city's greatness. Only after the Furies had been propitiated had Athena been able to impose the rule of law. In Nazi Germany, history too was the basis of politics. This history was not buried into an immutable past: the triumph of historicism had released the sanguinary Furies from their agreement with the goddess of civilization. The implacable law of blood had become, again, the contending law of history.

For Hitler the relationship between politics, history and the extermination of Jews was straightforward. "Politics is history in the making. History itself is the presentation of the course of a people's struggle for existence."[87] His view of history embraced the radical flank of the historicist view of the world. Its roots were in Herder's understanding of the unique nature of each *Volk*. In the preface to the 1938 edition of *Der Mythus des 20. Jahrhunderts* the Nazi Party ideologist Alfred Rosenberg (1893–1946) described Herder as "a teacher specially ordained for our time." Rosenberg

credited Herder with having discovered how a national consciousness
constituted the "life-endowed link" between the individual and the *Volk*.
"Herder consciously heaped scorn upon the pretentious savants of 'progress' who sought to measure the forms of life by the infantile scale of the
Enlightenment. He then uttered a phrase which is relevant to our own age
and our joyful message: '*Each nation has its centre of happiness within itself
as each sphere has its own centre of gravity.*' "[88] For Herder this nation had
been a linguistic community; for the Nazis it had become a racial *Volk*.
Under the influence of the political brand of Darwinism propagated by the
German zoologist Ernst Haeckel (1834–1919), the *Volk* had become a
biological entity. Haeckel had felt no hesitation to apply his insights into
the world of vegetation and animals to the history of civilization as such.
"None but the idealist scholar, who closes his eyes to the real truth, or the
priest, who tries to keep his spiritual flock in ecclesiastical leading-strings,
can any longer tell the fable of the 'moral ordering of the world.' It exists
neither in natural history, nor in the history of civilization. The terrible and
ceaseless 'Struggle for Existence' gives the real impulse to the blind course
of the world.[89] Haeckel had posited as a scientific truth that the laws of
nature taught that some races or nations were destined to surpass and even
to destroy others. These ideas influenced Hitler's understanding of world
history. Hitler ascribed to every organism a primeval sense of purpose
rooted in an unlimited instinct of self-preservation. Projecting billions
upon billions of these elemental aims and powers on the limited *Lebensraum* of a small and exactly measured sphere, he postulated that a basic
compulsion to engage in the struggle for existence framed a history understood as a turbulent process of becoming and the passing away of thousand
upon thousand of species from which man emerged to evolve in different
clans, tribes, peoples and states engaged in an eternal struggle because
they are subject to the iron dictate of fate which declared an eternal and
ferocious strife as the origin of culture and the basis of a moral order.
Following nineteenth-century German anthropological theory, Hitler
assumed that the measure of war which a people had faced in its history
determined the level of its development. Geographically isolated nations
had faced little challenge and were therefore apt to exhibit such characteristics as moronic indolence and physical lethargy. Nations exposed to
others could not afford mental inertness and want of activity. If they were
to survive, they had to rouse themselves from stagnation. Constant and
all-devouring war had been the fated tribulation of the German nation as
it lived in the exposed lands where the hordes from the east, the armies
from the west and the raiders from the north collided. Thus within the
empiricist comparison of stronger and weaker unfolded a rational analogy
of higher and lower which, in turn, petrified into the moral distinction of
good and evil. In this *Weltanschauung* the presence of *Kultur* implied the

victory of the stronger over a weaker foe. Hence the crystallization of a nation's elation in stone sanctioned and sanctified military conquest and political victory as the ascendancy of order over chaos and the good over the wicked.[90] In Herder's history of the world the nations had developed side by side; in Haeckel's evolutionary development they were engaged in universal strife. Nazi historiography described this struggle in gnostic terms: amid all the hostilities there was one war in which the relativism of opposing claims transcended into a global war between Evil and Good, Matter and Spirit. This war was the battle between the Jew and the Teuton.

The illusive and phantasmal understanding of history as a protracted Armageddon derived from Richard Wagner (1813–83)[91] and had been given its first full exposition by Wagner's son-in-law Houston Chamberlain (1855–1927). Chamberlain was a son of a British admiral who had moved to Germany in 1885 to become a staunch German patriot and a pan-German.[92] His qualifications as a historian were impeccable in an age that had preferred to see history as the study of the life and death of organisms: he had enjoyed a university education in the fields of systematic botany, geology, astronomy, anatomy and human physiology. In *Die Grundlagen des XIX Jahrhunderts* (1899)—published in 1912 in English as *The Foundations of the Nineteenth Century* (and the source of inspiration of Rosenberg's *Mythus*)—Chamberlain identified the achievements of antiquity as the soil in which the foundations of the modern age were sunk. Yet antagonism between the two heirs of antiquity constituted the actual foundations of the history of the West. In the chaos that followed the collapse of the Greco-Roman civilization towered, like "sharply defined rock[s] amid the formless oceans," two racially conscious peoples: the Jewish and the Teutonic races. Chamberlain believed that these two nations were in everything polar opposites. "To this day these two powers, Jews and Teutonic races, stand, wherever the recent spread of Chaos has not blurred their features, now as friendly, now as hostile, but always as alien forces face to face."[93] Their antagonism had intensified in what Chamberlain identified as the "Jewish Age": the nineteenth century. Invoking Herder's observation that the Jews were an "alien people," Chamberlain concluded that "this alien people has become precisely in the course of the nineteenth century disproportionately important and in many spheres actually dominant constituant of our life. . . . The Indo-European, moved by ideal motives, opened the gates in friendship: the Jew rushed in like an enemy, stormed all positions, and planted the flag of his, to us, alien nature—I will not say on the ruins, but on the breaches of our genuine individuality." Chamberlain admitted a certain admiration for the Jews, especially as they knew political, economic and cultural triumphs were only steps towards the more important and ultimately decisive biological victory.

The Jews deserve admiration, for they have acted with absolute consistency according to the logic and the truth of their own individuality, and never for a moment have they allowed themselves to forget the sacredness of physical laws because of foolish humanitarian day-dreams which they shared only when such a policy was to their advantage. Consider with what mastery they use the law of blood to extend their power: the principal stem remains spotless, not a drop of strange blood comes in; as it stands in the *Thora*, "A bastard shall not enter into the congregation of the Lord; even to the tenth generation he shall not enter into the congregation of the Lord" (*Deuteronomy* xxiii, 2); in the meantime, however, thousands of side branches are cut off and employed to infect the Indo-Europeans with Jewish blood. If that were to go on for a few centuries, there would be in Europe only one single people of pure race, that of the Jews, all the rest would be a herd of pseudo-Hebraic mestizos, a people beyond all doubt degenerate physically, mentally and morally.[94]

Thus Chamberlain thought to have rediscovered the structure of history. If, however, the "entrance of the Jew into European history had, as Herder said, signified the entrance of an alien element," the entrance of the Germanic people into the history of the world was to be "the very reverse. . . . It is only shameful indolence of thought, or disgraceful historical falsehood, that can fail to see in the entrance of the Germanic tribes into the history of the world the rescuing of agonizing humanity from the clutches of the everlasting bestial."[95] The Teuton had not yet completed his entrance into history. A final battle awaited him.

In the nineteenth century, as in all former centuries, but of course with widely different grouping and with constantly changing relative power, there stood side by side in Europe these "heirs"—the chaos of half-breeds, relics of the former Roman Empire, the Germanising of which is falling off—the Jews—and the Germans, whose contamination by mixture with the half-breeds and the descendants of other Non-Aryan races is on the increase. No arguing about "Humanity" can alter the fact that this means a struggle. Where the struggle is not waged with cannon-balls, it goes on silently in the heart of society by marriages, by the annihilation of distances which furthers intercourse, by the varying powers of resistance in the different types of mankind, by the shifting of wealth, by the birth of new influences and the disappearance of others, and by many other motive powers. But this struggle, silent though it be, is above all others a struggle for life and death.[96]

These were some of the conclusions which a man who defined himself as a "modest historian" thought proper to draw from his reading of history. His paltry musings on history found a well-prepared niche in Hitler's *Weltanschauung*.

Chamberlain's comprehensive and cogent reconstruction of a *Weltge-schichte* offered a Teutonic version of biblical history. Athens and Rome constituted Paradise, the fall of Rome the Fall, and the "Jewish Question" gave a providential order to the history that followed. Yet that history was essentially the story of the Teutons, as in the biblical view of the world the history of the world had been essentially the history of the Jews. Chamberlain believed that everything that had preceded the Teutonic contribution to history had been merely Prolegomena. "True history, the history which still controls the rhythm of our hearts and circulates in our veins, inspiring us to new hope and new creation, begins at the moment when the Teuton with his masterful hand lays grip upon the legacy of antiquity."[97] In Judeo-Christian historiography the history of the world first concentrated in the Jews, then in the remnant and finally in Christ; Hitler's reading of Chamberlain followed this pattern. The history of the world had become the history of the Teutons, and the history of the Teutons had become the history of Hitler. His hand was to be the "masterful hand" to undo the destruction of Athens and the fall of Rome.

Just as the perceived struggle for existence that had given structure to history had been waged on a biologically defined battleground, so the continuation of that war would follow racial principles. In practice this meant that Jews were sent to Auschwitz for the crime of being born from Jewish parents. For Pericles the Athenian necropolis stood for the Athenians who had bequeathed the city to his own generation. The stelai admonished the living not to forsake their responsibility to the past. In their effort to reconstruct the fivesquare city within a historicist perspective the Nazis built a gigantic necropolis in the form of amassed genealogical data. A person's fate was to be decided by her blood, and her blood by her family tree. Those who had been born from "Aryan" parents were fit to inherit the land; they could share in the blood of the sixteen (or 1,800,000) martyrs and take part in the Teutonic resurrection. As we have seen, the stela of their new order was the Blood Flag. Those who had been born from "non-Aryan" parents were excluded, enslaved and, if born from Jewish parents, doomed. The stela of their new order was to be a *stella*, the Latin word for "Star." Its epitaph read "Jude," "Juif," "Jood," . . . "Jew." It meant death. And as the Athenian necropolis had given access to the Asty, so the roads that ran through this European necropolis of racial designations led to the gate of the only real city that Nazism built.

The Acropolis

Auschwitz's Acropolis was of course the crematoria with their chimneys, the destiny of all those who arrived on the ramp, the destiny of all the inmates. In a fundamental sense it was also the destiny of Germany. The Nazi ideology claimed that the enduring basis of the life of the *Volk* was its struggle for existence, and therefore its true Acropolis was not the place where victory was preserved, but where it was created. The architecture of Germania, which celebrated the sacrifices of the past, was meaningless if not buttressed by the promise of the state's continued capability to kill in the future. The monument would only stand if supported by the instrumental logic of a modern bureaucratic system and the technological infrastructure of a modern industrial state. Architectonically this capability was expressed in the chimneys of the crematoria. The importance of the chimneys seems odd if seen from a purely pragmatic perspective. After all, most victims were killed in the underground gaschambers and not in the crematoria ovens. Yet gaschambers did not carry the metaphorical significance of the flue pipes: their very uniqueness preserved their singularity that did not allow for metaphorical connection or symbolic interpretation. The smokestacks of the crematoria belong to the common world. Their ordinariness allowed them to become emblematic for the extermination camps as such. They aptly evoked the industrial processes without which the war against the Jews could not have been waged or won. Therefore all efforts to come to terms with the Holocaust as a catastrophe of Western civilization (and not as a merely Jewish tragedy) ultimately centers on the chimneys. For Henry Feingold "the Final Solution marked the juncture where the European industrial system went awry; instead of enhancing life, which was the original hope of the Enlightenment, it began to consume itself." Therefore Auschwitz was "a mundane extension of the modern factory system."

> Rather than producing goods, the raw material was human beings and the end product was death, so many units per day marked carefully on the manager's production charts. The chimneys, the very symbol of the modern factory system, poured forth acrid smoke produced by burning human flesh. The brilliantly organized railroad grid of modern Europe carried a new kind of raw material to the factories. It did so in the same manner as with other cargo. In the gas chambers the victims inhaled noxious gas generated by prussic acid pellets, which were produced by the advanced chemical industry of Germany. Engineers designed the crematoria; managers designed the system of bureaucracy that worked with a zest and efficiency more backward nations would envy. Even the overall plan itself was a reflection of the modern scientific spirit gone awry.[98]

Feingold touched an essential aspect of Auschwitz. As a manifestation of Germany's technological prowess, bureaucratic discipline and ideological determination it attested to the leadership's confidence that the nation would persist in the face of the biological assault described by Chamberlain. The stacks were not only metaphors however. Their construction marked the final perfection of the death camp as an instrument of extermination.

The first death camps (Belzec, Sobibor and Treblinka) did not have the sophisticated smokestacked crematoria that were to become the symbol of the architectural contribution to the Nazi destruction of the Jews. The motivation that structured their design was the production of places where large groups of people could be killed efficiently. Yet soon after the first of these, Belzec, began operation it became clear that the real problem which was to face the managers of the death camps had not been addressed. In those early months of 1942 it became clear that the efficiency of a murder site was not measured by its capacity to kill, but its ability to clean up the resulting mess. Franz Stangl, who as commander of Sobibor and later Treblinka was to make great efforts to rationalize the process of destruction, recalled in an interview with Gitta Sereny how he had become aware of this problem. One month after Belzec had become operational, he had been ordered to report to Christian Wirth, the builder and first commander of Belzec and the inspector of the Operation Reinhard death camps (Belzec, Sobibor and Treblinka). On his arrival in Belzec Stangl found the whole operation in a state of chaos.

> "I can't describe to you what it was like," Stangl said; he spoke slowly now, in his more formal German, his faced strained and grim. He passed his hand over his eyes and rubbed his forehead. "I went there by car. As one arrived, one first reached Belzec railway station, on the left side of the road. The camp was on the same side, but up a hill. The Kommandantur was 200 meters away, on the other side of the road. It was a one-storey building. The smell . . ." he said, "Oh God, the smell. It was everywhere. Wirth wasn't in his office. I remember, they took me to him . . . he was standing on a hill, next to the pits . . . the pits . . . full . . . they were full. I can't tell you; not hundreds, thousands, thousands of corpses . . . oh God. That's where Wirth told me—he said that was what Sobibor was for. And he was putting me officially in charge."[99]

In a later interview, Stangl recalled some different aspects of his encounter with the mass graves.

> Wirth wasn't in his office; they said he was up in the camp. I asked whether I should go up there and they said, "I wouldn't if I were you—he's mad with fury. It isn't healthy to go near him." I asked what was the matter. The man I was talking to said that one of the pits had overflowed. They had put too many

corpses in it and putrefaction had progressed too fast, so that the liquid under-
neath had pushed the bodies on top up and over and the corpses had rolled
down the hill. I saw some of them—oh God, it was awful. A bit later Wirth
came down. And that's when he told me.[100]

The problem of the disposal of the corpses was never satisfactorily solved.
Originally the bodies were buried in large pits that were dug at some
distance from the gaschambers. The operation was labour intensive. SS-
Unterscharführer Franz Suchomel, employed in Treblinka, remembered
that "the bodies piled up around the gas chambers and stayed there for
days. Under this pile of bodies was a cesspool three inches deep, full of
blood, worms and shit."[101] But even if the bodies were buried in time,
there were problems. The disintegration of the corpses produced gasses
that destabilized the earth cover. Odours escaped and more and more dirt
had to be heaped on top of the graves. The earth refused to participate
in the crime. In the summer of 1942 the first full-scale cremation of the
bodies was attempted. The operation began as an effort to obliterate traces
of the mass shootings of Jews undertaken by the *Einsatzgruppen* of the SS in
the occupied parts of the Soviet Union. The leader of this operation, known
as "Sonderaktion 1005" was SS-Standartenführer Paul Blobel. He was
an architect by profession. After experimentation he found that the most
economical method of corpse-disposal was cremation in open fireplaces.
These fireplaces could be open pits or so-called "roasters," grates constructed of rails supported by concrete posts. The first death camp where
the Germans applied this method was Sobibor. In the summer of 1942
there was a long period of hot weather. The buried bodies started to swell,
and the soil that covered the mass graves started to rise above the surrounding fields. One of the Jewish prisoners, Leon Feldhendler, remembered that in that summer "out of the soil, blood and a bad odour of gas
began to surface; terrible smells spread over the whole camp, penetrating
everything. The water in Sobibor became rancid. This forced the Germans
to build a crematorium. It was a large pit with a roaster above it. The
bodies were thrown on the roaster. The fire was ignited from beneath, and
petrol was poured on the corpses."[102] In this way the burial pits were
slowly emptied. From then on great care was taken to cremate the corpses
of the new "arrivals" immediately after their extermination. This method
was consequently adopted in Treblinka and Majdanek.

Auschwitz–Birkenau was the only death camp where the process
of extermination received a consistent and, from the perspective of its
builders, largely satisfactory architectural solution. Unlike in the other
death camps, the building activities in Auschwitz were centrally planned in
Berlin and received the greatest possible professional attention. The Berlin

design office was Amtsgruppe C of the SS-Wirtschafts-Verwaltungshaupt-
ampt (Official Group C of the SS Economic–Administrative Main Office).
The chief architect of this office was SS-Gruppenführer Doctor Ingenieur
Hans Kammler. His deputy in Auschwitz was SS-Sturmbannführer Karl
Bischoff, a capable architect who arrived on October 1, 1941 to take
charge of the local Zentralbauleitung (Central Building Office) in Auschwitz. Bischoff oversaw large building activities: in 1942 and 1943 he
commanded a daily average of 8000 prisoners and roughly 800 civilian
workers. In 1942 most of the building activities concerned the creation of
a camp in Auschwitz–Birkenau with a capacity of 200,000 prisoners. The
combination of the design-skills of Amtsgruppe C, the Zentralbauleitung
and outside firms, and the availability of sufficient manpower, allowed
Bischoff to plan a final architectural solution to the problem of corpse
disposal. Having studied the procedures in the Operation Reinhard camps,
he and his colleagues prepared the designs for two large crematoria built
over large underground killing facilities and two smaller one-storey establishments. All four of them would be able to cremate large number of corpses quickly and relatively discreetly (the four crematoria were designed
to cremate 4,416 corpses in twenty-four hours). The designs were a compromise between capacity and fuel efficiency (which had become more
important because of the unreliable supply). In the summer of 1942 the
Zentralbauleitung invited the construction firms Hütte Hoch und Tiefbau
AG and Schlesische Industriebau Lenz & Co. AG in Katowice to submit
tenders for the project. The two firms had constructed buildings in Auschwitz before. They now were asked to undertake the building, while the
installations of the gaschambers and the ovens in the crematoria were to be
forwarded by the firm Topf and Sons from Erfurt, who were also to install
them on the spot. Lenz declined the invitation on the grounds of of shortage
of manpower. Therefore the Zentralbauleitung accepted the offer of the
firm Hütte with a construction estimate for 133,756.65 RM and asked
the firm to start building at once.[103]

The result was the four main crematoria at the western edge of Birkenau.
As long as the total number of victims per day remained below 4000, the
crematoria could handle the load, and the kind of jams and breakdowns
associated with the Operation Reinhard camps could be avoided. The
infamous selections on the ramp were to prevent an overloading of the
extermination machine. If, on occasions, the number of arrivals exceeded
the capacity of the crematoria (the gaschambers could "handle" a much
larger number of victims *per diem*), the excess was channelled into the
camp, which became a kind of safety valve or holding pen for the machinery of destruction. There were still doubts, however, that the combination
of the four crematoria and the holding pen would be sufficient in all situa-

tions. Even before the completion of the first of the new crematoria Bischoff began to prepare plans for an alternative safety valve. He envisioned a cheap and primitive arrangement that could be used in emergencies. Bischoff wrote a memorandum (12 february 1943) to the camp's commander Höss in which he suggested that a new type of crematorium should be developed that combined the immense capacity of the cremation pits with the fuel efficiency of the crematoria installed by the firm Topf and Sons.

> Referring to the conversation of your correspondent of Jan. 29, 1943, with Ing. Prüfer from the firm Topf and Sons, we have considered the possibility of constructing Crematorium VI (an open place of cremation 48,75 by 3,76 metres). The Central Building Section had, in connection with the project, commissioned the firm Topf and Sons to elaborate a plan for an open place of cremation, which plan you will find enclosed.[104]

The design of Crematorium VI was simple: it was to be shaped like an oven placed in a deep trench. It slopes were to be paved with fire-resistant bricks. In August, 1944 the anticipated bottleneck finally occurred. One day that month the total number of victims reached a peak of 24,000. The combined resources of the four sophisticated crematoria did not suffice. The Zentralbauleitung decided to return to the primitive methods developed by Blobel in the summer of 1942. They dug six huge pits beside Crematorium V and reopened old pits in the wood. Thus pit burning became the chief method of corpse disposal again. While not so sophisticated as the Crematorium VI that Bischoff had designed in collaboration with Ing. Prüfer, the pits were an improvement over those used two years earlier. They had indentations at one end from which the boiling human fat drained off. The Jewish inmates of the so-called "Special Squads" collected it, mixed it with oil and alcohol and poured it over the bodies. At intervals flamethrowers were brought in to destroy the rotten remains. Filip Müller, one of the prisoners in Auschwitz entrusted with the task to keep the corpses burning in the fall of 1944, recalled in his memoir that "the corpses in the pit looked as if they had been chained together."

> Tongues of a thousand tiny blue—red flames were licking at them. The fire grew fiercer and flames leapt higher and higher. Under the ever- increasing heat a few of the dead began to stir, writhing as though with some unbearable pain, arms and legs straining in slow motion, and even their bodies straightening up a little, hesitant and with difficulty, almost as if with their last strength they were trying to rebel against their doom. Eventually the fire became so fierce that the corpses were enveloped by flames. Blisters which had formed on their skin burst one by one. Almost every corpse was covered with black scorch marks and glistened as if it had been greased. The searing heat had burst open their

bellies: there was the violent hissing and spluttering of frying in great heat. Boiling fat flowed into the pans on either side of the pit. Fanned by the wind, the flames, dark-red before, now took on a fiery white hue: the corpses were burning so fiercely that they were consumed by their own heat. The process of incineration took five to six hours. What was left barely filled a third of the pit. The shiny whitish-grey surface was strewn with countless skulls.[105]

The open pits had made the chimneys obsolete within two years of their construction. The demonic symbols of industrial power and logistical planning had been superseded by the traditional iconography of the satanic. A few months later SS men mined the crematoria and their chimneys, and destroyed them before the Soviet liberation of the camp. Only rubble remained, and a few recently closed pits. It was the absence of the chimneys that was to reveal a second significance. While they stood, the chimneys proclaimed the total commitment of the struggle against the Jewish meta-enemy. Having disappeared, it became difficult to believe that what had happened actually had transpired. The destruction of the crematoria when they had ceased to be useful guaranteed that the only enduring legacy of the history that had passed within their boundaries would be disbelief and silence.

As we have seen, there were no crematoria in the first three death camps. Initially the bodies were buried in mass graves. The Germans were still confident that they would write the history of the war. While expediency dictated that the operations of the camps remain secret for the time being, the perpetrators believed that their contribution to the victory of Germany would receive in the future the laurels it deserved. Kurt Gerstein, the head of the Technical Disinfection Services of the military arm of the SS, recalled in 1945 the admonition given in 1942 by SS-Brigadeführer Odilo Globocnik, one-time architect and the leader of "Operation Reinhard" (the organization created with the specific task to exterminate the Jews in the General Government).

He [Globocnik] said: "This is one of our highly secret matters, you might even say the most secret. Anyone who talks about it will be shot. Yesterday two more who couldn't keep their mouths shut were shot." He then explained to us: "At present, there are three establishments:

1. Belzec, on the Lublin—Lvov road. Maximum per day 15,000 persons (seen)!

2. Sobibor; I don't know the exact location; not seen; 20,000 persons per day.

3. Treblinka, 120 km NNE of Warsaw, 25,000 per day; seen.

4. Maidanek, near Lublin; seen in preparation."

I made a thorough inspection of all these camps, accompanied by Police Superintendent Wirth, the head of all these death factories. . . . Globocnik said: "You will have to disinfect large quantities of clothing, ten or twenty times the quantity resulting from the *Spinnstoffsammlung* (collection of clothing and textile articles) which is only being done to obscure the source of clothing taken from the Jews, Poles, Czechs, etc. Your other duty will be to improve the service in our gas chambers, which function on diesel engine exhaust. What is wanted is a more toxic gas that works faster, such as prussic acid. The Führer and Himmler—they were here on August 15, that is, the day before yesterday—instructed me to act as personal escort to those who have reason to view these establishments." Professor Pfannenstiel then asked: "But what did the Führer say?" Globocnik replied: "The Führer has ordered all action to be speeded up. Dr. Herbert Lindner, who was with us yesterday, asked me: 'But wouldn't it be wiser to cremate the corpses instead of burying them? Another generation may perhaps judge these things differently!' I replied: 'Gentlemen, if there should ever be, after us, a generation so cowardly and so soft that they could not understand our work, which is so good and so necessary, then, gentlemen, the entire National Socialist movement would have been in vain. On the contrary, we ought to bury bronze tablets stating that it was we who had the courage to carry out this gigantic task!' The Führer then said: 'Yes, my good Globocnik, you are right!' "[106]

Thus in the early days of the extermination program, when it still seemed that Germany would win the war, there was confidence that later generations would venerate the sites of the camps as the hallowed places where the final Armageddon between good and evil had resulted in a triumph of the Teutonic knight over the Jewish monster. After El-Alamein and Stalingrad the mood changed. Camouflage was to serve the present and the future. With no corpses as evidence, nobody would believe that Auschwitz had been more than a strictly-run internment camp for Russian prisoners of war, or that the Operation Reinhard camps had been more than the present patches of forest, planted in the winter of 1943. At the end of Chapter Three I quoted Thucydides' observations on the purpose of the Athenian Acropolis. He claimed that its ruins would falsify history because it would suggest that Athens had been more powerful than Sparta, while in fact it had been the other way around. The chimneys fulfilled a similar purpose. They were an important tool in the anticipated distortion of history that was being wrought. Alexander Donat, who ascribed his survival of the Warsaw Ghetto uprising, Majdanek and Auschwitz to his sense of having been "charged with the sacred mission of carrying the Ghetto's history through the flames and barbed wire until such time as I could hurl it into the face of the world", recorded in his *The Holocaust Kingdom* how a fellow inmate in Majdanek, Dr Schipper, anticipated the difficulties the survivors would have in preserving their story. Even if some were to survive, and "write the history of this period of blood and tears—and I firmly believe we will—who will believe us? Nobody will *want* to believe us, because our disaster is the disaster of the entire civilized world. . . . We'll have the thankless job of proving to a reluctant world that we are Abel, the murdered brother. . . ."[107] The Italian survivor Primo Levi recorded in his *The Drowned and the Saved* the following admonishment that the SS guards enjoyed to give to the prisoners.

> However this war may end, we have won the war against you; none of you will be left to bear witness, but even if someone were to survive, the world will not believe him. There will perhaps be suspicions, discussions, research by historians, but there will be no certainties, because we will destroy the evidence together with you. And even if some proof should remain and some of you survive, people will say the events you describe are too monstrous to be believed: they will say that they are the exaggerations of Allied propaganda and will believe us, who will deny everything, and not you. We will be the ones to dictate the history of the Lagers.[108]

Initially the purpose of the chimneys was to erase all traces that a Jewish people had been. The soil that, at the beginning of history, had received Abel's blood to bear witness against Cain was to enter the thousand-year epoch that was to end history untarnished and undefiled. Therefore the chimneys were also to be destroyed once the so-called Jewish Problem had been solved. Their absence was to erase all traces of the Judeocide. Shortly before the Russians liberated Auschwitz the SS blew up the crematoria. Only their foundations remain today. Yet the void they have left has the same meaning as the much admired remains of the Parthenon. As the SS men intended, the revisionist writings of men like Paul Rassinier, Thies Christophersen, Franz J. Scheidl and Arthur R. Butz, who claim that the death camps and their gas chambers were a hoax created by Zionist and others for political purposes, all invoke the non-presence of the crematoria as crucial evidence to support their thesis.[109] We may be grateful for the courage of the French historian Jean-Claude Pressac, who has dedicated himself to the reconstruction of the true history of Nazi architecture. His first study on the architectural history of the crematoria has, however, been ignored by the architectural historical establishment.[110] Yielding to the Nazi ruse, they prefer to study the architectural and urban delusions of Germania. The reality of Nazi architecture has yet to find its place in the ever growing literature on the subject.

The Agora

Auschwitz had its agora also: its daily roll-calls offered a counter-assembly to the annual party rallies in Nuremberg. In Nuremberg the Führer mustered the German masses as a preparation for politics; in the camp his henchmen took account of the defeated foe. The Nuremberg laws had forged the legal connection between the two places of assembly, and the power of antisemitic propaganda had forged the historical link. The Nazi re-education of the population according to the *Weltanschauung* of *Mein Kampf* had brought about that split that assigned the attributes of veracity, righteousness and purity to the self and those of treachery, greed, cruelty, sadism and hostility to the Other, the Jew. It had bred the universal paranoia that transfigured one's Jewish neighbor into a malevolent conspirator, a demonic agent of dark forces or an immune bacillus-carrier of the plagues. Of course: neither Streicher nor Goebbels were always able to shake a person's conviction that his own neighbor was one of these rare exceptions to the rule—Himmler complained in his speech of October 4, 1943 that each German "has his one decent Jew. 'Sure, the others are swine, but this one is an A-1 Jew.'"[111] The insistence of the propagandists on the general validity of the thesis that assigned to the "Jewish Question" a worldhistorical significance engendered nevertheless that general sense of acquiescence which made people look in the other direction when their "A-1 Jew" was taken from her house. The editors of the antisemitic weekly *Der Stürmer*, the broadcasters of the Ministry of Propaganda and the Nazi teachers in the schools defined the horizon of what were and what were not the proper questions to ask and actions to take. Thus propaganda defined the practical determination of what belonged to the political, and what ought to be assigned to the fated.

The pragmatics of propaganda reflected the Nazi understanding of its conceptional significance. Hitler believed propaganda to be the foundation stone of the political. In *Mein Kampf* he argued that its assignment was the mobilization of the nation into a national community. Hitler believed that most people were simple-minded. Therefore propaganda had to be simple. "The more modest its intellectual ballast, the more exclusively it takes into consideration the emotions of the masses, the more effective it will be. . . . The receptivity of the great masses is very limited, their intelligence is small, but their power of forgetting is enormous. In consequence of these facts, all effective propaganda must be limited to a very few points and must harp on these in slogans until the last member of the public understands what you want him to understand by your slogan." Hitler asserted that the function of propaganda was "not to weigh and ponder the rights of different people, but exclusively to emphasize the one right which it has set out to argue for. Its task is not to make an objective study of the truth, in so far as it favours the enemy, and then set it before the masses with academic fairness; its task is to serve our own right, always and unflinchingly." The practical application of this principle was that it was correct to respond to catastrophe by loading "every bit of the blame on the shoulders of the enemy, even if this [does] not really correspond to the true facts."[112]

The elevation of propaganda to the level of *Realpolitik* and the consequent sanctification of intellectual falsehood into a civic truth radically challenged the Western understanding of politics. In ancient Athens public participation in government had emerged from trial by jury. The creation of legally constituted tribunals that were assigned the task to uncover the truth about the past and to mete out the right retribution for wrongs committed were the foundation of the political. The first office that was opened to the populace was that of juror. Having been given, as a collective body, the responsibility to judge the actions of men in the past, it was only a question of time before the commons would be invited to judge the prospective deeds of their leaders. Thus judicial practice begot democratic sentiment. In the ensuing history of suffrage, politics remained the handmaiden of justice; the Agora stayed in the shadow of the Areopagus. The politics of propaganda changed all of that. Accusation took the place of judgement; rambling prognostications took the place of a careful analysis of options and possibilities. This reversal brought about a transposition of guilt and retribution. In the traditional situation tribunals operated under the assumption that a crime engenders guilt, and that the ascertainment of guilt preceded the dispensation of punishment. In Hitler's Germany this changed: accusation acquired the reality of judgement and appropriated the power of punishment; people became guilty because the state saw fit to penalize them.

This seems absurd, yet it was not without precedent. Ten years before Hitler's ascent to power Franz Kafka (1883–1924) probed the Nazi transposal of crime and punishment. Kafka understood how this inversion had become possible. Appropriating a radical interpretation of historical relativism (which held that events in history are hermeneutically disconnected), Kafka applied the relativist logic (which had been developed to interpret events separated by generations) to the understanding of the momentary and the immediate. He challenged the traditional concept of progression, which derived from the epic, Greek drama and Judeo-Christian eschatology. He believed that if the narrative order of development (which assigns to the deed and the response to the deed a sequential order) did not apply to history at large any longer, then it did not apply to the story of our own lives. Thus Kafka matched relativist historiography with his narratives in which human life became a disjointed configuration of meaningless rituals and futile repetition. As he showed in *The Trial*, this relativist situation annulled the basis of jurisprudence.

The Austrian critic Günther Anders observed that Kafka's understanding of the repetitive nature of experience was radically different from Kierkegaard's existential appropriation of the possibility of repetition. "Kierkegaard found in 'repetition' a moral category of existence, and used the term to define the unremitting claim of old, but never imposed obligations, which are the reverse of the merely 'interesting.' What for Kierkegaard was the very principle of a morally valid existence is for Kafka the curse of an existence of endless, identical failures."[113] And he suggested Kafka's understanding of the nature of human activity in relativist time led to the inversion of guilt and crime that characterized Nazi politics.

> The paralysis of time is so complete that Kafka can—with an appearance of perfect naturalness—reverse the sequence of cause and effect. For example, *The Trial* begins with an accusation which remains utterly unsubstantiated, but plunges the accused, K., into guilt. . . . Behind this deeply disturbing inversion of guilt and punishment lies a wonderfully worked-out moral theology. Kafka's heroes are the victims of a kind of original sin, though not in the Christian sense. Simply because from the start they are shut out from paradise (which in their case is the world), they are guilty, and every culpable act is the result of this prior situation. In Kafka's world the Furies descend before instead of after the deed. They even drive the criminal to the crime, to "catch up" with his own retribution.[114]

Anders summarized Kafka's intellection of the rationality of the transposition of guilt and punishment succinctly. The process of reversal begins with the sudden exclusion of a person from society. This excision applies to space and time. As the result of a first act the protagonist ceases to share the world of other people and their destiny. He has become the Other. As a result of this relegation the individual loses a sense of where his obligations are. This ignorance gives rise to a bad conscience that, in turn, contributes to the feeling that he is without rights. "Since he has no rights he is in the wrong. Being in the wrong intensifies his moral anguish. His moral anguish places him outside the world." Anders concluded that "Kafka's entire work, where it is not concerned with describing this vicious circle of misery, is an attempt to escape the vertiginous sensation which it produces."[115] Summarizing the basis of the jurisprudence of the age of relativism Kafka declared "it is an essential part of the justice dispensed here that you should be condemned not only in innocence but also in ignorance."[116] Like modern (wo)man, the accused K. is not permitted to see the lawbooks that are scattered on the examining magistrate's desk—and when K. opens the book during a visit to the courtroom when the court is not sitting, he finds that the first lawbook is a collection of pornographic images and the second one a novel entitled *How Grete Was Plagued by Her Husband Hans*. Neither is K. allowed to know the content of the charge. And thus K. tries to negotiate life in the relativist epoch in which the accused is admonished not to make such an outcry about one's innocence, as it spoils the "not unfavourable impression" he made in other respects.[117]

This short excursion into Kafka's imaginary world allows us to get a better grasp on the world of German politics and what made it possible, *l'univers concentrationnaire*.[118] The legal, economic and finally physical effacement of the Jews was necessary to give validity to the accusation that they were the meta-enemy responsible for all of Germany's misfortunes— past, present and future. Their annihilation justified Nazi propaganda and therefore Nazi politics. The stages on the road to their final destination were carefully designed to give additional legitimacy to the acts of isolation, deportation and extermination. The ghettos and camps created a situation in which it became unavoidable that the crime would catch up with the retribution. When the Germans concentrated more than 400,000 Jews in an area of 403 hectares in Warsaw, they created a biological time-bomb. With a population density of 110,880 per square kilometre, the starving population tried to manage as best it could. Most people lived in utter degradation. For the Germans the common deprivation was a proof of Jewish depravity. As Alfred Rosenberg reported to the Reich press department on the conditions within the Warsaw ghetto, "The sights are so appalling and probably also so well-known to the editorial staffs that a description is presumably superfluous. If there are any people left who still somehow have sympathy with the Jews then they ought to be recommended to have a look at such a ghetto. Seeing this race en masse, which is decaying, decomposing, and rotten to the core will banish any sentimental humanitarianism."[119] The Kafkaesque inversion of retribution (the concentration of a huge population into a small area) and the crime (the physical and supposedly moral disintegration of the populace in that condition) did not trouble Rosenberg. And neither did it seem odd for the German population at large. The Nazi organisation "Strength through Joy" organized coach tours to the Warsaw ghetto. The tourists would be able to see first-hand what society looked if the Jews were left to manage their own (or, as was implied, German) affairs. And for those who could not join the trip there was always the film *Die Ewige Jude* (*The Eternal Jew*). Shot in the overcrowded ghettos, the film was the counterpart of Riefenstahl's *Triumph of the Will*. In a cinematographically accomplished manner it juxtaposed the diaspora of the Jews with the dissemination of rats.[120]

Auschwitz offered a more sophisticated example of an environment that allowed the crime to catch up with the retribution. In Chapter Three I quoted Pelagia Lewinska's discovery that the whole organization of the camp was geared towards the idea that the inmates would die in their own filth and drown in their own excrement. "They wished to abase us, to destroy our human dignity, to efface every vestige of humanity . . . to fill us with horror and contempt toward ourselves and our fellows."[121] The dreadful selections, the humiliating initiation rituals, the harassing roll-calls, the violent beatings, the oppressive overcrowding and the unbearable hunger were all the rudiments of an elaborate and sophisticated system that operated on the principle that the inmates were to blame themselves for the horrors they endured. The camps offered the inmates what William Styron labeled as Sophie's choice, or Lawrence Langer as the choiceless choice.[122] Whatever its name, the principle was always the same. The only choice which the Germans left to the inmates forced them to surrender the one thing that was left to them: their innocence. Having arrived on the Auschwitz camp, Mengele forces Sophie to choose which of her two children will be gassed. If she refused to choose, both would be killed. This was a fictional representation of an all too real dilemma. There were the prisoners who were given smaller or larger privileges, which gave them a greater chance to survive, but also forced them to become part of the totalitarian hierarchy of the camp that allowed the system of terror to remain intact. And then there were the so-called *Sonderkommandos* or "Special Squads" which were entrusted with the task of running the crematoria. The men selected to close the doors of the gaschambers, to extract the gold teeth from the jaws, to cut the women's hair and burn the corpses were Jews. Primo Levi agonized how "one is stunned by this paroxysm of perfidy and hatred: it must be shown that the Jews, the sub-race, the submen, bow to any and all humiliation, even to destroying themselves." And he judged that the conception and organization of the squads was National Socialism's most demonic crime. "Behind the pragmatic aspect (to economize on able men, to impose on others the most atrocious tasks) other more subtle aspects can be perceived. This institution represented an attempt to shift onto others—specifically, the victims—the burden of guilt, so that they were deprived of even the solace of innocence. It is neither easy nor agreeable to dredge this abyss of viciousness, and yet I think it must be done."[123] Levi maintained that no one may judge the members of the squads, "not those who lived through the experience of the Lager and even less those who did not."

I would invite anyone who dares to pass judgement to carry out upon himself, with sincerity, a conceptual experiment: Let him imagine, if he can, that he has lived for months or years in a ghetto, tormented by chronic hunger, fatigue, promiscuity, and humiliation; that he has seen die around him, one by one, his beloved; that he is cut off from the world, unable to receive or transmit news; that, finally, he is loaded onto a train, eighty or hundred persons to a boxcar; that he travels into the unknown, blindly, for sleepless days and nights; and that he is at last flung inside the walls of an indecipherable inferno. . . . The experiment I have proposed is not pleasant. Vercors tried to describe it in his story *Les armes de la nuit* (Albin Michel, Paris, 1953), in which he speaks of "the death of the soul," and which reread today seems to me intolerably infected by aestheticism and literary treachery. Undoubtedly, however, it deals with the death of the soul. Now nobody can know for how long and under what trials his soul can resist before yielding and breaking. . . . Therefore I ask that we meditate on the story of "the crematorium ravens" with pity and rigor, but that judgment of them be suspended.[124]

Levi's conclusion that the world of the camps discloses an *impotentia judicandi* recalls Sophocles' discovery that as politics is bounded by justice, justice, in turn, is bounded by an encompassing doom. If the extermination of the Melians terminated the greatness of Periclean Athens, our inability to judge the men of the *Sonderkommandos* brought an end to the assumption that the question of justice is a measurestick to assess our decisions in a world that encompasses Auschwitz, Sophoclean Thebes and Periclean Athens. In the end, there only remains an appeal for mercy, for them and for ourselves.

Yet were is She who will give it to them, to us?

At the Mind's Limits

This chapter is outside the dialogue that was the occasion of *Architectural Principles in the Age of Historicism*. It was included as an appendix to the text to account for the collapse of the dialogue at the end of Chapter Five. Discussing Sophoclean drama, it not only became clear that *Oedipus Tyrannus* marked the end of the Periclean assertion that rational politics can overcome doomed fate, but also that it was the effective limit of my faith in my own ability to recover some architectural principles from the past. Reflecting on Oedipus' fate it became more and more clear that it was impossible to restore a Judeo-Christian perspective on architectural history through a transposition of Athens for Golgotha. The reason for this collapse of confidence was to be found in my motivation to join Westfall in the debate. If the intellectual origin of my participation in that debate was an abstract issue of historiographic interest, its more visceral beginning was a profound sense of discomfort with the inability of architectural historians to respond to Auschwitz. This apprehension of our collective failure as a discipline shaped my exposition of the historiographical crisis in Chapter One. It guided me through Chapter Three to Jaspers. In his *The Origin and Goal of History* I recognized my own anguish *and* what seemed at that stage of our debate a—for the era of the Shoah—credible reclamation of a Judeo-Christian perspective on the past. I wrote Chapter Five confident that I had found as solid a foundation for a new architectural history and a new architectural theory as might be found in the Age of Historicism. Yet achievement turned into failure. Sophocles revealed a truth that arraigned the whole effort. The more I began to think about the implications of *Oedipus Tyrannus* for me, the more I began to see that the whole enterprise had been misdirected.

In those days I read again Jean Améry's magistral *At the Mind's Limits: Contemplations by a Survivor on Auschwitz and Its Realities* (1966). Born Hans Maier in Vienna in 1912, the highly assimilated and educated son of a Jewish father and a Catholic mother only faced his Jewishness late in 1935 when he read the text of the Nuremberg laws. At that moment "society, concretized in the National Socialist German state, which the world recognized absolutely as the legitimate representative of the German people, had just made me formally and beyond any question a Jew." Maier realized that he was from that moment on "a dead man on leave, someone to be murdered, who only by chance was not yet where he properly belonged. . . . Our sole right, our sole duty was to disappear from the face on the earth."[125] In 1938 Maier fled to Belgium, where he adopted the name Améry. He joined the resistance after the German invasion of Belgium, was arrested and tortured in 1943 and, on the discovery of his Jewish identity, shipped off to Auschwitz. He survived. Although Améry was unusually well-read in philosophy and literature at the time of his deportation, it was not until twenty-one years after his liberation that the first of several autobiographical investigations appeared which were to chart the chronicle of his own intellectual development as it "evolved in impassioned reaction to the philosophical and political turning points of an epoch that culminated in the monstrosity of the Third Reich."[126] The title of the first chapter of this book (originally entitled *Jenseits von Schuld und Sühne—Beyond Guilt and Atonement*) was "At the Mind's Limits," and its explicit purpose was to offer a reflection of Auschwitz as it was experienced by a cultivated person, an intellectual.

Améry defined an intellectual as a person "who lives within what is a spiritual frame of reference in the widest sense. His realm of thought is an essentially humanistic one, that of the liberal arts. He has a well-developed aesthetic consciousness. By inclination and ability he tends toward abstract trains of thought. Sequences of ideas from the area of intellectual history occur to him at every occasion." Améry proposed to confront such an intellectual with a borderline situation "where he has to confirm the reality and effectiveness of his intellect, or declare its impotence."[127] In other words he invited the reader to follow him into Auschwitz. The Hobbesian society in Auschwitz isolated the intellectual as intellectual. Learning had no social significance: it could not be shared, and lost its transcendence. The experience of one of Améry's fellow prisoners in Auschwitz, the psychiatrist Viktor Frankl, was paradigmatical. On his arrival in the camp he tried to keep only one of his possessions: a book he just had written.

> I tried to take one of the old prisoners into my confidence. Approaching him furtively, I pointed to the roll of paper in the inner pocket of my coat and said, "Look, this is the manuscript of a scientific book. I know that you will say, that I should be grateful to escape with my life, that that should be all I can expect of fate. But I cannot help myself. I must keep this manuscript at all costs; it contains my life's work. Do you understand that?"
>
> Yes, he was beginning to understand. A grin spread slowly over his face, first piteous, then more amused, mocking, insulting, until he bellowed one word at me in answer to my question, a word that was ever present in the vocabulary of the camp inmates: "Shit!" At that moment I saw the plain truth and did what marked the culminating point of the first phase of my psychological reaction: I struck out my whole former life.[128]

Frankl dropped all his learning at the camp's gate; Améry tried to preserve it, but he also learned that whatever significance a liberal education still had for the individual inmate, it could not be shared. He recalled how the intellectual would try to talk about books with his bunkmates. "But when for the thirtieth time he received the answer 'Shit, man!'—he left off. So it was that in Auschwitz everything intellectual gradually took on a doubly new form: on the one hand, psychologically, it became something completely unreal, and on the other hand, to the extent that one defines it in social terms, a kind of forbidden luxury." Culture lost its transcendence.

> I recall a winter evening when after work we were dragging ourselves, out of step, from the IG-Farben site back to the camp to the accompaniment of the Kapo's unnerving "left, two, three, four," when—for God-knows-what reason— a flag waving in front of a half-finished building caught my eye. "Die Mauern stehn / Sprachlos und kalt, im Winde / Klirren die Fahnen," I muttered to myself in mechanical association. Then I repeated the stanza somewhat louder, listened to the words' sound, tried to track the rhythm, and expected that the emotional and mental response that for years this Hölderlin poem had awakened in me would emerge. But nothing happened. The poem no longer

transcended reality. There it was and all that remained was objective statement: such and such, and the Kapo roars "left," and the soup was watery, and the flags are clanking in the wind. Perhaps the Hölderlin feeling, encased in psychic humus, would have surfaced if a comrade had been present whose mood would have been somewhat similar and to whom I could have recited the stanza. The worst was that one did not have this comrade; he was not in the work ranks, and where was he in the entire camp? If one ever did succeed in turning him up, then he was so alienated by his own isolation from all things intellectual that he no longer reacted. [129]

One of the most penetrating and moving analyses of the assault of the death camp on the fragile edifice of civilization follows. In the camp everything that had given value to human life became useless garbage. The so-called humanities ceased to be important in a domain designed to dehumanize even the strongest and the noblest. And even if a person did not turn into a staggering corpse—"a bundle of physical functions in its last convulsions"—then it was still impossible to apply a rigorous discipline of thought to the environing situation. For example the intellectual who had pondered the problems of historical relativism at home found himself in the camp confronted with the question whether the SS who were preparing to destroy him were actually in the right. "Absolute intellectual tolerance and the methodical doubting of the intellectual became factors in his autodestruction. Yes, the SS could carry on just as it did: there are no natural rights, and moral categories come and go like fashions. A Germany existed that drove Jews and political opponents to their death, since it believed that only this way could it become a full reality. And what of it? Greek civilization was built on slavery and an Athenian army had run wild on the Island of Melos as had the SS in Ukraine. . . . The Via Appia had been lined with crucified slaves and over in Birkenau the stench of cremated bodies was spreading. . . . That is the way history was and that is the way it is."[130] And if one's historical education tended to collaborate with the system, one's philosophical cultivation proved meaningless. Even the ponderous metaphysics of death, disclosed in German Romantic poetry, developed in German nineteenth-century philosophy and dilated in the Wagnerian opera, were out of place. "For death in its literary, philosophic, or musical form there was no place in Auschwitz." Death, Améry observed, had vanished from sight because of the omnipresence of dying. "The entire problem was reduced to a number of concrete considerations. For example, there was once a conversation in the camp about an SS man who had split open a prisoner's belly and filled it with sand. It is obvious that in view of such possibilities one was hardly concerned whether, or *that*, one had to die, but only *how* it would happen. Inmates carried on conversations about how long it probably takes for the gas in the gas chamber to do its job. One speculated on the painfulness of death by phenol injections. Were you to wish yourself a blow to the skull or a slow death through exhaustion in the infirmary?" In short: "the reality of the camp triumphed effortlessly over death and over the entire complex of the so-called ultimate questions. Here, too, the mind came up against its limits."[131]

At the mind's limits Améry ran into the philosopher who so readily had called in the early thirties for a radical new beginning with all its strangeness, darkness and insecurity, the man who, since the mid-forties, so unremittingly refused to address the eerie, dismal and perilous reality that he witlessly and wrongly had endorsed. Améry recalled how at occasions "that disquieting magus from Alemannic regions came to mind who said that beings appear to us only in the light of Being, but that man forgot Being by fixing on beings. Well now, being. But in the camp it was more convincingly apparent than on the outside that beings and the light of Being get you nowhere. You could *be* hungry, *be* tired, *be* sick. To say that one purely and simply *is*, made no sense. And existence *as such*, to top it off, became definitively a totally abstract and thus empty concept."

To reach out beyond concrete reality with words became before our eyes a game that was not only worthless and an impermissible luxury but also mocking and evil. Hourly, the physical world delivered proof that its insufferableness could be coped with only through means inherent in that world. In other words: nowhere else was reality so real. In no other place did the attempt to transcend it prove so hopeless and shoddy. Like the lyric stanza about the silently standing walls and the flags clanking in the wind, the philosophic declarations also lost their transcendency and then and there became in part objective observations, in part dull chatter. Where they still meant something they appeared trivial, and where they were not trivial they no longer meant anything. We didn't require any semantic analysis or logical syntax to recognize this. A glance at the watchtowers, a sniff of burnt fat from the crematories sufficed.[132]

In Conclusion

Améry's thoughts clarified why *Architectural Principles in the Age of Historicism* was misdirected. I do not think that Améry's discovery of the futility of the inherited wealth of Western civilization as a means to subsist in the death camps implies that an intellectual after Auschwitz cannot turn to the riches of Aeschylus, Thucydides, Pericles and Sophocles to find a useful if restricted perspective on the challenge of the camps to his or her domain of scholarly and undoubtedly also scholastic concern. But his experience suggests that all the edifices of learning that scholars erect are doomed to remain castles in the air. To be more than that there must be a foundation of trust. A historian who turns to the past in search for architectural (or political, or other) principles can only do so when she believes that there are such norms to be found. She must, in short, have a trust in the world and a trust in the power of the mind to discover the universal within the contingent.

Améry believed that the Jew after Auschwitz must "get along without trust in the world."

> My neighbour greets me in a friendly fashion, *Bonjour, Monsieur*; I doff my hat, *Bonjour Madame*. But Madame and Monsieur are separated by interstellar distances; for yesterday a Madame looked away when they led off a Monsieur, and through the barred windows of the departing car a Monsieur viewed a Madame as if she were a stone angel from a bright and stern heaven, which is forever closed for the Jew. . . . As a Jew I go through life like a sick man with one of those ailments that cause no great hardships but are certain to end fatally. He didn't always suffer from that sickness. When he attempts, like Peer Gynt, to peel his self out of the onion, he doesn't discover the malady. His first walk to school, his first love, his first verses had nothing to do with it. But now he is a sick man, first and foremost and more deeply than he is a tailor, a bookkeeper, or a poet. Thus, I too am precisely what I am not, because I did not exist until I became it, above all else: a Jew. Death, from which the sick man will be unable to escape, is what threatens me. *Bonjour, Madame, Bonjour, Monsieur*, they greet each other. But she cannot and will not relieve her sick neighbour of his mortal illness at the cost of suffering to death from it herself. And so they remain strangers to one another.[133]

I believe that *Monsieur* is not necessarily a Jew: he can be Japanese, or Sri Lankan, or Senegalese. He can be you, or me. He is, in short, Post-Auschwitz Man. Like *Monsieur*, we are all in a certain sense dead people on leave, beings to be betrayed and murdered. And do Architectural Principles matter when we really belong to the world explored in this chapter?

To live without trust in the world means to live without trust in the mind. I believe that the intellectual after Auschwitz is doomed to discover sooner or later that the foundations of her learning are sunk in an abyss of despair. When she discovers that the ground on which she stands is cursed with an unredeemable past, she will surrender to apathy or to that form of despair which Kierkegaard identified as defiance. Kierkegaard defined defiance as the despair of him who "wants to begin a little earlier than do other men, not at and with the beginning, but 'in the beginning'; he does not want to put on his own self, does not want to see his given self as his task—he himself wants to compose his self by means of being the infinite form."[134] It is clear that the search for Architectural Principles after Auschwitz, undertaken in the odd-numbered chapters of this book, was such an act of defiance. Not trusting the cursed ground on which I stand and the cursed past from which I come, those pages are the record of an attempt to re-create, so to speak, the world of space and time. "In despair the self wants to enjoy the total satisfaction of making itself into itself, of developing itself, of being itself; it wants to have the honour of this poetic, masterly construction, the way it has understood itself. And yet, in the final ana-lysis, what it understands by itself is a riddle; in the very moment when it seems that the self is closest to having the building completed, it can arbitrarily dissolve the whole thing into nothing."[135] Indeed: if the debate which provided the occasion for this book was in a mundane sense an act of defiance against the principles which rule the current architectural-his-torical discourse, then the (partial) outcome of the debate fits this begin-ning. The author of this chapter feels that the trust in the genuineness of his concern, the validity of his method and the admissibility of any answer—that the confidence so carefully constructed in years of graduate education—will not return.

Notes

Prolegomenon

1. Rudolf Wittkower, *Architectural Principles in the Age of Humanism*, Studies of the Warburg Institute, vol. 19 (London: The Warburg Institute, 1949), p. 135; see also Henry A. Millon, "Rudolf Wittkower, *Architectural Principles in the Age of Humanism*: Its Influence on the Development and Interpretation of Modern Architecture," *Journal of the Society of Architectural Historians* 31 (1972), pp. 83–91.

2. Harry Ritter, *Dictionary of Concepts in History* (New York, Westport, Connecticut and London: Greenwood Press, 1986), p. 183.

3. As quoted in Aristotle's *Nicomachean Ethics* (1155b2–6); see Jonathan Barnes, ed., *Early Greek Philosophy* (Harmondsworth etc.: Penguin Books, 1987), p. 115.

4. Thomas Hardy, "In Tenebris ·II," in *The Complete Poems*, James Gibson ed. (London: Macmillan, 1976), p. 168.

5. The term "parataxis" has been popularized in recent years in the criticism on the poetry of Friedrich Hölderlin. See: Theodor W. Adorno, "Parataxis," in *Neue Rundschau* 75 (1964), pp. 15–46; the chapter "parataktische Denken" in Pierre Bertaux, *Friedrich Hölderlin* (Frankfurt am Main: Suhrkamp, 1980) and Eric L. Santner, *Friedrich Hölderlin: Narrative Vigilance and the Poetic Imagination* (New Brunswick and London: Rutgers University Press, 1986).

6. John Emerich Edward Dalberg-Acton, *Selections from the Correspondence of the First Lord Acton*, ed. John Neville Figgis and Reginal Vere Laurence (London: Longmans, Green & Co., 1917), p. 214.

7. Leo Strauss, *The Rebirth of Classical Political Rationalism*, ed. Thomas L. Pangle (Chicago and London: The University of Chicago Press, 1989), pp. 72f.; 270.

Chapter One: Heraclitean Heritage

1. See: Ernst Troeltsch, *Der Historismus und seine Probleme*, vol. 3 of *Gesammelte Schriften von Ernst Troeltsch* (Tübingen: J.C.B. Mohr, 1922); Ernst Troeltsch, *The Absoluteness of Christianity and the History of Religions*, transl. David Reid (Richmond Va: John Knox Press, 1971); Friedrich Meinecke, *Historism: The Rise of a New Historical Outlook*, transl. J.E. Anderson (London: Routledge & Kegan Paul, 1972); for a contemporary assessment of the Troeltsch's thought see: J. Klapwijk, *Tussen Historisme & Relativisme: Een Studie over de Dynamiek van het Historisme en de Wijsgerige Ontwikkelingsgang van Ernst Troeltsch* (Assen: van Gorcum & Comp., 1970). Anyone who desires to get an initial grasp of the complexities of historicism and relativism should turn to the following two works. Written fifty and thirty-five years ago by a philosopher and a theologian, they are because of their wide and humanistic scope still the classical introductions to the field: Ernst Cassirer, *The Problem of Knowledge: Philosophy, Science, and History Since Hegel* (New Haven: Yale University Press, 1950); Rudolf Bultmann, *History and Eschatology: The Presence of Eternity* (New York: Harper & Row, 1957); for a

more unusual perspective on the problem of relativism see Chapter Two in Strauss's *The Rebirth of Political Rationalism.*

2.   Friedrich Meinecke, "Geschichte und Gegenwart," *Zur Theorie und Philosophie der Geschichte,* ed. Eberhard Kessel; vol. 4 of *Friedrich Meinecke Werke,* ed. Hans Herzfeld, Carl Hinrichs, Walther Hofer (Stuttgart: K.F. Koehler Verlag, 1959), p. 97

3.   Neil Jackson's *Report on Architectural History Education in Undergraduate Departments of Architecture,* which appeared in 1989 under the sponsorship of the Society of Architectural Historians, reflects the manner in which architectural historians discuss the place of their discipline vis-à-vis architectural education very well. It limited a fundamental discussion to the following observation. "Changes in attitude during the last twelve years offer an opportunity for a clarification of this definition [of architectural history]. J. Mordaunt Crook's article on 'Architecture and History' in *Architectural History* 27 (1984), drew a distinction between architectural history and the history of architecture, analogous to that between economic history and the history of economics (p. 555). The present writer believes that such a definition is crucial to the role which the study of old buildings plays within the undergraduate curriculum in architecture. The history of architecture seeks to display the subject as an unfolding chronology of monuments and men. Architectural history, on the other hand, offers an explanation of societal and cultural developments through the medium of buildings, whether monumental or vernacular. For students of architecture, whose future role will be to shape the nature, and determine the direction, of society through their own architecture, this surely is a much more relevant approach" (Neil Jackson, *Report on Architectural History Education in Undergraduate Departments of Architecture; Report prepared for the Society of Architectural Historians* [Philadelphia, 1989], p. 2). Surely so. But why? Reading the report one encounters information about the number of programs, the number of duly qualified professors of architectural history, the number of credit hours required, the number of classes with more than a certain number of students, the number of libraries with a rare book collection, the number of slide libraries with small or large number of slides, and so on. And still grinding more statistics one finds oneself suddenly in the Conclusion of the report. It begins hopefully with the remark that "the teaching of architectural history in undergraduate departments of architecture is considerably stronger than it was in 1977. This is good" (p. 10). The report continues with the suggestion that this positive development makes it necessary to consider "the real nature of architectural history education for students of architecture. It is no longer adequate to consider architectural history either as an adjunct of art history courses or as a cultural education course for designers. The role of architectural history in the 'post-Modern' world is too important. Whether architectural history is used to encourage architectural students to respond in a historicist manner, or to respond in an ahistoricist manner, matters little. What is important is that they respond knowledgeably and to do so they must have a working knowledge of the past. For it is only through the past that the future can be understood. Thus this writer would encourage architecture departments to develop their architectural history courses so that they meet the needs of the designers of tomorrow" (p. 10). The observations are both vague (what does it mean to respond in a historicist or an ahistoricist manner?) and commonplace (only through the past can the future be understood). They certainly do not reflect critical insight into the basic debate concerning historicism and relativism. The recommendations which follow are straightforwardly pedestrian: reduce class sizes; reduce the breadth of the program and develop a few in-depth courses; develop courses which meet the special needs of the undergraduate architecture students (which needs?); hire only architectural historians who have a proper PhD; demand that each department of architecture appoint at least two architectural historians and so on. The final three paragraphs of the Conclusion suggest that architectural historians should be given ample leave of absence and sabbatical leaves to conduct research and that they should have "equal opportunity for promotions, raises, tenure, and for providing leadership and responsibility." In short, in the opinion of the Society of Architectural Historians Education Committee, which judged the report fit for publication, this defines the discussion on "the real nature of architectural history education for students of architecture."

4.   Troeltsch, *The Absoluteness of Christianity,* p. 47.

5.   C.S. Lewis, *The Screwtape Letters / Screwtape Proposes a Toast* (New York: Macmillan, 1961), pp. 139f.

6.   Erich Frank, *Philosophical Understanding and Religious Truth* (London, New York & Toronto: Oxford University Press, 1945), p. 116.

7.   Edmund Burke, *Reflections on the Revolution in France* (Harmondsworth and London: Penguin Books, 1982), p. 119.

8.   Ibid., p. 120.

9.   See also the excellent analysis of Burke's understanding of the customary society in Bruce James Smith, *Politics & Remembrance: Republican Themes in Machiavelli, Burke, and Tocqueville* (Princeton: Princeton University Press, 1985), pp. 102–154.

10.   Edmund Burke, "An Abridgement of English History," *The Works of Edmund Burke*, 8 vols. (London: George Bell & Sons, 1894), vol. 4., p. 203.

11.   Norman Hampson, *The Enlightenment: An evaluation of its Assumptions, Attitudes and Values* (Harmondsworth and London: Penguin Books, 1987), p. 71.

12.   John Locke, *An Essay Concerning the Understanding, Knowledge, Opinion, and Assent*, ed. Benjamin Rand (Cambridge Mass.: Harvard University Press, 1931), pp. 17f.

13.   Ibid., p. 84.

14.   See Hampson, op. cit., pp. 73–96; also Carl L. Becker, *The Heavenly City of the Eighteenth-Century Philosophers* (New Haven: Yale University Press, 1932), pp. 63–70.

15.   Joseph Addison, "Essay 413," in Joseph Addison and Richard Steele, *The Spectator*, ed. Gregory Smith, 4 vols. (London and New York: Dent & Dutton, 1945), vol. 3, pp. 283f.

16.   Friedrich Hölderlin, "Hyperion's Song of Fate," in *Poems and Fragments*, transl. Michael Hamburger (London: Routledge & Kegan Paul, 1966), p. 79.

17.   See Chapter Ten "Progress or Return?" in Strauss's *The Rebirth of Classical Political Rationalism*; for a general history of the idea of progress see J.B. Bury, *The Idea of Progress: An Inquiry into Its Origin and Growth* (London: Macmillan, 1920).

18.   R.G. Collingwood, *The Idea of History* (Oxford: Oxford University Press, 1961), p. 82.

19.   Becker, op. cit., p. 87.

20.   Ibid., p. 108.

21.   Ibid., pp. 97f.

22.   Hampson, op. cit., pp. 186ff., 239ff.

23.   Johann Gottfried Herder, *Outlines of a Philosophy of the History of Man*, transl. T. Churchill (New York: Bergman Publishers, s.d.), p. viii.

24.   Ibid., pp. 230f.

25.   For a critical assessment of Herder's thought and significance see Meinecke, *Historism*, pp. 295–372.

26.   Herder, op. cit., pp. 233f.

27.   Johann Wolfgang von Goethe, *Goethe's Autobiography: Poetry and Truth from My Own Life*, transl. R.O. Moon (Washington DC: Public Affairs Press, 1949), pp. 222f.

28.   Becker, op. cit., p. 96.

29.   Quoted in M.A. Fitzsimons, *The Past Recaptured: Great Historians and the History of History* (Notre Dame and London: University of Notre Dame Press, 1983), p. 199.

30.   Numa Fustel de Coulanges, *The Ancient City: A Study on the Religion, Laws, and Institutions of Greece and Rome* (Baltimore: Johns Hopkins Press, 1980), p. 3.

31.   Fitzsimons, op. cit., p. 198.

32.   Leo Strauss, *The Rebirth of Classical Political Rationalism*, ed. Thomas L. Pangle (Chicago and London: The University of Chicago Press, 1989), p. 12.

33.   Goethe, op. cit., p. 337.

34.   Ibid., p. 446.

35.   Gottfried Semper, "On Architectural Styles: A Lecture Delivered at the Rathaus in Zürich," in *The Four Elements of Architecture and Other Writings*, transl. Harry Francis Mallgrave and Wolfgang Herrmann (Cambridge: Cambridge University Press, 1989), pp. 268f.

36.   Ibid.

37.   Marvin Trachtenberg and Isabella Hyman, *Architecture: From Prehistory to Post-Modernism / The Western Tradition* (New York / Englewood Cliffs: Abrams / Prentice Hall, 1986), p. 41.

38.   Martin Heidegger, "Building Dwelling Thinking," *Poetry, Language, Thought*, transl. Albert Hofstadter (New York etc.: Perennial Library, 1975), p. 146f.

39.   Heidegger, "The Origin of the Work of Art," op. cit., p. 42.

40.   Friedrich Hölderlin, "In Lovely Blue . . ." in *Hymns and Fragments*, transl. Richard Sieburth (Princeton: Princeton University Press, 1984), pp. 249–51.

41.   Heidegger, ". . . Poetically Man Dwells . . ." op. cit., pp. 220f.

42.   Ibid., p. 227.

43. Hölderlin, "Half of Life," in *Hymns and Fragments*, p. 47.

44. Eric L. Santner, *Friedrich Hölderlin: Narrative Vigilance and the Poetic Imagination* (New Brunswick and London: Rutgers University Press, 1986), p. 85.

45. Michael Hamburger, *Contraries: Studies in German Literature* (New York: E.P. Dutton, 1970), p. 269; as quoted in Santner, op. cit., p. 86.

46. Santner, op. cit., p. 89.

47. See Victor Brombert, *Victor Hugo and the Visionary Novel* (Cambridge Mass. and London: Harvard University Press, 1984), pp. 84f.

48. Victor Hugo, *Notre-Dame de Paris*, transl. J. Carroll Beckwith, 2 vols. (Philadelphia: George Barrie, 1892), vol. 1, p. 130.

49. Ibid.

50. For a history of the idea that the architecture of the Temple of Solomon is a secret code see my own *Tempel van de Wereld: de kosmische symboliek van de tempel van Salomo* (Utrecht: Hes Uitgevers, 1984).

51. Hugo, op. cit., vol. 1, p. vii.

52. Ibid., vol. 2, p. 96.

53. Kenneth Clark, *Civilization: A Personal View* (New York and Evanston: Harper & Row, 1969), p. 347.

54. Nikolaus Pevsner, *An Outline of European Architecture* (Harmondsworth: Penguin, 1945), p. 220. First published in 1943.

55. Brombert, op. cit., pp. 51f.

56. Ibid., p. 55.

57. Victor Hugo, *Ninety-Three*, transl. Jules Gray, Philadelphia: George Barrie, 1894, pp. 317f.

58. Ibid., p. 318.

59. Karl Jaspers, *The Origin and Goal of History*, transl. Michael Bullock (New Haven: Yale University Press, 1953), p. 269.

60. Barnes, op. cit., p. 114.

Chapter Two: Politics

1. Bernard Bosanquet, *A History of Aesthetic* (New York: Meridian Books, 1957), p. ix.

2. Edmund Burke, *Reflections on the Revolution in France* (Harmondsworth and London: Penguin Books, 1987), p. 184.

3. The allusion is to Robert Venturi and the quotation is from his *Complexity and Contradiction in Architecture* (New York: Museum of Modern Art, 1966), p. 19.

4. See Karl Raimund Popper, *The Poverty of Historicism*, 3rd ed. (London: Routledge & Kegan Paul, 1961).

5. Leo Strauss, *The City and Man* (Chicago and London: University of Chicago Press, 1964), pp. 10–11.

6. See the extremely useful essay by Arthur Lovejoy, " 'Nature' as Aesthetic Norm," in *Essays in the History of Ideas* (Baltimore: Johns Hopkins Press, 1948), pp. 69–77.

7. For this and other material on this point see Hadley Arkes, *First Things* (Princeton: Princeton University Press, 1986), especially Chapter Four.

8. Burke, op. cit., p. 38.

9. This last point based on Jean-Pierre Vernant, *The Origins of Greek Thought* (Ithaca, NY: Cornell University Press, 1982), p. 103.

10. Leo Strauss, *Natural Right and History* (Chicago and London: The University of Chicago Press, 1953), p. 88.

11. Arkes, op. cit., pp. 83–84.

12. Thomas Jefferson, "Letter to Samuel Kercheval," July 12, 1816, in Merrill D. Peterson, ed., *The Portable Thomas Jefferson* (Harmondsworth and London: Penguin Books, 1977), p. 559.

13. This idea is an expansion of suggestions of two rather different authors: Wolfgang Braunfels (e.g., in "Institutions and Their Corresponding Ideals," in *Smithsonian Annual II: The Fitness of Man's Environment*, [Washington DC: Smithsonian Institute, 1968]; *Monasteries of Western Europe*, transl. Alastair Laing [Princeton: Princeton University Press, 1972]; and its complement, *Urban Design in*

Western Europe: Regime and Architecture, 900–1900, transl. Kenneth J. Northcott [Chicago and London: The University of Chicago Press 1988 (the paperback edition contains various corrections)]), and Norris Kelly Smith (e.g., in *Frank Lloyd Wright: A Study in Architectural Content*, revised ed. [Watkins Glen, N.Y.: American Life Foundation & Study Institute, 1979], esp. p. 22).

14. For a discussion of institutions defined a little differently, but one that is quite useful for some of its general ideas, see Samuel P. Huntington, "Political Development and Political Decay," in *World Politics* (April, 1965), pp. 386–430. For a very different but more familiar definition that is not useful in this context, see Raymond Williams, *Keywords: A Vocabulary of Science and Society*, 2nd ed. (New York: Oxford University Press, 1983), s.v. Institution.

15. Ernst Gombrich, *In Search of Cultural History* (Oxford: Clarendon Press, 1967, 1969); and in *Ideals and Idols* (Oxford: Phaidon, 1979), pp. 24–59.

16. Lewis Mumford, *The City in History* (New York: Harcourt, Brace & World, 1961), pp. 571 and 576.

Chapter Three: Prophetic Remembrance

1. Friedrich Meinecke, *Historism: The Rise of a New Historical Outlook*, transl. J.E. Anderson (London: Routledge & Kegan Paul, 1970), p. liv.

2. For a concise discussion of the history of the formula that history is the teacher of life see the essay entitled "Historia Magistra Vitae: The Dissolution of the Topos into the Perspective of a Modernized Historical Process," in Reinhart Kosselleck, *Futures Past: On the Semantics of Historical Time*, transl. Keith Tribe (Cambridge Mass.: MIT Press, 1985), pp. 21–38.

3. L.B. Alberti, *I libri della famiglia*, transl. R.N. Watkins (Columbia, SC: University of South Carolina Press, 1969), p. 60.

4. C.W. Westfall, "Thoughts on Freedom and Architecture in the Constitution's Bicentennial Year," *Journal of Architectural Education* 40 (1987), p. 90.

5. Karl Löwith, *Meaning in History* (Chicago and London: The University of Chicago Press, 1949), pp. 4ff.; Charles William Fornara, *The Nature of History in Ancient Greece and Rome* (Berkeley: University of California Press, 1988); Cynthia Farrar, *The Origins of Democratic Thinking* (Cambridge: Cambridge University Press, 1988), pp. 126ff.

6. Thucydides, *History of the Peloponnesian War*, transl. R. Warner (Harmondsworth: Penguin, 1972), p. 48.

7. Barry Cooper, *The End of History: An Essay on Modern Hegelianism* (Toronto, Buffalo and London: University of Toronto Press, 1984), p. 47.

8. For a good introduction to the Christian view of history see the various essays collected in *God, History and Historians: Modern Christian Views of History*, ed. C.T. McIntire (New York: Oxford University Press, 1977); See also Rudolf Bultmann, *History and Eschatology: The Presence of Eternity* (New York: Harper & Row, 1962); Karl Löwith, op. cit., see especially pp. 137–90. A good study on the biblical view of history is Simon J. De Vries, *Yesterday, Today and Tomorrow: Time and History in the Old Testament* (Grand Rapids: Eerdmans, 1975). A most accessible theological consideration can be found in Part V, "History and the Kingdom of God" of Paul Tillich's *Systematic Theology*, 3 vols. (Chicago and London: The University of Chicago Press, 1957–63), vol. 3, pp. 297–423. Of (cultural) historical interest are R.A. Markus, *Saeculum: History and Society in the Theology of St. Augustine* (New York: Cambridge University Press, 1970) and C.A. Patrides, *The Grand Design of God: The Literary Form of the Christian View of History* (Toronto: University of Toronto Press, 1972).

9. Hermann Cohen, *Religion of Reason: Out of the Sources of Judaism*, transl. Simon Kaplan (New York: Frederick Ungar, 1972), pp. 261f.

10. Ibid., pp. 249f.

11. Søren Kierkegaard, *Philosophical Fragments or A Fragment of Philosophy: by Johannes Climacus*, transl. David F. Swenson (Princeton and New York: Princeton University Press/American–Scandinavian Foundation, 1946), p. 70.

12. Ibid., p. 6.

13. Ibid., p. 13.

14. Søren Kierkegaard, *The Concept of Anxiety*, transl. Reidar Thomte and Albert B. Anderson (Princeton: Princeton University Press, 1980), pp. 88f.

15. Ibid., p. 89.

16. Ibid., p. 90.

17. Kierkegaard, *Philosophical Fragments*, pp. 63f.

18. Ibid., pp. 65f.

19. Ibid., p. 111.

20. Haggai 1: 1–15.

21. Richard Elliott Friedman, *Who Wrote the Bible?* (New York: Summit Books, 1987), pp. 136–49.

22. I Kings 9: 1–9.

23. II Kings 21: 71–3.

24. Johann Gottfried Herder, *Outlines of a Philosophy of the History of Man*, transl. T. Churchill (New York: Bergman Publishers, s.d.), p. 453.

25. Ibid., p. 123.

26. Ibid., p. 442.

27. Friedrich Schiller, *On the Aesthetic Education of Man in a Series of Letters*, transl. E.M. Wilkinson and L.A. Willoughby (New York: Oxford University Press, 1967), p. 35.

28. Friedrich Hölderlin, "As on a Holiday...," in *Poems and Fragments*, transl. Michael Hamburger (London: Routledge & Kegan Paul, 1966), pp. 375–7.

29. Hölderlin, "The Archipelago," in op. cit., p. 227.

30. Ibid., pp. 227–9.

31. Ibid., pp. 217, 221–5.

32. On the origin of the linguistic distinction see Koselleck, op. cit., 27ff.; the distinction became important in the theological debate on the relationship between the Jesus of History and the Christ of Faith. The first study to adopt the distinction between *historisch* and *geschichtlich* as the basis of a theological thesis was Martin Kähler's essay *Der sogenannte historische Jesus un der geschichtliche biblische Christus*, translated in 1964 as *The So-Called Historical Jesus and the Historic Biblical Christ* (Philadelphia: Fortress Press, 1964). The distinction was popularized by Rudolf Bultmann, who maintained that Christian faith should not be based on a knowledge of the historical Jesus, but in a faith in the historic significance of the Christ event. See especially his *Faith and Understanding*, transl. Louise Pettibone Smith (New York and Evanston: Harper & Row, 1969). For a concise introduction to Bultmann's understanding of history see Morris Ashcraft, *Rudolf Bultmann* (Waco, Texas: Word Books, 1972), pp. 35–41.

33. While not dealing explicitly with the distinction between *Historie* and *Geschichte*, James Carse's *Finite and Infinite Games* (New York: The Free Press, 1986) provides some useful and poetic insights into their differences. See especially pp. 99–113.

34. Isaiah 60: 19–20.

35. Benedetto Croce, *History as the Story of Liberty*, transl. Sylvia Sprigge (London: George Allen & Unwin, 1941), p. 227.

36. Ibid., p. 279.

37. Bultmann, op. cit., pp. 143.

38. Croce, op. cit., p. 280.

39. Ibid., pp. 247f.

40. Jeremiah 7: 1–11.

41. This modernist "discovery" denies Westfall's understanding of the good life, and, consequently, his doctrine of the city. In the preceding chapter Westfall defined the good life as the art of living together in order to perfect the nature of each individual. Westfall's treatment of the good life suggested that our inclination to live together and our desire to perfect ourselves bear a natural relationship. Aristotle, who was the first to define the good life in those terms, had never any illusions that it was anything more than a compromise which linked the ideal of the philosophical (contemplative) and the necessity of the ethical (active) life in an often shaky and often contradictory unity (*Nicomachean Ethics*, X, 7–8). This compromise can take a better or a worse form, yet it will be always less than the ideal of the contemplative life, and therefore the ought of the good life will always contain within it an element of misgiving which propels the timeless ideal into the contingency of the historical world. This apprehension has become a central theme of twentieth-century thought. We interpret Aristotle's (or Westfall's) understanding of the good life in terms of the dynamism of the twofold duty we face as human beings. The first part of that duty is to become ourselves, or, as Westfall would phrase it, to attain virtue

through the cultivation of our faculties. The second part of that duty is to resist an unwelcome side-effect of our search for self-consciousness. We have learned that no understanding of the self can emerge without acquiring a sense of what is different or other—*alienum* in Latin—and that therefore the price we must pay for our selfhood is a certain measure of alienation from the world. To live a human life implies therefore to see the world *sub specie alienationis*. We may hope to strike a balance between the conflicting movements of withdrawal and integration, yet history teaches us that this has proven exceedingly difficult. Even if one does not agree with Freud's assessment of the relationship between man and society as sketched in his *Civilization and Its Discontents*, then it is still important to acknowledge at least the relevancy of Freud's pessimistic account of the way the civilizations we create and the cities we build alienate us from ourselves. Having discovered the unconscious as the deposit of our personal and collective histories, we cannot return anymore to the Aristotelian conception of an ahistorical human nature. See Walter Kaufmann's essay entitled "The Inevitability of Alienation," in Richard Schacht, *Alienation* (Garden City, NY: Doubleday & Company, 1970), pp. xv–lviii.

42. Norman O. Brown, *Life Against Death: The Psychoanalytical Meaning of History* (Middletown Connecticut: Wesleyan University Press, 1959), p. 283.

43. The literature on the idea that the resurrection is the end of history is immense. A good introduction to the theme is Reinhold Niebuhr, *Faith and History: A Comparison of Christian and Modern Views of History* (New York: Charles Scribner's Sons, 1949).

44. Oscar Cullmann, *Christ and Time: The Primitive Christian Conception of Time and History*, transl. Floyd V. Filson (Philadelphia: The Westminster Press, 1950), pp. 145f.

45. Niebuhr, op. cit., p. 149.

46. See Jonathan Z. Smith, *To Take Place: Toward Theory in Ritual* (Chicago and London: The University of Chicago Press, 1987), pp. 74–83.

47. Eusebius of Caesarea, *Vita Constantina* 3.28; quoted in Smith, op. cit., p. 81.

48. See especially Stephen G. Nichols, *Romanesque Signs: Early Medieval Narrative and Iconography* (New Haven and London: Yale University Press, 1983); also Carol Heitz, *L'Architecture religieuse carolingienne: les formes et leurs fonctions* (Paris: A. et J. Picard, 1980).

49. Nichols, op. cit., p. 107.

50. Mark 9: 1–9. See also Matthew 17: 1–8 and Luke 9: 28–36.

51. Nichols, op. cit., p. 15.

52. Rodolphus Glaber, *Historiarum sui Temporis Libri Quinque*, Book III, chapter 4. Quoted in Nichols, op. cit., pp. 16, 209.

53. For an introduction to Christian typological thought see Leonhard Goppelt, *Typos: The Typological Interpretation of the Old Testament in the New*, transl. Donald H. Madvig (Grand Rapids: Eerdmans, 1982); Alan C. Charity, *Events and Their Afterlife: The Dialectics of Christian Typology in the Bible and Dante* (Cambridge etc.: Cambridge University Press, 1987); see also J.C.K. von Hofmann, *Interpreting the Bible* (Minneapolis: Augsburg Publishing House, 1959), pp. 169–80.

54. Epistle to the Hebrews, 9: 1–5.

55. For a comprehensive history of the allegory of the Tabernacle see my own *Tempel van de Wereld: De Kosmische Symboliek van de Tempel van Salomo* (Utrecht: Hes Uitgevers, 1984).

56. Epistle to the Hebrews, 9: 6–10.

57. Oscar Cullmann, *The Christology of the New Testament*, transl. Shirley C. Guthrie and Charles A.M. Hall (Philadelphia: The Westminster Press, 1959), pp. 86f.

58. Epistle to the Hebrews, 9: 11–12.

59. Genesis 14: 17–19.

60. Epistle to the Hebrews, 7: 1–10.

61. Van Pelt, op. cit., pp. 133ff.

62. W. Robert Connor, *Thucydides* (Princeton: Princeton University Press, 1984), p. 235.

63. Ibid.

64. Thucydides, *History of the Peloponnesian War*, transl. R. Warner (Harmondsworth: Penguin, 1972), pp. 401f.

65. Dionysius of Halicarnassus, *On Thucydides*, transl. W. Kendrick Pritchett (Berkeley, Los Angeles and London: University of California Press, 1975), p. 31.

66. Connor, op. cit., p. 155.

67. Thucydides, op. cit., pp. 407f.

68. G.W.H. Lampe, "The Reasonableness of Typology," in G.W.H. Lampe and K.J. Woolcombe, *Essays on Typology* (Naperville, Ill.: Allenson, 1957), p. 34.

69. Ibid., p. 35.

70. Leopold von Ranke, *History of the Latin and Teutonic Nations, 1494–1535*; as found in the anthology *The Varieties of History from Voltaire to the Present*, ed. F.R. Stern (New York: Meridian Books, 1957), p. 56.

71. A. Robert Caponigri, *History and Liberty: The Historical Writings of Benedetto Croce* (London: Routledge & Kegan Paul, 1955), p. 4.

72. Nicolas Berdyaev, *The Meaning of History*, transl. George Reavey (New York: Charles Scribner's Sons, 1936), p. 1.

73. See C.T. McIntire, "Introduction: The Renewal of Christian Views of History in an Age of Catastrophe," in *God, History, and Historians*, pp. 3–26.

74. Bultmann, op. cit., pp. 129f.

75. Karl Jaspers, *The Origin and Goal of History*, transl. Michael Bullock (New Haven: Yale University Press, 1953), p. xiii.

76. Ibid., p. 1.

77. Ibid., p. xv.

78. Oscar Cullmann, *Christ and Time: The Primitive Christian Conception of Time and History*, transl. Floyd V. Filson (Philadelphia: The Westminster Press, 1950), pp. 115ff.; see also Löwith, op. cit., p. 183.

79. Jaspers, op. cit., p. xv.

80. Ibid., p. 262.

81. Ibid., p. 1.

82. Ibid., p. 2.

83. The preponderence of one specific temple in the Judahite and Jewish religion, the result of the centralization of the religious cult under kings Hezekiah and Josiah, explains why the spiritual breakthrough initiated by Isaiah, Jeremiah and Second Isaiah (and in a sense completed by Jesus) could not but acquire an anti-architectural character.

84. Jaspers, op. cit., p. 262.

85. Martin Heidegger, *An Introduction to Metaphysics*, transl. Ralph Mannheim (New Haven and London: Yale University Press, 1959), p. 155.

86. Jaspers, op. cit., pp. 126ff.

87. Ibid., p. 139.

88. The term *homo hostilis* derives from Sam Keen's *Faces of the Enemy: Reflections of the Hostile Imagination* (San Francisco: Harper & Row, 1988), pp. 10f.; scholars who have explored the normative relevance of the Promethean Age for our own self-understanding as agents of change are Ernest Becker, *Escape from Evil* (New York: The Free Press, 1975); Andrew Bard Schmooker, *The Parable of the Tribes: The Problem of Power in Social Evolution* (Boston: Houghton Mifflin, 1984); of special interest for architects is Peter J. Wilson, *The Domestication of the Human Species* (New Haven and London: Yale University Press, 1988).

89. Jaspers, op. cit., p. 140.

90. Ibid., p. 5.

91. Ibid., pp. 147f.

92. Karl Jaspers, *Die Schuldfrage* (Heidelberg: Verlag Lambert Schneider, 1946); *The Question of German Guilt*, transl. E.B. Ashton (New York: Dial Press, 1948).

93. Jaspers, *The Origin and Goal of History*, p. 148.

94. Ibid.

95. Elie Wiesel, *Legends of Our Time* (New York: Schocken, 1982), p. 190.

96. Emil Fackenheim, *To Mend the World: Foundations of Future Jewish Thought* (New York: Schocken, 1982), p. 273.

97. Ibid., p. 234.

98. Ibid., p. 233.

99. Pelagia Lewinska, *Twenty Months at Auschwitz*, transl. Albert Teichner (New York: Lyle Stuart, 1968), pp. 41f.; see also Terrence Des Pres, *The Survivor: An Anatomy of Life in the Death Camps* (Oxford, New York etc.: Oxford University Press, 1980), pp. 53ff.

100. Fackenheim, op. cit., p. 239.

101.   Leo Strauss, *Studies in Platonic Political Philosophy* (Chicago and London: The University of Chicago Press, 1983), p. 168.

102.   Carl Schmitt, *The Concept of the Political*, transl. George Schwab (New Brunswick NJ: Rutgers University Press, 1976), p. 26.

103.   Leo Strauss, "Preface to the English Translation," *Spinoza's Critique of Religion*, transl. E.M. Sinclair (New York: Schocken, 1965), p. 31.

104.   Strauss, *Studies in Platonic Political Philosophy*, p. 168.

105.   Fackenheim, op. cit., p. 277.

106.   Leo Strauss, *The Rebirth of Classical Political Rationalism* (Chicago and London: The University of Chicago Press, 1989), p. 89.

107.   Ibid., pp. 100f.

108.   Strauss, "Preface to the English Translation," *Spinoza's Critique of Religion*, p. 2.

109.   Fackenheim, op. cit., p. 262. For a reply of a follower of Strauss to Fackenheim's charge see Kenneth Blanchard, "Philosophy in the Age of Auschwitz: Emil Fackenheim and Leo Strauss," in *Remembering for the Future: Working Papers and Addenda*, ed. Yehuda Bauer e.o., 3 vols. (Oxford etc.: Pergamon Press, 1989), vol. 2, pp. 1815ff.

110.   Fackenheim, op. cit., p. 263.

111.   Connor, op. cit., p. 242

112.   Ibid., p. 246.

113.   Ibid., p. 249.

114.   Jonathan Barnes, ed., *Early Greek Philosophy* (Harmondsworth etc.: Penguin Books, 1987), pp. 103, 104.

115.   Thucydides, op. cit., p. 529.

116.   Ibid., p. 135.

117.   John Dunne, *The City of the Gods: A Study in Myth and Mortality* (New York and London: Macmillan, 1973), p. 84.

118.   Thucydides, op. cit., pp. 76f.

119.   Ibid., p. 162.

120.   Ibid., p. 148.

121.   Ibid., p. 48.

122.   Strauss, *The Rebirth of Classical Political Rationalism*, pp. 86ff.

123.   Thucydides, op. cit., p. 244.

124.   Ibid., p. 536.

125.   Ibid., p. 148.

126.   Heidegger, op. cit., pp. 151f.

127.   Ibid., p. 152.

128.   Ibid., pp. 152f.

129.   Thucydides, op. cit., p. 41.

Chapter Four: Building Types

1.   The term "type" is a conventional term used for convenience and is meant to be synonymous with alternative usages according to context, as, for example, sort, class, category or other word of that kind, or, in other contexts, universal building, a design's essence, a building in principle, an ideal design, the building's nature.

2.   Van Pelt made important contributions to the historical content of this section.

3.   "diverse forme di Tempij antichi & moderni;" see: Sebastiano Serlio, *Tutte l'opere d'archi-tettura* (Venice: Giacomo de'Franceschini, 1619), fol. 202ʳ (Book V).

4.   "molti modi de'tempij disegnati in diverse forme;" ibid., fol. 126ʳ (Book IV).

5.   "cinque maniere dell'edificare, & de gli ornamenti suoi;" ibid., fol. 126ʳ (Book IV).

6.   René Descartes, "Discourse on Method," in *Descartes: Selected Philosophical Writings*, transl. John Cottingham, Robert Stoothoff and Dugald Murdoch (Cambridge: Cambridge University Press, 1988), p. 29.

7.   See now Mark Jarzombek, *On Leon Baptista Alberti: His Literary and Aesthetic Theories* (Cambridge Mass and London: MIT, 1989).

8. Descartes, op. cit., p. 29.

9. Francesco Milizia, *Principii di architettura civile*, I, iv; in *Opere complete* (Bologna: Cardinali e Frulli, 1827), vol. VI, p. 50.

10. Ibid., I, iv; VI, p. 53.

11. Ibid., I, iv; VI, p. 51.

12. Ibid., II, iv; VII, pp. 62–4.

13. Marc-Antoine Laugier, *Essai sur l'architecture* (Paris: Duchesne, 1753) Intro.; for an English edition of his work see Marc-Antoine Laugier, *An Essay on Architecture*, transl. Wolfgang and Anni Herrmann (Los Angeles: Hennessey & Ingalls, 1977), p. 12.

14. Ibid., III, intro., p. 115; ed. Herrmann, p. 68.

15. Ibid., III, iii, p. 155; ed. Herrmann, p. 90.

16. Marc-Antoine Laugier, *Essai sur l'architecture*, 2nd ed. (Paris: Duchesne, 1755), p. 299.

17. Laugier, *Essai sur l'architecture*, first edition, II, vii, p. 105; "The five Orders are not suitable for every kind of building because they involve expense which not everybody is able to afford and require a facade of a scale feasible for few buildings" (ed. Herrmann, pp. 61f.).

18. Ibid., Intro.; ed. Herrmann, p. 12.

19. Ibid.

20. J.N.L. Durand, *Recueil et parallèle des édifices en tout genre* (Paris: A l'École polytechnique, [1800]); *Précis des Leçons d'architecture donneés à l'École Polytechnique* (Paris: Bernard, 1802–5).

21. See the discussion in Anthony Vidler, "The Idea of Type," *Oppositions* 8 (1977), pp. 106–7.

22. Immanuel Kant, *The Critique of Judgement*, transl. James Creed Meredith (Oxford: Clarendon Press, 1928), p. 67.

23. The point about the grid and axis is stressed in Rafael Moneo, "On Typology," *Oppositions* 13 (1978), p. 29.

24. Vidler, op. cit., p. 110.

25. A quick glance at the titles of the first-year courses listed in the 1989/90 calender of the University of Waterloo's School of Architecture illustrates the problem. Arch 112: Mathematics in Architecture; Arch 124: Introduction to Landscape Design; Arch 142: Iconography I: Conventions; Arch 143: Iconography II: A Survey of the Symbolic Nature of the Environment; Arch 163: Statics and Structural Analysis; Arch 171: Theories and Technologies of Building; Arch 172: Building Construction; Arch 192: Design Fundamentals and Workshop, Design Studio; Arch 193: Design Fundamentals and Studio. A similar point cannot be made from the University of Virginia's not because its program is so very different but because its undergraduate program leads to a liberal arts degree rather than to a professional degree.

26. See for example Carroll L.V. Meeks, *The Railroad Station: An Architectural History* (New Haven: Yale University Press, 1956); Michael Forsyth, *Buildings for Music: The Architect, the Musician, and the Listener from the Seventeenth Century to the Present Day* (Cambridge Mass.: MIT Press, 1985).

27. Delivered as the A.W. Mellon Lectures in the Fine Arts in 1970 and published in the Bollingen Series by Princeton University Press in 1976. For an analysis of Pevsner's place and role in the writing of the history of architecture, see Part III of David Watkin, *Morality and Architecture* (Oxford: Oxford University Press, 1977). Watkin's book was written before Pevsner's *A History of Building Types* was available.

28. Quotations here and in the following from Anthony Vidler's translation of Quatremère's article entitled "Type"—published originally in the *Encyclopédie méthodique: Architecture* (Paris: Panckoucke, 1788–1825), vol. 3, p. 543; see *Oppositions* 8 (1977), pp. 148–50.

29. Vidler, op. cit., p. 105.

30. Aldo Rossi, *The Architecture of the City*, transl. Diane Ghirardo and Joan Ockman (Cambridge Mass. and London: MIT Press, 1982), p. 41.

31. Rafael Moneo, "On Typology," *Oppositions* 13 (1978), p. 23.

32. Ibid., p. 38; see also Micha Bandini, "Typology as a Form of Convention," *AA Files* 6 (1984), pp. 73–82.

33. Because in making that discovery they depended upon discourse (dialectic), because to have discourse presumes the existence of a society, and because a society that uses discourse to inquire into the best things is called a polity, it is clear that nature sheltered the first societies and that polities preceded buildings. The types of buildings useful to people in society were discovered in that same nature.

34.   The meanings discussed in two recent excellent studies of classical architecture operate in the realm of conventional symbolism; see George Hersey, *The Lost Meaning of Classical Architecture* (Cambridge Mass.: MIT Press, 1988); and John Onians, *Bearers of Meaning* (Princeton: Princeton University Press, 1988).

35.   Plural: *tholi*; literal: dome, cupola, rotunda. This and the subsequent definitions are adapted from Charlton T. Lewis and Charles Short, *A Latin Dictionary Founded on Andrews' Edition of Freund's Latin Dictionary* (Oxford: Clarendon Press, 1879).

36.   Plural: *templa*; literal: a space marked out, in particular, in augury: an open place for observation; a consecrated or sacred place, a sanctuary; a place dedicated to some particular deity, a fane, temple, shrine.

37.   Plural: *domus*; literal: house; home; one's native place; contrast *casa, -ae*, a simple or poorly built house, cottage, hut; and contrast *regia*, discussed below.

38.   Plural: *tabernae*; literal: hut, booth, stall, shop; workshop, inn.

39.   Plural: theatra; literal: playhouse, theater; place of exhibition.

40.   Plural: *regiae*; literal: royal palace, castle, fortress, residence, the court, in particular, the royal palace of Numa on the Sacra Via in the forum (used as the residence for the *pontifex maximus*); also: a basilica, a colonnade, portico, hall.

41.   Note: for reasons to be discussed later, the range must be consulted in that order, and not in its reverse.

42.   For such an explanation, see Charles Burroughs, "Palladio and Fortuna: Notes on the Sources and Meaning of the Villa Rotunda," *Architectura* 18 (1988), pp. 59–91.

Chapter Five: Athenian Assurance

1.   M.I. Finley, *Economy and Society in Ancient Greece*, ed. Brent D. Shaw and Richard P. Saller (London: Chatto & Windus, 1981), p. 20.

2.   A good introduction to the function, form and purpose of the oldest cities is the part entitled "Go to, let us build us a city and a tower!" in A. Leo Oppenheim, *Ancient Mesopotamia: Portrait of a Dead Civilization*, revised edition completed by Erica Reiner (Chicago and London: The University of Chicago Press, 1977), pp. 74–142.

3.   James Dougherty, *The Fivesquare City: The City in the Religious Imagination* (Notre Dame and London: University of Notre Dame Press, 1980), p. 2.

4.   Paul Wheatley, *The Pivot of the Four Quarters: A Preliminary Enquiry into the Origins and Character of the Ancient Chinese City* (Chicago: Aldine Publishing Company, 1971).

5.   Revelation, 21: 22–3.

6.   The literature on the history of Athens's urban form is vast. One of the most useful introductions to the topic is R.E. Wycherley, *The Stones of Athens* (Princeton: Princeton University Press, 1978); John Travlos, *Pictorial Dictionary of Ancient Athens* (New York: Praeger, 1971) offers a wealth of pictorial material. Useful are also I.T. Hill, *The Ancient City of Athens: Its Topography and Monuments* (London: Methuen, 1953) and J.S. Boersma, *Athenian Building Policy from 561/0 to 405/4* (Groningen: H.D. Tjeenk Willink, 1970).

7.   John Dunne, *The City of the Gods: A Study in Myth and Mortality* (New York and London: Macmillan, 1973), pp. 1–15; see also Robert Jay Lifton and Eric Olson, *Living and Dying* (New York and Washington: Praeger, 1974), pp. 93ff.

8.   Alexander Heidel, *The Gilgamesh Epic and Old Testament Parallels* (Chicago and London: The University of Chicago Press, 1949), pp. 16f.

9.   François de Polignac, *La naissance de la cité grecque: cultes, espace et société VIIe–VII siècles avant J.-C.* (Paris: Éditions la Découverte, 1984).

10.   Jacques Ellul, *The Meaning of the City*, transl. Dennis Pardee (Grand Rapids: Eerdmans, 1970), pp. 150f.

11.   Chester G. Starr, *The Economic and Social Growth of Early Greece 800–500 B.C.* (New York: Oxford University Press, 1977), p. 166; see also Ellen Meiksins Wood, *Peasant–Citizen–Slave: The Foundation of Athenian Democracy* (London and New York: Verso, 1988) and Robin Osborne, *Classical Landscape With Figures: The Ancient Greek City and Its Countryside* (London: George Philip, 1987).

12.   W.J. Woodhouse, *Solon the Liberator* (Oxford: Oxford University Press, 1938), p. 7.

13. Ibid., pp. 207f.

14. Plutarch, *The Rise and Fall of Athens: Nine Greek Lives*, transl. Ian Scott-Kilvert (Harmondsworh etc.: Penguin Books, 1960), p. 96.

15. Robert Garland, *The Piraeus: From the Fifth to the First Century B.C.* (London: Duckworth, 1987), pp. 83ff.

16. Thucydides, *History of the Peloponnesian War*, transl. R. Warner (Harmondsworth: Penguin, 1972) p. 91.

17. Ibid., pp. 133, 135.

18. Ibid., p. 155.

19. Oppenheim, op. cit., p. 116; see also Hans J. Nissen, *The Early History of the Ancient Near East: 9000–2000 B.C.*, transl. Elizabeth Lutzeier and Kenneth J. Northcott (Chicago and London: The University of Chicago Press, 1988), pp. 141f.

20. For a clear if not altogether undisputed account of the Greek understanding of the distinction and relationship between the public and the private realms see Hannah Arendt, *The Human Condition* (Chicago and London: The University of Chicago Press, 1958), pp. 22–67.

21. Ibid., p. 38.

22. Dunne, op. cit., p. v.

23. Arendt, op. cit., pp. 61, 65.

24. Woodhouse, op. cit., pp. 173f.

25. J.M. Edmonds, *Greek Elegy and Iambus*, Loeb Classical Library, 2 vols. (London and Cambridge Mass.: Heinemann and Harvard University Press, 1968), vol. 2, p. 151.

26. Ibid., pp. 150f.

27. Pseudo Dicaearchus I.i; quoted in Bertha Carr Rider, *The Greek House: Its History and Development from the Neolithic Period to the Hellenistic Age* (Cambridge: Cambridge University Press, 1916), p. 210.; see also Wycherley, *The Stones of Athens*, pp. 237ff.

28. Arendt, op. cit., p. 70.

29. Lifton and Olson, op. cit., p. 94.

30. Ibid., p. 95.

31. Arendt, op. cit., p. 19.

32. Thucydides, op. cit., p. 160.

33. See especially Nicole Loraux *The Invention of Athens: The Funeral Oration in the Classical City*, transl. Alan Sheridan (Cambridge Mass. and London: Harvard University Press, 1986).

34. For an assessment of the political significance of the Athenian funeral orations see Loraux, op. cit.; A good introduction to the various customs pertaining to burial etc. is Robert Garland, *The Greek Way of Death* (Ithaca NY: Cornell University Press, 1988). Also Emily Vermeule, *Aspects of Death in Early Greek Art and Poetry* (Berkeley, Los Angeles and London: University of California Press, 1979) and Donna Carel Kurtz and John Boardman, *Greek Burial Customs* (London: Thames & Hudson, 1971).

35. Pausanias, *Guide to Greece*, transl. Peter Levi, 2 vols. (Harmondsworth etc.: Penguin, 1971), vol. 1, pp. 84ff.

36. For a description of the canonic parts of the Greek funeral see Garland, *The Greek Way of Death*, pp. 21ff; for the Athenian public funeral see Loraux, op. cit., pp. 17ff.

37. Thucydides, op. cit., p. 143.

38. Ibid., p. 149.

39. Ibid.

40. Loraux, op. cit., pp. 145.

41. Thucydides, op. cit., p. 148.

42. Plutarch, op. cit., p. 63.

43. Garland, *The Greek Way of Death*, p. 104.

44. Ibid.

45. R.E. Wycherley, *How the Greeks Built Cities* (London: Macmillan & Co: 1962), pp. xix, xxi.

46. My observations on the architectonic character of the stela are based on Hans van der Laan, *Architectonic Space: Fifteen Lessons on the Disposition of the Human Habitat*, transl. Richard Padovan (Leiden: Brill, 1983).

47. Fernand Robert, *Thymélè: recherches sur la signification et la destination des monuments circulaires dans l'architecture religieuse de la Grèce* (Paris: Boccard, 1939); William L. MacDonald,

The Pantheon: Design, Meaning, Progeny (Cambridge Mass.: Harvard University Press, 1976); Louis Hautecoeur, *Mystique et architecture: symbolisme du cercle et de la coupule* (Paris: A. et J. Picard, 1954); Florian Seiler, *Die Griechische Tholos: Untersuchungen zur Etnwicklung, Typologie und Funktion kunstmässiger Rundbauten* (Mainz am Rhein: Verlag Philipp von Zabern, 1986).

48.   Georg Wilhelm Friedrich Hegel, *The Philosophy of History*, transl. J. Sibree (New York: Dover, 1956), p. 253.

49.   Loraux, op. cit., p. 329.

50.   Thucydides, op. cit., pp. 145f.

51.   Plutarch, op. cit., pp. 29f.

52.   Ibid., p. 179.

53.   As we have seen, the Kleisthenic reforms of 508/7 BCE completed the constitutional project begun by Solon through the establishment of ten new tribes. To name the tribes, Kleisthenes sent the names of 100 ancient Athenian heroes to the oracle in Delphi. The oracle chose ten, after whom the tribes were named. These heroes, who lend their names to the tribes (hence *eponymous*, which means to give one's name to something), were honored with a monument on the Agora. This monument served as the city's public notice board. See John M. Camp, *The Athenian Agora: Excavations in the Heart of Classical Athens* (London: Thames & Hudson, 1986), p. 97ff.

54.   Vincent Scully, *The Earth, the Temple and the Gods: Greek Sacred Architecture*, revised edition (New Haven and London: Yale University Press, 1979), pp. 171.

55.   Ibid., p. 172.

56.   Ibid., p. 183.

57.   Norman O. Brown, *Life Against Death: The Psychoanalytical Meaning of History* (Middletown Connecticut: Wesleyan University Press, 1959), p. 283.

58.   Thucydides, op. cit., pp. 160ff.

59.   Plutarch, op. cit., pp. 177f.

60.   Scully, op. cit., p. 184.

61.   Johann Gottfried Herder, *Outlines of a Philosophy of the History of Man*, transl. T. Churchill (New York: Bergman Publishers, s.d.), p. 230.

62.   James Stuart and Nicholas Revett, *The Antiquities of Athens; and other Monuments of Greece*, second (pocket) edition (London: Crossly, Tilt & Bogue, 1841), pp. viii, xii.

63.   Scully, op. cit., p. 185.

64.   The basic work on the Agora is H.A. Thompson and R.E. Wycherley, *The Agora of Athens: The History, Shape, and Uses of an Ancient City Center*, vol. 14 of *The Athenian Agora: Results of Excavations Conducted by the American School of Clasical Studies at Athens* (Princeton: The American School of Classical Studies in Athens, 1972); see also Camp, op. cit.; neither study includes the Areopagus in its discussion of the Agora. For a consideration of the various meeting places around the agora see William A. MacDonald, *The Political Meeting Places of the Ancient Greeks* (Baltimore: Johns Hopkins Press, 1943) and Stephen G. Miller, *The Prytaneion: Its Function and Architectural Form* (Berkeley: University of California Press, 1978).

65.   A good introduction to the political and constitutional structure of the polis is Victor Ehrenberg, *The Greek State*, revised edition (London: Methuen, 1969); also C. Hignett, *A History of the Athenian Constitution to the End of the Fifth Century B.C.* (Oxford: Clarendon Press, 1952).

66.   This location of the "Old Agora" is the consensus of those connected to the American School of Classical Studies in Athens, which has done most of the excavations on the Agora. Some believe that the older Agora was on the south slope of the Acropolis. This theory was first proposed by E. Curtius in his *Attische Studien*, 2 vols. (Göttingen: In der Dieterichsen Buchhandel, 1862–65), vol. 2; a most recent defense of this position is A.N. Oikonomides, *The Two Agoras in Ancient Athens: A New Commentary on Their History and Development* (Chicago: Argonaut Inc. Publishers, 1964); for a review of the problem of the "Old Agora" see R.E. Wycherley, "Archaia Agora," *Phoenix* 20 (1966), pp. 288–93.

67.   In 480 BCE there were between 25,000 and 30,000 Athenian citizens. Together with their families this group came to between 80,000 and 100,000 people. Added to this were a group of between 9000 and 12,000 foreigners with their families and between 30,000 and 40,000 slaves. Consequently one fifth of all the inhabitants of Athens could attend and vote in the Assembly. These figures are taken from Ehrenberg, op. cit.

68.   Thompson and Wycherley, op. cit., p. 25.

69.   George Thomson, *Aeschylus and Athens: A Study in the Social Origins of Drama* (New York: The Universal Library, 1968), p. 272.

70.   Aeschylus, *The Eumenides*, in *The Oresteia*, transl. Robert Fagles (Harmondsworth etc.: Penguin Books, 1984), p. 234.

71.   Ibid., p. 262.

72.   E.T. Owen, *The Harmony of Aeschylus* (Toronto: Clarke, Irwin & Company, 1952), p. 128.

73.   Aeschylus, op. cit., p. 271.

74.   Plutarch, op. cit., p. 96.

75.   Rhys Carpenter, *The Architects of the Parthenon* (Harmondsworth etc.: Pelican Books, 1970).

76.   Aristotle, *The Athenian Constitution*, transl. P.J. Rhodes (Harmondsworth etc.: Penguin, 1984), p. 89f.

77.   Jean-Pierre Vernant, *The Origins of Greek Thought* (Ithaca, NY: Cornell University Press, 1982), p. 101.

78.   Dunne, op. cit., pp. 29ff.

79.   Aristotle, op. cit., pp. 43f.

80.   Vernant, op. cit., pp. 41f.

81.   Ehrenberg, op. cit., p. 98.

82.   Scully, op. cit., p. 191.

83.   J.J. Coulton, *The Architectural Development of the Greek Stoa* (Oxford: Clarendon Press, 1976), pp. 12f.

84.   Fragment 44, quoted in Jonathan Barnes, ed., *Early Greek Philosophy* (Harmondsworth etc.: Penguin Books, 1987), p. 105.

85.   Plutarch, op. cit., p. 88.

86.   Garland, *The Piraeus*, pp. 21f.

87.   Jean-Pierre Vernant, "Tensions and Ambiguities in Greek Tragedy," *Interpretations*, ed. Charles S. Singleton (Baltimore: Johns Hopkins University Press, 1969), p. 108.

88.   Karl Jaspers, *Tragedy Is Not Enough*, transl. Harald A.T. Reiche, Harry T. Moore and Karl W. Deutsch (London: Victor Gollancz, 1953), p. 31.

89.   Ibid., p. 41.

90.   Ibid., pp. 78f.

91.   Just when *Architectural Principles in the Age of Historicism* went into production I obtained a copy of J. Peter Euben's *The Tragedy of Political Theory: The Road not Taken* (Princeton: Princeton University Press, 1990). This book, as well as the earlier collection of essays edited by Euben—*Greek Tragedy and Political Theory* (Berkeley, Los Angeles and London: University of California Press, 1986)—, often support, at times critically engage and always amplify my analysis concerning the quintessential political significance of Attic tragedy. Euben summarized the purpose of tragedy as follows. "In the theater of Dionysus, during the festival honoring the god who confounded the divisions and inequalities deemed central to public life, tragedy put the city's dearly bought cultural accommodations on trial before itself. There and then the putatively normal and natural stood revealed as fictive imperatives that more often than not entailed violation of nature, city, household and self. From inside the polis tragedy questioned the divisions between inside and outside. Part of the city's order, it 'problematized' the idea of order, contesting as it constructed, challenging what it helped to sustain, and presenting trangressions, paradoxes, and archaisms to disrupt civic teleologies which it eventually reaffirmed." (*The Tragedy of Political Theory*, p. 29)

92.   Jaspers, *Tragedy is not Enough*, p. 102.

93.   Alan M.G. Little, *Myth and Society in Attic Drama* (New York: Columbia University Press, 1942), p. 27.

94.   Froma Zeitlin, "Thebes: Theater of Self and Society in Athenian Drama," in *Greek Tragedy and Political Theory*, pp. 116f.

95.   Gerard Else, *The Madness of Antigone*, Abhandlungen der Heidelberger Akademie der Wissenschaften: Philos.-Histor.-klass. Abhandelungen, pt. 1 (Heidelberg: Carl Winter, 1976), p. 12.

96.   Sophocles, *The Three Theban Plays: Antigone, Oedipus the King, Oedipus at Colonus*, transl. Robert Fagles (Harmondsworth: Penguin Books, 1984), p. 112.

97.   Ibid., p. 115.

98.   Cedric H. Whitman, *Sophocles: A Study of Heroic Humanism* (Cambridge, Mass.: Harvard University Press, 1951), p. 233.

99.   Bernard Knox, "Introduction: Oedipus the King," in Sophocles, op. cit., p. 150.

100. Sophocles, op. cit., p. 233.

101. Karl Reinhardt, *Sophocles*, transl. Hazel Harvey and David Harvey (New York: Barnes & Noble Books, 1979), pp. 133f.

102. Knox, op. cit., p. 140. .

103. Ibid., p. 133.

104. Ibid., p. 153.

105. See George Steiner, *Antigones* (New York and London: Oxford University Press, 1984), pp. 66ff; Emery E. George, *Friedrich Höolderlin: An Early Modern* (Ann Arbor: The University of Michigan Press, 1972).

106. Friedrich Hölderlin, "Oedipus," from his *Sämtliche Werke [Grosse Stuttgarter Ausgabe]*, ed. Friedrich Beissner and Adolf Beck, 8 vols. (Stuttgart: Cotta, 1943–85), vol. 5, pp. 197, 198, 200; as quoted in David Constantine, *Hölderlin* (Oxford: Clarendon Press, 1988), pp. 294, 387.

107. Friedrich Hölderlin, "Remarks on Oedipus," from *Essays and Letters on Theory*, ed. Thomas Pfau (Albany: State University of New York Press, 1988), p. 102; see also the chapter entitled "The Caesura" in Philippe Lacoue-Labarthe's *Heidegger, Art and Politics*, transl. Chris Turner (Oxford and Cambridge Mass.: Basil Blackwell, 1990), pp. 41–6; also Andrzej Warminski, *Readings in Interpretation: Hölderlin, Hegel, Heidegger* (Minneapolis: University of Minnesota Press, 1987), pp. 17ff.

108. Hölderlin, op. cit., p. 102.

109. Sophocles, op. cit., p. 183.

110. Hölderlin, op. cit., p. 107.

111. Friedrich Hölderlin, "Hyperion's Song of Fate," in *Poems and Fragments*, transl. Michael Hamburger (London: Routledge & Kegan Paul, 1966), p. 79.

112. Hölderlin, "As On a Holiday . . .," in *Poems and Fragments*, p. 377.

113. Hölderlin, "Bread and Wine," in *Poems and Fragments*, p. 249.

114. Steiner, op. cit., p. 79.

115. Hölderlin, *Essays and Letters*, p. 108.

116. Lacoue-Labarthe, op. cit., pp. 44f.

117. Steiner, op. cit., p. 86.

118. Mark 15: 34.

119. Little, op. cit., p. 49.

120. Aristophanes, *The Birds*, in *The Knights/Peace/The Birds/The Assembly Women/Wealth*, transl. David Barrett and Alan H. Sommerstein (Harmondsworth etc.: Penguin Books, 1978), p. 159.

121. Ibid., p. 187f.

122. A.W. Pickard-Cambridge, *The Theatre of Dionysius in Athens* (Oxford: Clarendon Press, 1946).

123. Aristophanes, op. cit., p. 206.

124. Edmund Burke, *Reflections on the Revolution in France* (Harmondsworth etc.: Penguin Books, 1982), p. 299.

125. Aristophanes, op. cit., p. 188.

126. Thucydides, op. cit., pp. 403ff.

127. Ibid., p. 402.

128. Connor, op. cit., p. 157.

129. Emmanuel Levinas, *Ethics and Infinity: Conversations with Philippe Nemo*, transl. Richard A. Cohen (Pittsburgh, Duquesne University Press, 1985), p. 86.

130. Ibid., pp. 105f.

131. Emmanuel Levinas, "Philosophy and the Idea of Infinity," in *Collected Papers*, transl. Alphonso Lignis (Dordrecht, Boston and Lancaster: Martinus Nijhoff, 1987), p. 58.

132. Emmanuel Levinas, "God and Philosophy," in *Collected Philosophical Papers*, p. 167f.

133. Ibid., p. 170.

134. Sophocles, *Oedipus at Colonus*, in *The Three Theban Plays*, p. 289.

135. Ibid., p. 299.

136. Ibid., p. 318.

137. Ibid., p. 375.

138. J. Peter Euben, "Introduction," in *Greek Tragedy and Political Theory*, p. 11.

139. John D. Caputo, *Radical Hermeneutics: Repetition, Deconstruction and the Hermeneutic Project* (Bloomington and Indianapolis: Indiana University Press, 1987), p. 2.

140. Søren Kierkegaard, *Fear and Trembling/Repetition*, transl. Howard V. Hong and Edna H.

Hong (Princeton: Princeton University Press, 1983), p. 131.

141. Elie Wiesel, *Messengers of God: Biblical Portraits and Legends*, transl. Marion Wiesel (New York: Schocken, 1976), p. 32.

142. Pat Bigelow, *Kierkegaard & the Problem of Writing* (Tallahassee: The Florida State University Press, 1987), p. 174.

143. Kierkegaard, *Repetition*, p. 149.

144. Ibid., p. 302.

145. Caputo, op. cit., p. 30.

146. Kierkegaard, *Repetition*, p. 307.

147. Numa Fustel de Coulanges, *The Ancient City: A Study on the Religion, Laws, and Institutions of Greece and Rome* (Baltimore: Johns Hopkins Press, 1980), p. 3.

148. Friedrich Hölderlin, "Mnemosyne," in *Hymns and Fragments*, transl. Richard Sieburth (Princeton: Princeton University Press, 1984), pp. 117–9.

149. Hölderlin, "I Want to Build," in *Hymns and Fragments*, p. 245.

150. See Peter Szondi, "Überwindung des Klassizismus: Der Brief an Böhlendorff vom 4. Dezember 1801," *Hölderlin-Studien. Mit einem Traktat über philologische Erkenntnis* (Frankfurt am Main: Insel Verlag, 1967), pp. 85–104; also Andrzej Warminski, op. cit., pp. 27ff.

151. Warminski, op. cit., pp. 26f.

152. Hölderlin, "Letter to Casimir Ulrich Böhlendorff," in *Essays and Letters on Theory*, pp. 149f.

153. See the important discussion on the relationship between Egypt, Greece and Germany in Warminski, op. cit., pp. 17ff.

154. Hölderlin, "Letter to Casimir Ulrich Böhlendorff," in *Essays and Letters on Theory*, p. 151.

Chapter Six: Architectonics

1. My understanding of this topic has been profoundly affected by Demetri Porphyrios; see, for example, his "Imitation and Convention in Architecture," *Architectural Design Profile 71, The New Classicism in Architecture and Urbanism* (London and New York: Architectural Design, 1988), pp. 14–21.

2. For this see most recently the *Architecture Design Profile 75, Imitation and Innovation*, ed. Lucien Steil (London and New York: Architectural Design, 1988).

3. See Norris Kelly Smith, "Crisis in Jerusalem," *Late Entries to the Chicago Tribune Tower Competition*, ed. Stanley Tigerman (New York: Rizzoli, 1980), vol. 2, pp. 106–10.

4. A standard handbook states "Balloon framing . . . is the term given to that system of construction in which the skeleton, or framework, of a building is spiked together with butt joints, and depends almost entirely for its strength and stability upon its exterior covering and the manner in which the covering is applied." *International Library of Technology: A Series of Textbooks . . . Masonry, Carpentry, Joinery,* (Scranton: International Textbook Company, n.d. [1899]; reprinted Chicago: William L. Lavicka, 1977), vol. 2, p 100; see also p. 31 for the definition contrasted with that of braced-frame construction. A standard current source for Western framing is Robert T. Packard, ed., *Ramsey/Sleeper Architectural Graphic Standards*, 7th ed. (New York, etc.: John Wiley, 1981), "Light Wood Framing," pp. 319–33. The first edition of Charles Ramsey and Harold Sleeper's handbook appeared in 1932. For a highly colored discussion of the origins of this distinctly American construction see Sigfried Giedion, *Space, Time and Architecture* (Cambridge, Mass.: Harvard University Press), 1941, pp. 269ff. See now the excellent discussion in Edward R. Ford, *The Details of Modern Architecture* (Cambridge Mass. and London: *MIT Press*, 1990), Chapter 5.

5. This should not be understood to suggest that architecture is language, a topic to which I shall return in Chapter Eight.

6. An important topic entailed within this is one that need not be presented in full on this occasion, viz., the ability to differentiate between actual and fictive derived from the same understanding of actual things and the appearance of them that allowed Brunelleschi to discover the rules of perspective. Perspective is to vision as the rules of grammar and dialectic are to speech. Perspective design makes architecture articulate. For a different discussion of the importance of apparent structural representation in classical architecture, see Geoffrey Scott, *The Architecture of Humanism*, 2nd. ed. (New York and London: Norton, 1974), esp. chapters 4 and 8.

7.   See John Onians, *Bearers of Meaning* (Princeton: Princeton University Press, 1988), passim.

8.   Sigfried Giedion, op. cit., caption to fig. 156, p. 269.

9.   Kent C. Bloomer and Charles W. Moore, *Body, Memory, and Architecture* (New Haven and London: Yale University Press, 1977), pp. 115–9. The college had to be built cheaply because "the budget . . . was based on the colleges being in genuine competition with the cheap developer's housing for students which was springing up near the campus." There was nothing in the required cheapness of construction that led necessarily to the evocation of the shopping center and settlement. The contrast with another complex serving as a residential college and called a village by its designer, Thomas Jefferson, hardly needs citing. For my earlier comments on the approach to design embodied in Kresge College see "Adam and Eden in Post-Modern Chicago," *Threshold: Journal of the School of Architecture, University of Illinois at Chicago*, 1982, pp. 102–19; p. 105.

10.   See also C.W. Westfall, "On Razing the Primitive Hut," *Art Criticism* (Department of Art, State University of New York at Stony Brook), vol. 3, no. 1, 1986, pp. 11–26.

11.   L.B. Alberti, *Ten Books on Architecture*, transl. James Leoni (London: Tiranti, 1955), VI, ii, p. 113; Rykwert et al. transl., p. 156: "ut sit pulchritudo quidem certa cum ratione concinnitas universarum partium in eo, cuius sint, ita ut addi aut diminui aut immutari possit nihil, quin improbabilius reddatur." Ibid., *de re aedificatoria*, ed. Giovanni Orlandi, 2 vols. (Milan: Polifilo, 1966), VI, ii, p. 446.

12.   John Onians, op. cit., p. 330.

13.   George Hersey, *The Lost Meaning of Classical Architecture* (Cambridge Mass. and London: MIT Press, 1988), p. 149.

14.   Ed. cit., IX, v, p. 194; Rykwert et al. p. 302. "Ut vero de pulchritudine iudices, non opinio, verum animis innata quaedam ratio efficiet." Ed. cit., IX, v, p. 813.

15.   See Immanuel Kant, *The Critique of Judgment*, transl. James Creed Meredith (Oxford: Clarendon Press, 1928), sections 32–40; for this I found the following especially useful: Joan Gadol, *Leon Battista Alberti* (Chicago and London: University of Chicago Press, 1969), pp. 107 and 235; David Summers, *The Judgment of Sense* (Cambridge: Cambridge University Press, 1987), esp. pp. 106f. and 132–7; and Claudia Brodsky, "Architecture and Architectonics: The Art of Reason in Kant's *Critique*," *Canon/The Princeton Journal: Thematic Studies in Architecture* (Princeton, Princeton Architectural Press, 1988) pp. 103–17.

16.   For more on this topic, see the classic discussion in Rudolph Wittkower, *Architectural Principles in the Age of Humanism*, 3rd ed. (London: Tiranti, 1962), Part IV; see also George Hersey, *Pythagorian Palaces* (Ithaca and London: Cornell University Press, 1976). Note that what Alberti calls finishing we generally call proportion and that we generally think that what we call proportion somehow satisfied all aspects of beauty as it was understood by classical theorists and architects. The presentation here should make clear the inadequacy of that understanding.

17.   Ed. cit., IX, vii, p. 201; Rykwert et al., p. 310.

18.   Latin: *concinnitas*; in English, concinnity: "Skilful and harmonious adaptation or fitting together of parts; harmony, congruity, consistency." OED lists examples from 1531 to 1886.

19.   Alberti, ed. cit. IX, v, p. 195; Rykwert et al., pp. 302–3 (here with revisions). The key passage: "hoc est absoluta primariaque ratio naturae. . . . Hanc ipsam maiorem in modum res aedificatoria sectatur; hac sibi dignitatem gratiam auctoritatem vendicat atque in precio est." Ibid., ed. cit., IX, v, p. 817.

Chapter Eight: Cities

1.   The most useful recent source is Joseph Rykwert, *The Idea of a Town* (Princeton: Princeton University Press, 1976). See also the still current classic, Numa Fustel de Coulanges, *The Ancient City: A Study on the Religion, Laws, and Institutions of Greece and Rome* (Baltimore: Johns Hopkins Press, 1980).

2.   The word probably derives ultimately from *temenos* which in Greek usage was a shrine, especially one associated with the enduring presence of a founding hero or heroes. See Joseph Rykwert, op. cit., pp. 45–6.

3.   Ibid., p. 117, quotes Ovid in a passage referring equally well to boundaries (*termini*; see above for van Pelt's discussion of Greek *horoi*) and to *mundi*:

A ditch was dug down to the firm clay
Fruits were thrown to the bottom,
And earth from the neighboring fields.
The ditch was filled again and an altar put on it.
And the new hearth
Was decked with kindled fire.

4.   And with awareness of Sallust. See Donald Earl, *The Moral and Political Tradition of Rome* (Ithaca and London: Cornell University Press, 1967), pp. 123–4.

5.   "Outside the service of the Republic there existed no public office and, therefore, strictly speaking, no *gloria*, no *nobilitas*, no *auctoritas*, no *virtus*." Donald Earl, op. cit., p. 35.

6.   For a discussion of this design within the frame of reference being developed here, see my analysis in "Purpose and Form in the Renaissance Palace," *Roma, centro ideale della cultura dell'Antico nei secoli XV e XVI: da Martino V al Sacco di Roma, 1417–1527*, ed. Silvia Danesi Squarzina (Milan: Electra, 1989), pp. 316–336, pp. 331ff.

7.   See Leon Battista Alberti, *On Painting*, transl. John Spencer (New Haven and London: Yale University Press, 1956); and his *On Painting and On Sculpture*, ed. and transl. Cecil Grayson (London: Phaidon, 1972).

8.   See Marvin Trachtenberg, "What Brunelleschi Saw: Monument and Site at the Palazzo Vecchio in Florence," *Journal of the Society of Architectural Historians* 47 (1988), pp. 14–44. For an earlier discussion, which includes a discussion of relational aspects of Roman (precinct) space, see Lisa Bek, *Towards Paradise on Earth: Modern Space Conception in Architecture*, Analecta Romana Instituti Danici 9, Supplement (Odense, Denmark: Odense University Press, 1980).

9.   The corollary is this: it is probably not an object with an interior extending outward beyond its boundary, as van Pelt suggests his stoa to be.

10. Homo = Greek *homo* = same; morphic = Greek *morphe* = form.

11. Ernst Gombrich, *Art and Illusion* (Princeton: Princeton University Press, 1961), p. 257.

12. See the brief comments in Alberto Pérez-Gómez, *Architecture and the Crisis of Modern Science* (Cambridge Mass. and London: MIT Press, 1983), pp. 100, 114–5, 160, 174f. where, unaccountably, issues raised in the fifteenth century are treated as if they are seventeenth- century issues.

13. A suggestion of what constitutes the substance of this argument has been a *Leitmotif* in the works of Ernst Gombrich. See for example his *Art and Illusion* and "The Renaissance Conception of Artistic Progress and Its Consequences," *Norm and Form* (London and New York: Phaidon, 1966), pp. 1–10.

14. Jacob Burckhardt, *The Civilization of the Renaissance in Italy*, transl. S.G.C. Middlemore (New York and Evanston: Harper Torchbooks, 1958), p. 107; for the earlier point, see his letter to Louise Burckhardt, 25 September, 1841, "there is only *one* remedy against the threatening decline of a people, and that is: to renew its links with its origins" (original emphasis; in the diction of this presentation for origins read beginnings); and the letter to Albert Brenner, 17 October, 1855, "Once we really break off relations with the great and the infinite, we are utterly lost and caught in the wheels of the present age." *Burckhardt: The Civilization of the Renaissance in Italy and Other Selections*, ed. Alexander Dru (New York: Washington Square Press, 1966), pp. 292 and 303.

15. William L. MacDonald, *The Architecture of the Roman Empire*, vol. 2: *An Urban Appraisal* (New Haven and London: Yale University Press, 1986), p. 3.

16. As at Palmyra; see William L. MacDonald, op. cit., figs. 16 and 17; for the foursquare structures, see pp. 87ff.

17. Jaquelin Robertson has provided a suggestive catalogue: "The street, the tree, the yard, the public green; the fence, and sidewalk, and backyard; the formal park and the green square; the irregular intrusions of natural terrain and the ever-present backdrop of the continent; . . . together with the central presence of the travel machine and the house. . . ." "In Search of an American Urban Order, Part I: The Nagasaki Syndrome," *Modulus* 16 (The University of Virginia Architectural Review), 1983, pp. 2–15. Also important in forming my thought on this topic has been the work of Boston architect and critic Robert Campbell, and the explorations in the American Urbanism Studio at the University of Virginia conducted by Robert Dripps, III.

18. Among the most fruitful suggestions for further directions of inquiry are the following: J. Robertson, op. cit.; "Part II: The House as the City," *Modulus* 19, 1989, pp. 138–59; the entire

Architectural Design Profile 54 edited by Demetri Porphyrios, Leon Krier: Houses, Palaces, Cities (London: AD Editions, 1984; also cited as Architectural Design, 54, nos. 7/8, 1984), with contributions by D. Porphyrios, Colin Rowe and J. Robertson; Michael Dennis, Court & Garden: From the French Hôtel to the City of Modern Architecture (Cambridge Mass. and London: MIT Press, 1986); the same author's "Excursus Americanus," Modulus 16, 1983, pp. 110–25; and Andres Duany, "Traditional Towns," Reconstruction and Deconstruction: An Architectural Design Profile 81 (London: Academy Editions, and New York: St Martin's Press, 1989; also cited as Architectural Design, 59, nos. 9/10, 1989), pp. 60–4.

19. See Wolfgang Braunfels, Mittelalterliche Stadtbaukunst in der Toskana (Berlin: Verlag Gebr. Mann, 1966).

20. For a European view which in many ways is compatible with this one to the extent allowed by political differences, see Leon Krier, "Urban Components," in Houses, Palaces, Cities, ed. Demetri Porphyrios; Architectural Design Profile 54 (1984), pp. 40–50, and elsewhere in his important writings.

21. A comprehensive history of the Northwest Ordinance is yet to be written. For an indication of its adaptability to changing circumstances, see Benjamin Horace Hibbard, A History of the Public Land Policies (New York: Macmillan, 1924); Roy M. Robbins, Our Landed Heritage: The Public Domain, 1776–1970, 2nd ed. (Lincoln and London: University of Nebraska Press, 1976); and Hildegard Binder Johnson, Order Upon the Land: The U.S. Rectangular Land Survey and the Upper Mississippi Country (New York etc.: Oxford University Press, 1976).

22. See John R. Stilgoe, Common Landscape of America: 1580–1845 (New Haven and London: Yale University Press, 1982), "Landscape."

23. See Hermann G. Pundt, Schinkel's Berlin: A Study in Environmental Planning (Cambridge Mass.: Harvard University Press, 1972), chapter IV.

24. Robert W. Berger, Versailles: The Château of Louis XIV (University Park and London: Pennsylvania State University Press, for the College Art Association of America, 1985), p. 1.

25. My understanding of this point is based on discussions with Professor Egon Verheyen, who also supplied the information about the terms used to refer to the rotunda.

26. Quoted in Lois Craig et al., The Federal Presence: Architecture, Politics, and Symbols in United States Government Building (Cambridge Mass. and London: MIT Press, 1978), p. 136. See also Bates Lowry, Building a National Image: Architectural Drawings for the American Democracy, 1789–1912 (Washington: National Building Museum, 1985), chapters 2–3.

Chapter Nine: Apocalyptic Abjection

1. See Michael E. Zimmerman, Heidegger's Confrontation with Modernity: Technology, Politics, Art (Bloomington and Indianapolis: Indiana University Press, 1990); Philippe Lacoue-Labarthe, Heidegger, Art and Politics, transl. Chris Turner (Oxford and Cambridge Mass.: Basil Blackwell, 1990); a dissenting vision is given in Luc Ferry and Alain Renaut, Heidegger and Modernity, transl. Franklin Philip (Chicago and London: The University of Chicago Press, 1990); for an account of Heidegger's formal involvement with Nazism see Victor Farías, Heidegger and Nazism, ed. Joseph Margolis and Tom Rockmore transl. Paul Burrell and Gabriel R. Ricci (Philadelphia: Temple University Press, 1989).

2. Martin Heidegger, An Introduction to Metaphysics, transl. Ralph Mannheim (New Haven and London: Yale University Press, 1959), pp. 105ff.

3. Martin Heidegger, "Remembrance of the Poet," Existence and Being, Werner Brock ed. (Washington DC: Regnery Gateway, 1988), p. 233.

4. Martin Heidegger, Hölderlins Hymnen "Germanien" und "Der Rhein": Freiburger Vorlesung Wintersemester 1934/35, ed. Susanne Ziegler, vol. 39 of Martin Heidegger: Gesamtausgabe (Frankfurt am Main: Vittorio Klostermann, 1980), p. 293.

5. Heidegger, An Introduction to Metaphysics, pp. 38f.

6. Martin Heidegger, "The Self-Assertion of the German University: Address, Delivered on the Solemn Assumption of the Rectorate of the University of Freiburg," transl. Karsten Harries, Review of Metaphysics 38 (1985), pp. 471ff.

7. Martin Heidegger, "The Rectorate 1933/34: Facts and Thoughts," transl. Karsten Harries, Review of Metaphysics 38 (1985), p. 483.

8.   Ibid., p. 498.

9.   Franz Neumann, *Behemoth: The Structure and Practice of National Socialism, 1933–1944* (Toronto, New York and London: Oxford University Press, 1944), pp. 62ff.

10.   Heidegger, *An Introduction to Metaphysics*, pp. 152f.

11.   Martin Heidegger, "Deutsche Studenten," *Freiburger Studentenzeitung* 15 (Nov. 3, 1933), p. 1; quoted in Farías, op. cit., p. 118.

12.   According to Dr Werner, the chairman of the presiding council of the German Evangelical church, Hitler was a *Wundermann Gottes*, "a man of miracles sent by God." He, and other German theologians, celebrated Hitler as a German messiah sent by God to guide the German nation to salvation. German Protestants were urged to bring thanks to God for having sent Hitler to them. For a shocking account of the German Protestant vision of Hitler see Günther Brakelmann and Dieter Beese, *Kirche im Krieg: Der deutsche Protestantismus am beginn des II. Weltkrieges* (Munich: Kaiser, 1979), pp. 100ff.

13.   Adolf Hitler, *Mein Kampf*, transl. Ralph Manheim (Boston: Houghton Mifflin, 1971), p. 3.

14.   Michael D. Ryan, "Hitler's Challenge to the Churches: A Theological Political Analysis of *Mein Kampf*," *The German Church Struggle and the Holocaust*, ed. Franklin H. Littell and Hubert G. Locke (Detroit: Wayne State University Press, 1974), pp. 152f.

15.   Ibid., p. 153.

16.   Quoted in: Eberhard Jäckel, *Hitler's World View: A Blueprint for Power* (Cambridge Mass. and London: Harvard University Press, 1981), pp. 62f.

17.   Hitler, *Mein Kampf*, pp. 122f.

18.   Quoted in J. Noakes and G. Pridham, *Nazism 1919–1945: A Documentary Reader*, 3 vols. (Exeter: Exeter University Publications, 1983–88), vol. 1, p. 33.

19.   Alfred Rosenberg, *Portrait eines Menschheitsverbrechers: nach dem hinterlassenen Memoiren des ehemaligen Reichsministers*, ed. Serge Land and Ernst von Schenck (St. Gallen: Zollikofer, 1947), p. 274; as quoted in Robert R. Taylor, *The Word in Stone: The Role of Architecture in the National Socialist Ideology* (Berkeley, Los Angeles and London: University of California Press, 1974), p. 147.

20.   Wilhelm Lotz, "Das Reichsparteitagsgelände in Nürnberg," in Anna Teut, ed. *Architektur im Dritten Reich: 1933–1945* (Berlin, Frankfurt am Main and Vienna: Ullstein, 1967), p. 190.

21.   Gerdy Troost, *Das Bauen im Neuen Reich* (Bayreuth: Gauverlag Bayerische Ostmark, 1938), p. 10.

22.   As quoted in Taylor, *The Word in Stone*, p. 147.

23.   Klaus Vondung, *Magie und Manipulation: Ideologischer Kult und Politische Religion des Nationalsocialismus* (Göttingen: Vandenhoeck & Ruprecht, 1971), pp. 159ff; Simon Taylor, *Prelude to Genocide: Nazi Ideology and the Struggle for Power* (London: Duckworth, 1983), pp. 177ff. Taylor's description of the Ninth of November celebrations contains a number of errors as to the places where specific parts of the liturgy were celebrated, and should therefore be used with care.

24.   Eberhard Wolfgang Möller, "Die Verpflichtung," *Volksspieldienst nr. 5*, (Berlin, 1935), pp. 15ff.; quoted in Taylor, *Prelude to Genocide*, p. 181.

25.   Herbert Böhme, *Gesänge unter der Fahne*, (Munich 1935), p. 59; quoted in Taylor, *Prelude to Genocide*, p. 180.

26.   Böhme, op. cit., p. 44; quoted in Taylor, *Prelude to Genocide*, p. 183.

27.   Adolf Hitler as quoted in the *Völkischer Beobachter*, November 10, 1935; quoted in Taylor, *Prelude to Genocide*, p. 179.

28.   *Völkischer Beobachter*, November 10, 1935; quoted in Taylor, *Prelude to Genocide*, p. 178.

29.   *Völkischer Beobachter*, November 10, 1935; quoted in Taylor, *Prelude to Genocide*, pp. 177f.

30.   Heidegger, "The Origin of the Work of Art," *Poetry, Language, Thought*, p. 77.

31.   Vondung, op. cit., pp 180ff.

32.   Jost Dülffer, Jochen Thies and Josef Henke, *Hitlers Städte: Baupolitik im Dritten Reich*, (Cologne and Vienna: Böhlau Verlag, 1978), p. 36; *see also* Jochen Thies, *Architekt der Weltherrschaft: Die "Endziele" Hitlers* (Düsseldorf: Droste Verlag), 1976.

33.   Elias Canetti, *The Conscience of Words*, transl. Joachim Neugroschel (London: Pan Books, 1987), p. 74.

34.   Ryan, op. cit., pp. 160f.

35.   Carl Schmitt, *The Concept of the Political*, transl. George Schwab (New Brunswick: Rutgers University Press, 1976), p. 46.

36. Quoted in Raul Hilberg, *The Destruction of the European Jews*, revised and definitive edition, 3 vols. (New York and London: Holmes & Meier, 1985), vol. 3, p. 1021.

37. The English translation of the full text of this and the other laws discussed can be found in Lucy S. Dawidowicz, ed., *A Holocaust Reader* (New York: Behrman House, 1976), p. 47.

38. Hilberg, op. cit., vol. 1, p. 70.

39. Dawidowicz, op. cit., pp. 46f.

40. Judith Ryan, *The Uncompleted Past: Postwar German Novels and the Third Reich* (Detroit: Wayne State University Press, 1983), p. 25.

41. For a useful account of this history see Taylor, *The Word in Stone*, pp. 210–18.

42. Wolf Braumüller, *Freilicht-und Thingspiel: Rückschau und Forderungen* (Berlin: Volksschaft-Verlag für Buch, Bühne und Film, 1935), p. 45; as quoted in Taylor, *The Word in Stone*, p. 213.

43. Richard Euringer, "Thingspiel—Thesen I," *Völkischer Beobachter*, June 20, 1934; quoted in Joseph Wulf, *Theater und Film im Dritten Reich: Eine Dokumentation* (s.l.: Sigbert Mohn, 1966), pp. 168f.

44. Eugène Wernert, *L'art dans le IIIeme Reich: une tentative d'esthetique dirigée* (Paris: Centre d'études de politiques étrangers, 1936), p. 100; quoted in Taylor, *The Word in Stone*, p. 218.

45. Felix Emmel, *Theater aus deutschem Wesen* (Berlin: Georg Stilke, 1937), pp. 22f.

46. Friedrich Hölderlin, "Remarks on 'Oedipus'," from *Essays and Letters on Theory*, ed. Thomas Pfau (Albany: State University of New York Press, 1988), p. 102.

47. Hölderlin, "Remarks on 'Antigone'," *Essays and Letters on Theory*, p. 110.

48. Emil Fackenheim, *To Mend the World: Foundations of Future Jewish Thought* (New York: Schocken, 1982), pp. 238f.

49. Arthur A. Cohen, *The Tremendum: A Theological Interpretation of the Holocaust* (New York: Crossroad, 1981), p. 1.

50. Ibid., pp. 4f.

51. Ibid., pp. 18f.

52. Ibid., p. 52.

53. Ibid., p. 20.

54. Ibid., p. 53.

55. Ibid., p. 97.

56. David Tracy, "Foreword," in Cohen, *The Tremendum*, p. vii.

57. Richard L. Rubenstein and John K. Roth, *Approaches to Auschwitz: The Holocaust and Its Legacy* (Atlanta: John Knox Press, 1987), p. 334.

58. Extract of this unpublished lecture is quoted in Lacoue-Labarthe, op. cit., p. 34.

59. Ibid., p. 35.

60. Ibid., pp. 45f.

61. Ibid., p. 46.

62. Emil Fackenheim, "Holocaust and *Weltanschauung*: Philosophical Reflections on Why They Did It," *Holocaust and Genocide Studies* 3 (1988), p. 204.

63. Hitler, op. cit., pp. 288f.

64. Fackenheim, op. cit., p. 206.

65. W.H. Auden, "The Poet & The City," in *The Dyer's Hand and Other Essays* (New York: Vintage International, 1989), pp. 84f.

66. Steve Wasserman, "Interview with Hans-Jürgen Syberberg," *The Threepenny Review* (Summer, 1980), p. 4.

67. Hans-Jürgen Syberberg, *Hitler, A Film from Germany*, transl. Joachim Neugroschel (New York: Farrar, Straus & Giroux, 1982), p. 234.

68. Raul Hilberg, "The Holocaust," *Facing Evil: Light at the Core of Darkness*, ed. Paul Woodruff and Harry A. Wilmer (LaSalle, Ill.: Open Court, 1988), p. 107.

69. Lacoue-Labarthe, op. cit., p. 58.

70. Richard L. Rubenstein, *The Cunning of History: The Holocaust and the American Future* (New York etc.: Harper Colophon Books, 1978), pp. 94f.

71. Irving Abella and Harold Troper, *None Is Too Many: Canada and the Jews of Europe, 1933–1948* (New York: Random House, 1983), p. v.

72. Kitty Hart, *I Am Alive* (London, New York and Toronto: Abelard-Schuman, 1961), pp. 85ff.

73. Ibid., pp. 92f.

74.   Tadeusz Borowski, *This Way for the Gas*, transl. Barbara Vedder (New York: Penguin, 1976), p. 30.

75.   A good introduction to the purpose and function of "Kanada" can be found in Hermann Langbein, *Menschen in Auschwitz* (Vienna: Europaverlag, 1972), pp. 158–68; see also Józef Garliński, *Fighting Auschwitz: The Resistance Movement in the Concentration Camp* (London: Julian Friedmann Publishers, 1975), pp. 90ff.

76.   Peter J. Haas, *Morality After Auschwitz: The Radical Challenge of the Nazi Ethic* (Philadelphia: Fortress Press, 1988), pp. 169f.

77.   Quoted in Lucy S. Dawidowicz, ed., *A Holocaust Reader* (New York: Behrman House, 1976), p. 131.

78.   Ibid., pp. 132ff.

79.   Norman O. Brown, *Life Against Death: The Psychoanalytical Meaning of History*. (Middletown Connecticut: Wesleyan University Press, 1959), p. 280.

80.   Quoted in Dawidowicz, op. cit., p. 131.

81.   Hilberg, *The Destruction of the European Jews*, vol. 3, p. 934.

82.   Quoted in Benjamin B. Ferencz, *Less Than Slaves: Jewish Forced Labor and the Quest for Compensation* (Cambridge Mass. and London: Harvard University Press, 1979), pp. 77f.; epigraph.

83.   Borowski, op. cit., pp. 130f.

84.   Taylor, *The Word in Stone*, pp. 231f.

85.   Charlotte Beradt, *The Third Reich of Dreams*, transl. Adriane Gottwald (Chicago: Quadrangle Books, 1968), p. 21.

86.   Ibid., p. 9.

87.   Adolf Hitler, *Hitler's Secret Book*, ed. Telford Taylor, transl. Salvator Attanasio (New York: Grove Press, 1983), p. 5.

88.   Alfred Rosenberg, *Selected Writings*, ed. Robert Pois (London: Jonathan Cape, 1970), pp. 88f.

89.   Ernst Haeckel, *The Evolution of Man*, 2 vols. (New York: D. Appleton, 1896), vol. 1, pp. 11f.

90.   Hitler, *Hitler's Secret Book*, pp. 6f.

91.   Richard Wagner, "Judaism in Music," *Richard Wagner's Prose Works*, transl. William Ashton Ellis, 8 vols. (London: Kegan Paul, Trench, Trübner & Co., 1894), vol. 3, pp. 75–122.

92.   See Geoffery G. Field, *Evangelist of Race: The Germanic Vision of Houston Stewart Chamberlain* (New York: Columbia University Press, 1981).

93.   Houston Stewart Chamberlain, *Foundations of the Nineteenth Century*, transl. John Lees, 2 vols. (London and New York: John Lane, 1912), vol. 1, pp. 253, 257.

94.   Ibid., pp. 330f.

95.   Ibid., pp. 494f.

96.   Ibid., pp. 577f.

97.   Ibid., p. 257.

98.   Henry L. Feingold, "How Unique Is the Holocaust?", *Genocide: Critical Issues of the Holocaust*, ed. Alex Goodman and Daniel Landes (Los Angeles: The Simon Wiesenthal Centre, 1983), p. 398; for a general discussion on the relationship between Auschwitz and modern technological civilization see Zygmunt Bauman, *Modernity and the Holocaust* (Ithaca NY: Cornell University Press, 1989). At occasions the comparison is "pushed too far." An illustrative example of this is Frank Parker's interpretation of Majdanek. He described its efficiency in terms of a Mercedes-Benz factory. "Everything was so neat, clean and functional. In one case, the starting material is a hulk of metal, cloth, wood and other materials; the end product turns out to be a shiny roadster. In the other case, the starting material was a healthy human being guilty only of displeasing the Nazis. The end product turned out to be the ashes of a totally worked out, recently dead cretin." Parker noticed in the Polish death camps "a slickness of design there that was never matched in the camps built in the Fatherland" (in fact, no death camps were built in the Fatherland). And he continued his reverie with the observation that "if Majdanek had resembled an American prison of the same era, it would not have seemed so disturbing. Places of misery that they are, the San Quentins and Sing Sings can be rated as functionally and architecturally ridiculous. Wasted, impractical mountains of concrete abound. Very little space is productively utilized. Large numbers of guards are needed to supervise prisoners. The American prison architects must have been misfits. Designing an outhouse appears beyond the ca-

pacities of most of them. Majdanek is in a different league. Every inch of space was utilized. Every building was placed in a logical functional succession. Intelligent men constructed it. Many of the same men today built houses, roads, and hospitals in Germany and Austria. Clearly, their on-the-job training helped." Frank S. Parker, "A Visit to Majdanek," *When God and Man Failed*, ed. Harry James Cargas (New York and London: Macmillan, 1981), p. 3.

99.   Gitta Sereny, *Into That Darkness: An Examination of Conscience* (New York: Vintage Books, 1983), p. 11.

100.   Ibid., p. 112.

101.   Franz Suchomel in interview with Claude Lanzmann; quoted in Claude Lanzmann, *Shoah: an Oral History of the Holocaust* (New York: Pantheon, 1987), p. 56.

102.   Quoted in Yitzhak Arad, *Belzec, Sobibor, Treblinka: The Operation Reinhard Death Camps* (Bloomington and Indianapolis: Indiana University Press, 1987), p. 172.

103.   Danuta Czech, "Most Important Events in the History of the Concentration Camp Auschwitz–Birkenau," *From the History of KL–Auschwitz*, ed. Kazimierz Smoleń, transl. Krystyna Michalik (New York: Howard Fertig, 1982), pp. 193f.

104.   Smoleń, Ibid., pp. 22f.

105.   Filip Müller, *Eyewitness Auschwitz: Three Years in the Gas Chambers* (New York: Stein and Day, 1979), pp. 136f.

106.   Kurt Gerstein's report dated April 26, 1945; quoted in Saul Friedländer, *Counterfeit Nazi: the Ambiguity of Good*, transl. Charles Fullman (London: Weidenfeld & Nicolson, 1969), pp. 104f.

107.   Alexander Donat, *The Holocaust Kingdom* (New York: Holocaust Library, 1978), pp. 183, 211.

108.   Primo Levi, *The Drowned and the Saved*, transl. Raymond Rosenthal (New York: Summit Books, 1988), pp. 11f.

109.   The following four titles are but a small selection of the increasingly large body of so-called revisionist writings on the Holocaust. Central thesis of many of these books is that the gaschambers either did not exist, or if they did, that they were used for the disinfection of clothes or, as Butz suggests, that these spaces were like large carburetors necessary to run the crematoria where the bodies of those inmates who had died a natural death were cremated. As an architectural historian I felt obliged to read an important part of this revisionist literature. Those hours were among the worst I have had in my professional work. The revisionist literature is an insult to the intellect; their "evidence" is doctored, and in their attempts to reveal a great "conspiracy" to blot the reputation of Germany, these "scholars" either ignore half of the evidence, and that part of the evidence they attempt to discredit they butcher and mutilate beyond recognition. Paul Rassinier, *Debunking the Genocide Myth: A Study of the Nazi Concentration Camps and the Alleged Extermination of European Jewry*, transl. Adam Robbins (Los Angeles: The Noontide Press, 1978); Thies Christophersen, *Die Auschwitz-Lüge: Ein Erlebnisbericht* (Mohrkirch: Kritik-Verlag, 1973); Franz J. Scheidl, *Die Wahrheit über die Millionenvergassung von Juden, Geschichte der Verfemung Deutschlands*, vol. 4 (Vienna: Dr.-Scheidl-Verlag, n.d.); Arthur R. Butz, *The Hoax of the Twentieth Century* (Richmond: Historical Review Press, c.1976); Fred A. Leuchter Jr., *An Engineering Report on the Alleged Execution Gas Chambers at Auschwitz, Birkenau and Majdanek—Poland* (Boston: Fred A. Leuchtner, 1988). For an effective reply to this revisionist trash see Georges Wellers, *Les chambres à gaz ont existé* (Paris: Gallimard, 1981). See also: Anti-Roeder-Arbeitskreis, *"NSDAP"-Propagandisten unter der Lupe: Dokumentation antisemitischer, antidemokratischer und offener NS-Provokationen der Schönborn-Roeder-Christophersen-Bände und ihre Deckung seitens staatlicher Organe* (Hamburg: J. Reents-Verlag, 1978).

110.   Jean-Claude Pressac, "Les 'Krématorien' IV et V de Birkenau et leurs chambres à gaz: construction et fonctionnement," in *Le Monde Juif* 38, new series, no. 107 (1982), pp. 19–131. Shortly after the manuscript of *Architectural Principles in the Age of Historicism* was closed I received a copy of Pressac's monumental *Auschwitz: Technique and Operation of the Gas Chambers*, transl. Peter Moss (New York: The Beate Klarsfeld Foundation, 1989). The publication of this 564 pp. folio work is without doubt the most exciting and important architectural historical publications of the last decade.

111.   Quoted in Dawidowicz, op. cit., p. 133.

112.   Hitler, *Mein Kampf*, pp. 180–2.

113.   Günther Anders, *Franz Kafka*, transl. A. Steer and A.K. Thorlby (London: Bowes & Bowes, 1960), p. 37.

114.   Ibid., p. 38.

115. Ibid., pp. 30f.

116. Franz Kafka, *The Trial*, transl. Willa and Edwin Muir (New York: Schocken, 1968), p. 50.

117. Ibid., p. 12.

118. The term "l'univers concentrationnaire" was coined by David Rousset. See his *L'univers concentrationnaire* (Paris: Les Éditions de Minuit, 1965).

119. Quoted in J. Noakes and G. Pridham, *Nazism 1919–1945: A Documentary Reader*, 3 vols. (Exeter: Exeter University Publications, 1983–1988), vol. 3, p. 1071.

120. Régine Mihal Friedman, *L'image et son Juif: le Juif dans le cinéma nazi* (Paris: Payot, 1983), pp. 70f.

121. Pelagia Lewinska, *Twenty Months at Auschwitz*, transl. Albert Teichner (New York: Lyle Stuart, 1968), pp. 41f.

122. Langer used an event taken from the history of another camp to explain the dimensions of this choiceless choice. Transports of new prisoners arrived each day. But the supply of food did not increase. The camp commander was a man of the rules, who thought it to be important that each man got his proper ration. And as there were every day too many mouths to feed, he instituted a daily ballot. "The following morning the losers did not go to work. At noon they were led out behind the barbed-wire fence and shot." And he continued with the observation that "few examples could illustrate more effectively the notion of choiceless choice. The victims are offered an option that is no option, since the results of a lottery are governed by chance, not choice. And obviously, anyone who refused to participate in the macabre game certified his execution the next day. Refusal to participate in the ritual of extermination was not a meaningful alternative for the victim because he shared no responsibility for the situation that condemned him to such an existence. He lacked the power to act physically in behalf of his own survival, and without this power . . . no mere control of attitude or feeling of spiritual inviolability could salvage his moral self. Since the deathcamp universe eliminated conditions that support worth, the victim could not 'choose' extermination and remain human, while the survivor could not 'choose' life and remain human. He could strive for life and, if lucky, remain *alive*, but this was a struggle between states of being, not competing values." See Lawrence L. Langer, "The Dilemma of Choice in the Deathcamps," *Echoes from the Holocaust: Philosophical Reflections on a Dark Time*, ed. Alan Rosenberg and Gerald E. Myers (Philadelphia: Temple University Press, 1988), pp. 125f.

123. Levi, op. cit., pp. 52f.

124. Ibid., pp. 59f.

125. Jean Améry, *At the Mind's Limits: Contemplations by a Survivor on Auschwitz and Its Realities*, transl. Sidney and Stella P. Rosenfeld (New York: Schocken, 1986), pp. 85f.

126. Sidney Rosenfeld, "Jean Améry: The Writer in Revolt," in Améry, op. cit., p. 105.

127. Améry, op. cit., p. 2.

128. Viktor E. Frankl, *Man's Search for Meaning: An Introduction to Logotherapy* (New York: Simon & Schuster, 1984), p. 27.

129. Améry, op. cit., p. 7.

130. Améry, op. cit., p. 11.

131. Ibid., pp. 17f.

132. Ibid., pp. 18f.

133. Ibid., pp. 94f.

134. Søren Kierkegaard, *The Sickness Unto Death: A Christian Psychological Exposition for Upbuilding and Awakening*, transl. Howard V. Hong and Edna H. Hong (Princeton, Princeton University Press, 1983), p. 68.

135. Ibid., pp. 69f.

Index